SPORTING GOODS

Sporting Goods

Sports equipment and clothing, novelties, recreative science, firemen's supplies, magic lanterns and slides, plays and joke books, tricks and magic, badges and ornaments

---

PECK & SNYDER
1886

Illustrated Catalog and Historical Introduction

AMERICAN HISTORICAL CATALOG COLLECTION

THE PYNE PRESS
Princeton

All Rights Reserved

Copyright © 1971 by The Pyne Press

No part of this publication may be reproduced
or transmitted in any form or by any means,
electronic or mechanical, including
photocopy, recording, or any information storage
and retrieval system, without permission
in writing from the publisher.

First edition

Library of Congress Catalog Card Number 78-162361

ISBN 0-87861-014-6

Printed in the United States of America

Note to the reader. Reproduction of copy and line drawings is as faithful to the original as is technically possible. Broken type and lines which are uneven can be spotted; these are original! The reader will also note a number of repetitions in the listing of items. These, too, are original with Peck & Snyder.

Customers will please read the following notice carefully :
GOODS SENT BY EXPRESS, C. O. D.

We send goods in this manner when the order amounts to $2.00 or more. On shipments to extreme points, North, South, East or West, or on shipments of goods of great weight or bulk, and of small value, we shall require a remittance of 25 per cent. with order.

GOODS BY MAIL.

Most goods in our catalogue can be sent by mail as merchandise, at the rate of one cent per ounce. Customers ordering goods by mail must enclose stamps for postage, unless goods are advertised post-paid in catalogue. We copy the following from the present Postal Law, with some hints of our own in addition :

First.—Glass, Liquid, or Sharp-pointed Tools are unmailable unless mentioned otherwise.

Second.—Packages over four pounds in weight, or more than thirty-six inches long, are unmailable.

Third.—We are not responsible for goods sent by mail not registered.

Fourth.—Merchandise packages can be registered for ten cents each extra besides postage.

Fifth.—To seal a merchandise package secure and tight subjects it to letter postage.

Sixth.—To place a letter or writing in a package subjects it to letter postage.

Seventh.—Tie your packages with string, but use no paste or mucilage unless the ends are left open.

Eighth.—Do not place stamps over the string or edge of wrapper, as that virtually seals the package.

Avoid enclosing coin in letters, it is liable to drop out.

Do not stick the stamps to the letter. We do not take Canada or Foreign stamps in payment for our goods. Persons ordering goods to be sent by mail to Canada, or any other Post Office outside the United States and in the Postal Union, must send additional 10 cents for every 8 ounces, and each package not to exceed 8 ozs.

Goods sent by mail to Post Offices, not belonging to the Postal Union must send the full letter postage.

We will accept U. S. postage stamps of any denomination and quantity, in payment for our goods, but at retail price only. We prefer 1 or 2 cent stamps, and in sheets.

N. B.—Our own advice : Persons sending goods to us by mail, will please observe the Postal Law, and not seal a package. Secure it so that it can be easily examined at the Post Office, without breaking the wrapper. Do all your corresponding by letter or postal card, and never inclose any writing in or on a package sent by mail; if detected at the Post Office, the receiver would have to pay full letter postage, and the sender is liable to a fine of $25.00. All such packages sent to us, the goods will be forfeited by the sender, unless the sufficient amount is sent us to redeem them.

Never write, print or stamp *anything* upon the stamped side of a Postal Card, except name and address, as it will be subject to five cents extra postage to the party to whom addressed.

We do not hold ourselves responsible for money sent us through the mails, and lost in transit. Nor do we hold ourselves responsible for the safe delivery and in good condition of goods sent by mail. If the loss is occasioned by our own employees, we will be responsible.

All goods sent out by mail are at our patrons' own risk, we do our best for their safe and quickest delivery.

We prefer that remittances be made to us (when possible) by Express Money Orders, which are absolutely safe, and can be obtained at any office of the American, Wells, Fargo & Co., or United States Express Co., at the following rates : 1 cent to $5, 5 cents ; over $5 to $10, 8 cents ; over $10 to $20, 10 cents ; over $20 to $30, 12 cents ; over $30 to $40, 15 cents ; over $40 to $50, 20 cents ; over $50, proportionately. Where these Companies have no offices, or if more convenient, remittances may be made by Bank Draft, Post Office Order or Registered Letter. Always make payable to the order of PECK & SNYDER, New York.

Customers are requested to give exact directions, for shipping or mailing of goods, as packages occasionally miscarry from improper directions. Every order received by us is registered in a book kept for that purpose with the date of receipt and mailing, so that any person not receiving from us at once the goods ordered, can be sure of receiving satisfaction upon dropping us a line. The system with which we conduct this branch of our business is a guarantee against delay or dissatisfaction.

We are all liable to make mistakes. We try to do our part faithfully. We often receive letters dated, for instance : Fairview, giving no state. On referring to the Post Office Guide, we find 28 places of that name in as many different states. We often receive elaborate letters, couched in language more forcible than elegant, wanting to know if we ever intend to send the goods for the money sent. On referring, we find that our indignant friend forgot to sign his name to his order, hence the trouble.

In issuing this special catalogue, we are confident, we are meeting a long felt want. Customers receiving this will be able to order intelligently, and may rely on getting only first-class goods at the lowest market price. A good part of these goods are manufactured at our own factories, and we can guarantee the quality to be right, and the workmanship the best.

Our knit goods, of which we carry the Largest Assorted Stock of any dealer in the world, are made from best Silk and Worsted yarns and are positively Fast Colors, and full regular made. We carry in stock 36 different colors, and can usually fill orders same day as received. This is a great advantage to out of town buyers—and the saving of time will be appreciated by our customers.

Confident that we can meet your wants in a satisfactory manner, and soliciting your favors,

We remain, yours respectfully,   PECK & SNYDER.

PECK & SNYDER'S PRICE LIST
OF
Base Ball, Gymnasium, Boating, Firemen, Cricket, Archery, Lawn Tennis and Polo Implements, Guns, Skates, Fishing Tackle, Manly Sporting Goods, Novelties, &c.

N. B.—Prices in this Catalogue, Cancel all others previously issued by us.

Being manufacturers of most of the goods mentioned in this catalogue, we offer them to clubs and dealers believing our low prices, for the superior grade of goods we offer, will secure your patronage.

Please, when ordering goods, do not cut the book, but send the *number* or *name*, and all will be correct; and never neglect to send size of Belts, Caps, Shoes, Shirts, Pants, &c., as directed, with each article. We will not be responsible, nor will we exchange any goods that do not fit if measures are not sent with the order.

In ordering Belts please order by numbers, and send waist measurements; we can then send just what will fit. Firemen must invariably send their measures, as lettered belts cannot be exchanged or made large or small. Style No. 104 to 109 are principally made to order for Firemen, and are not as desirable for Base Ball Clubs, Boating or Gymnasiums as the Web Belts, the prices of which we quote on the following pages. Parties ordering by the half dozen or more are entitled to our dozen rates.

		Per doz.	Each.
No. 100.	Boys' Plain Black, Patent Leather, 1¾ inches wide; lengths, 24 to 32 inches	$1 50	$0 20
" 101.	Men's " " " 2 " " 30 to 38 "	3 00	0 30
" 102.	Boys' Red, White or Blue, P. L. Belts, 1¾ inches wide; lengths, 24 to 32 inches	3 00	0 30
" 103.	Men's " " " " 2 " " 20 to 38 "	4 00	0 40
" 104.	Black Patent Leather, half lined, with name of Company in any color block letter, in sunk panel of any color, with initials or number on side loop to match. (Sizes to measure). (See cut, belt Eagle)	9 00	1 00
" 105.	Red, White or Blue Patent Leather, made same style as No. 104	11 00	
" 106.	Black Patent Leather, full lined with fine enameled leather, and fancy stitched with around the edges, name of company on back, and number on side loop. (See cut, belt Enterprise)	13 00	
" 107.	Red, White or Blue Patent Leather, made same style as No. 106	11 00	
" 108.	Black Patent Leather, full lined and bound with scalloped edge, red, white, or blue Patent Leather, name on back, etc., same style as No. 106. (See cut, belt Active Hose)	17 00	
" 109.	Red, White or Blue Patent Leather, made same style as No. 108	19 00	
Name painted on Belts Nos. 100, 101, 102, 103, any color, extra		3 00	3 50

PRIZE BELTS AND TRIMMINGS.

We always keep an assortment on hand, or make to order, for Firemen, Boat Clubs, Base Ball, Pedestrians Fairs, etc. We have made and sent our Prize Belts to London, Scotland, Ireland, Paris, Germany, China, Japan and all over the United States and Canada, and in all cases they have given perfect satisfaction.

		Per doz.	Each.
No. 110.	Any color Patent Leather, very fancy stitched with silk, representing scroll work, bound with scalloped edge colored leather, and in other ways same as No. 109....		$4 50
" 111.	Made same as No. 110, but with double sunk panel and slide loop. This is the neatest belt we make. (See illustration)................		6 00
" 112.	Made same as No. 110, but with silver or gold gilt letters (German text letters)......		7 50
" 113.	Metal clasps with figure in centre, to use on belts in place of straps and buckles, to use with any of the above belts	$9 00	1 00
" 114.	Metal Letters, extra make, and heavy gold or silver gilt (German text style) ¾ inch ..	2 50	0 25
" 115.	" " cheapergrade................	1 00	1 10
" 116.	Gymnast Belt. Made of fine English worsted web, 3½ inches wide, blue or white or red and white stripe, russet leather finish, double straps, etc.................		1 25
" 117.	Lunge belts. For turning somersaults with, made of same web as No. 116, but with extra heavy straps and buckles, with a ring on each hip.................		3 50
" 118.	Trapeze Belts, made of same material and finish as No. 116, but with one ring in centre of the belt.................		2 50
" 119.	Police Belts, made of heavy black Enameled Leather, full lined and stitched with silk, with metal clasp and leather frog for holding club; silver plated clasps for privates	24 00	2 25
" 120.	Same as No. 119, but with gold gilt clasps for officers.................	28 00	2 60
" 121.	Cord Tassels, any color silk, for police belts and clubs	6 00	50
" 122.	Wreath and numbers complete for privates' caps, German silver.................	3 00	30
" 123.	" " " " officers' caps, gold embroidery	1 50	2 50
	" " " " " gilt "	1 00	2 00
" 144.	English Worsted Web Belts, 2 inches wide, in blue red, three and red and white stripes (mostly), russet leather finish, 1 buckle.................	5 00	0 50
" 145.	English Worsted Web Belts, same as No. 143, with Gold Gilt Clasp, with base ball emblems.................	6 50	0 65
" 146.	Base Ball Clasps, as used on belt No. 145.................	2 00	0 25

AMERICAN UNION WEB BELTS.

Of this grade of Webbing we make but two styles. It is 2¼ inches wide, very strong, with leather finish; strap and buckle, made in lengths 24 to 36 inches long.

No. 148.	Red Centre, white narrow border.................	3 00	0 30
" 149.	Blue " " "	3 00	0 30
" 150.	Cartridge Waist Belts, made of strong russet leather, strap to go over the shoulder, loops for holding firm, from 30 to 40 cartridges, of from 10 to 12 calibre. (See cut No. 150).................	2 50 to	3 50
" 151.	Trout Basket Belts, made of Web and Leather. Length of web 20x2¼ inches wide; leather strap 36 inches long. Two qualities................each	0 40 and	0 60

RIBBON BADGES AND ROSETTES, for Base Ball Clubs, Parties and Societies.

(These illustrations are half exact size.)

Any colored ribbon badges with emblem or name stamped on fine silk ribbon, not less than one dozen at a time, per doz................. $2 00

The above with the following emblems thereon at the same price, viz.: Anchor, Yacht (under sail), Eagle, Masonic or Odd Fellows, Base Ball, Boating, etc. Monograms cut to order will cost $1.00 a letter; special emblems to order at a low price, according to design. Badges for Societies, Balls, or special occasions, elaborate design, in any colored silk, embossed in gold, trimmed with rosettes and gold or silver tassels, according to finish, from $3.00 to $6.00, $9.00, $12.00, $15.00 and $18.00 per dozen, special prices for quantities of fifty or more at a time.

Ribbon Rosettes for Societies, Pic-Nics, Clubs, Committees, &c., &c.—We furnish raised rosettes of any colored satin ribbon, with gold or silver star in centre; each, 50 cts....... ....per dozen, $4 00

We make a very elaborate rosette trimmed with two silver or gold tassels, by mail, each, 75 cents; Per dozen.................$8 00

BASE BALL BELTS. IMPORTED ENGLISH WORSTED WEB FOR BELTS.

Imported Worsted Web Belts. These belts have become extremely popular among ball players, gymnasts, and the boating fraternity where it is necessary that nothing should impede the motion of the body in the various attitudes. This has been the objection to heavy leather belts, and thus these are preferable. These belts are made of the best material, 2¼ inches wide, russet leather finish, Single or Double Straps, ⅞ and ⅝ inch buckles, and made any length to suit size of waist. We always keep several hundred dozens on hand. We keep in stock the following styles:

No.	Description	Price
125.	White Centre, 2 inches wide, red edges ½ inch wide. (See cut.)	
126.	" " " blue " " "	
128.	" " ½ inch " " 1 inch "	
129.	" " 1 inch " red and blue edge, each ¼ inch wide	$4.00 per doz.
B.	Solid Brown, 2 inches wide	40 cts. each.
B½.	White Centre, 2 inches wide, brown edge ½ inch wide	
130.	Solid Red, 2¼ inches wide	
131.	" Blue, " "	
132.	" White, " "	
133.	" Green, " "	
134.	Blue Centre, 2 inches, white edge, ½ inch wide	
136.	Red and White Cross Bars	
141.	White Centre, 2 inches wide, red edges, ½ inch wide, with name Captain worked in red block letters on back. (Extra fine Web)	8 00 0 75
142.	White Centre, 2 inches, blue edges, ½ inch wide, with name Captain worked in blue block letters on back. (Extra fine Web)	8 00 0 75

Cotton Web Belts, assorted colors. Red, white, blue, navy. Blue and white stripes, and red and white stripes. 25 cents each, $2 50 dozen.

BASE BALL SHOES. Best Quality.

The superior grade of shoes that we offer our customers are made expressly for our trade, and are much better than most canvas goods that are offered.

	Per Doz. pair without spikes.	Per Pair without spikes.
No. 1.—Professional Calfskin Leather Shoe. A handsome and serviceable shoe	$30 00	3 00
No. 2.—Our League Club Base Ball Shoe. Made of extra heavy white canvas, foxed all around with russet calf trimmings, extra instep strap and toe strap. The most durable canvas shoe that we make. (If with spikes, add price of spikes as per list)	24 00	2 50
No. 3.—Our Standard Base Ball Shoe. Made of strong, white canvas, with extra calf-trimmed toe and instep straps. A good, honest shoe. (Add price of spikes)	18 00	1 75
No. 4.—Our Popular Brown Canvas Shoe. The best low-priced shoe made	12 00	1 25

FOOT-BALL SUITS. JACKETS.

No. A 1.—Canvas Jackets, made from finest quality goods; all seams double-stitched with silk; patent gusset at arm-hole, affording ease of motion; improved pattern throughout, same Jacket used by Yale, Harvard, Princeton and all the large colleges......each $2 00

FOOT-BALL PANTS.

No.	Description	Price
A 2.—Canvas Knee Pants, same goods as Jackets		per pair $2 00
A 3.—Grey Flannel " medium quality		" 2 00
A 4 " " best quality		" 3 00
A 4½—Brown or Drab Corduroy, good quality		" 2 75
A 5 " " best quality		" 3 50
A 6.—Tight-fitting Worsted, all colors		" 3 00

FOOT-BALL JERSEYS.

No.	Description	Price
A 7.—Worsted Jerseys, best quality, with Collar, all colors	each $4 00
A 8 " " " striped	" 4 25
A 9 " " without Collar, plain	" 3 50
A 10 " " " striped	" 4 00
A 11 " heavy weight, blue or white	" 3 50

FOOT-BALL STOCKINGS.

No.	Description	Price
A 12.—Best ribbed Worsted Stockings, extra long, all colors	per pair $1 50
A 13—P. & S. Brand Special " " "	" 1 00
A 14—Heavy Cotton Ribbed " " "	" 0 50

These are the three leading styles. We have several other grades on hand at all times, and are constantly adding new colors and styles. The Worsted Stockings come in grey, navy blue, cardinal, seal brown, royal blue, black, and garnet.

FOOT-BALL CAPS.

No.	Description	Price
80.—Tight-fitting Short Worsted Caps	each $0 75
81 " " " striped	" 0 85
85 " Long " plain	" 1 50
86 " " " striped	" 1 75

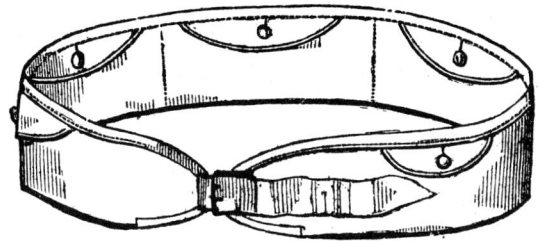

No. 124. Money Belts, made of good solid Chamois Skin and Silk Elastic Web in middle of belt, bound all around with silk ribbon, and with six to eight pockets to hold gold, silver and paper money $1 00

IMPORTED ENGLISH WORSTED WEB FOR BELTS.

Imported Worsted Web Belts. These belts have become extremely popular among ball players, gymnasts, and the boating fraternity where it is necessary that nothing should impede the motion of the body in the various attitudes. This has been the objection to heavy leather belts, and thus these are preferable. These belts are made of the best material, 2¼ inches wide, russet leather finish, Single Straps, ⅞ buckles, and made any length to suit size of waist. We always keep several hundred dozens on hand. We keep in stock the following styles:

Cut No. 3.

STOCKING SUPPORTERS.

See Cut No. 3.

Better than anything yet invented, of great value to Bicycle Riders, Lawn Tennis and Base Ball players and on any occasion where knee breeches are worn. Always keeping the Stocking in place, and positively preventing the Stocking slipping down that so often occurs, when it is not properly fastened. Made up neat and strong, with band around waist. Per pair, 35c.

Without waist band.................. " 25c.

The Waist Garter is better adjusted to use for long Stockings, as the weight is equally distributed around the waist, and does not come all in one place, as is the case with those without the waistband. These Supporters are made of best elastic web, with adjustable slides and patent fastenings.

We also make them in Silk, a very handsome and durable Supporter. Price, per pair, $1 00

SHIRT FRONTS, SHIELDS, INITIALS, MONOGRAMS.

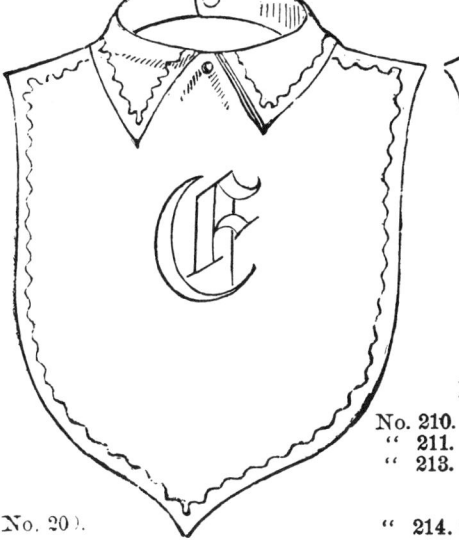

No. 209.

No. 214.

No. 209. Peck's Combination Shirt Front. This is the best substitute for a shirt ever made. It is neat, showy and sure to fit. It is made of the very best flannel, and bound with the finest braid, with initial letter of the club on front, any color to suit. For measure and size of collar worn, see cut No. 209.

Per doz............$6.00
Each............ ...60c

	doz.	each
No. 210. Initial letters for shirt fronts, any color......	$1 50	15
" 211. Monogram letters for shirt fronts, any color..	3 00	30
" 213. Shirt fronts made of the best flannel and bound with braid, any color wished, and with initial or number of club on..........	4 00	40
" 214. Shirt fronts, any color flannel or pattern to suit, with full name across front. (See cut.).	5 00	50

PECK & SNYDER, Importers and Dealers in every variety of Ladies' and Gent's Lawn Tennis, Bathing and Gymnasium shoes, also for Base Ball, Cricket, Yachting, Boating, Running, Pedestrian, Fencing and Shoes for all Sporting purposes.

For description and prices of these Shoes, see following page.

BASE BALL, CRICKET, BOATING, LAWN TENNIS, GYMNASIUM SHOES, &c.

The superior grade of shoes that we offer our customers are made expressly for our trade, and are much better than most canvas goods that are offered.

	Per doz. pair without spikes.	Per pair without spikes.
No. 1.—**Our Professional Walking Shoe.** These shoes are of Drab Canvas, with calf trimmings and hand sewed throughout, with extra broad low heels and broad soles; they make a most desirable shoe for summer tramping	$42 00	$4 00
No. 2.—**Our League Club Base Ball Shoe.** Made of extra heavy white canvas, foxed all around with russet calf trimmings, extra instep strap and toe strap. The most durable canvas shoe that we make. (If with spikes, add price of spikes as per list)	24 00	2 50
No. 3.—**Our Standard Base Ball Shoe.** Made of strong, white canvas, with extra calf-trimmed toe and instep straps. A good, honest shoe. (Add price of spikes)	18 00	1 75
No. 4.—**Our Popular Seaside Canvas Shoe.** Made of blue canvas with russet leather trimmings. A very desirable shoe	12 00	1 25
Boys' and Youths' sizes of the above, Nos. 10, 11, 12, 1, 2, 3 and 4	10 00	1 00
No. 5.—**Our Summer Oxford Boating or Base Ball Shoe.** Made of white canvas with extra instep and toe straps, with heavy sole and heel as in (No. 3)	18 00	1 75
No. 6.—**Our Popular Boating Shoe.** Same as No. 5, only with a light weight single sole and single lift on heels for boating	18 00	1 75

	Per pair.
No. 7.—**Our Popular French Slipper** white canvas uppers and rubber soles, which we warrant to hold fast. (See illustration)	$1 25
No. 8.—The same in blue, brown or gray, extra heavy	1 75
No. 9.—**Our Standard Domestic Tennis Shoe,** of strong white or brown canvas, with corrugated rubber soles, (See illustration)	2 00
No. 10.—**Our Superior Hand Sewed American Made Shoe,** equal in most respects to the best imported. Made in brown or white canvas, with russet calf trimmings and Pyramid rubber soles, (Same style as No. 9)	3 00
No. 11.—**Imported London Made Tennis Shoes,** with russet trimmings, corrugated soles in brown or white canvas, (See illustrations)	5 00
No. 12.—**Our Finest Imported Shoe,** in blue, brown or white canvas, with russet calf trimmings, hand sewed, with pliable pyramid soles. (See cut)	6 00
No. 13.—**Gents' or Ladies' Low Cut,** Calf or Alligator Skin, russet or maroon color, hand sewed, with pyramid soles (Style same as No. 12	6 00
No. 14.—**High Cut,** brown canvas hand sewed with pyramid soles. A popular shoe. (See cut).	4 00

In addition to the above regular line, we have on hand and make to order various styles and widths of Ladies' and Gent's Shoes. When ordering by mail, send size usually worn. Sizes exchanged if not satisfactory. Sample pairs can be sent by registered mail for 35 cents in addition to the price which must accompany the order. New soles put on old shoes as good as new..................Per pair, $2 00

No. 22.	Fencing Shoes, made of tan colored leather; fancy trimmed and bound, with rough leather soles to prevent slipping	$4 00
" 23.	Gymnasium or Theatrical high cut shoes, made of white canvas, and bound with colored leather. (See cut)	1 50
" 24.	Gymnasium or Theatrical high cut Shoes, made of black Morocco Kip	3 00
" 25.	Peck & Snyder's Gymnasium low cut Slippers, made of white canvas, with shir string to tighten at the ankle. Hand Sewed.............$7 50	0 75
" 26.	Gymnasium or Theatrical Slipper, same pattern as No. 25, but made of Black Morocco or Kip 15 00	1 50
" 27.	Yachting Shoes, Oxford low cut, made of fine canvas, leather trimmed toes, insteps and heels; patent hard rubber soles, with suction so as not to slip on wet decks, English make, imported	6 00
" 28.	English Running Shoes made of black kid leather uppers, oak-tanned soles, with steel spikes inserted between the soles. Imported, (see cut)	5 00
" 29.	American Running Shoes after the style of English, of black calfskin leather, with English spikes. A desirable shoe for amateurs	3 00
" 30.	American Running Shoes same as 29, in every respect, but without spikes	2 50
" 31.	English Running Shoe Spikes (imported) per set of 10	0 50

PECK & SNYDER'S UMPIRE'S ASSISTANT.

This New Counter no doubt will become an Invaluable Assistant to Umpires in keeping a correct Tally of Balls and Strikes, without confusing one with the other. It is made of Brass, Nickle-plated, and exact size of this illustration, it is a convenient size for the pocket and is not liable to get out of order.

Sent by Mail, on receipt of price, 50 cents.

SHOE SPIKES FOR CRICKET, BASE BALL, RUNNING, ETC.

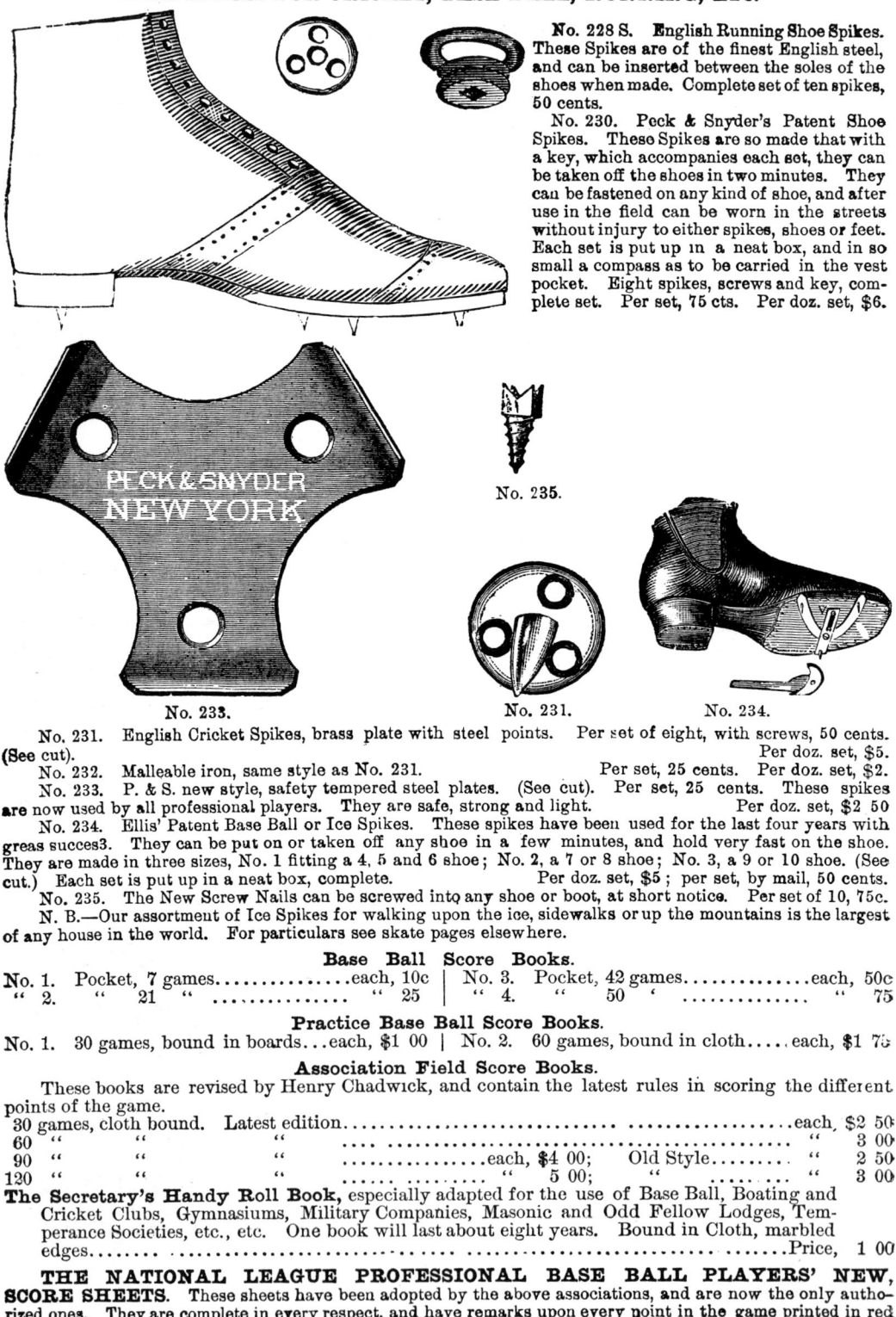

No. 228 S. English Running Shoe Spikes. These Spikes are of the finest English steel, and can be inserted between the soles of the shoes when made. Complete set of ten spikes, 50 cents.

No. 230. Peck & Snyder's Patent Shoe Spikes. These Spikes are so made that with a key, which accompanies each set, they can be taken off the shoes in two minutes. They can be fastened on any kind of shoe, and after use in the field can be worn in the streets without injury to either spikes, shoes or feet. Each set is put up in a neat box, and in so small a compass as to be carried in the vest pocket. Eight spikes, screws and key, complete set. Per set, 75 cts. Per doz. set, $6.

No. 231. English Cricket Spikes, brass plate with steel points. Per set of eight, with screws, 50 cents. (See cut). Per doz. set, $5.

No. 232. Malleable iron, same style as No. 231. Per set, 25 cents. Per doz. set, $2.

No. 233. P. & S. new style, safety tempered steel plates. (See cut). Per set, 25 cents. Per doz. set, $2 50. These spikes are now used by all professional players. They are safe, strong and light.

No. 234. Ellis' Patent Base Ball or Ice Spikes. These spikes have been used for the last four years with great success. They can be put on or taken off any shoe in a few minutes, and hold very fast on the shoe. They are made in three sizes, No. 1 fitting a 4, 5 and 6 shoe; No. 2, a 7 or 8 shoe; No. 3, a 9 or 10 shoe. (See cut.) Each set is put up in a neat box, complete. Per doz. set, $5; per set, by mail, 50 cents.

No. 235. The New Screw Nails can be screwed into any shoe or boot, at short notice. Per set of 10, 75c.

N. B.—Our assortment of Ice Spikes for walking upon the ice, sidewalks or up the mountains is the largest of any house in the world. For particulars see skate pages elsewhere.

Base Ball Score Books.

No. 1. Pocket, 7 games..............each, 10c | No. 3. Pocket, 42 games..............each, 50c
" 2. " 21 " .... " 25 | " 4. " 50 " .... " 75

Practice Base Ball Score Books.

No. 1. 30 games, bound in boards...each, $1 00 | No. 2. 60 games, bound in cloth.....each, $1 75

Association Field Score Books.

These books are revised by Henry Chadwick, and contain the latest rules in scoring the different points of the game.

30 games, cloth bound. Latest edition..each, $2 50
60 " " " ..... " 3 00
90 " " " ....each, $4 00; Old Style......... " 2 50
120 " " " .... " 5 00; " " 3 00

The Secretary's Handy Roll Book, especially adapted for the use of Base Ball, Boating and Cricket Clubs, Gymnasiums, Military Companies, Masonic and Odd Fellow Lodges, Temperance Societies, etc., etc. One book will last about eight years. Bound in Cloth, marbled edges. ....Price, 1 00

THE NATIONAL LEAGUE PROFESSIONAL BASE BALL PLAYERS' NEW, SCORE SHEETS. These sheets have been adopted by the above associations, and are now the only authorized ones. They are complete in every respect, and have remarks upon every point in the game printed in red and black, upon good, heavy paper, and bound in pads of 50 each. Size, 8 x 10½ inches.

Price of pad, by mail, 65 cents.

IMPROVED WATER-PROOF CATCHERS' GLOVES.

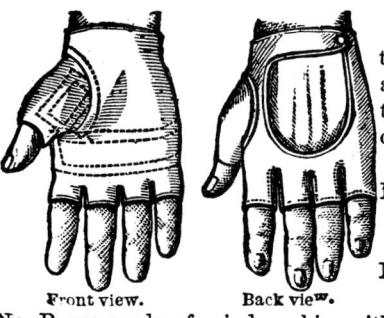

Front view.   Back view.

Sizes of gloves are 7¼ to 10. These gloves are made open up the back of the hand, so as not to confine the hand in any way, and are made in sizes the same as a kid glove. The leather that these gloves are made of is soft and pliable to the hand, and cannot be made hard with water or perspiration.

Per Pair.

No. A x, or Professional are made of extra heavy buckskin, with half fingers, and palm of hand full padded.. $2 50
No. A, are made of Indian tanned buckskin, with half fingers and palm of hand full padded......... 2 00
No. B, are made of reindeer skin, with half fingers, and palm of hand full padded.......... 1 50
No. C, are made of soft fine tan leather, half fingers, padded palm........................... 1 00
No. D, are made of soft tan color leather, same pattern as above, but palm not padded........ 75
No. E. A good stout Boys' Glove... 50
No. F. Boys' Catcher Gloves... 25

We can furnish A x, A, B and C with left hand glove made full size with fingers if wanted.
Any of the above gloves sent by mail, postage paid, upon receipt of price.

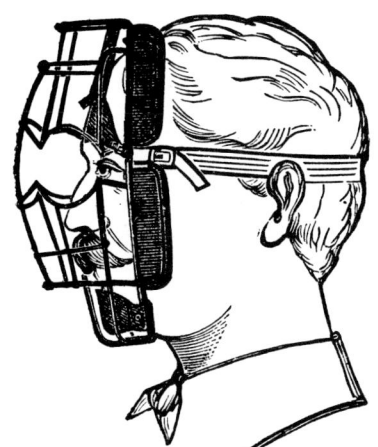

PECK & SNYDER'S IMPROVED CATCHER'S MASK.

This Mask has been in use for the past two years, and is pronounced by our most prominent Catchers the best made.

They are made of wire, in such a manner that they can be bent or shaped to fit any size face, with eye holes so as not to obstruct the vision, and padded with soft leather cushions, with chin and forehead rests and are light, and easy to adjust.

Each.

No. 1, Youth's $1 75
" 2, Men's 2 00
" 3, Professional............................... 3 00

PRIZE.

THE CHAMPION BASE BALL BADGE.

(CUT EXACT SIZE AND PATTERN.)

This is one of the showiest and neatest Badges made, and without exception the cheapest. Is made solid and Nickel Plated.

Each, 10 cents, 3 for 25 cents, 9 for 50 cents, 60 cents per dozen.

Sent by mail, postage paid, upon receipt of price.

THE PRIZE BASE BALL BADGE.

(CUT EXACT SIZE AND PATTERN.)

Prices and terms same as the "Champion Badge."

CHAMPION.

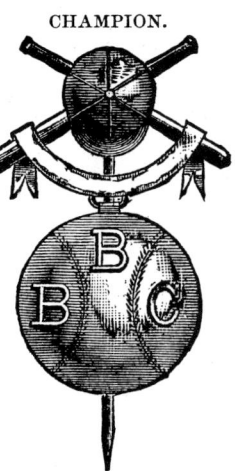

N. B.—We will send one each Popular Base Ball Belt, Cap, and Base Ball Badge by Mail, postage paid for 25 cents.

Front View.

Back View.

PECK & SNYDER'S PROFESSIONAL CATCHER'S GLOVES.

No. 1. Made of extra heavy buckskin, full padded Left hand glove has sole leather finger tips, to protect fingers from low curved balls. Right hand glove is made open back and half fingers. (see cut) .... Per Pair, $5 00

No. 2. Made same style as No. 1, excepting quality of leather, which is lighter............................... Per Pair, $4 00

No. 3. Same as No. 1, without sole leather finger tips......... Per Pair, $3 00

No. 4. Same as No. 2, without sole leather finger tips .... Per Pair, $2 50

No. 15.

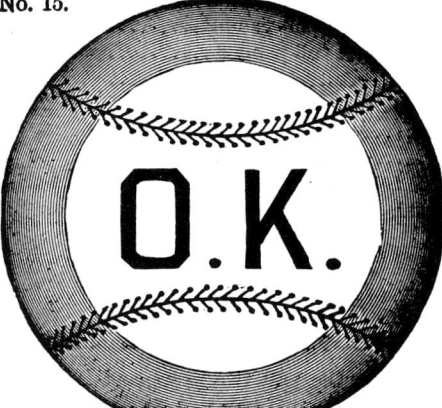

PECK & SNYDER'S POPULAR BASE BALLS.

This is the best Ball in the market at the price.

No. 15. Price, each 5 cents, per dozen 50 cents. These we do not send by mail.

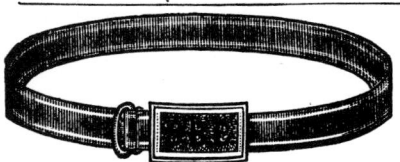

BOYS' POPULAR BASE BALL BELTS.

No. 1, in red and white, with buckle like cut.
No. 2, same as above, in blue and white.

Price, 10 cents each, 3 for 25 cents, 9 for 50 cents, 60 cents per dozen.

Sent by mail, postage paid, upon receipt of price.

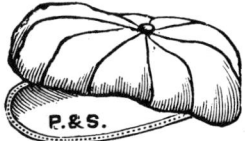

BOY'S POPULAR BASE BALL CAPS.

No. 1. Red and White.
" 2. Blue and White.

Price, 10 cents each, 3 for 25 cents, 9 for 50 cents, 60 cents per dozen.
Sent by mail, postage paid, upon receipt of price.

Peck & Snyder's Safety Steel Shoe Spike.

These spikes have been in use among the most prominent players for the past five years, and are now pronounced the lightest, cheapest and best Spike in use.

Price, complete, per doz. sets with screws, each set in an envelope.

$2.00 per dozen, 20 cents per pair.

CANVAS BASES.

Complete sets, consisting of 3 Bags, 3 Straps, 3 Pins and Staples, and the Regulation Marble Home Plate.

No. 277.—1st quality, per set complete.. $4 00
No. 277 —2d quality, per set complete.. 3 50

FIELD SCORE BOOKS.

ASSOCIATION FIELD SCORE BOOKS.

30 games, cloth bound.............. ..each, $1 50
60 " " " .... " 2 00
90 " " " .... " 3 00
120 " " " .... " 4 00

PRACTICE B. B. SCORE BOOKS.

No. 1. 30 games, bound in boards..... each, $1 00
" 2. 60 " " " cloth....... " 1 50
Score Pads, 50 games .... " 50

POCKET SCORE BOOKS.

No. 1. Pocket, 7 games.............. each, $0 10
" 2. " 21 " .... " 25
" 3. " 42 " .... " 50
" 4. " 60 " .... " 75
Score Cards.... 3
" ....per 100, 1 00

BASE BALL UNIFORMS COMPLETE.

In addition to our three grades of Uniforms, that met with such general favor last season, we have this spring added two new lines: One at $13.50, and one at $5.00. The 13.50 grade as our best, and the $5.00 grade as our lowest-priced uniform. These, combined with our $7.00, $8.50 and $10.00 uniforms, make a line of suits, in quality and price, that must afford satisfaction to all.

COMPLETE UNIFORM "X" $13.50. Consists of

Extra Quality, Heavy Flannel Shirt, | Best Quality, English Worsted Belt,
" " " Knee Pants, | " " Fine Calfskin Shoes, Professional,
" " Hat or College Cap, | " " Safety Steel Plates.
" " Ex. long Ribbed Worsted Stockings, |

COMPLETE UNIFORM "A" $10.00, Consists of

Best Quality Heavy Flannel Shirt, | Best Quality, English Worsted Web Belt,
" " " Knee Pants, | " " Professional Canvas Shoes, best made.
" " Hat or College Cap, | " " Safety Steel Plates.
" " Ex. long Ribbed Worsted Stockings. |

COMPLETE UNIFORM, "B" $8.50, Consists of

Good Quality, Medium weight Flannel Shirt, | Good Quality Worsted Web Belt,
" " " " Knee Pants, | " " Canvas Shoes,
" " Hat or College Cap, | Best " Safety Steel Plates.
" " Ex. long Ribbed Cotton Stockings, |

COMPLETE UNIFORM "C" $7.00, Consists of

Second Quality, Flannel Shirt, | Second Quality Cotton Belt,
" " " Knee Pants, | " " Blue Canvas Shoes,
" " Worsted or Cotton Stockings, | Best " Safety Steel Plates.
" " College or Regatta Caps, |

Please mention when ordering Shoes, if you wish high or low cut.

COMPLETE UNIFORM "D" $5.00, Consists of

Fair Quality Flannel Shirt, | Good Quality Cotton Belt,
" " " Knee Pants, | " " Brown Canvas Shoes,
" " Cotton Stockings, | Best " Safety Steel Plates.
" " College Cap, |

This grade of Suit is made of Cotton and Wool mixture, and makes a very strong Suit.

SACK COATS FOR ANY OF THESE SUITS MADE FROM SAME MATERIAL, AS FOLLOWS:

No. X Quality...$6 00 Each.
" A " .... 4 75 "
" B " .... 4 00 "
" C " .... 3 00 "
" D " .... 2 25 "

Cut good shape and well made.

DIRECTIONS FOR SELF-MEASUREMENT.

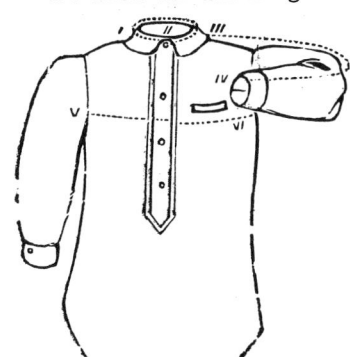

Give exact Measurement.
We allow for Shrinkage.

Please be particular and give full instructions as to how you want each article made and trimmed, color of trimmings, style and number of cap or hat, whether pockets in pants or not, etc., so there can be no chance of misunderstanding your order. By following these instructions, you will insure prompt attention, and your order will be filled to your satisfaction.

For Shirt, size of collar worn; length of arm from center of back to wrist, 3 to 4; size around chest, 5 to 6.

For Pants—Size around waist, 1 to 2; length of outseam, 3 to 4; length of inseam, 5 to 6.

For Coat—Same as Shirt measure.

Prices for Suits include 4 inch letter or initial on Shirt front.

Complete name of Club in two-inch letters on shirt. 5 cents each letter.

Base Ball Shirts are made either laced, buttoned, pleated or shield fronts.

REEVE'S ERYTHROXYLON COCO TROCHE.—Invaluable to Base Ball Players, Cricketers, Rowers, Gymnasts, Athletes, and Sportsmen in general. These Troches are prepared with the pure Extract of the Erythroxylon Coco Leaves. "as used by Weston the American Pedestrian," Cavill, the champion swimmer, and others; carefully selected from Bolivia, which has the reputation of producing the best. Combined with the Extract of Coco is a small proportion of phosphate of lime and other ingredients, which are well-known to have great tonic and invigorating powers. The Troches are convenient and exceedingly pleasant to take, and are now acknowledged throughout the world to be the greatest tonic extant. The proprietor (T. L. Reeve) is now having a pamphlet published containing many testimonials and interesting details from athletes and eminent men, including Sir Robert Christison, M.D., Edinburgh, who has had experience with the Coco and obtained marvelous results. The Pamphlet, when complete, will be forwarded to any address on application. The Troches may be given to delicate children with great advantage. Dose, according to age.

Price, per box, by mail, 25 cents.

PECK & SNYDER, 126, 128 & 130 NASSAU STREET, NEW YORK.

C. C., No. 5.
The Pleated Adirondack Flannel Shirt, in White and Light Weight Mixtures.

C. C., No. 3.
Orient, White Flannel, Buttoned Shirt.

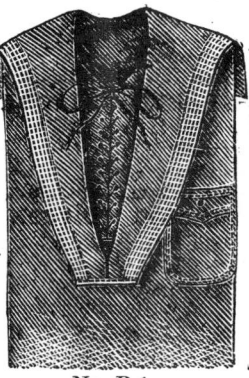

No. B-1.
Yachting Shirt. Fast Color, Navy Blue.

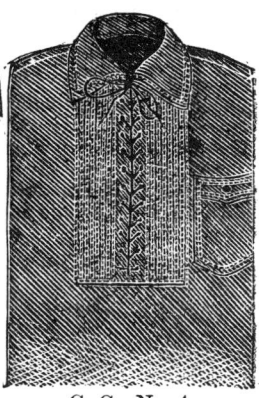

C. C., No. 4.
"Orient" Laced Tennis Shirt, White and Colors.

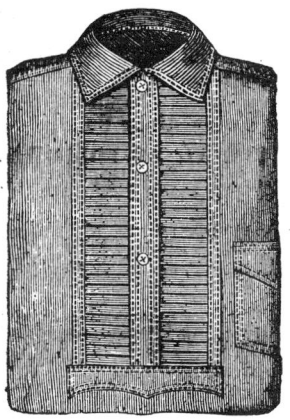

C. C., No. 9.
The "Cavalier," Cross Pleated Shirt, All Colors.

C. C., No. 10.
Lawn Tennis, Patent Laced Shirt. All Colors.

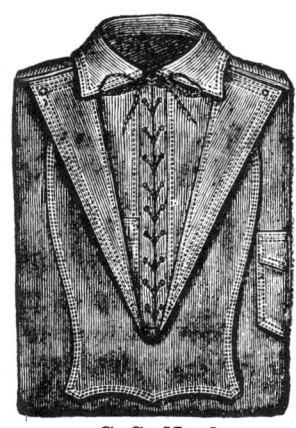

C. C., No. 8.
The "Newport." New Style Yachting and Tennis Shirt. All Colors.

A. A., No. 1.
Pleated Norfolk Jackets. All Colors.

X, No. 2.
Corduroy Bicycle Coats. All Colors.

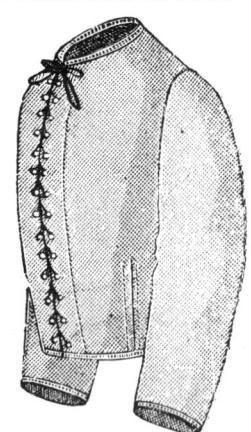

A, No. 1.
Canvas Foot Ball Jackets.

Manufacturers of Every Style of Sporting Shirts, Blouses, Jackets, Etc.

TENNIS, TOURISTS' AND CRICKET SUITS FOR THE LAWN, THE SEASIDE AND THE MOUNTAIN.

Of these suits we have in stock a large and complete assortment of low, medium and high priced goods. All colors and weights in coats, pants, knickerbockers, suits, hats, caps, stockings, belts, etc. Particular attention given to our order department. Suits made in two or three days. Prices right.

No. AA.—NORFOLK JACKETS.—*See illustrated pages.*

No.	Description	Price
1	Pleated Norfolk Jackets. Navy Blue. Fast Color. Good quality....each	$6 50
2	" " " " " " " Best " "	8 00
3	" " " Grey or Brown. " " "	8 00
4	" " " White Flannel. " " "	9 50
5	" " " Assorted Colors. Serge. " " "	12 00

No. BB.—SACK COATS. (4 Buttons.)

No.	Description	Price
1	White Flannel. Sack Coats. Good quality....each	$6 00
2	" " " " Best " "	8 00
3	Navy Blue Flannel. Sack Coats. Good quality. "	6 00
4	Striped Flannel. " " Neat Patterns. Good Quality. "	6 00
5	" " " " Polka Dots, Stripes, etc. "	8 00

No. CC.—SHIRTS. (Flannel.)—*See illustrated pages.*

No.	Description	Price
1	Fine Light Weight. Striped Button Shirts. Neat and attractive designs....each	$3 00
2	" " " " " " Best Quality. Very Fine Pattern "	3 50
3	"Orient Brand" Fine White Buttoned Shirts	3 50
4	" " " " " Laced "	3 50
5	"The Adirondack" Fine White Pleated and Buttoned Shirts	3 75
6	"The Feather Weight" Pleated and Buttoned Shirts, Light Mixtures	3 50
7	"The Adirondack" Pleated Flannel Shirts in Grey and Colors.	3 25
8	"The Newport" Laced " " " " " "	3 00
9	"The Cavalier" " Cross Pleated in Grey and Colors	2 75
10	The Lawn Tennis Patent Laced Shirts in all Colors	3 00
11	White Flannel Buttoned or Lace Shirts.	2 50
12	The "Demet" White Flannel Laced Shirt	1 00

We have in stock, and are constantly adding, new lines and styles of shirts—making the largest assortment to be found at any one establishment.

No. DD.—WORSTED TENNIS JERSEYS.—*See illustrated pages.*

These popular garments are made in all colors and styles. No extra charge for making to order of any special color.

No.	Description	Price
1	Laced Tennis Jerseys. Best Worsted. Any Color....each	$5 00
2	" " " " " Striped Collars and Cuffs "	5 00
3	" " " " " " Body, Collars and Cuffs. "	5 00
4	Closed " " " Standing Collar. Any Color. "	4 00
5	" " " " " " Striped "	4 25
6	" " " " Rolling " Any Color "	4 00
7	Pure Silk Jerseys (to order only)....each $20 00 to	25 00
8	A Good Worsted Jersey in Navy Blue or Maroon	3 00

No. EE.—TROUSERS.

No.	Description	Price
1	Orient Brand. White Flannel Trousers....per pair	$3 50
2	Best Quality Heavy Flannel Trousers in White, Yale Grey, Blue Mixed and Navy Blue. "	5 00
3	Best Quality English Flannel Trousers. White. "	8 00
4	" " " " Navy Blue Serge Trousers "	6 00
5	Good " Flannel Trousers in Navy Blue, Grey, or Brown "	3 50
6	" " " " in White or Grey "	3 00
7	Corduroy " Brown or Drab. "	5 00

No. FF.—KNEE PANTS.

No.	Description	Price
1	"Orient" Brand White Flannel Knee Pants....per pair	$3 00
2	Best Quality Heavy Flannel " " in White, Yale Grey, Navy Blue, Blue Mixed "	4 00
3	Best Quality English Flannel Knee Pants in White. "	6 25
4	" " " Serge " " in Navy Blue. "	4 50
5	Good " Flannel Knee Pants. Navy Blue, Grey or Brown "	3 00
6	" " " " in Grey or White "	2 25
7	Corduroy Knee Pants. Brown or Drab. "	3 50
8	Knit Worsted Knee Pants. Brown, Black or Navy. Very fine. "	4 00

No. GG.—TENNIS STOCKINGS.—*See illustrated pages.*

No.	Description	Price
1	Best Quality. Ribbed Worsted Hose. All Colors....per pair	$1 50
2	" " " " " Extra Heavy. English Mixture. "	2 00
3	"Our Special" Make. Ribbed Worsted Hose. All Colors. "	1 00
4	" " " " Cotton Hose. All Colors "	50
5	Heavy Silk Ribbed Hose. " Very Fine "	5 00

X 39.	Cloth Helmets, patent ventilated, in colors. Navy Blue, Grey, Brown	$1 50
X 40.	Canvas and Linen Helmets	75c., $1 00 and 1 50
X 42.	Cloth Hats, Grey, Blue, White, etc.	$1 00 " 1 50
X 43.	Canvas " White and Drab	75c. " 1 00
X 44.	"Pull-over" Caps. Checks and Stripes	$1 00 " 1 50
X 45.	Gold or Silver Initials for Caps, 7c. each.	

No. P P.—BICYCLE STOCKINGS.—See illustrated pages.

X 46.	Heavy Ribbed Worsted Stockings, English mixtures	pair	$2 00
X 47.	" " Plain Colors	"	1 50
X 48.	"Our Special" Make Worsted Stockings, Plain Colors and Grey	"	1 00
X 49.	" " " Cotton " " " "	"	50
X 50.	Heavy Silk Ribbed " " "	"	5 00
X 51.	Stocking Supporters, with Waistband, 35c. Without Waistband, 25c.		

A special price to Clubs ordering in quantities, and estimates furnished for every desired style of uniform.

BASE BALL SHIRTS, PANTS, Etc.—Separate.

BASE BALL SHIRTS.—See illustrated pages.

Made either in laced, buttoned or shield fronts, and trimmed any color desired.

No. X.	—Best Quality Heavy Flannel. White, Blue, Grey, etc.	per doz.	$48 00
A.	Fine " " " White, Blue, Grey, Brown, etc.	"	36 00
B.	" " " Good Weight Flannel. Grey, White, Blue, etc.	"	30 00
C.	" " " Cotton and Wool mixed Flannel. White, Grey and Brown	"	24 00
D.	Good Strong Cotton mixed Flannel. Brown, White and Grey	"	16 50

BASE BALL PANTS.—See illustrated pages.

Made to buckle or button at knee, trimmed to match shirts.

No. X.	—Best quality goods to match Shirts	per doz.	$48 00
A.	Fine " " " " "	"	36 00
B.	" " Good Weight. To match shirts	"	30 00
C.	" " Cotton and Wool mixed. To match Shirts	"	24 00
D.	Good Strong Cotton mixed. To match Shirts	"	16 50

Pants and Shirts may be made of different colors in same grade suit if preferred.

BASE BALL COATS.—See illustrated pages.

No. X.	—Flannel Sack Coat. Same material as Suits. Each	$6 00
A.	" " " " " " " "	4 75
B.	" " " " " " " "	4 00
C.	" " " " " " " "	3 00
D.	" " " " " " " "	2 25

BASE BALL HATS AND CAPS.—See illustrated pages.

No. 1.	—Our Popular "College Cap." Square crown	Each,	75c.	Doz.	$8 00
2	" " 2d Quality "College Cap." Square crown	"	60c.	"	6 00
3	" " Rage Cap. Eight cornered. Pull over visor	"	75c.	"	8 00
4	" " " 2d Quality. Eight cornered. Pull over visor	"	50c.	"	5 00
5	" Cheap Rage Cap. 3d " " " " "	"	35c.	"	3 50
6	Jockey Shape Caps. All colors. Leather visor	"	75c.	"	8 00
7	No. 300 Base Ball Hat. All colors, trimmed with silk	"	$1 50	"	15 00
8	No. 300 P " " Same Hat, but without lining	"	1 25	"	12 00

BASE BALL STOCKINGS.

MADE EXTRA STRONG, ESPECIALLY FOR OUR TRADE.—See illustrated pages.

No. 1.	—Best Heavy Ribbed Worsted Stockings, all Colors	Pair	$1 50	Doz.	$16 00
2.	—Our Special " " " " " "	"	1 00	"	10 00
3.	—No. 237 Medium Weight " " Navy, Red, Brown or Blue	"	75	"	8 00
4.	—Our Special " " Cotton " " " " " "	"	50	"	5 00
6.	—" " Striped Worsted " " (to order only)	"	1 50	"	15 00
7.	—Any Special Color to order. Average price	"	1 50	"	15 00

We have in stock a Job Lot of Odd Colors in All Wool Stockings at 35c. a pair; good value at 75c. A good chance for clubs who want a Low-priced Stocking.

BALL PLAYERS' ELASTICS.—See illustrated pages.

We are now manufacturing a full line of Silk Elastic Goods, especially adapted to the use of base ball players, athletes, gymnasts, etc., for all parts of the arm or leg. They are invaluable in cases of sprains, weak joints, varicose veins, tired muscles, etc. Being direct manufacturers we are able to offer this line of goods at prices that will bring them within reach of all.

No. 1.—Silk Elastic Wristlets	Each, $ 75	No. 5.—Silk Elastic Shoulder Cup	Each,	$2 25
" 2.— " " Elbow Cup	" 1 50	" 6.— " " Knee	"	2 00
" 3.— " " Muscle	" 1 25	" 7.— " " Stocking	"	4 50
" 4.— " " Forearm	" 1 00	" 8.— " " Ankle	"	3 00

6 Stocking Supporters, with Waist Band	per pair	$0 35
7 " " without Waist Band	"	25

All of these Stockings come in following colors: Navy Blue, Royal Blue, Seal Brown, Black Cardinal, Grey and Garnet.

No. HH.—TENNIS HATS AND CAPS.—*See illustrated pages.*

No. 1.—Our "Popular." White Flannel Tennis Hat	each	$1 50
2 " " Tennis Hat in Blue, Brown or Grey	"	1 25
3 " " " " in Brown or Drab Corduroy	"	1 50
4 " " " " in Striped Flannels	"	1 50
5 Light Weight Felt Tennis Hat in all Colors	"	1 25
6 White or Drab Duck Hat	75c. and	1 00
7 English Tennis Caps. Flexible Visors, in White, Checks and Stripes. All Colors	$1 00 and	1 50
8 "Over Land and Water" Tennis Hat in Red, Blue, Grey or White	"	1 25
9 Tam O'Shanter Worsted Caps. All Colors	"	1 50

Other patterns and styles in stock and to order. Caps and Hats made to match suits.

No. II.—BELTS.—*See illustrated pages.*

Best English Web Belts. One or two straps. All Colors	each	$0 40
" Cotton " " " " "	"	25
" Silk Belts. Metal Clasp. All Colors	"	1 25

No. JJ.—WHEELMEN'S SUITS. COATS.

X 1. Corduroy Coats. Standing Collar	each	$8 50
X 2. " " Rolling "	"	8 50
X 3. Navy Blue. Flannel Coats. Standing or Rolling Collar	"	6 50
X 3. Best " " " " "	"	8 00
X 4. Grey Mixed Cloth " " " " "	"	8 00
X 5. Brown " " " " " "	"	8 00
X 6. White Flannel Cloth " " "	"	9 50

No. KK.—BICYCLE KNEE PANTS.—*See illustrated pages.*

X 7. Corduroy Knee Pants	per pair	$3 50
X 8. Navy Blue " " Good Quality	"	3 00
X 9. " " " " Best Quality	$3 50 and	$4 50
X 10. Grey Mixed Cloth " "	per pair	3 50
X 11. " Flannel " "	"	3 00
X 12. Brown " " "	"	3 00
X 13. " Cloth " "	"	3 50
X 14. Knit Ribbed Worsted Pants. Best Quality in Navy, Black and Brown	"	4 00

All of these Suits made of "*Fast Color*" material, and all the pants excepting the worsted are reinforced. The Corduroy is "odorless," and particular attention is paid to the sewing on of the Buttons, etc.

No. LL.—BICYCLE SHIRTS.—*See illustrated pages.*

X 15. Patent Laced Shirts, all colors	$3 00
X 16. "The Adirondack" Pleated Shirt, buttoned. All colors	3 25
X 17. "The Tourists'" buttoned Shirts, in Stripes	3 00
X 18. " " " " Checks and Stripes	3 50
X 19. " " " " Plain Colors	3 00
X 20. "Indigo" Blue Laced Shirts, Color Warranted	3 00

No. MM.—KNIT BICYCLE JERSEYS.—*See illustrated pages.*

X 21. "The Coolest and Healthiest Garment for Wheelmen."	
X 22. Best Worsted Jerseys. Fast Colors. Standing or Rolling Collar	4 00
X 23. Good Quality Worsted Jerseys. Navy Blue and Garnet only	3 00
X 24. Best Worsted Laced Jersey. All colors	5 00
X 25. " " " " Striped Collar and Cuffs	5 00
X 26. " " " " Body, Collar and Cuffs	5 00

No. NN.—BICYCLE RACING SUITS.—*See illustrated pages.*

X 27. Cotton Long Sleeve Shirts in Flesh, Black or White	1 50
X 28. " Tights " " " "	1 50
X 29. " Sleeveless Shirts " and White	50
X 30. " ½ Sleeve " " "	50
X 31. Worsted Long Sleeve Shirts, all colors	3 50
X 32. " ½ " " "	3 50
X 33. " Sleeveless " "	3 00
X 34. " Tights " "	3 50
X 35. " Knee Tights " "	3 00

No. OO.—BICYCLE CAPS AND HELMETS.—*See illustrated pages.*

X 36. Navy Blue Cloth Bicycle Cap, "Regulation Style."	1 25
X 37. Grey " " " "	1 25
X 38. Corduroy " " "	1 25

HATS AND CAPS.

A sample hat will be sent by mail to any address, on receipt of price, or we will send one dozen by mail, on receipt of price, with 50 cents extra for postage. Caps and Hats also sent by express, C.O.D.

Jockey-Shaped Caps, with Star on Top.

No. 158. Jockey, solid white, blue star, white button.
" 160. Jockey, solid red, white star, blue button.
" 162. Jockey, B. & W. alternate, red star, white button.
" 166. Jockey, R. & W. alternate, blue star, white button.

No. 166¼. Red, white and blue alternate.
" 159. Jockey, blue and white alternate. (See cut).
" 159R. Jockey, red and white alternate.
" 161. " solid blue, white corded seams.
" 163. " " white, blue "
" 167. " " " red "

Made of Best Merino, any style.................................per doz. $9 00; by mail, each, $0 85
Made of Best Opera Flannel, any style.......................... " 8 00; " " 75
Made of Best Uniform Flannel, any style...................... " 7 00; " " 65

N. B.—Besides the above style of Jockeys, we make some twenty other styles for the different Trotting Associations throughout the States; and, if required, we make them elastic backs, so that they are sure to fit any head.
No. 195. Silk Jockey Caps, any color, to order.....................................Each, $4 00

TENNIS HATS AND CAPS.

No. 1. Our popular white flannel tennis hat.........................$1 00 & $1 50
" 2. " " blue, brown and light or dark gray hat.........................1 25
" 3. " " brown or drab corduroy hat.........................1 50
" 4. " " striped flannel.........................1 50
" 5. Light weight felt tennis and hammock hats, all colors.........................75c. & 1 25
" 6. White or drab duck hats.........................75c. & 1 00
" 7. English pull over tennis caps in colors, stripe and check.........................1 00 " 1 50
" 8. Land and water felt tennis hats, red, white, navy, gray or brown.........................1 50
" 9. Tam O'Shanter worsted caps, all colors.........................1 50

BASE BALL HATS AND CAPS.

No. 300.—**New Style Base Ball Hats.** (See cut No. 1). Which we get up in the finest manner; they are neat, light, and richly made; the material is a fine quality flannel, bound and trimmed with fine silk ribbon. Price, per dozen, $15.00; each, $1.50

No. 300 P. Made same shape as No. 300, but without lining; it weighs only 1½ ounces, and can be carried in the pocket with ease; will always keep its shape. Per dozen, $12.00; each, $1.25.

No. 301. Same as No. 300, but with flat top. In ordering, state color of flannel and ribbon desired.

No. 1. **New Style College Cap.**—Made of best flannel any desired color, and bound the match, with sweat leather linings. (See cut).....................Price, each, 75c.; per doz., $ 8 00
With satin ribbon badge, with name of club printed in gold.................... " 10 00
Or with name stamped on fine silk badge ribbon, gold letters.................. " 13 50

The above badges can be worn on the cap or the coat, and are quite appropriate for visiting clubs and their members. Special prices for badges given in quantities.

No 3. "Rage," eight cornered base ball caps, with or without star, all colors, each, 75c.; per doz., $8 00
" 4. " " " 2nd quality base ball caps, with or without star, all colors.
Each, 60c.; per doz., 5 00
No. 5. "Rage," eight cornered 3rd quality base ball caps, with or without star, all colors.
Each, 35c.; per doz., 3 50
No. 6. Jockey shaped base ball caps, with or without star, all colors......Each, 75c.; per doz., 8 00

BICYCLE CAPS AND HELMETS.

No. 36. Navy Blue Cloth Regulation Bicycle Caps...........................Each, $1 25
" 37. Gray " " " " .... " 1 25
" 38. Corduroy " " " " .... " 1 25
" 39. Cloth Helmets, all colors.. " 1 50
" 40. Canvas Helmets...Each, 75c. to 1 75
" 41. " " Cork Lined.. " 2 25
" 42. Straw Helmets, Patent Ventilated.................................... " 1 00

YACHTING CAPS.

No. B. 7. Navy Cloth Caps, best quality fast colors...............................$1 50
" B. 8. " " " good " " 1 00
" B. 9. White Duck, " best, " two covers........................... 1 00
" B.10. " " " 2d. " " " 1 00

In ordering, please state whether you want straight or turn down visor.

CANOE MATTRESS AND LIFE PRESERVER.

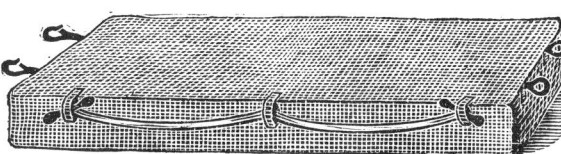

This Mattress serves also as a cushion, the tick is 50 inches long that may encircle the chest, 18 inches wide and 4 inches deep, it is divided lengthwise into 3 compartments by 2 partition strips of muslin 6 inches wide sewn on upper and under side of the Mattrass. Fine cork shavings about 1¼lbs. are put into each compartment, it is a good non-conductor of either the cold or the moisture of the earth, made of Ida Canvas, being porous and a non-conductor.

Price, $5.00 each.

BASE BALL, CRICKET, ARCHERY, LAWN TENNIS, BOATING, YACHTING, NAVY, POLO AND HORSE RACING CAPS.

No. 191.   No. 194.   No. 196.
No. 192.   No. 193.   No. 81.

Patent Solar Cork Hats.—We beg leave to call your attention to our Patent Solar Cork Hat, adapted especially for wear during the heated term.

The body of this hat consists of concrete cork, and is therefore a non-conductor of heat. It is also water-proof, and can be worn without injury to its shape in any kind of weather.

The peculiar arrangement of the sweat renders the ventilation perfect and keeps the head perfectly cool in the warmest weather.

It is particularly desirable as a summer uniform for Clubs, Societies, Pic-nic Parties, &c.

This Hat has been adopted as a standard for Summer Helmets for the U. S. Army, and has given satisfaction in every respect.

We can supply these Hats in any quantity and of any quality desired, at prices proportionate to materials and finish.

No. 1, Drab or White Linen Helmets, Fancy Band, Green Linen Underbrim................each, $2 00
" 2, Serge Helmets in Drab or Slate,   "   "   "   .... "   2 50
" 3, Satine   "   "   "   Green Linen Underbrim .... "   3 00
Sailor—Same as No. 3... "   3 00

We can put plain bands on above, if desired. Sent by mail upon receipt of 25 cents extra.

No. 191.—Yachting, or Navy Caps.

	Per doz.	Each.
Fine White duck, with leather peak, (very light) see cut...........................	$10 00	$1 00
Of best flannel, of any color...	9 00	1 00
Fine Navy Blue cloth...	12 00	1 25
White duck skull caps, no peak..	9 00	85
Glazed covers, for any of the above, extra......................................	2 50	25

No. 191 X. New skeleton or double cover Yachting Cap, made on a skeleton frame. Made of best white duck, and has two covers, which can be taken off and washed. (See cut.)
Per dozen, 15.00; each, $1.50.

Gold embroidered names for boat clubs, on cloth, per letter, 8 cents.
Gold wreaths embroidered on cloth, for boating clubs, each, $1.50; per doz., $15.00.

No. 81.—Polo or Lawn Tennis Cap. Made of best twilled flannel, with band on side and top, of different color, or, if desired, can have with two narrow bands on side. A large variety always on hand, or made to order. Per dozen, $10.00; each, $1.00.

Special styles of caps, different to what we here describe, made to order. In ordering caps, send size of your own cap worn.

No. 196. **English Cricket Caps,** London make, imported assorted colors, (see cut).
Per dozen, $10 00; each, $1.00.

No. 194. **The Creedmoor Shooting and Hunting Cap.** With cape to cover the neck and shoulders, made of best brown or white linen, (see cut). Each, $1.25.

GRAY'S PATENT BODY PROTECTOR.

The most useful device ever invented for the protection of catchers or umpires, and renders it impossible for the catcher to be injured while playing close to the batter. Made very light and pliable, and does not interfere in any way with the movements of the wearer, either in running, stooping or throwing. No catcher should be without one of these protectors.

Price, each, $10 00

Jockey-Shaped Caps, with Star on Top, or Corded Seams.

No. 158. Jockey, solid white, blue star, white button.
" 160. Jockey, solid red, white star, blue button.
" 162. Jockey, B. & W. alternate, red star, white button.
" 166. Jockey, R. & W. alternate, blue star, white button.

No. 166¼. Red, white and blue alternate.
" 159. Jockey, blue and white alternate. (See cut.)
" 159 R. Jockey, red and white alternate.
" 161. ' solid blue, white corded seams.
" 163. " " white, blue '
" 167. " " " red "

Made of Best Merino, any style ......per doz. $9 00 ; by mail, each, $0 85
Made of Best Opera Flannel, any style.................. " 8 00 ; " " 75
Made of Best Uniform Flannel, any style................ " 7 00 ; " " 65

N. B.—Besides the above style of Jockeys, we make some twenty other styles for the different Trotting Associations throughout the States ; and, if required, we make them elastic backs, so that they are sure to fit any head. Price, per dozen, $10 00

YACHTING SHIRTS.

No. B 1.—Blue, White or Grey Flannel, best quality................ $4 00
B 2 " " " good quality................ 3 50
B 3.—Grey or White " medium quality................ 3 00

YACHTING PANTS.

No. B 4.—Best Navy Blue Flannel Pants, fast color................ $5 00
B 5.—Good quality Navy Blue Flannel Pants, fast color................ 3 75
B 6 " White, Grey or Blue................ 3 50

YACHTING CAPS.

No. B 7.—Navy Cloth Caps, fast color................ $1 50
B 8 " Flannel Caps................ 1 00
B 9.—White Duck Caps, 2 covers................ 1 25
B 10.— " " 2d quality................ 1 00

YACHTING SHOES.

No. B 11.—Rubber Sole Canvas Shoes................per pair $1 25
B 12 " " better quality................ " 2 00
B 13 " " best quality................ " 3 00

SAILORS' JERSEYS.

No. B 14.—Heavy Knit Worsted Jerseys, Navy blue................ $3 50
B 15 " " white................ 3 50
B 16.—Knit Worsted Yacht Caps................ 1 55

BATHING SUITS.

We manufacture a large assortment of Bathing Suits, in both worsted and cotton. Best quality worsted suits can be made in any color, plain or striped.

Light Weight Worsted Two-piece Suits, consisting of short sleeved Shirt and Knee Pants $6 00
" " Two-piece Suits, striped two colors................ 6 50
" " " " three " 7 00
" " Union One-piece Bathing Suit 7 00
" " " " striped................ 7 50
Worsted Two-piece Bathing Suit, in maroon or navy blue 2 50
" Union One-piece Suit, navy blue................ 3 00
Cotton Bathing Suits, one piece, fancy colors, striped ....$1 00 and 1 50

BATHING TRUNKS.

Best Worsted Trunks, all colors ....per pair $1 75

COTTON TRUNKS.

No. A.—Fancy Striped Cotton Bathing Trunks 0 25
B " " " 0 35
C " " " 0 40
D " " and Solid Colors Bathing Trunks 0 50

TOWELS.

X Rough Turkish Towels, medium size................each $0 25
XX " " " large size................ 0 35
XXX " " " best quality................ 0 50
XXXX " " " " extra large................ 0 75
No. A1 " " " extra fine and large................$1 00 and 1 50

For use after exercising, rubbing down, etc. Essential to every athlete and gymnast.

No. W. BLANKET ROBES.

No. 1.—Heavy Blanket Robes, good quality $8 00
2 " " " better " .... $9 00 to 12 00
3 " " " extra fine, fancy patterns................ 12 00 to 15 00

For the bath, for wear after exercising, etc. Made up in the best manner, and in plain and fancy patterns.

PECK & SNYDER'S
TRADE MARK REGULATION BASE BALL BATS.

Clubs when ordering Bats from us, can depend upon receiving fine stock, clear of knots or imperfections. When you order, order by numbers as given below; also the length required. Men's Bats are 35, 36, 37 and 38 inches long, and Boys' Bats are from 24 to 34 inches long.

The following list comprises the best selling bats in the market; particular attention is called to our hand-turned Trade Marked Bats, which for style, finish, balance and uniformity are not surpassed.

		Clubs Per Doz.	Retail Each.
No. 1	Peck & Snyder's Trade marked Ash hand turned, in various approved models, finished in shellac and selected..................	$3 00	0 35

No. 1-X.

This Bat is finished in polished French shellac, and being the desirable shape among Professional Batters it has met with great favor with the Trade. We offer it less than one-half the price of a similar finished Bat of other makers.

No. 1-X.	Peck & Snyder's New League Model selected Ash Bats, 33, 34 and 35 inch..................	$5 00	0 50
2.	Peck & Snyder's Trade Mark Basswood Bat, light, selected timber, varnish finish..................	2 50	0 25

No. 3.

No. 3.	Peck & Snyder's Trade Mark oiled Georgia Pine Bat, made of second growth selected stock; a good light Bat..................	$3 00	0 35
" 4.	Peck & Snyder's Trade Marked Cherry Bat, of selected stock. A good, durable Bat, in weight between that of Bass and Ash........	3 50	0 35

No. 5.

No. 5.	Peck and Snyder's Trade Marked Willow Bat, very light and durable, highly finished, each Bat in a paper bag..................	$5 00	0 50
" 6.	Full Polished Ash, with wound handle; a very durable Bat..........	6 00	0 75

No. 7.

No. 7.	Peck & Snyder's Waxed Ash Bat, with wound and waxed handle.....	$4 00	0 50
" 8.	Peck & Snyder's light-weight Polished Willow, with wound handle, the most durable light Bat made..................	6 00	0 75
" 9.	Men's Plain Ash Bats, seasoned stock..................	2 00	0 20
" 10.	" Bass " " "	1 50	0 20
" 11.	Boys' Plain Ash " assorted, 24 to 34 inch..................	1 25	0 15
" 12.	" Bass " " "	1 00	0 10
" 13.	Boys' Trade Marked Cherry..................	2 00	0 25
" 14.	" " " Ash..................	2 00	0 25
" 15.	" " " Willow..................	2 00	0 25

The above Nos. 13, 14 and 15 are the same style and finish as our Men's Trade Marked Bats.

Clubs supplied C. O. D., or on receipt of price.

PRIZE BALLS AND BATS.
Appropriate as Prizes at Fairs, and Encouraging to Local Contests on the Field.

No. 245. Heavy Silver-plated Prize Ball, engraved as to represent a stitched ball, *regulation size and weight*, with Morocco and Satin-lined case, as represented in annexed cut............$8 00

No. 246. Heavy Silver-plated Prize Ball only, engraved as to represent a perfect stitched ball, *regulation size and weight*......$5 00

No. 247. Morocco Prize Ball Case only. Satin-lined............$3 00

ENGRAVING ON PRIZE BALLS, PER LETTER.

Script, 6 cents; Old English, small, 8 cents; Old English, large, 14 cents; Block, 8 cents; Scroll or Ornament, extra.

No. 248.	Prize Bat, in Morocco case, satin-lined as per above cut, Solid Rosewood Bat highly polished, with two beautifully engraved, silver-plated bands, and a silver-plated inscription plate in centre, complete	$25 00
" 250.	Solid Rosewood Bat, French polished, not mounted....................................	4 00
" 251.	" " with one band only, no plate......................................	7 00
" 252.	" " with two bands only...	10 00
" 253.	" " with Engraved Inscription Plate only.......................	12 00
" 254.	" " " " " and two bands.......................	13 00
" 255.	Morocco Prize Bat Case, Satin-lined..	12 00

BASE BALL BAT BAGS.

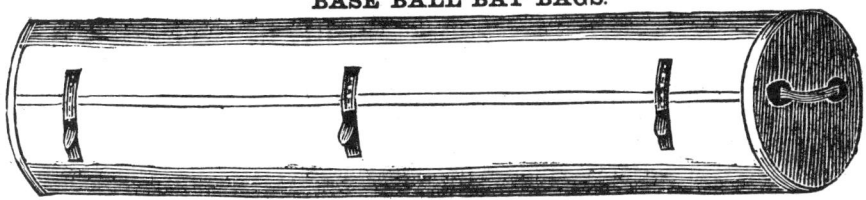

No. 280. Best Sail Canvas Bags, for holding 2 dozen bats, leather top and bottom, with leather handles for carrying, etc...$5 00
" 281. Best Sail Canvas Bags, for holding 1 dozen bats, leather top and bottom................. 3 50
Name of club painted on bat bag, extra 0 50

1885.

PECK & SNYDER'S STANDARD BASE BALLS.

We respectfully call the attention of the Base Ball Clubs of the country to the following *Reduced Price List* of our superior Balls which for finish, durability and superior workmanship are not surpassed by those of any other manufacturer. Our new "Gut Stitch" League Ball, which gave such general satisfaction the past season we can highly recommend for its lasting qualities. The Gut Stitch should not be used in wet weather.

						Clubs. Per Doz.	Retail Each.
No. 1.	Superior League (White or Red) Gut Stitched............					$15 00.	$1 50
" 2.	" " " " " Flax Thread Stitched..............					15 00.	1 50

No. 3. Our Treble Match Ball (Red or White).

Clubs. Per Doz.	Retail. Each.
$12 00.	$1 25.

NOTE.—Sample Balls by Mail Postage paid on receipt of price.

No. 4. Professional Match Ball, 1 oz. Moulded Rubber Red or White.

Clubs. Per Doz.	Retail. Each.
$10 00.	$1 00.

Fig. 1.

Fig. 2.

PECK & SNYDER'S
NEW
SEAMLESS LEAGUE

We introduce this Seamless Ball to the public, believing it to be the best wearing Ball that has ever been offered; the stitch being a blind one, the seam is not exposed to wear, and there is nothing to injure the hands of the player. The inside is composed of the very best material, and the cover is of selected Buckskin, tanned by a special process that renders it soft to the hand and yet hard enough to stand the severest batting. Fig. 1 shows the complete Ball with the blind seam exposed. Fig. 2 shows the Ball in the process of manufacture, before the blind seam is finally drawn into position. Every Ball warranted not to rip.

No. 1 X.—Seamless League, White.........

Club Price, Per Doz.,	Retail, Each,
$15.00.	$1.50.

PECK & SNYDER'S INDIVIDUAL BAT BAG,

Used by Professional and Amateur Players for carrying their own Bats. Made of strong canvas, leather ends, handle and straps for holding two Bats............................Price each, $1 25
Individual Bat Bag for two Bats, all leather... " 3 50

No. 5

PECK & SNYDER'S
POPULAR BASE BALLS.

No. 5.—The Amateur Dead Ball is put up one Dozen in a box and each Ball in a seperate box rolled in Tissue paper and Tin Foil, this keeps each Ball clean and fresh which is very desirable for the retail trade.

	Club. Per Doz.	Retail. Each.
No. 5. Amateur White, Dead..........	$8 00	$0 75
No. 6. Amateur Red,	8 00	0 75

No. 7.

No. 7.—**THE BOUNDING ROCK BALL.**

This Ball is of selected stock, put up in Tin Foil and is one of our best selling Balls at the low price it is offered.

	Club. Per Doz.	Retail. Each.
No. 7. Bounding Rock in White only......	$5 00	$0 50

No. 8.

No. 8.—**THE "ATLANTIC" BALL.**

This Ball is in all respects the same as No. 7. put up in the same manner, the name being a very popular one with Ball Players and the trade.

	Club. Per Doz.	Retail. Each.
No. 8. Atlantic, in White only..........	$5 00	$0 50

No. 9

PECK & SNYDER'S
NEW
Popular Base Balls.

The demand for a first-class Horsehide covered Ball for Boys has induced us to manufacture this Ball. It is made in the best manner and being somewhat smaller and lighter, is better adapted to the hands of the Youth than the larger Balls.

Put up each Ball in a box with tin foil &c.

	Clubs. Per Doz.	Retail. Each.
No. 9.—Youths' League,	$5 00	$0 50

No. 10.

No. 10.—THE BOY'S LEAGUE.

This Ball being the same in size and weight as No. 9, the cover is of selected Sheepskin, a good hand Ball, but not as durable for batting as the Youths' League.

	Clubs. Per Doz.	Retail. Each.
No. 10.—Boy's League,	$2 50	$0 25

No. 11.

This Regulation Ball is one of the most popular brands, and as a low priced Ball has met with popular favor.

No. 11.—New York Regulation,

Clubs. Per Doz.	Retail. Each.
$2 50	$0 25

No. 12.

PECK & SNYDER'S
NEW
Popular Base Balls.

A Reliable Ball at a Low Price.

	Club. Per Doz.	Retail. Each.
No. 12.—"Practice" Ball,	$2 00	$0 20

No. 13.

A very good Ball for the price.

	Club. Per Doz.	Retail. Each.
No. 13.—Boy's Dead,	$1 50	$0 15

No. 14.

This is the largest and best Ball ever offered at the price, we decline filling Trade orders on this Ball only unless accompanied with orders for other styles.

	Club. Per Doz.	Retail. Each.
No. 14.—Young America,	$1 00	$0 10

THE POPULAR GAME OF LA-CROSSE.—Since the first appearance of that interesting article on Canadian Sports in the August number of *Scribner's Magazine*, by George W. Beers, Esq., the game of Lacrosse has rapidly grown into public favor among colleges and clubs as a rival of foot ball during the early spring or in the fall of the year when the bracing air makes it uncomfortable to play the less active games of base ball or cricket. PECK & SNYDER have recently republished the rules and by-laws of the Montreal Lacrosse Club, together with the latest revised rules of the Rugby Foot Ball Union of London, including also the latest price lists of all articles used in the game.

By mail, post-paid, 25 cents.

	Per doz.	Each.
Lacrosse Bats, Canadian make, men's sizes	$18 00	$1 75
Lacrosse Bats, Boy's size	9 00	1 00

Per set of Four.

Lacrosse goal flags, complete with poles.........................$5 00

French Lacrosse shoes, white canvas with rubber soles. Per pair.........$1 50

LACROSSE BALLS.

The Balls that have been offered by the trade are too small to meet the requirements of the rules. We have these made to order for the purpose, and they meet the requirements, and have been adopted by all the leading Clubs as the Regulation Ball.

Price each, 50 cents. Per dozen, $5 00

Lacrosse uniforms, of any pattern, etc., made to order, either of worsted or flannel goods.

EQUESTRIAN POLO.

Regulation Polo Mallets, each..$1 50
"   "   "   per dozen..15 00

Polo Mallets made to order to special patterns.

Regulation Polo Balls, each..25 cents.
"   "   "   per dozen...$2 00
The Rules of Polo, by mail..10 cents.

WICKET-KEEPING GAUNTLETS AND GLOVES.

White or Buff, Patent Ventilated Palm. (See Cut No. V.)	per pair,	$4 00
" " plain	"	3 50
Batting Gloves, Grey Tubular Vulcanized Rubber. (See Cut No. B.)	"	3 50
Batting Gloves, Patent Sponge Rubber. (See Cut No. 4.)	"	4 00
Batting Gloves, all England Patent Clasp. (See Cut No. 2 A.)	"	3 75
Batting Gloves, Registered, the Bat is grasped with the naked hand, backs of hands well protected with Rubber. (See Cut No. F.)	"	3 75

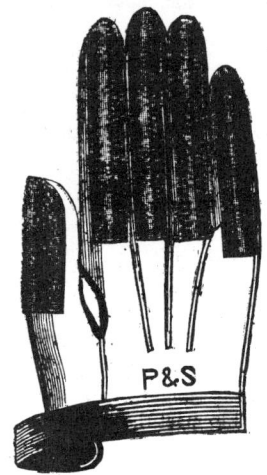

No. 4.—Paten Sponge Rubber.

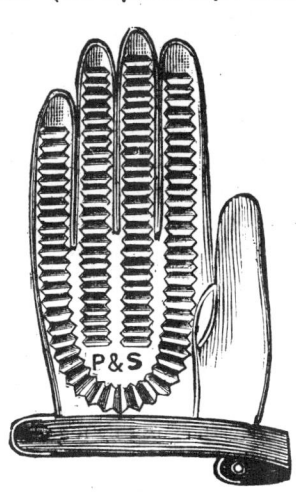

No. 2 A.—All England.

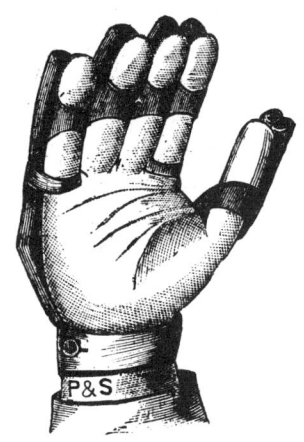

No. F.—Registered.

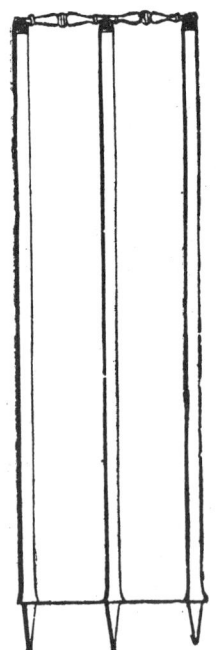

No. 2.

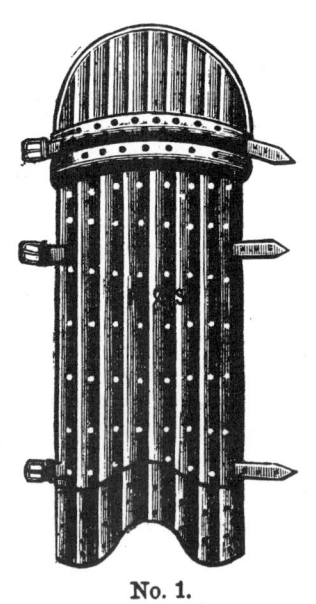

No. 1.

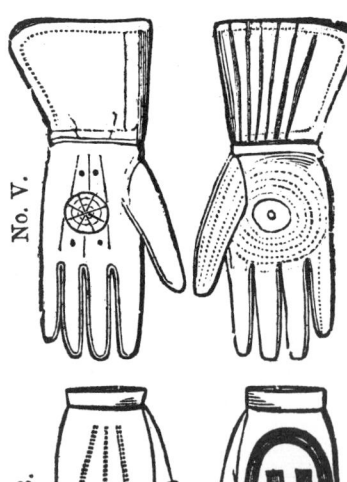

No. V.

No. B.

BUCK LEG GUARDS.

No. 1.	Best Buck, match, patent flexible, stuffed, straps and buckles, (See Cut No. 1.)	per pair,	$4 50
" 2.	Best Buff, " " "	"	4 00
" 3.	Best Muslin, match, flexible, stuffed, with straps	"	3 50
" 4.	Best Youths' " " "	"	3 00

ENGLISH CRICKET GOODS.

N. B.—We would respectfully call the attention of all Cricketers in America, that all goods we sell are imported from London, and that we are the Sole Agents for the United States for the sale of Jeffries & Co's (Woolwich) London Cricket Goods, Yachting and Gymnasium Shoes and Footballs. We shall always keep a full supply on hand. Parties when ordering $25 at one time of Cricket Goods, will receive a discount of 10 per cent.

PLAIN MATCH BAT. — No. 2, Cricket Bat.

DOVE TAILED BAT. — No. 5, Cricket Bat.

SINGLE CANE-HANDLE BAT. — No. M, Cricket Bat.

SUPERIOR ALL CANE-HANDLE BAT. — No. I, Cricket Bat.

Spring Handle Cricket Bats.

M.	Single Cane Bats, French Polished, 5 pieces of cane. (See cut)				Each, $5 00
A.	Double " " " 10 " "				5 50
L.	Treble " " " 15 " "				6 50
I.	All cane, superior " " 20 " ' (See cut)				7 00
5.	Best dove-tailed Match Bat, polished, regulation size. (See cut)				4 00
4.	Men's best Practice Bat, ash handle, dove-tailed and polished				4 00
3.	" Club " polished handle and bat one piece of willow				3 50
2.	Men's best Match Bat, polished, handle and bat one piece willow. (See cut)				3 00
1.	College Bat, strong and useful				2 00
6.	Youths', half cane				4 00
Heavy Green Baize Bags for Bats, each...........75c.	Green Flannel Bags					0 50

Boys' Cricket Bats, a full assortment always in stock :

No	1,	2,	3,	4,	5,	6,	7,
Each	50c.	65c.	75c.	$1.00	$1.25	$1.50	$1.75

Cricket Bats of other London makers at about same prices as Jeffries & Co's.

Stumps or Wickets with Bails.

		Per Set.
No. 1.	Polished Rock Maple, Plain	$2 00
2.	" " brass-ringed. (See Cut.)	2 50
3.	" " brass-capped	3 00
Lillywhite's Cricketers' Guide and Yearly Annual		each, 0 50

CRICKET SCORE BOOKS, Latest and Improved Styles,..................each, 25c., 50c., $1.00

Cricket Shirts, Belts, Shoes, Spikes and Caps, same price as Base Ball, when made of American goods.

Cricketers' Book of Rules (English) by John Wisden	0 25
Cricket Nets, 18x6 feet, for Practice	3 50
Cricket Nets, 42x6 feet	5 00
No. 147. English Elastic Webb Belts, two inches wide, assorted colors, gold gilt clasp, with Cricket emblems of different patterns, very showy............per doz., $7.00; each,	0 75

Samples of prices furnished upon application, for uniforms or imported flannels.

Cricket Balls.

	Each.
J. & Co. Patent Cat Gut, treble seamed (Gold Crown stamp)	$3 50
J. & Co. Superior Cat Gut, treble seamed (See cut)	3 00
J. & Co. Practice Cat Gut, double seamed	2 50
J. & Co. Small Practice Ball, double seams, for boys	2 00
Duke or Dark's extra fine xxx seam	3 50
" " best xxx seam	3 00
Double Seamed Practice Balls.................................75c., $1.00 and $1 25	

BOYS' CRICKET BALLS.

No. 4.	Double Seam	Each, $0 50
" 5.	Fine Double Seam	" 0 75
" 6.	Trebled "	" 1 00

ARCHERY BOWS AND ARROWS AND FIXTURES.
(For description and prices see following page.)

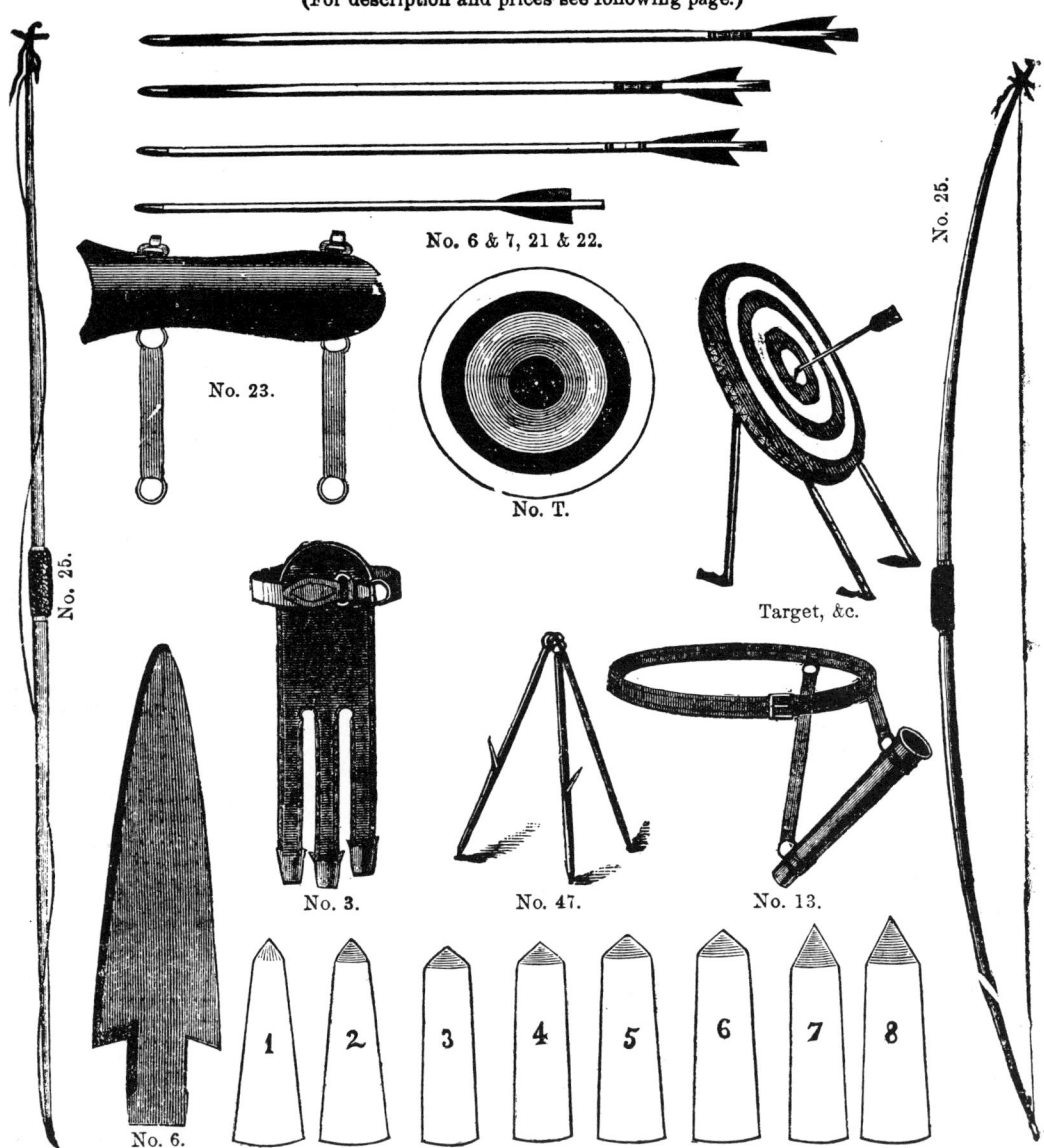

The popular demand for Archery Goods last season was something without precedent, and we can safely assert, that not more than ten per cent. of the orders for implements were filled. This year domestic goods will be placed on the market from all quarters, by men who know no more about bow making than a Yankee does about making a cricket bat. Bow making is a trade that we may learn by patient application and experience; but until we master the art, we will still continue to act as sole agents for Philip Highfield, of London, who is without doubt, the best Bow-maker in the world; and we caution our customers against trash which will be offered, corresponding in numbers to those advertised by us, but of very inferior quality.

We add the following hints for the observance of parties favoring us with their orders:

1.—In England, a claim for breakage of Bows is unknown, from the fact that no bow is guaranteed not to break.
2.—Bend Bows with flat side out.
3.—When a Bow is strung, do not allow it to be strung without an Arrow of the proper length for the Bow.
4.—We test every Bow before shipping.

5.—As we have no redress, we cannot make good any breakage after Bows leave our store.
6.—As most Bows are broken through not properly observing the rules of handling them, we have published a book of rules, styled the "Modern Archer," giving all information. Blue Cloth Binding, 32 Pages. Illustrated. By mail, 25 cents.

FINE ARCHERY FROM AUCTION. Having recently purchased at a great bargain the entire production of a large manufacturer, consisting of over five thousand fine two piece Bows, metal or horn tips, best linen strings, 5 feet 6 inches and 6 feet long and to pull from 30 to 60 pounds. These Bows have formerly sold for five and six dollars each, we are now closing them out for the low price of one dollar each, or six for $4.50

On orders to the amount of Ten Dollars, we allow 25 per cent. discount from the following prices:

No.	Length.	BOWS.	Each.
5	3 ft. 3 in.	Polished	$ 20
6	3 ft. 9 in.	"	30
7	4 ft. 3 in.	"	40
8	4 ft. 9 in.	Stained and polished........	50
9	5 ft. 0 in.	" "	75
10	5 ft. 6 in.	" "	1 25
11	6 ft. 0 in.	" "	1 50
12	4 ft. 0 in.	Horn-tipped "	1 00
13	4 ft. 6 in.	" "	1 25
14	5 ft. 0 in.	" "	1 50
15	5 ft. 6 in.	" "	2 00
16	6 ft. 0 in.	" "	2 25
17	4 ft. 0 in.	Superior plush handles and Flemish Strings...............	1 25
18	4 ft. 6 in.	Superior plush handles and Flemish Strings...............	1 50
19	5 ft. 0 in.	Superior plush handles and Flemish Strings (see cut)......	2 25
20	5 ft. 6 in.	Superior plush handles and Flemish Strings...............	2 25
21	6 ft. 0 in.	Superior plush handles and Flemish Strings...............	2 50
22	4 ft. 0 in.	Best self lancewood, made to weight....................	2 25
23	4 ft. 6 in.	Best self lancewood, made to weight....................	2 75
24	5 ft. 0 in.	Best self lancewood, made to weight....................	3 50
25	5 ft. 3 in.	Ladies' self lancewood, made to weight (see cut).............	4 00
26	6 ft. 0 in.	Gents' self lancewood, made to weight..................	5 00
27	5 ft. 3 in.	Ladies' lemonwood, made to weight....................	5 00
28	6 ft. 0 in.	Gents' lemonwood, made to weight (see cut)...........	6 00
28	6 ft. 0 in.	Lemonwood, the hunter's Bow, (new) to pull 60 to 80 lbs....	10 00
29	5 ft. 3 in.	Ladies' lance and hickory......	5 00
30	6 ft. 0 in.	Gents' " "	7 00
31	5 ft. 3 in.	Ladies' fancy wood backed Bows	7 00
32	6 ft. 0 in.	Gents' " " "	8 50
33	5 ft. 3 in.	Ladies' three piece Bows.......	8 50
34	6 ft. 0 in.	Gents' " "	10 00

No.	ARROWS AND FIXTURES.	Per dozen.
1	12 in. Arrow.................	$ 25
2	15 in. "	50
3	20 in. Sharp points, glued feathers........	75
4	21 in. " three "	1 00
4a	21 in. Painted and polished...............	1 50
5	24 in. Polished	1 75
5a	Painted and polished	2 00
6	25 in. ¼ Knocks, painted and polished..(cut)	2 25
6a	21 in. " " " "	2 00
7	28 in. " " " " ..(cut)	2 50
8	25 in. ¼ " " " "	3 00
9	28 in. " " " "	3 50
10	22 in. Youths' best pine painted and gilt...	3 50
11	25 in. Ladies' " " " "	4 00
12	21 in. Gents' " " " "	5 00
15	25 in. Old Deal, painted, gilt and painted between the feathers...............	6 00
16	28 in. Old Deal, painted, gilt and painted between the feathers (see cut).......	6 75
17	25 in. Ladies' best Pine Footed.............	7 00
18	28 in. Gents' " " "	8 00
21	25 in. Best Footed, with parallel points, painted and gilt, and painted between the feathers........(see cut)	8 50
22	28 in. Gents' Best Footed, with parallel points, painted and gilt. and painted between the feathers....(see cut)	9 00
T	28 in. Thompson's Model Hunting Arrows, with Indian Spear points..........	3 00
6	Steel-pointed Indian Arrow Heads (see cut exact size)....	1 00
	28 in. Steel, blunt-point, hickory arrows, feathered	3 00
	Target points for arrows...........35 and 50	
	Superior Parallel Steel Points, Plates	1 00
	When ordering Points, please state if for Ladies' or Gents' Arrows.	
	Horn Tips for bows .... per pair,	50
	Hickory Arrows (Indian make)..18 21 24 27 in. per doz. 60c. 80c. $1.00 1.25	
	Scoring Cards for round tablet ....per doz.	30
	Patent Leather Tablet, square, with card "	60
	Ebony Scoring Tablet, round, with card and pricker ....each,	75

TARGETS of Canvas Facings, painted in gold, blue, red, black and white, and mounted on platted straw. Target Facings, not mounted, one-quarter price of above. (See cut No. 36).

Diameter........ 12 in.	15,	18,	21,	24,	30,	36,	42,	48,
Each............... $1 00	1 25	1 75	2 00	2 50	3 00	4 00	5 00	6 00

MISCELLANEOUS.

No.		Each.
2	Ladies' Gloves, round top................	$1 00
3	" " lace tips (see cut)........	1 25
7	" Arm Guards, plain green	1 25
8	" " lined and stitched.....	1 50
9	" " silk lined...........	1 75
13	" Quiver Belts, with slides (See cut)...	2 00
14	" " stitched	2 50
17	Gents' Gloves, plain, round top............	1 00
18	" " lace tips.............	1 25
22	Gents' Arm Guards, plain elastic bnnds....	1 25
23	" " lined and stitched (See cut)...................	1 50
25	" Buff Leather Quiver and Belts.......	2 00
26	" " " " extra quality	2 50
33	Ladies' Green Worsted Tassels	50
34	Gents' " " "	75
40	Wood Grease Cups, with lids.............	50
41	Ivory " " "	1 00
42	Gents' Best White Flemish Strings, whipped	60
43	Ladies' " " " " "	50
44	Heavy Green Baize Bow Covers	1 00

No.		Each.
46	5 ft. Iron Target Stands. portable.........	$2 50
47	5 ft. 6 in. " "	2 75
48	6 ft. " "	3 00
50	Peck & Snyder's American Bow Strings, 25, 40	50
51	Extra strong strings, suitable for Hunting Bows	60
52	Archery Score Books......... 75c. $1 00,	1 50
54	Modern Archery Complete Book on Rules..	25

The Witchery of Archery, a complete manual of Archery, with many chapters of adventures by field and flood, and an appendix containing practical directions for the manufacture and use of Archery Implements, by Maurice Thompson, bound in green cloth, gold gilt, 259 pages, fully illustrated. Price, $1 50

The Book of Archery (English), being the complete history and practice of the art, ancient and modern, interspersed with numerous interesting anecdotes and an account of the existing Toxophilite Societies, by George A. Hansard, containing 15 full page steel plate engravings, also 139 smaller ones. 504 pages, bound in cloth, gold gilt. Price, $3 00

Gents' Archery Uniforms.—In stock, or made to order.

THE NEW FRENCH COMBINATION BOXES OF GAMES for LAWN AND PARLOR.

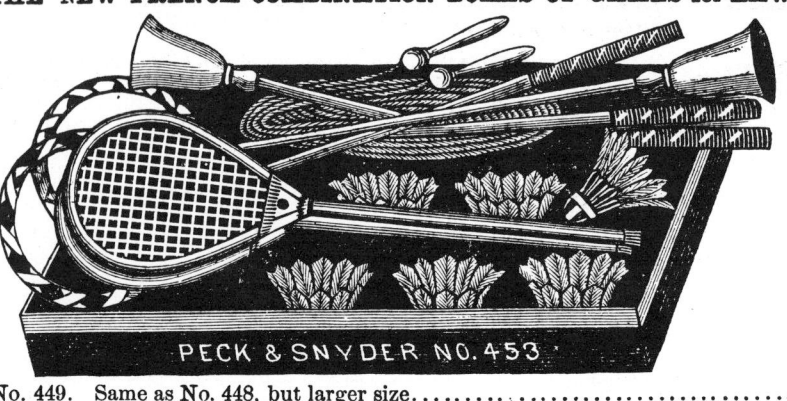

Each set is put in a heavy fancy pasteboard box, wood frames.

No. 1091. Contains 2 Battledores, handles covered with fancy leather, and four Shuttlecocks.
Price, per set, $2 50

No. 448. Contains 2 Battledores, handles covered with fancy colored leather, and six Shuttlecocks.
Price, per set, $3 25

No. 449. Same as No. 448, but larger size... 3 50
No. 450. Same as No. 448. Battledores, frame and handle covered with fancy lecther, fancy ornamented in gold, and six Shuttlecocks... 4 50
No. 451. Same as No. 450, but larger size... 5 00
No. 452. Same size and style of battledores and shuttlecocks as No. 451, also 1 jumping rope, 2 fancy bound grace hoops, 4 fancy bound handles, and 2 long catch cups for shuttle-cock (see cut). Set complete 6 00
No. 453. Same size and style as No. 452, but battledores, frame and handles covered with colored leather, fancy ornamented in gold. Complete... 7 00

No. 579.   **THE NEW FRENCH RAPID SHUTTLECOCK.**
A New Parlor Toy.   (Patented).

The Rapid Shuttlecock, owing to its great simplicity, is beyond all that has been made till now. It is more elegant than the battledore and besides has the advantage of being a very attractive parlor toy. Either one person or several ones together may use it to play at shuttle-cock, at cup and ball or to shoot at a target as the players choose.

The cup or bowl is made of heavy tin, nickel plated, black ebony handle, and fancy colored shuttlecock complete in box with directions.   Each 50c.

LE GRACE HOOPS, FRENCH MADE.
Colored Sticks with Velvet covered Hoops, per set, 4 Sticks and 2 Hoops.

Nos.	249	250	251	252
Per Set.	30c.	50c.	60c.	75c.
Nos.	253	254	255	256
Per Set.	85c.	$1 00	$1 25	$1 50

FRENCH BATTLEDORES
Threaded with Catgut, Fancy Frames.

Nos.	257	258	259	260	261	263
Per Pair	40c.	50c.	60c.	75c.	85c.	$1 00
Nos.	264	255	266	267	269	270
Per Pair	$1 25	1 50	1 75	2 00	2 50	2 75

French Make Shuttle Cock.   (See Cut No. 2.)
188. 17 White Feathers, rubber bottom, fancy bound, per pair, $0 30
189. 19 White Feathers, rubber bottom, fancy bound, per pair......... 0 40
190. 24   "   "   "   "   " 0 75
191. 24 Asstd. Colrd. Feathers "   per pair........ .... 1 00

Genuine London Make Battledores.
Made of best seasoned wood handles and spoons of Battledores, wound with red leather and gilt striped.

Best make Parchment Drum, both sides, (see cut 1)

Nos.	1	2	3	4	5
Per Pair.	75,	85	1 15	1 25	1 50

Best make Parchment Drum one side Catgut, strung the other. (See cut No. 2.)

Nos.	1	2	3	4	5
Per Pair.	1 25	1 50	1 75	2 25	2 75

Best Vellum, Drum both sides.

Nos.	1	2	3	4	5
Per Pair.	1 00	1 25	1 75	2 25	2 75

Best Vellum Drum, one side Catgut, strung the other.

Nos.	1	2	3	4	5
Per Pair.	1 50	1 75	2 00	2 50	3 00

French make Shuttle Cocks, with fancy velvet heads.   (See cut No. 1.)
No. 283. 16 White Feathers, per pair..........20c. | No. 285. 20 White Feathers, per pair..........40c.
 " 284. 18   "   "   "   ....30c. | " 286. 24   "   "   "   ....50c.

THE REGULATION TENNIS BALL, 1886.
Patented September 22d, 1885.

This Ball has been adopted by the United States National Lawn Tennis Association, and by the Intercollegiate Association, as the Regulation Ball to be used in all match games. The Ball for 1886 is much superior to any Ball that we have heretorore manufactured, and superior to any ever offered.

The *Cyclist and Athlete*, of Feb. 12th, 1886, in speaking of the new Ball, says:—"The contrast between the old and new Balls is very marked. Cut one of the old Balls in half and turn it 'inside out'—but very little manipulation is required to split the quarters and loosen the strips. Cut one of the new Balls in half, turn it 'inside out' and no amount of manipulation will either split the quarters or loosen the re-enforcing ribs—thus proving that the defects of the first Ball have been fully overcome. As to the playing qualities of the new Ball a trial will demonstrate that it possesses in a high degree all the qualities which are desirable in a perfect Lawn Tennis Ball, especially in the qualities of quickness and accuracy in responding to the blow given it by the racket. This year Peck & Snyder will place on the market the new Ball. It should not be confounded with the Ball of 1885. If ever imported balls are superseded in this market by American balls, it will be by this 1886 Ball."

		Price each.	Per doz.
No. 1.	Best Felted Cloth Cover, Cemented......	$0 50	$5 00
No. 2.	" Plain Rubber, for wet weather...	25	2 50

COVERED TENNIS BALL.

This Ball, which we offer without our name or recommendation, is a good playing Ball for Amateurs, not as elastic as the 1886 Ball, but a very good Ball for the price.

Covered with Felt and Cemented.

Per half dozen, $1.50; per dozen, $3.00

Lawn Tennis Handle Covers, Rubber.........Each, 50 cents.

THE NEW LAWN TENNIS SCORE BOOK.

With complete Instructions for keeping a correct Score. By HENRY CHADWICK.—The only data on which a correct estimate of a player's skill can be based in Lawn Tennis is that which gives the figures of the score of aces by service and returns. This is the only correct Score Book published, and is endorsed and used by all prominent clubs. Price, in flexible cloth, each, 25 cents.

PECK & SNYDER'S LAWN TENNIS SCORE CARD.

These cards are ruled on slate and are indestructible. Score can be washed out and the card used for years. Two pages, pocket form. By mail, each, 10 cents.

PECK & SNYDER'S CELEBRATED RACKETS.

"THE FRANKLIN," Expert, No. 1.
Patented Feb. 12, 1884.

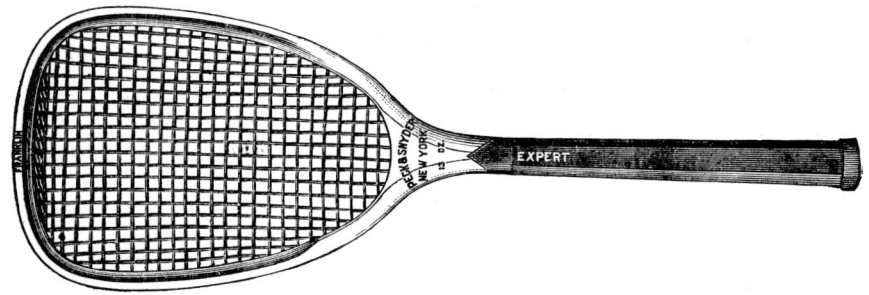

The "Expert" Franklin, which we offer this year for the first time must commend itself to Tennis players who know a good Racket when they see and use it. We have spared no expense in selecting and paying the price for the best gut that can be produced. The selection of the frame and the style of finish will recommend itself.

With octagon California Redwood Handle and patent concave beveled frame........Price, each, $5 50
  With Cork or Rubber Handle, 50 cents each additional.
With Inlaid Handles, Fancywoods..Price, each, $8 00

THE "FAR AND NEAR," No. 4.
Patented Feb. 12, 1884.

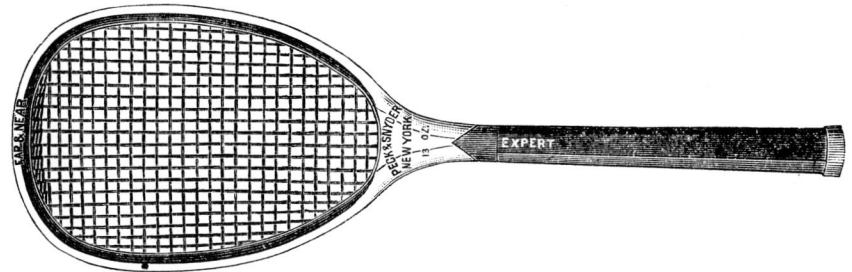

A first-class Racket, in all respects the same as our Expert Franklin, (excepting shape) with our Patent Concave Beveled Frame, size of face 8 x 12 inches, weights from 12 to 16 oz.

Price Each.
With Roughened Octagon California Redwood Handle................................$5 50
  " Octagon Cork or Rubber   " 6 00
  " Fancy Inlaid Handle... 8 00

THE "FRANKLIN," Junior, No. 9.
Patented Feb. 12, 1884.

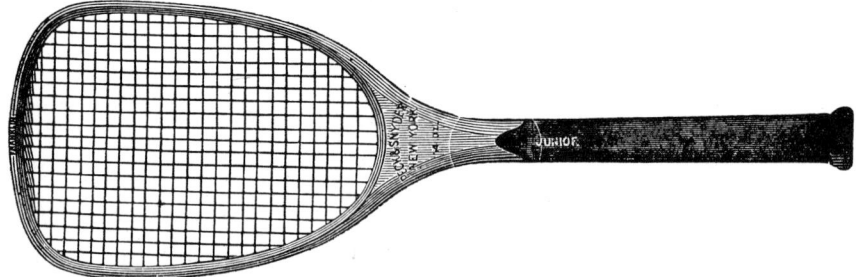

This Racket is the same in construction and stringing as our 1885 Franklin, at a reduction of 1.00 on each racket. The Franklin Junior must become very popular. The construction of the beveled frame enables us to produce an extra large face, with reliable stringing and light weight. They are all made full size, 7 x 11¼ inches, in weight varying from 12 oz. to 16 oz., 13½ and 14 oz. being the best weights for the general demand.

With octagon California Redwood Handle..............................Price, each, $4 50
  " Cork or Rubber Handle...   "   "   5 00

THE "STATEN ISLAND," No. 5.

This desirable shape has met with popular favor for the past three years, straight frame with reliable stringing, the face measurement is 7¼x10¾ inches, weights from 12 to 16 ounces.

	Price Each.
With California Redwood Handle	$3 50
" Cork or Rubber "	4 00
" Fancy Inlaid "	6 00

THE "POPULAR."

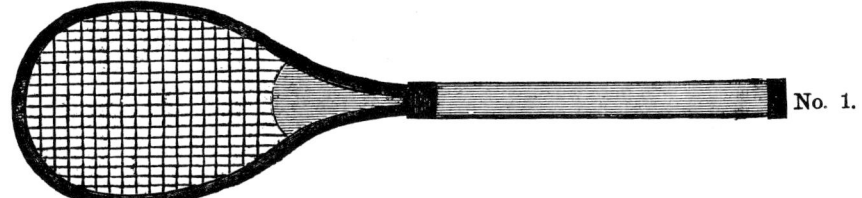

No. 1.

This is a desirable Racket for beginners, with medium grade of stringing, face measurement, 6½x9 inches..........................Price, each, $2.00

THE "PRACTICE" RACKET.

No. 2.

This Practice Racket is made with a medium size face, the stringing surface measures 6½x9 inches, weights from 11 to 13 ounces..........................Price, each, $2.50

TENNIS RACKET BAGS.

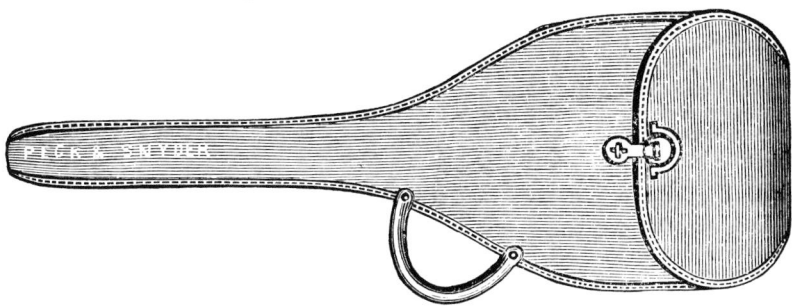

It will preserve the stringing of your Racket by always keeping it in the Bag when not in use.

	Each.
No. 1.—Made of Best Felt Cloth, various colors	$1 00
No. 2.— " " Brown Canvas, Flannel Lined	1 00
No. 3.— " " Split Russet Leather, "	1 50
No. 4.— " " Grain Calf Russet Leather, Flannel Lined	3 00

DIRECTIONS.—Put the pieces forming handles together as shown in the cut. You will find that the pieces are marked with punch marks; put them together as marked and screw them up tight. Then fasten the handles to the powder holder with the bolts provided, screw them up tight also. Oil all the bearings. The machine will now be ready for use. Fill the powder holder with the powdered marble, and bear down on the handles so as to lift the front wheel off the ground, and run the machine to the court where you wish to commence marking. Now lift the handles so that the whole weight of machine comes on the front wheel; be careful, however, not to lift so high that the cover of the front wheel comes on the ground, as in that case it will work very hard. Drive the machine ahead and it will leave a distinct mark behind it. When you come to a corner bear down on the handles again and turn the machine on the rear wheels; if you turn on the front wheel you will be apt to clog up the chain so that it may not make a good mark. So continue where you want the marks to extend.

Care should be exercised to keep the marble dust dry, as when wet it is apt to cake. It is considered advisable to line out the court with a string the first time it is marked, so as to be sure of making perfectly straight lines.

Price, boxed, complete, each...$ 8 00
Marble dust, per 100 lbs.. 1 00
    "   "   per barrel, 350 lbs... 2 00

COLUMBIA LAWN MARKER.

DIRECTIONS FOR USE.—See that the Belt is *flat* around *under* Left Wheel, *over* Guide Rollers, and *under* Tension Wheel in Reservoir. Experience shows that whitewash from fresh slaked lime is the best, most distinct, and most durable marking material. Fill Reservoir to within two inches of top with whitewash, of consistency of thin cream, previously prepared. Stretch a white cord taut where desired to mark. Follow cord with belt wheel. To shift *without* marking, tip Marker slightly, so as to run on free wheel. Move to new point, then set belt wheel on line. To cleanse, empty the wash, and dash a pail or two of water into and over machine and empty. Oil wheels and rollers occasionally.

Price, each, $6.00

THE ROTARY LAWN TENNIS COURT MARKER.

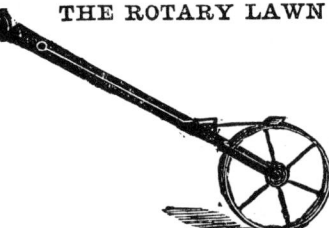

The most simple and effective Court Marker made, suitable for grass or asphalte courts; also Base-Ball and Cricket grounds with complete directions. No. 1, Each, $3.50.
No. 2, P. & S. Improved Model, extra large wheel, 2½ inches wide.
Each, $5.00.

No. 1.   No. 2.

THE EUREKA TENNIS COURT MARKER.

PRICE, $1.50.

This is a "Dry Marker" and requires no mixing of material with water to get ready for use. Push back slide A and put in any powdered material such as marble dust, air-slacked lime, plaster paris or ground plaster, such as is used for fertilizing purposes, flour, &c. Fill the wheel about two-thirds full, which is amply sufficient for once marking the Court. By using a sprinkler immediately after marking, or marking at eve, before the dew falls, a more permanent result will be obtained.

LAWN TENNIS NETS.

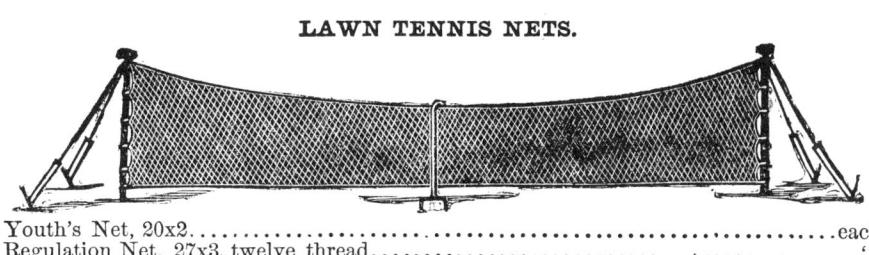

No. 0. Youth's Net, 20x2	each,	$1 00
No. 1. Regulation Net, 27x3, twelve thread	"	1 50
No. 2. " " 33x3, fifteen thread	"	2 00
No. 3. " " 36x3, " "	"	2 50
No. 4. " " 42x3, " "	"	3 00
No. 5. " " extra heavy, 42x3, twenty-one thread	"	4 50
Nos. 4 and 5. Bound on top with white drilling, to show two inches on each side, $1.50 extra.		
Back Stop Nets, 50x7	"	5 00
8 feet brass-tip ash poles for Stop Nets	"	1 00

THE IMPROVED TENNIS FORK.

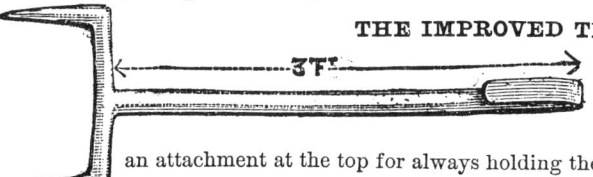

This device has long been required to hold the net exactly three feet high at the centre. It is made of Wrought Iron, is forced in the ground at the bottom with an attachment at the top for always holding the net in position. Price, each, $1 00.

LAWN TENNIS POLES.

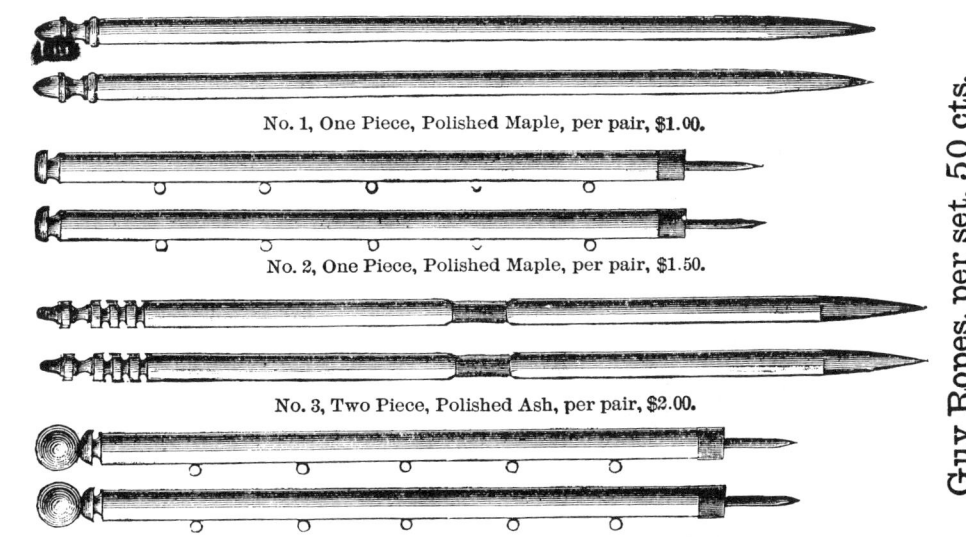

No. 1, One Piece, Polished Maple, per pair, $1.00.

No. 2, One Piece, Polished Maple, per pair, $1.50.

No. 3, Two Piece, Polished Ash, per pair, $2.00.

No. 4, One Piece, Polished Ash, Fancy, per pair, $2.50.

Guy Ropes, per set, 50 cts.

GUY ROPES, RUNNERS AND PINS, COMPLETE..................Per set, 50 cents.

LAWN TENNIS MAHOGANY PRESSES.

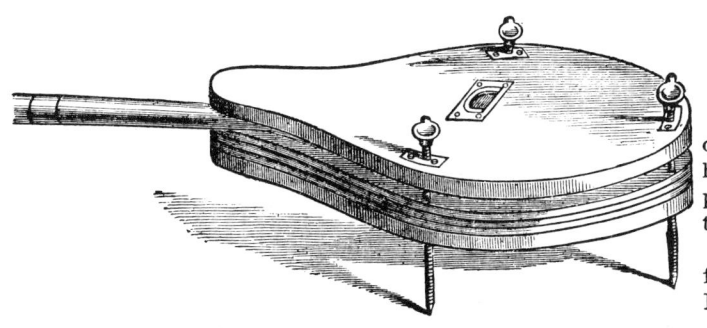

(London make.) Imported.

These presses are made of thoroughly seasoned woods, the mahogany being very highly French polished, and the wood keepers thin, strong and well seasoned.

With brass screw, keepers, etc., for holding four or six Tennis or Racket Bats.........Each, $5 00

COMPLETE SETS OF LAWN TENNIS.

The list below comprises complete Sets of Tennis. We will make up sets to order, omitting any item given in the sets, or substituting other styles of items, as may be desired.

No. 1—POPULAR SET—Consists of 4 of our own Popular Rackets, Medium size, Gut strung, 4 Plain Balls, 1 pair Polished Jointed Poles, 1 Net, 27x3, 1 set Guy Ropes, 1 set Guy Pins, 1 Mallet, Book of Rules, complete in Box. Per Set, 12.00

No. 2—PRACTICE SET—Consists of 4 of our new practice Rackets, 6 Covered Tennis Balls, 1 pair Polished Portable Poles, 1 Net 33x3, 1 pair Guy Ropes and Pins, 1 Mallet, 1 Book of Rules, complete in Box. Per Set, $17.00

No. 3—FAMILY SET—Consists of 4 Selected Rackets, 6 Covered Balls, 1 Net 33x3 feet, 1 pair Polished Ash Poles, 1 Set Guy Ropes, 1 Set Guy Pins, 1 Mallet, 1 Book of Rules, all complete in a large Box. Per Set, $18.00

No. 4—STATEN ISLAND SET—Consists of 4 Staten Island Rackets, 6 Covered 6 Plain Balls, 1 Net 42x3, 1 pair Extra Polished Jointed Poles, 1 Set Guy Pins, 1 Mallet, 1 Book of Rules, complete in Box. Per Set, $25.00

No. 5.—FRANKLIN (Junior) SET—Consists of 4 Franklin (Junior) Rackets, 1 dozen Covered Balls, 1 Net 42x3, 1 Pair Best Poles, 1 Set Guys, 1 Set Guy Pins, 1 Mallet, 1 Book of Rules. Price, complete in Box, $30.00

No. 6.—FAR AND NEAR (Expert) SET—Consists of 4 Far and Near Rackets, 1 dozen Best Covered Balls, 1 Net 42x3, 1 Pair Best Poles, 1 Set of Peck & Snyder's Marking or Boundary Plates, Guys, Guy Pins, Mallet and Rules, complete, with Box. Per Set, $35.00

No. 7.—FRANKLIN (Expert) SET—Consists of 4 Franklin (Expert) Rackets, 1 dozen Covered Balls, 1 Pair Polished Jointed Poles, 1 Extra heavy Net 42x3, 1 Set Guy Ropes and Pins, 1 Mallet, Book of Rules, 1 Tennis Fork, 1 Set of Peck & Snyder's Marking or Boundary Plates, complete in Box. Per Set, $35.00

No. 8.—PRIZE SET—Consists of 4 Prize Fancy Handle Rackets, 1 dozen Covered Balls, 1 Extra 42x3 Net, 1 Pair Best Poles, 1 Tennis Fork, 1 Set of Marking or Boundary Plates, 1 Mahogany Racket Press, Guys, Mallet, Rules, &c., complete in Box. Per Set, $50.00

CORRECT DIAGRAM OF A DOUBLE TENNIS COURT, showing the position and mode of placing our boundary plates. DIRECTIONS FOR USING.— When measuring the Courts, put one Pin at each angle as shown in the above diagrams. Press them down nearly flat in the ground, put the line round them, and run the marker on the inside of each line, so that the mark finishes exactly at the end of each Pin. Then take off the line and press them flat into the ground, where they remain. The consequence is, that if heavy rain sets in and washes out the marking, it is only necessary to raise the Pins a little out of the ground, put the line round, and then re-mark, *thus saving any remeasuring. Being flat with the ground, they do not in the least interfere with the play,* or with mowing.

Price, complete set, $1.00

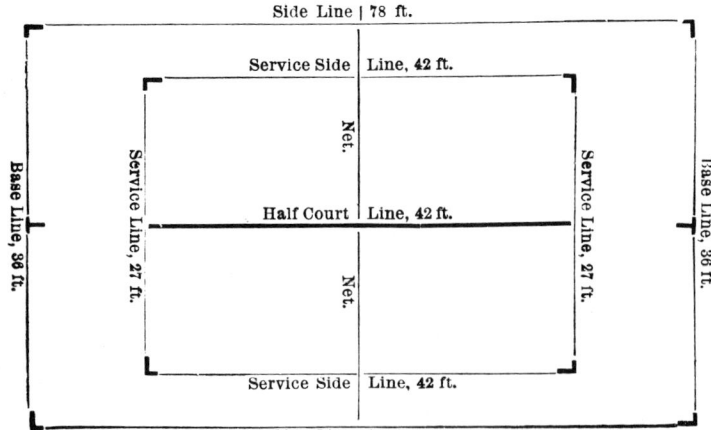

SUPERIOR ENGLISH OR DOMESTIC TENNIS SHOES.

No. 7.—Our Popular Slipper.—This Shoe is made of White or Brown Canvas, with a Pyramid Ruber Sole, moulded on the upper. We can warrant them not to come off. Price, per pair, $1 25

No. 7.　　　　　　　　　　　　　No. 8.

No. 8.—Same style and make as No. 7, only High Cut, white or brown.　　Price, per pair, $1 50

STANDARD DOMESTIC TENNIS SHOES.

No. 9.—Machine Sewed Corrugated Rubber Sole, per pair, $2 00
10.—Same style as No. 9.—Superior hand sewed Shoe, with best pyramid sole, per pair.... 3 00

No. 9.　　　　　　　　　　　　　No. 10.

SUPERIOR ENGLISH TENNIS SHOES.

No. 11.—Brown or White Corrugated Soles............................$5 00
" 12.—Our Finest Imported Shoe in Blue, Brown or White Canvas, with Pyramid Soles... 6 00
No. 13.—Lady's or Gent's Low or High Cut Calf or Aligat or Skin Shoes, superior make................ 6 00
No. 14.—Gent's or Lady's High Cut Balmorals in Brown Canvas, with Pyramid Soles....... 4 00
Pyramid Soles put on old Shoes, per pair..... 2 00

No. 14.　　　　　　　　　　　　　No. 12.

LAWN TENNIS FIXTURES

PECK & SNYDER'S LAWN TENNIS MARKING PINS.

Price per Set of 10 Pins, $1.00.

The Pins are eight in number and are made of Malleable Iron, painted white.

The way to use them is as follows:—When measuring the Courts, put one Pin at each angle as shown in the subjoined diagram, ⌐ press them down nearly flat in the ground, put the line round them, and run the marker on the inside of each line, so that the mark finishes exactly at the end of each Pin. Then take off the line and press them flat into the ground, where they remain. The consequence is, that if heavy rain sets in and washes out the marking, it is only necessary to raise the Pins a little out of the ground, put the line round, and then re-mark, *thus saving any re-measuring.* Being flat with the ground, they do not the least interfere with the play or with mowing.

LAWN TENNIS WELLS AND BALL CARRIERS.

The Lawn Tennis Wells and Ball Carriers, indispensable to every Lawn Tennis Court, by which all stooping for balls is avoided and the game not interrupted. It is also most convenient for carrying ball to the court; it is likewise convenient for all lawn games, to hold the implements in, such as Croquet, Le Grace, Battledore, Archery. Made of neatly turned wood frames, polished, with strong canvas well. Will fold up and take to pieces.　　Per pair, $3 50

UNION WEB HAMMOCKS.

These Hammocks are all made of very best quality cord, by the most improved machinery, and equal in finish to the finest hand work. In every Hammock there are between 1000 and 2000 meshes. They are handsomely dyed in the brightest colors (warranted fast), and will not soil the finest fabric. We have made improvements on all our grades of hammocks this season, and with specialties added to our list, we claim to have the most complete assortment in the United States, from which any dealer can easily make a selection best suited to his trade.

For use in the Woods.

For use in the House and Lawn.

For use on Yachts, Ships, &c.

Empress, Assorted Colors—length, 10½ feet; length of bed 6 feet; width of bed, 8 feet, each,		$1.00
Beatrice, Assorted Colors—length, 11 feet; length of bed, 6 feet; width of bed, 8 feet,	"	1.00
BB, Variegated Colors—length, 11 feet; length of bed, 6 feet; width of bed, 10½ feet,	"	1.25
Marchioness, length, 11 feet; length of bed, 6 feet; width of bed, 10 feet, with rope for hanging,	"	1.50
Paragon, length, 12 feet; length of bed, 6½ feet; width of bed, 11 feet,	"	1.75
Blue Grass, New and very desirable, closely resembling the Mexican Grass, variegated colors—length, 15 feet; length of bed, 7 feet; width of bed, 12 feet,	"	2.00
AB, Variegated Colors, with Patent Horseshoe Fastening—length, 12 feet; length of bed, 6 feet; width of bed, 12 ft.,	"	2.00
AA, Variegated Colors, with Patent Horseshoe Fastening, made of AA web,—length, 12 feet; length of bed, 7 feet; width of bed, 17 feet,	"	3.00
AAA, Our best style, Variegated Colors, with Patent Horseshoe Fastening, made of double web—length, 12 feet; length of bed, 7 feet; width of bed, 17 feet,	"	5.00

PECK & SNYDER'S LAWN TENNIS CHAIRS.

Made of white rock maple, strong and fancy Carpet Seats, each section is fastened with a bolt, secured with nut and double washers, so as to work free. For durability, strength, &c., it is the cheapest chair in the trade. It folds up in a neat parcel, and can be easily packed or carried in a trunk. Price each, $1.25

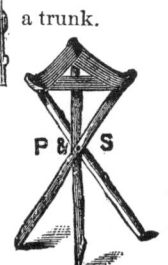

PORTABLE CAMP STOOL.

THE CHEAPEST AND BEST STOOL MADE.

For camp meetings, picnics, base ball, fishing, hunting, etc. When open for use, it is large and strong enough to sustain 300 pounds. Price by mail, post paid, 75 cents.

ROUND OR LAWN TENT.

Tents any size and shape made to order. Send for estimates.

Size.	Drill.	Size.	Stripe.
8 Feet Diameter	$ 6.50	8 Feet Diameter	10.00
9 " "	7.00	9 " "	11.00
10 " "	8.50	10 " "	13.00
11 " "	10.00	11 " "	15 00
12 " "	11.00	12 " "	16.00

The above prices include Pole, Stakes and Bag, complete.

Hammock Awning and Canvas Hammock.

Hammock Awning, Made of Fancy Colored Striped Goods, with Scolloped Curtain, Rods and Guys complete, one size only; it is 7 ft. long and 3 ft. 7 inches wide. **$3 50**

THE IMPROVED CANVAS HAMMOCK.

Made of Duck specially designed for this purpose. A great improvement over the old Canvas Hammocks, and far superior to the Net Hammocks. Most comfortable, durable and handsome hammock in the market. Light Drab Color with Blue Border, Brass Rings, Colored Clew Lines. **$4 00 each.**
Old Style, Plain White.............. $3 00 each. | Hammock Pillows................. 25 "
Hammock Spreaders................ 25 " | Hammock Hooks, to screw in wood... 15 "

SHADE, OR HAMMOCK TENT.

These are intended for Lawns, and are made with scolloped curtains or border, and furnished with poles, guys, and pins, complete.

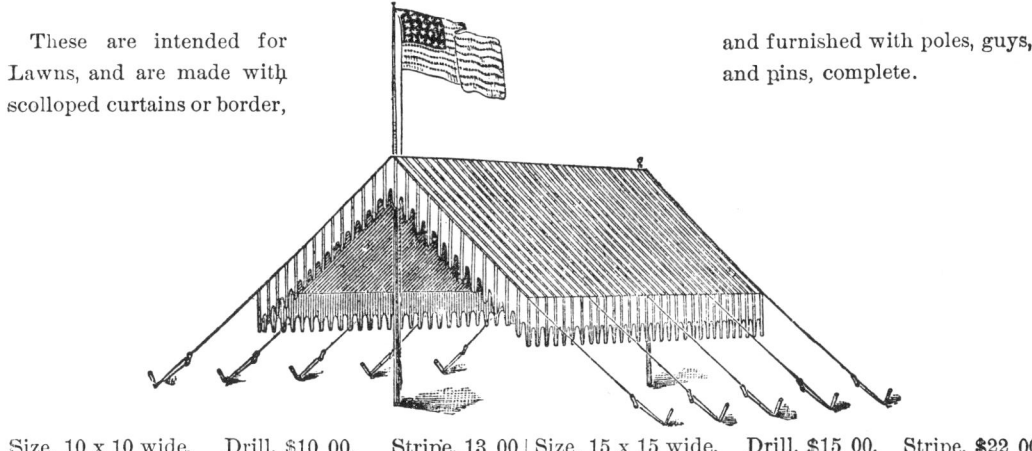

Size, 10 x 10 wide,	Drill, $10 00,	Stripe, 13 00	Size, 15 x 15 wide,	Drill, $15 00,	Stripe, $22 00
" 10 x 12 "	" 11 00,	" 14 00	" 15 x 22 "	" 17 00,	" 23 50
" 10 x 15 "	" 12 00,	" 16 00	" 15 x 25 "	" 19 00,	" 25 00
" 12 x 15 "	" 13 25,	" 19 00			

THE TUXEDO PARK GRASS HAMMOCKS.

These Hammocks are all made of the best-selected Mexican Grass. They are all hand-made by the Mexicans, and to special orders. They are made in plain and fancy bright colors, warranted fast, and will not soil the finest fabric. Full length, 14 feet; length of bed, 8 feet; width of bed, 6 feet; 1 inch meshes; about 4,000 meshes to each hammock; full weight, 5½ pounds; 195 strands. Sent by express only. Prices, plain, each, $5 00; colored, each, $6 00

THE NEW METAL HAMMOCK SPREADER.

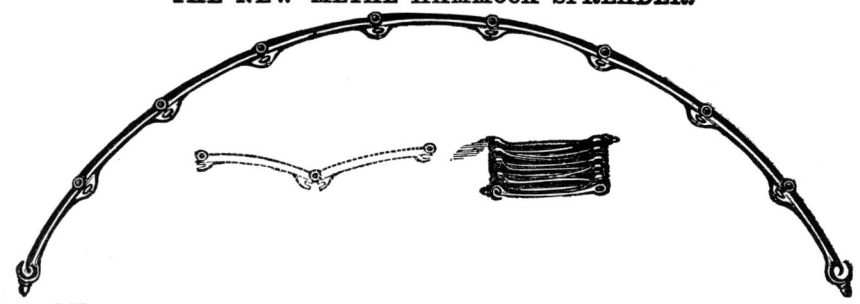

A metal Hammock Spreader, known as the "Grace Hammock Spreader," which is indestructible, being malleable iron. It folds up in space 5 x 2 inches, and can be carried in your pocket. It cannot get out of order. Is used on the under side of the Hammock, and is an ornament. Are finished in japan, bronze, galvanized and nickeled.

Japanned Spreaders..................each, $0 20 | Bronzed Spreaders..................each, $0 25
Galvanized   "   ....   "   25 | Nickel Plated Spreaders..... .... "   75

FOLDING CHAIRS, NEAT, GOOD, CHEAP AND DURABLE.

No. 1.—The Popular Lawn Stools. This Lawn Stool is made of second growth White Ash, the strongest and most beautiful of our native woods. The seat is heavy cotton sail duck. The frame is put together with bolts and screws, and without glue, so that rain does not injure it. It shuts up more compactly, weighs less than any four-post stool in market. While it is much the cheapest and it is equal to the best in use. Dealers in such goods in all places will get them to fill the demand. They weigh two pounds each, and will be sent by mail on receipt of the price and 43 cents for postage.   Samples each, 25 cents; per doz., $2 50

No. 2.—The Alexandria Chair. Made of second growth Ash or Maple neatly turned, and with strong cotton duck seat all put together with screws, and capable of holding persons of any weight. Folds up into as small a parcel as No. 1.   Each 50 cents; per dozen, $5 00

No. 3.—The Newport Folding Chair. For Piazzas, Lawns, Beaches, Hotels, Offices, etc., or any place requiring a compact, handy, and easy-sitting chair. When folded, occupies less than one cubic foot of space. Light, strong and large enough for comfort. Finished in light or red. Handsome, durable, easy, clean. The material of which the seats of these chairs are made, is strongest fibre of manilla and jute put together under great pressure and finished in a variety of deep rich colors, by a process similar to that in the manufacture of upholstery leather, which it very closely resembles. It will wear and keep its shape better than leather, it is perfectly durable, clean, cool, free from moths, and too tough to be cut with a knife.   Each, $1 25

HUNTING OR CAMPAIGN LEGGINS.

A splendid article for Street Parades, Hunting, Fishing or Camping purposes. They keep the dust and dirt from the ankles when worn with low shoes, also to preserve the pant legs. Made of Linen Duck in the best manner.

Four Sizes, 6s, 7s, 8s and 9s, per dozen pairs,...... ......$4.50

Price per pair, by mail, 50 cents.

Very liberal terms to Clubs when buying by the 100 pairs.

THE PALMETTO LAWN TENT.

10 feet square, 10 feet high in centre. Complete.

No. 1.—Made of best striped or plain awning goods, $20.00

No. 2.—Made of extra striped or plain awning goods, $25.00

THE NEW PORTABLE HAMMOCK CHAIR.

In which Ease, Luxury, Comfort, Rest, &c., can be enjoyed for a little money.

No. 1.	Plain White Duck Varnished Chair Ash Frame.........................each,	$2 00
" 2.	" Brown " " " .... "	2 25
" 3.	With Brussels Carpet Seat.. "	4 00
" 4.	Duck Seat with Foot-rest (see cut).. "	4 00
" 5.	Brussels Carpet Seat (see cut).. "	6 00

The above are all ash frames. If painted red or black, 50 cents each chair additional.

THE PORTABLE BED COT, WITHOUT CANOPY.

The frame is strong, light and very springy, which allows the canvas to conform to the body as agreeably as a hammock, and is more comfortable, as the occupant lies straight. Folded or opened instantly, self-fastening; just the thing for Hotels, Offices, Cottages, Camp Meetings, Sportsmen, Steamboats, Military Camps, &c.

Good for the lawn, piazza, or the "coolest place in the house." Splendid for Invalids, or spare beds, and *especially* adapted for Children.

No. 1.	Not Painted, White Duck.......each,	$2 00	No. 4.	Painted Frame, Red, Fancy Duck.....	$3 00
" 1½.	White Duck (extra strong)...... "	2 50	" 5.	" " " Creton Cover	3 50
" 2.	Painted Frame, Red, White Duck "	2 25	Mosquito Frame and Canopy		2 25
" 3.	" " " Brown " "	2 50			

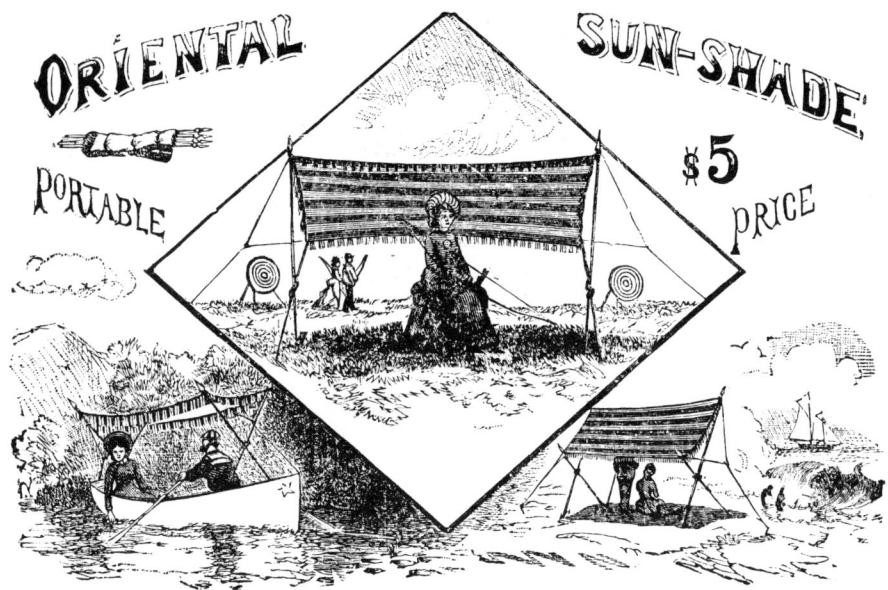

A COMBINED LAWN, BEACH AND BOAT CANOPY, Patented, March 9. 1880. Highly oranmental and useful. DIMENSIONS: length of awning 8 feet, width of awning 3½ feet, height of adjustable poles 6 feet, length when folded, 3 feet. Can be packed in your trunk when travelling.

At the low price of $5 00 which we have put this Canopy on the market, it must meet with a large demand, as it is pronounced by every one to be an almost indispensable article for the tourist. It makes a perfect shield from the sun's rays for ten persons; can be put up to withstand a gale within two minutes, and tilted to any pitch when the sun is low; can be folded to a neat package, weighing but 4 lbs., and carried in the hand. It is suitable for archery, tennis and other lawns. Most desirable for the sea-beach or artist's shelter, and can be adjusted to any boat as quickly as to the lawn or beach. Affords the protection of a tent, and is more convenient than an umbrella.

Price, complete, by express, C. O. D. .... $5 00 | Price, complete, by mail, post-paid by us $5 50

No. 3. Boys' Tent, 7 feet square, 7 feet high.. ....$ 9 00
Wedge Tent set without Poles, No. 4. 7 feet square, 7 feet high.................................... 9 00
    "   "   "   "   " 5. Extra heavy canvas... 10 00

Tents made to order of any desired design or pattern. Estimates cheerfully furnished.

HAMMOCKS.

Made of Best Quality Cord. As durable as Mexican Grass, and less in price.

No. 1. Large full length, 14 feet, length of Bed, 8 feet..each, $1 50
No. 2. Medium full length, 13 feet, length of Bed, 7 feet...each, 1 25
No. 3. Same size as No. 2, but not so heavy.....each, 1 00
    " 1 will hold 500 lbs., and No. 2, 300 lbs. safely.
Cotton Hammocks, extra size and weight. Each $3.50 to $4.50

MEXICAN GRASS HAMMOCKS.

No. 850, White, length, 14 feet..................each, $2 00
 " 850½, Colored, " 14 " .... " 2 25
Mexican Grass Hammocks, extra long, fine mesh and fancy ....each, $5 00 to $25 00

Sample Hammocks mailed, post-paid for price, and 25c. extra for postage.

PEERLESS HAMMOCK ATTACHMENTS,

Improved, *Patented, November* 18, 1879.

THEY CAN BE APPLIED TO ANY HAMMOCK.

They consist of two adjustable spreaders, and a yielding head-rest or pillow.

The SPREADERS are made from hard wood, bent bow shape. They are provided with hooks on the lower edge, which fasten into the netting of the hammock and holds the spreaders firmly in position. These spreaders are placed at each end of the Hammock, as shown in cut.

The PILLOW consists of a strip of cotton duck, 18 inches long and 6 inches wide; it is provided with hooks at each end, and is shorter than that part of the Hammock over which it extends, so that it will be drawn tight when the Hammock is properly suspended, and thereby elevated above the central part of the Hammock, constituting thus a yielding head-rest, and is very cool for the head.

The spreaders keep the Hammock open like a cot, and removes its cramping propensities entirely.
Ladies and Children can use the Hammock without danger of overturning.
The attachments make the Hammock a complete luxury.
They are neat and strong, and add greatly to the beauty of the Hammock.

Complete set, 2 Spreads and 1 Pillow..Price complete, 75c.
"   "   2 Spreaders only..   "   50c.
"   "   Anchor and Hammock Rope Adjuster..............................   "   50c.

Hammock Hooks made of galvanized iron, screw ends, and will hold any weight from 200 to 1000 lbs.
Price per pair, 40 cents.

A, OR COMMON TENT.

Size, feet,	6 x 6	6 x 9	7 x 7	7 x 9	9 x 9
Made of Drill,	$6.00	$7.00	$7.50	$8.50	$9.50
Stripe or Duck,	7.50	9.50	11.00	13.00	15.00

The above prices include Poles, Stakes and Bag complete.

WALL OR CAMPING TENT.

Length and Breadth.	Height of Pole.	Height of Wall.	Price. Drill.	Duck or Stripe.
6 x 6 Ft.	6 Ft.	3 Ft.	$7.00	$.900
7 x 7 "	7 "	3 "	9.00	13.00
10 x 12 "	9½ "	4 "	18.00	27.00
12 x 15 "	9½ "	4 "	22.00	34.00

The above prices include Poles, Stakes and Bag complete.

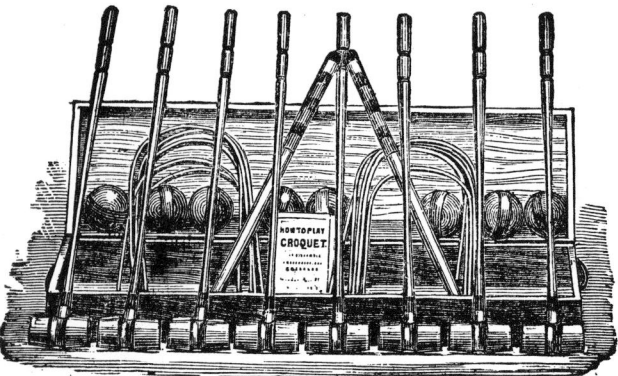

FIELD CROQUET.

The Best Line of Croquet for Quality and Price ever offered. Good. Cheap, Durable.

	Per Set by Express.
No. 4, Turkey Boxwood. The most durable set made. Mallets of selected Turkey Boxwood. Club pattern, with Young Sapling Ash Handles. Balls of choice Turkey Boxwood. Stake of fancy design, polished and painted. Arches of extra heavy galvanized steel wire. All packed in wide chestnut case, dovetailed, and with separate compartments for the Balls. With book. An elegant set; are unequaled for service..................................	$12 00
No. 5, Turkey Boxwood. Second quality of No. 4 set. Same style as No. 4, put up same way, and in all respects similar, excepting having imperfections in wood, which in many cases hurt only the appearance—for service often being fully as good as the No. 4 set. The cheapest Boxwood set ever offered	8 00
No. 6, Selected Rock Maple. Same style as Boxwood set. White wood box instead of chestnut. A beautiful set, and for a higher priced set, one of the best ever offered.............	5 00
No. 7, Fine Rock Maple. All varnished. Balls and Mallets of finest rock maple, young ash handles, Mallets design pattern with fancy turning, painted stripes on head of mallets. Balls with one white and four narrow stripes. Stakes fancy finished and painted. Arches of heavy galvanized steel wire. White wood box, dovetailed, extra strong with book. A very attractive and durable set, only...	4 00
No. 8, Rock Maple. All varnished. A very similar set to No. 7. Same general style, but with less ornamentation on Balls and Mallets. Arches of heavy steel wire, coppered with book. A fine durable set, and low priced, at	3 00
No. 9, Rock Maple. All varnished. Cylinder-shaped Mallets, with fancy turning and painting on head. Balls with one wine and two narrow stripes. Fancy turned stakes. Arches of heavy steel wire, coppered. Dovetailed box, with book. Complete set................	2 50
No. 10, Rock Maple. All varnished. Complete set, eight balls, eight mallets. Full size. Mallets design shaped with three stripes around head. Ash handles. Ball with one wide and two narrow stripes. Two stakes. Arches of steel wire, coppered. Dovetailed box, with book. A fine, durable and showy set......	2 00
No. 11, Hard Wood. All varnished. Full set, eight balls, eight mallets. Mallets design shaped with three stripes on head. Balls striped; two stakes. Arches of steel wire, coppered, in dovetailed box. The best set for the money ever offered, only..	1 75
No. 0, Hard Wood. All varnished. Full size, full set, eight balls, eight mallets. Mallets barrel shape. Arches and stakes complete, in hinged cover box. The cheapest all varnished set we have ever offered, only..	1 50
No. X, Hard Wood. Full set, eight balls, eight mallets. Well finished, arches and stakes complete. All packed in full sized, hinged cover box. The cheapest good full set ever offered. Only	1 50
No. XX, Hard Wood. Full set, full size, hinged cover box, style similar to No. X, except stock not so carefully selected, only	1 25
No. 13, Three-Quarter Set. In hinged cover box. Six balls, six mallets, ten arches, two stakes. All hard wood. Good finish. A very good set, and low prices, at...	1 00
No. 15, Half Set. In neat hinged cover box. Four balls, four mallets, ten arches, two stakes. All hard wood. Good finish, only..	0 75

PRICE LIST OF ODD PARTS OF CROQUET SEPARATELY

One Set....Nos.	4.	5.	6.	7.	8.	10.	11.
8 Mallets	$6 00	$3 00	$1 75	$1 25	90c.	65c.	50c.
8 Balls	6 00	3 00	1 40	1 20	90	65	50
10 Arches	60	60	60	60	35	30	30
2 Stakes	45	45	45	45	30	20	20

Sockets for Croquet Arches 50 cents per set of 20.

The other numbers of Croquet on our list we do not break.

PROFESSIONAL CROQUET MALLETS.
OF BEST BOXWOOD.

Each,	75c.	$1.00	$1.00	$1.25
Length of Mallet,	6in.	6¼in.	7in.	7¼in.
Each,	8in.	8¼in.	9in.	10in.
Length of Mallet,..	$1.25	$1.25	$1.25	$1.50

The same bound with Metal Bands on each end to prevent splitting, 50 cts. each, additional.

Best Boxwood Balls, each,........75c.
" Lignumvitæ " " ....75c.

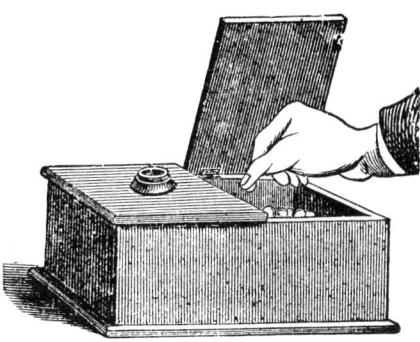

No. A.
THE SECRET BALLOT BOX.
Made of Black Walnut, Fine French Polished and Lined. Can be used for Base Ball, Cricket, Archery, Foot Ball, Boating and all other Sporting Clubs; also for Masonic and Odd Fellow Lodges, Temperance and all other societies Size 9x6x4¼ inches..each. $5 00

No. C.
BALLOT BOX,
Made of Black Walnut, Finely polished. Used for same purposes as No. A. Size, 9¼x6x3¾. Each, $2 50
N. B.—Each Box, Nos. A, B and C, are furnished with 12 white and 6 Black Balls.
White Ballot Balls, extra, per hundred........$0 40
Black   "   "   "   " 0 60
Black Ballot Cubes   "   " 1 00

BALLOT BOX,
No. B. Made of Black Walnut, finely polished, latest style. Used for same purposes as No. A. Size, 9½ x 5½ x 3¼ inches.
Each $3 50
No. 1, Plain,....................... 1 50
"   2   " with Drawer......... 2 00

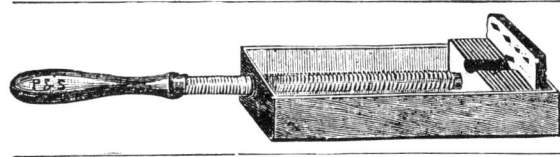

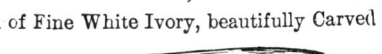

CARD PRESSES.
No. H. For Club rooms. Will hold 6 packs of cards; made of Black Walnut, with thread screw handles to press and keep the cards in shape. Size 9¾x3x5.
Each $1 00

GAVELS, For Societies, Clubs, &c.
No. D. Made all of Fine White Ivory, beautifully Carved and Polished........Each, $10 00
No. E. White Ivory Gavel, carved and Polished Rosewood Handle..........Each, $8 00
No. F. Gavels. Made of Rosewood, Boxwood or Ebony, beautifully carved, of different styles and highly French Polished................................Each, 1 00
No. G. Gavels. Made of Polished Black Walnut, carved........................... "   0 50
Striking Blocks for Societies, etc., made to order.

POLICE CLUBS.—Made of Rosewood or Lignumvitæ Woods.

8 in.	10 in.	12 in.	14 in.	16 in.	18 in.	20 in.	22 in.	
50	60	70	75	$1 00	1 10	1 25	1 50	each.

EBONY POLICE CLUBS.

10 in.	12 in.	14 in.	16 in.	18 in.	20 in.	22 in.	
$1 00	1 25	1 35	1 50	1 60	1 75	2 00	each.

Rosewood Billeys 8 to 15 inch..75c.   "
Ebony   "   8 to 15 " ....$1 00 "
Locust Night Clubs...65c.   "
Police Nippers, Chain, Nickel-Plated...per pair, $1 25
   "   "   Patent Spring, the best made............................   "   2 00
Hand-Cuffs..Polished, per pair, $4 00; Nickel-Plated, $5 00
Hand-Cuffs, for conveying three prisoners together.......... "   "   6 00;   "   7 00
Leg Irons.. "   "   6 50;   "   8 00

PECK & SNYDER,
MANUFACTURERS OF
FIREMEN'S SUPPLIES,
126, 128 & 130 NASSAU STREET, N. Y.

NOTE.—To Fire Companies contemplating purchasing Equipment, we will furnish samples of Shirts, Caps, Belts, etc., for inspection to responsible parties, they to pay all charges, and if required to leave a deposit.

Fire Pictures.—These "Fire Scenes" are fine lithographs, handsomely colored by hand, and are just the thing to decorate the walls of an engine house. Prices do not include frames.

THE LIFE OF A FIREMAN.
Size 25x36 inches.

"Start her lively, Boys!"..................$3 00
"Jump Her, Boys!"........................ 3 00
"The Fire! Shake Her Up!"................ 2 00
"Steam and Muscle,"..................... 3 00
"The Metropolitan System,"............... 3 00

FIRE PICTURE.—THE AMERICAN FIREMAN.
Fine Lithographs.

"Always Ready,"   sizes 20x36 inches........ $1 25
"Rushing to the Fire,"   "   " 1 25
"To the Rescue,"   "   " 1 25
"Facing the Fire,"   "   " 1 25

PATENT LEATHER BELTS FOR FIREMEN'S USE.
Per doz.

No. 101. Plain Black Patent Leather Belts, assorted sizes..$ 3 00
" 104. Black Patent Leather, half lined, with name of Company in any color, block letter, and in sunk panel any color, with initials or numbers on slide loop to match (sizes to measure) see cut 9 00
No. 105. Red, white or blue patent leather, same style as No. 104 ....11 00

The above cut represents styles No. 104 and 105, the difference being in the color of the leather only; red, white or blue leather costing more than the black.

Per doz.
No. 106. Black patent leather, full lined with fine enameled leather, and fancy stitched with silk around the edges, name of Company on back, and number on slide loop (see cut)................. $11 00
" 107. Red, white or blue patent leather, made same style as No. 106................................ 13 00

The above cut represents style Nos. 106 and 107. the difference being in the color of the leather only.

No. 108. Black patent leather, full lined, and bound with scalloped edge, red, white or blue patent leather, name on back (see cut)...per doz., $17 00
" 109. Red, white or blue patent leather, made same style as No. 108................. . "   19 00
New York Regulation Belt, made of the best leather, with a spring nickel-plated clasp, socket to carry spanner, and side strap with spring to catch on the ladder while using the pipe at a fire. They have saved many a fireman's life. All complete...each, 3 10

FIRE DEPARTMENT BUTTONS, three sizes, nickel and gilt, and **POST OFFICE BUTTON** 2 sizes, Coat and Vest.

No. 1. Fireman's Parade Shirts.　　　　　　　　　　　　　No. 2. Fireman's Service Shirts.

Coat for Post-office..................per doz., $1 00	Large size, Coat Button.....gross, $7 50; doz., 90c.
Vest " " " .... " 50	Medium size, Shirt Button... " 5 50; " 75c.
	Small size, Vest Button..... " 4 00; " 50c.

FIREMEN'S SHIRTS.—We get up several different styles and patterns of Shirts, both long and in jacket form.

The prices of these shirts depends on the market price of flannel, and also on the quality of the goods. We can make these shirts plain, from $24 to $30 per dozen, and those with fancy trimming and monograms, or figures on breast, from $30 to $40 a dozen. The Buttons used on most of the Fire Shirts are made of wood molds covered with flannel, to match Shirts, but the latest and most attractive are those of Silver Plated Metal, and Gold Plated for the Officers. They add very much to the Beauty of the Shirt, and only (for one dozen shirts) $5 extra, (about the actual cost of the buttons). We do not ask a profit on the buttons as they always help the sale of our shirts. We place ten on the breast and two on each cuff.

Worsted Scarfs, or Tippets for collar..........$2 50 per doz.
Leather Rings, with figure for tippets......... 2 50 "

Firemen's Parade Shirts. Made of red, white, blue or gray opera flannel, handsomely trimmed, and bound on collar and cuffs, with monogram or figure on front. Per doz., $33 00

Firemen's Service Shirts. Best flannel, with figure or monogram............ " 30 00
Very good flannel, with figure or monogram.. " 27 00

Firemen's Shirts and Jackets. Shirt Jacket, with figure or monogram on front, of best flannel, per dozen, $30.00; the same, of cheaper flannel....................... " 27 00

THE MERRIMAN GRADUATE WATER BELT.

Invented by Captain C. S. MERRIMAN, Inventor and Patentee of the suit used by the noted swimmer PAUL BOYTON, and supplied to the United States Government and all European Life Saving Stations.

With the Merriman Graduate Water Belt the timid and inexperienced person can learn to swim without an instructor, and enjoy the exhilarating sensation of floating with perfect safety in the deepest water, and the wearing or carrying of the belt cannot be noticed.

In quiet water, a gentleman can bathe and swim and keep his cigar lighted, or a lady need not wear oiled silk to keep her head dry ! !

The Swimmer has a safeguard against cramp ; his muscle movements are not hampered nor his progress retarded. Captain Merriman always uses one, and has saved many persons from drowning.

A very important feature of the belt is that it makes a RELIABLE POCKET LIFE PRESERVER, and being always present, always ready, and PERSONAL PROPERTY, it is a precautionary measure, invaluable to travelers on the water.

Full printed description accompanies each belt.

They are made in 4 sizes from the Youth of 75 pounds to the heavy person of 200 pounds weight.
All sizes, price each,.....................　　　　　　　　..............................$3.00

FIREMEN'S BADGES FOR SERVICE USE AND PRIZES.

No. 283.

No. 284.

No. 285.

No. 286.

No. 287.

These styles of Badges are adopted by a great many cities, and are made up very handsome for Engines, Hose or Truck Companies. They are made of German silver or gilt metal. These cuts represent Badges the exact size.

No. 823.—This is the most approved badge now in use, and is the same shape as the New York Fire Department.

Badges in either German silver or gold, gilt styles, Nos. 284, 286, 287 and 823, with same name and number of company engraved on top and bottom. Per doz. $12 ; Per 100, $75 00

Style No. 285, all gold or all silver gilt, with name on top and number or company on bottom or design of Engine, Hose Carriage, Hook and Ladder Truck or number in piece.
Per doz. $12 00; Per 100, $75 00

Or we can furnish the No. 285 badge, with a silver border and gold centre at the same price: we cannot sell less than 50 at the 100 price as given. We will mail sample badges on receipt of price for approval.

MONTGOLFIER BALLOONS.

A splendid article for public and private display, variegated colors, with new floating attachments (patented). No more alcohol, kerosene or stove-pipes to be used.

Circumference.		Circumference.	
5 feet	per doz., $2 00	15 feet	per doz., $7 00
6 "	" 2 50	20 "	" 10 00
8 "	" 3 25	25 "	" 14 00
10 "	" 4 25	30 "	" 18 00

Animal Figure Baloons.—A great novelty; being Baloons inflated with hot air in the same manner as the ordinary Paper Balloons- They are made of strong Tissue Paper, and in the shape of mammoth Pigs, Elephants, Fishes and other animals, and different figures; being very easy to inflate and send up, they present in the air a life-like representation of the animal, causing great merriment to all who may see the ascension. Animal Figure Baloons Per doz. $18 00

FIREMAN'S LEATHER AND CLOTH CAPS FOR SERVICE AND FATIGUE DUTY.

No. 171.—LEATHER BADGES. The above badges are designed for either the helmet or fatigue caps. Made of black leather.

Lettered, with panel for firemen's caps, per doz. $7 00
" in panel, half lined and stitched " 9 00
" in panel, full lined and stitched " 11 00

The above of red, white or blue patent leather, extra.................... per doz. $1 00

No. 172.—HELMET CAP. Made of black enameled leather, with best leather peaks, with seams corded with leather; a very nice, light, durable hat, without badges..................Per doz., $20 00
Red, white or blue patent leather, without badges... " 22 00
Red, white, blue, or black enameled cloth, with imitation leather peaks, without badge...... " 15 00
For price of badges, see illustration and description of No. 171.

No. 173.—FATIGUE CAPS. Best cloth caps, leather peaks, silk lined..........Per doz.; $15 00
Best flannel caps, leather peaks, well lined.. " 12 00
Gold gilt or silver gilt wreaths, with number of company, same as shown on cap No. 174, are 25c additional.
Campaign Caps, the above shape or military shape, made of enameled cloth, any color suitable for parades not lined, and made cheap... Per doz., $6; per 100, $25

No. 174.—N. Y. REGULATION. This style, made of the best blue cloth, lined throughout with leather and hair cloth, with spring top, so as to retain shape, trimmed with Fire Department buttons. This is the finest cap that can be made...Price, per doz., $21 00
The same shape, of red, white or blue enameled leather............................... " " 23 00
Wreaths in gold or silver gilt, as shown in the illustration, are 25 cents a cap additional. For price of leather lettered badges for the above, see No. 171.
Gilt embroidered wreaths, with name for officers, etc............................each, $1 50

No. 179.—EIGHT-CONE FIRE HELMET.

Black, with front.......................................Per Dozen, $48 00

Fancy colored, with front..................................... " 51 00

No. 175. **Jockey-Shaped Fire Cap.** (See Cut.)

Best enameled leather, black.......................................Per dozen, $20 00
" " red, white or blue....................................... " 22 00
Enameled cloth, red, white, black or blue....................................... " 12 00
Lettered fronts for the above are $7, $9 and $11 per dozen extra.

No. 176. (See cut). This Hat is made of Sole Leather like our eight-Cone, and can be finished up black luster varnish or painted any color. We have them of light, medium or heavy weight; they resemble the eight cone Regulation, with exception of not having the four small cones between the four large ones. We put on any color frontispiece and either of our five metal tips, same as we offer with the eight cones. Price, if black, 48.00 per dozen; colored, 54.00 per dozen.

No. 177. (See cut). No Hat made for use in the Fire Department has excelled this one. It has been in use about fifty years, and for real service and durability has proven superior to all the many styles of Helmets, Derbys, Skull Hats, and others under fancy names, all of which, more or less, have failed to be of an equivalent and practical service.

To properly equip a Company to appear and really be Duty Firemen this is the best Hat, as it will last for years, and has saved many valuable lives from falling timbers and other burning property. By reversing it at hot fires it will prevent the heat from injuring the face. Many suppose that the more Cones there are in a hat the stronger it is; this is not so, as Hats having a larger number of cones are made of lighter leather, and in consequence not as durable for duty. Our Hats are finished in the best manner, and have a sufficient ventilation.

Prices for Light, Medium, or Service weight, with Eagle, Tiger, Hound, Fox or Fireman Tip, Black $54.00 per dozen. White, Blue or any color, $60.00 per dozen.

No. 178. **Fancy Cone Hats.** For Officers of Departments, with the regular hand-made Cones; not the imitation pressed ones.

These are for Officers, Presentation and Fairs. When made with Fancy Embossed Rim, Gold Leather Fronts, Painting of Steamer, Hose Carriage or Truck. 16 to 200 cones each, $12 to $70 each.

Send size, colors to be painted, etc., and allow time for their proper manufacture.

Officer's fronts, without hats, in white leather with Leather Lettering, Silk Stitching, $1 25 to $2 00 each. Gilded Fronts with painting of Steamer, Truck or Carriage, $4 00 each,

HATTER'S SIZE MEASURE. To obtain the correct size of the head, use a strip of paper—newspaper will do. Draw it tightly around the largest part of the head, and have the ends just meet. Then measure the length of the paper and the figures below will give you the size according to hatter's measure. An eighth of an inch either way will make no difference. The measures will answer for any style of hat or cap we make, and which we advertise in this catalogue.

18¾ inches is	5⅞	20¾ inches is	6½	22½ inches is	7⅛	24 inches is	7⅝
19 "	6	21 "	6⅝	23 "	7¼	24½ "	7¾
19⅜ "	6¼	21⅛ "	6¾	23⅜ "	7⅜	25 "	7⅞
19¾ "	6⅜	21⅞ "	6⅞	23¾ "	7½	25¼ "	8
20¼ "	6¼	22¼ "	7				

No. 120. **FIREMEN'S LANTERNS AND TORCHES.**

This lantern is now used exclusively by the Fire Departments of New York and Brooklyn and other cities. Furnished with either oil or kerosene burners.

Brass.......................................each, $3 50

Nickel plated throughout....................................... " 5 00

Lighted and regulated without removing the oil cup. We have other styles besides, price from $3 00 to $4 00.

Lanterns with blue or red glass, $1 00 each, extra. Names ground in glass, $1 00 each.

Police Rattle, or Philadelphia Stop Thief. No family should be without one of these Rattles, to call Fire, Police, Watchman or your Neighbors. You have merely to twirl the Rattle around a few times in your hand, and it makes a noise that can be heard a distance of half a mile. Made of Hickory and Ash woods, and are not liable to get out of order. See cut and description elsewhere.......................Price, each, $1 25

TORCHES FOR CAMPAIGN, PARADE AND SPORTING USE.

Manuf'rs Office, 126—130 Nassau St., N.Y.

RALLY FOR THE CAMPAIGN!

PRICES ARE COMPLETE WITH STICKS AND WICKS.

THE PATENT IMPROVED

EUREKA TELESCOPE TORCH,

THE ONLY PERFECT TORCH EVER INVENTED.

Neat, Compact, Light, Clean, Convenient, Cheap.

Price, per 100, complete with Wick, &c., **$40.00**

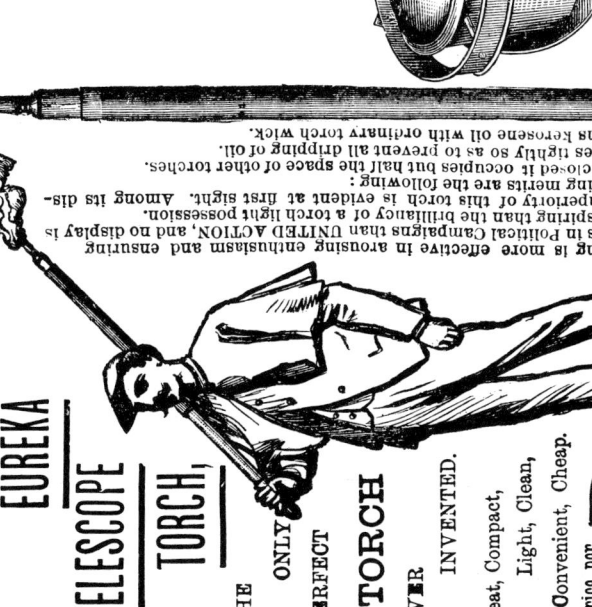

Nothing is more effective in arousing enthusiasm and ensuring victories in Political Campaigns than UNITED ACTION, and no display is more inspiring than the brilliancy of a torch light possession. The superiority of this torch is evident at first sight. Among its distinguishing merits are the following:

When closed it occupies but half the space of other torches.
It closes tightly so as to prevent all dripping of oil.
It burns kerosene oil with ordinary torch wick.

Its beauty and convenience makes it an excellent substitute for the musket for drilling in the Manual of Arms. Nearly 20,000 of these torches were sold outside of this city and Brooklyn in the last Presidential Campaign.

PECK & SNYDER, Owners of Patent.

		Per 100
No. 1. Tin Torch		$14 00
" 2. " Large		20 00
" 4. " Stamped		20 00
No. 5. Cap Lamp to fasten on front of Cap, Hat or Helmet, Nickel Plated, Red, White and Blue Glass, Oil Burner......complete per Dozen, $5 00		

No. 288. Fireman's Duty Trumpet.

FIREMEN'S DUTY TRUMPETS.

Brass	16 inches,	each,	$3 50
"	18	"	"	4 00
"	20	"	"	4 50
" nickel plated	16	"	"	5 50
" " "	18	"	"	6 00
" " "	20	"	"	6 50

No. 289.

PRESENTATION OR PARADE TRUMPETS.

16 inches chased and plated	each,	$15 00
18 " " " "	"	18 00
20 " " " "	"	21 00
16 " extra chased and plated, bell and mouth-piece gold lined, each	"	21 00
18 " "	"	26 00

CORD AND TASSELS (For Trumpets).

Silk	$2 00
Silver	3 00

GERMAN SILVER KEY CHECKS, &c., Nos. 70 to 83, with Name and Address, each 25c.
BRASS BAGGAGE or **SATCHEL CHECKS** Nos. 85 to 89, per 100, Plain, $1.30 to $3.00. Numbering, per 100, extra, $1.00. Name on, extra, ½ ct. per letter.

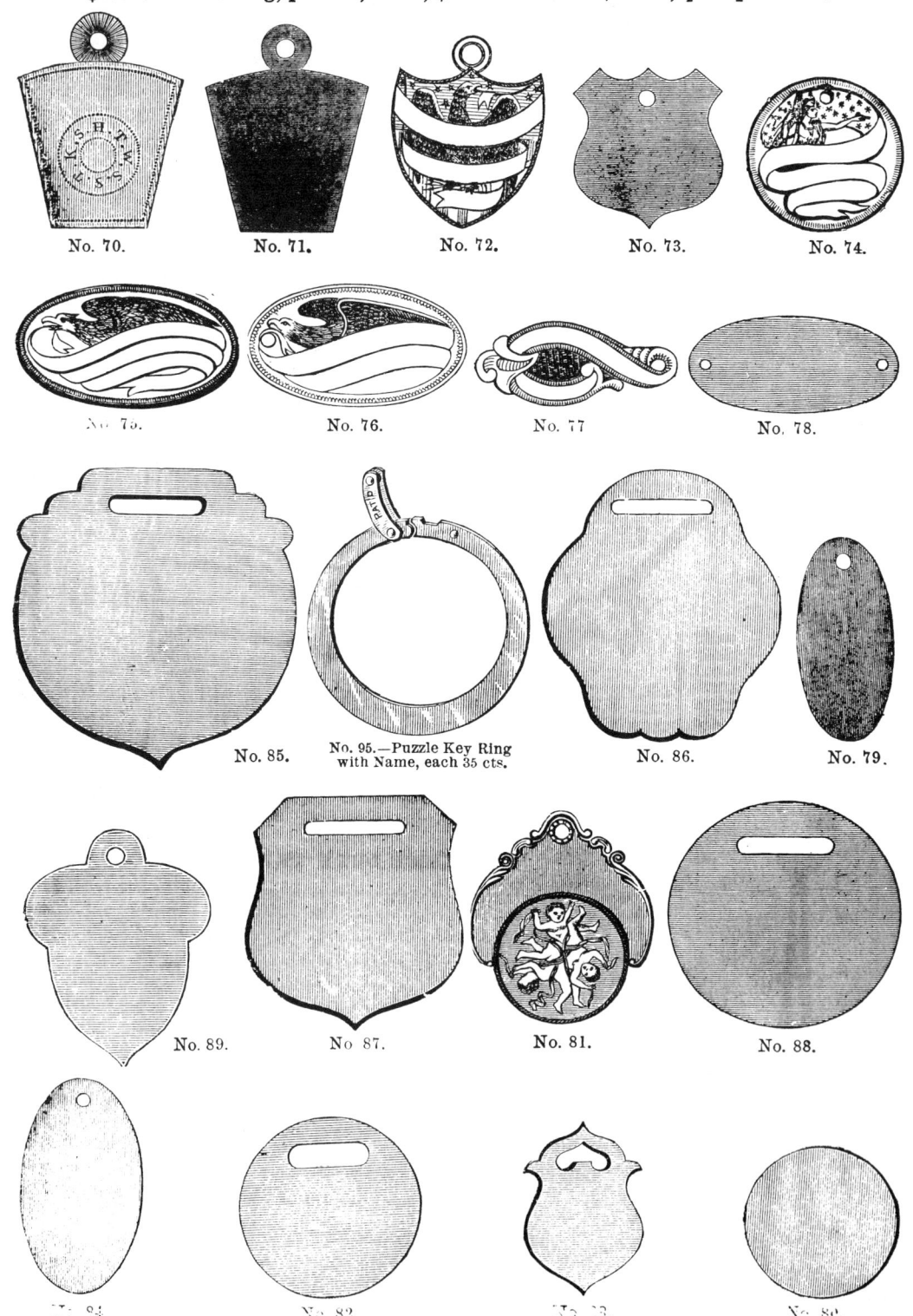

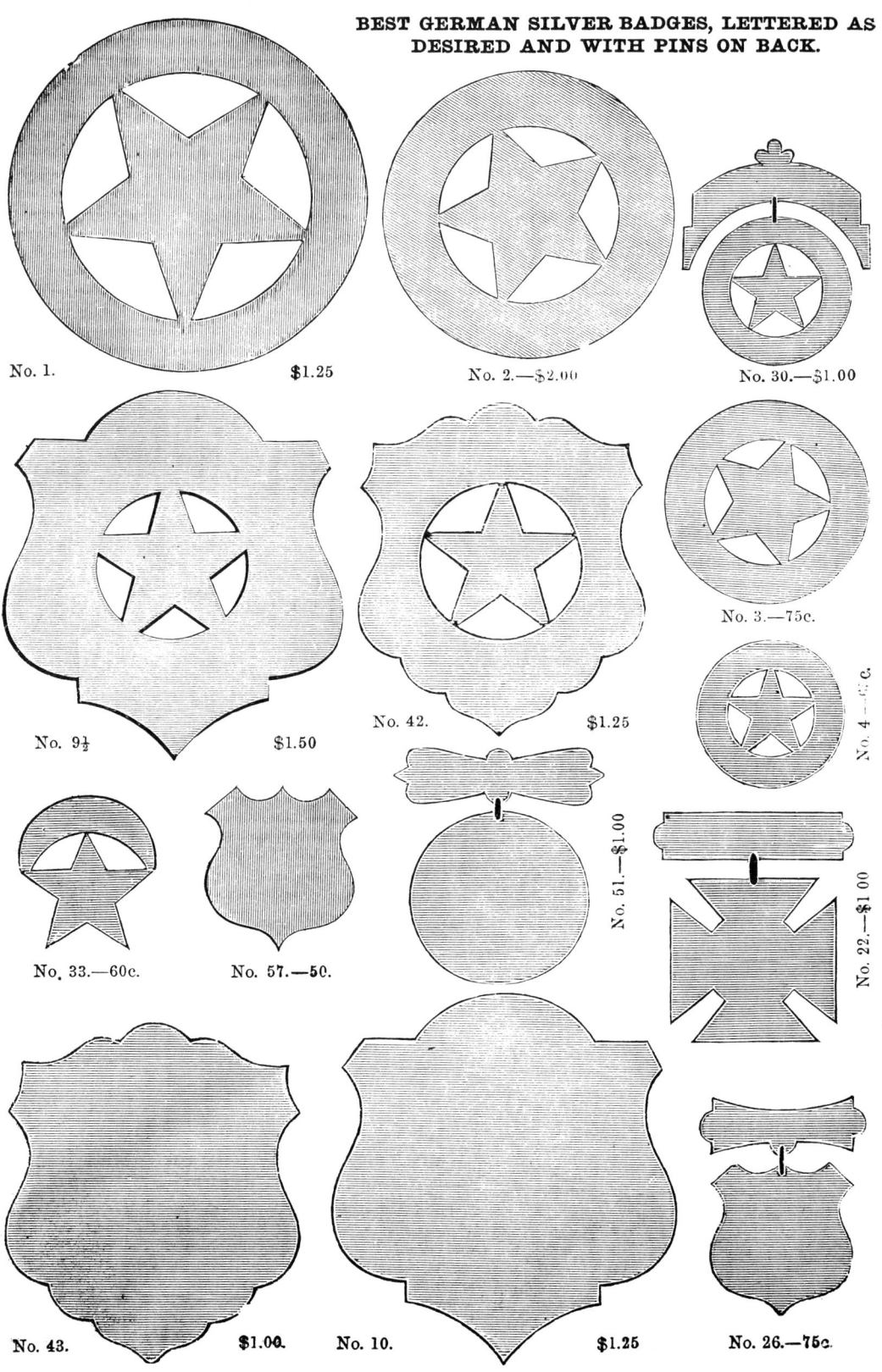

GERMAN SILVER BADGES.

Finest quality of German Silver Badges, for Railroad Companies, Fire Companies, Special Officers, Deputy Sheriffs, Special Police, Detectives, Reporters, Ushers, Athletic Clubs, Societies, Pleasure Clubs, &c. They are highly polished and equal in appearance to Coin Silver. The Pins are all fastened with hard solder.

We manufacture to order, from Coin Silver, any of the Designs herein shown, or such Special Designs as may be wanted, but cannot quote prices until we know the Style, Quantity and Lettering for each Badge.

We also manufacture to order, **Gold and Gold Plated Badges.**

When ordering, do not mutilate the Catalogue by cutting out the illustrations, simply mention the Number of the Badge wanted. These Badges and Plates are stamped to order with any desired lettering.

No. 60.—Conductor's Badge,............each, 30 cts.

No. 61.—Brakeman's Badge,...............each, 30 cts.

No. 62.—Baggage Master's Badge,........each, 30 cts

No. 64.—Conductor's Badge, with name..... each, 50 cts.

No. 65.—Trunk Plate, with name........ each, 50 cts.

No. 66.—Trunk Plate, with name........each, 30 cts.

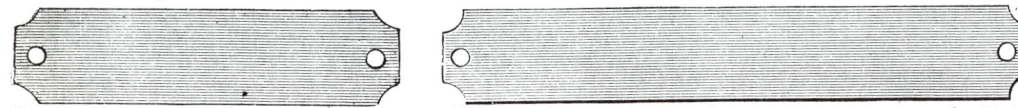

No. 67.—Carriage Plate,.....each, 40 cts.

No. 68.—Carriage Plate, with name............each, 50 cts.

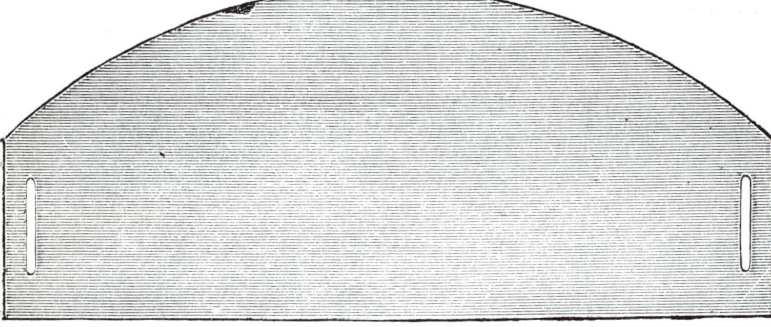

No. 69.—Porter's or general Badge, these can be made of different shapes as desired.

Each, with name. $1.00

SOMETHING NEW AND ORIGINAL, THE IMPROVED "PUZZLE" KEY RING.

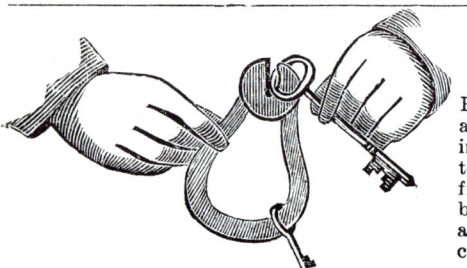

Its Novelty, Durability, Security and Ingenuity Increased. Puzzling and Amusing! Never fails to interest and excite attention. Unsurpassed by anything of the kind ever before invented for the purpose. All the parts are strongly riveted together. They cannot become lost, nor broken, nor the key from accidental or other causes work off in the pocket, or become otherwise lost. This ring can be stamped with the name and address of the purchaser, making a key check and key ring combined. Per dozen by mail, $1.25. Each, 25 cents.

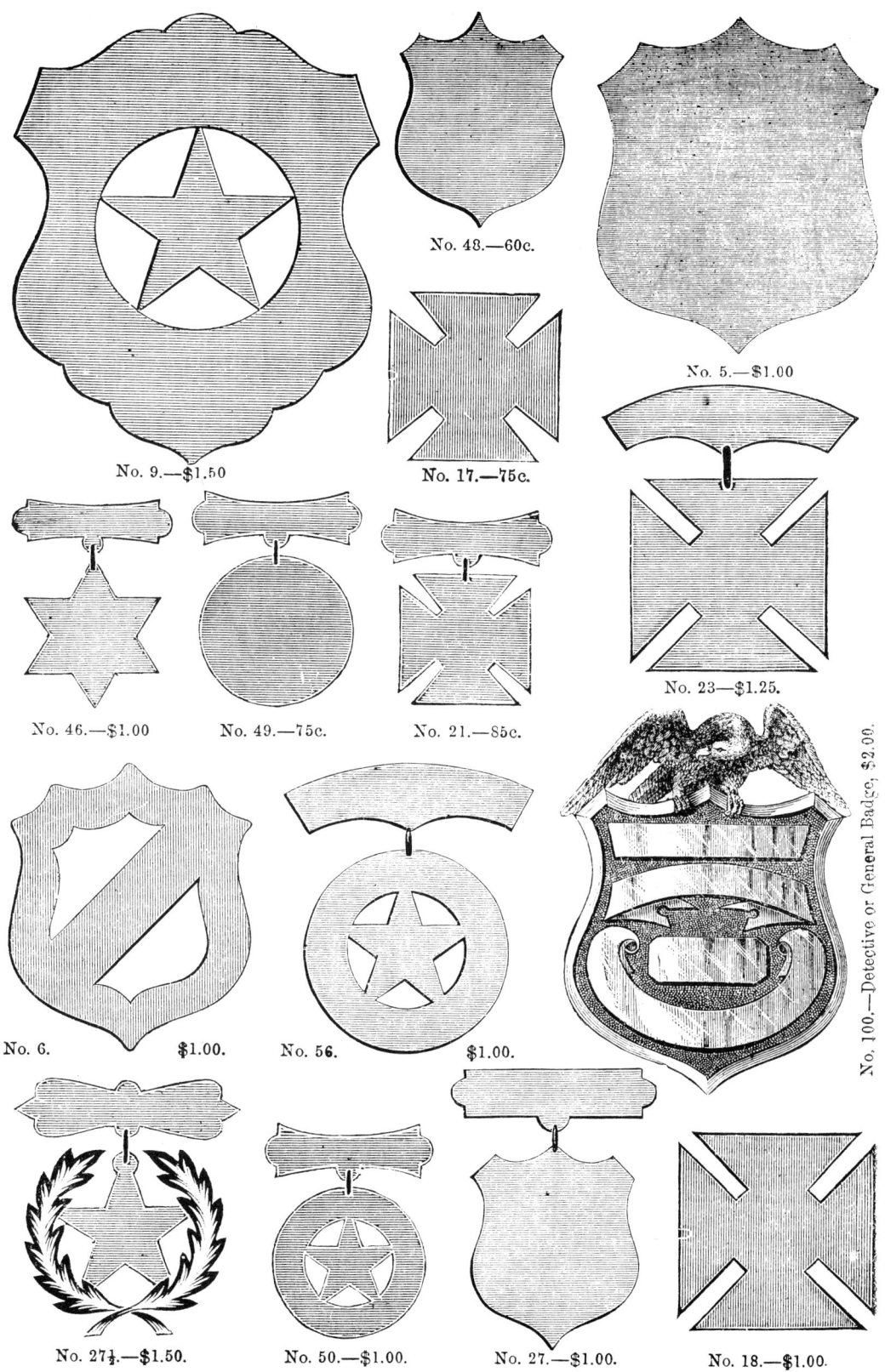

WORSTED GOODS, FOR BOATING, GYMNASTS, BASE BALL, THEATRICAL, &c., KNIT FASHIONED AND TIGHT FITTING. (For prices see following pages).

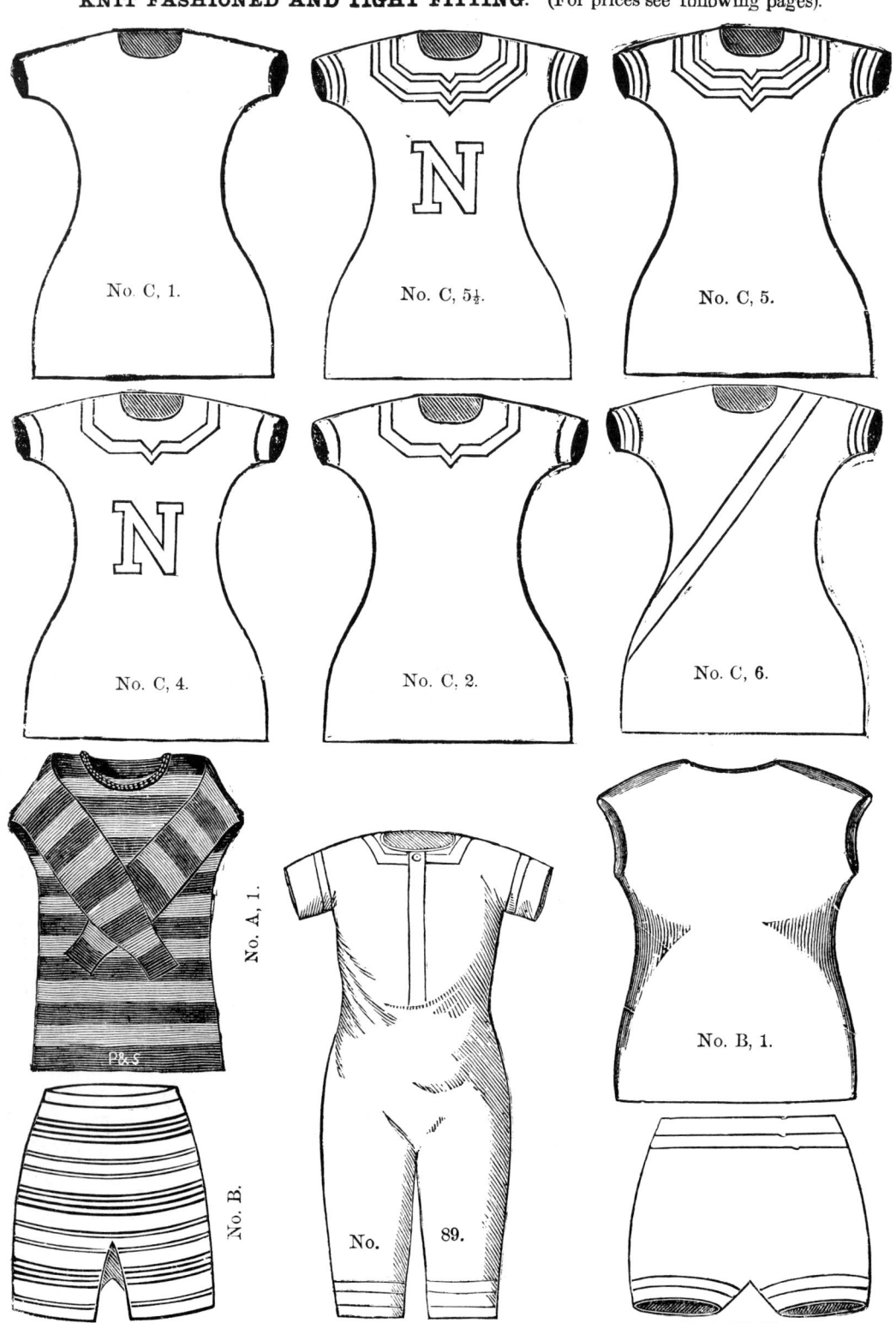

ROWING SUITS.

In stock at all times a large and well assorted stock of Boating Suits, in both plain colors and stripes. All goods in our best grade warranted *fast colors*. This fact will be appreciated by any oarsman who has been unfortunate enough to have worn a suit in which the color came off on his body. To make the color fast is to make the goods expensive, and on this account cheap goods are not fast in color.

No extra charge for making suits to order of any special color.

In ordering these goods the only measurement required is size around chest, waist and length of inseam.

No. A.—SWEATERS.

No. 1.—Fine Wool Sweaters.	White. Best quality		$5 00
2 " " "	Colored (to order only)		6 00
3 Good Quality "	Navy blue or white		3 50
4 Med. " "	" "		3 00
5 Heavy Worsted	" "		4 50
" "	Striped		5 00

No. B.—SLEEVELESS WORSTED SHIRTS.

No. 1.—Sleeveless Worsted Shirts.	Any solid color. Best quality	each	$3 00
2 " " "	Any color. Stripe around neck and arm	"	3 25
3 " " "	" " Star or letter on breast	"	3 25
4 " " "	" " Stripe neck and letter on breast	"	3 50
5 " " "	" " Diagonal sash across breast	"	4 25
6 " " "	Any two colors. Striped around	"	3 25
7 " " "	Any three " " "	"	3 50
8 " " "	Good quality. Colors, Navy blue or maroon	"	1 25

This grade in above colors only. Cannot be made striped.
4-in. letters in these shirts 25c. each ; 2-in. 6c. each.

No. C.—QUARTER SLEEVE SHIRTS.

No. 1.—Quarter Sleeve Worsted Shirts.	Any solid color. Best quality	each	$3 50
2 " " " "	Stripe around neck	"	3 75
3 " " " "	Star or letter on breast	"	3 75
4 " " " "	Stripe on neck and letter on breast	"	4 00
5 " " " "	Two stripes around neck	"	4 00
6 " " " "	Diagonal sash across chest	"	4 75
7 " " " "	Two colors striped around	"	3 75
8 " " " "	Three " " "	"	4 00

(In ordering striped shirts please state width of stripe desired.)

9   Good Quality Worsted   Quarter Sleeve Shirts in colors. Navy blue or maroon ..... " 1 25

This grade in these colors only, and cannot be made in stripes.
Letters or stars on these shirts 25c. each for 4-in. letters, and 6c. each for 2-in letters.

No. D.—ROWING PANTS.

No. 1.—Worsted Knee Tights.	Any solid color. Best quality	per pair	$3 00
2 " " "	Any color, stripe top and bottom	"	3 00
3 " " "	Two colors, striped around	"	3 25
4 Chamois Seats, in knee tights		each	75
5 Pig Skin Seats, " "		"	1 00
6 Flannel Knee Pants.	Navy blue, white or gray	per pair	2 50
7 Worsted "	Good quality. Navy blue or maroon	"	1 25

No. Dx.—ROWING CAPS.

No. 1.—Worsted Scull Caps.	Any color	each	75
" " "	Stripe around bottom	"	75
" " "	Striped around	"	85
" " "	Star in crown	"	1 00
Flannel " "	Made plain or striped. Two colors, with visor	"	75

Special shapes made to order.

No. E.—STOCKINGS.

No. 1.—Long Cotton Hose.	Black, brown, navy, garnet and blue	per pair	50
2 " Worsted Hose.	" " " " "	"	1 00

For other styles of hose see "Tennis Stockings."

No. F.—COTTON SHIRTS AND PANTS.

No. 1.—Sleeveless Cotton Shirts.	White or pink	each	50
2 Quarter Sleeved Cotton Shirts.	White or pink	"	50
3 Cotton Knee Pants.	White or pink	"	50

Any of these shirts or pants, trimmed any color, 25c. each extra. 4-in. letters on these shirts, each 25c. 2-in. 6c.

Cotton goods in above colors *only*.

No. G.—BARGE SHIRTS.

No. 1.—Flannel Barge Shirts.	Good quality	each	$3 00
2 " " "	Better "	"	3 50
3 " " "	Best "	"	4 50

WORSTED GOODS FOR GYMNASTS, BOATING, THEATRICAL & KNIT FASHIONED AND TIGHT FITTING.
For prices see following page.

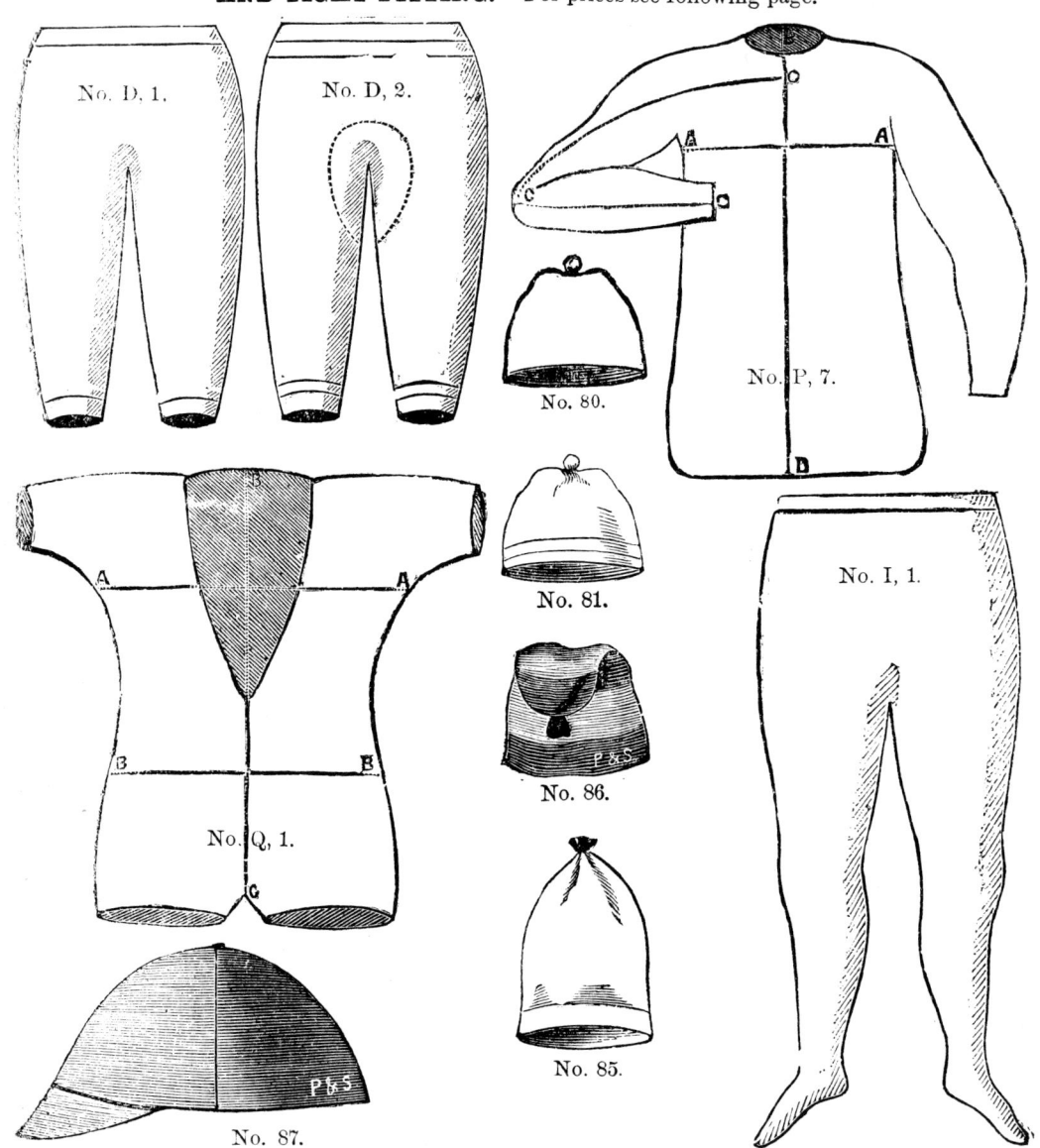

Directions for Self-Measurement for Worsted Goods.

No. P, 7, Gymnasium or Equestrian Shirt.—Around the chest, A to A; length of body, D to D; length of sleeve from centre of back, C to C.

No. Q, 1. The Leotard or Gymnast's dress.—Around the chest, A to A; around the waist, B to B; length from back of neck to crotch, C to C.

No. I, 1. Equestrian or Gymnasium Tights.—Around the waist, A to A; length of inside seam, B to B; length of outside seam, C to C; length of foot, D to D.

No. D, 1. Knee Tights for Boating, Gymnastics, etc.—Around the waist; length of inside seam to knee; length of outside seam to knee; size of leg below knee.

No. 61. Trunks for Boating, Gymnastics, Swimming, etc.—Size around the waist.

No. 13. Saratoga Shirts, ¼ sleeves.—Around the chest; length of body; around the neck.

No. 2. Rowing and Regatta Shirts, no sleeves.—Around the neck; length of body; around the chest.

Bathing Suits. (Full Size).

No. 88.	Cotton, solid or striped, fancy colors	$1 50 and 2 00
" 89.	Worsted, plain, any plain color, (see cut,)	7 50
" 90.	" stripe on neck, sleeves and bottom	8 00
" 91.	" stripe around, any two colors	8 00

ATHLETIC SUITS.

For the Gymnasium, Athletic Games, Boxing, Running, etc.

No. I.—TIGHTS.

No.					
1.—Worsted Tights.	Best quality.	Any desired color	per pair	$3 50
2 " "	Good "	" " "	"	3 25
3 Cotton "	Best "	Colors, Black, flesh, and white	"	1 50

No. J.—ANKLE TIGHTS.

No. 1.—Worsted Ankle Tights. Best quality. Any desired color .... per pair $3 50
    2 " " " Good " " " " .... " 3 00
    3 Cotton " " Best " Black, flesh, and white .... " 1 50

No. K.—KNEE TIGHTS.

No. 1.—Worsted Knee Tights. Best quality. Any desired color .... per pair $3 00
    2 " " " Good " " " " .... " 2 75
    3 " " " Medium quality. Navy blue or maroon .... " 1 25
    4 Cotton " " Good " White and flesh, only .... " 50

No. L.—KNEE PANTS.

No. 1.—Flannel Knee Pants. Navy blue, white or gray .... per pair $2 00
    2 " " " " " Best quality .... " 3 00
    3 Canton Flannel Knee Pants. Blue or white. " " .... " 1 25

No. M.—SHORT RUNNING PANTS.

No. 1.—Best Quality. Satin Running Pants. Any color, to order only .... per pair $5 00
    2 Good " " " " " " " " .... " 3 50
    3 Best " Silk " " " " " " .... " 5 00
    4 Good " " " " " " " " .... " 3 50
    5 Flannel " " " " .... " 2 00
    6 " " " " Second quality .... " 1 50
    7 Silesia " " White or blue .... " 75

Above Pants are loose fitting and come above knee. In ordering state length of inseam required.

No. N.—TRUNKS.

No. 1.—Worsted Trunks. Best quality. Any desired color .... per pair $1 75
    2 " " Good " " " " .... " 1 50
    A Cotton " For bathing, swimming, etc. Fancy stripes .... " 25
    B " " " " " " " .... " 35
    C " " " " " " " .... " 40
    D " " " " " " Solid colors .... " 50

No. O.—VELVET TRUNKS.

Used by all gymnasiums and athletic clubs. Forming a handsome finish to the suit and being made full around the hips. Preventing the person from the exposure attendant on all tight fitting suits. A very handsome and dressy garment. Should be used whenever public exhibitions are given.

No. 1.—Best Quality, Velvet Trunks. Garnet, black or blue .... per pair $1 50
    2 " " " " Any other color to order only .... " 1 75

These Trunks are cut full and are necessary to all who frequent the gymnasium.

No. P.—WORSTED AND COTTON SHIRTS.

No. 1.—Sleeveless Worsted Shirts. Best quality. Any desired color .... each $3 00
    2 " " " Medium quality. Navy blue or maroon .... " 1 25
    3 " Cotton " Good " White and flesh .... " 50
    4 Quarter Sleeved Worsted Shirts. Best quality. Any desired color .... " 3 50
    5 " " " " Medium quality. Navy blue or maroon ..... " 1 25
    6 " " Cotton " Good " White and flesh .... " 50
    7 Long Sleeved Worsted " Best quality. Any desired color .... " 3 50
    8 " " " " Good " " " " .... " 3 25
    9 " " " " Medium quality. Navy blue or maroon ...... " 1 50
   10 " " Cotton " Good " White, black and flesh ...... " 1 50

No. Q.—LEOTARDS.

No. 1.—Worsted Leotards. Best quality. Any desired color .... each $3 75
    2 " " " " To button under crotch .... " 3 50
    3 " " " " Different color around opening .... " 4 25

No. R.—SWEATERS, LONG SLEEVES.

No. 1.—Fine Lambs Wool Sweaters. Ex. heavy. Pure white .... each $5 00
    2 " " " " " Colored. To order only .... " 6 00
    3 Good quality " " White .... " 3 50
    4 Medium quality " " " .... " 3 00
    5 " " " " Navy blue .... " 3 00

No. S.—LONG STOCKINGS.

No. 1.—Long Cotton Stockings. Navy, garnet, brown, black and blue .... per pair $ 50
    2 " Ribbed Worsted Stockings. All colors including gray .... " 1 00
    3 " " " " Ex. heavy. All colors .... " 1 50

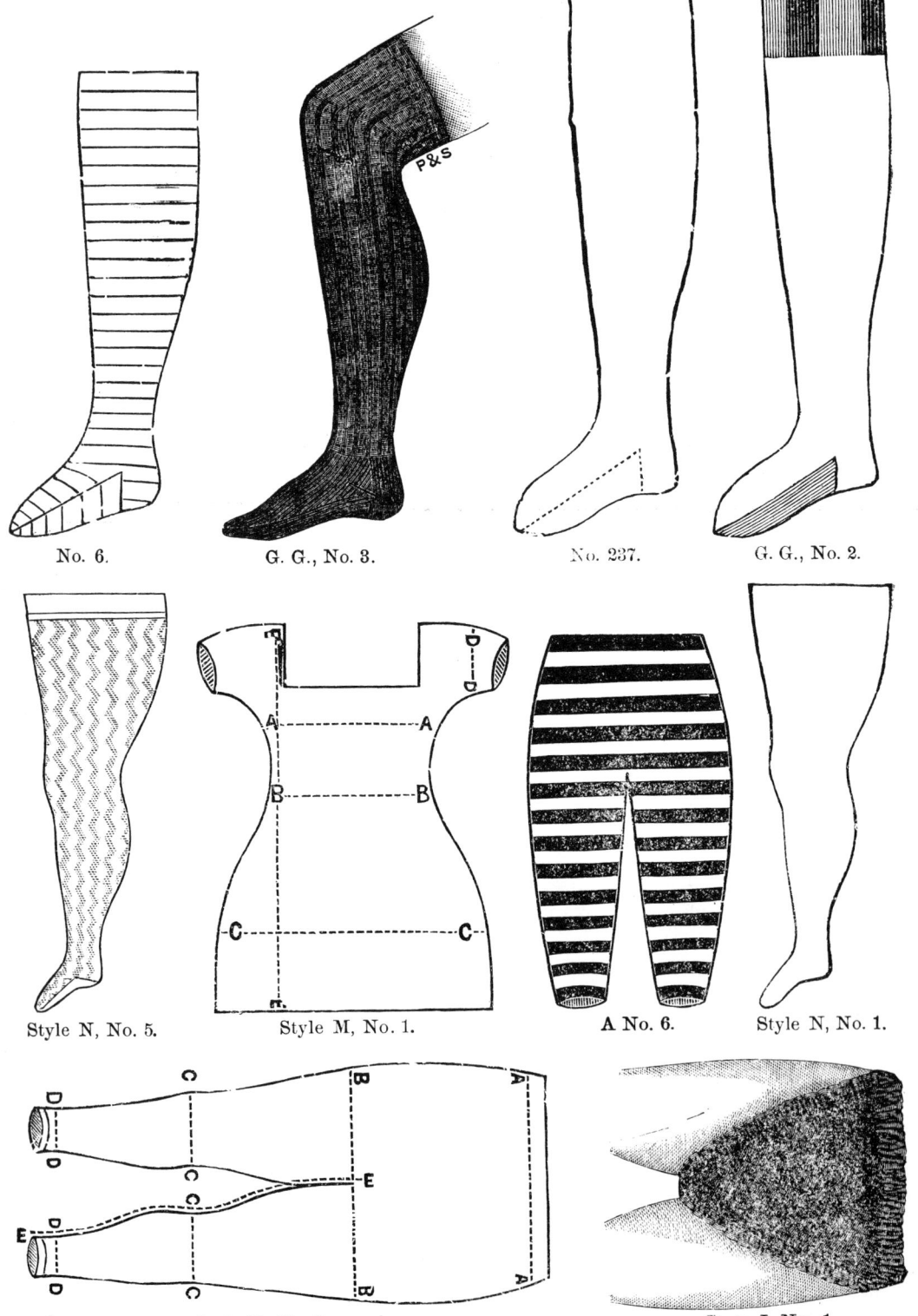

Style A.—Silk Tights.

No. 1. All Silk Tights, best quality, all colors...........per pair, $10.00
    2.   "   "   "   "   2 colors, striped................." " 11.00
    3. Silk Tights, cotton tops, all colors.................." " 9.00
    4.   "   "   "   2 colors, striped..............." " 10.00
    5. Perforated Silk Tights, all colors, (see cut)........" " 18.00
    6.   "   "   "   2 colors........................" " 20.00
    7. Ankle Tights same price as full Tights. Special designs to order.

Style B.—Worsted Tights.

No. 1. First Quality Worsted Tights, heavy weight, any color, (see cut).....per pair, $3.50
    2.   "   "   "   "   "   2 colors, striped ...." " 3.75
    3.   "   "   "   "   light weight, any color............" " 3.25
    4.   "   "   "   "   2 colors, striped ...." " 3.50
    5.   "   "   "   "   heavy weight, 1 inch perpendicular strip..." " 16.50
    6.   "   "   "   "   "   2 inch   "   "   "......" " 14.00
    7.   "   "   "   Fools' Tights, each leg different color,......" " 4.00
    8. Ankle Tights same price as full Tights. Fancy designs and patterns to order. Spangling to order. (See cut.)

Style C.—Cotton Tights.

No. 1. Heavy English Cotton Tights, white..................per pair $1.50
    2.   "   "   "   "   flesh ...." " 1.50
    3.   "   "   "   "   black ...." " 1.50

Cotton Tights in these Colors only as we cannot recommend Cotton goods in high Colors. Lisle Thread Tights we do not keep. Preferring to sell our light weight Worsted Tight, which presents an almost silky appearance, and is much more elastic and durable. Lisle Thread Tights made only to order.

Style D.—Silk Shirts.

No. 2. All Silk Equestrian Shirts, best quality, any color............each $10.00
    2.   "   "   "   "   2 colors, striped..............." 11.00
    3. Silk Shirts, cotton bottoms, any color ...." 9.00
    4.   "   "   "   "   2 colors, striped ...." 10.00
    5. Fancy designs and patterns to order.
    5. Perforated Silk Shirts, any color ...." 18.00
    7.   "   "   "   2 colors ...." 20.00

Style E.—Equestrian Worsted Shirts.

No. 1. First Quality Worsted Shirts, heavy weight, any color, (see cut))......each $3.50
    2.   "   "   "   "   "   2 colors, striped..............." 3.75
    3.   "   "   "   "   light weight, any color............" 3.25
    4.   "   "   "   "   "   2 colors, striped.............." 3.50
    5.   "   "   "   "   heavy weight, 1 inch perpendicular stripe.." 16.50
    5.   "   "   "   "   "   "   2 inch   "   "   " 14.00
    7.   "   "   "   Fools' Shirts, 2 colors........................." 4.50

Style F.—Equestrian Cotton Shirts.

No. 1. Heavy English Cotton Shirts, white·..................each $1.50
    2.   "   "   "   "   flesh........................" 1.50
    3.   "   "   "   "   black........................" 1.50

Style G.—Silk Leotards and Body Dresses.

No. 1. Silk Leotards, any color.............................each $10.00
    2.   "   "   2 colors.............................." 11.00
    3. Silk Body Dress, laced in front, any color..........." 13.50
    4.   "   "   "   "   "   2 colors............." 15.00

Style H.—Worsted Leotards and Body Dresses.

No. 1. Best Quality Worsted Leotards, any color, (see cut)..........each $3.75
    2.   "   "   "   2 colors............................." 4.00
    3.   "   "   Body Dress, any color, (see cut).........." 4.00
    4.   "   "   "   "   2 colors........................." 4.25

Style I.—Silk Trunks.

No. 1. Best Quality Silk Trunks, any color..........................per pair $6.50
    2.   "   "   "   "   striped around......................" " 7.00

Style J.—Velvet Trunks.

No. 1. Best Quality Velvet Trunks, any color.......................per pair $1.75
These Trunks are puffed and handsomely made. Indispensable to Circus Riders, Leapers, Tumblers, &c.

Style K.—Worsted Trunks.

No. 1. Best Worsted Trunks, any color.............................per pair 1.75
    2.   "   "   "   light weight.........................." " 1.75
    3.   "   "   "   any color, fashioned hips................" " 2.00
    4.   "   "   '   striped............................" " 2.00

N. B.—Any of the above goods can be sent either by mail or express. Persons wishing them in a hurry and to be sent by mail, will please remit 25 cents in addition to the advertised price, and for safety in carriage, 10 cents extra for registering package.

Equestrian Tights. Scale of Sizes for Ordering from Self-Measurement.

Size.	Around the Waist, AA.	Length of Inseam, BB.	Length of Outside Seam, CC.	Length of Feet, DD.
00,	28 in.	26 in.	35 in.	8½ in.
0,	30 "	28 "	38 "	9 "
1,	32 "	30 "	41 "	9 "
2,	34 "	32 "	43 "	9½ "
3,	36 "	33 "	45 "	10 "
4.	38 "	34 "	47 "	10½ "

Trunks measure the same in the waist as Tights.

Equestrian Shirts. Scale of Sizes for Ordering from Self-Measurement.

Size.	Around the Chest, AA.	Length of Body, BB.	Length of Sleeve from Centre of Back, CCC.
00,	26 in.	22 in.	21 in.
0,	28 "	25 "	23 "
1,	31 "	27 "	25 "
2,	33 "	29 "	27 "
3,	36 "	31 "	28 "
4,	38 "	33 "	30 "

The "Leotard" Dress. Scale of Sizes for Ordering from Self-Measurement.

Size.	Around the Chest, AA.	Around the Waist, BB.	Length from Back of Neck To Crotch, CC.
0,	28 in.	26 in.	24 in.
1,	31 "	28 "	25 "
2,	33 "	30 "	27 "
3,	36 "	32 "	29 "
4,	38 "	34 "	31 "

Body Dress. Scale of Sizes for Ordering from Self-Measurement.

Size.	Around the Chest, AA.	Length of Sleeve from Center of Back, BBB.	Length from Back of Neck To Crotch, CC.
0,	28 in.	23 in.	24 in
1,	31 "	25 "	25 "
2,	33 "	27 "	27 "
3,	36 "	28 "	29 "
4,	38 "	30 "	31 "

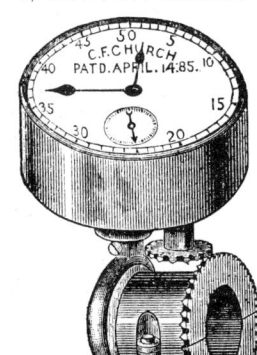

THE CHURCH BICYCLE AND TRICYCLE CYCLOMETER.

From the principle of construction, the correct registering of this machine cannot be disputed. It deals with positive motion only, and when adjusted to a Bicycle becomes part of it, and no motion can be given to the Bicycle, without being registered. There are no balls, or springs to get out of order, the whole machine consisting of nine cog wheels, the large wheel of the Bicycle forming the tenth. It has the following points in its favor.

1st. Absolutely correct in the registering of distances.
2d. Simplicity of construction.
3d. Can be read from the saddle.
4th. Can be adjusted to any machine.
5th. Has lamp attachment.
6th. The only machine in the market, that deals with *positive motion only*

DESCRIPTION.

The dial is like that of a watch in size and shape, except that the figures run by fives, from one to fifty, the minute hand going around once a mile, the hour hand once in fifty miles, and the second hand once in one thousand miles. It is full nickel plated, and weighs with ball attached about ten ounces. The ball can be detached, and a lamp attached, making a cyclometer and lamp combined.

In ordering give size and make of wheel. Price each, $9.00

PECK & SNYDER'S NEW HOME GYMNASIUM.

The "Home Gymnasium" embodies all the virtues to be derived from attending a regular gymnasium, but far more beneficial in its results, as the tendency in a gymnastic school is to overdo, and thus neutralize the otherwise good results of judicious muscular exercise.

There are several objects sought to be attained by a course of gymnastic training.

One is to call into use certain parts of the body that are not otherwise brought into sufficient action, as, for instance, the muscles of the arms, chest, etc.

Another is to exercise parts that are weak, such as the lungs, back, stomach, etc.

To know when, just how much, and what kind of exercise to take so that the most benefit may be had, is the problem for us to determine.

The "Home Gymnasium" consists of pulleys, cords and weights such as have been used in our best gymnasiums for many years and is considered the most valuable device among many of various kinds, but to which valuable improvements have been added and the whole thing perfected and arranged in elegant form, appropriate to be put in any room in the house. It can be put up in five minutes ready for use, is not in the way, and will last a lifetime.

The weights accompanying it range from two to sixteen pounds, the lightest being for delicate children, the heaviest for a strong man.

The principles embodied in its use are, that by its use it is nearly impossible to overdo, as the system is not called upon to exert any sudden efforts, as in the health lift, but the exercise is begun gradually with smaller to greater weights, and only continued until slightly wearied, devoting more and more time and heavier weights until the maximum of time and weights are arrived at, and if strength comes with each succeeding day, will not health come? Are not strength and health convertible terms? And are they not worth all the wealth to mankind, and bring true happiness.

The "Home Gymnasium" also embraces the whole Swedish Movement, and makes it fascinating and interesting. Each machine is put up complete with an illustrated and descriptive catalogue, with instructions how to use, and is the cheapest and most complete apparatus of its kind made. Price, $5.00

Swinging Rings for Children and Adults, of Maple and Black Walnut.

Glued together and polished, cannot break.

3 inches outside diameter, pair,				$0 40
4 " " " "				0 50
5 " " " "				0 60
6 " " " "				0 80
7 " " " "				1 00
8 " " " "				1 20

Exercising Rings for Schools, made of polished maple, in one piece.

Special prices on orders of 25 pairs, or more, for schools or gymnasiums.

5 inches outside diameter, pair,				$0 40
6 " " " "				0 50

Galvanized Wrought Iron Swinging Rings.

6 inches in diameter, per pair				$1 00
8 " " " "				1 50
10 " " " "				2 00
12 " " " "				2 50

The attention of Oarsmen and the Public is called to the New
EUREKA PARLOR ROWING MACHINE, WITH HEALTH LIFT AND CHEST EXPANDER COMBINED.

This Machine gives an axcellent and excellent and exact representation of Rowing. It has the sliding seat movement, and its propelling action is with oars (as in a boat). It is simple in construction and durable, and it packs so small that it can be stowed away in almost any cupboard or closet, and can be put up and worked in any ordinary sized bedroom. It is excellent for oarsmen to train and practice on when the weather or any other cause prevents them reaching the river. A beginner can learn on it to be a good sculler as well as increase his muscular and physical development. By shifting the chain links attached to the lever it can be adapted to the strength of any person, or used and worked by a child twelve years of age. It has been used by a number of ladies with great benefit to their general health. It has been adopted by athletes and recommended by physicians generally. It is the most economical and perfect machine ever made, being sold for $10.00, with all the above-named apparatus included, thus forming a complete Home Gymnasium.

Sent on receipt of postal order or money, to any part of the world. For further particulars send stamp for descriptive circular, with testimonials from prominent athletes who have used them

Coiled Steel Springs, can't wear out. Price, complete, $10 00

PECK & SNYDER, 126, 128 & 130 NASSAU STREET, N. Y.
Manufacturers and Dealers in Gymnasium Goods of every description.
Gymnasiums fitted up and estimates given.
GOODYEAR'S POCKET GYMNASIUM OR HEALTH PULL.

The movements employed in using the Pocket Gymnasium are many and graceful. They are adapted to the old and young of both sexes, and of all degrees of muscular development. The feeble invalid may use them in a small way, and gain new strength day by day. The little child may be taught some graceful movements, and will rapidly acquire strength of limb, erectness of posture, and the rosy tint of health. The mother, the father, brothers and sisters, each member of the household, will employ these life-giving tubes with keen satisfaction and increasing benefit. In this good work we have the co-operation of scores of the best people—ministers, doctors, heads of hospitals, editors and public men. Teachers commend it to pupils, and instruct them in its use.

The Pocket Gymnasium.—Price List.

No. 1. For Children from 4 to 6 years......$1 00
" 2.   "   "   6 to 8 "...... 1 10
" 3.   "   "   8 to 10 "...... 1 20
" 4.   "   "   10 to 14 "...... 1 30

No. 5. For Ladies and Children, 14 years and upward..........................$1 40
" 6. For Gentlemen of moderate strength. 1 50
" 7. Used by Ladies, Children or Gents... 2 00
" 8. For Gentlemen of extra strength..... 2 50

Nos. 7 and 8 are fitted with a screw-eye and hook to attach to the wall or floor. A pair of No. 7, ($4), or 8 ($5), make a complete gymnasium. Extra hooks, 5 cents each, or 60 cents per dozen. We send these goods to any address, post paid, on receipt of price.

Black Walnut Wands, for Exercising with, Beautifully Turned.

4 feet long......................per doz. $3 00 | 5 feet long......................per doz. $4 50
4½   "   .... " 3 50

Blood and Breath. By Professor J. E. Frobisher, author of "Voice and Action," a system of true exercise, illustrated with outline movements, to accompany Goodyear's Pocket Gymnasium. Price, 25c.
The Modern Fencer (new), 40 illustrations of accurate positions, boards, 100 pages.........$0 50
The Modern Gymnast (new), 120 practical illustrations, boards, 125 pages................ 50
Manly Exercises, 42 illustrations, boards... 25
Gymnastic Exercises, 42 illustrations, boards...................................... 50
Pedestrianism, Running, Jumping, etc., 16 illustrations............................. 10
Athletic Sports for Boys. A repository of graceful recreation for youth. Containing complete instruction in gymnastic and limb exercises, skating, swimming, rowing, sailing, riding, driving, angling fencing and broadsword exercises, illustrated with 194 wood cuts, bound in boards. Price, 75c.

HEALTH AND MUSCLE. HOW TO PROMOTE LONGEVITY OF LIFE. THE COLUMBIA PARLOR EXERCISING AND ROWING MACHINE.

It is a duty we owe ourselves and our Maker to give our physical as well as our mental constitution a fair chance for growth, health and improvement; for as Thomson sings:

> "Ah! What avail the largest gift of Heaven
> When drooping health and spirits go amiss
> How tasteless then whatever can be given
> Health is the vital principal of bliss;
> And exercise of health."

Takes the place of the old pulley-weights and rowing machines which have been in use in all the gymnasiums throughout the world; combining every movement of both in the small space of six inches, whereas the old pulling machines are large and cumbersome, taking up to much space for either the Parlor or Gymnasium; besides the operator is obliged to try both before getting all the movements of this machine. It can be disconnected and set under a chair or table when not in use. A miniature gymnasium cannot be surpassed in its excellence for the developing of health, strength and muscle, or in its simplicity of action, throughout the world, and may be used for the following methods of exercise: On the Parlor Gymnasium there are about 30 motions in the various ways of exercising—pulling down, up, right and left, with both and one arm; in to the chest, arms, out to the full extent; one arm up, and one down. All these motions may be made with back towards the machine. Used also for Dumb-bell and Club. The whole machine includes about 40 other motions. Rowing, Lifting, Tug of War, Floor Motions, Pulleys from the floor and several other motions. For illustrations see opposite page.

The Parlor Exercising Machine complete .... $ 5 00
The Rowing and Exercising Machine in one, complete $10 00

RING MOTION.   PUNCHING BAG.   RING MOTION.

THE COLUMBIA INSTANTANEOUS DOORWAY GYMNASIUM AND PARLOR EXERCISING AND ROWING MACHINE.

Superior to anything of the kind in the World.

Each apparatus is complete in itself, and they are stout and strong, being made out of the best ash and hickory. The reader will bear in mind that some fifty different motions, similar to these shown here, can be performed on the apparatus. The benefits of exercise:—Brightens the eye, quickens the hearing, increases the wind, elevates the mind, increases the appetite, causes good digestion and regular action of the bowels, prevents sickness and bad vices. All the good qualities which by its means may be secured, certainly make a man more fit and able to attend to his ordinary avocation, whatever it be, while at the same time it enables him to act with more decision in any case of sudden emergency than he otherwise would be. To quicken the mind and give power and agility, proper nourishment with good care of the body is the only true way.

PRICES OF PARTS FOR ADULTS.

Horizontal Bar, with Brackets Nickeled......$1 50	Low Horizontal Bar.........................$0 50
Gymnastic Eye Rings, Leather Covered, and Snap Hooks with Extension Ropes 2 50	Canvas Punching Bag, hair lined............. 4 50
Horizontal Bars, Chest Bars, and Substitute for Parallel Bars, with Brackets 6 00	Leather Punching Bag, extra 8 50
	Trapeze...................................... 1 00
	The whole complete as above.... ....14 50

PRICES OF PARTS FOR BOYS AND GIRLS.

Horizontal Bar, with Brackets...............$1 50	Independent Bar and See Saw..............$3 00
Trapeze, additional... .... 1 00	Tug of War and Climbing Ropes............. 1 00
Chair Swing 1 00	

THE NEW SPARRING BAG for PROFESSORS & AMATEURS.

PECK & SNYDER'S LIVELY SPARRING BAG COMPLETE $5.00.

Gymnasts all know that it is useless to enter into any contest where strength, skill, and quick action is necessary without a proper training of the arms, back and shoulders, there is no course of training that will develop the form for Sparring, Rowing, Tennis and other Athletic Sports as well as our lively Bag. It is used by Sullivan and other hard hitters of lesser note. The Bag is of the best Foot Ball Leather with a Rubber Bladder inside for inflation, we make them either Round or Egg shape, with Galvanized ring in top for suspending. Samples, by Express, on receipt of price,................................. $5 00

Extra Large Size.. 6 00

PECK & SNYDER'S MODEL AND POPULAR INDIAN CLUBS.

PECK & SNYDER'S MODEL INDIAN CLUBS.

The above Model Clubs are made of selected and seasoned maple and finely French polished, from 1 to 12 pounds.

Sizes......	1 lb.	2 lbs.	3 lbs.	4 lbs.	5 lbs.	6 lbs.	7 lbs.	8 lbs.	9 lbs.	10 lbs.	12 lbs.
Per pair....	$1 00,	1 25,	1 50,	2 00,	2 50,	2 50,	3 00,	3 00,	3 50,	4 00,	5 00.

PECK & SNYDER'S POPULAR INDIAN CLUBS.

These Clubs are made of maple, not fine polished, finished in wax, and quite as good for service as the finer finished.

Sizes......	1 lb.	2	3	4	5	6	7	8	9	10	12
Per pair.....	75c.,	$1 00,	1 00,	1 25,	1 50,	1 50,	1 75,	1 75,	2 00,	2 00,	2 50.

Kehoe's model Clubs made to order, of any desired length or weight.
Wheelwright's Instructions in Indian Club Exercises, ten new illustrations, paper............... 25
Kehoe's Indian Club Exercises, containing thirty illustrations from life, bound in cloth, large size, 1 00
Indian Club, Dumb bell and Sword Exercises, by Professor Harrison, illustrations, in boards..... 25

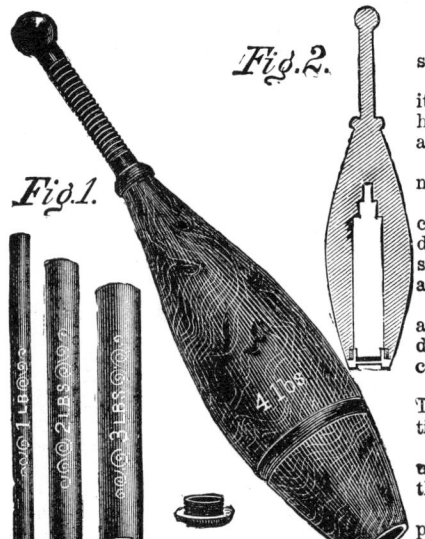

FOLK'S ADJUSTABLE WEIGHT INDIAN CLUB.

Patented March, 12, 1878, and Patent allowed May, 16, 1882, seven pair in one. 4, 5, 6, 7, 8, 9, and 10 lbs.

Fig. 1. is a representation in perspective of the club proper, with its three accompanying weights and detached chamberhead, said head being provided with a rubber plate on the inner side to afford a uniform bearing for the weights.

Fig. 2. is a longitudinal section showing the internal arrangement with the chamber-head attached.

This club is the same externally as the ordinary article, but is chambered in the larger end for the reception of detachable cylindrical weights which are readily, firmly, and noiselessly secured, singly or combined, in sockets in the inner end of the chamber, by a threaded metallic head.

It embraces all the sizes used by ladies, gents, misses, and youths, and is adapted to increasing strength, various movements, and different persons, being equivalent to seven pair of single weight clubs.

It is carefully turned out of the best maple, and finely polished. The weights are made of cast iron, and coppered. The other fittings are neatly set and dressed.

Club swinging is a well tried and established institution and is universally recognized as one of the best methods for developing the muscles of the body, improving the circulation, digestion, etc.

This Club with its many advantages must add greatly to the popularity of this beneficial exercise, and fully merits the favor with which it is being received.   Price $5.00 per pair.

Peck & Snyder's New and Improved Horizontal Bars, for Gymnasium, Stage or Parlor.

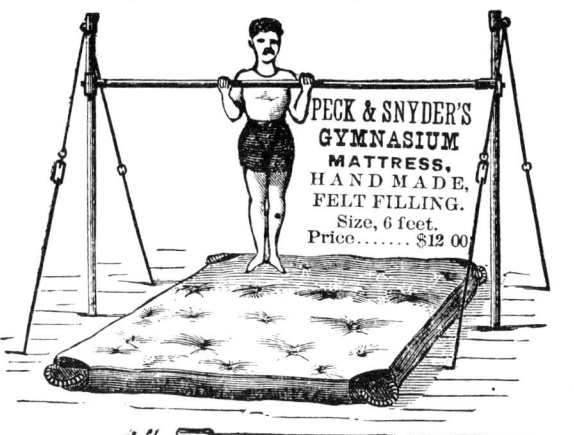

There has long been felt in families (especially where there are young children), the **want of a simple but effective means of physical culture**, now universally admitted to be so essential to health. It is confidently believed that the above apparatus will efficiently supply this want, as it will be found in the highest degree simple, strong, portable, light, neat, well finished and cheap. It can be fixed easily in a few minutes in any room, and as quickly removed; and is adapted for both sexes and all ages. The fastenings are most ingeniously arranged to adjust the bar to any height. Height of upright, 7 feet 8 inches; it can be adjusted as low as 4 feet, and regulated to use from a four to a six-foot bar. The Guy ropes, or side regulators, are made of iron rods. Weight only 68 pounds, without Steel Core, with Steel Core, 80 pounds.

Price of everything complete, plain Hickory Bar, packed ready to ship................$25 00
Price, complete, with Steel Core Bar........................ 35 00

Length in feet..................	4	4½	5	5½	6	6½
Plain Hickory Bars...............	$1 25	$1 50	$1 75	$2 00	$2 25	$2 50
Hickory Bars, Steel Core........				9 50	10 00	10 50

All Horrizontal Bars are made of the best young hickory and finely finished.

PECK & SNYDER'S GYMNASIUM MATTRESSES

Made of extra heavy white canvas, filled with two-inch felt and tufft, heavy leather corners, with round handles, all hand-made, and will last for years with common care. Size, 6 by 5 feet. Price, $12 00. Any size made to order, and prices furnished upon application.

WOODEN WANDS AND RINGS FOR PHYSICAL EXERCISE.

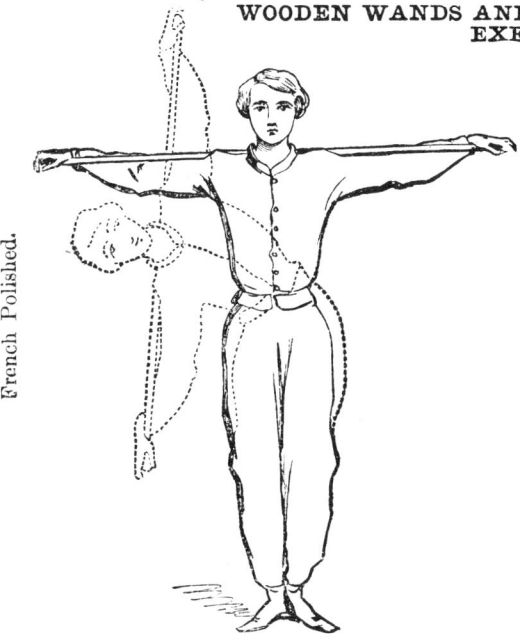

Black Walnut or Cherry Wood Wands, smooth turned and French Polished.

Prices, Black Walnut or Cherry Wood Wands.
4 feet long.............per doz., $3 00
4½ "   "   "   3 50
5 "   "   "   4 50
Wooden Balls for Wands, extra, 1 dozen pair, $2.00.

STEEL CORE TRAPEZE BARS.

Made of the best second growth Hickory, with Steel Core running entirely through and improved Brass Cups to receive ropes. Length between Cups, 20 and 26 inches, weights, 4 and 4½ pounds.
Without Ropes.....................each, $4 00
We make to order any length wanted up to 4 feet. These bars are very desirable for double trapezes. Price quoted upon application.

GIFFORD BROTHERS' HOME GYMNASIUM;
OR
HEALTH EXERCISING APPARATUS.

Fig. 5. Direct Chest Movements.
To Deepen the Chest and Draw the Shoulders Back.

Fig. 6. BICYCLE MOVEMENT.
To Strengthen the Legs, Back and Hips.

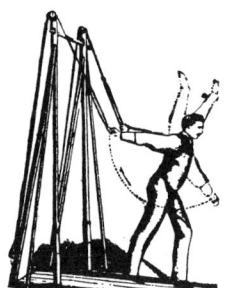

Fig. 7. PULLING WEIGHTS.
To Expand the Chest and Draw the Shoulders back.

Fig. 8. PULLING WEIGHTS
For the Arms, Back and Abdominal Muscles.

Fig. 9. CURVED BOARD.
To Strengthen the Back, Neck, Abdominal Muscles, and Expand the Chest.

Fig. 10. LEG EXERCISE.
To Strengthen the Legs, Hips and Abdominal Muscles.

Fig. 11. Horizontal Bar Exercise.
To Elevate the Ribs and Strengthen and Straighten the Spine.

Fig. 12. Adjustable Trapeze

Fig. 13. STRIKING BAG.
Develops Arms, Chest, and strengthens Lungs.

Fig. 14. HAND ROLLER.
To develope the Hand, Wrist and Forearm.

Fig. 15. CHILD'S SWING.

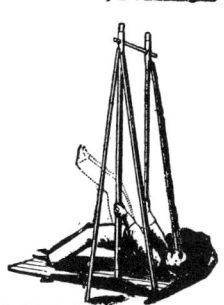

Fig. 16. Back and Stomach Roller
For Kneading and Strengthening the Back and Abdominal Muscles.

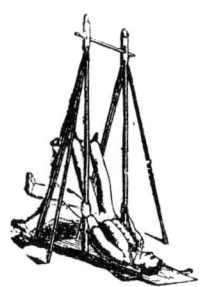

Fig. 17. POSTURAL BOARD.
For the Treatment of Female Diseases, Hernia, etc. and Strengthening the Back, Loins and Abdomen.

Fig. 18. SPRING BOARD.
To Equalize the Circulation, and produce an easy carriage of the Body.

Fig. 19. Combination Bar & Weight Exercise.—Bringing into action at once nearly every Muscle of the body.

Fig. 20. Adjustable Parallel Bars.
To develope the Arms, Chest and the upper portion of the body.

The Illustrations numbered from 1 to 32 show the Principal Combinations which can be made on this Apparatus.

Gifford Brothers' Exercising Apparatus.

A PERFECT GYMNASIUM IN ONE MACHINE.

IT MAKES OVER 30 DIFFERENT COMBINATIONS.　　　　　**EXERCISES EVERY MUSCLE OF THE BODY.**

A sound mind in a sound body is the grandest possession mortals can have; better than power or position. Which is the way to get both and to keep them? Good education, moral and intellectual, serves for the one—good air, temperate living and healthful exercise serve for the other.

Gifford Brothers' Health Exercising Apparatus supplies a want long felt, and brings within the reach of every thinking person the means of acquiring a thorough physical education.

Systematic and healthful exercise consists in frequent changes in the position of the body, bringing into action at each change a different set of muscles, thereby strengthening and symmetrically developing every part of the body. Thus exercise may become an exhilarating pleasure, instead of a tiresome and exhausting labor. By using light weights at first and frequently changing the movements, the weights and amount of exercise can be gradually increased without fatigue.

The attention of physicians need only be called to the variety of movements this Apparatus combines to enable them to see at once that it will prove a valuable adjunct in the treatment of many diseases and a great benefit to the over-worked in their own profession. Aside from the cumulative exercise it furnishes for the young as well as the old, it makes a number of combinations especially adapted for the amusement and instruction of children.

The Gifford Apparatus is superior to all others. Particular attention is called to the rowing machine and pulling weights. The use of ropes and weights give a uniform pull from the start to the finish, instead of starting with little tension and finishing the stroke with a jerk that instantly naps the rower back again to the start—this being the action of rubber straps, spiral or other springs. It is a great improvement over all the old methods, as practiced in gymnasiums; also over all the recent inventions that claim to be rowing machines, but use weights with a perpendicular fall. These weights give to the return the same jerking motion. This obstacle is entirely overcome by having the weights on this Apparatus slide upon inclined tramways, thereby giving an easy gliding motion, which enables the rower to follow them back without being pulled, giving the muscles a chance to relax naturally, and making the recovery of the stroke the same as in rowing.

It is plain that every inch the tramways are placed out of perpendicular retards the fall of the weights. In order to make a rowing machine and pulling weights for natural or practical exercise, it is absolutely necessary to have the ropes and weights separate; this compels each hand and arm to do its work independently, obviating every chance of doing the work with the stronger arm. Independent and separate action of the ropes and weights gives the operator perfect freedom of motion, enabling him while moving his arm in one direction to pull in exactly the opposite direction with the other, giving the reverse action with each arm and set of muscles. *It is absolutely impossible to get this freedom of action and motion with both hands pulling upon one weight.* The foot-rest and height of pull can be accurately adjusted to correspond with the position taken by the rower in his own boat; he can row with every variety of movement. Instead of using ordinary weights, that are unavailable for any other purpose, this Apparatus is constructed with saddles which slide on inclined tramways that will hold the largest or smallest dumb bells. These can be instantly changed to suit the strength of a small child or powerful athlete, and can also be used for other exercises. The rowing seat moves upon convex wheels, which run in grooves in the platform, and are placed at such an angle as to obviate all possibility of tipping when leaning backward with the hands pulling over the shoulders.

Nothing will equalize the circulation and action of the whole system, remove the weariness of an over-taxed brain, like GENERAL *light exercise.* It will divert the mind, and prove the old adage, that a "change of work is rest." Remember, *the more strength and power you have, the less wear there is upon you.*

Ask the majority of people if they exercise, and they will answer, "Yes; we walk a great deal." But ask them if they are sick in the legs, and they will invariably answer, "No." Use the other muscles of the body as much as those used in walking, and you will find, in an incredibly short time, weakness and ill health disappearing. This has been the experience of scores of people, and the personal experience of the inventors. The Apparatus is placed before the public on its own merits, and good results have invariably followed its use.

DR. CHAS. H. GIFFORD.　} *Inventors and*
J. H. GIFFORD.　　　　　　 *Patentees.*
A. C. GIFFORD.

LIST OF PRICES.

The main part of each Apparatus includes the following exercises, and combines a greater number of movements, both preventative and curative of disease, than can be obtained from the use of TWELVE separate machines, each requiring as much room as this single Health Apparatus: *Rowing Machine, Chest Bars, Horizontal Bar, Pulling Weights* (High Chest Motions, Direct Chest Motions, Low Chest Motions, Floor Motions), *Curved Board* (for Back, Chest, Neck and Abdominal Muscles), *Leg Weights, Bicycle Motions, Health Lift, Trapeze and Spring Board.*

Apparatus to stand close to wall, in 2 ft. space, combining the above exercises (except Rowing and Spring Board),	$15 00
Rowing Attachment (with Sliding Seat) and Spring Board, for Wall Apparatus, extra,	5 00
Two pairs of dumb bells furnished with this Apparatus.	
Main Apparatus (2 ft. by 22 in. wide, 7 ft. high, combining all the above exercises,	35 00
Main Apparatus (4 ft. by 22 in. wide, 7 ft. 6 in. high, combining all the above exercises,	40 00
This size Apparatus, made to extend 4 feet, for 4-foot Horizontal Bar,	45 00
Three pairs of dumb bells furnished with each of the above machines. Extra dumb bells (best quality, japanned), 6 cents per pound.	
Parallel Bars (adjustable to any angle or height,	$10 00
Extra Attachments, for special exercises and the curative treatment of many diseases, at the following prices:	
Back and Stomach Roller, with Adjustable Postural Board, for kneading and strengthening the back and abdominal muscles, also for the preventative and curative treatment of female diseases, &c.,	5 00
Hand Roller (for strengthening the hand, wrist and forearm,	2 00
Striking Bag, $2 00　Tilting Board,	2 00
Swing, 2 00　Blackboard,	2 50
Easel Rests,	1 50

An Illustrated Chart showing how to adjust the Apparatus and take all the exercises, will be sent with each Apparatus.

Fig. 1. CHEST BARS.

Wall Apparatus.

Fig. 2. ROWING—Start & Finish.
To develope the Arms, Legs and Back.

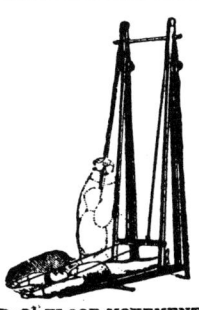

Fig. 3. FLOOR MOVEMENTS
To strengthen the Back, Arms and Abdomen.

Fig. 4. HEALTH LIFT.
For Back, Legs and Arms, to equalize the circulation.

JAPANNED AND NICKEL-PLATED IRON DUMB BELLS, LEATHER COVERED, WOOD HANDLES, AND SOLID WOOD.

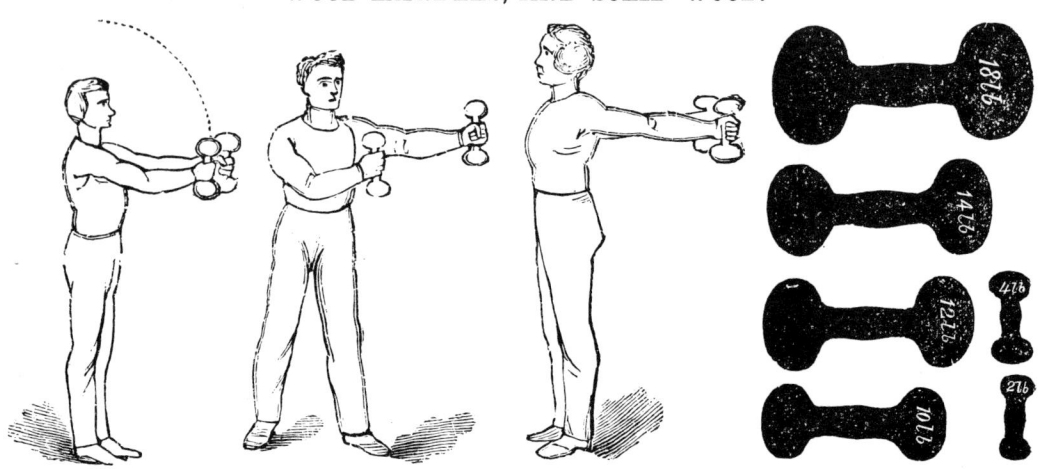

Plain Cast Iron Dumb Bells, nicely Japanned, weights from 1 to 50 lbs. each, always in stock. Larger sizes made to order (on three days' notice). Price per pound, 5 cents.

NICKEL PLATED IRON DUMB BELLS.

Made from pure Grey Iron and then polished very smooth, so as to be free from all blotches, &c., then very heavily Nickel Plated. As well as useful, they are very ornamental.

1 lb. each, $1 75 pair.	2 lbs. each, $2 00 pair.	3 lbs. each, $2 25 pair.	4 lbs. each, $2 50 pair.	5 lbs. each, $2 75 pair.
6 lbs. each, $3 00 pair.	7 lbs. each, $3 50 pair.	8 lbs. each, $3 75 pair.	10 lbs. each, $4 00 pair.	12 lbs. each, $4 50 pair.

PECK & SNYDER'S NEW PATENT DUMB BELLS.

They consist of two metallic heads, with a handle of wood fastened together with a wrought iron bolt which passes through the whole and is secured at one end by a small iron nut. It is symmetrical in form, cannot break by falling, and is much more agreeable to handle than the old patterns. The castings are very smooth, and altogether are very neatly made. Made from two to twenty pounds each. Price, per lb., 10 cents.

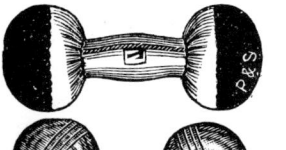

Plain Cast Iron Dumb Bells, covered with leather or chamois, one to six pounds each, extra per pair, 50 cents; seven to twelve pounds, each, extra per pair, 75 cents.

WOODEN DUMB BELLS OF POLISHED MAPLE.

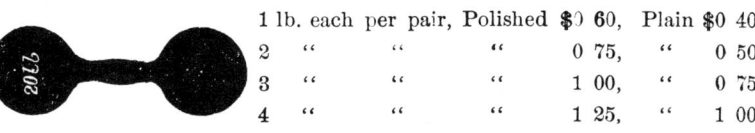

	Polished	Plain
1 lb. each per pair,	$0 60	$0 40
2 " " "	0 75	0 50
3 " " "	1 00	0 75
4 " " "	1 25	1 00

"SYRACUSE" SUSPENSORY BANDAGE.

With Self-Adjusting Sliding Loop at Back of Pouch.

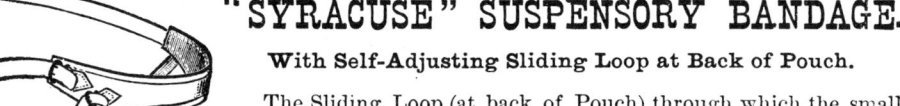

The Sliding Loop (at back of Pouch) through which the small strap passes works freely on the strap, and thereby allows the scrotum to adjust itself just as the movement of the body or clothing requires, and consequently our Suspensory will fit while the person wearing it is in motion. The Sliding Loop makes Suspensory self-adjusting, and gives freedom of movement. Prevents pulling, cording and chafing. Gives support without restraint of motion, renders displacement impossible. Makes our Suspensory perfect fitting, and affords comfort and relief to wearer. Price, 75 cts.

PROF. D. L. DOWD'S HOME EXERCISER.

The "Home Exerciser," patented, is the desideratum for Physical Culture at home.

REASONS.

1. It takes up but six inches square of floor room.
2. It is an ornament.
3. It is noiseless; has a swivel top, and can be put up in the corner of the room.
4. It cannot get out of order.
5. Can be adapted instantly to the use of any one over 4 years of age.
6. No other apparatus is necessary.
7. The work on the "Exerciser" is the most fascinating form of exercise ever devised.
8. Especially adapted to bring about the cure of billiousness, dyspepsia, constipation, and, above all else, weak lungs, or even the first stages of consumption.

The following are the principal exercises explained and illustrated in the book of instruction that accompanies the "Home Exerciser."

SHOULDER PULLEY.
1. Broadening Chest.
2. Deepening Chest.
3. " " No. 2.
4. Triceps muscle, or back of upper arm.
5. Muscles of the neck.
6. Upper pectoral or breast muscle.
7. Lower pectoral or breast musele.
8. Posterior Deltoid, or back of shoulder.
9. Fore arm, front and back.
10. Rectus Abdominis or muscles in front of abdomen.
11. Obliqus Abdominis or muscles of sides of abdomen.
12. Middle Trapezius, and muscles between shoulder blades.
13. Latissimus Dorsi, muscle of the side and back.
14. Striking Muscles.

FOOT PULLEY.
15. Outer Deltoid, or shoulder muscle.
16. Biceps of arm.
17. Anterior Deltoid, front of shoulder.
18. Loins of back, Rectus Spinalis.
19. Gluteus Maximus, or hip muscle.
20. Biceps, or back of thigh.
21. Abductors, inner side of thigh.
22. Abductors, outer side of thigh.
23. Calf of leg.
24. Front of leg.
25. Front of thigh.

Each exercise is a distinct movement, and is calculated to develop the part of the body named in the exercise.

The work on the "Exerciser" not only strengthens the muscular system, but has a wonderfully beneficial effect in strengthening the internal organs, lungs, stomach, liver, etc., and this increases the vital powers. There are certain movements that will invariably cure constipation and billiousness, and others that will strengthen weak lungs, etc.

The book of instruction contains illustrations of the muscular system of the human body that enables one to understand the exercises as given above and the reasons for them.

The following Letters are taken from the hundreds we receive commending the "Home Exerciser."

This letter was received from Mr. Wiliam Blaikie, Author of *"How to Get Strong," "Sound Bodies for Our Boys and Girls,"* etc.

Law Office of WILLIAM BLAIKIE, (Com'r of U. S. Court of Claims),
PROF. D. L. DOWD, 206 BROADWAY, NEW YORK, Dec. 5th, 1884.

My Dear Sir:—At odd moments daily for a year or more, I have used your "Exerciser," and am much pleased with it- I have seen many "home gymnasiums," *but never saw any other that I liked half as well.* In compactness (for it takes almost no room), ample strength for its work, lightness and grace of construction, and more important than all, in its power to allure one to do a little daily, brisk and telling work, it is an admirable appliance. For him with a weak, flat or hollow chest it is so valuable a friend that ten minutes a day at the side and front chest exercises with it (breathing as you direct), are likely add many years to his life. For the maiden who is eager to become "deep breasted as Juno" this is the weapon.

If there was one in every bedroom in the United States you would be one of the nation's benefactors.

Yours sincerely, WM. BLAIKIE.

Dr. Dio Lewis says of it: "It is without a doubt the best thing I have ever seen on the market."

If the "Exerciser" be attached to the window casing it can be covered from sight by the curtain when not in use. The change from one attachment to another is almost instantaneous. There are over 30 different movements given for the "Exerciser." The weight used can be varied, according to the strength of the user, from 4 to 15 pounds or more.

We make three grades of the "Home Exerciser." Prices (with book of instructions, entitled "Physcal Culture at Home," by W. E. Forest, M. D.), $8, $10 and $12. The $12 one will make an ornamein in any room. The weights and all the iron work is nickel plated and highly polished, the wood work is neatly shellaced. The $10 is made as good in every respect—the only difference is the iron work is japanned instead of nickeled. The $8 one is made up plainly, but just as durable as the others—the only difference is in the appearance of them—the system of exercise remains exactly the same.

PECK & SNYDER, 126, 128 & 130 Nassau Street, New York.
Dealers in all Goods beneficial to Health and Exercise.

THE PNEUMATIC PARLOR ROWING MACHINE.

IMITATES ROWING PERFECTLY.

STROKE HARD AT THE BEGINNING.
EASY AT THE FINISH,
RECOVERY UNASSISTED

MACHINE FOLDED.

DESCRIPTION.

A cylinder made of brass, having a closed end and a highly polished interior, is placed in front of the oarsman, as shown in the illustration. The piston rod of the cylinder is connected with the short oars by means of a whiffletree and connecting rods.

The act of taking a stroke draws the piston away from the closed end of the cylinder, produces a vacuum, and the pressure of the atmosphere upon the piston simulates the resistance that is afforded by the water in rowing a boat. The cylinder (a sectional view of which is shown below), is provided with a series of small holes commencing about half way from the closed end, which allow the atmosphere to enter, and as the piston is drawn past them gradually relieve the vacuum. Hence the stroke is hard at the beginning, when the vacuum is perfect, and gradually becomes easier as these holes are passed. The air thus accumulated in the cylinder, finds free exit through a large opening in the closed end, as it is pushed before the piston in the "recovery." This opening is closed by a valve automatically upon the commencement of a new stroke. There is, therefore, neither *assistance* nor *resistance* to recovery. The oars turn so as to allow of feathering. Adjustable to any strength.

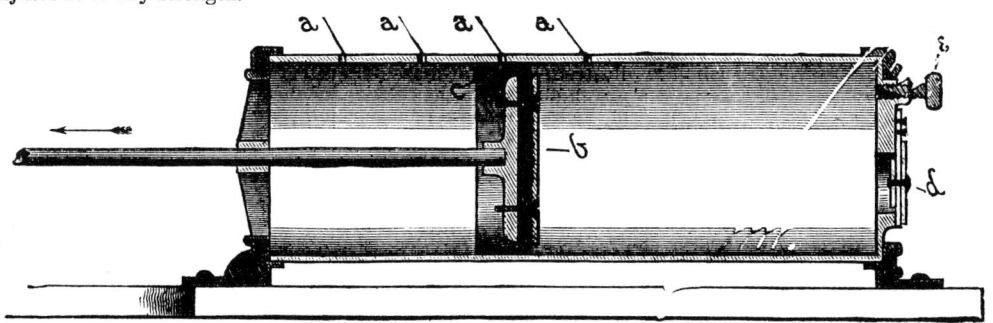

SECTIONAL VIEW OF THE CYLINDER.

a a a.—Holes in the cylinder for the admission of air. As the piston is drawn past them, the vacuum is relieved.
b.—The piston.
c.—Leather cup or packing of the piston.
d.—Valve covering the large opening in the closed end of the cylinder. This valve closes automatically upon the commencement of a stroke and opens to allow free exit for the air accumulated in the cylinder as the piston is pushed back in the recovery.
e.—Screw filed away on one side, by unscrewing which a small or large opening is made, as described.

The machine will be sent to any part of the world on receipt of the price. In remitting send check on this city, postal money order, or by registered letter.

PRICE OF PARLOR MACHINE, $15.00.

NEW YORK, OCTOBER 28th, 1882.

DEAR SIR:—I have one of your PNEUMATIC PARLOR ROWING MACHINES, and find it the most perfect rowing machine I have ever tried. The motion is exactly like that of an oar, and the use of the machine will develop the same muscles that are called into play in rowing, and to the same extent. It is an excellent substitute for the water, and I gladly recommend it to professional and amateur oarsmen, and others. Hoping you will meet with the success you deserve,   I remain, yours truly,

EDWARD HANLAN,
(Champion Oarsman of the World.)

THE PNEUMATIC ROWING MACHINE.

The above illustration represents the machine in "sweep" or single oar form, adapted for use by College and Professional Crews and Gymnasiums. It is made heavier and stronger than the machine intended for parlor use and calculated to stand very hard usage. The cylinder is longer and has greater power. Each "sweep" is complete in itself, including a cylinder, sliding seat, foot rest, oar and stands, all hansomely decorated.

Price of Machine Complete (for each Sweep), $20.00.
COST OF CASING EXTRA.

NEW YORK ATHLETIC CLUB, NEW YORK, FEB'Y 29th, 1884.

DEAR SIR:—During the past winter we have had nine of the PNEUMATIC ROWING MACHINES in constant use in our gymnasium. The imitation of rowing is perfect; the catch, finish, and in fact the entire stroke being as near the actual thing as it is possible to obtain by artificial means, the tapering off of the stroke being a special feature not obtained in any other machine that we have tried. It is invaluable in training crews, as the coach can detect faults and weaknesses in individual members that would pass unnoticed in a boat. We find the machine very durable and always ready for use, requiring very little attention to keep it in perfect order. Every one of our members who has tried it, unite with us in saying that it is the best rowing machine made.   Yours truly,
OTTO SARONY, Captain N. Y. Ath. Club.
DAVID ROACH, Coach N. Y. Ath. Club.

COLUMBIA COLLEGE, NEW YORK, May 1st, 1883.

DEAR SIR:—The eight Pneumatic Rowing Machines which you furnished the Columbia College Boat Club, have been used daily at the College Gymnasium since the first of March, by the University and Class Crews, and have proved to be admirably adapted to the purpose for which they were designed. The imitation which the machine gives of rowing is as perfect as it seems possible to obtain by mechanical means. We consider it far superior to any machine now in use. You may refer to us, and we shall take pleasure in recommending your machine for its admirable qualities.
    Yours truly,   JASPER T. GOODWIN.
J. A. B. COWLES.
A. HOWARD VAN SINDEREN.

19 CONGRESS ST., BOSTON, DEC. 31st, 1883.

DEAR SIR:—You are liberty to refer to me, as considering the PNEUMATIC ROWING MACHINE better than any machine I have ever tried. It resembles rowing more closely than I supposed it possible for any machine, and my judgment is, that I could teach a novice with it better and in less time than by any I have seen. I have tested it thoroughly and find it always ready for use, requiring very little care; and as well as I can judge after several months hard use, should say it is remarkably durable, and not likely to need repairing.   Yours truly,   R. C. WATSON, (of Harvard College).

CELTIC ROWING CLUB, BUFFALO, FEB'Y 20, 1884.

DEAR SIR:—The PNEUMATIC ROWING MACHINES which we purchased of you some time ago have been in almost continual use since their arrival. The workings of the machines resemble a boat as near as possible, we think, and, to use the expression of those who have seen them "all that is needed is water to make the similarity complete." For the special purpose for which we use them, that is the training of crews, they are unexcelled. With the "Sweep" machine the coach is given even a better chance to instruct amateurs, and to detect and correct any bad habits contracted by an experienced oarsman, than he could possibly get with a boat. The main feature in making up first-class fours is to have the men as evenly matched as possible. For this purpose we consider the "Sweep" machine far superior to the boat, in that the weak man or men can be more easily detected and weeded out. For these reasons and for the many physical benefits which the use of the machines furnish to members in need of exercise, we heartily recommend them to every rowing club.   Yours respectfully,   JAMES MURPHY
J. F. KIMBEL,
T. J. MURPHY,
FRED. KULL,
Racing Committee, Celtic Rowing Club.

The genuineness of these letters is guaranteed.
    PECK & SNYDER.

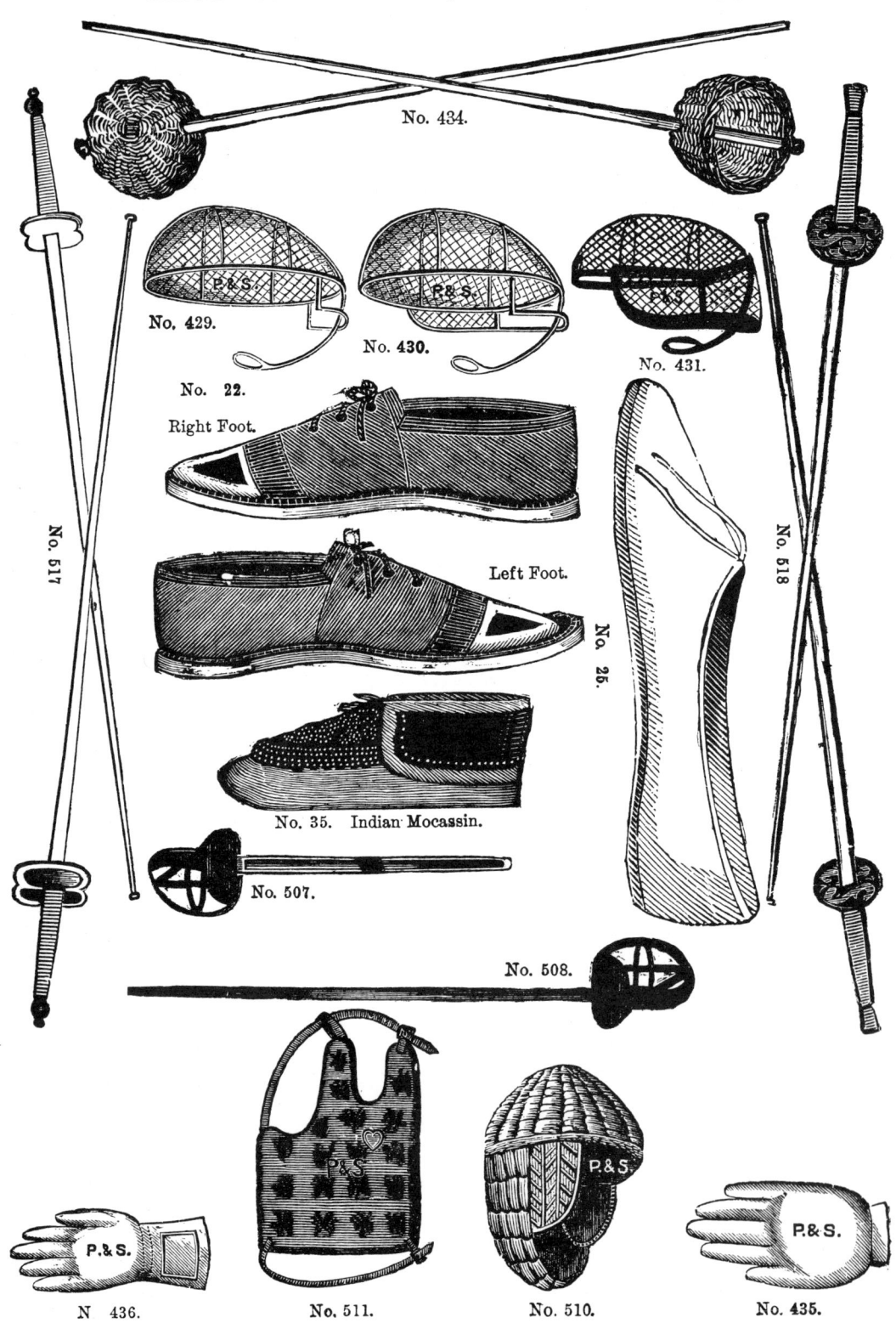

EASTMAN'S CALISTHENICS.

A complete system of Calisthenic Exercises brought within the compass of a single instrument of not above a pound in weight, and seeming more of the nature of ornament than use—as the simplest and most helpful and attractive means for the complete development of muscular strength and the attainment of graceful movement and manly bearing.

The handles are of iron, japanned or nickel plated, and connected with rubber bands which enables you to go through various graceful and health-giving motions.

No. 1. Japanned, with book of instructions..per pair, $0 50
" 2. Nickel plated, with book of instructions.. " 1 00
"Eastman's System of Calisthenic Culture and Manual," 22 pages, illust., by mail, post-paid on receipt of 1 00

BACON'S HOME GYMNASIUM.

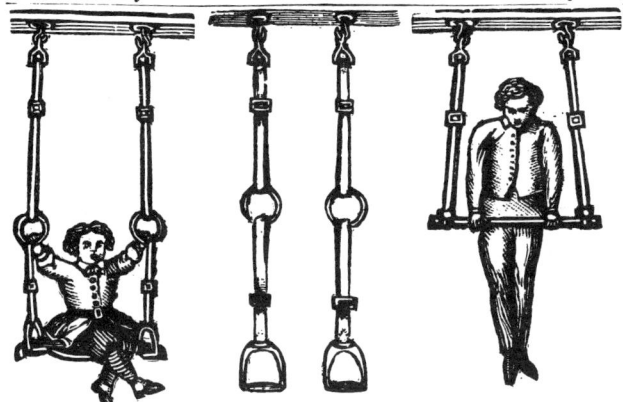

The apparatus is supported by two strong screw hooks in the ceiling, about eighteen inches apart and screwed five inches into the joist. It can also be used out of doors by erecting a framework, such as is used for swings. The straps are of the strongest linen, handsomely colored. The rings are of the patent bent wood, about six inches in diameter. By an ingenious device, the rings and stirrups can be instantly raised or lowered to any desired height, or the stirrup straps removed, or the rings removed for the insertion of the trapeze bar. The apparatus can be put up in any room, and removed in a moment, leaving only the two small eyes in the ceiling visible. It can be used in different rooms at pleasure, by having extra set of hooks for the ceiling. A space six or eight feet wide is ample for any of the exercises.

To Clergymen, literary men, and all persons of sedentary occupation, it is particularly adapted. The exercises are especially invigorating to the digestive and respiratory organs.

In using the trapeze bars the rings are removed, and the bar placed in the upper strap.

The Swing consists merely of a seat, which can be easily constructed to fit into the stirrups.

The Best and Cheapest in the World for the price. Highly recommended by the Medical Faculty.
Price complete ready to put up only, $5 00

FOR DESCRIPTION OF FENCING GOODS, SEE OPPOSITE PAGE.

No.	Description	Price
507.	Combat Swords, made of Fine English Steel, per pair	$6 00
508.	Haute Rapier, " " " "	6 00
509.	Wire Helmets, English pattern and make, for Combat or Broad Sword, Rapier or Foil exercise. Per pair	10 00
510.	Cane Helmets, English pattern and make, for stick practice, &c., (See cut)	6 00
511.	Plastroons, for protection of the chest when fencing; made of fine chamois skin and full padded. (See cut.) Each	2 50
		Per pair.
512.	Buffalo Hilts for single sticks	4 00
514.	Fencing Foils, with fine steel blades, iron mounted handles. (See cut.)	1 50
515.	" " " " " " curved handles. (See cut)	2 00
516.	Foil Blades, for Nos. 514 and 517, extra	1 25
517.	Fencing Foils with brass mounted handles, wound with fancy colored leather. (See cut)	2 50
518.	Fencing Foils, best steel Solingen blades, highly finished brass mountings, curved handle, wound with fancy leather. (See cut)	3 50
519.	Foil Blades, for Nos. 515 and 518, extra	1 50
429.	Wire Fencing Masks, plain, French pattern. (See cut)	2 50
430.	Wire Fencing Masks, with ear protectors. (See cut)	3 00
431.	" " " " and forehead protectors. (See cut)	4 00
432.	Fencing Foils, of the best Solingen blades, highly finished, and curved handle, neatly bound with velvet, and wound with gilt cord, blades engraved	6 00
433.	Fencing Foils, of the best Solingen blades, highly finished, etc., in other ways same as No. 432, but without improved handles and engraved blades	5 00
434.	Cane Wicker Basket Hilts, with sticks	1 50
435.	Fencing Gloves, made of fine buckskin, and full padded with curled hair. (See cut)	2 00
436.	Fencing Gauntlets, made of fine buckskin, full padded, and trimmed tastefully with fancy colored leather. (See cut)	3 50

The Modern Fencer (new), with the most recent means of attack and defense when engaged with an adversary, and figures showing the various positions of the body. Bound in cloth, 94 pages, 25 full-page illustrations. By Captain T. Griffiths, Professor of Fencing, Gymnastics, &c., for the London Schools and Colleges.
Price, 50 cts.

Sword Exercises, Indian Clubs and Dumb Bells, fancy paper cover, 34 illustrations, 64 pages. By Professor Harrison, of London..Price, 25 cts.

Fencing, Broadsword and Archery, board covers, 34 illustrations, 91 pages. By Stonehenge and the Rev. J. G. Wood, of London..Price, 25 cts.

THE NARRAGANSETT EXERCISING APPARATUS AND HOME GYMNASIUM.

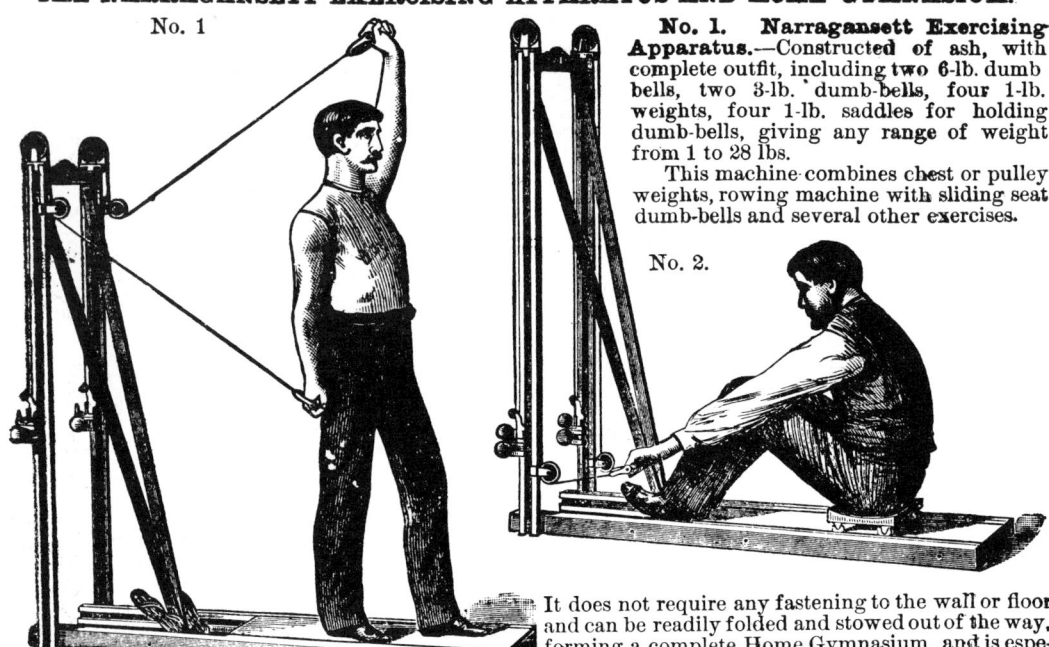

No. 1

No. 2.

No. 1. Narragansett Exercising Apparatus.—Constructed of ash, with complete outfit, including two 6-lb. dumb bells, two 3-lb. dumb-bells, four 1-lb. weights, four 1-lb. saddles for holding dumb-bells, giving any range of weight from 1 to 28 lbs.

This machine combines chest or pulley weights, rowing machine with sliding seat dumb-bells and several other exercises.

It does not require any fastening to the wall or floor and can be readily folded and stowed out of the way, forming a complete Home Gymnasium and is especially adapted for the use of societies, clubs, &c., where it is desirable to use the room occupied by the apparatus for other purposes. Price, complete, $15 00

No. 3. Narragansett Exercising Apparatus.—Single upright bar, double handles, (see cut), constructed of Ash with complete outfit, including two 6-lb. Dumb-bells, two 1-lb. saddles for holding Dumb-bells, four 1-lb.-weights, giving any range of weight from 2 to 20 lbs. (See Cut.)

This machine combines the chest or pulley weights, Rowing-weights, Dumb-bells, and the several other exercises, which may be obtained by moving the adjustable pulley to any desired position on the bar. Price, $5 00

No. 4, same as No. 3, constructed of Black Walnut. " 6 00

NOTE.—For Rowing weights the handles may be removed by slipping the ropes from the ends of the cross-bar.

No. 5. Narragansett Exercising Apparatus.—This machine consists of two upright bars similar to Nos. 3 and 4, connected at the top by an ornamental iron brace. It is secured to the wall and floor in the same manner as Nos. 3 and 4, thus forming the regulation chest or pulley weights, improved by our adjustable pulleys and weight holders. Constructed of ash, with complete outfit, including two 3-lb. Dumb-bells, four 1-lb. Saddles for holding Dumb-bells, four 1-lb. weights...$9 00

This machine combines chest or pulley weights, Dumb-bells, Rowing weights, and the many other exercises which may be obtained by moving the adjustable pulleys to any position on the bars.

No. 6, same as No. 5, constructed of black walnut.................$10 00

Nos. 3, 4, 5, 6, Stationary Apparatus may be had extra length, thus forming upper and lower Back Weights in addition to the other exercises, at the following prices:

No. 3, Single Bar, Ash	$ 5 50
No. 4, " Black Walnut	6 50
No. 5, Double Bar, Ash	10 00
No. 6. " Black Walnut	11 00
Extra Saddles for holding dumb-bells	0 8
" 1-lb. weights, each	0 8
Dumb-bells, any weight, per lb	0 6

All our weights and dumb-bells are made from the best grey iron nicely enameled.

NOTE.—In making the various changes on all our machines nothing is detachable except the weights, thus preventing the loss of any of the working parts.

Cut No. 2 shows the apparatus used as a Rowing machine. The same apparatus can be used by ladies and children with the same benefit as for gentlemen.

All these machines are made of selected wood nicely finished in oil. All the iron work is finely enameled and ornamented. The ropes used are the best Silver Lake braided cord. Hardwood fibre seats secured by brass-headed tacks, are used on our improved rowing seat, and the workmanship is first-class throughout.

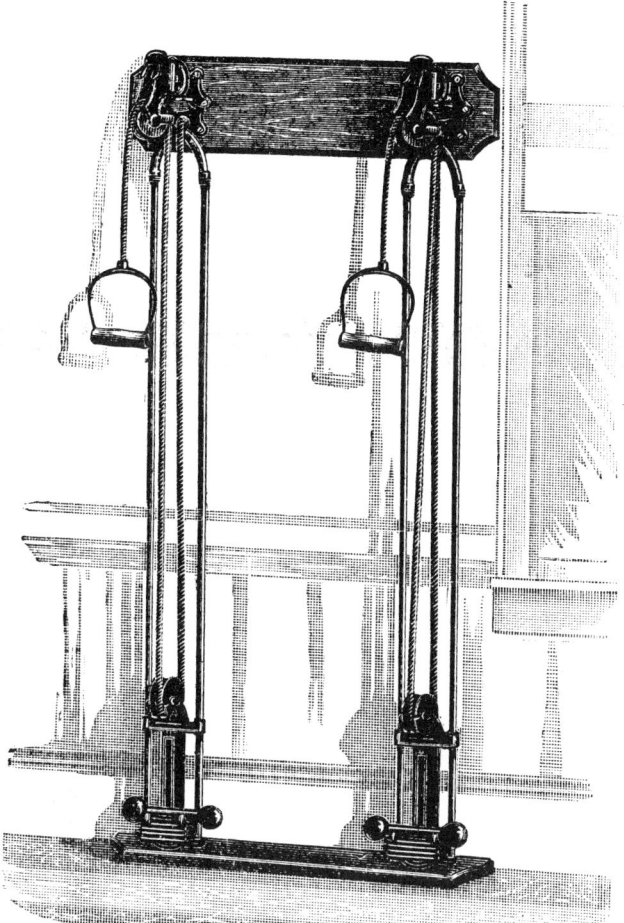

Standard Chest Weight.

Pat. Jan. 6, 1885 and Aug. 14, 1885.

SPECIAL FEATURES OF THE STANDARD APPARATUS.

It has a compound or double rope which allows twice the usual movement of the handles, and makes the weight twice as quick in action.

It has our swivel block, which allows movement in any direction.

It is absolutely noiseless, and requires no grease or oil.

Its lightness and elegance fit it for the home. Its strength and durability for the gymnasium.

All of these features are possessed only by the Standard Apparatus.

TO GYMNASIUMS.

The Standard Apparatus is specially adapted for gymnasiums, either as chest weights or in the construction of giant pulleys, chest expanders, chest developers, wrist machines, or any pulley weight apparatus used in a gymnasium. The swivel blocks may be used in any position, either on the wall, floor or ceiling. It is the only complete line of pulley weight apparatus ever made.

They are now used by most of the leading colleges and gymnasiums in the U. S.

No. 10. Mounted on black-walnut, finished in enamel and gold, ebonite wheels, drab silver lake braided cord, etc., with one pair 3 pound dumb bells, four 1 pound weight, two 1 pound dumb bell holders. Price, $10.00

No. 11. Single weight holder and block, with cross-bar and two handles, similar in finish to No. 10. Price, $5.00.

Full Particulars on Application.

THE PATENT IMPROVED STRIKING BAG, FOR PHYSICAL CULTURE.

Refines, elevates and enobles; adds to our courage, zeal and health and thereby to our happiness. The bag is intended to strengthen the arms, wrists, shoulders, back, loins, and particularly the muscles of the abdomen, and will teach the striker how to deal a blow. It is of inestimable value to every one, especially those whose business requires confinement.

PRICES COMPLETE WITH RINGS AND HOOKS.

No. 1. 20 lbs. covered with Buff Leather	Each.	$12 00
No. 2. 25 lbs. " "	"	14 00
No. 3. 20 lbs. " English Buck	"	16 00
No. 4. 25 lbs. " "	"	18 00
No. 5. 10 lbs. " Canvas	"	10 00
No. 6. 15 lbs. " "	"	12 00
No. 7. 6 lbs. " Buff Leather	"	8 00
No. 8. 4 lbs. " Canvas	"	5 00

MODEL JAPANNED IRON QUOITS.

2 lbs. each .... per set of 4 Quoits,	$0 50
2½ "	0 65
3 "	0 80
4 "	1 00

SUPERIOR FORGED STEEL QUOITS.

These are very superior, turned true, and made to proper weights, warranted not to break.

	Polished.	Nickel Plated.
2½ lbs. each per set of 4 Quoits,	$3 00	$4 00
3 " " "	3 25	4 25
3½ " " "	3 50	4 50
4 " " "	4 00	5 00
Wrought Iron Pins for the above. Per pair,	0 50	

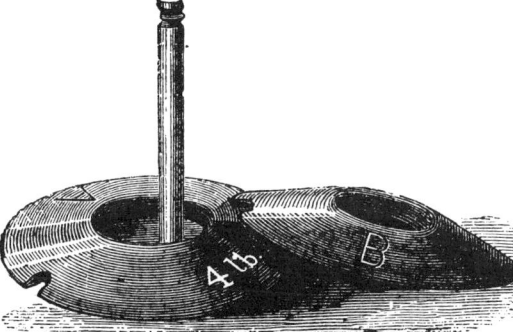

Prof. RUMSEY'S HEALTH EXERCISING PATENT ELASTIC STRIKING AIR-BAG.

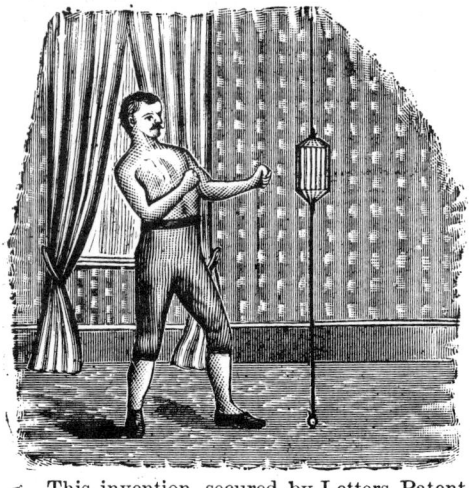 

This invention, secured by Letters Patent of the United States, Canada and Great Britain, is certainly the most important contribution to the science of Athletics which has been introduced for twenty years, combining as it does, in the most simple form, all of the advantages which may be derived from the use of dumb bells, Indian clubs, ropes and rings, rowing machines, pulley weights, and even the boxing glove itself. It is made of an outside canvas cover and inside rubber bladder, being of a conical shape (giving it strength), same as the canvas, with screw eyes, rope, &c., all complete, at the following prices: No. 1, Men's, $6.00; No. 2, Ladies', $5.50; No. 3, Children's, $5.50. No. 4, Square Bag, $6.00; No. 5, Gynasium Size, Extra strong, $7.00.

GYMNASIUM ROPES AND RINGS.—Rings of 6 Inch Galvanized Iron.

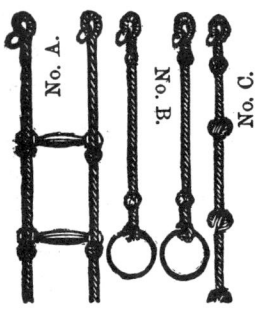

See Cut No. B.   Per pair.

No. 1.	5ft. Ropes with Iron Rings		$2 00
" 2.	6ft. " "		2 25
" 3.	7ft. " "		2 50
" 4.	8ft. " "		2 75
" 5.	9ft. " "		3 00
" 6.	10ft. " "		3 25
" 7.	11ft. " "		3 50
" 8.	12ft. " "		3 75

Rings covered with leather............per pair, extra, 1 00
The above sets are all complete, with Wrought Iron Galvanized Ceiling Hooks.
Wrought Iron Galvanized Ceiling Hooks, extra per pair.................. 0 40
Knotted Rope, any length required (see cut C.), per running foot........ 0 20
Trapezes, from 20 in. to 26 in. with improved Brass Cups to receive the ropes and steel center... 6 00
Rope Ladders (see cut A.)...per foot. 0 40

Gymnasium Mattresses of extra heavy Duck, with Leather Handles and Corners, to order, size 6x5 feet.

        Filled with 2 inch Felt, $12.00; unfilled, $6.50.

Trapeze Bars made of the best young hickory and finely finished.

Per Set.

No. 1.	2½ft. Bar,	5ft. Ropes		$2 00
" 2.	3 ft. "	6ft. "		2 25
" 3.	3½ft. "	7ft. "		2 50
" 4.	4 ft. "	8ft. "		2 75

We make any length ropes to order.............................per foot, extra, 0 15

PECK & SNYDER'S NEW PORTABLE PARALLEL BARS.

These Bars are the only ones made that can be taken apart with ease and safety. They are now being used throughout the country, in gymnasiums, societies, schools, and for private use; they can be packed and shipped with safety and can be put up ready for use upon any stage or parlor floor in a few minutes; they are made of seasoned oak and hickory woods, and first class workmanship every way.

Price of Parallel Bars and Platform complete, 8 feet long,
                                                                              $18 00

A COMPLETE BOWLING ALLEY.

TEN PIN BALLS AND PINS FOR BOWLING ALLEYS.
REDUCED PRICES.

The balls of our manufacture are of the best selected Lignumvitæ: pins of polished maple. A complete set for one alley consists of 12 balls, assorted sizes, and one set of 10 pins. Make your selection from the following list of sizes:

Diameter of ball,	4 in......	each,	$1 00
"	"	4½ in......	"	1 25
"	"	5 in......	"	1 50
"	"	5½ in......	"	1 75
"	"	6 in......	"	2 00
"	"	6½ in......	"	2 50
"	"	7 in......	"	2 75
"	"	7½ in......	"	3 50
"	"	8 in......	"	3 75
"	"	8½ in......	"	4 25
"	"	9 in......	"	4 75
"	"	9½ in......	"	5 25

Maple Pins, per set of 10.......... 5 00

Ten Pin Score Book.—Just published a neat and improved book for the use of all clubs. Splendid Title Page with blank spaces for club name and officers.

No. 1.—Bound in Cloth, size 9 x 11¼ ins. 60 Games, price.................$1 25

No. 2.—Bound in Cloth, size 9 x 11¼ ins. 120 Games, price $1 75

IMPLEMENTS FOR ATHLETIC GAMES.—All of the latest regulation weight, size, etc.

Iron Hammer with Hickory Handle.

Lbs............................	12	16	20
Each............................	$2 25	2 50	2 75

Hammer only. .... each 12 lbs, $1 25; 16 lbs., $1 50; 20 lbs, $2 75

SOLID SHOT.

Lbs......................................	12.	16.
Each......................................	$1 25	$1 50

The 56 lb. weight..... ....Each, 5 00

ENGLISH IMPORTED FOOT BALLS AND FIXTURES.

At greatly reduced prices.

Style A.   Style B.   Style C.

They are made of the best vulcanized India-rubber bladder, with outside leather case; are warranted to stand any climate, and to outlast three or more ordinary ones; they are properly inflated before shipped, and they will keep so until worn out.

    Style A. The Association, or round Foot Ball (English), consists of a rubber bladder and outside leather case.

    Style B.—The Rugby, or oval-shaped Foot Ball (English), consists of a rubber bladder and outside leather case.

    When ordering, state whether you want the Rugby oval-shaped or the Association round ball.

The sizes and prices of style A and B foot balls and bladders:

Nos.	2.	3.	4.	5.	6.
Inches in circumference	19.	22.	24.	27.	30.
Each	$2.00	$2.50	$3.25	$4.00	$5.00
Prices for bladders only: Nos.	2.	3.	4.	5.	6.
Each	$1.00	$1.25	$1.50	$1.75	$2.00

    N. B.—No Foot Ball bladders will be taken back after once sold, as they are all tested and found perfect before leaving our store. Never inflate a bladder unless in the leather case.

    Style C. The American Foot Ball is made of heavy canvas, thoroughly saturated with rubber, very strong, so to be blown up with key, which goes with each one.

Nos.	1.	2.	3.	4.	5.	6.
Inches in circumference	20.	22.	24.	26.	28.	30.
Each	$.75	$1.00	$1.25	$1.50	$1.75	$2.00

Extra Keys for American Foot Balls, each .... 10 cents.

    We send Foot Balls by mail, post paid on receipt of price.

    For prices of Pants, Shirts, Stockings, Caps, Foul Flags and Belts, see Base Ball outfits and Worsted Goods, or send for prices.

    Peck & Snyder's Foot Ball Book of Rules, reprinted from the latest English editions. Together with the latest rules of Lacrosse as played by the Canadian Clubs. Bound in Blue blue cloth, and gold, illustrated Price .... 25 cents.

    The American College Rules of Foot Ball, as adopted by the Association .... each, 15 cents.

THE NEW PATENT FOOT BALL INFLATOR.

These inflators are far superior, in every respect, to the old style large brass pumps With them the largest ball can be inflated to its fullest capacity in five minutes time, while the old way took half an hour. It is not advisable to inflate Foot Balls with the breath, as the moisture that collects in them soon rots the bladder, you will always keep the bladder dry by using the new Foot Ball Inflator, it is easily carried in the pocket and not liable to get out of order.

Price only $1.00

THIS CUT ONE-THIRD SIZE.

No. 5. FOOT-BALL JACKETS.

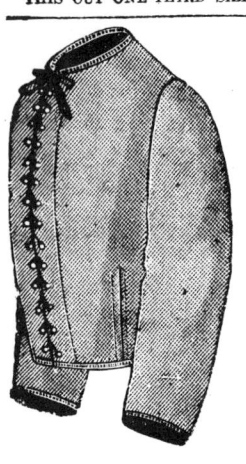

We are now manufacturing for foot-ball teams, a superior Canvas Jacket.

Price, each, $2.00   Per doz. $21.00

When ordering, send the following measurements, &c., Neck, Chest, Waist, Arms, Yoke, Length down back.

No. 3. FOOT-BALL SHOES.

We have three styles Foot-Ball Shoes, with sole leather ribbed soles, as shown in the illustration.

Per pair.

No. 1. White Canvas $3 00
" 2. Light Russet Leather 6 00
" 3. " French Russet Calf 7 00

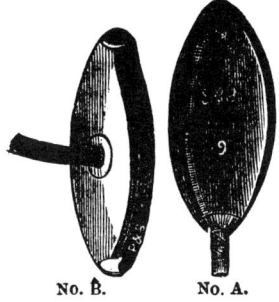

RUBBER BLADDERS FOR ENGLISH LEATHER CASE, FOOT BALL OR OVAL SHAPES.

No. B, for Rugby Ball, are made of the best vulcanized India rubber, and has tube fixed in the side of bladder, so that it will expand and fill up properly the space in the case.

No. A, for the Association or round shaped ball, made of same material as No. B, but with the tube on the end. Prices for either of the make of Bladders, are:

Size ball, Number	2	3	4	5	6
Each	$1 00	1 25	1 50	1 75	2 00

FOOT-BALL SHIN GUARDS.

No. 1.—Made in Buff Leather, with Cane, and fastened with elastic and buckles; thin, light, and a great protection; can be worn under the stocking weighing under six ounces per pair
Per pair, $2 00
No. 2.—White Chamois, ditto, ditto................... " 2 50

FOOT-BALL SUNDRIES.

Waterproof Dubbin, prepared especially for Foot-Balls and Boots, in tins, with instructions. Per tin, 75 cents.
Solution for repairing Bladders, in tins, including Sheet of Rubber, with instructions..................................per doz. 50 cents
Foot-Ball Scoring Books, for 25 Matches..................each, 25 "
" " " " 50 " .... " 50 "

LUNN & CO'S LAWN TENNIS, SCORING DIALS. (New.)

This cut shows the dial, ½ exact size, and asite an be affixed to any racquet. There are two dials affixed, one for keeping your own score, the other your opponents. They are made of metal, very strong, light, durable and nickel plated, ivory knobs on gilt hand, all put in round wooden box with screws, directions, &c.
All complete, per set, by mail, $1 00

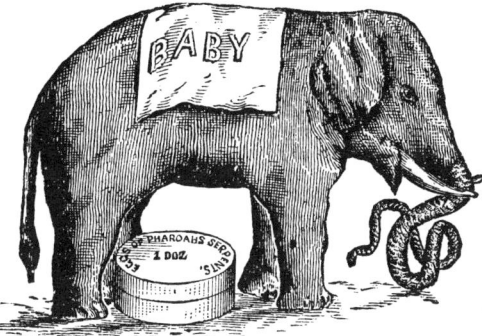

No. 69-2.—THE BABY ELEPHANT, WITH THE MAGIC TRUNK.

This little novelty consists of a perfect representation of the Baby Elephant, made of iron, but without its trunk. Insert one of the Eggs of Pharaoh's Serpents, in the opening where the "Trunk ought to be," light it with a match, the result will be that the Trunk will grow rapidly and form many curious shapes. Baby Elephant with Box of Eggs.....Price, complete, $0 25

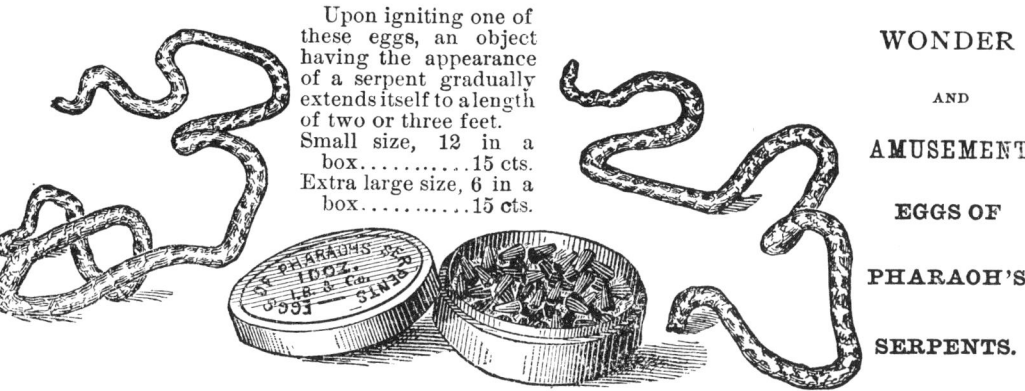

Upon igniting one of these eggs, an object having the appearance of a serpent gradually extends itself to a length of two or three feet.
Small size, 12 in a box..........15 cts.
Extra large size, 6 in a box..........15 cts.

WONDER

AND

AMUSEMENT

EGGS OF

PHARAOH'S

SERPENTS.

FLESH GLOVES, BRUSHES, PADS & BATH STRAPS OF ENGLISH & FRENCH MAKE.

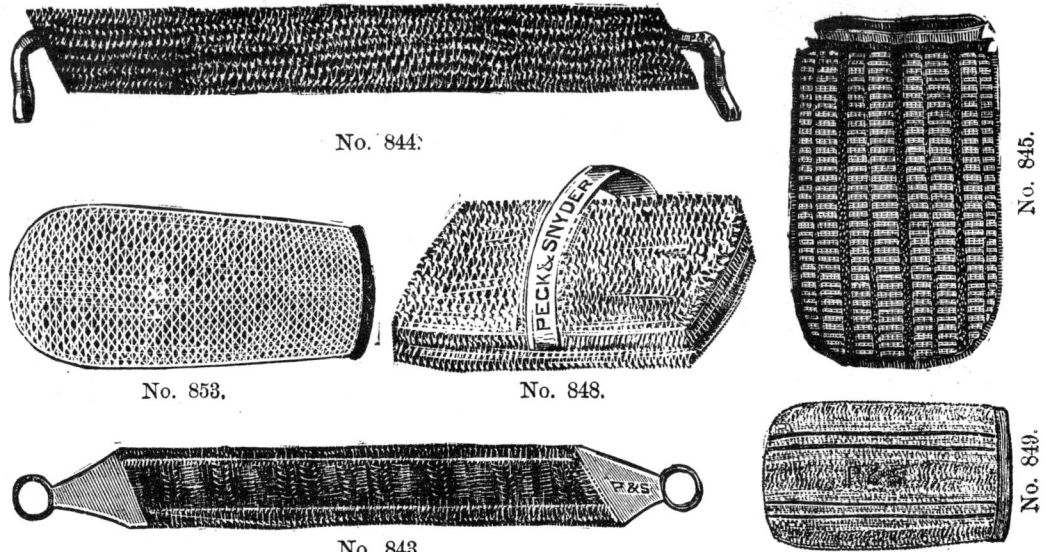

Flesh Gloves, Brushes, Pads and Bath Straps, for wet or dry use.—Highly recommended by the medical profession, for imparting a natural vigor to the nervous system, for strengthening weak limbs, and for the prevention and relief of Gout, Rheumatism, &c., also very beneficial for use to Pedestrians, Gymnasts, Base-Ball, Tennis and Cricket Players, Rowers and Sporting men in general.

NOTICE TO THE PUBLIC IN GENERAL.—Never until we began importing and keeping a full stock and assortment of these goods on hand, were they to be obtained anywhere, unless made to order, and then at very high prices. Our goods are all of the best material and workmanship, and sold at prices within the reach of all classes.

Lawrence & Co.'s Patent Improved Flesh Gloves and Straps for producing a healthy state of the system by friction, without the risk of tearing the skin, as all the ordinary horse-hair gloves are liable to do.

The great value of the Horse-hair Renovator as a therapeutic agent, when applied to the human body, is now too well known to everyone who has paid the least attention to the importance of a healthy action of the Skin, to require further comment.

The superior advantages of the Patent Flesh Gloves and Straps, are that, by a peculiar process in the machinery employed in their manufacture, the points of the hair are brought perpendicularly to the service, thereby removing the liability to tear the Skin (a very general complaint against the ordinary kind), rendering them more pleasant to use. at the same time enabling the process of friction to be much more effectually performed; they are, indeed, a positive luxury to use, apart from their salutary effects.

The peculiar fabric manufactured expressly for the use of Ladies deserves their special attention; it has been highly recommended by the most eminent of the medical profession, and given universal satisfaction to those who have used it.

No. 843.	Bath Straps, for wet or dry use...	Each, $2 50
No. 844.	Bath Straps, for wet or dry use...	" 2 00
No. 853.	Ladies' Honeycomb gloves, front and back, white, for tender skin...........	" 40
No. 850.	Ladies' and Children's Brush, white, red striped, wood back................	" 1 00
No. 852.	Ladies' and Children's brush, long handle, white, red striped, wood back...	" 1 50
No. 849.	Alexandria Flesh Gloves, double, with red and white stripes................	" 1 25
No. 847.	Scrubbers or Pads, double...	" 85
No. 845.	Flesh Gloves, extra quality, without thumbs...............................	" 1 00
No. 846.	Flesh Gloves, extra quality, with thumbs..................................	" 85

No. 848. The Oxford Washing Pad, (to be used with soap).—This article, suggested by an "Oxford Man," for the special use of Sportsmen, for removing Stains from the Hands, being found to thoroughly answer the purpose, has established fair pretensions to become of universal use, which it is rapidly doing. Hair both sides, with a regulating strap. Each, $1.25

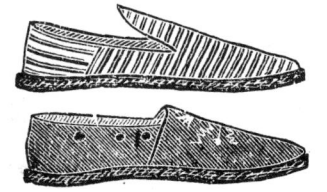

THE NEW FRENCH BATHING SLIPPERS.

No. 1. Plain and striped linen uppers, closely roped soles.
                                                                        Per pair, 50 cents.
No. 2. Plain linen uppers, embroidered, closely roped soles,
                                                                        Per pair, 75 cents.
No. 3. The American sample pattern, as No. 2, but made of light weight canvas, bound around with colored braid, composition cork sole, covered.
                                                                        Per pair, 50 cents.

No A.
THE SECRET BALLOT BOX.
Made of Black Walnut, Fine French Polished and Lined. Can be used for Base Ball, Cricket, Archery, Foot Ball, Boating and all other Sporting Clubs; also for Masonic and Odd Fellow Lodges, Temperance and all other societies Size **9x6x4¼** inches..each. $5 00

No. C.
BALLOT BOX,
Made of Black Walnut, Finely polished. Used for same purposes as No. A. Size, 9½x6x3¾. Each, $2 50

N. B.—Each Box, Nos. A, B and C, are furnished with 12 white and 6 Black Balls.

White Ballot Balls, extra, per hundred........$0 40
Black   "   "   " 0 60
Black Ballot Cubes   "   " 1 00

BALLOT BOX,
No. B. Made of Black Walnut, finely polished, latest style. Used for same purposes as No. A. Size, 9½ x 5½ x 3¼ inches.
Each....................$3 50
No. 1, Plain,............ 1 50
 " 2 " with Drawer.... 2 00

CARD PRESSES.
No. H. For Club rooms. Will hold 6 packs of cards; made of Black Walnut, with thread screw handles to press and keep the cards in shape. Size 9¾x3x5.
Each..............................$1 00

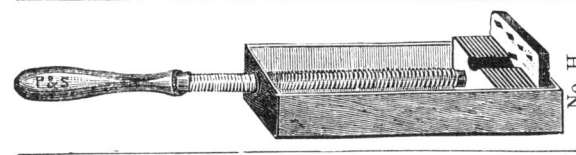

GAVELS, For Societies, Clubs, &c.
No. D. Made all of Fine White Ivory, beautifully Carved and Polished........Each, $10 00
No. E. White Ivory Gavel, carved and Polished Rosewood Handle........Each, $8 00
No. F. Gavels. Made of Rosewood, Boxwood or Ebony, beautifully carved, of different styles and highly French Polished............................Each, 1 00
No. G. Gavels. Made of Polished Black Walnut, carved................. "   0 50
Striking Blocks for Societies, etc., made to order.

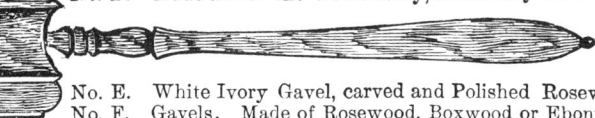

POLICE CLUBS.—Made of Rosewood or Lignumvitæ Woods.

8 in.	10 in.	12 in.	14 in.	16 in.	18 in.	20 in.	22 in.	
50	60	70	75	$1 00	1 10	1 25	1 50	each.

EBONY POLICE CLUBS.

10 in.	12 in.	14 in.	16 in.	18 in.	20 in.	22 in.	
$1 00	1 25	1 35	1 50	1 60	1 75	2 00	each.

Rosewood Billeys 8 to 15 inch...75c.   "
Ebony   "   8 to 15 " ....$1 00   "
Locust Night Clubs..65c.   "
Police Nippers, Chain, Nickel-Plated.............................per pair, $1 25
    "   Patent Spring, the best made......................   "   2 00
Hand-Cuffs..Polished, per pair, $4 00; Nickel-Plated, $5 00
Hand-Cuffs, for conveying three prisoners together..........   "   "   6 00;   "   7 00
Leg Irons..   "   "   6 50;   "   8 00

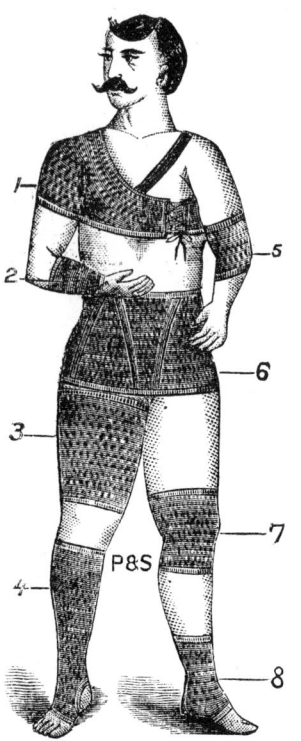

BASE BALL PLAYERS' ELASTICS.

We are now manufacturing a full line of Silk Elastic Goods, especially adapted to the use of Ball Players, Athletes, Gymnasts, etc·, for all parts of the arm, body or leg. Recommended by the medical fraternity, in all cases of sprains, weak joints, varicose veins, weak or tired muscles, etc.

Being manufacturers, we are able to offer these goods at a lower price than any other house.

Directions for Measurement.

No. 1. Silk—Shoulder Cup, laced across the chest........... $4 50
"   "   "   "   "   "   with strap. 2 25

Circumference around Arm and Chest separately:

No. 2—Silk Wristlet—circumference around wrist............   75
" 2½. Silk Muscle Cup,   "   "   muscle 1 25
" 5. Elbow Cup, circum. around arm, above and below elbow, 1 50
" 5¼. Fore arm   "   "   fore arm...... .... 1 00
" 3. Thigh piece, around leg above knee, around thigh, and length from crotch to knee.... .... 4 00
" 4. Knee Stocking. circumference around leg at knee, calf, ankle and instep—length from knee to bottom of heel, 4 50
" 6. Abdominal Belt, circumference around waist and above and below bowels............................. ... 6 00
" 7. Knee Cup, circumference around, above and below knee, 2 00
" 8. Anklet, circumference around ankle and instep—also length from sole of foot to above ankle.......... ... 3 00

We do not quote prices on Cotton Elastic Goods, as there is very little difference in the price, and the Silk Goods being much handsomer, more durable and satisfactory.

Attention is called to above explicit directions for measuring Elastic Stockings, etc. By carefully observing them, an accurate fit can always be secured, and a fresh and reliable article can always be depended upon.

SILK SPONGE TOWELS,

Every fibre of these Silk Towels guaranteed to be pure Silk, without mixture. Useful and beneficial to all gymnasts and sporting men in every way.

Bathing.—For removing the secretions of the pores of the skin, leaving a healthy surface, Silk Towels are as effective as a bath brush, and do not irritate the skin. They should be used as a Sponge, with soap and water, or Bay Rum and like washes. There is no better FACE CLOTH than the Silk Sponge Towel.

For General Household and Hotel Use, wet with pure water (no soap required), in wiping Table Glassware, Cleaning Paint, Cleaning and Polishing Windows, Cleaning Linoleum Carpets, Cleaning Metal Signs, Cleaning Furniture, Mirrors, and Washing Dishes, they are a success. They are very durable.

Soft as a NEW CHAMOIS, never getting hard to scratch the most highly polished furniture. The Silk Sponge Towel can be easily washed, and is then as clean as new. They are an absolute necessity to those who take a pride in their housekeeping. Price, 25 cents each.

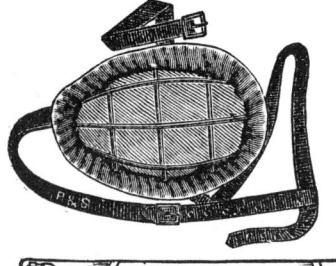

ABDOMEN MASK.

This is almost another indispensable article for Base Ball Catchers. It is easily adjusted and can be worn with comfort and not interfering with your play. It has been highly recommended by those who have used them. They are made of strong wire and neatly covered with chamois, and padded.. ....Each, $2.00

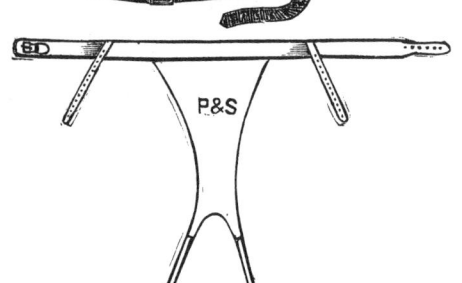

No. 950.—THE LATEST IMPROVED JOCK STRAP OR SUPPORT.

A great benefactor for Gymnasts, Rowers, Bal Players, Bicycle Riders, Horse back riding, Runners, and all Athletic Sports. It is considered one of the best of the kind. Made of Chamois leather, linen, lined, Each, $1.50. Made of all Linen, each, $1.00

SUSPENSORY BANDAGES and JOCK STRAPS, FOR MEN'S USE.

These Cuts are about 1-5 the exact size of the Suspensories, &c.

No. 808. No. 809. No. 810. No. 910. No. 900.

The above goods are of French, English and American make. They are all of the best, simplest and most useful styles to be had; are in three sizes—small, medium and large bag, and when ordering please mention which size you wish, and send size around waist for strap (prices the same for all sizes). They are especially adapted for the use of pedestrians, equestrians, gymnasts, base-ball, cricket, polo and lawn tennis players, bicycleists, rowers, boxers, hunters, and sportingmen in general; also for men who stand or walk a great deal. All these persons will find great relief and comfort in wearing either of the above suspensories.

No. 808.—Suspensory Bandage made with cotton band to buckle, and fine cotton bag, closely knit, with shir string, to tighten at will. Price, 25 cents.

No. 809.—Suspensory, same as No. 808, but in place of shir string has straps, which button on band. Price, 25 cents.

No. 810.—Suspensory Bandage, made of fine elastic band; to fasten with a new style of hook and eye, same to regulate for size of waist, with closely knit cotton bag, to shir and tighten at pleasure. Price, 60 cents.

No. 811.—Suspensory, same as No. 809, but band, which is one-half of fine elastic web, and which gives freely to the movement of the body. Price, 40 cents.

No. 910.—Suspensory, a full elastic band with eyelet holes and hooks, fine net bag, trimmed with silk; same can be taken off of band and washed, as it is fastened with small and neat hooks and eyes. Price, 75 cents.

No. 900.—Jock Strap, used more by gymnasts, athletes, rowers, etc., made of fine cotton band, bag of sateen lined with fine cotton; size of band regulated with buckle, and strings, to tighten the bag, by fastening through eyelet holes. Price, 50 cents.

N. B.—The buckles and hooks on all our Suspensories are so fastened as not to touch the flesh, are very secure, and work with great ease.

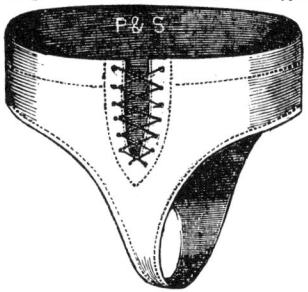

THE NEW ATHLETE'S SUPPORTER.

This is considered the best Supporter now made, and it answers for a combination of beneficial uses. They are sure to fit, as they are made in different sizes to fit all size waists; are made of a fine quality of Canton flannel with regulated laced front. It is also very beneficial to those who are troubled with kidney or spinal difficulties, or a weak or sprained back. When ordering send size of waist. Price, 50 cts.

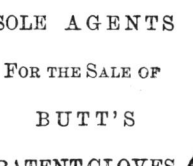

BOXING AND CONTEST GLOVES.

Patented September 3d, 1878.

WE ARE SOLE AGENTS FOR THE SALE OF BUTT'S PATENT GLOVES

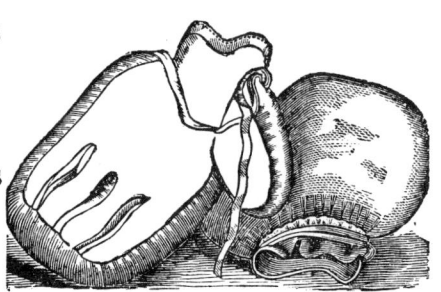

Which are used exclusively by all the prominent athletes throughout the country. These gloves are made with solid palms; the fingers are made by stitching double fourchettes inside of the glove, and with one half the stitching that is required in an old style Glove; and no stitching comes inside to touch the hand in any part, to rot out with perspiration, thus causing them to rip.

No. A.—Boys', are made of soft tan leather palms, and chamois coverings, and stuffed with curled hair.
Price per set, two pair, $2 50

No. B.—Men's, made of the same as above, but better quality leather and hair. Price per set, two pair, $3 00

No. C.—Made of extra tan leather, palms and wrists bound with blue fancy leather and strings to tighten around the wrist, stuffed with curled hair, and sewed in with an extra band of leather, with double stitching to keep the hair in place. Price per set, two pair, $3 50

No D.—Same as No. C, only heel padded.. $4 00

No. E.—Are made with white kid palms with blue fancy leather cuffs, and elastic to tighten around the wrists; extra soft coverings, stuffed with curled hair, and double sewn in with an extra band of leather, with ventilated palms..$4 50

No. F.—Same as No. E, only heel padded... 5 00

No. G.—Are made with soft tan dog-skin palms, with red fancy leather cuffs, and elastic to tighten around the wrists, and extra fine soft covering, stuffed with curled hair, and double sewn in with an extra band of leather, with ventilated palms..Price, per set, $5 50

No. H.—Same as No. G, only heel padded... 6 00

No. I.—Peck & Snyder's Professional Sounding Gloves are made with reindeer, Indian tanned palms: with white kid coverings, and with red, white and blue cuffs of fancy leather; stuffed with the best curled hair, and double sewn in with an extra band of leather, and with ventilated palms................Price per set, $6 50

No. P.—Same as No. I, only heel padded... 7 00

No. K.—Are made of imported white French kid; palms and coverings of the very best material; finished with long red, white, and blue fancy leather cuffs, nicely stitched with silk, &c., with ventilated palms.
Price per set, 7 50

No. L.—Same as No. K, only heel padded 8 00

No. M.—Or the Marquis of Queensborough Professional Contest Gloves.
This Glove is made to lace up at the back under the hair in order to tighten it to any size hand, with white kid covering. The tops of the fingers are outside, so the hand can be closed as easily as in a kid glove.
Price per set, two pair, $6 00

Sample sets, by express, on receipt of price, or by registered mail, at our risk, on receipt of price and 50 cents per pair additional for postage and registering.

Boxing Made Easy; or the complete manual of self-defense, clearly explained and illust'd. Price, 15c.

The Science of Self-Defense. By Edmund Price. 130pp. Illust'd. and bound. By mail, " 75c.

The Art of Boxing. By Ned Donnelly, Professor of Boxing to the London Athletic Club. 35 double figure illustrations with others..Cloth bound, 50c., paper cover, 25c.

This is the most complete work on the subject yet published.

N. B.—Owing to the great demand for a cheap kid and chamois Boxing Glove, we offer the following, which for cheapness and quality cannot be surpassed.

No. OO.—Boys, made of soft Tan Leather palms, Chamois Covering and stuffed with curled hair, a good cheap glove, price, per set, two pairs, $2.00.

No. O.—Men's, made same as No. OO, but better goods and hair, price per set, two pairs, $2.50.

No. EE.—Reindeer palms and white kid covering, stuffed with hair, price, per set, two pairs, $5.00.

No. CC.—Dog Skin palms, kid covering, stuffed with hair, cheapest kid glove made, price, per set, two pairs, $4.50.

All the above Boxing Gloves are warranted not to harden by water or perspiration.

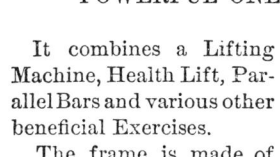

PECK & SNYDER'S NEW AND IMPROVED HEALTH LIFT.

THE CHEAPEST, BEST AND MOST POWERFUL ONE MADE.

It combines a Lifting Machine, Health Lift, Parallel Bars and various other beneficial Exercises.

The frame is made of second growth Ash, with Malleable Iron and Steel fittings, which makes it very strong and durable.

Price, complete, $6 00

The object of this invention is to contrive a simple arrangement of apparatus whereby a machine with only one pair of handles or levers may be readily converted into an arrangement for producing the same result by bearing downward on said handles or levers, or one by which the said result may be effected by bearing down on one handle or lever by one hand and lifting on the other handle by the other hand; or both levers may be secured in a fixed position for use as parallel bars.

The essential feature of the invention consists of a duplex pivotal connection of the working levers or handles and a detachable brace, together with an adjustable connection of the rods with said levers, which couple them to the platform, whereby the fulcrum is readily shifted from one side to the other of said connection, as it is desired to raise the platform by lifting or pressing down; and there is a locking device in connection with the platform, connecting rods, levers and brace, by which said levers are secured in the position of parallel bars.

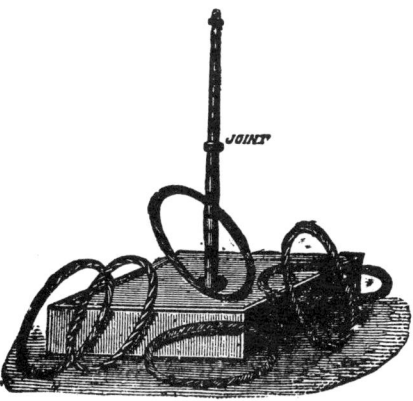

RING TOSS, FOR PARLOR OR FIELD.

This ever-pleasing game is here brought out in a new and attractive design. There are several rings or hoops, some large and some small. The game is to throw these over the standard or target-post at a given distance. The hoops are made of rattan, graded in size and wound with fancy colored webbing, thus presenting a beautiful appearance, and at the same time being perfectly harmless to the wall or furniture when played in the house. Equally adapted to the lawn. It is a healthful and fascinating game. The stake is jointed and can be placed in the box when not in use. This is a great advantage in packing.

Price, per set, $1 00

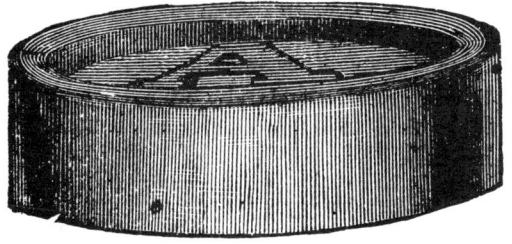

THE IMPROVED SHUFFLEBOARD WEIGHT.

No. 500.—The annexed cut represents the exact size, are solid cast and of the best iron, finely finished, 8 in a set, four letters A and 4 B, or letters C and D, or O and K, as parties wish. Price of set complete, $3 50

SCANDINAVIAN PADLOCK AND CHAIN FOR LOCKING BICYCLE.

Is also used to secure valise to seat in car when traveling.

They are very neat and handsome.

No. 1.   Finished in Brown..$0 65
No. 2.   "   in Gilt... 1 00

Cut is half the size of Lock.

SPOKE GRIP OR WRENCH.

Every Wheelman needs a good strong spoke wrench, one that will not mar his spokes. This one will be found to answer every purpose. Has a full cut steel screw and forged steel clamp.

Nickel Plated...Price, each, $0 75

BICYCLE WRENCH.

The best Wrench made for a Bicycle; is adjustable. Drop forged from Norway iron and bar steel. Finished in a thorough manner and case hardened. Length of Wrench when closed, 4 inches.

Nickel Plated...Price, each, $1 00
Blued.. "   "   75
Plain Finish.. "   "   35

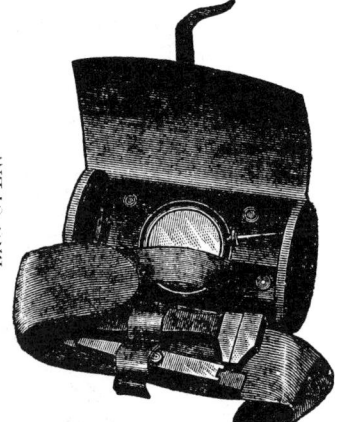

THE BUFFALO TOOL BAG.

HAND MADE.
    NEW DESIGN.
        BEST MATERIAL.
SMALLEST.
    NEATEST.
        HANDIEST.
MULTUM IN PARVO.   BAG CLOSED.

Does not rattle. Without doubt the most complete in the market.

Price, $2 00

THE EUREKA PATENT BICYCLE LAMP, JUST OUT,

Is considered the best and most convenient Lamp made. It gives a very strong light, and is so made as to fit almost every style of Bicycle. Also combines all the latest improvements that are wanted in a good lamp. They are made in two sizes—Nickel plated and Japanned—have red and green side lights, also two red lights on back, with nickel plated reflectors. The small size has a heavy white glass bull's eye 2¼ inches in diameter; the large size, 3¼ inches.

No. 1, small Japanned, each..$3 00
No. 2, large Japanned, each... 4 00
No. 3, small Nickel plated, each.. 4 00
No. 4, large Nickel plated, each.. 5 00

BICYCLE AND TRICYCLE BELLS.

No. 6.　　　No. 7.　　　No. 10.　　　No. 9.　　　No. 8.

In ordering Bells, give the name of the machine, except in the following cases, when orders by number will be sufficient : Nos. 1 to 6 inclusive.　　　Price each, $3.00

No. 1. Standard Columbia. (*Attaches to head*).
No. 2. Harvard, Yale, D. H. F. Premier, Harvard Special.
No. 3. Special Challenge, D. H. F. Singer, Extraordinary Challenge, Humber, Expert Columbia, Harvard Special, Harvard.
No. 4. Special Columbia, Ordinary, Mustang, Standard Columbia, Ideal. (*Attaches to break*).
No. 5. American Star.
No. 6. Royal Challenge, Club, Special Club, British Challenge, Shadow, Rudge, Matchless, Yale, Expert Columbia, American Club, Sanspareil, American, Victor, Royal Mail.

No. 6. **The Automatic Alarm**—Introduced in 1878, is the most successful Bicycle Bell ever made, its use having extended to all districts in this country where the wheel is known and to foreign countries as well.

The Automatic Alarm is handy when wanted. Out of the way when not wanted. Cannot strike when machine falls. Does not interfere with attachments. Does not interfere with coasting. Has a remarkably loud, clear tone. Commands instant attention. Is elegantly finished. Is handsome. Improves the machine.　　　Price of Alarm, $3 00

No. 7. **Tricycle Alarm.**—For the Tricycle there has been felt a want of an alarm equal in effect to our Automatic on the Bicycle. To meet this, we offer our No. 7. It is operated by pulling a chain which lies in a grooved flange surrounding the edge of the gong, the rotation thereof causing a hammer to strike the gong. At the end of the chain is a hard rubber ring which comes in position to allow the forefinger of the left hand to operate the alarm without moving the hand. By pulling more or less and faster or slower, one stroke or a series of strokes may be had at will, and the effect is practically the same as the *Automatic* on the Bicycle, the tone being equally loud and clear. We have found it out of the question to adapt a bell operated by contact with the tire, to the tricycle, but though we have substituted a pull bell for this, it will be found very efficient and satisfactory.

It has a 3 inch gong. The back is closed by a plate, and a simple clip admits of fastening to any size handle rod. It is equally adapted to the Humber pattern tricycle, being attached to the handle bar and pulling in a horizontal direction.

It is finely polished and plated all over, and by far the handsomest bell ever made.
　　　Price of Alarm, $3 50

No. 10. **Hill & Tolman Stop Bell.**—We confidently offer this as a PERFECT STOP BELL. Its simplicity, lightness, freedom from possibility of rattle, its neat appearance on the machine, the ease, convenience and certainty of stopping, its out-of-the-wayness when not wanted, and above all its remarkable sensitiveness and loud ringing, will satisfy all who try it, of the propriety of our claim.

It has the spring hammer similar to No. 8, but being inside the gong it is protected from injury. It is stopped by shifting the projecting handle as shown in cut, the stopping contrivance being a single piece of wire. This bell will ring freely on the smoothest roads, and on ordinary roads is nearly equal to our Automatic in effect. It can be used on handle bar, but will generally be preferred on brake upright, in which case the head of the upright will be found a convenient stop for the handle of the bell. If used on handle bar, remove the gong and turn the hammer round to hang down.

The screws in clamp are set at an angle so that in putting on the bell the screw driver avoids the head of the machine, thus doing away with the necessity of removing the brake.

It has a 3 inch gong, and is finely finished and plated.　　　Price, $1 25

No. 9. **Peerless Stop Bell.**—This is the same as No. 8, with the addition of a second hammer. The ringing is more full, continuous and musical. More hammers can be added if wanted. 2½ inch Gong.　　　Price, 85 cents. Extra Hammers, each, 15 cents.

No. 8. **Peerless Stop Bell.**—This is a modified and improved form of bell which was known as the "Peerless Alarm." The hammer is hung on a sensitive steel spring which responds to the slightest jar of the machine, giving a clear musical ring. The bell is stopped by catching the hammer over the edge of the gong as in cut, a touch from the finger releasing it for action. Equally adapted to brake or handle bar. *When to be used for the latter, loosen the screw and turn the hammer into a vertical position.*

Especially recommended for boys to use on Bicycles and Velocipedes, and in cases where a bell is carried simply to meet the requirements of town or city ordinance.　　　2½ inch Gong, Price, 75 cents.

PECK & SNYDER, N. Y.

Dealers in all styles of Bicycle and Tricycle Bells, Lamps, Cyclometers Saddles, Tool Bags, Locks, Wrenches, Uniforms, Rubber Cement and all kinds of Sundries.

BOYS' PATENT VELOCIPEDES.

BOYS' VELOCIPEDE.

This style of Velocipede has been greatly improved and simplified this season, and the price has been reduced nearly one-half. We claim its superiority to anything of the kind in the market. The reaches and saddle are made of selected hard wood, finished and polished in its natural state. Axles are made of the best Swedish iron; all castings of malleable iron highly tinned; the seat is neatly covered with carpet, which adds greatly to appearance and comfort; the wheels are made of well seasoned and selected stock, and have welded oval tires. This Velocipede presents an elegant appearance.

No. 1 has 16 in. front wheel and 12 in. hind wheels. Price, $3.00
No. 2 has 20 in. front wheel and 16 in. hind wheels. Price, $4.00
No. 3 has 24 in. front wheel and 20 in. hind wheels. Price, $5.00
No. 4 has 28 in. front wheel and 24 in. hind wheels. Price, $6.00

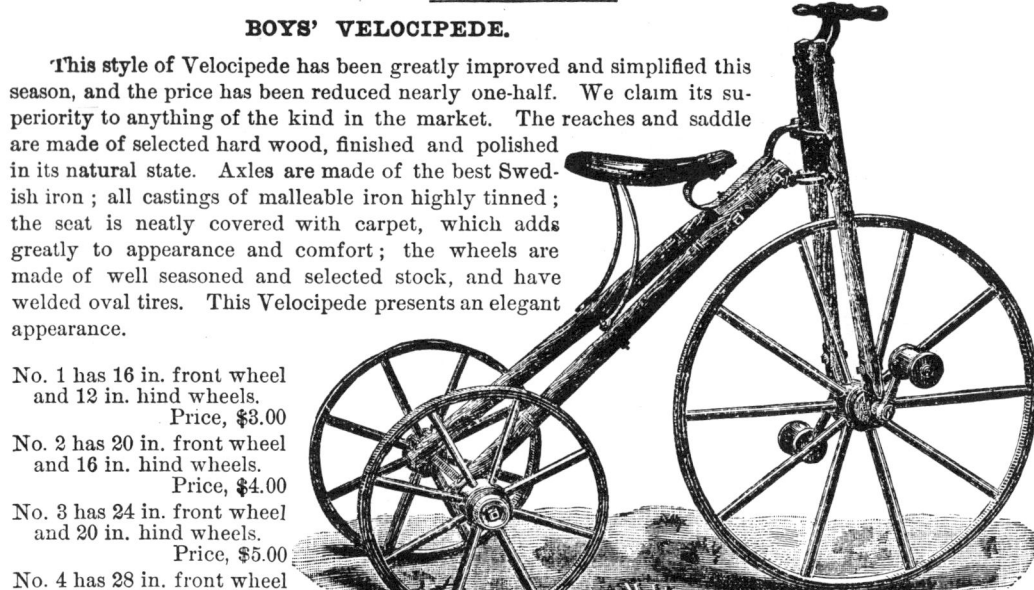

IRON VELOCIPEDE.
WOOD WHEEL.—PATENTED.

The above is an entirely new improvement, which we feel satisfied will prove to be the most stylish and practical machines ever offered to the trade. The frames are made of malleable iron, well braced and finished; the saddle is covered with leather, and is supplied with an elastic spring; the wheels are made of well seasoned and selected stock, and have welded oval tires.

No. 5 has 16 in. front wheel and 12 in. hind wheels. Price, $4 00
No. 6 " 20 in. " " 16 in. " " 5 00
No. 7 " 24 in. " " 20 in. " " 6 00
No. 8 " 28 in. " " 24 in. " " 7 00

IRON VELOCIPEDE.
STEEL WHEEL.—PATENTED.

The frame of this Velocipede is the same as our Wood Wheel Velocipede, but has steel wheels, made of the best quality of wrought iron, with steel wire spokes.

No. 9 has 16 in. front wheel and 12 in. hind wheels. Price, $5 00
No. 10 has 20 in. front wheel and 16 in. hind wheels. Price, $6 00
No. 11 has 24 in. front wheel and 20 in. hind wheels. Price, $7 00
No. 12 has 28 in. front wheel and 24 in. hind wheels. Price, $8 50

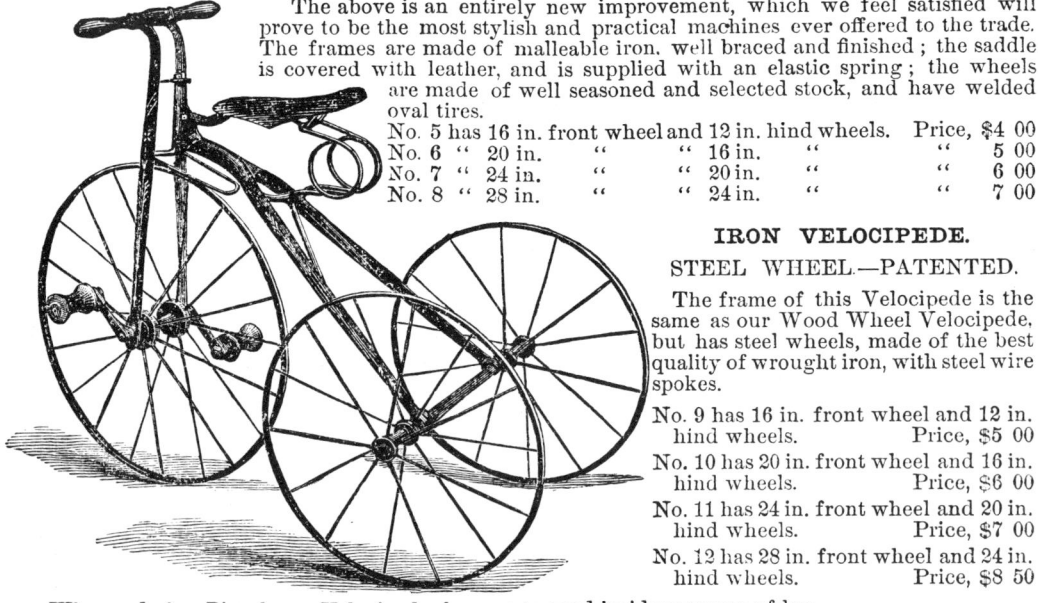

When ordering Bicycles or Velocipedes be sure to send inside measure of leg.

CONTINUOUS ALARM BELL.

This is the most popular Bicycle or Tricycle Bell in use. By simply pressing the fingers on the lever it rings continuously with a nice chime.

Price, each, $2 00

THE POPULAR PETITE TRICYCLES.

PETITE WOOD TRICYCLE.
PATENTED.

Our PETITE TRICYCLE has proved to be the most popular article ever made by us; it has entirely taken the place of all the girls' velocipedes and so called tricycles in the market. The above cut represents our PETITE WOOD WHEEL TRICYCLE. The frame is constructed of wrought iron pipes; seat is adjustable, and rests on springs; adjustable foot cranks to take up slack in chain; power is derived by combination of foot cranks, sprocket wheels and endless chain. The front or guide wheel is controlled by handles in front of rider. The machine is neatly painted and presents an elegant appearance.

No. 1 has wooden wheels 14 in. front and 24 in. hind.   Price, $7 50
No. 2 has wooden wheels 14 in. front and 28 in. hind.   Price, $10 00
No. 3 has wooden wheels 14 in. front and 32 in. hind.   Price, $12 50

PECK & SNYDER,
Dealers in all styles of Bicycles, Tricycles and Velocipedes for Boys and Girls.

PETITE STEEL TRICYCLE.
PATENTED.

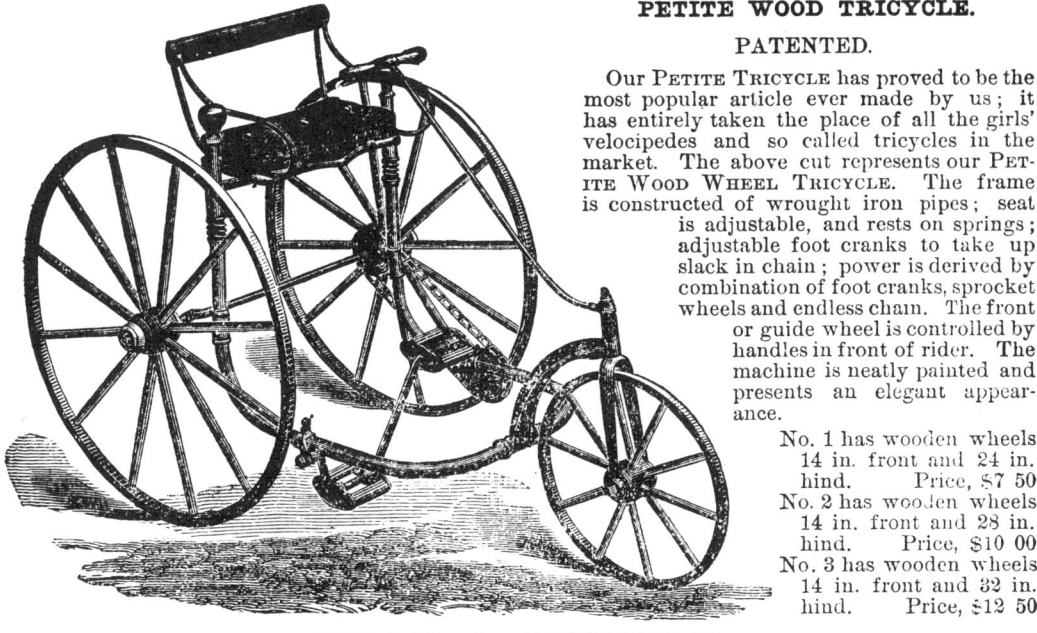

Petite Steel Wheel Tricycle is same make and style as Nos. 1, 2 and 3, but has steel wheels.

No. 4 has steel wire wheel 14 in. front and 24 in. hind.
   Price, $9 00
No. 5 has steel wire wheel 14 in. front and 28 in. hind.
   Price, $12 00
No. 6 has steel wire wheel 14 in. front and 32 in. hind.
   Price, $15 00

PETITE RUBBER TRICYCLE.
PATENTED.

Petite Rubber Tricycle is same make and style as the others, but has steel wire wheel with molded rubber tires of the best quality.

No. 7 has steel wire wheels with rubber tires, 14 inches front and 24 inches hind.
   Price, $18 00
No. 8 has steel wire wheels with rubber tires, 14 inches front and 28 inches hind.   Price $25 00.
No. 9 has steel wire wheels with rubber tires, 14 inches front and 32 inches hind.   Price $30 00.

PRICE LIST OF
FLAGS, POLES, PAPER LANTERNS, BALLOONS, &c.

SEWED BUNTING FLAGS. (American.)

Width.	Length.	Per Piece.	Width.	Length.	Per Piece.
2	by 3 feet	$1 25	10	by 18 feet	$22 00
2½	" 4 "	2 25	10	" 20 "	23 50
3	" 5 "	3 00	12	" 18 "	25 00
4	" 6 "	4 25	12	" 20 "	28 00
4	" 7 "	4 75	13	" 21 "	32 00
5	" 8 "	6 00	13	" 23 "	35 00
6	" 9 "	8 00	15	" 24 "	40 00
6	" 10 "	8 75	16	" 26 "	46 00
6	" 12 "	10 00	20	" 30 "	65 00
8	" 12 "	12 75	20	" 36 "	75 00
8	" 15 "	15 00			
9	" 18 "	18 50			

SEWED BUNTING FLAGS. (American.)
WITH PRINTED CANVAS JACKS.

Width.	Length.	Per Piece.	Width.	Length.	Per Piece.
2	by 3 feet	$0 90	6	by 9 feet	$6 00
2½	" 4 "	1 50	6	" 10 "	6 75
3	" 5 "	2 00	6	" 12 "	8 00
4	" 6 "	3 00	8	" 12 "	10 50
4	" 7 "	3 50	8	" 15 "	12 75
5	" 8 "	4 75			

SEWED MUSLIN FLAGS. American.)

Fast Colors with Printed Jacks. (Imitation Bunting Flags.)

Width.	Length.	Per Piece.	Width.	Length.	Per Piece.
4	by 6 feet	$1 75	6	by 10 feet	$3 25
4	" 7 "	1 85	6	" 12 "	3 75
5	" 8 "	2 50	8	" 12 "	4 25
6	" 9 "	3 00	8	" 15 "	4 75

With Sewed Jacks (for Decorators).

10	by 15 feet	9 00	10	by 20 feet	$11 75
12	" 18 "	12 50	12	" 24 "	16 00

FLAG POLES, Complete.
WITH TRUCKS, HALLIARDS AND METAL BALLS.

6 feet	$1 00
8 "	1 25
10 "	1 50
12 "	1 75
14 "	2 00

BRACKETS or POLEHOLDERS.

No. 1,	1⅞ in. bore	$ 90	No. 7,	⅞ in. bore	$ 45
" 2,	1¾ "	85	" 8,	¾ "	20
" 3,	1½ "	75	" 9,	⅝ "	15
" 4,	1⅜ "	65	" 10,	½ "	10
" 5,	1⅛ "	60	" 11,	7-16 "	07
" 6,	1 "	55			

SEWED SILK FLAGS. American.

Width.	Length.	Per Piece.	Width.	Length.	Per Piece.
3	by 5 feet	$12 00	5	by 8 feet	$25 00
4	" 6 "	15 00	6	" 9 "	35 00

6 " 6½ feet Regulation Company Flags. ... 25 00

DYED SILK FLAGS.
ON NICELY FINISHED STAFFS, WITH SPEARS.

Width. Length.	Per Piece.
12 by 18 inches	$ 50
16 " 24 "	75
24 " 36 "	1 25
30 " 48 "	2 00

SMALL SILK FLAGS.
WITH STAFFS AND ACORNS.

2½ inches long....................50 cts. per doz.
3½ " " ....75 " "

AMERICAN SHIELDS,

Width. Length.	Per Dozen.
24 by 36, on lined pasteboard	$2 00

PRINTED AMERICAN FLAGS.
ON GOOD MUSLIN, IN FAST COLORS, ON STICKS.

No.	1	2	3	4	5	6
Length, inches	3	5	6	7½	9½	14
Per dozen	5c.	8c.	10c.	15c.	20c.	30c.
No.	7	8	9	10	11	12
Length, inches	18	27½	36	43	50	66
Per dozen	40c.	$1.00	$1.50	$2.00	$2.50	$6.00

MUSLIN FLAGS, Assorted Nations.
12 NATIONS IN A SET.

36 inches long, on sticks..............$2.00 per set.

Pin Flags, American...............50c. per gross.
" Assorted Nations,........50c. "

GRAND ARMY REPUBLIC FLAGS.
ON STICKS.

Length.	Per Dozen.
24 inches	$1 00
36 "	2 50

Letters "G. A. R.," printed on any size Muslin Flag at a moderate charge.

KNIGHTS TEMPLAR FLAGS.
ON STICKS.

36 inches long.	Per Dozen.
Cross (In hoc signo vinces)	$2 25
Maltese Cross	2 25
Cross and Crown	2 25

CHRISTMAS PAPER FLAGS.
WITH STAFF AND SPEAR.

10 inches long......................50 cts. per dozen.

MUSLIN CHRISTMAS BANNERS.

With Staff and Spear,......No. 1, $1 00 per dozen.
" " " ...... " 2, 1 25 "

PECK-SNYDER, N.Y.
PECK & SNYDER,
126, 128 & 130
Nassau Street, N. Y.

PAPER BUCKET LANTERNS.
IMPROVED AGAINST CATCHING FIRE.

	Per 100.
6 inches Diameter,	$2 25
7¼ " "	2 50
9 " "	3 50
12 " "	7 50

BALL LANTERNS.

	Per 100.
Diameter 11 inches	$10 00

LANTERN STICKS.

	Per 100.
60 inches long,	$4 50
40 " "	2 50

CANDLES.

	Per 100.
Parafine Candles, for Bucket Lanterns or Transparencies	$4 00
Adamantine Candles, for Bucket Lanterns or Transparencies	3 00

PAPER BALOONS.

Circumference.	Per Doz.	Circumference.	Per Doz.
6 feet	$1 50	15 feet	$5 00
8 "	2 25	20 "	7 50
10 "	2 50	25 "	10 00
12 "	4 00	30 "	12 00

NEW OTTO IMPROVED BICYCLE.

With Rubber Tires.

The above cut represents our New Otto Improved Bicycle. This machine is made of the best material, elegantly finished. It has the cylindrical head. Nos. 3-5 have detachable slotted cranks, adjustable step. Has heavy rubber tires and cow horn handle bar. We finish these machines, partly nickeled, as follows: Top of fork, brake, handle bar, crank, pedals, spring, footstep, and has rubber handles; balance of machine enameled and highly ornamented, also has tool bag, wrench and oil can.

No.	Diameter of Front Wheel.	Diameter of Hind Wheel.	Length of leg inside measurement to sole of foot.	Weight.	Price.
1	28 in.	12 in.	23 in.	16 lbs.	$12 50
2	32 "	12 "	26 "	19 "	18 00
3	36 "	14 "	28 "	27 "	25 00
4	39 "	14 "	29 "	30 "	30 00
5	42 "	14 "	30 "	32 "	35 00

OTTO SPECIAL BICYCLE.
With Rubber Tires.

Our Otto Special is made of the best material and elegantly finished; it has the cylindrical head, long parallel front bearings, detachable and slotted cranks, adjustable step and heavy rubber tire, together with many other valuable improvements. Any one who is a judge of Bicycles will appreciate its merits.

We finish these machines partly nickel plated, as follows: Top of fork, brake handle bar, crank, pedals, footstep and has rubber handles; balance of machine enameled and highly ornamented, also has tool bag, wrench and oil can.

No.	Diameter of Front Wheel.	Diameter of Hind Wheel.	Length of leg inside measurement to sole of foot.	Weight.	Price.
6	44 in.	16 in.	31 in.	40 lbs.	$45 00
7	46 "	16 "	32 "	42 "	50 00
8	48 "	16 "	33 "	46 "	55 00
9	50 "	16 "	34 "	48 "	60 00

Bicycle Stockings, English Mixture, Heavy Worsted, per pair................$2.00
Bicycle Stockings, Solid Colors, Heavy Worsted, 1.50
"Our Special" Stockings, Solid Colors, Worsted, 1.00
"Our Special" Stockings, Solid Colors, Cotton 0.50
Heavy Silk Stockings, Solid Colors, to order__5.00
Bicycle Coats, Plain or Pleated......6.00 to 12.00

Bicycle Knee Pants, Corduroy, Cloth or Worsted, $3.50 to 6.00
" Jerseys, Worsted, all Colors___1.50 to 5.00
" Flannel Suits, Plain Checks and Strips, 1.00 to 5.00
Caps, 1.00, 1.25; Helmets, 0.75, 1.00, 1.50.
Special Prices on Club Uniforms. For complete list see "Wheelman's Suits."

HARWOOD'S PATENT DETACHABLE BICYCLE STEPS.

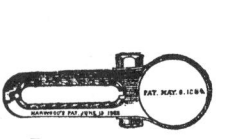
No. 1.

Harwood's Detachable Safety Bicycle Step.

No. 2.

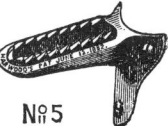
No. 5

By this improved step a firm and positive foot hold is secured when mounting or dismounting, and danger of *cutting* the leg is *obviated* by the projecting safety flange. The edges of the *teeth* are so *beveled* that they will not catch or *tear* the *clothing*, in case of a miss-step or fall. The steps are easily applied, are light and strong, are an ornament to the bicycle. Five styles are made, varying in height, and with brackets so shaped as to admit of application to any make of bicycle without drilling new holes in the backbone.

No. 1 is adapted to the "Standard" or "Special Columbia," "Boston" or "Yale," 50c.
No. 2 to the "Harvard," Expert Columbia," "Club," or "Premier," 75c.
No. 3 is designed to replace the old style "Harvard" Step, 50c.
No. 4, a new pattern, adopted by Stoddard, Lovering & Co.) is made for the "British Challenge,"—though equally applicable to the "Matchless," 50c.
No. 5 is made expressly for the "American Sansparel" and "Rudge Roadster," 75c.

The plain finish has been discarded as it is believed the crocus polish or nickel will meet all requirements. Order by No. Clearly indicate the style of finish, and if holes for screws are to be drilled, give the name of machine, and if of English make send pattern of step bracket, with position of screw holes indicated.

The safety step does not mar the backbone, no screws being used in attaching it. A rubber pad is placed between the step and backbone, and cemented there, which prevents scratching or slipping. Seven sizes of bands are made, increasing by 1-16 inch from 15-16 to 1 5-16 inch inclusive. Two bands are sent with each step. In ordering, give diameter of backbone at height of step, and state whether round or oval.

Price, $1.00, extra bands, 10 cents each.

LAMSON'S LUGGAGE CARRIER.
THE NEW DETACHABLE FORM FOR BOOKS OR ANY OTHER BUNDLE.

This carrier is made detachable, so that it may be removed from the Bicycle without undoing the bundle. Simply unbuckle the strap which holds it down in front and unhook it behind the bar, fasten the hook again and you have a perfect Shawl Strap.

Students using the "Wheel" will find this arrangement invaluable in carrying their books to and from school. (Made in two widths, 3¼ and 4⅝ inches between the arms). For sale by all Bicycle dealers. Sent by mail on receipt of Price, each, **$1 00**.

THE LATEST THING IN CYCLOMETERS. EXACT SIZE. WARRANTED ACCURATE.
LAMSON'S PRACTICAL CYCLOMETER,

For Bicycles and Tricycles. Weight about two ounces. The action is REALLY POSITIVE and the Cyclometer cannot fail to operate at any rate of speed on any road. It is attached to a spoke and operated by a neat clip on the inside of the right fork, which works a lever on the back of the Cyclometer. On the end of the lever is a small rubber covered roller, so that the action is noiseless, and the arrangement is so that the little roller does not project between the spokes far enough to hit the fork, and is entirely out of the way. The Cyclometer is easily put on by any one, and is out of the way of a hub lamp, is dust and water-proof, strong and durable. No springs that can get out of order. Made by a practical watchmaker, and every Cyclometer warranted.

Registers up to TEN THOUSAND MILES before commencing again at zero. The dial is easily read, and the Cyclometer is an ornament to any wheel. This Cyclometer will soon be on the market, and every effort will be made to make it the most perfect as well as the CHEAPEST Cyclometer in the world. Orders taken and filled in turn.

In ordering, give size and make of wheel. Price, each, **$5 00**

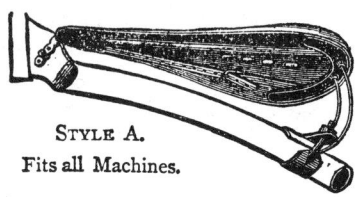

STYLE A.
Fits all Machines.

Prince's Record of 2.39 was made on a Duryea.
Used also by Hendee, Sellers, Howell, Woodside, Corey, Dolph, Landy, Jenkins, Brooks, Eck, Morgan, Higham, Yates; also, Mlles. Armaindo and Sylvester, and all the flyers and long-distance riders.

Fits any Machine. (State what machine you ride.) Is Low, Neat, Comfortable, Adjustable and Cheap. Try it once, and You will Use no other; it makes Road Riding a Luxury.

Prices, Japanned, **$3.00**; Nickeled, **$3.75**.

PRICE LIST OF FISHING TACKLE AND FIXTURES.

The price-list of fishing tackle published on the following pages is the most complete that has ever been offered. Fishermen ordering their supplies direct from us, can rely on getting just what they order, and at the lowest market price as quoted. Such articles as hooks, lines, flies, spoons, etc., can be sent by mail, on receipt of price. Goods sent, C. O. D., by express, to all parts of the country.

No. 320. Trout and Black Bass Rods, Brass Mounted.

			Description	Length Feet	Each
A.	3	Piece,	Trout Rod, single ferrules, made of ash	10½	$0 25
B.	3	"	Bass Rod, single ferrules and guide rings, made of ash	10½	0 35
C.	3	"	Trout Rod, double ferrules and guide rings	10½	0 50
D.	3	"	Trout Rod, double ferrules and guide rings, stained dark	10½	0 75
E.	4	"	Trout Rod, double ferrules, guide rings, stained dark and polished	12	1 00
F.	3	"	Trout Rod, double ferrules, reel bands guide rings and good finish	10½	1 00
G.	4	"	Trout Rod, double ferrules, reel bands, guide rings, and very good finish	12	1 25
H.	3	"	Trout Rod, double ferrules, reel bands, guide rings and good finish	12	1 00
I.	4	"	Trout Rod, full mounted, stained and polished	12	1 50
J.	3	"	Mountain Trout Rod, full mounted and fine finish	9½	2 00
K.	4	"	Heavy Trout or Black Bass Rod, full mounted and fine finished	12	2 25
L.	4	"	Heavy Trout or Black Bass Rod, hollow butt, extra tip and finish	12	2 50
M.	4	"	Trout Rod, full mounted, hollow butt, extra tip and fine finish	12	3 00
N.	4	"	Trout Rod, full mounted, hollow butt, extra tip and very fine finished	12	5 00
O.	3	"	Black Bass Rod, full mounted	10½	1 50
P.	3	"	Black Bass Rod, full mounted and good finish	10½	2 00
Q.	3	"	Black Bass Rod, full mounted and fine finish	9	2 50
R.	3	"	Black Bass Rod, full mounted, hollow butt, extra tip and finish	9 and 10½	3 00
S.	3	"	Black Bass Rod, full mounted, solid reel plate, hollow butt, extra tip and finish	9 and 10½	3 75
T.	3	"	Black Bass Rod, full mounted, solid reel plate, hollow butt, extra tip, and fine finish, mountings all plated	9 and 10½	4 00
U.	3	"	Black Bass Rod, full mounted, fine ferrules, whipped butt, extra tip, finish and mountings	10½	6 00

No. 321. Trunk or Combination Rods, Brass Mounted.

			Description	Each
A.	5	Piece,	Double mountings, each joint 2 feet	$1 50
B.	6	"	Double mountings, each joint 2 feet, a very good rod	2 75
C.	6	"	Full mounted, for Trout and Bass fishing, each joint 2 feet	3 50
D.	6	"	Full mounted, hollow butt, extra tips, for Trout and Bass fishing, each joint 2 feet fine finish	4 00
E.	6	"	Full mounted hollow butt, solid reel plate, extra tips for Trout and Bass fishing, each joint 2 feet, fine finish	5 00
F.	6	"	Full mounted, hollow butt, extra tips for Trout and Bass fishing, each joint 2 feet, solid reel plate, fine finish and plated mountings	6 50

No. 322. Black Bass Rods, German Silver Mounted.

			Description	Length Feet	Each
A.	3	Piece,	Lake Bass Rod, full mounted	9	$6 00
B.	3	"	Lake Bass Rod, full mounted, extra tip and extra fine ferrules, fine	10½	12 00
C.	3	"	Lake Bass Rod, whipped butt and hollow, with extra tip, fine mountings	9	12 00
D.	3	"	Lake Bass Rod, whipped butt, extra tip, with bamboo case for spare tip, very fine mounting and finish	10½	15 00
E.	3	"	Lake Bass Rod, split bamboo, extra tip with bamboo case for tips, best	9½ and 10½	16 00
F.	4	"	Lake Bass or Trout Rod, extra tip, fine finish and fine mountings	12	10 00
G.	4	"	Lake Bass or Trout Rod, hollow butt, extra tip, very fine finish and fine mountings	12	12 00
H.	6	"	Trunk Rod for Trout or Bass fishing, hollow butt, with extra tips, best mountings and fine finish. Length of joint, 28 inches		16 00

No. 323. Fly Rods, Brass Mounted.

			Description	Length Feet	Each
A.	3	Piece,	Full Mounted, Mountain Trout Rod, for Fly or Worm fishing	10½	2 50
B.	3	"	" " " Fly Rod, nicely stained, and good finish extra tip	10½	4 00
C.	3	"	Peck & Snyder's Excelsior Fly Rod, whipped butt, extra tip, and fine finish	11	8 00
D.	4	"	" " " " " " " " " "	12	8 00
E.	4	"	" " " " " hollow " with extra tip, and fine finish	12	10 00
F.	4	"	California General Rod, hollow butt, with extra tips for Lake Bass and Trout fishing	12½	5 00
G.	4	"	" " " " " " " " " "	12½	7 00

No. 324 C.

No. 324. Fly Rods, German Silver Mounted.

			Description	Length Feet	Each
A.	3	Piece,	Mountain Trout Rod, for fly or worm fishing, with fine mountings	9½	$5 00
B.	3	"	Peck & Snyder's Excelsior Fly Rod, whipped butt, extra tip and finish	11	10 00
C.	4	"	" " " " " " " " " (See cut.)	12	10 00
D.	4	"	" " " " General Rod hollow butt, with extra tip, very fine finish	12	12 00
E.	3	"	" " " " " whipped butt, bamboo case for extra tip, fine ferrules and finish	11	15 00
F.	4	"	California General Rod, with extra tips for Lake Bass and Trout fishing, extra good ferrules and fine finish	12½	15 00
G.	3	"	6 splice, Split Bamboo Fly Rod, bamboo case to hold extra tip, fine finish and extra good mountings	10½ and 11½	16 00
H.	3	"	6 splice, Split Bamboo Patent Ferrules, a very fine Rod	10½ and 11½	25 00

No. 325. Bass or Weakfish, and Blackfish Rods, Brass Mounted.

			Feet	Each
A.	3	Piece, Double ferrules, reel bands and guides	10½	$1 00
B.	3	" " " " " " " good finish	9	1 25
C.	3	" Full mounted, good finish	9	1 50
D.	3	" " " a very strong rod, and good finish	9	1 75
E.	3	" " " Lancewood tip, and good finish	9	2 00
F.	3	" " " " " a good, strong rod, and good finish	9	3 50
G.	3	" " " " " extra good ferrules and finish	9½	4 50
H.	4	" " " " " good finish	12	3 00
I.	4	" " " hollow butt, with extra tip and good finish	12	3 50
J.	4	" " " " " " " " extra good ferrules and fine finish, a very fine rod	12	10 00
K.	3	" " " double guides, extra good ferrules and extra heavy tip, good finish	9	6 00
L.	3	" " " Newport Bass Rod, double guides, extra good ferrules, extra tip, and fine finish	9½	10 00
M.	4	" " " hollow butt, with extra tip, and heavy tip to fit second joint, best ferrules and fine finish	12	12 00
N.	3	" " " hollow butt, with extra tip, extra good ferrules	9	3 50
O.	3	" Newport Bass Rod, single guides, solid reel plate, extra tip, and extra strong	9	5 00

No. 326. Bass or Weakfish and Blackfish Rods, German Silver Mounted.

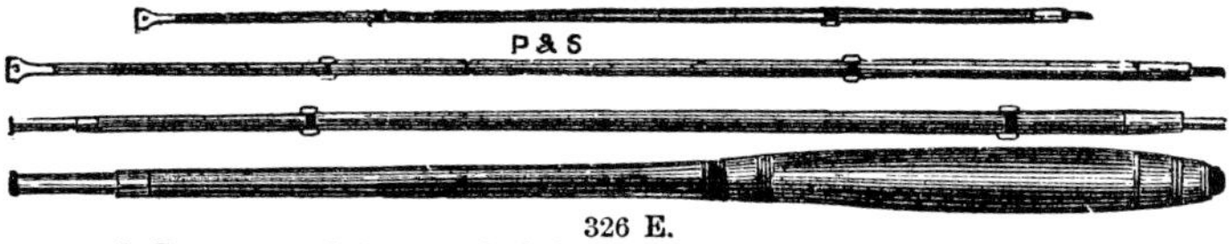

326 E.

			Feet	Each.
A.	3	Piece, Full mounted, Lancewood tip, good finish	9	$5 00
B.	3	" " " Lancewood tip, extra good ferrules and good finish	9	7 00
C.	3	" " " double guides, extra good ferrules, fine finish, solid reel plate	9	10 00
D.	3	" " " " " hollow butt with extra tip, extra good ferrules and finish	9	11 00
E.	3	" " " " " extra good ferrules and extra tip, fine finish (see cut)	9	12 00
F.	4	" " " " " hollow butt, with extra tip, extra good ferrules and fine finish	12	14 00
G.	3	" Split Bamboo Newport Bass Rod, double guides, solid reel plate, extra tip, extra fine mountings and finish	9	16 00

No. 327. Bamboo Rods, Brass Mounted.

A.	2	Piece, Double ferrules, guide rings and reel bands for Blackfish and Bass Fishing, 8 feet long	$2 50
B.	3	" " " " " " " " " " about 10 feet	2 50
C.	3	" " " " " " " for Lake Bass, Trout and Perch Fishing, 10 feet long	2 50
D.	3	" Double ferrules with guides and reel bands for Bass and Perch Fishing, 14 feet long	2 50
E.	4	" " " " " " " Lake Bass, Trout and Perch Fishing, 14 to 16 and 18 feet long	3 50
F.	2	" Full mounted, swelled butt for Black Fish and Bass Fishing, 8 to 9 feet long	4 00
G.	3	" Walking Cane Rod, for Trout and Perch Fishing, 10 feet long	3 50
H.	4	" " " " " " " 12 "	5 00

Split Bamboo Salmon Rods, and Rods made to order. Mountings of all kinds. Ferrules, Reel Bands, Guides and Tips.

Split Bamboo Grilse or Salmon Rods.

Mounted in German Silver, with Waterproof Ferrules, Capped and Rimmed and Solid Metal Reel Seat.

3 Pieces,	14 and 15 feet long, weight, 23 and 25 ounces, has 2 Tips, in Grooved Wood Form and Partition Bag .... Each,	$35 00
3 "	16 and 17 feet long, weight, 27 and 30 ounces, has 2 Tips, in Grooved Wood Form and Partition Bag .... Each,	50 00

No. 328. Common Brass Dip Reels.

			Each.
A.	15 yards,	1½ in. diameter of Plates	$ 40
B.	25 "	1¾ " " "	50
C.	40 "	$1\frac{15}{16}$ " " "	60
D.	60 "	$2\frac{1}{8}$ " " "	75
E.	15 "	1½ " Common Brass Click Reels	50
F.	25 "	1¾ " " " " "	70
G.	40 "	$1\frac{15}{16}$ " " " " "	80
H.	60 "	$2\frac{1}{8}$ " " " " "	90

No. 329. Brass Reels, with Stop.

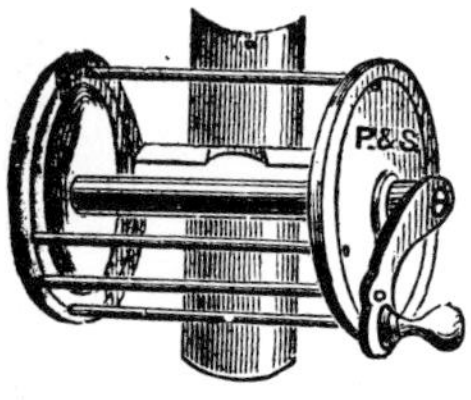

A.	15 yards,	1½ in. Diameter of Plates	$ 50
B.	25 "	1¾ " "	70
C.	40 "	$1\frac{15}{16}$ " "	80
D.	60 "	$2\frac{1}{8}$ " "	90
E.	80 "	$2\frac{5}{16}$ " "	1 00

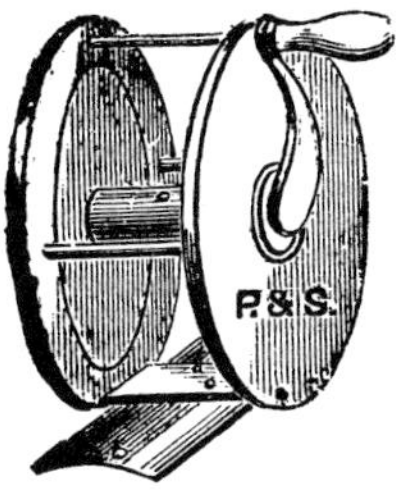

No. 330. Brass Plain Click Reels.

			Each
A.	15 yards, $1\frac{1}{2}$ in. Diameter of Plates		$ 75
B.	25 "	$1\frac{3}{4}$ " "	1 00
C.	40 "	$1\frac{15}{16}$ " "	1 15
D.	60 "	$2\frac{1}{8}$ " "	1 25
E.	80 "	$2\frac{5}{16}$ " "	1 35

Peck & Snyder Brass Click Reels. Nickel Plated.

F.	25 yards, $1\frac{5}{8}$ in. Diameter of Plates		$2 50
G.	40 "	$1\frac{15}{16}$ " "	2 75
H.	60 "	$2\frac{1}{8}$ " "	2 85
I.	80 "	$2\frac{5}{16}$ " "	3 00

No. 330 X. Salmon Reels.

Diameter.		
J.	$3\frac{1}{2}$ inch, 150 yards English Salmon Rubber Click Reel	$10 00
K.	4 " 200 " " " "	11 00
L.	$4\frac{1}{2}$ " 250 " " " "	12 00

No. 332. Brass Reels, Balance Handle, Multiplying.

	Yards.		Diam. Plate.	Each.
A.	25.	Peck & Snyder, N. Y.	$1\frac{3}{4}$ in.	$1 75
B.	40.	" " "	$1\frac{15}{16}$	2 00
C.	60.	" " "	$2\frac{1}{8}$	2 25
D.	80.	" " "	$2\frac{5}{16}$	2 50
E.	100.	" " "	$2\frac{1}{2}$	2 75
F.	150.	Peck & Snyder, N. Y.	$2\frac{3}{4}$	$3 00
G.	200.	" " "	$2\frac{15}{16}$	3 50
H.	250.	" " "	$3\frac{1}{8}$	3 75
I.	300.	" " "	$3\frac{3}{8}$	4 00
		Any of the above reels plated, extra		1 00

No. 333. German Silver Click Reels.

	Yards.		Diam. Plate.	Each.
A.	25.	Peck & Snyder, N. Y.	$1\frac{3}{4}$ in.	$4 25
B.	40.	" " "	$1\frac{15}{16}$	4 50
C.	60.	" " "	$2\frac{1}{8}$	5 00
D.	80.	" " "	$2\frac{5}{16}$	5 50
E.	25.	Brass, Rubber Click Reels	$1\frac{3}{4}$	$2 00
F.	40.	" " "	$1\frac{15}{16}$	2 25
G.	60.	" " "	$2\frac{1}{8}$	2 35
H.	80.	" " "	$2\frac{5}{16}$	2 50

No. 334. German Silver Reels, Balance Handles, Multiplying.

	Yards.		Diam. Plate.	Each.
A.	25.	Peck & Snyder, N. Y.	$1\frac{5}{8}$	$3 50
B.	40.	" " "	$1\frac{15}{16}$	4 00
C.	60.	" " "	$2\frac{1}{8}$	4 50
D.	80.	" " "	$2\frac{5}{16}$	5 00
E.	100.	" " "	$2\frac{1}{2}$	5 75
F.	150.	Peck & Snyder, N. Y.	$2\frac{3}{4}$	$ 6 50
G.	200.	" " "	$2\frac{15}{16}$	7 50
H.	250.	Steel pivot and patent cap	$3\frac{1}{8}$	17 00
I.	300.	" " " "	$3\frac{3}{8}$	18 00
		Any of the above reels with drag, extra		1 00

No. 335. Trout Baskets.

A.	French or English made	Each	$0 90
B.	" "	"	1 00
C.	" "	"	1 25
D.	" "	"	1 75
E.	" "	"	2 00
F.	" "	"	2 25

No. 336. Leather and Web Straps for Trout Baskets.

Each..35 and 50 cents.

No. 337. Square Fish Baskets.

A.	New York make	each $2 00
B.	" "	" 2 25
C.	New York make	each $2 50

No. 338. Trout Flies, London and New York Make.

Best quality, all colors	per doz.	$0 75
" Brown and Black Hackle	"	75
" Red Ibis and Professor	"	1 00
" Lake Flies Bluejay and Silver Doctor	"	2 00

No. 339. Salmon and Bass Flies, London and New York Make.

Scarlet Ibis and White Miller Bass Flies	per doz.	$2 50
Professor and Montreal Bass Flies	"	2 50
Best Salmon Flies	per doz.,	$3 50 to 5 00

No. 340. Trout Leaders, Single Gut.

		Each.
A.	1 yard best Trout Gut, white or colored	.15
B.	2 " " " "	.30
C.	3 " " " "	.40
D.	1 " Salmon Gut "	.20
E.	2 " " "	.40
F.	3 yard Salmon Gut, white or colored	.60
G.	1 " " extra strong	.30
H.	2 " " "	.50
I.	3 " " "	.75

Fishing with Hook and Line, a Manual for Anglers, 64 pages, illustrated..........25 cts.

Fur, Fin and Feather; or Game Laws of every State in the Union and Canada. Published annually, 200 pages..........50 cts.

No. 341. Bass Leaders Double Gut.

		Each			Each
A.	2 feet Best Gut, white or colored	.15	D.	6 feet Best Gut, white or colored	.50
B.	3 " " " "	.20	E.	9 " " " "	.75
C.	4 " " " "	.30			

No. 342. Bass Leaders Treble Gut.

		Each			Each
A.	1 foot Best Gut, white	.10	C.	3 foot Best Gut, white	.30
B.	2 " " " "	.20	D.	4 " " " "	.40

No. 343. Silk Worm Gut.

Best Trout Gut, per hundred....$1 00, 1 50 to 2 00 | Best Salmon Gut, per hundred.......$2 50 to 3 00

No. 344. Best Trout Lines. Waterproof taper braided Silk Lines.

Yards	20,	25,	30,	40,	50,	120
Each	$1 50	2 00	2 25	3 00	4 00	10 00

No. 345. Oiled Silk Lines, Braided.

Yards	25,	50,	75	100	
Each, No. 5	$0 50	1 00	1 50	2 00	Trout Line.
Yards	25,	50,	75	100	
Each, No. 4	$0 75	1 50	2 25	2 75	"
Yards	25,	50,	75	100	
Each, No. 3	$1 00	1 75	2 60	3 50	Bass Line.

No. 346. Laid Silk Lines, White, Green or Mottled.

No. 1.	Silk Trout Line	per yard, 2c.	No. 4.	Silk Bass Line	per yard, 4½c.
" 2.	" " "	3c.	" 5.	" " "	5c.
" 3.	" " "	4c.			

No. 347. Silk and Hair Trout Lines.

Yards	10,	15,	20,	25,	30,
Each	$0 50	0 75	1 00	1 25	1 50

No. 348. Grass Lines.

Nos	1,	2,	3,
Per Hank	50c.	50c.	50c.

No. 349. Braided Silk Lines.

Nos	1,	2,	3,	4,	5,
Each 50 yards	$2 50	2 00	1 65	1 35	1 00

No. 350. Braided Linen Lines.

Nos:	1,	2,	3,	4,	5,
Each 50 yards	65c.	65c.	65c.	65c.	65c.

No. 351. Peck & Snyder's Hard Braided Linen Lines.

Nos	1,	2,	3,	4,	5,
Each 50 yards	85c.	85c.	85c.	85c.	85c.

No. 352. Laid Linen Trout Lines.

A. 100 feet Linen Reel Line.................25c. | B. 100 yards Linen Reel Line................65c.

No. 353. Parker's Pocket Scales for Weighing Fish.

Weighing from 2 ozs. to 8 lbs ....Each 25c.

No. 353

No. 354. Laid Linen Bass Lines.

C.	100 feet,	9 thread Reel Line	$0 30
D.	100 yds.	9 " "	0 75
E.	100 feet,	12 " "	0 40
F.	100 yds.	12 " "	1 00

No. 355. Best Laid Cuttyhunk Line.

G.	100 yards, 12 thread Reel Line	$1 00	I.	100 yards, 18 thread Reel Line	$1 50
H.	100 " 15 " "	1 25	J.	100 " 21 " "	1 75

No. 356. Hall's Best Laid Linen Bass Line.

A.	200 yards, 9 thread Reel Line	$2 50	D.	200 yards, 18 thread Reel Line	$3 75
B.	200 " 12 " "	3 00	E.	200 " 21 " "	4 00
C.	200 " 15 " "	3 50			

No. 357. Cable Laid Linen Pickerel Line.

K.	100 feet, 18 thread Reel Line	$0 50	M.	100 feet, 21 thread Trolling Line	$0 75
L.	100 " 18 " Heavy Reel Line	0 60	N.	100 " 27 " "	1 00

No. 358. Cable Laid Linen Lines on Block.

O. 100 feet Reel Line.................$0 50 | P. 100 yards Reel Line.................1 50

No. 359. Hand Bass Lines on Block.

Length	100 feet.	50 feet.	25 feet.
Each	25c.	15c.	10c.

No 360. Cable Laid Cotton Blue Fish Lines.

Q.	75 feet, White Trolling Line	$0 25	Braided Cotton, No. 1. 84 feet Trolling Line	$0 35
R.	75 " " " "	0 30	" " " 2. 84 " " "	0 30
S.	75 " " " "	0 35	" " " 3. 84 " " "	0 25
T.	75 " " " "	0 40	" " " 4. 84 " " "	0 20
			" Cod Line, 150 " " "	0 65

No. 361. Linen Hank Lines, Assorted Colors.

Length	15 feet.	25 feet.	50 feet.
Each	5c.	10c.	15c.
Per dozen	40c.	75c.	$1 00

No. 362. Hooks Mounted on Gut.

Size 1, 2, 3, 4, 5, 6, 7, 8, Limerick, Carlisle, Aberdeen, New York Trout and McKensey Hooks, on best Per doz.
   Single gut... $0 30
Limerick Hooks, curved or straight on second quality gut................................ 0 30
Size, 1-0, 2-0, 3-0, Carlisle or Limerick Hooks, on double gut for Bass or Weak Fish.... 0 50
  " 4-0, 5-0, 6-0, "   and "   "   " treble "   "   " 0 60
  " 1, 1-0, 2-0, 3-0, Aberdeen Hooks on double gut, for Lake Trout and Lake Bass Fishing............ 0 50
  " 4-0, 5-0, 6-0, Aberdeen Hooks on treble gut, for large Trout and Bass Fishing.............. 0 75
  " 7-0, 8-0, Carlisle and Curved or Straight Limerick, on best treble gut for large Bass or Weak Fish.. 1 00
  " 1-0, 2-0, 3-0, Sprout Bend and O'Shaughnessy Hooks, on best double gut for Bass fishing......... 0 50
  " 4-0, 5-0, Sprout Bend and O'Shaughnessy Hooks, on best treble gut, for large Bass fishing........ 0 75
  " 4, 5, 6, 7, 8, Blackfish and Chestertown Hooks, on best treble gut....................... 0 60

No. 363. Hooks on Gimp.
(Best Hollow Point, Limerick, curved or straight, for Pickerel or Bass Fishing).

No. 1-0 to 3-0................per dozen, $0 75 | No. 6-0 to 7-0......................per dozen, $1 50
  " 4-0 to 5-0..................... "   1 00 |

No. 364. Black Fish and Limerick Hooks on Lines.

No. 1 to 6, Limerick..............per dozen, $0 25 | No. 3 to 6, Black Fish, curved or straight
  " 1-0 to 5-0, Limerick........... "   0 35 | Per dozen, $0 40

No. 365. Bait Boxes.

No. 1. Padlock, brown, green and blue..each, $0 20 | No. 3. Oval, green and blue............ "   0 20
  " 2. Basket.......................... "   0 20 | " 4. Crescent....................... "   0 25

No. 366. Minnow Gangs.

No. 1. On Gut, one swivel..............$0 35 | No. 3. On Gimp, with extra swivel............ 0 50
  " 2. On Gimp, one swivel.............. 0 35 |

No. 367. Cork Floats, Bound.

Barrel Shaped	3 in.	3½ in.	4 in.	4½ in.	5 in.	5½ in.	6 in.
Each	25	25	35	35	40	50	60c.

5 to 6 inch Hollow Wood Floats, each, 35 cents.

No. 368. Cork Floats, Bound.

Egg Shaped	1 in.	1½ in.	2 in.	2½ in.	3 in.	3½ in.	4 in.
Each	10	15	20	25	25	35	40c.

No. 368A. Wood Floats.

Egg Shaped	1¼ in.	1½ in.	2 in.	2½ in.	3 in.	3½ in.
Each	5	5	8	10	15	20c.

No. 369. Quill Floats.

Common Quill, for Trout and Perch Fishing... $0 10 | Porcupine, for Trout and Perch Fish___g.......$0 10
Varnished Plug, for Trout and Perch   "   ... 0 15 |

No. 370. Furnished Lines on Wood and Cane.

No. 2, 12 feet Furnished Line, on wood, one wood Float, Hook and Sinker, for Perch Fishing.......... $0 05
  " 5, 12   "   "   "   "   "   "   "   "   "   "   " 0 08
  " 6, 12   "   "   on cane   "   "   "   "   "   " and Trout Fishing. 0 12
  " 9, 12   "   "   "   "   "   "   "   "   "   "   " 0 20
  " 10, 15   "   "   "   one cork   "   "   on Gut and Sinker, for Trout and Perch
       Fishing..... 0 25

No. 371. Canvas and Leather Bass Books.

Canvas 3½ in. wide, 6 in. long,........Each, $0 75 | Leather, 3½ in. wide, 6 in. long,........ Each, $1 75
   "   3½   "   " 7 "   " .... "   1 00 | "   3½   "   " 7 "   " .... "   2 00

No. 372. Fly Books.

Plain Bound..............Each, 50c. to $1 50 | Morocco Leather, bound........Each, $4 00 to 5 00
Extra Bound and Large .... " $1 75 to 3 00 |

No. 373. Squids for Bass and Weak Fish.

No. 1. Block Tin................Each, $0 10 | No. 2, Pearl....................Each, $0 30

No. 374. Peck & Snyder's Spinning Squid for Bass and Weak Fish.

Nickel-plated, surpassing everything ever before offered to the public for Sea and Lake Fishing

No. 1 and 2. Single Hook............Each, $0 50 | No. 5. Florida Bait.................Each, $1 25
  " 3. Triple Hook, for Lake & River Bass "   0 65 | " 6. Single Hook for Blue Fish...... "   1 50
  " 4 and 5. Single Hook for Blue Fish. "   1 00 | " 0. Triple Hook for Lake Bass...... "   0 35
  " 4. Triple Hooks for Pike........... "   1 00 |

No. 376. Block Tin, Blue Fish Squid.

Nos.	1	2	3	4	5
Each	25	30	35	40	60

No. 375. The Novelty Pocket Scale.

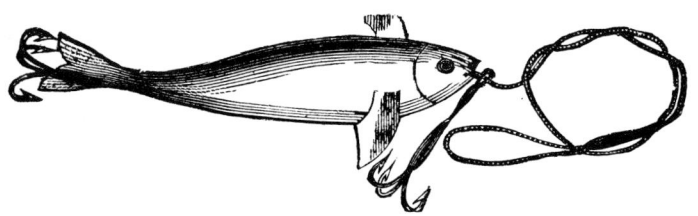

A Scale for Surgeons, Hunters, Fishermen, Sharpshooters and family use. The scale is graduated to weigh 15 pounds by two ounces, and is warranted correct. It is handsomely plated on the best quality of Nickel Silver, and with proper care will last a lifetime. We can vouch for the success of every agent that honestly employs his time selling it. We send them to any part of the country. One dozen, by mail, $3 50 Six dozen, by express, $18 00.

Price, each, by mail, 35 cents.

No. 377. Caledonian Minnows.

Nos.	1, 2, 3,	4, 5,	6, 7,	8, 9,
Each	65c.	65c.	75c. 85c.	$1 00

No. 377 X. Trolling with the Dead Gorge Bait.

As the only dead-bait snap-tackle of any value is that used in spinning, so the only dead-bait gorge tackle which can be similarly described is that employed in the method of pike fishing, commonly known as trolling.

Double Gorge Hook, with lead, each............15c.

No. 378. Phantom Minnows.

Nos.	1, 2, 3,	4, 5, 6,	7, 8,	9,
Each	75c.	75c. 85c.	$1 00	$1 25

No. 379. Peck & Snyder's Improved Rubber Insects for Trout and Black Bass.

These cuts represent the exact size of each article.

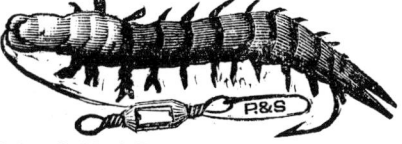

Dobson's Black Bass Bait, per doz., $5.00

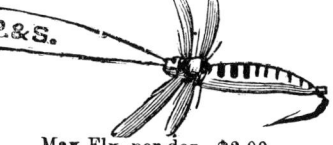

May Fly, per doz., $2.00

Wasp, per doz. $2.50

Small Frogs for Black Bass, per doz. $3.00
Large   "   "   "   5.00

Humble Bee, per doz., $3.00

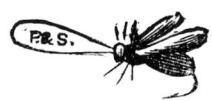

House Fly, per doz., $2.00

Grasshopper, per doz., $3.00

Cockchafer, per doz., $3.00

Cricket, per doz., $3.00

Artificial Worm, per doz., $3.00

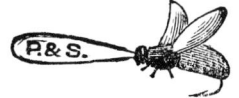

Blue Bottle. per doz., $3.00

No 380. Spoon Baits, Plain Single Hooks.

| Nos | 1, | 2, | 3, | 4, | 5, | 6, each, 25 cents. |

No. 381. Copper and Silver-Plated Triple Hooks.

| Nos. | 1, | 2, | 3, | 4, | 5, | 6 each, 50 cents. |

No. 382. Copper and Silver-Plated Triple Hook, Fly Spoon.

Nos.	1,	2,	3,	4,	5,	6,
Each	75	75	50	50	50	50c.

FISHING SPOON AND BAITS FOR TROLLING IN GREAT VARIETY.

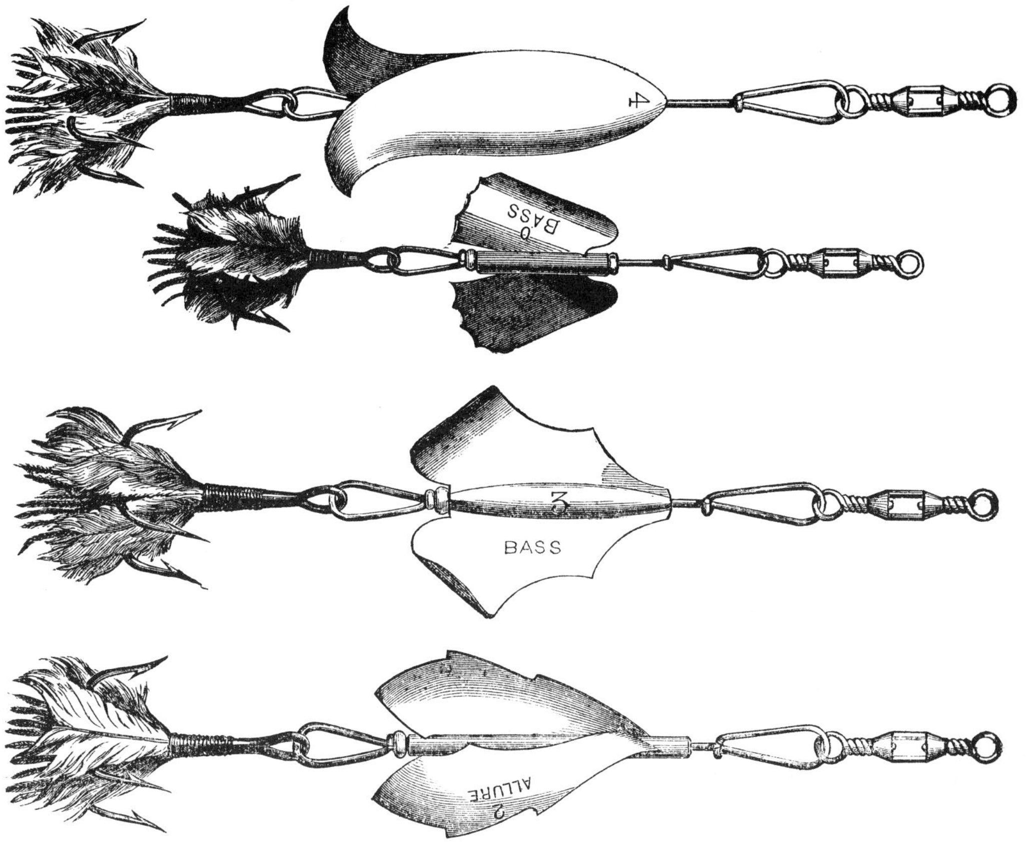

No. 378x. Minnow Propellers and Bass Baits for Bass, Pike and Pickeral Fishing.

Propellers	No 2.	No. 3.	No. 4.	No. 5.
Each	85c.	75c.	65c.	60c.
Bass Bait	No. 0.	No. 1.	No. 2.	No. 3.
Each	65c.	85c.	75c.	75c.
Allure Bait	No. 2-0.	No. 1-0.	No. 1.	No. 2
Each	$1 00.	85c.	75c.	65c.

No. 383. Bass & Pickerel Fly Spoon Baits.

Nos	1	2	3	4	5	6	7
Each	75	75	50	50	50	50	50c.

No. 384. Bass and Pickerel Fly Spoon Baits, Gold-plated.

Nos	2	3	4	5	6	7
Each	$1 00	1 00	75	75	75	75c.

No. 385. Pearl Spoon Bait.

Nos	1	2	3	4
Each	$1 50	1 25	1 25	1 00

No. 386. Muskallonge Bait.

Nos. 1, 2, 3, each $1 00

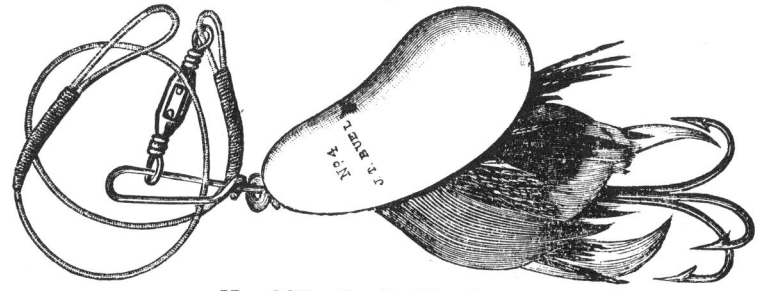

No. 387. Buel's Fly Spoons.

Nos	2-0	1-0	1	2	3	4	5	6	7
Each	75c.	75c.	60c.	60c.	60c.	50c.	50c.	50c.	50c.

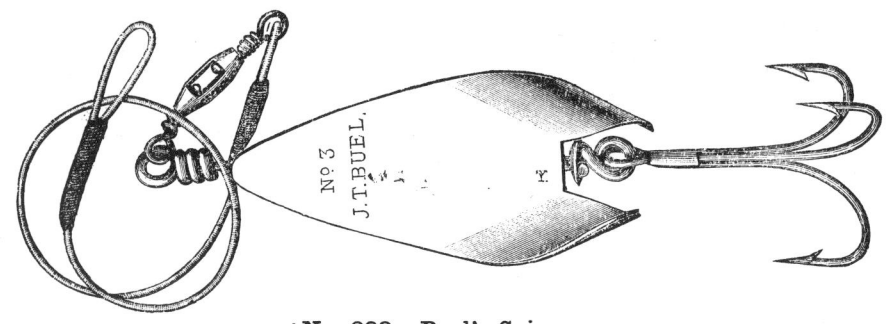

No. 388. Buel's Spinners.

Nos.	2-0	1-0	1	2	3	4	5	6
Each.	75c.	75c.	60c.	60c.	60c.	60c.	60c.	60c.

No. 389. Landing Nets Rings.

2 Joint Folding	Brass Ring, with net and jointed handle						$3 50
2 "	"	Plated	"	"	"	"	4 50
3 "	"	Brass	"	"	"	"	4 00
3 "	"	Plated	"	"	"	"	5 00

No. 1 OUTFIT.—This outfit consists of one Rod, 6 pieces, each piece 2 feet long; brass mounted. 1 reel, 1 linen line, 1 float, 2 sinkers, 6 hooks on gut, 3 flies, and one three-foot leader. This Rod can used for trout, perch and bass fishing. Complete, in varnished case, $3.00; by mail, $3.50.

No. 2 OUTFIT.—Same case, with flies, leader, hooks, float and sinkers. Fine finished Rod, with solid reel plate mountings plated, and plated click-reel, with 25 yards oiled silk line.
Complete, $8.00; by mail, $8.50.

PATENT FLY BOOK.

This Book is the most complete of any that has ever been made. It is so easy to take the flies out and put them in book without injuring them in any way. Every angler should have one to keep his tackle in good order. This Fly Book is made of the best material, and will last for years. Price, $4.00; by mail, $4.15.

Furnished with one dozen trout flies, half dozen bass flies, two six-feet single leaders, two four-feet double leaders, half-dozen hooks on single gut, for trout fishing, and half-dozen hooks on double gut for bass fishing.
Complete, $7.50.

No. 331. Brass Reels, Plain Balance Handle.

	Yards.		Diameter of Plates.	Each		Yards.		Diameter of Plates.	Each
A.	25.	Peck & Snyder, N. Y.	1¾ in.	$0 65	F.	40.	Plain Multiplying Reels with drag	1 15⁄16	$1 15
B.	40.	" " "	1 15⁄16	0 75					
C.	60.	" " "	2⅛	0 85	G.	60.	Plain Multiplying Reels with drag	2⅓	1 25
D.	80.	" " "	2 5⁄16	1 00					
E.	25.	Plain Multiplying Reels with drag	1¼	1 00	H.	80.	Plain Multiplying Reels with drag	2 5⁄16	1 50

No. 389. 0.

0.	Wood ring, with net and handle	$1 50
1.	Crab net, ring and handle	40
1.	" " jointed handle	1 00

No. 390. Crab Nets.

No. 1.	Cotton, 16 inch	0 15
" 2.	" 18 "	0 20
" 3	" 20 "	0 25

No. 391. Minnow Nets

No. 1.	Linen, 16 inch	each,	0 50
" 2.	" 18 "	"	0 60
" 3.	" 20 "	"	0 75
" 4.	" 24 "	"	1 00

No. 0.

No. 392. Landing Nets.

No. 1. Linen, 20 inch	each, $0 75	No. 3. Linen, 30 inch	each, $1 50
" 2 " 24 "	" 1 00	" 4. " 36 "	" 2 00

No. 393. Trout Sinkers.

Split Shot in flat tin cases........each, $0 10 | Split Shot in round plated tin case......each, $0 15

THE WONDERFUL EAGLE CLAW.

It is the most ingenious device ever invented for catching all kinds of Fish or Game. Will spring in any position. It is a great triumph, over the uncertain fish hook. The best article we ever used.

Editorially endorsed by the leading Sporting Papers of this country and Europe. Nothing can escape until released. This done without soiling the hands. Easy to set. Suited to any bait.

No. 1, by mail, post paid...35 cts
No. 2, "   "   ....50 "

PECK & SNYDER, 126–130 NASSAU STREET, N. Y., THE PLACE TO BUY GOOD FISHING TACKLE CHEAP.

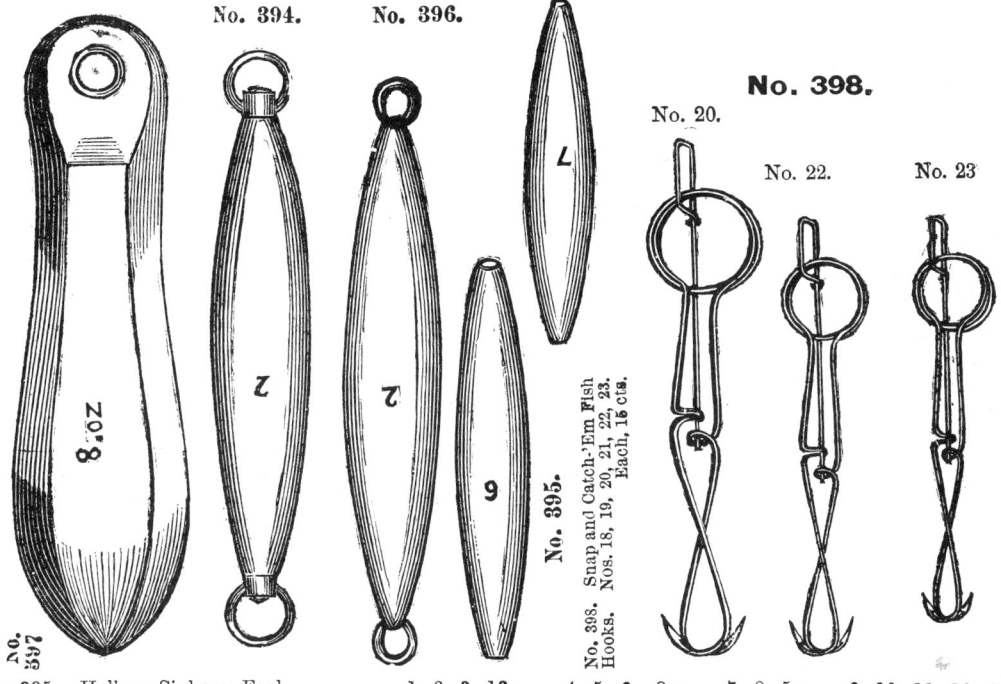

No. 394. No. 396. No. 398. No. 20. No. 22. No. 23.

No. 395.

No. 398. Snap and Catch-'Em Fish Hooks. Nos. 18, 19, 20, 21, 22, 23. Each, 15 cts.

No. 395. Hollow Sinkers, Each	1, 2, 3, 12c.			4, 5, 6, 8c.			7, 8, 5c.		9, 10, 11, 12, 3c.		
No. 396. Ringed Sinkers	1	2	3	4	5	6	7	8	9	10	11	12
Each	12c.	12c.	12c.	8c.	8c.	5c.	5c.	5c.	3c.	3c.	3c.	3c.
No. 394. Swivel Sinkers	1		2	3		4	5		6	7		8
Each	15c.		15c.	15c.		10c.	10c.		10c.	10c.		10c.
No. 397. Common Sinkers	15 oz.	12 oz.	10 oz.		8 oz.	6 oz.		4 oz.		2 oz.		1 oz.
Each			15c.			10c.		5c.		3c.		2c.
No. 398. Egg Sinkers	1		2	3		4	5		6	7		8
Each	12c.		10c.	8c.		5c.	5c.		3c.	3c.		3c.

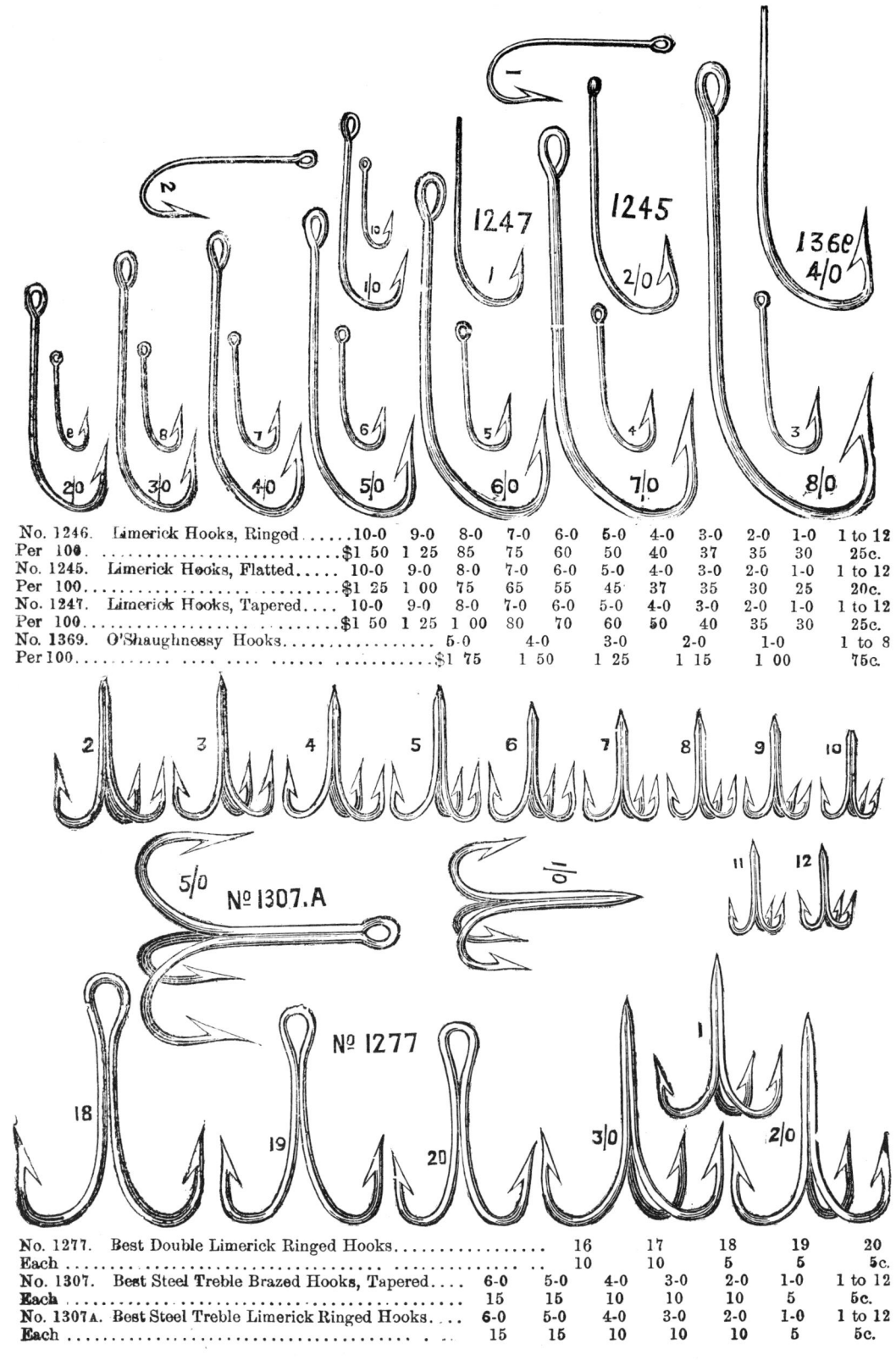

No. 1246.	Limerick Hooks, Ringed	10-0	9-0	8-0	7-0	6-0	5-0	4-0	3-0	2-0	1-0	1 to 12
Per 100	$1 50	1 25	85	75	60	50	40	37	35	30	25c.
No. 1245.	Limerick Hooks, Flatted	10-0	9-0	8-0	7-0	6-0	5-0	4-0	3-0	2-0	1-0	1 to 12
Per 100	$1 25	1 00	75	65	55	45	37	35	30	25	20c.
No. 1247.	Limerick Hooks, Tapered	10-0	9-0	8-0	7-0	6-0	5-0	4-0	3-0	2-0	1-0	1 to 12
Per 100	$1 50	1 25	1 00	80	70	60	50	40	35	30	25c.
No. 1369.	O'Shaughnessy Hooks				5-0	4-0	3-0	2-0	1-0	1 to 8
Per 100	$1 75	1 50	1 25	1 15	1 00	75c.

No. 1277.	Best Double Limerick Ringed Hooks					16	17	18	19	20
Each						10	10	5	5	5c.
No. 1307.	Best Steel Treble Brazed Hooks, Tapered	6-0	5-0	4-0	3-0	2-0	1-0	1 to 12
Each	15	15	10	10	10	5	5c.
No. 1307A.	Best Steel Treble Limerick Ringed Hooks	6-0	5-0	4-0	3-0	2-0	1-0	1 to 12
Each	15	15	10	10	10	5	5c.

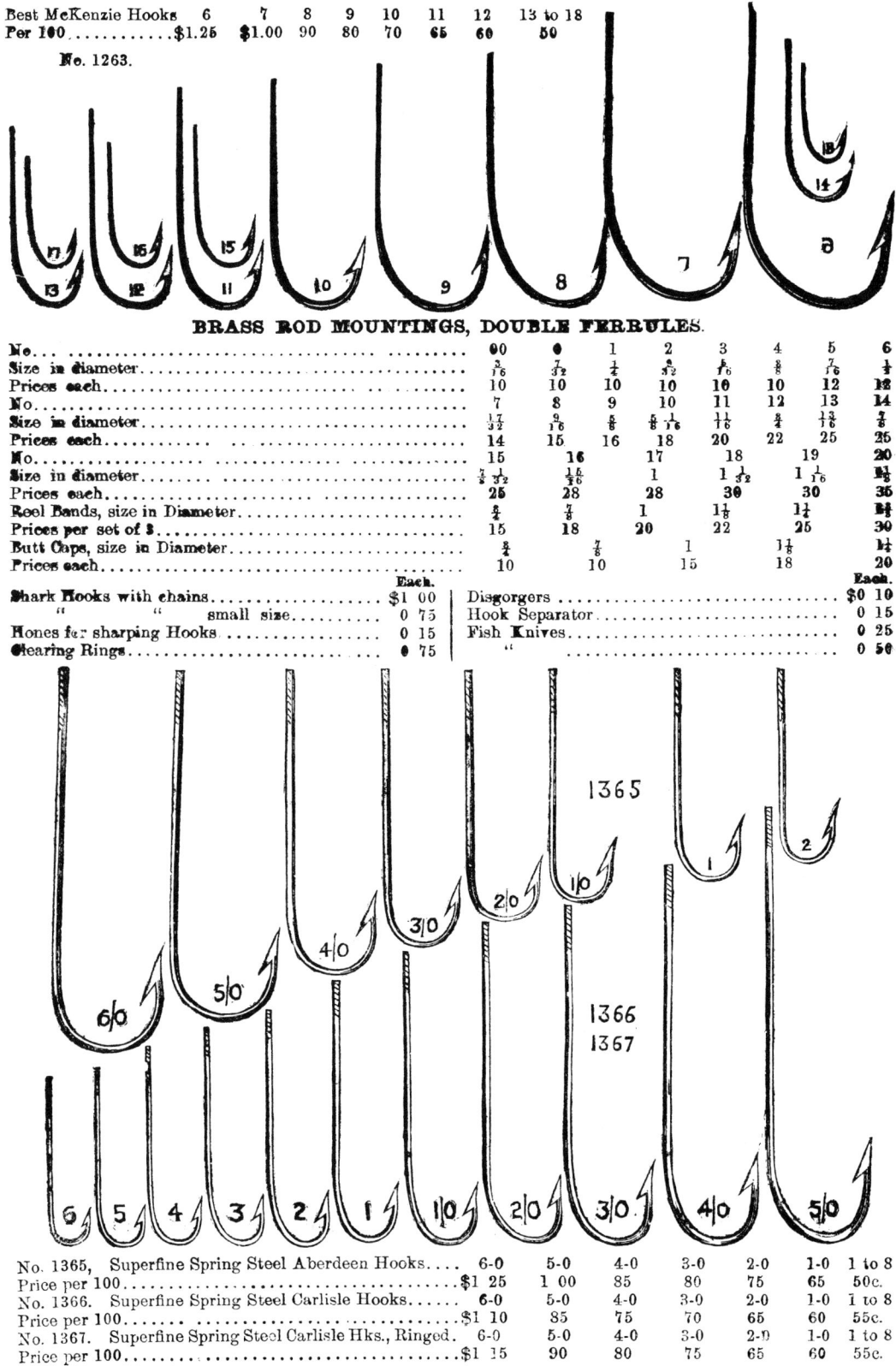

Best McKenzie Hooks	6	7	8	9	10	11	12	13 to 18
Per 100	$1.25	$1.00	90	80	70	65	60	50

No. 1263.

BRASS ROD MOUNTINGS, DOUBLE FERRULES.

No.	00	0	1	2	3	4	5	6
Size in diameter	$\frac{3}{16}$	$\frac{7}{32}$	$\frac{1}{4}$	$\frac{9}{32}$	$\frac{5}{16}$	$\frac{3}{8}$	$\frac{7}{16}$	$\frac{1}{2}$
Prices each	10	10	10	10	10	10	12	12
No.	7	8	9	10	11	12	13	14
Size in diameter	$\frac{17}{32}$	$\frac{9}{16}$	$\frac{5}{8}$	$\frac{11}{16}$	$\frac{11}{16}$	$\frac{3}{4}$	$1\frac{3}{16}$	$\frac{7}{8}$
Prices each	14	15	16	18	20	22	25	25
No.	15	16	17	18	19	20		
Size in diameter	$\frac{15}{32}$	$\frac{15}{16}$	1	$1\frac{1}{32}$	$1\frac{1}{16}$	$1\frac{1}{4}$		
Prices each	25	28	28	30	30	35		
Reel Bands, size in Diameter	$\frac{3}{4}$	$\frac{7}{8}$	1	$1\frac{1}{8}$	$1\frac{1}{4}$	$1\frac{1}{4}$		
Prices per set of 3	15	18	20	22	25	30		
Butt Caps, size in Diameter	$\frac{3}{4}$	$\frac{7}{8}$	1	$1\frac{1}{8}$	$1\frac{1}{4}$			
Prices each	10	10	15	18	20			

	Each.			Each.
Shark Hooks with chains	$1 00	Disgorgers		$0 10
" " small size	0 75	Hook Separator		0 15
Hones for sharping Hooks	0 15	Fish Knives		0 25
Clearing Rings	0 75	"		0 50

No. 1365, Superfine Spring Steel Aberdeen Hooks	6-0	5-0	4-0	3-0	2-0	1-0	1 to 8
Price per 100	$1 25	1 00	85	80	75	65	50c.
No. 1366. Superfine Spring Steel Carlisle Hooks	6-0	5-0	4-0	3-0	2-0	1-0	1 to 8
Price per 100	$1 10	85	75	70	65	60	55c.
No. 1367. Superfine Spring Steel Carlisle Hks., Ringed	6-0	5-0	4-0	3-0	2-0	1-0	1 to 8
Price per 100	$1 15	90	80	75	65	60	55c.

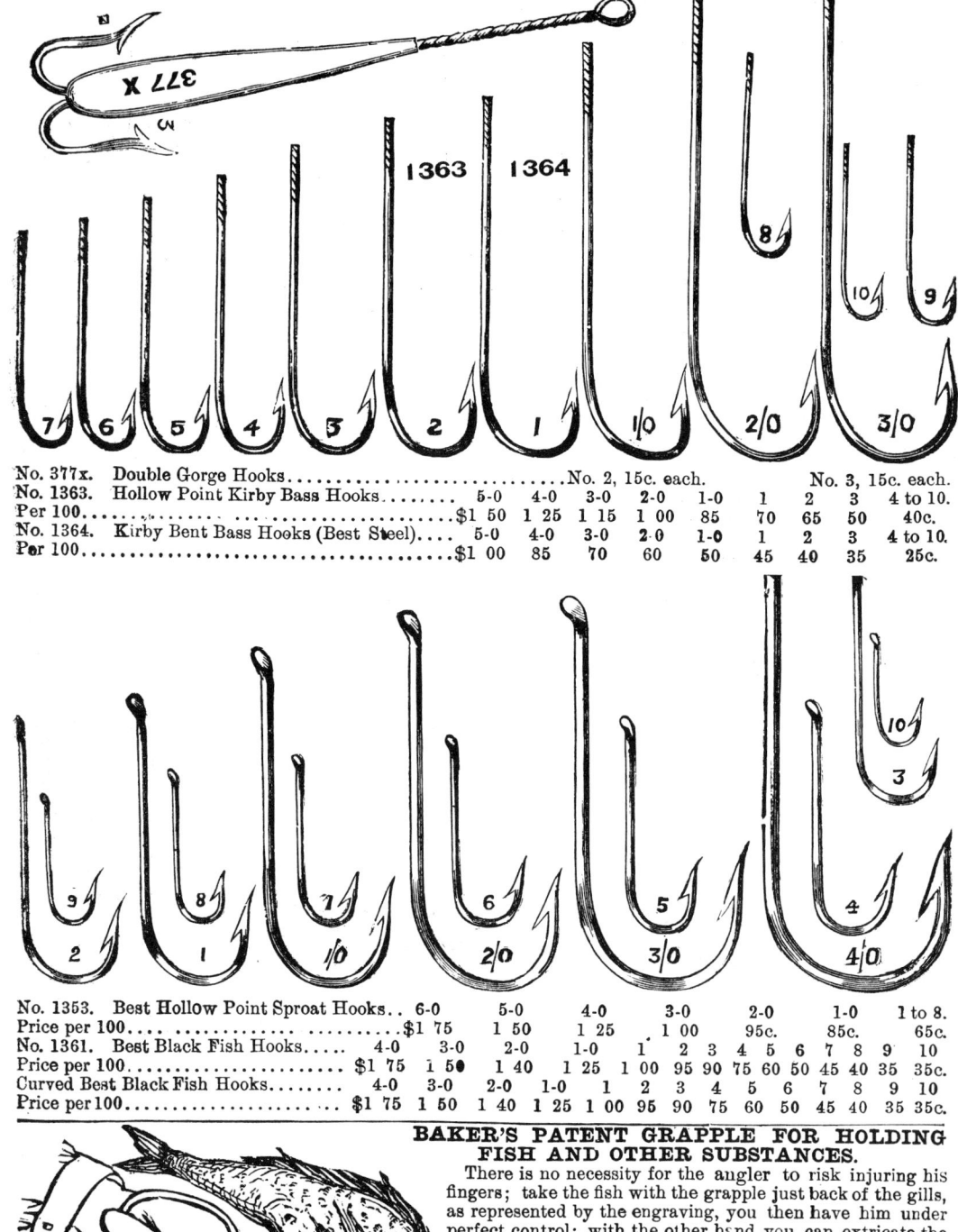

No. 377x.	Double Gorge Hooks					No. 2, 15c. each.				No. 3, 15c. each.	
No. 1363.	Hollow Point Kirby Bass Hooks	5-0	4-0	3-0	2-0	1-0	1	2	3	4 to 10.	
Per 100	$1 50	1 25	1 15	1 00	85	70	65	50	40c.		
No. 1364.	Kirby Bent Bass Hooks (Best Steel)	5-0	4-0	3-0	2-0	1-0	1	2	3	4 to 10.	
Per 100	$1 00	85	70	60	50	45	40	35	25c.		

No. 1353.	Best Hollow Point Sproat Hooks	6-0	5-0	4-0	3-0	2-0	1-0	1 to 8.			
Price per 100	$1 75	1 50	1 25	1 00	95c.	85c.	65c.				
No. 1361.	Best Black Fish Hooks	4-0	3-0	2-0	1-0	1	2	3	4	5	6	7	8	9	10
Price per 100	$1 75	1 50	1 40	1 25	1 00	95	90	75	60	50	45	40	35	35c.
Curved Best Black Fish Hooks	4-0	3-0	2-0	1-0	1	2	3	4	5	6	7	8	9	10
Price per 100	$1 75	1 50	1 40	1 25	1 00	95	90	75	60	50	45	40	35	35c.

BAKER'S PATENT GRAPPLE FOR HOLDING FISH AND OTHER SUBSTANCES.

There is no necessity for the angler to risk injuring his fingers; take the fish with the grapple just back of the gills, as represented by the engraving, you then have him under perfect control; with the other hand you can extricate the hook without trouble. It is admirably adapted for the securing of eels. Anglers are fully aware of the trouble and annoyance the eel imposes on them, especially when the hook is swallowed; and strange to say, the pressure of the grapple on the spine or vertebra produces a kind of paralysis which keeps him quiet, while you liberate the hook.

Price, ... 50c. each
By Mail, ... 60c. "

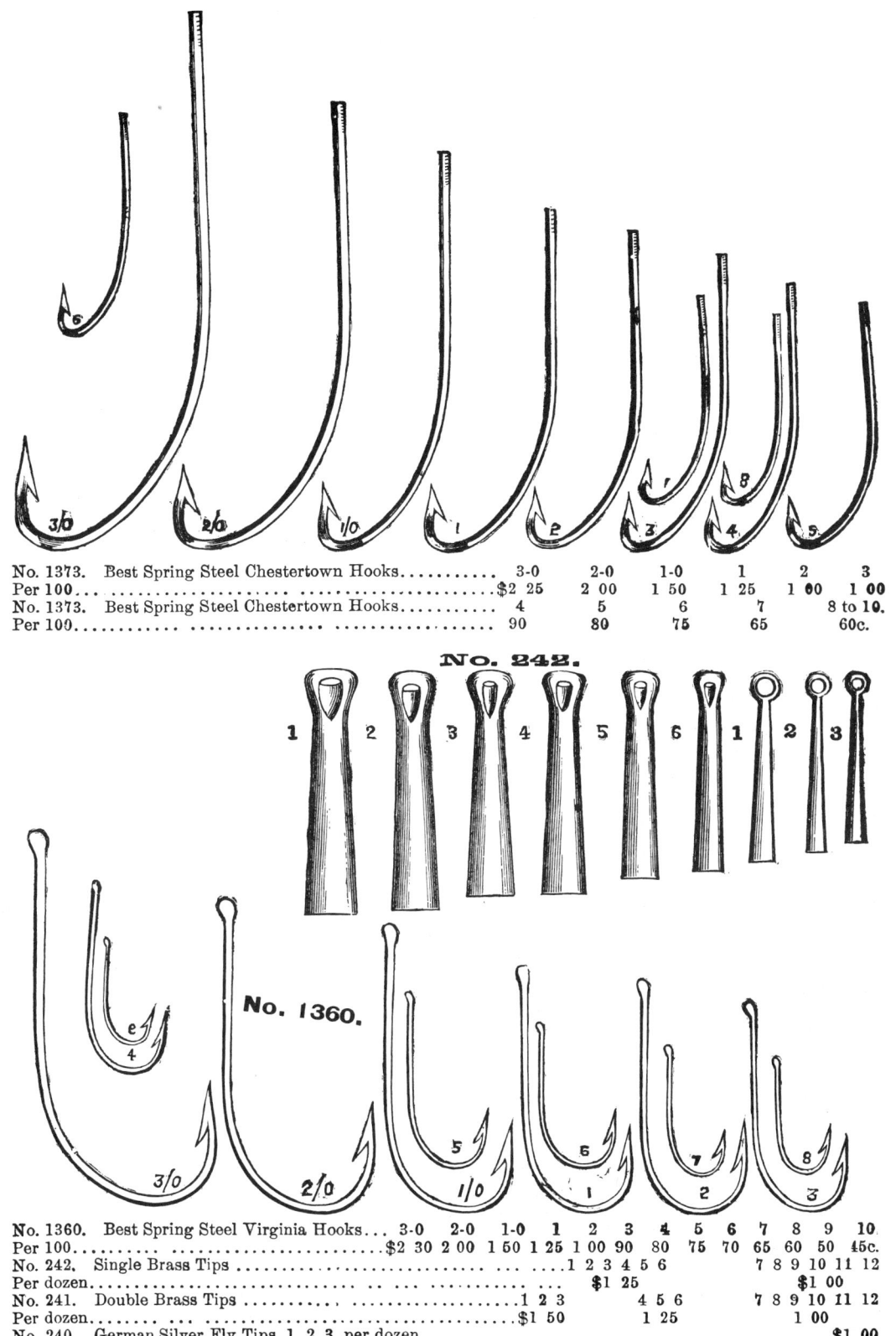

No. 1373. Best Spring Steel Chestertown Hooks	3-0	2-0	1-0	1	2	3
Per 100	$2 25	2 00	1 50	1 25	1 00	1 00
No. 1373. Best Spring Steel Chestertown Hooks	4	5	6	7	8 to 10	
Per 100	90	80	75	65	60c.	

No. 1360. Best Spring Steel Virginia Hooks	3-0	2-0	1-0	1	2	3	4	5	6	7	8	9	10
Per 100	$2 30	2 00	1 50	1 25	1 00	90	80	75	70	65	60	50	45c.
No. 242. Single Brass Tips			1	2	3	4	5	6	7	8	9	10	11 12
Per dozen					$1 25						$1 00		
No. 241. Double Brass Tips			1	2	3		4	5	6	7	8	9	10 11 12
Per dozen			$1 50					1 25				1 00	
No. 240. German Silver Fly Tips, 1, 2, 3, per dozen													$1 00

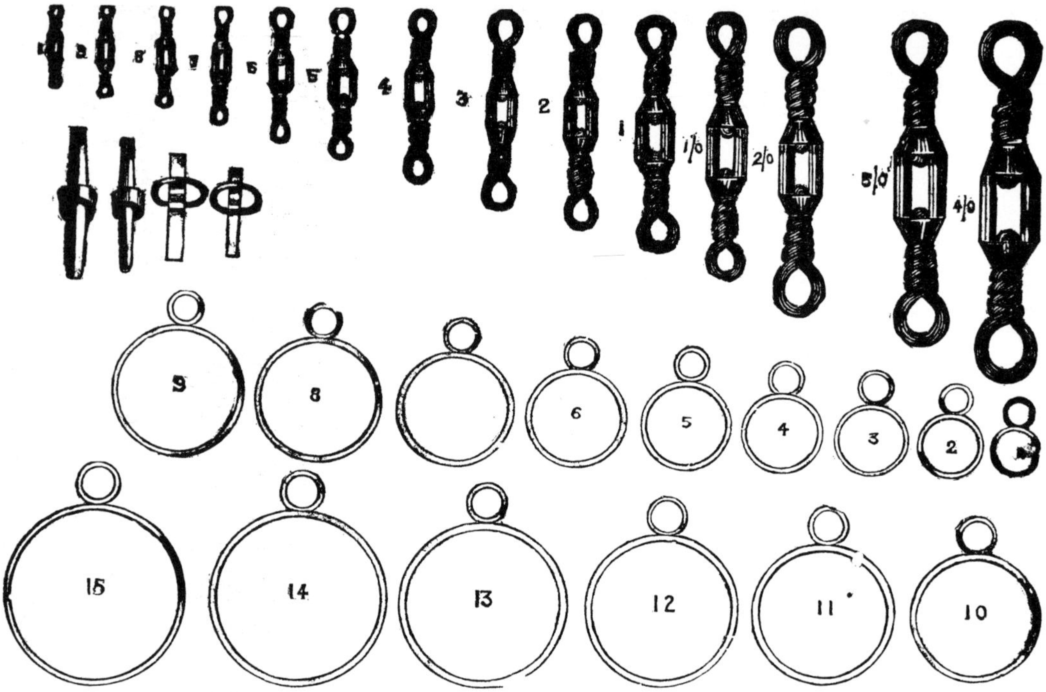

No.										
"	238.	Brass Tie Guides..Per doz.,							$0 50
"	237.	Rod Rings and Keepers...							"	0 15
"	243.	Single Brass Guides, Nos. 15, 14, 13, 12, 11, 10, 9, 8, 7, 6, 5, 4, 3, 2, 1....							"	0 50
"	243x.	Double Brass Guides, Nos. 15, 14, 13, 12, 11, 10, 9, 8, 7, 6, 5, 4, 3, 2, 1...........							"	1 00
"	569.	Best Box Brass Swivels................	5-0	4-0	3-0	2-0	1-0		1 to 10
Each..			20c.	15c.	15c.	10c.	10c.		5c.

PECK & SNYDER, 126, 128 & 130 NASSAU STREET, N. Y., IMPORTERS & DEALERS IN EVERY VARIETY OF FISHING TACKLE.

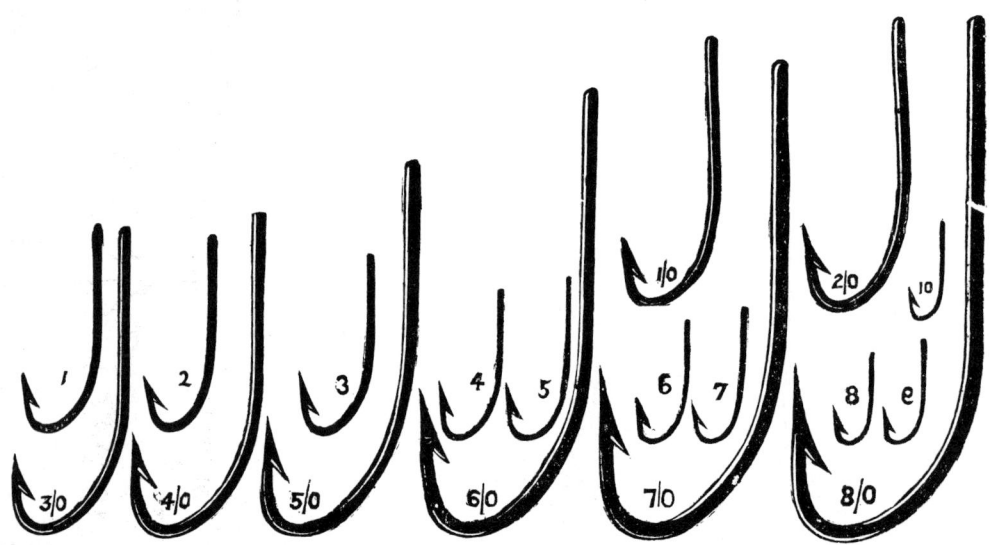

No. 1250.	Hollow Point Limerick Hooks, Marked,	10-0	9-0	8-0	7-0	6-0.	5-0	4-0	3-0	2-0	1-0	1 to 12
Per 100..		$2 00	1 75	1 50	1 25	85	75	65	60	55	50	45
No. 1368.	Hollow Point Curved Limerick Hooks Marked	10-0	9-0	8-0	7-0	6-0	5-0	4-0	3-0	2-0	1-0	1 to 12
Per 100..		$2 00	1 75	1 50	1 25	85	75	65	60	55	50	45

THE EDGAR PATENT BARBLESS HOOKS.

(PATENTED, OCTOBER 30, 1877.)

Will catch quicker than the ordinary barbed hook, and is sure to hold every Fish hooked.

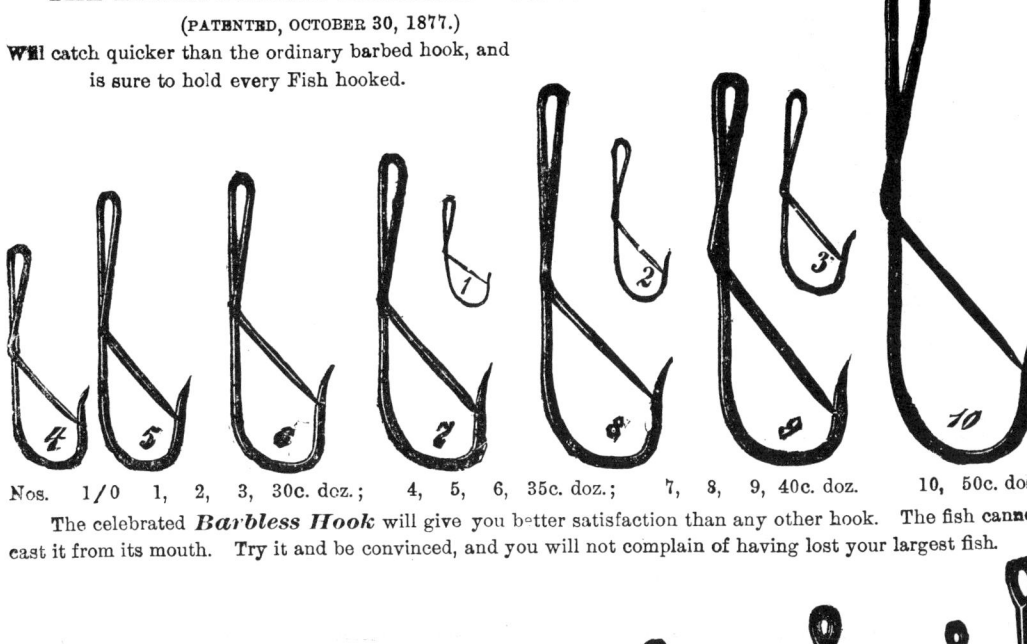

Nos. 1/0 1, 2, 3, 30c. doz.; 4, 5, 6, 35c. doz.; 7, 8, 9, 40c. doz. 10, 50c. doz.

The celebrated **Barbless Hook** will give you better satisfaction than any other hook. The fish cannot cast it from its mouth. Try it and be convinced, and you will not complain of having lost your largest fish.

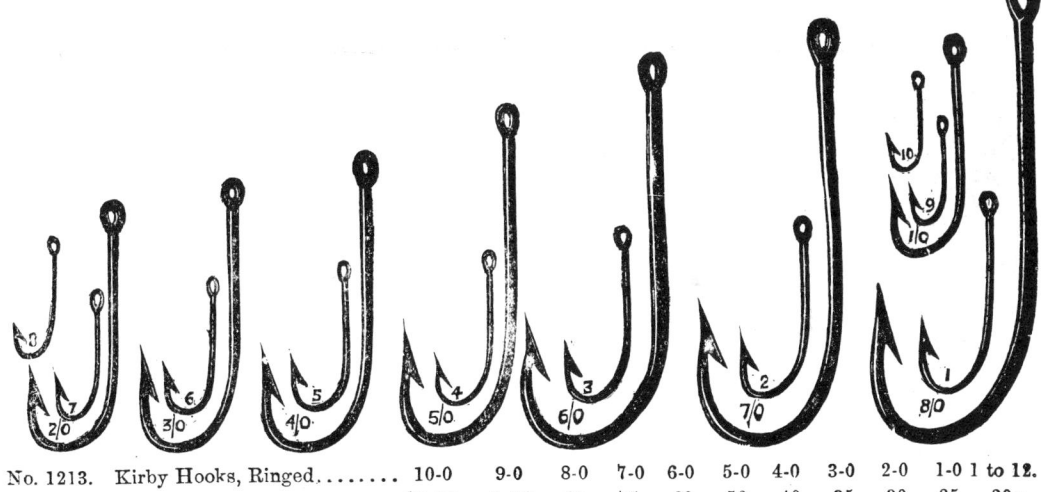

No. 1213. Kirby Hooks, Ringed	10-0	9-0	8-0	7-0	6-0	5-0	4-0	3-0	2-0	1-0	1 to 12.
Price per 100	$1 25	1 00	85	75	60	50	40	35	30	25	20c.

STANDARD PORTABLE CAMP STOVE.

Entirely new, a complete Stove for Tourists, Sportsmen, Private Families, Picnics and Students, will cook a meal for 2 or 3 persons in 15 minutes, and at the same time if in cold or chilly weather, will heat an ordinary sized room. Outfit consists of Kettle, Tea Pot and Sauce Pan, (each holding over one pint), and Fry Pan, 4 lamps by which a person can cook one or four dishes at a time. The cooking utensils are made of the best double tin and the Stove of sheet iron, with perforated sides and all of the best workmanship. In the stove there is plenty of room to pack Knives, Forks, Spoons, Pepper, Salt and Spice, Dishes packed in wood case, size, 7 x 9 x 4 inches, weight 4¼ lbs. Price, $1 75.

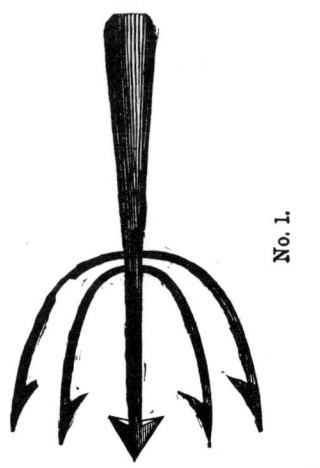 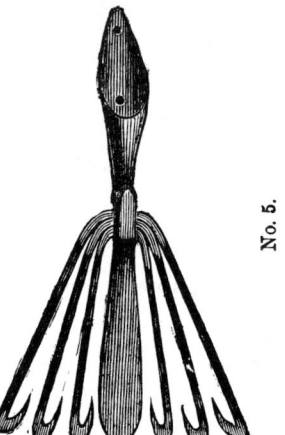 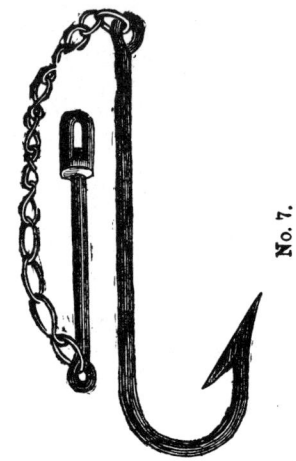

No. 1.—FISH SPEARS. (See cut).

No. 1.—3 Prong.............. Each, 75 cents. | No. 3.—5 Prong, heavy............... " 1 50
" 2.—5 " ....Each, $1 25

No. 5.—EEL SPEARS. (See cut).

Each.... ....$2 00

No. 7.—SHARK HOOKS. (See cut).

Nos.	8.	7.	6.	5.	4.	3.	2.	1.
Each	65 cts.,	75 cts.,	85 cts.,	$1 00,	$1 25,	$1 50,	$1 75,	$2.00

THE FOLLETT REEL. Patented.

This Reel is very simple in construction, and durable, stamped out of brass, nickel plated, and holds 150 feet of Trout Line, will not get out of order, and will last a long time with proper care.   Price, each, $1 50

EXCELSIOR BAIT PAIL! THE FISHERMAN'S FRIEND.
Patent Applied for.

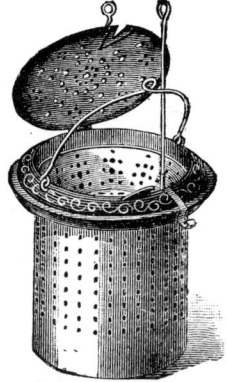

This Pail is Substantially Made of Heavy Tin, and Handsomely Japanned.

The inside pail can be removed and placed in the water the same as a "fish car," thus keeping the bait alive for an indefinite time. The pan which fits in the inside pail can be raised and lowered, thus affording an easy selection of bait without wetting the hand. The bait is kept alive during transportation (the critical time) by the continuous flowing of the water through the perforations, thus causing a never failing supply of fresh air.

This is the only practical bait pail in the market, and no fisherman can afford to be without one.

PRICES.
8 Quart, each............$2.75 Securely packed.
12   "   "   .... 3.50   "   "

PAIL COMPLETE.   Inside Pail Removed.

No. 10 FISHING TACKLE BOX.

Size of Box, Length 9¼ in., Width, 6¼ in., Depth, 3 in.: One Tray, Length, 6 in., Width, 4 in., Depth, 1¾ in. Four partitions in the Tray; five partitions in the Box, making nine places in the Box. For Lines, Hooks, Sinkers, Spoons, Reel, Fly Hooks, &c. This Box has Hasp and Staple, for Padlock.   Price, each $2 50

No. 20. Fishing Tackle Box.

This Box is approved by the practical piscatorial professors who have investigated its perfections. It is nicely painted and ornamented with fish pictures. Size of Box, Length, 12in. Width 7½ in. Depth 4¼ in. 4 Trays, Length 7¼ in. Width 4 in, Depth, 1 to 1¾ in. Size of Top Tray, Length 11¾ in. Width 7in. depth 1½ inches.—This Box has Lock and Key. Three partitions in each small Tray, eight in large Tray; two compartments in box, making twenty-four places for lines. hooks, sinkers, spoons, reels, fly-hooks, etc., in which disciples of Isaac Walton delight.   Price, each, $4 50

No. 2 Tackle Case.

Contains 1 large Tray, 1 small Tray, handle on Top, space for Reel, &c.

SIZE OF CASE OUTSIDE.

10 inches long,   8 inches wide,   6 inches high.

Price, $7.50

NEW AND IMPROVED SEAMLESS-EDGE BRIDLE LEATHER REEL AND TACKLE CASES.

Patented July 12, 1881, and March 27, 1883.

No. 1 Tackle Case.

Contains Two Trays and space for Reel, &c., has strap all around case which can be used as shoulder strap or handle, as desired.

SIZE OF CASE OUTSIDE.

13 inches long,   6 inches wide,   7 inches high.

Price, $7.50

Reel Cases, Lined throughout with Velvet.

	Each
No. 0—00 .... Price,	$2 50
No. 1— 2 .... "	2 25
All Multiplying Click Reel Cases .... "	2 25
Small Click Reel Cases .... "	1 75

Sole Leather Fishing Rod or Gun Cases.

Prices according to the size. Estimates will be furnished for the same on sending measurement. In ordering, give circumference at largest part of butt, also at the tip, and the length in inches.

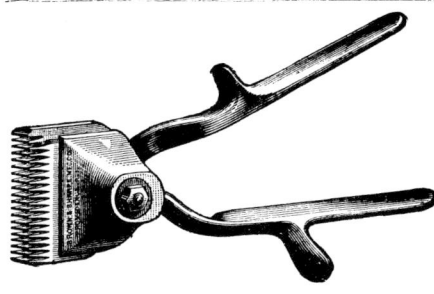

HAIR CLIPPERS, FOR BARBERS' USE.—Patented July 1st, 1879.—These clippers are carefully made, and are of such a quality and form as to work with smoothness and ease. The shearing plates are thick enough to allow of repeated sharpening, which should be done only by the makers, or some person having a suitable machine for grinding flat surfaces. Never apply files or grindstones to the clippers, as it only increases the cost of repairing. Keep them well oiled when laid away, as well as when in use. Have the nut adjusted just tight enough to have the clippers clip the hair well and work easily. Each clipper is nickel plated and put up in a paper box, with a wrench to use in adjusting the nut, also one extra spring.

	Each
Prices, No. 1, To cut hair one-eighth of an inch long	$4 00
No. 2, To cut hair one-quarter of an inch long	4 50
No. 3, To cut hair five-sixteenths of an inch long	5 00
We also make a clipper (No. 0) to be used only for cutting the hair very short about the neck, & about equal to shaving	3 50

Sent per mail on receipt of price and fifteen cents for postage, Springs .... 10 cents each.

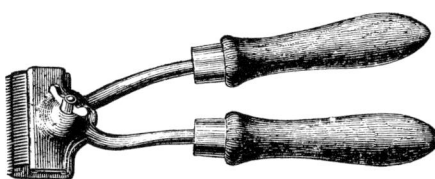

IMPROVED HORSE CLIPPERS.—Patented July 1st, 1879.—These clippers are made in a superior manner, of the best materials, and work with great smoothness and ease. The shearing plates are thick enough to allow of repeated sharpening, which should be done only by the makers or some person having a suitable machine for grinding flat surfaces. Never apply files or grindstones to the clippers, as it only increases the cost of repairing. Keep them well oiled when laid away, as well as when in use. Have the nut adjusted just tight enough to have the clippers clip the hair well and work easily. Take the clipper apart frequently, clean out the dirt and hair that gathers between the plates. Each clipper is nickel plated and put up in a paper box.

Price $3 50 ; sent by mail on receipt of $3 75.

OLRY'S GLASS POCKET FLASKS With and Without Cups,

Covered with Roan, Hogskin, Morocco and Russian Leathers; also **Britannia Metal Flasks**, lined with or without Glass. All with metal Screw Tops, fastened without Cement.

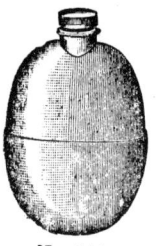  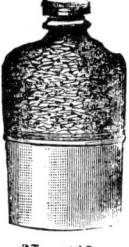   

No. 840.   No. 842.   No. 843.   No. 844.   No. 845.   No. 846.

Nos.	Description.		¼ Pint.	½ Pint.	¾ Pint.	Pint.
840.	All metal	Each,	$1 00	$1 25		
841.	Metal, glass lined	"	1 35	1 75	$2 00	
842.	Turkey Morocco, assorted colors	"	1 00	1 25		$2 00
843.	Hogskin	"	1 15	1 25	1 50	2 00
844.	Russia Leather, open sides	"	1 35	1 75	2 00	2 50
845.	Russia Leather, Grecian pattern	"	1 75	2 25	2 50	3 00
846.	Turkey Morocco, engraved and silver-plated metal	"	2 50	3 00	3 50	4 00

N. B.—All of the above Flasks are warranted not to injure the liquor in any way.

READY FOR USE.

CAMPING AND MINING STOVE.
(Patented June 22, 1875.)

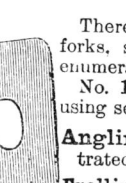

To our numerous patrons who delight in hunting, fishing, camping out, etc., we now present for the first time the New Portable Traveling Stove (No. 1), weighing only 27 pounds, very durable, and which will cook for 8 or 10 persons. This stove is especially adapted for camping purposes. The ware consists of 8-quart Kettle, 6-quart Tea Kettle, 2-quart Coffee Pot, Fry Pan, round Tin Pan, 2 square Pans, Dipper, Gridiron, Tent Collar, and 8 feet funnel, and an oven that will roast 15 pounds of beef.

There is room for packing half a dozen plates, knives, forks, spoons and drinking cups, in addition to articles enumerated above.

No. 1 A—Packed size, 12x12x20. Full directions for using sent with each stove. Price, complete, $15.00.

Angling; or How to Angle, and Where to Go. Full illustrated. Post-paid..........$0 50

Trolling; or Pike, Salmon, and Trout Fishing. With directions on the selection of hooks, etc. Fully illustrated. Post-paid.......... 50

Bottom or Float Fishing. With suggestions on the necessary outfit. Fully illustrated. Post-paid.... 50

Fly Fishing and Worm Fishing, For Salmon, Trout, and Grayling. Post-paid.......... 50

Fishing with Hook and Line, a Manual for Anglers, 64 pages, illustrated.......... 25

GAME BAGS.
No. 576, fine......each, $1 50, $2 00, $2 50, $3 50, $5 00

No. 666. **Houchin's Pocket Cook Stove.**

No. 576.   No. 666.

The annexed cut represents the stove in operation, **with the** boiler placed upon it, by which enough water can be boiled in five minutes to make a cup of tea, coffee, chocolate and other hot drinks. Is convenient to boil or scramble eggs, make an oyster stew, etc. This cut represents the stove stand, boiler and gridiron placed inside the box; size, 4 in. square, 1¼ in. high; weight 13 ounces, including Boiler. Just the thing for **travelers**, tourists, camp meetings and family use.

Samples by mail, post-paid, on receipt of price.   Price, $1; Nickel-plated..........$1 75

CURB CHAIN DOG COLLARS.
No. 40, single, 16 to 20 in. long..........$1 00 | No. 40, double, 16 to 20 in. long..........$1 25

DOG WHIPS.
No. 2453..........each, 30, 50, 75c., $1 00, $1 25, $1 50

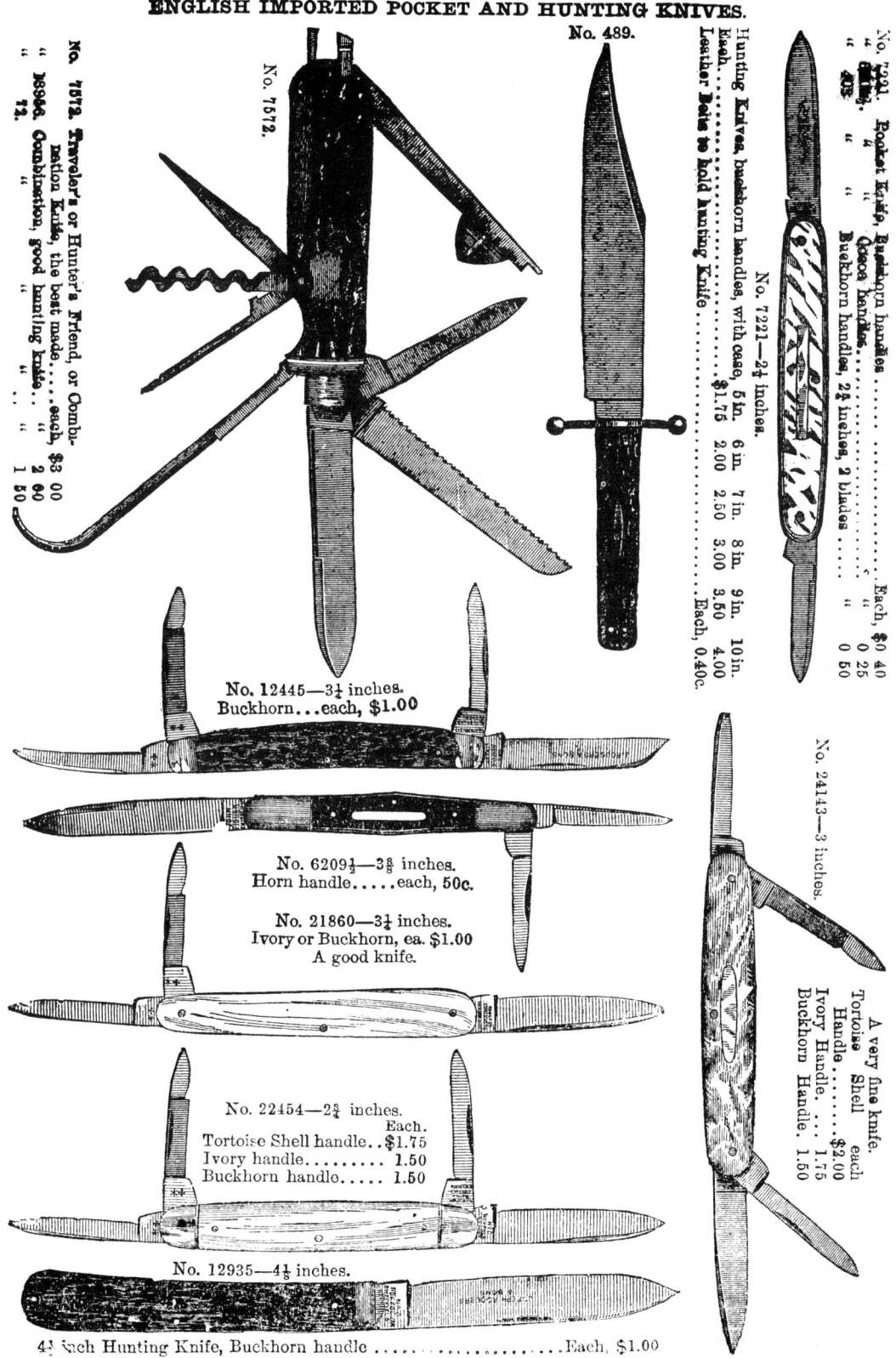

THE NOVELTY POCKET LANTERN.

No. 944.

No. 250.   No. 350.

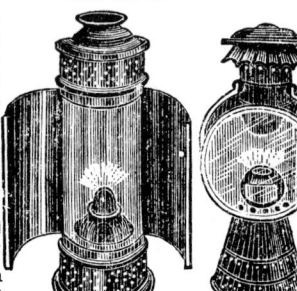

Cheap, Durable, Brilliant, Convenient.—This new lantern is the most compact and perfect that has ever been introduced. It being only 5½ inches high, 2½ in. wide and 1¼ inches thick. It may be carried in the pocket. This little lantern will throw a larger volume of light than most lanterns of five times the size; the inside being an oval shape and heavily nickled plated, makes a durable and brilliant reflector. Price, each, 75 cts

No. 250.—Small Pocket Lantern. Nickel Plated. Height, 6 inches, diameter, 2½ inches weight 10 ounces. Burn either Sperm or Lard Oil Price, each, $2 50

No. 350.—Dash Lantern. Height, 10 inches, weight, 23 ounces, 4 inch reflector. Burns a candle. Price, each, $3 50

940

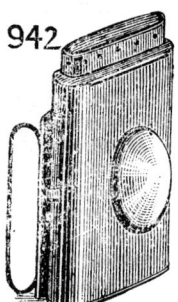

DASH LAMP

Made of Tin and Painted.

Can also be used for Hunting and Fishing.

Small size, 4 inches reflector....................$3.00
Large size, 6 inches reflector....................$5.00

941

The New French Bull's Eye POCKET LANTERN.

Same as used by the Police in Paris, it can be used also as a Skating Lantern. It is the smallest and most powerful Lantern made.

Small size 2 inch, Bull's Eye, nickel plated.............$2.00
Large size 2½ inch, Bull's Eye, 2.50

942

FLAT POLICE,
OR
DARK LANTERN,

Made of Tin & Painted,

Can be carried in the pocket and used for skating.

Small size, 2 inch. Bull's eye.........................$1.00

943

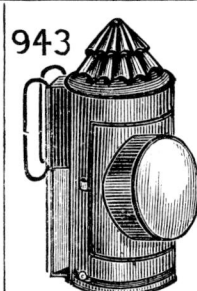

ROUND POLICE.
OR
Dark Lantern,

MADE OF TIN & PAINTED,

Can be used for Skating.

Small size, 2¾ inch. Bull's Eye....................$1.00
Large size, 3 inch. Bull's Eye....................1.50

PECK & SNYDER, 126, 128 & 130 Nassau St., N. Y., Manufacturers and Importers.

SUPERIOR DUCK AND SNIPE DECOYS.

Solid Wood Decoy Ducks....Per dozen, $9 00
"   "   "   Snipes.... "   3 50

SYPHON FILTERS.

For Fishing, Hunting, Travelers, Etc.

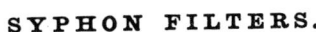

Shows the small Army or Camp Filter, which may be carried in the vest pocket and water taken up clean by it from even some of the most unclean pools by the person using it. Hunters, soldiers, woodmen and travelers should never be without them.

The cut represents about two-thirds of full size with wood mouth-piece and Rubber Tube attached to stone. It is cleaned by blowing through the mouth-piec

Each, by mail, 40 cents., larger size, 75c.

DOG CALLS OR WHISTLES.

Each illustration is the exact size of the article mentioned. Beautifully carved Ivory Whistles on hand, from 75c. to $1.50 each. Any of these sent by mail on receipt of price.

No. 299. Polished Metal, With Rattle, 30c.

No. 302. Railroad Call. Polished Metal, 35c.

No. 303. Conductor's Whistle, double, 50c.
One for Starting, One for Stopping, Polished Metal.

No. 298. Polished Metal, 25c.
" 297. " " 20c.

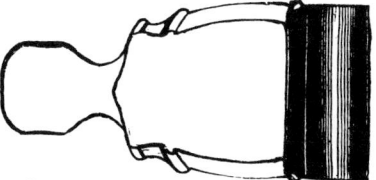
No. 300. Double Polished Metal with Rattles, 40c.

No. 301. Police Call, Polished Metal, 35c.

No. 305. Horn, 25c. 306, 35c.
" 307, Large, 40c.

No. 308. Ivory Whistles. 75c. 309. Large, 85c.
" 310. " " Fine, $1.00

No. 304.

THE PUZZLE WHISTLE.

The best and cheapest whistle of the age, it will frighten away a whole army of burglars with one blow, the noise being so loud and shrill. You can hand it to your friends and if they do not know the secret they can not make any noise at all.

Cut exact size, nickel plated.

Per doz., 75c.; each by mail, 10c.

THE PERFECTION TOY BELL.

For bird cages, cats, dog collars &c. They are made of the best metals, heavy gold or silver gilt and beautifully chased (cut exact size).

Small..each 15c.
Medium.. " 20c.
Large.. " 25c.

MICROSCOPIC CHARM.

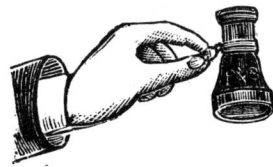

This is a very pretty and useful ornament for the watch chain; it is made of Ivory and exact size of illustration, with a very powerful microscope lenz and photo picture, of which we supply a variety, such as heads of distinguished personages, landscapes, buildings, statuary, all the different Centennial Buildings in Philadelphia, the Creed, the Lord's Prayer, Ten Commandments, etc., etc.; the natural size of these pictures is scarcely larger than the period dot at the end of this sentence. But by the powerful lenz it is magnified about 10,000 times, and stands out with great distinctness, and the Lord's Prayer is read as easily as this description. Each, 15 c.; 2 for 25c

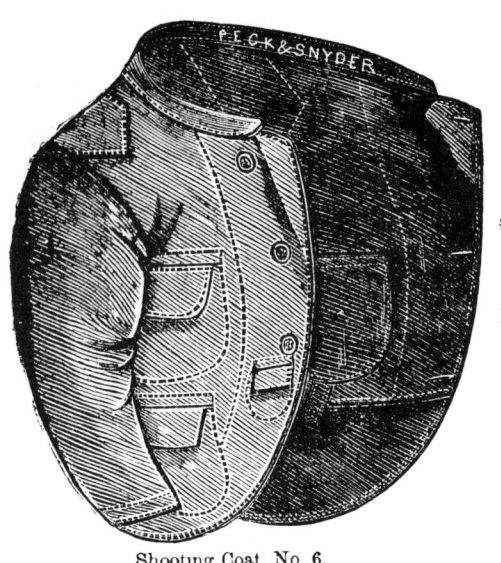

Shooting Coat, No. 6.

Vest No. 11.

WATER-PROOF SHOOTING AND HUNTING SUITS.

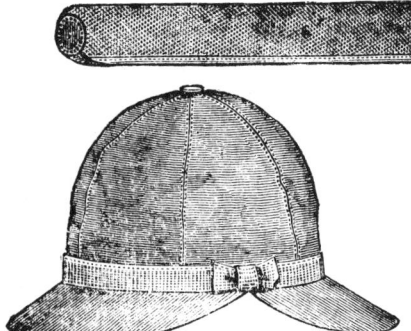

No. 60.

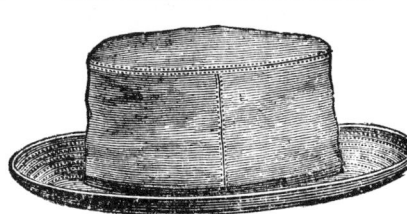

Cap No. 12. Hat No. 14.

Made of extra quality duck, (waterproof by the celebrated paraffine process), making the best and cheapest suit ever offered to American Sportsmen.

*No. 5 Shooting Coat............................ $3 00	*No. 8, Coat without, and vest with sleeves, made of heavy duck and in best style......... $8 00
*No. 6 Shooting Coat, heavier duck than No. 5, and better made throughout............. 4 00	No. 9, Shooting Pants....................... 2 00
*No. 7 Shooting Coat, same as No. 6, but lined throughout with pliable leather, making the warmest and best coat for cold weather shooting ever known................. 9 00	No. 10, Shooting Knee Breeches............. 2 00
	No. 11. " Waistcoat or Vest........... 2 00
	No. 12, Shooting Cap....................... 1 25
	No. 14, Shooting Hat....................... 1 50

*These Coats have two large cartridge pockets on back that are not shown on cut.

RULES FOR SELF-MEASUREMENT.—Send breast measure and length of sleeve from middle of back to waist, with arm raised and bent for coat; breast measure for vest, waist and inseam measure for Pants; size of head for Hat or Cap.

No. 60. Extra heavy waterproof canvas, lined with flannel, with binding and handle............ $1 00
No. 63. Black or Russet bag leather, Victoria-shaped cover, not lined........................ 3 25
No. 64. Extra heavy waterproof canvas, lined with flannel, Victoria-shape, folded stock on barrels, with binding and handles.. 1 25
No. 65. Superior quality of very heavy canvas, reinforced with leather, and having pocket for cleaning rod, same style as 64.. 1 75

Fishing, Hunting or Camp Blankets.

Camp Blankets, on Sheeting, 45 x 72 inches, weight 2¼ lbs..........................each, $2 00
" " " 45 x 72 " with hole in the centre, to be used as cape if necessary, weighing 2½ lbs.. " 2 50
" " flannel lined, 52 x 78 inches, weighing 3¼ lbs........................ " 3 50
" " " 63 x 78 " " 4 " .... " 4 00
" " " 78 x 78 " " 4½ " .... " 4 50

These are invaluable for protection from dampness while lying on the ground, and also very useful for wrapping purposes.

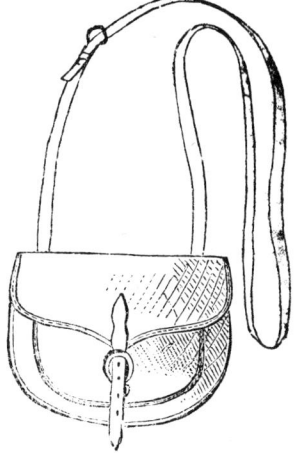

No. 80. No. 69.

FISHING STOCKINGS.

Fishing Stockings on ordinary black rubber, weighing 2 pounds ....per pair, $4 50
"   "   light drab cloth, weighing 1¾ pounds.................... "   7 50

FISHING PANTS.

Fishing Pants on ordinary black rubber, weighing 3¾ pounds........................per pair, 6 00
"   "   light drab cloth, weighing 3½ pounds................... ..... "   12 00

These Stockings and Pants are made with feet, over which are worn leather shoes to prevent their destruction while walking upon rough substances. The drab cloth, of which one of the styles is made, is similar to the English McIntosh, but more serviceable. The sizes from 6 to 11 correspond with the leather boot worn by the person using them, and when ordering all that is necessary is to give us the size of the foot

FISHING BOOTS.

Fishing Boots, with long black tops..per pair, $6 00
These are made in the same style as the Fishing Stockings, excepting in place of the foot there is attached a pair of light or heavy Rubber Boots. Sizes, 6 to 11.
Rubber Short Boots, light or heavy, 17 inches, length of leg.........................per pair, $5 00
"   Knee   "   "   "   24   "   "   " 5 50

CARTRIDGE BELTS.

No. 80.   Leather loop, with shoulder to prevent cartridge from falling through, lined and stitched,
              with strap to go over shoulder..Each, $1 50
" 81.   Same as No. 80, except with extra heavy water-proof canvas body............... "   1 25
" 83.   Leather loop for sporting rifle cartridge.. .... 1 10

CARTRIDGE BAGS.

No. 69.   Extra heavy waterproof canvas, holds seventy rounds.........................Each, $1 00
" 70.   "   "   "   "   "   fifty rounds .... "   0 75
" 71.   Bag leather, with pocket, holds one hundred rounds....:.................... "   2 00
" 72.   "   "   "   "   seventy rounds...... .... "   1 75
" 73.   "   "   "   "   fifty rounds.............................. "   1 50

POCKET DRINKING CUPS.

ONE HALF THE REGULAR SIZE.

Each Cup is packed in a neat box convenient for the pocket.

                                                                                Each.
No. 847. Telescope Metal Cup, Nickel plated................. 30c.
" 849.   "   Hard Rubber Cup........................ 65c.
" 850.   "   "   "   " Screw Cover.............. 85c.
" 851. The Vest Pocket Leather Drinking Cup .... 25c.

The above Cups will be sent by mail, postage paid, on receipt of price.

CLEANING RODS AND IMPLEMENTS. (Three Jointed.)

Including Swab, Scratch Brush, Wormer and Wiper.

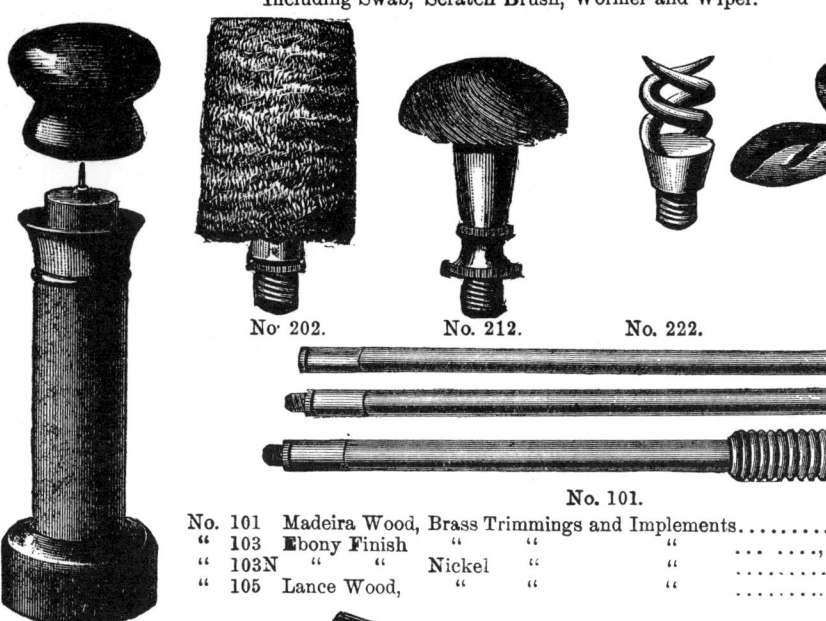

No. 202.   No. 212.   No. 222.   No. 232.

No. 101.

No. 101	Madeira Wood, Brass Trimmings and Implements	....	Each,	$1	25
" 103	Ebony Finish " " "	....,.....	"	1	50
" 103N	" " Nickel "	....	"	1	75
" 105	Lance Wood, " " "	....	"	2	00

No. 1149

No. 760. Duck Call, Cocobolo Wood and Nickeled Tip .... Each, 75 cts.
" 765. Turkey Call, Cocobolo Wood and Horn Tip .... " 75 "

RELOADING TOOLS AND BENCH CLOSERS.

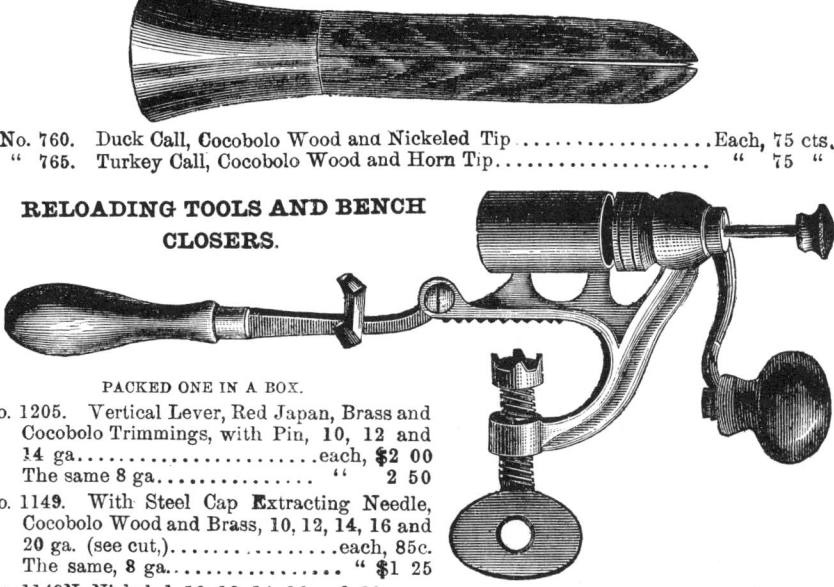

PACKED ONE IN A BOX.

No. 1205. Vertical Lever, Red Japan, Brass and Cocobolo Trimmings, with Pin, 10, 12 and 14 ga. .... each, $2 00
The same 8 ga. .... " 2 50

No. 1149. With Steel Cap Extracting Needle, Cocobolo Wood and Brass, 10, 12, 14, 16 and 20 ga. (see cut,) .... each, 85c.
The same, 8 ga. .... " $1 25

No. 1149N. Nickeled, 10, 12, 14, 16 and 20 ga. .... each, 90c.
The same, 8 ga. .... " $1 50

No. 765.

POWDER AND SHOT MEASURES.

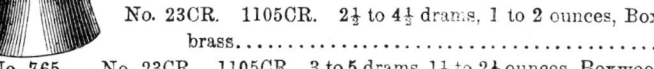

No. 23CR. 1105CR. 2½ to 4½ drams, 1 to 2 ounces, Boxwood Rammer, brass .... each, 50 cts.
No. 23CR. 1105CR 3 to 5 drams, 1⅓ to 2⅓ ounces, Boxwood Rammer, brass ..... each, 60 cts.

GENUINE NEWHOUSE STEEL TRAPS.

Universally known as superior to any and all other Traps, in strength, lightness and durability. Every Trap Warranted. The established reputation of the Newhouse as the best Trap in the World leaves little to by said about its quality. We will only add that the Newhouse Trap for 1883 will be equal if not superior to the make of any previous season, and that no pains will be spared to sustain its well-earned reputation.

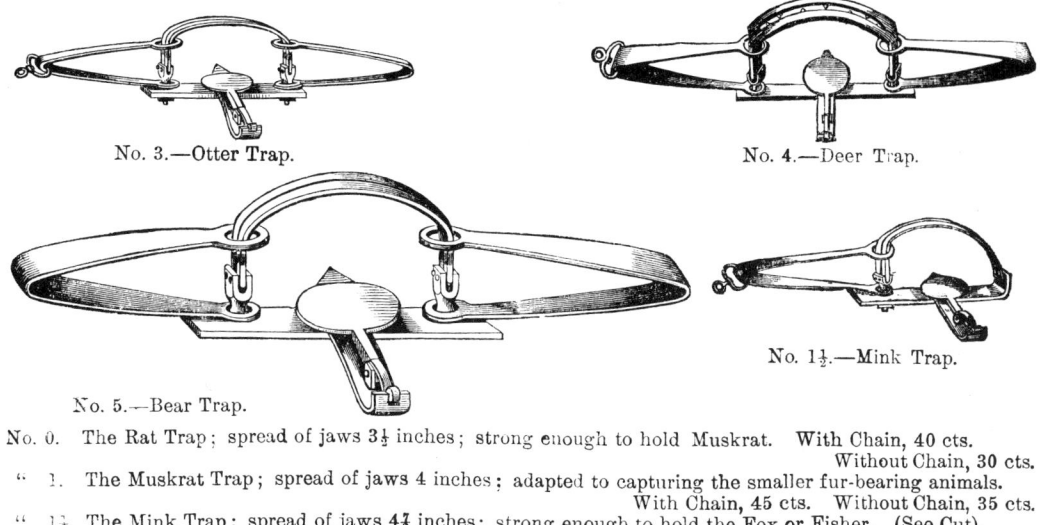

No. 3.—Otter Trap.   No. 4.—Deer Trap.   No. 1½.—Mink Trap.   No. 5.—Bear Trap.

No. 0. The Rat Trap; spread of jaws 3½ inches; strong enough to hold Muskrat. With Chain, 40 cts. Without Chain, 30 cts.

" 1. The Muskrat Trap; spread of jaws 4 inches; adapted to capturing the smaller fur-bearing animals. With Chain, 45 cts. Without Chain, 35 cts.

" 1½. The Mink Trap; spread of jaws 4⅞ inches; strong enough to hold the Fox or Fisher, (See Cut). With Chain, 65 cts. Without Chain, 50 cts.

" 2. Fox Trap, with double spring; spread of jaws, 4⅞ inches; strong enough to hold an Otter. With Chain, 90 cts. Without Chain, 80 cts.

" 3. The Otter Trap, double spring; spread of jaws, 5½ inches. " $1 25. " $1 10
" 4. The Beaver Trap, " " " 6½ " " 1 50. " 1 30
" 4. Deer Trap, " " " 6½ " " 1 60. " 1 45
" 5. Beaver Trap; spread of jaws, 11¼ inches; weight of each spring, 6 lbs. 10 oz.; weight of Trap, 17 lbs; suitable for taking the common Black Bear. Only, with Chain, each, $12 00

" 6. Bear Trap, large size, spread of jaws, 16 inches; weight of each spring, 6 lbs. 10 oz; weight of Trap 42lbs.; made throughout, except the pan, of wrought iron and steel—strong enough to hold the Moose or the Grizzly Bear. Only, with Chain, each, $24 00

A Swivel is attached to every Trap, and Chains are furnished when desired. Springs warranted to stand under water.

No. 260.   No. 330.   No. 265.   No. 335.   No. 425.   No. 661.   No. 676.   No. 606.

COPPER SHELL POWDER FLASKS.

	Each.		Each.
No. 260. 8 oz. common	$0 75	No. 1 S T. 8 oz. fine quality	$2 00
" 330. " medium	1 00	" 2 " 10 " "	2 50
" 365. 10 oz. common	1 25	" 3 " 12 " "	2 75
" 335. 8 oz. medium	1 50	" 1250 W. 12 oz. German Silver top	5 00

The above Flasks can be furnished with or without Cords.

LEATHER SHOT POUCHES.

No. 425, 2½ lbs. ...... $0 75   No. 425. 4 lbs. $1 50
" 3 " ...... 1 00   " 5 " 2 00

LEVER TOP SHOT BELTS.

No. 661, double ...... $2 00   No. 676, double Oregon best $4 00
" 661, " best ...... 3 50   " 606, single " 1 25
" 676, " Oregon ...... 3 00   " 606, " best 2 00

NEW YORK CITY OR BERGH'S CRUELTY TO ANIMALS' MUZZLE.

They are made of the best Tinned Wire, in nine different sizes as per measurement below:

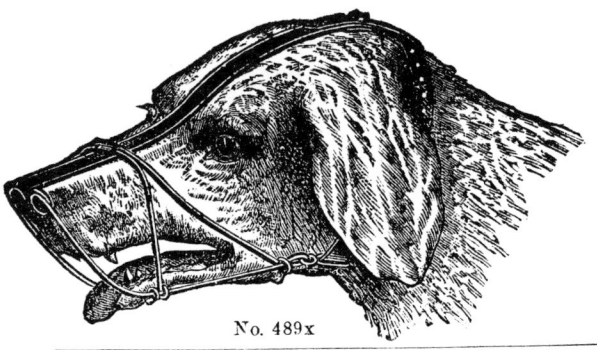

No. 489.

	Around Nose at 2.	Around Head at 3.	From 2 to 4.	Each
No. 1....	6 inches..........	7½ inches..........	6 inches............	$0 50
" 2....	6½ "	.... 8½ "	.... 7 "	50
" 3....	7 "	.... 9½ "	.... 8 "	50
" 4....	7½ "	........10 "	.... 8¾ "	75
" 5....	8 "	........10½ "	.... 9 "	75
" 6....	8¼ "	........11 "	.... 9¼ "	75
" 7....	9 "	........12¼ "	............10 "	1 00
" 8....10	"	........13¼ "	............11 "	1 00
" 9....11½	"	........15 "	............12 "	1 00

Strap around neck can be lengthened at pleasure.

No. 489x

SAFETY DOG MUZZLES.

	Each
Small................	30c.
Medium..............	40c.
Large................	50c

To avoid mistakes, order by our exact numbers.

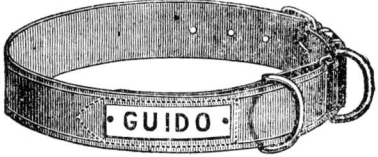

DOG COLLARS,

In great variety of styles and prices.

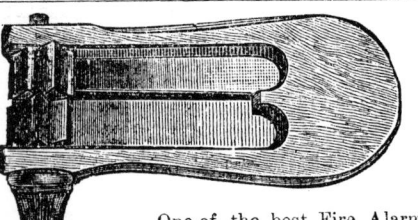

No. 135. Extra heavy leather, nickel plated trimmings, buckle, locks with a key; cannot be taken from the dog's neck without cutting; finest leather collar made, (See cut Death). Price, $2 00
No. 136. Made of heavy bridle leather, nickel plated buckle D, and name plate, (See cut Dash.) Price, $0 75
No. 137. Combination slip and straight collar, made of heavy bridle leather, with nickel plated Buckle, D's and name plate. Impossible for dogs to slip this collar, as it tightens with pulling and loosens as soon as the strain is off, (See cut Guido.) Price, $1 00
No. 138. Made of heavy bridle leather, polished wire buckle, and D, with German silver name plate, 0 50
No. 139. Made of heavy bridle leather, polished wire buckle and D, no name plate. 0 40
No. 140. Heavy bridle leather, nickel plated trimmings, screw collar, fastened with screw instead of buckle. Price, $0 75

Nos. 135, 136 and 137 will be stamped with name of dog or owner, same as cut, if so ordered, at same price. Give size of dog's neck in inches.

BURGLAR ALARM OR WATCHMEN'S RATTLE.

One of the best Fire Alarm Signals invented for country and suburban use; well made. Good to protect the house when the head of the family is away. Good to leave with the watchman, to protect our lives our valuables, and our property. A man traveling through the country throwing away half dollars could not collect any greater a crowd than you can with this Rattle. Not dangerous but always reliable and sure of action. Also excellent for masquerades.

Price, each $1 25

SPRING AND KEY PADLOCKS FOR DOG COLLARS. (Cuts exact size.)

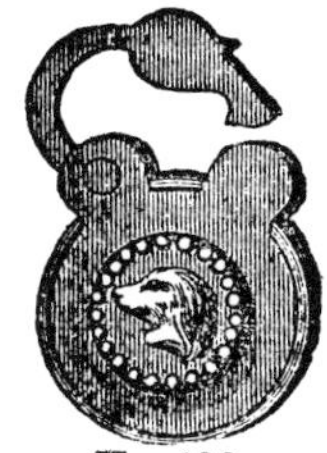

No. 486.

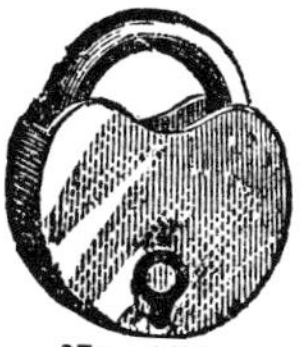

No. 490.

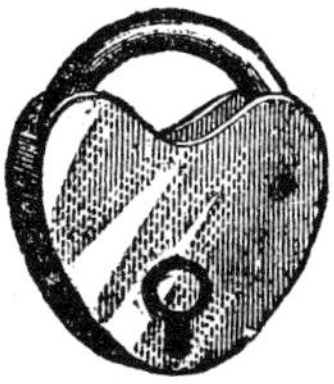

No. 490.

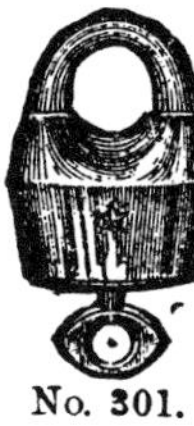

No. 301.

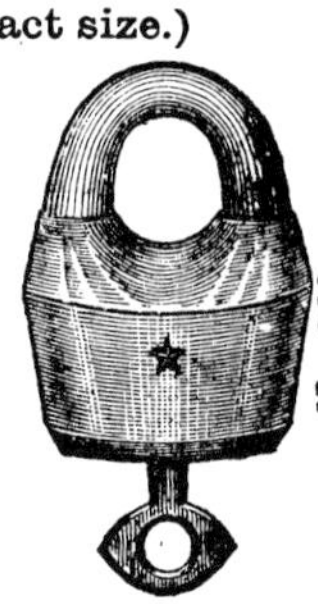

No. 302.

Spring Padlocks.

No. 486. $\frac{5}{8}$ inch, Brass Spring Padlocks, each... 15c.
$\frac{3}{4}$ " " " " ....15c.

No. 486. $\frac{5}{8}$ inch, Nickel Plated Padlocks, each...25c.
$\frac{3}{4}$ " " " " ...25c.

No. 487. Chain Dog Leaders, of steel or iron, or linked, assorted sizes, 30 cents, 40 cents, and 50 cents each.
" 488. Dog Leaders, of plaited leather, with and without tassels, assorted sizes, 25, 50 and 60 cents each.

Padlocks with Key.

No 490. $\frac{5}{8}$ Brass........................each, 20c.
$\frac{3}{4}$ " .... " 20c.

No. 490. $\frac{5}{8}$ Nickel Plated ....each, 30c.
$\frac{3}{4}$ " .... " 30c.

Scandinavian Padlocks.

No. 301. $\frac{5}{8}$ Gilt.... .... 30c.
" 302. $\frac{3}{4}$ " .... 50c.

No. 301. $\frac{5}{8}$ Nickel.............................. 40c.
" 302. $\frac{3}{4}$ " .... 60c.

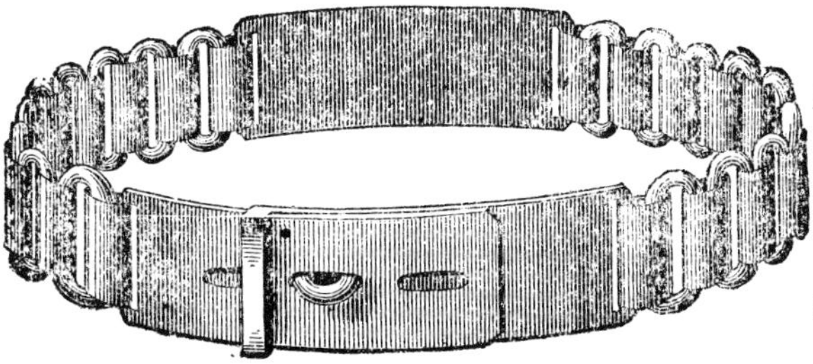

NICKEL-PLATED CHAIN DOG COLLARS.

			Each
No. 50,	$\frac{1}{2}$ in. wide,	9, 11, 13, 15 in. long,	$0 50
" 65,	1 "	14, 16, 18, 20 "	0 85
" 80,	1 "	14, 16, 18, 20, 22 "	1 00
" 60,	$\frac{1}{2}$ "	9, 11, 13, 15 "	0 65

Nickel-Plated Chain Dog Collars.

Lined with enameled leather in fancy colors.

No. 170, $\frac{5}{8}$ in. wide, 9, 11, 13, 15 in. long... $1 00
" 180, 1 " 14, 16, 18, 20, 22, 24 in. long, 1 50

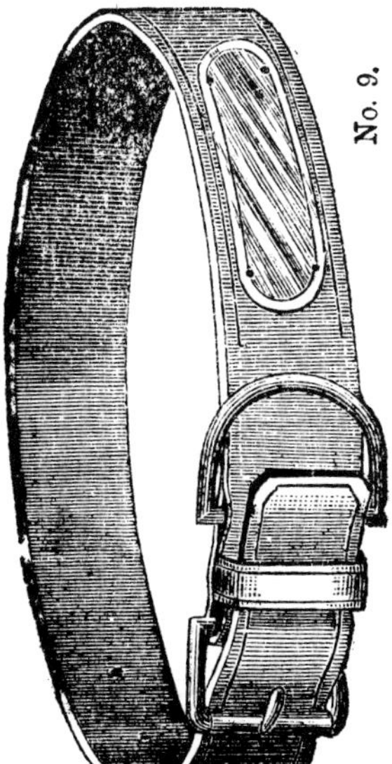

No. 9.

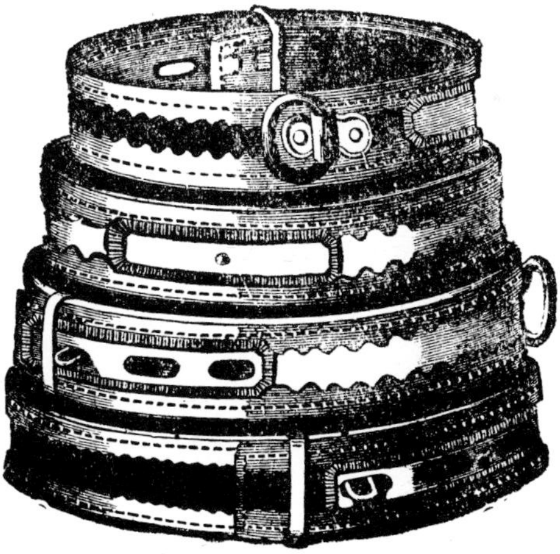

Nos. 41, 25, 28, 30.

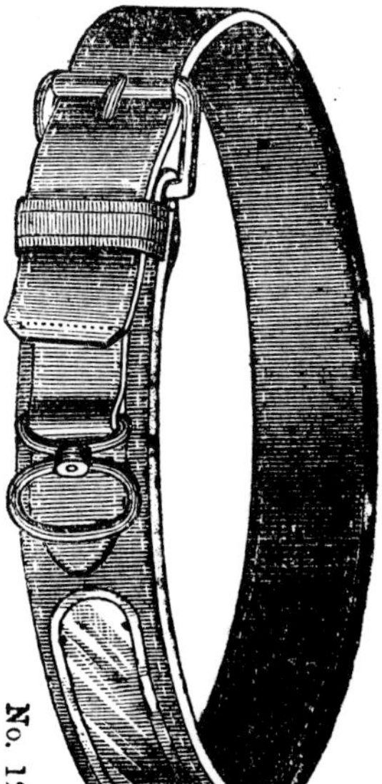

No. 12.

FANCY COLORED LEATHER DOG COLLARS, NICKEL TRIMMINGS.

No. 41. $\frac{5}{8}$ inches wide, 9, 11, 13, inches long. $ 35
" 25. $\frac{1}{2}$ " raised edges, 9, 11, 13, inches long.......................... 50

No. 28. 1 inch wide, raised edges, 14, 16, 18, 20 inches long,................. 85
" 30. 1 inch wide, raised edges, 18, 20, 24 inches long,..................... 1 50

PLAIN LEATHER DOG COLLARS.

No. 9. 1 inch wide, 18 to 22 inches long........40c. No. 12 $1\frac{1}{2}$ inch wide, 22 to 26 inches long......75c.

Engraving name on Collars, 5 cents a letter. When ordering, state exact length required. Sent by mail, post-paid, on receipt of price.

OARS AND ROW LOCKS.

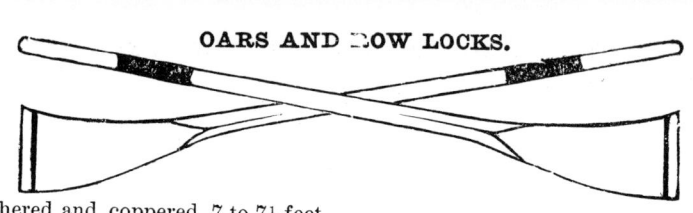

Spoon Oars, leathered and coppered, 7 to 7½ feet...	per pair,	$4	00
" " " 8 to 9 "	"	4	75
" " " 10 "	"	5	00
" with buttons, rights and lefts, etc., 9 to 10...	"	7	00
" " " " 11 to 12...	"	12	00
Plain Oars, of Spruce..	per foot,		20
" of Ash..	"		15

Measure all Row Locks at the narrowest part of the opening.

SOCKET ROW LOCKS.
Galvanized (Malleable Iron).

No. 0	1¾ inch opening.................................	per pair	$0	50
" 1	2 " "	"	0	60
" 2	2¼ " "	"	0	75
" 3	2½ " "	"	1	00
" 4	3 " "	"	1	25

Brass (Finished).

No. 1	2 inch opening.................................	per pair	$1	75
" 2	2¼ " "	"	2	50
" 3	2½ " "	"	3	50
" 4	3 " "	"	4	50

SURFACE SWIVEL ROW LOCKS.
Galvanized (Malleable Iron).

No. 101	2 inch opening.............	per pair	$1	0
" 102	2¼ " "	"	1	25

Brass (Polished).

No. 101	2 inch opening.............	per pair	$3	25
" 102	2¼ " "	"	3	75

"HARLEM RIVER" ROW LOCKS,
Galvanized (Malleable Iron).

No. 9. 2¾ inch Opening, Plate 7 inches long, ⅞ inch wide, with Side Plate same as Engraving, per pair.................... $1 00
No. 10. 2¾ inch Opening, Plate 10 inches long, 1 inch wide, no Side Plate, per pair,... 1 00

Brass (Finished).

No. 9. 2¾ inch Opening, Plate 7 inches long, ⅞ inch wide, with Side Plate, same as Engraving, per pair.................... 2 25
No. 10. 2¾ inch Opening, Plate 10 inches long, 1 inch wide, no Side Plate, per pair.... 2 25

WORKS ON YACHTING, BOATING, SCULLING, STEERING, &c., &c.

The Yachtsman's Handy Book.—Signals for Pilot Distress, Stations and Semaphores, Navigation, Nautical Astronomy, Log Book, and how to keep it, Chart, Sextant, Iron Yachts' Compasses, International (Commercial,) Colored Code of Signals, Questions and Answers in Rock and Mortar Apparatus, Fore and Aft Seamanship, &c. Useful to all Yachtsmen, whether intending to work up for a Certificate, or only desirous of understanding the Chart and Instrument work of a Coasting Voyage, International Steering and Sailing Rules, full of illustrated Charts, &c., bound in cloth, blue and gold, by W. H. Rosser..................$1.75

Fore and Aft Seamanship for Yachtsmen, with Names of Ropes, Spars and Sails in a Cutter, Yawl or Schooner, with Plate, illustrated in boards..................50c.

Model Yacht Building and Sailing.—A Treatise on the Construction, Rigging and Handling of Model Yachts, Ships, and Steamers, with Remarks on Cruising and Racing Yachts and the Management of Open Boats; also Lines for a Racing Cutter, suitable for a 5 to 20 tonner, full of illustrations, Drawings, Plans, &c., by Biddle..................$2.00

The Practical Guide to the use of Marine Steam Machinery and internal management of small Steamers, Steam Yachts and Steam Launches, fully illustrated, bound in cloth and gold, by James Donaldson, Engineer..................$2 00

Drawing and Rough Sketching.—For Marine Engineers, with proportions, Instructions, Explanations and Examples intended for the use of Sea-going Engineers and others in preparing Working Sketches and Rough Drawings as required for H. M. Navy and Board of Trade examinations, also how to design Engines, Boilers, Propeller, Paddle Wheels, Shafts, Rods, Valves, &c., &c., and information useful as a reference to those concerned in the construction of Marine Machinery, illustrated with 19 single, double and treble pages of designs, bound in cloth and gold, by J. Donaldson, Engineer, $2 00

Stellar Navigation—With new A, B, and C Tables, for finding by easy methods Latitude, Longitude and Azimuths; Latitudes and Declinations, ranging to 68° North or South, large 4 to. size, illustrated, bound in cloth and gold, by W. H. Rosser..................$1.75.

Knots, Bends and Splices.—How to make them; for the use of young seamen and Yachtsmen, full of illustrations, bound in boards; by T. E. Biddle..................50 cents.

Sailing Vessels—Varieties of them and names of Masts, Spars, Sails, standing and running Rigging. Watches and time on board ship, words used with shipping, &c., also how to learn to box the Mariners Compass, fully illustrated, bound in boards..................50 cents.

Standards and Flags of all Nations.—Yacht Club Flags, Pilots, Distant, Boat, Semaphore Storm Marryatts and Commercial Code Signals, standing and running Rigging, Sails of a Ship and Shipping explanation of terms used regarding Ships, Navies of principal Nations, &c., 255 Colored Flags and many others, bound in boards..................50 cents.

Amateur Yacht Designing.—Hints to Beginners, with lines for a single handed Cruiser and a 5 to 10 ton Cutter or Yawl, full of illustrations, large four page drawings and designs, bound in cloth and gold, by T. E Biddle..................$1.25.

The Corinthian Yachtsman or Hints on Yachting.—Yachting as a National Sport, Progress of Naval Architecture, Buying and Building, Preparing to Start, Extended Cruises, Racing, &c., Dictionary of principal terms used in Yacht Sailing, &c., bound in cloth and gold, by T. E. Biddle,...$2 00

Model Yacht Building and Sailing.—A Treatise on the Construction, Rigging and Handling of Model Yachts, Ships and Steamers, with remarks on Cruising and Racing Yachts, and the management of open boats; also Lines for various Models and Cutter Yachts, full of illustrations and designs, bound in cloth and gold, by T. E. Biddle..................$2.00

Practical Canoeing—A Treatise on the management and handling of Canoes, definitions and classifications for different Canoes, fully illustrated, bound in cloth and gold, by Ziphys..................$2 50

Law of Storms, considered Practically.—History of the Development of the Law of Storms: Early Notices of Hurricanes prior to 1830; Subsequent Views, Redfield, Reid, Piddington, Thom, Keller, &c.; Latest Views, Meldrum, Buys Ballot, Russell, Lay, Loomis, Blasius, Blanford, Buchan, Wilson, &c., Investigation by Continental Authors; Hurricane Season; Region of the Typical Hurricane. West Indies, South Indies, South Indian Ocean, Bay of Bengal, Arabian Sea, China Sea; Hurricanes in all the Oceanic Areas; The Circular Theory, and Rules for Management of Ships in reference to that Theory; The Incurved Spiral Theory, and Rules relating thereto; How to distinguish Hurricanes from ordinary Gales, and how to avoid the vortex, and profit by outlying winds; General Cautions; fully illustrated, bound in cloth, blue and gold, by W. H. Rosser..................$2.50

Rowing, Sculling and Yachting, 64 pages, illustrated paper covers..................25 cents.

The Sailing Boat.—A complete treatise on English and American Boats and Yachts; also the form and peculiarities of Sails, Rigs, &c., of the vessels of every nation, 130 illustrations........ 7 00

The Arts of Rowing and Training (by Argonant), illustrated..................2 00

The Modern Oarsman; a compendium of information on Rowing, Sculling, Steering, Feathering, Coaching, Sliding Seats, Trimming and Sitting a Boat, Dimensions of Work, Analysis of Faults, together with the principal Sculling Matches and Championship Contests to date in both hemispheres; Portraits of the most noted Oarsmen of the World: Rules of Boating, professional and amateur, &c., compiled by Ed. James. 60 pp., illustrated paper covers..................50 cents each.

POCKET, BOAT AND HUNTING COMPASSES.

These cuts represent the exact size of each article. We send them by mail upon receipt of price.

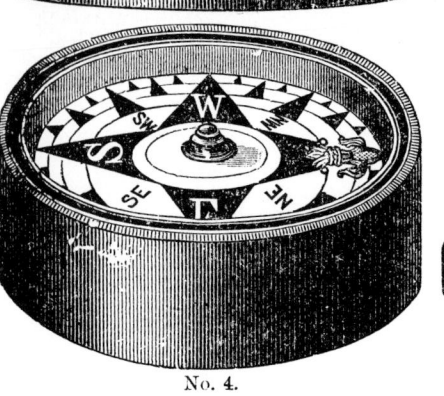
No. 4.

No. 11.

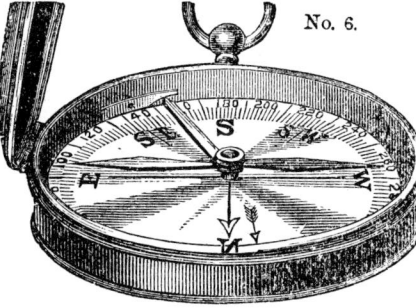
No. 6.

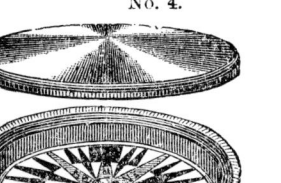
No. 1.

No. 8.

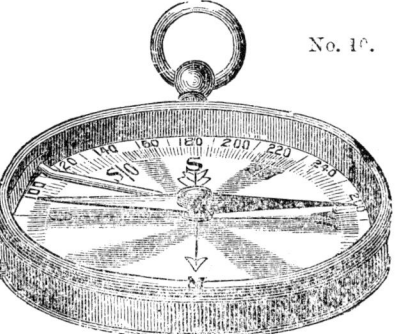
No. 10.

No. 1.	Floating Dial Compass, 1¼ inch in diameter, brass case, see cut					each,	$1 00
No. 2.	"	"	1¾	"	"	"	1 15
No. 3.	"	"	2	"	"	"	1 25
No. 4.	"	"	2½	"	" see cut	"	2 75
No. 5.	"	"	3½	"	"	"	3 00
No. 6.	Hunting Case Compass, with stop, 1½ inch in diameter, see cut					"	1 75
No. 7.	"	"	2	"	"	"	2 00
No. 8.	Hunting and Fishing Compass, 1⅜ inch in diameter, open face, see cut					"	0 75
No. 9.	"	"	1¾	"	"	"	1 00
No. 10.	2 inches in diameter, Agate Pivot with Stop, see cut					"	1 50
No. 11.	Charm Compass, Gold Plated, ½ inch in diameter, see cut					"	0 25
No. 12.	"	"	¾	"	"	"	0 40
No. 13.	"	"	13-16th inch in diameter, fine			"	0 65

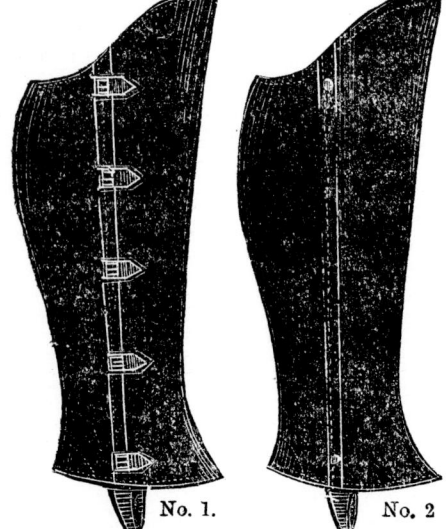
No. 1. No. 2.

HUNTING, RIDING, FISHING and BICYCLE LEGGINGS.

Made of Heavy Grain Leather and Heavy Waterproof Canvas. Tan Color.

No. 1 Heavy Grain Leather with Buckles.....$3 50 per pair.
" 2 " " " " Side Springs, (See cut)............................ 4 00 "
" 3 Heavy Canvas, Tan Color, No. 4 with Buckles............................ 2 50 "
" 5 Heavy Canvas, Tan Color, No. 4 with Buckles............................ 2 25 "
" 1, No. 4 Heavy Canvas, Tan Color with Side Springs.................... 3 60 "

Rules for Self Measurement. Send Measurement of largest part of Calf, and Diameter from Heel to top of same

THE AMERICAN PATENT CIGARETTE MAKER. (New.)

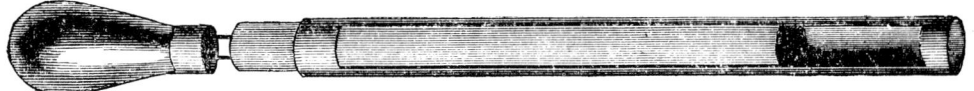

This Cut shows with Cigarette made. The simplest and most complete device ever introduced for making Cigarettes. Every smoker is enabled to select tobacco best suited to his taste, and with the aid of the Cigarette Machine can make his own cigarettes in a speedy and satisfactory manner. The advantage of being able to select one's own tobacco is an advantage every smoker will doubtless appreciate. A book of cigarette paper accompanies each machine, and a person of quick movements can make easily 1,500 cigarettes a day. Plain finish, per dozen by mail.....$1 10; each, 15c | Nickel plated, per dozen, by mail....$2 00; each, 25c.

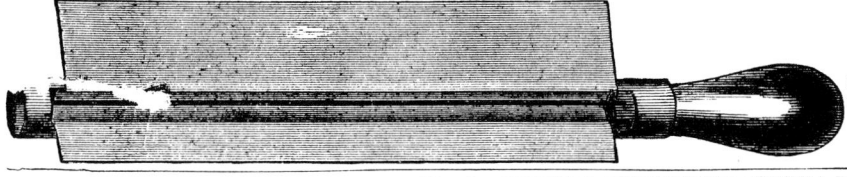

This cut shows the maker with paper ready for tobacco.

No. 7. PECK & SNYDER'S HOME FAVORITES.

This is an entirely new article and is supposed to represent a box full of Segars, it is made the exact size and counterfeit of a box to hold 50 genuine Segars, with assorted fancy picture labels designating the brand. The first layer of Segars, are a perfect imitation of the genuine ones and are fastened on a cover that lifts out, and underneath is a receptacle for holding Segars, Tobacco or any fancy articles. It is one of the best jokes to play on your friends or company. When they call on you, you pass them the box, (cover open) and ask them to try one of your new Segars which you consider very choice, and upon their going to take one, they see you have got the joke on them, and may stand treat for the genuine ones all around. Price per box complete, by mail, 60 cents.
Peck & Snyder's Joke Segars (new) being a fac-simile of the genuine Henry Clay Segar, with label around Segar, and it opens in the centre and is all hollow. Will hold 2 or 3 Cigarettes, or small articles or candies. By mail per dozen, 60 cents.

No. 8. THE DECEITFUL TOBACCO BOX.

This trick Box is made of tin, with the word "Tobacco" on the side and is the proper size for holding a small paper of tobacco or cigarettes The box may be filled full and exhibited by the owner, when a friend may ask for a chew, it may be handed to him, who will open it to find it perfectly empty, while the owner may take tobacco from it at pleasure. It is almost impossible for the spring that opens the secret slide to be found without directions.
Price by mail, postage paid, on receipt of................25 cents.
(CUT ½ THE SIZE.)

MOSQUITO SHIELD FOR THE HEAD,

A sure protection from Mosquitoes, Gnats, Black and Sand Flies, an indispensable article of comfort by night or day, in localities infested with these insects, no Fisherman, Hunter, Traveller or Sportsman should be without one. Can be worn by women as well as men, also to be used in the house where infested with these insects. No difficulty whatever in breathing when in use. Price, by mail, each $1 00.

THE JAPANESE HAMMOCK PILLOW.

Made of fine matting and pillow shape on a strong light frame, size 22 inches, 5 inches square on end ....each, $1 00. By mail, $1 15

PECK & SNYDER, 126-130 Nassau Street, N. Y.,

Dealers in all goods for the use of Fishermen, Hunters and Sporting Men in general.

THE ECONOMY TAPE MEASURE, (New.)

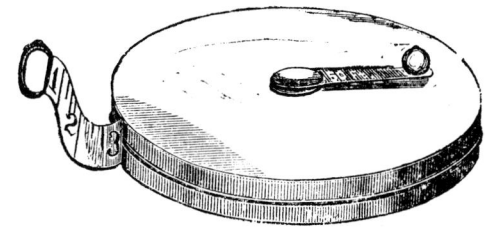

This is something cheaper and more substantial than has been offered to the trade or public yet, and so cheap that it comes within the reach of every family. Measures 50 feet Is suitable for Real Estate and Lumber Dealers, Miners, and all who have use for measuring House Lots, Roads, Rooms, Base Ball, Cricket, Croquet and Lawn Tennis Grounds, &c., &c. The tape is of the best quality; the cover heavy tin, nickel-plated. Price by mail............each. 50c.

THE SMOKER'S POCKET COMPANIONS.

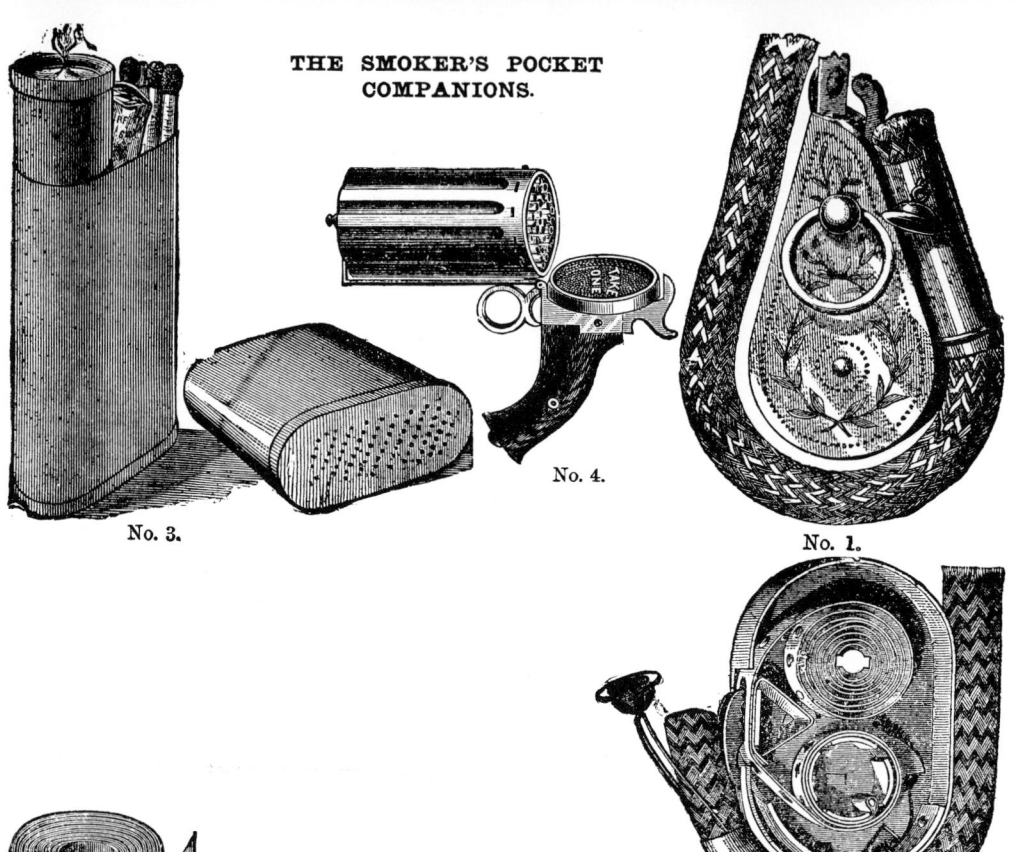

No. 1.—**The Erie Cigar Lighter.** Cut Exact Size. Pushes the tape up to the Hammer, where the Pellets are struck and the tape torn off. The fuse is drawn up by a Hook and Chain Stopper, and pulled back by the hanging end. Price, 25 cents each; $2 50 per dozen.
Patent igniting Tape, 100 Pellets to a Roll, (See cut No. 6.) .... 5 cents per Roll.
Best Prepared Fuse or Wick .... 10 " " Yard.
 "   "   " by the Piece of 18 yards. .... 75 cents.

No. 2.—**The Universal Cigar Lighter.** Allows one end of the Fuse to hang loose, and any length can be used. Feeds the Patent Tape by a winding wheel, and confines the used tape, positive motion, sure light, no tearing of tape, no Refuse, Patent Fuse Stopper, will operate the Fuse both ways, it is turned up when lighting the Cigar. Price, 35c. each; per dozen, $2 75.
Pat. Igniting Tape, 100 Pellets to a Roll, 5c. per Roll. | Best Prepared Fuse or Wick, piece of 18 Yds....75c.
Best Prepared Fuse or Wick .... 10c. per Yard. | Full Instructions with each Lighter.
This cut shows the Universal Segar Lighter with cover removed.

No. 3.—**Combination Pocket Match Safe and Candle Holder.** This cut represents the new Combination Pocket Match Safe and Candle Holder. The Candle, which may be lit at any time, is raised with a spring until entirely burned out. Price, complete, with box of candles, 25c.; extra candles, box of ½ doz., 15c.
Sent by mail, post-paid, on receipt of price. This cut is the exact size of the Match Safe and Candle Holder.

No. 4.—**Take One.** It is a perfect fac-simile of an eight-barrelled revolver. It will scare a burglar or cut-throat, as well as sell your best friend. It is large enough to hold a bunch of cigarettes. Above cut explains it thoroughly. It is nickel-plated, handsome and stylish. Dealers will find it a desirable article to add to their list of attractions, necessary to draw attention, these hard times. It sells at sight. Sample sent by mail, postage paid, price, $1 25. N. B.—These goods are amongst some of the best selling for agents, by the dozen or quantity we allow a great reduction, they are all first-class make and always saleable.

CANOE MATTRESS AND LIFE PRESERVER.

This Mattress serves also as a cushion, the tick is 50 inches long that may encircle the chest, 18 inches wide and 4 inches deep, it is divided lengthwise into 3 compartments by 2 partition strips of muslin 6 inches wide sewn on upper and under side of the Mattrass. Fine cork shavings about 1¼lbs. are put into each compartment, it is a good non-conductor of either the cold or the moisture of the earth, made of Ida Canvas, being porous and a non-conductor.
Price, $5.00 each.

THE TRICK CIGAR.

AMUSING,
BOOMING,
CONFOUNDING,
DEFYING,
EXCITING,
FASCINATING.
SOMETHING
ENTIRELY
NEW

And never fails to excite harmless and pleasant surprise when the trick is practiced upon the unsuspecting victim.

It consists of a light, strong metal shell, the size and shape of a common cigar, wrapped with tobacco-colored paper so as to perfectly resemble one, and has a spiral spring concealed within that may be released, at the will of the operator, by slightly pressing a trigger that is attached to the small end of the Cigar. One end of the spring is permanently fastened in the shell and the other end, which is projected when released, has a cork attached for the purpose of retaining it in the shell. When the spring is released it will fly out from twelve to fifteen inches with a slight rattling noise, so quickly that while the person towards whom it is pointed can see something coming and hear something, he cannot tell just what has happened until after he has made a big effort to dodge a small joke. Perhaps not until he can "see a man" who can explain the matter.

Each one upon whom the trick is played, will immediately buy one or more of the Trick Cigars and go for his friends with the least possible delay. Unlike most cheap novelties this Cigar is so durably made that it will last until the purchaser is tired of it   It is so harmless that it may then be safely given a child to play with.   1 dozen $2.00, 3 dozen $4.50 by mail   Sample, by mail, 25 cents.

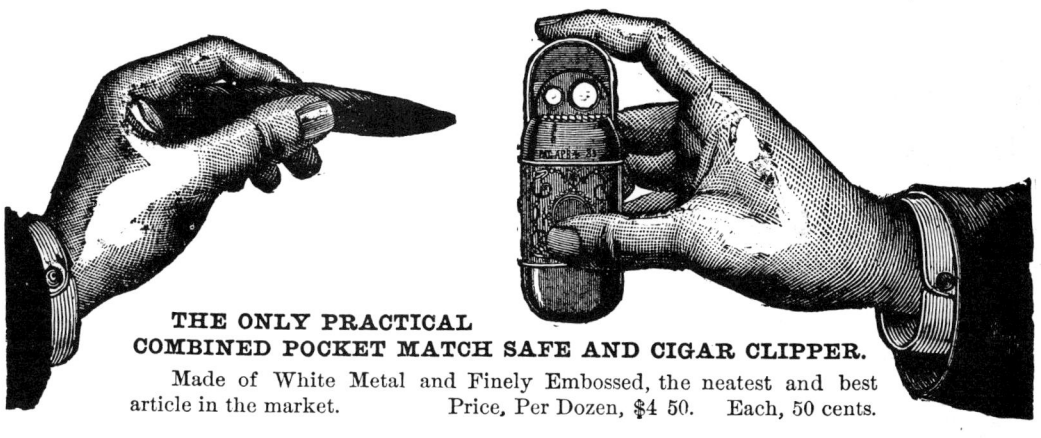

THE ONLY PRACTICAL COMBINED POCKET MATCH SAFE AND CIGAR CLIPPER.

Made of White Metal and Finely Embossed, the neatest and best article in the market.   Price, Per Dozen, $4 50.   Each, 50 cents.

QUACKENBUSH'S NEW COMBINATION AIR GUN.

Full length of Gun, 36 inches. Weight, 6½ pounds.
A Fire Arm and Air Gun in one. Shooting a regular 22-100 Cartridge, "TT" Shot, or 21¼-100 Dart and Slugs. Name either Combination or No. 5.

This Air Rifle is the most complete arrangement ever offered. As a cartridge rifle it is as handy, shoots as strong and accurate as those more expensive, besides it is equally perfect as an air gun. It can be instantly changed from one to another. As an air gun it has an accurate range of 60 feet, and will shoot a slug or shot with sufficient force to penetrate ⅜ inch pine.

This gun has a steel barrel, rifled; all the parts are extra heavy, and so constructed of best material to stand continous service, making the most durable gun manufactured, and worth more than the price asked, and is by far the most practical *long range* air gun ever made for gallery or field.

Full Nickel or Brown Finish, each,...$18.00
Smooth Bore as Air Gun only,   " 16.50
Extra, if fitted with Globe and Peep Sights,... 3.50
Accompanying each gun we send 6 Darts and 100 Felted Slugs

PATENT MECHANICAL GALLERY TARGETS

No. 2.—Drummer Girl, beating Drum and raising a flag in a very natural manner when bull's-eye is hit. Nickel-plated drums, finely painted. (See cut.)
Iron covered, for cap and shot................$30 00   Heavy Iron covered, for 22 cartridges........$35 00
Size, 2 feet wide. 6 feet high. Set by a rope from stand.

No. 5.—Ballet Girl, raising arm and leg and ringing a gong very naturally when the bull's-eye is hit. Finely painted. (See cut.)   Iron covered, for cap and shot, $20; heavy iron covered, for 22 cartridges, $25.

No. 6.—Bugler, raising arm to mouth with trumpet and playing a bugle call in a very life-like manner when the bull's-eye is hit. Finely painted. (See cut.)
Iron covered, for cap and shot...............$50 00   Heavy iron covered, for 22 cartridges.......$55 00
Size, 2 feet wide, 6 feet high. Set by a rope from stand.

No. 8.—Plain Round 18-inch Target, with 12-inch iron plate, for cap and shot, comic figure rising and ringing a gong when bull's eye is hit. Nicely painted. (See cut.) Set by a rope from stand...........$5 00

No. 9.—Eagle, opening his wings and ringing a bell when bull's eye is hit. Finely painted. Iron covered, for 22 cartridges. Size, 28x28 inches. (See cut.) $7 00

No. 9½.—Hussar, falling back and ringing a gong when bull's-eye is hit. Very natural. Nicely painted. Entirely of iron, for cap and shot. (See cut.) Size, 23x28 inches. Set by a rope from stand.......$9 00

No. 10—Indian Hunter, falling back when bull's-eye is hit. Made entirely from iron, for cap and shot, nicely painted $6 00

No. 11.—Falling Birds and Stars, falling back when hit. Made for out-door shooting. (See cut.)
Entirely of iron, for cap and shot, nicely painted $5.50   Entirely of iron, for 22 cartridges...........$6 00
Set by a rope from stand.

No. 12.—Rooster, small chick springing on his back when bull's-eye is hit. Nicely painted. (See cut.) Entirely of iron, for 22 cartridges. Size, 14x16 inches...$3 00

No. 18.—Deer, falling over when bull's-eye is hit. Nicely painted. (See cut.)
Entirely of iron, for cap and shot..............$3 00   Entirely of iron, for 22 cartridges..........$3 50

No. 20.—The New York Clockwork Targets.—This cut represents the New Style Bell Target, which is run by clock-work. When the bull's-eye is struck the bell works the same as an alarm or electric bell. The bull's-eye may be struck twenty times with one winding. They are easily fastened to any board or wall.
This cut represents the back view of the target, the front being painted with corrugated rings numbering from 1 to 12; size of target, 11 inches in diameter.
Iron face, for bullets or shot..................$5 00   Wood face, for darts only................ 5 00

DENNISON'S STANDARD TARGETS, PADS AND PASTERS.

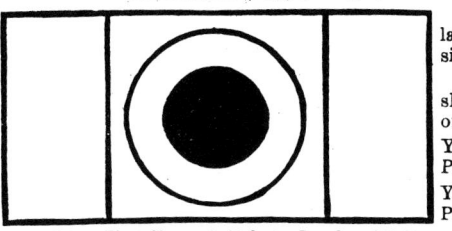

1000 Yds.—First Class—6x12 feet. Per doz. $22.00
500 Yards.—Second Class. 6x9 feet. Per doz. $10.50
200 Yds. Third Class. 8x4 feet. Per doz. $4.

We are prepared to supply Creedmoor Targets f the regulation 1000, 500, and 200 yards, and the accurately reduced sizes, for the other Ranges indicated on the annexed price list.

These Targets being of very tough, strong paper, on whole sheets are as useful and convenient as though made of canvas or other material, and at much less cost.

Yards	25	50	75	100
Prices per doz. Targets	$0.15	$0.25	$0.50	$0.85
Yards	200	500	1000	
Prices per doz. Targets	$4.00	$10.50	$22.00	

A Sample Package, containing 1 Target of each of above (5 Targets in all) will be forwarded by mail upon the receipt of $1.00; or sample 100-yard Target upon the receipt of 10c , together with printed rules for private practice.

Shot Gun Targets and Pads.

Standard Targets, for testing Pattern......per dozen, 65c.
" Pad, for testing Penetration...... " 75c.

Dennison's Premium Score Pad.

Combining all Ranges. Adopted by the National Rifle Association as the best.

Per Dozen Pads..............$2 50 | A sample Pad sent by mail for....25c.

Dennison's Target Pasters.—Black or White.

Are put up in a neat box and ten boxes in a carton.

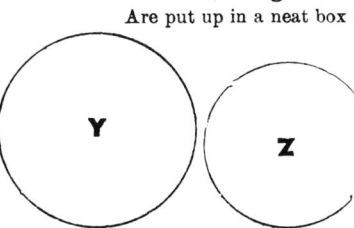

Per 1000 X	$1 00
" Y	75
" Z	50
Per 100	15
"	12
"	10

Any of the above will be sent by mail on receipt of price.

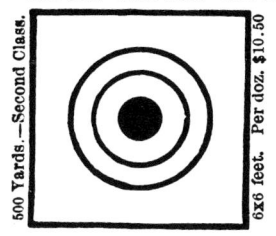

QUACKENBUSH'S SAFETY CARTRIDGE RIFLE,
Something entirely new.
The Cheapest Accurate Rifle Yet Offered.
Whole length 33 inches ; Weight, about 4½ lbs., 22-100 calibre.

We would call your attention to our Safety Cartridge Rifle, in the confident belief that you will find it, upon trial, to possess the essential requisites of cheapness, accuracy, durability and ease and rapidity of operating, with absolute safety.

This rifle has a rifled steel barrel and automatic cartridge extractor, and shoots a 22-100 cartridge, long or short ; also "BB" cap cartridge ; its stock is of black walnut, handsomely finished, and so fastened to the barrel that the two may be easily and quickly separated, making the arm handy to carry in a trunk, valise or package. The barrel and all parts are well and durably nickeled, and the breech block is case hardened in colors.

Taken as a whole, this rifle is equal to the higher priced fire arms, and is so constructed, as to workmanship and material, that it will bear incessant use without impairing its efficiency in the least degree.

It is a capital rifle for the shooting gallery, target practice, and for small game.

Price, boxed	$7 00
If sent by mail	8 00
BB Cap Cartridges, per 1,000 $2 00	Box of 250 0 60
22-100ths Short " " 3 00	" 100 0 35
" Long " " 3 60	" 100 0 40

THE PATENT HARMLESS GUN.

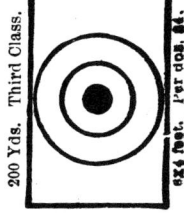

Fires a Hollow Rubber Ball. No danger. No Ram Rod, Arrow, Dart, Powder or Cap. Can't break windows, nick furniture or do harm. The King of Toys

Each one in a nice box, with three Hollow Rubber Balls free. Two grades, for large and small boys Elegantly finished, highly ornamented ....Price, $1 00
Balls extra, per Dozen, by Mail...................25 cents.

SMITH & WESSON'S NEW MODEL.
Nos. 38 & 32.

With Patent Automatic Ejector; Five shot; weight, 16 oz. Calibre, 38-100; Length of Barrel, 3 and 1 4 inches.

Blue....................................Each, $12 00
Nickel-plated....................... "   12 00
Self-acting.......................... "   14 00

32-100. With Patent automatic Ejector, Five-shot · 12 oz; Length of Barrel, 3 inches.

Blue....................................Each $11 00
Nickel-plated....................... "   11 00
Self-acting.......................... "   12 00

No. 3. NEW RUSSIAN MODEL.

With Patent Automatic Ejector, Six-shot; weight 2 5-8 lbs. Calibre, 44-100. Length of Barrel, 7 inches.
Blued..................................Each $18 50   Nickel-plated..................Each $20 00

THE DEFIANCE, OR ROBIN HOOD REVOLVER.

This Revolver has the advantages of the latest improvements; can be loaded or unloaded without removing the cylinder may be removed in an instant. It is very neat and well made; weight 8 oz. We send to any address, express paid, for..$1 50

COLT'S OLD MODEL SEVEN-SHOT REVOLVER.

Shoots 22 long or short cartridge, and warranted. Weight 8 oz. Full length, 6 inches. Price, express paid, $3 00; full nickel, $4 00

Seven-shot; weight, 8 ounces; Wrought Iron Frame, Rosewood Stock; Calibre, 22-100. Length of Barrel, 3 inches.

No. 1. POCKET PISTOL.

Smith & Wesson, Blued, No. 1—7 shot, 22-100..........................$ 8 00
"   "   Plated,   7 shot, 22-100............................ 8 50
Terror, Self-acting, weight,   13 oz., 32-100............................ 5 50
Bull Dog,   "   "   14 "   38-100............................ 6 00
Swamp Angel,   "   12 "   41-100............................ 7 00
Colt's New Model, half nickel-plated, 7 shot Revolver, 22-100........... 4 00
"   "   full   "   "   "   22-100.............. 4 50

YOUNG'S PATENT FOLDING POCKET SCISSORS.

In act of opening Scissors.   The Scissors closed for Pocket.

We are pleased to inform our customers that we have made arrangements which enable us to supply the great demand for Young's Patent Folding Scissors, and to facilitate ordering, we name the following styles and send them by mail on receipt of the following prices:

No. 1. Large size, pointed blades................................Length, 4¾ inches, $1 50 each.
"   2.   "   half pointed... "   "   1 50 "
"   3.   "   blunt.. "   "   1 50 "
"   4. Small size, pointed, with nail files............................. "   3 10/16 inches, 1 00 "
"   5.   "   half pointed... "   "   1 00 "
"   6.   "   blunt.. "   "   1 00 "
"   7.   "   embroidery.. "   "   1 00 "
"   8. Buttonhole... "   "   1 50 "
"   9. Pruning and nail scissors... "   "   1 50 "
"   10. Lace point or sewing machine.................................... "   "   1 50 "

The material used in the manufacture of these goods is the very best. All are nickel-plated, and furnished with a neat morocco case. These prices being as low as those for plain scissors of the same quality, will place them within the reach of all.

J. STEVENS & CO'S BREECH-LOADING RIFLE.

Cut represents either No. 3 or 4 Rifle, 24 in barrel.

Breech-Loading Sporting Rifle—Nickel Frame. 32, 38 and 44 Caliber.

	No. 1 Oiled Stock, Open Sights.	No. 3 Varnished Combined Sights.
24 in. Barrel, weight 6 to 8 lbs.	$20 00	$23 00
26 " " " " " "	21 00	24 00
28 " " " 6½ to 8½ lbs.	22 00	25 00
30 " " " " " "	23 00	26 00

Shooting Gallery Rifles—Nickel Frame, 22 Caliber.

	No. 2 Oiled Stock, Open Sights.	No. 4 Varnished Combined Sights.
24 inch Barrel, weight 6 to 8 lbs.	$20 00	$23 00
26 " " " " " "	22 00	25 00
28 " " " 6½ to 8½ lbs	24 00	27 00
30 " " " " " "	26 00	29 00
Vernier sight (to hinge down) back of the hammer on any rifle, extra		4 50

BEDFORD'S EUREKA AIR PISTOL.
The only Air Pistol a Lady can Load.

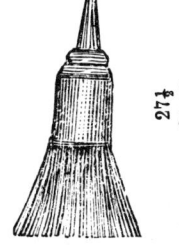

It is the only Air Pistol that has ever been made with a stationary barrel, which we claim as a very great advantage, and is fitted perfectly air-tight. It is easy to load. Each pistol is tested, so that we can warrant every one to be accurate, and by practising with Bedford's Eureka Air Pistol, one can become proficient in the use of a gun, revolver, and fire-arms generally. This Pistol has become a favorite parlor amusement in this and many other countries.

Bedford's Patent Self-Adjusting Bell Target is a valuable adjunct to the pistol. Wholesale price of Pistol, with Gunstock, Darts, Slugs, Targets, etc., **$5.00** each. Nickel-plated, **$6.00** each. Bell Target, **$1.50** Darts, 60 cents per dozen. Slugs, 15 cents per 100.

DARTS FOR AIR GUNS AND PISTOLS. (Exact Size.)

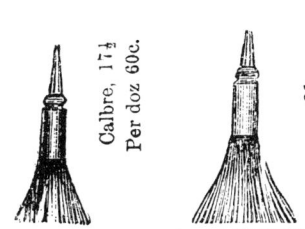

Calbre, 17¼ Per doz 60c.   21 60c.   21¼ 60c.   25¼ 75c.   27¼ $1.00.

SHOOTING GALLERY OUTFITS.
For Fair Grounds, Picnics and Galleries.

FLOBERT SALOON RIFLE.

No. 1 Rifle, polished mountings, loads at breech with small percussion cartridges, will shoot 250 feet with accuracy and force... $5 00
No 2. Rifle, finely Case Harden mountings ... 8 00
There is scarcely any report and no smell from these Rifles, making them very appropriate for parlor use, picnics and fairs.
No. 3 Rifle, fine finished, with Remington system on breech; will shoot 22-100 cartridges, 200 yards, with accuracy, rifled barrel... 10 00
Heavy barrel and rifled... 12 00
Either of the above full nickel-plated... extra 3 00
Cartridges for these Rifles, per 1000 ... $2 00; box of 250... 60

Darts, per dozen. 21-100	$0 60	Colored Paper Targets, 7 in. Diam. per doz.,	15
Burred Slugs, per hundred, 21-100	10	Plain " " 8 " " " "	10
Felted	15	" " 12¾ " " " "	20

Darts or targets sent by mail on receipt of price, and slugs four cents per hundred extra, for postage.

BALLARD RIFLE, BEST GALLERY GUN MADE.

Representing Nos. 2, 3 and 4.

No. 2 Sporting Rifle.—Octagon Barrel, Rocky Mountain Sights. The 32 and 38 calibres have reversible firing pins, using 32 and 38 long cartridges, either rim or center fire. The 44 calibre use centre fire cartridges 44 Winchester.

Calibre	Barrel	Weight	Price
32 Calibre,	26 inch.	8 lbs.	$18 00
32 "	28 "	8¼ lbs.	18 00
38 "	28 "	8½ lbs.	18 00
38 "	30 "	8¾ lbs.	18 00
44 "	30 "	9 lbs.	18 00

No. 3 Gallery Rifle.—Octagon Barrel, using 22 cal. long or short cartridges, rim fire, and ball caps, For shooting galleries, target and home practice. A 22 calibre Rifle is the most difficult to make to shoot with positive accuracy; we have overcome all the difficulties, and the Ballard Gallery is without question the best, and for several years past the demand has exceeded the supply.

Barrel	Weight	Price
24 inch,	7½ and 8¼ lbs.	$18 00
26 "	7 and 8 lbs.	19 00
28 "	9¼ lbs.	20 00

No. 4 Perfection Rifle.—Octagon Barrel, Rocky Mountain Sights, Extra heavy Wrought Frame. 32—40 and 40—63. 30 inch, 9¼ lbs. $20 00. Is intended either for a Hunting or Target Rifle.

Globe and Peep Sights for Ballard Rifle...Extra, $5 00

21-100 Cal.

THE NEW IMPROVED AIR GUN FOR TARGET PRACTICE AND SHOOTING SMALL GAME.

By far the best Gun made for the money. Shoots Darts and Slugs with force and accuracy equal to the most expensive air guns made. It can be operated rapidly, and with perfect ease. There is no pumping, pulling, or any tedious labor required to load it. The amount of compressed air is equal each time; consequently it shoots alike. A person practicing with it can become a DEAD SHOT. No caps or percussion used. The material and workmanship are of the best. It is made ENTIRELY OF METAL, except the stock, which is black walnut, handsomely finished. It can be also instantly taken apart, for the convenience of carrying it in your trunk or valise, by simply unscrewing the front piece that holds the barrel. Each Gun is neatly boxed, with six Patent Darts, six Paper Targets, one hundred Slugs, together with a Combined Claw and Wrench.

Price, blued, $9.00   Full nickeled, $10.00

No. 1, NEW MODEL AIR GUN.

22-100 Cal.

Shoots Darts and Slugs. (Full Length 37 inches.)

Weight, 70 ounces with appurtenances, 93 ounces. Similar in construction and same in operation as the "IMPROVED AIR RIFLE." except the barrel is heavier and held in the frame by a spring guard, the drawing back of which will allow the barrel, piston and spring to be instantly withdrawn, when necessary, for boxing, cleaning, and giving access to each part.

Each gun is neatly boxed with Six Patent Darts, Six Paper Targets, One Hundred Slugs, together with a Claw. Price.. $12 00

If sent by mail $1 additional.

No. 2, Shot Air Gun, same as No. 1 in construction, but shooting only No. F. shot.

This is the cheapest, accurate strong shooting Air Gun in the market. It can be loaded and discharged fifteen times a minute with ease. It is extremely simple in construction, well made and not liable to get out of order. The barrel is steel and held in the frame by a spring guard, the drawing back of which will allow the barrel to be instantly withdrawn when necessary for boxing, cleaning and giving access to each part. Full Nickel Plated.

The gun shoots a common No. F shot, 22-100 inch diameter, making it the most economical gun to use.

Weight, 70 ounces; length, 37 inches. Price, complete.. $12 00

If sent by mail........................... $13 00   No. F Shot, a bag of 5 lbs................... 50

MAGAZINE SHOT AIR GUN.

22-100 Cal.

This Gun is one of the finest and most handy of any on the market. It is the same every way as the one above, except that it has a Magazine attached for holding 20 "F" Shot, making a desirable improvement,

The Magazine can be quickly filled and operated, making the Gun always ready, and saves the inconvenience and delay of handling the shot each time.

Price, boxed, with 6 Colored Targets and 200 "F" Shot, ... $15 00

5 lb. Bags "F" Shot. 50 cents.

TALLYING REGISTERS.—Never makes an Error.

This cut represents our No. 0 Register, or Tallying Machine, as held in the hand to be used. At the back of the instrument is fixed a ring through which a finger is passed to bring the machine in the right position that the pusher may be operated by the thumb. The machine is about two inches in diameted, registers as high as 1,000, and when it has reached that number, it commences over again. This register can be set back to zero, or to any number desired, in a moment, by operating the pusher till the units dial shows 0; then set the tens and hundredths disk to 0 by turning the set back knobs at the back of the machine *in the direction opposite* to which the dials turn when counting.

This machine is intended for general tallying purposes; as, for instance, upon docks where vessels are being loaded or nloaded; in factories; among stock men; for pedestrians; base ball umpires; boating men; in fact, wherever it is desired to keep tally, it will be found to be more convenient and *far* more reliable than the old method with pencil and paper. This register is especially adapted for detective's use on street cars, or in counting persons entering places of amusement, as it is small and can be easily concealed while being operated. Nickel-plated, $2.50

KAHNWEILER'S NEVER SINK CORK JACKET.

If you own a Yacht, Sail or Row Boat see at once that you are provided with Cork Jackets, or if taking a trip on the Ocean see that you have one packed up with your baggage, they are light and take up but little space. To Ocean passengers they are worth more than ten times their value, in giving them a contented mind and an insurance of a sense of security in case of accident.

They are the safest and cheapest Life Saver in existance, are approved and adopted by the U.S. Board of Supervising Inspectors. Also, approved and used by all the Steamship Companies, Pilot Boats and others sailing out of New York, Boston or Philadelphia harbors. Price complete, only, $2.00

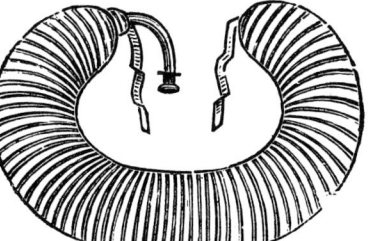

Learn how to Swim with
THE ENGLISH LIFE-PRESERVER, (new).

Cut represents it blown up ready for use. It is made of a strong rubber tubing especially prepared and covered with a fancy woven tight-fitting bag. When not inflated, can be rolled up and put in a neat rubber-cloth bag (which accompanies it), and carried in the pocket. With one of these on, it would be almost an impossibility to sink when tied around the neck. Price, each $1.50 and $2.00

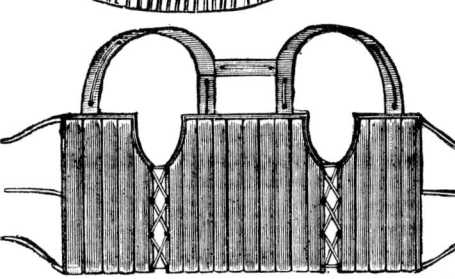

No. 1.—LIFE SAVING JACKETS.

Life Jackets are made so as to be adjusted to the size of the wearer. In the excitement of disaster it is proverbial that large men seize small and ill-fitting Jackets and small men grab large and loose ones, with the bulk on the front causing them to be thrown on the back, or a preponderance on the back which pitches them on the face. This is obviated in the Alaska Down Life Preserving Jacket by having equal and exact weight on front and back, with lacings at the side to fit it to the form of any person. This can be done before sailing, when it will be ready for use.
Weight, 2 lbs. 12 oz. Price complete, $5.00.

No. 2.—Life Saving Jacket made similar to No. 1, only of cheaper material, to new beginners this affords a support sufficient to encourage the most timid in first lessons of Swimming and a sure Preserver in case of disaster. Weight, 12 oz. Price, $1.50.

PATENT BOAT CUSHIONS.

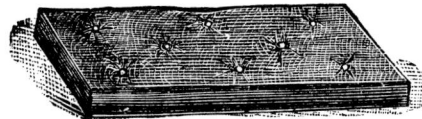

Boat Cushions made of this material are superior to Curled Hair, being soft and comfortable, and possessing *four times the buoyancy of cork*, covered with a beautiful dark imitation leather, combining a luxuriant cushion and superior Life-Boat.

Made to order to fit any Boat, Yacht or Steamer at about the same rates, by sending exact measurement and drawing. Weight, 3½ lbs. Measurement Surface, 13x33 inches, Thickness, 4 inches.
It requires only ten lbs. buoyancy to support a live person in the water. No rowing or sailing boat should be without the cushions Price each, $3.00, In case of capsizing, they afford support until rescued.
Patent Life Mattresses with life lines attached, made of same material. ....Each, $10.00
Life Buoys of same material.. " 5.00

THE SCIENCE OF
SELF-DEFENCE
OR
The Art of Sparring or Boxing Taught Easily Without a Master.
WITH 40 LARGE ILLUSTRATIONS,

SHOWING ALL THE DIFFERENT POSITIONS, BLOWS, STOPS & GUARDS.

By NED DONNELLY, Professor of Boxing to the London Athletic Club, &c.

EDITED BY J. M. WAITE,

Professor of Fencing, late of the Second Life Guards.

The whole theory and practice of the science of Self-Defence taught by two of the best boxers in the world. How to hit and hit hard; how to stop quickly and easily; and how "to get away" without even stopping a blow, are all explained plainly, so that one can easily learn to be a perfect boxer without taking lessons. But to make it still more plain, 40 pictures show every possible attitude for blow, feint, stop, dodge, or "get away." Everything is here plainly told that can make a gentleman so good a sparrer, that he can defend himself, and punish his attacker, while all that qualifies a game man to win in a prize fight, is explained by pictures as well as by words. A man is no less a good citizen because he knows how to guard his life, without a dagger or a revolver. **PRICE 25 CENTS.**

READY-MADE
AUTOGRAPH ALBUM VERSES.

As everybody wishes to oblige his lady friends here is the very book that must be acceptable to everybody.

Expressive of Almost Every Human Feeling and Sentiment, Such as Love, Friendship, Respect, Admiration, Good Wishes, etc., Including a Great Number of Acrostics for Proper Names, all Entirely Original.

No Gentleman, young, middle aged or old, can go at all into society without having some fair lady's **Book of Autographs** plumped into his hands. He feels that to refuse would stamp him a downright bear. He must comply. Left to himself he would probably write "himself down an ass." But this book will take him out of the dilemma. Here he will find something to write at once eloquent and appropriate—to suit every phase of feeling, sentiment or humor. Any article that he may copy from this book will stamp him a gentleman in the best meaning of the term.

PRICE 25 CENTS.

Tricks and Diversions with Cards

How to Avoid being Cheated at Cards.

Contains all the Tricks and Deceptions with cards ever invented, including the latest Tricks of the most celebrated conjurors, Magicians, and Prestidigitators popularly explained, simplified and adapted for **Home Amusement and Social Entertainments.** To lovers of the marvelous and ingenious this book will be a perpetual source of delight. The **rare Tricks Performed with Sleight-of-Hand.—By Mental Calculation.—By Memory.—By the Arrangement of the Cards.—By the Aid of Confederates.—By the Aid of Mechanical Contrivances.** The whole so elucidated that any one can, with a little practice, perform the most difficult feats, to his own satisfaction and to the wonder and admiration of his friends. There is also added a **Complete Exposure of all the Card Tricks made use of by Professional Card Players and Gamblers.** Shows how "Skin" Gamblers cheat and win money by their infernal "palm filing," and other tricks. It contains also the **ART OF FORTUNE TELLING BY CARDS.** These features make it the best work ever published on Card Tricks. It is handsomely gotten up, and illustrated with numerous engravings. **PRICE 25 CENTS.**

THE AMERICAN BUSINESS MAN
AND
Book-Keepers' Practical Guide.
A Complete Guide to all Kinds and Forms of Commercial and Mercantile Transactions, Including a Dictionary of all the terms and Technicalities used in Commerce and Business Houses.

There is also added many new and valuable methods of finding the cost of merchandise, and getting the solution of many matters constantly occurring in trade. Correct legal forms are given of Bills, Deeds, Notes Drafts, Cheques, Agreements, Receipts, Contracts and other instruments of writing constantly necessary to every one, no matter what calling he follows. Not only does it tell how to do business, but it is a complete book of legal knowledge. Its use will save many a dollar in lawyers' fees, and save much uncertainty and embarrassment to all who have occasion to give or receive anything in Writing. It tells **How to do Business. How to Conduct Mercantile Transactions by Sea or Land, at Home or in Foreign Countries. How to keep a Bank Account. How to make out Notes of all Kinds. How to Write an Agreement. How to Draw up Articles of Copartnership. How to Write a Bond. How to find out Profit and Loss on Goods. How to make out a Deed. How to mark Goods (private). How to Write a Contract for Building. How to Write a Lease. How to keep Books.** To the young man desirous of bettering his condition in life by engaging in mercantile, this book is worth its weight in gold. It is just what he needs. Its instructions will enable him to become proficient in the language of mercantile men, and also render him thoroughly competent to perform any duties that may devolve upon him in the banking house, the store or the office. **MIND THIS.**—If you want to get into a store or a bank, there are a hundred things you've got to know, no odds how much schooling you have. By studying **this** book you will often save yourself from "looking like a fool." **Price 25 Cts.**

"Grace was in all her steps."
BALL-ROOM DANCING
WITHOUT A MASTER
AND BALL-ROOM MANUAL.

Dancing as an elegant accomplishment has ever stood prominent, because no other art or exercise can give the individual that graceful demeanor and easy deportment so essential to a correct appearance in cultured society. As it is not always convenient to have recourse to a teacher of dancing, this work aims to supply the deficiency. In this it has been very successful. By a series of practical and lucid instructions the art of dancing is so simplified that any one can become proficient in the art **Without the aid of a Master.** In addition to specific detailed instructions as to **How to Dance,** it gives some very valuable information relating to **Organizing a Ball, Ball-Room Toilet, Etiquette of the Ball-Room, Managing and Arranging the Ball-Room. All the Popular Dances** are given, and the whole is illustrated by numerous cuts and diagrams, making the art so simple that the most ignorant can become experts in it.

PRICE 25 CENTS.

Book of Useful Receipts
AND MANUFACTURERS' GUIDE.
BY PROFESSOR JOHNSON.

For conciseness, reliability and cheapness, this work is superior to any published. Not only does it contain a vast number of reliable and practical receipts and processes relating to the **Fine Arts, Trades and General Manufactures,** but it gives full and explicit instructions for acquiring and successfully practicing numerous arts and professions, among which are **Electrotyping and Electroplating, Making and Working an Electric Telegraph, Monochromatic and Crayon Painting, Vitremaine,** and many others of equal value and importance. The portion relating to **Domestic Economy and Household Science** is very comprehensive and valuable, and cannot fail to be of great utility and profit to every housekeeper, as it gives explicit rules and methods, many of them new, for **Dyeing, Preserving, Cooking, Gardening, Repairing and Making Articles of Domestic Adornment.** Any person of common sense, without much learning, can make up things from this book, that will give him or her a fortune. It has been done and can be done again. This comprehensive and useful work is a complete and reliable book of reference, for the **Mechanic, Artist, Manufacturer, Merchant, Farmer, Housekeeper and Amateur Artisian,** and may be considered an **Authority** and **Guide** in all matters pertaining to the occupations of every-day life. **Price 25 Cents.**

Copies of the above Books sent by Mail, Postpaid, to any Address, on receipt of Price.

THE Young Wife's Own Cook Book

A practical and reliable guide to every-day cookery
By an Experienced Housekeeper.

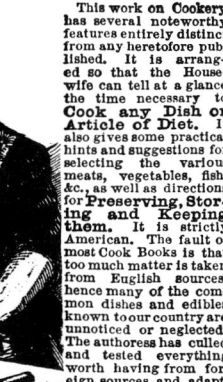

This work on Cookery has several noteworthy features entirely distinct from any heretofore published. It is arranged so that the Housewife can tell at a glance the time necessary to **Cook any Dish or Article of Diet.** It also gives some practical hints and suggestions for selecting the various meats, vegetables, fish, &c., as well as directions for **Preserving, Storing and Keeping them.** It is strictly American. The fault of most Cook Books is that too much matter is taken from English sources, hence many of the common dishes and edibles known to our country are unnoticed or neglected. The authoress has culled and tested everything worth having from foreign sources, and adapted them to the wants and habits of the American people. Special attention is paid to economy, and an effort is made to remove the reproach which justly clings to American Cookery, of being extravagant and wasteful without being palatable and healthful. Full instructions are given to prepare all kinds of Pies, Puddings, Cakes, Jellies, &c., as well as preparing and cooking all kinds of Meats, Soups, Gravies, Fish, Vegetables, &c., in an Economical and Appetizing Manner.

There is also much other information given relating to domestic economy and household comforts, including many important Receipts for Washing, Scouring, Cleaning, &c., and a variety of others equally useful and necessary to the Housekeeper or Cook. These features make this work the best, most practical, and Popular Cook Book ever issued. Illustrated.

PRICE 25 CENTS.

The Favorite Pictorial, Defining and Pronouncing Dictionary of the English Language

Containing Upwards of 30,000 Words, Orthography, Pronunciation, and Definition, According to Webster and Other Lexicographers, With an Appendix Containing Abbreviations, Foreign Words and Phrases, etc. Illustrated with Over 200 Engravings.

This book is a complete epitome of valuable explanations and definitions of difficult English and foreign words, phrases and expressions, with the correct pronunciation of each word. It aims to afford the general reader and man of business with an instant and concise definition of those abbreviations, technical terms and words, appropriated from foreign languages which continually occur in the literature and conversation of the day. Much care has been bestowed upon the sound of words, so as to give an accurate and simple method of pronunciation. Strongly bound in cloth.

PRICE 25 CENTS.

INCIDENTS OF AMERICAN CAMP LIFE.

A collection of Tragic, Pathetic and Humorous Events Actually Occurring During the late Civil War.

No war ever abounded in such feats of desperate bravery; ne--r were there more noble instances of patriotic devotion than in this state, in which "Brother's swords were wet with brother's blood." Yet never were there camps more full of boisterous hilarity when the soldier laddies were off duty. This book brings all scenes visibly before us. **PRICE 15 CENTS.**

HONEST ABE'S JOKES.

A Collection of Authentic Jokes and Squibs of Abraham Lincoln.

Grand as Lincoln stands before us as a statesman and a ruler, we like better to contemplate him as a genial Humorist. This work is "chock-full" of all his **Button-Bursting Anecdotes,** "humly" stories, and quaint but apt illustrations which often "start up" some gassy Congressman or squelched some office-seeking politician. This book is chock-full of the best things "Old Abe" ever got off. **PRICE 25 CENTS.**

Common Complaints
And How To Cure Them.
A PRACTICAL AND RELIABLE FAMILY DOCTOR.
By Thomas Faulkner, M. D.

This admirable treatise is concise and practical, and adapted to the comprehension of ordinary men and women. Its use in accidents and in cases of sickness would save an untold amount of suffering. Common ailments and injuries are detailed and treated in a plain, practical and certain manner—so that any one can, by easy reference to the book, apply the remedies. The directions are stripped of all unnecessary verbiage and medical technicalities, and tells what to do and how to do it in the plainest possible manner. Illustrated. **Price 25 Cents.**

HOW TO KEEP A GOOD HORSE. HOW TO SAVE MONEY IN BUYING. HOW TO MAKE MONEY IN SELLING.

THE AMERICAN HORSE OWNER'S GUIDE.

And Practical Farrier and Doctor.

No person who owns, cares for, or works a horse, can afford to be without this work. It is just the handy, complete and practical manual that has long been needed by horse owners. It is written by a well-known veterinary surgeon and horse dealer of great experience, so that no matter of importance relating to the horse in all stages of its existence is neglected. This work thoroughly informs you about the **Kind of Horse to Buy —How to Detect Horse Jockey Tricks—How to Manage a Horse—How to Shoe a Horse—How to Break and Train Horses—How to Cure all kinds of Diseases of Horses.** There is nothing relating to **Buying, Breeding, Rearing, Training, Shoeing, Feeding, Taming, Breaking and Doctoring Horses** but is thoroughly detailed. In addition is given the **Art of Training and Taming Horses** by a new method. And it tells **How to make a Horse lie down—To Catch a Wild Horse—To Drive the Wildest Horse—To Teach a Horse to Pace—To Make a Horse Stand—To Make a Horse Sit on its Haunches—To Make a Horse Come Down for Mounting—To Make a Horse Follow You—To Make a Horse Stand Still without Hitching—To Prevent a Horse Running Away.** This great practical work on the horse is only **25 CENTS.**

How to Write Short-Hand.

Being the Only Concise yet Full Exposition of the Elements of the Latest and Most Improved Methods of Stenographic Writing.

Illustrated by Numerous Plates, Having Printed Keys for the Use of Students.

BY ELIZA BOARDMAN BURNS.

This work is based wholly upon a system that has been reduced to every-day practice. A Boy of twelve by this method will learn in a week what it would take an adult a year to learn by other systems. It is hardly necessary to point out the advantages of Phonic Shorthand writing. Every young man about to start in the world will find this art of immense service to him. To say nothing of its absolute necessity to an editor, a press or legal reporter, it is valuable to clerks, lawyers, travelers and merchants. In short, a man in any profession thoroughly posted in Phonic Shorthand, has his capacity for business almost doubled, if it is merely to record at once in his memorandum-book transactions and conversations and agreements. **PRICE 25 CENTS.**

"Too Funny for Anything!"
JOLLY TIT BITS FOR MIRTHFUL MORTALS.

"Josh Billings, Bret Harte, and Mark Twain Rolled into One."

It is not too much to say that this book contains the Choicest Humor in the English Language. Its size is mammoth, containing more than one thousand of the Raciest Jests, Comical Hits, Exhilarating Stories, Flowers of Wit, Excruciating Jokes, Uproarious Poems, Rollicking Songs, Laughable Sketches, Darky Comicalities, Clown's Efforts, Button-bursting Conundrums, Endmen's Jokes, Plantation Humor, Funny Caricatures, Hifalutin' Dialogues, Curious Scenes, Kute Sayings, Ludicrous Drolleries, Peculiar Repartees. In fact it is a complete "Joe Miller" and "Tom Brown" in one volume. All the Great Comic Stars refer to it, because they can find in it something to "touch the funny-bone" every time. It contains an immense collection of Irish Bulls, Dutch Comicalities, and Yankee Yarns, affording fun for a lifetime. Humorously illustrated by lots of Komikal Kuts. **PRICE 25 CENTS.**

Copies of the above Books sent by Mail, Postpaid, to any Address, on receipt of Price.

GILBERT'S BOOK OF PANTOMIMES!

Acting Charades, Parlor Theatricals and Tableaux.

This is the very best book of the kind ever devised to amuse a household with instructive, captivating performances, in which young, middle aged and old "can all take a hand in." Illustrated with numerous **Fine Engravings**, showing exactly how everything should be done. The fullest instructions are given as to the **Dresses, Scenes, Positions, Lights, &c.** The Publishers feel a just pride in presenting this book to the public, as they know it to be the best of its class ever printed. The numerous pieces are all by masters of their peculiar lines. Some of the pieces are deeply pathetic, stirring up every good feeling of the heart, and teaching priceless moral lessons in an affecting but pleasing manner. Numerous other pieces are brim full of fun of the healthiest and heartiest description. Wild, jolly, rollicking fun, that can be joined in by the youngest and the oldest alike. Here is a brief epitome of the contents of this charming book:—**Shadow Pantomimes; Ghosts, and How to Raise Them; The Gallanty Show; Compliments of the Season; Bandoline, the Bloodless; Wild Wolf of Tartary; Ever-so-little-Bear; White Rose of the Plantation; Charades in Action. 50 Tableau Vivants or Animated Pictures**, from the most simple to the most complicated. Persons who have never seen any of these things acted can easily arrange them, so full and plain are the directions in this book. For Church Fairs, School Exhibitions and Parlor Entertainments, they are just the thing, being easily produced and giving excellent opportunities for young and old to participate. Although this book contains 120 pages, the price is **ONLY 25 CENTS.**

THE Taxidermist's Guide
——OR, THE——
Art of Collecting, Preparing, Mounting and Preserving all kinds of Animals, Birds, Fishes, Reptiles, Insects, etc.

This is a truly valuable and indispensable work for the use of the Naturalist, Traveler and Amateur, or anyone who delights in observing the interesting and multifarious products of Nature. It gives plain directions for skinning, stuffing and mounting all animals, from a mouse to an elephant. Also, how to Catch, Skin, Preserve and Mount all kinds of Birds, both land and water. Also, the best methods of **PRESERVING BIRDS' NESTS AND EGGS;** it teaches the art of **Skinning, Preserving and Setting up Reptiles, Fishes and Molluscous Animals**, including Tortoises, Turtles, Crocodiles, Lizards, Serpents of all kinds, Frogs and Toads. It also gives the best methods of Collecting, Preserving and Polishing all kinds of Land, Marine and Fresh Water Shells; the art of **Breeding and Rearing Insects and Preparing Skeletons**, including a number of the best receipts used by the most eminent Taxidermists for the preservation of animals. Illustrated. **PRICE 25 CENTS.**

OUR KNOWLEDGE BOX;
OR,
Old Secrets and New Discoveries.

It tells all about **Electrical Psychology**, showing how to biologize any person, and while under the influence, he will do anything you may wish him, no matter how ridiculous it may be, and he cannot help doing it.

It tells how to **Mesmerize**. Knowing this, you can place any person in a mesmeric sleep, and then be able to do with him as you will. This secret has been sold over and over again for $10.00.

It tells how to make persons at a distance think of you—something all lovers should know.

It tells how to charm those you meet and make them love you, whether they will or not.

It tells how spiritualists and others can make writing appear on the arm in blood characters, as performed by Foster and all noted magicians.

It tells how to make a cheap galvanic battery; how to plate and gild without a battery; how to make a candle burn all night; how to make a clock for 25 cents.

HOW TO DETECT COUNTERFEIT MONEY, how to banish and prevent mosquitoes from biting; how to make yellow butter in winter;

Circassian curling fluid; sympathetic or secret writing ink; Cologne water; artificial honey; stammering; how to make large noses small; to cure drunkenness; to copy letters without a press; to obtain fresh-blown flowers in winter; to make good burning candles from lard.

It tells how to make a horse appear as though he was badly foundered; to make a horse temporarily lame; how to make him stand by his food and not eat it; how to cure a horse from the crib or sucking wind.

How to put a young Countenance on the Horse. How to cover up the heaves; how to make him appear as if he had he glanders; how to make a true-pulling horse balk; how to nerve a horse that is lame, etc., etc. These **Horse Secrets are being continually sold for One Dollar each.**

It tells how to make the eggs of Pharaoh's serpents, which, when lighted, though but the size of a pea, there issues from it a coiling, hissing serpent, wonderful in length and similarity to a genuine serpent.

Old Secrets and New Discoveries is worth FIVE DOLLARS to any person, but it will be mailed to any address on receipt of only **25 Cents.**

HAWTHORNE'S
JUVENILE SPEAKER AND READER.

Prepared Expressly and Carefully
FOR
The Use of Young Children.
Containing a large number of Pieces, some cunning and simple enough
TO PLEASE INFANTS;
While all are sure to
DELIGHT AND IMPROVE
CHILDREN OF EVERY AGE.

Every thoughtful person likes to see children happy and this book will be a wellspring of delight to both the little ones and their elders. It is full of pieces in which virtuous lessons are encrusted with a coating of honeyed sweetness. **Price 25 Cents.**

CHOICE VERSES

FOR
VALENTINES, ALBUMS,
AND
Wedding Celebrations.
Containing Original and Selected Verses applicable to
Wooden, Tin, Silver, Golden and Diamond
WEDDING ANNIVERSARIES,
Bouquet and Birth-Day Presentations, Autograph Album Verses and Acrostics,
And a variety of Verses and Poems adapted to
SOCIAL ANNIVERSARIES AND REJOICINGS.

Every person moving in respectable society may be at any moment called on to be present as a guest, or a principal, in one of these occasions, or to write in some kind of album. Here is everything handy that can be said, sung or written appropriately. It comprises the best contents of any dozen similar books. **Price 25 Cents.**

Genteel Behavior.

A Complete Handbook of Modern Etiquette, for Ladies and Gentlemen.

A perusal of this work will enable every person to rub off the rough husks of ill-breeding and neglected education, and substitute for them gentlemanly ease, and graceful, ladylike deportment (as the case may be), so that their presence will be sought for, and they will not only learn the great art of being thoroughly *at home* in polite society, but will have the rarer gift of making everybody around them feel easy, contented, and happy. This work is fully up to the requirements of the times. It describes (what all should learn)—

How to Enter a Room and how to Leave it. —How to Accost or Notice Ladies or Gentlemen on the Street.—How to Dress Well, and yet not Garishly.—How to Give and Receive Introductions.—What kind of Cards to Have, and how to Present or Send them.—The proper Mode of Giving Presents.—How to Shake Hands and Bid Good Bye.—How to Begin, Conduct, and End a Conversation.—How to Accompany Acquaintances on the Promenade.—How to Seek a Partner in the Dance, and how to Decline an Invitation.—How to Behave at Dinners, either as Host or Guest.—How to Behave During Courtship and Marriage.—How to "play the affable" at Church, at Parties, &c.

Get this Greatest Handbook of Modern Etiquette.
PRICE 25 CENTS.

Personal Beauty,

OR THE WHOLE ART OF ATTAINING
Bodily Vigor, Physical Development, Beauty of Feature and Symmetry of Form, with the Science of Dressing with Taste, Elegance and Economy.

To those to whom Nature has been sparing in her gifts, suggestions are here offered that will enable them to overcome all defects, and to become beautiful, elegant, and graceful, and to be admired and sought after by the opposite sex.

Among numerous other matters, it tells—
How to improve the Complexion, Make Cosmetics, Remove Freckles, Make the Eyes Beautiful, Cause the Eyelashes and Eyebrows to Grow Long, Prevent the Hair Falling Off, Prevent Gray Hair, Cause the Beard and Mustache to Grow, Cure Baldness, Remove Superfluous Hair, Preserve the Teeth, Cure the Toothache, Have White Hands, Cure Corns, Cure Pimples, Invigorate the System, Improve the Memory, Prolong Life, Cure Nervous Ailments, Increase the Vital Forces, Produce Physical Vigor, &c.

The book also gives a vast amount of other equally important information, the details of which can not be enumerated here. Illustrated. **Price 25 Cents.**

The Best in the World.
HOW TO WRITE A LETTER.

A Complete Letter-Writer for Ladies and Gentlemen.

This book is not a mere collection of letters and examples, as is generally the case with all "Complete Letter-Writers now in use, but it is a book which actually tells how to write a letter upon any subject, out of the writer's "own head." It gives much very necessary information relating to PUNCTUATION, SPELLING, GRAMMAR, WRITING FOR THE PRESS, LEGAL IMPORTANCE OF LETTERS, LOVE, COURTSHIP AND MARRIAGE.
It also contains the Art of Rapid Writing, by the abbreviation of Longhand, and a DICTIONARY OF ABBREVIATIONS. This book its worth its weight in gold to all. No one can fail to be benefited by some of the information it contains. It embraces all the points and features that are in other Letter-Writers with very much that is new, original and very important, and which cannot be found in any other book. **Price 25 Cents.**

Key to Composition.
Or, How to Write a Book.

A complete guide to authorship, and practical instructor in all kinds of literary labor. As an aid and instructor to those who desire to follow literary pursuits permanently for profit, or to those who write for recreation and pleasure, this book is indispensable. **Price 25 Cents.**

Hunters' & Trappers' Guide
A Practical Manual of Instruction in the Art of Hunting, Trapping and Fishing.

This book will be found very valuable to those who have not had any experience in these healthy, manly and profitable pursuits. A boy who has never handled a gun or set a snare, or caught fish, or cured a skin, can learn to do all these things, without any teacher but this book. The mystery of making, setting and baiting traps successfully is shown. The best methods of catching all kinds of fish, either in the sea, lake or river, is told practically and understandingly. The whole art of managing and training dogs for sporting purposes, and all about the care of skins and furs, so that they will bring the highest market price, is given, with a vast amount of other valuable information relating to the Hunter's craft.

ABSTRACT OF CONTENTS.
The Art of Gunning.—The Rifle and How to Use it.—Rabbit, Snipe, Partridge, Woodcock, and Wild Fowl Shooting.—Deer and Buffalo Hunting.—How to Make Traps.—Setting and Baiting Traps.—Specific Directions for Trapping and Snaring all Kinds of Birds and Animals.—Fishing, Baits, Hooks, Lines, and Rods.—Stretching and Curing Skins.—Dressing and Tanning Skins and Furs.—Coloring and Dyeing Skins and Furs. &c., &c.

The book is indispensable to all who delight to Fish, Hunt or Trap, either for sport or profit. The instructions will enable any one to become easily and thoroughly expert in the sports and pastimes of the river, field or forest. Illustrations are given where needed, as in the construction of traps, &c.

PRICE 25 CENTS.

PARLOR PASTIMES,
or, THE WHOLE ART OF AMUSING.
FOR PUBLIC OR PRIVATE ENTERTAINMENTS.

An entirely new work by the celebrated Professor RAYMOND, on **MAGIC, CONJURING, LEGERDEMAIN, AND PRESTIDIGITATION.**
This work is a complete exposé of the Wizard's Art. No trick or illusion of importance is left unnoticed; and the instructions and explanations are so simple and exhaustive that a child could perform them. This book thoroughly elucidates and explains all the mysteries associated with BLACK MAGIC, WHITE MAGIC, NATURAL MAGIC, GALVANISM, LEGERDEMAIN, ELECTRICITY, PRESTIDIGITATION, ALCHEMY, JUGGLERY, SLEIGHT-OF-HAND, NECROMANCY, CARTOMANCY, CHEMISTRY, &c. This book tells how to make, operate, and perform with COINS, CARDS, FIREWORKS, MECHANICAL DEVICES, AND MAGNETIC CONTRIVANCES. It also contains a large collection of RIDDLES, CONUNDRUMS, CHARADES, ENIGMAS, TRANSPOSITIONS, REBUSES, PUZZLES, ACROSTICS, ANAGRAMS, PARADOXES, AND PROBLEMS.
If you desire to shine as a star at parties, instead of sitting like a drone and a dummy, get this book and learn a few tricks in a few hours. Give a little more time, and you can equal Blitz, or Hermann, or Heller.

PRICE 25 CENTS.

PRACTICAL MAGICIAN
—AND—
VENTRILOQUIST'S GUIDE.

CAN MAKE A GOOD LIVING, IF NOT A FORTUNE, BY WHAT YOU CAN LEARN IN THIS BOOK.
To those desirous of learning the Art of Magic, a work is now for the first time offered that will impart the necessary instruction. By a series of systematic lessons the learner is conducted through the whole field of MAGIC, CONJURING AND LEGERDEMAIN. The whole science is so simplified that a few lessons will enable any one to perform the most perplexing and wonderful tricks and illusions equal to any of the great Wizards, Magicians and Prestidigitators o tthe day. There is also given complete instructions for acquiring

THE ART OF VENTRILOQUISM.
The instructions are so very simple and practical that no one can fail to acquire this amusing art, and become a Proficient Ventriloquist and Polophonist. Illustrated. **Price 25 Cents.**

THE AMERICAN REFERENCE BOOK.

A Manual of Facts. Containing a Chronological History of the United States; the public lands; everything about the constitution, debt, revenue, productions, wealth, population, railroads, exemption, interest, insolvent and assignment statutes of the U. S. Also valuable information about the rulers, debts and productions of various nations, and a concise list of Mythological and Classical names. **Price 25 Cents.**

Copies of the above Books sent by Mail, Postpaid, to any Address, on receipt of Price.

THE AMERICAN POPULAR DICTIONARY.

CONTAINING

EVERY USEFUL WORD IN THE ENGLISH LANGUAGE,
WITH ITS CORRECT SPELLING, PROPER PRONUNCIATION, AND TRUE MEANING.

ALSO, A VAST AMOUNT OF

ABSOLUTELY NECESSARY INFORMATION
UPON

Science, Mythology, Biography, American History, Constitutions, Laws, Growth of Cities, Colleges, Army and Navy, Rate of Mortality, Land Titles, Insolvent and Assignment Laws, Debts, Rates of Interest, and Other Useful Knowledge.

BEING

A PERFECT LIBRARY OF REFERENCE IN ONE HANDY VOLUME.

512 pp., 12mo. Cloth. Gilt. Illustrated. Price 50 cents.

☞ **RAPID FORTUNES EASILY MADE.** ☜

THE GREAT BOOK OF
MONEY-MAKING SECRETS
Or, 500 Ways to Get Rich.

To persons who work hard for a living and then don't get it, we have a few plain words to say. Every person wants to make money, and wants to make it **fast and easy.** This book will **tell them how,** as sure as sunrise makes day. Many worthy people grow gray with hard work, and have nothing to show for it. It is such people we address. Among the **five hundred valuable secrets** in this really great book are many plainly explained, **requiring no capital,** but little labor, and no special ability. By any one of these you can make money ten times easier than by hard work, and be your own master at that. This book is crammed full of wonderful ways of **becoming rich quickly.** Not by peddling, and forcing sales, but by making things that nearly everybody will readily buy. We know hundreds that have made from $1000 to $10,000 by secrets learned out of the greatest book of "**Money-making Secrets**" in the world. No such word as "*fail*" about it. No machinery, no chemical works, needed. All the operations can be done in city or country. No "gift of gab" needed. Things will sell themselves. **No capital needed to begin. The money rolls in from the start.**

Besides collecting secrets from the highest-priced books, we have bought up all the rapid, **sure ways of making fortunes easy,** paying as high as $300 for some. But it pays us; for so many people have written telling how much they have made by taking up even *one* of the secrets we divulge, they have prospered from the start. It is not only women and men, but also girls and boys, who have bought the book, and write us that they are more than satisfied, for they are now on the **highway to fortune.** A lady can quietly make things at home, and the great profits alone would tell the story. An outlay of 25 cents for this great book will probably start you right on the road to a fortune, and will **surely tell how to make money fast and easy.**

☞ As there are some spurious books of this kind, of no good whatever, be sure to write for the great book of "**Money-making Secrets; or, 500 Ways to Get Rich.**" Price **25** cents, or five copies for **$1**.

THE
AMATEUR PAINTER.

A Manual of Instruction in the Art of
PAINTING, VARNISHING and GILDING.

With plain rules for the practice of every department of House and Sign Painting.

CONTENTS.

Colors, and How to Mix them—Compound Colors—Oils—Varnishes—Polishes—Gilding Materials—Miscellaneous Materials—Grinding and Washing Colors—Cleanliness in Working—Practice of Painting—Practice of Varnishing and Polishing—Practice of Gilding—Instructions of Sign Writing—Harmony of Colors—Birds-Eye Maple in Distemper—Satin Wood—Mahogany in Distemper—Mahogany in Oil—Rose Wood.

This book is thorough in detail in every branch of Painting. By its aid every man can become his own Painter, in whatever kind of work he desires to undertake. **PRICE 25 CENTS.**

MOTHER GOOSE'S MELODIES.

This is not one of the new-fangled, modernized volumes for young ladies and gentlemen; but the regular old-fashioned rhymes that Grandma used to sing to her dear little girls and boys. It has all the old favorites from "Sing a song of Sixpence," to "Goosey, Goosey, Gander." Besides more than fifty pretty, quaint, comical, pictures. **Price 10 Cents.**

GYPSY FORTUNE-TELLER

A GUIDE TO LUCKY DREAMS AND SPEEDY FORTUNE.

Containing the only true methods of Fortune-telling and Divination. Also, a Complete Dictionary of Dreams; the Art of Palmistry; a Full Collection of Charms, Spells, and Incantations; and much other matter relating to the Occult Arts, now for the first time made public.

This is the plainest Fortune-teller ever published. It gives correct rules for foretelling what is going to happen. It contains all that was ever made known by Madame Normand, Mother Shipton, or any of the old sybils. Any one that can read can, with this book, tell all about the future. With this book you can tell your own or another person's fortune far better than any astrologer, clairvoyant, or medium can tell it for you. It foretells exactly what will happen to you. It gives the **Hindoo Secrets of Love,** and how to manage, what to say, and what to do, to gain the heart and hand of the one you desire to marry. It gives the art of Telling Fortunes by the Lines of the Hand.—It contains a Complete Dictionary of Dreams, by which you can easily and truly interpret any Dream as soon as you hear it.—It tells you a Charm to protect you from Danger.—It teaches how to make the Lucky Dream Rose.—Who your future Wife or Husband will be,—The Love-letter Charm,—How to know the Sex of Children before birth,—To know how soon you will marry, —To know what fortune you will have,—The Lover's Charm,—The only True Method to Tell Fortunes by Tea or Coffee Cup,—To know if your love of a person will be mutual.—It tells your Lucky Days,—Fortune-telling by Cards,—What you will be successful in,—What your absent Husband or Wife is doing,—What your Future Destiny is,—Whether your Wife, Husband, or Intended is true to you,—Whether you will ever marry,—Whether you will have Money left you,—Whether your Marriage will be happy,—How to be Successful in your Love affairs,—Whether you will die rich or Poor,—Seven Signs of Speedy Marriage,—How to Choose a Good Husband or Wife.

These are only a few of the mysterious revelations unfolded in the pages of this wonderful book. Anything you are troubled about, or anything you want to know, can be solved and ascertained by consulting this great book. Price **25** cents, or **five** copies for **$1**.

MARRIAGE MADE EASY;

Or, the Mystery of Love-making made plain.

The whole Art of being Successful with the Ladies, and also Giving Important Counsels to a newly married pair.

With most people marriage is "a leap in the dark." So thick is the curtain drawn before its mysteries, that persons smart in everything else are left to grope blindfold on the threshold of the bridal chamber. This should not be. What captain would think of entering an unknown sea without a map or a quadrant? Ladies look with contempt upon a "greeny." Marriage is a mighty event in every person's life, whether man or woman. But courtship is quite as important. To win a suitable mate is often as difficult as to keep one. This book explains **everything** in relation to winning a woman's love. Nothing is left untold by which affection can be stimulated, and virtuous love crowned with connubial happiness. Much information will be found in these pages that has heretofore been sealed and hidden; but we break the seals, and reveal the secrets. Married folks, we think wrongfully, make a sort of masonic secrecy of what must be known first or last,—and the sooner the better. No one who becomes thoroughly posted from this book need fear to try his luck with the most haughty and icy fair one, be she **maid** or **widow,** for he will be in possession of the "Open, Sesame!" that will not fail under any circumstances. The ladies will also doubtless like to read this interesting work,—and we suppose they will. Reveals hidden Secrets, Married People should know—will bring back a fickle husband, and keep him true. Shows surely how to gain your choice. The book is worth 1000 times 25 cents, for it will bring thousands into wedlock. Posts you thoroughly how to behave in **Courtship** and **Marriage**—no Secrets kept back. Price **25** cents, or five copies for **$1**.

The American Hoyle; or, Gentleman's Hand-Book of Games. Containing all the Games Played in the United States, with Rules, Descriptions and Technicalities. Adapted to the American Methods of Playing. By TRUMPS. Thirteenth Edition: Illustrated with Numerous Diagrams and Engravings. This work is designed and acknowledged as an *Authority on all Games as played in America*, being a guide to the correct methods of playing, and an arbiter on *all disputed points*. In each of the previous editions the work was subjected to careful revision and correction; but this, the Thirteenth Edition, is entirely new, and re-written from the latest reliable sources. It includes an Exhaustive Treatise on Whist, with all the latest essays on the Modern Game, by CLAY, POLE, DRAYSON, &c., &c. Also, a lucid description of all the Games now in vogue in America, with the Laws that govern them, revised and corrected to conform to present usages; and embraces an elaborate and practical analysis of the DOCTRINE OF CHANCES. 12mo, cloth, 536 pages..$2.00

The Complete Poker Player. A practical Guide-Book to the American National Game; containing mathematical and experimental analyses of the probabilities at Draw Poker. By JOHN BLACKBRIDGE, Actuary and Counselor-at-Law. This, as its title implies, is an exhaustive treatise on the game of Draw Poker, giving minute and detailed information on the various chances, expectations, possibilities and probabilities that can occur in all stages of the game; with directions and advice for successful play, deduced from actual practice and experience, and founded on precise mathematical data. New Edition, thoroughly revised. Small quarto, 142 pages, paper cover..50 cts.
Cloth..$1 00

The Modern Pocket Hoyle. Containing all the Games of Skill and Chance, as played in this country at the present time; being "An authority on all disputed points." By "Trumps." Tenth Edition. This valuable manual is all original, or thoroughly revised from the best and latest authorities, and includes the laws and complete directions for playing one hundred and eleven different Games—comprising Card Games, Chess, Checkers, Dominoes, Backgammon, Dice, Billiards, and all the field games. 16mo, 388 pages, paper cover...50 cts.
Boards..75 cts.
Cloth, gilt sides...$1 25

The Laws of Athletics. How to Preserve and Improve Health, Strength and Beauty; and to correct personal Defects caused by want of Physical Exercise. How to train for Walking, Running, Rowing, &c., with the systems and opinions of the Champion Athletes of the World. Including the latest Laws of all Athletic Games and how to play them. A thorough and comprehensive work on all the Athletic Exercises and Sports of the present day. By William Wood, Professor of Gymnastics, Calisthenics and Physical Training. 18mo, paper cover..25 cts.
Flexible cloth cover.. 50 cts.

The Science of Self Defence. A treatise on Sparring and Wrestling. Including Complete Instructions in Training and Physical Development, also several remarks upon a course prescribed for the reduction of Corpulency. By Edmund E. Price. Illustrated with Explanatory Engravings. 16mo, bound in boards..75 cts.
12mo, cloth..$1 25

The American Card Player. Containing clear and comprehensive directions for playing the games of Euchre, Whist, Bézique, All Fours, French Fours, Cribbage, Casino, Straight and Draw Poker, Whiskey Poker and Commercial Pitch, together with all the Laws of those Games. 150 pages, bound in boards, with cloth back.. 50 cts.
Bound in cloth, gilt side... 75 cts.

Marache's Manual of Chess. Containing Preliminary Games for Beginners, fifty Openings of Games, giving all the latest discoveries of modern masters, with best Games and Copious Notes, Endings of Games, Numerous Problems, Diagrams, etc. By N. Marache. 16mo, cloth, gilt side............. 50 cts.
Bound in boards, cloth back.. 75 cts.

Spayth's American Draught Player; or, the Theory and Practice of the Scientific Game of Checkers. Simplified and Illustrated with Practical Diagrams. Containing upwards of 1,700 games and positions. By Henry Spayth. Sixth edition, with over 200 Corrections and Improvements. 12mo, cloth...$3.00

Spayth's Draughts or Checkers for Beginners. Being a comprehensive Guide for those who desire to learn the Game, this treatise was written by Henry Spayth, the celebrated player, and is by far the most complete and instructive elementary work on Draughts ever published. 16mo, cloth..............75 cts.

Spayth's Game of Draughts. Containing over 500 Games and Positions; Full Instructions; the Move and its Changes; Laws of the Game, &c. By Henry Spayth. 12mo, cloth...........................1.50

The Game of Draughts or Checkers Simplified and Explained. With Practical Diagrams and Illustrations, together with a Checker-board numbered and printed in red. Containing the eighteen standard games, with over 200 of the best variations. By D. Scattergood. 16mo, bound in cloth, with flexible cover... 50 cts.

Walker's Cribbage Made Easy. Being a new and complete Treatise on the Game in all varieties. By George Walker, Esq. 16mo, 142 pages, bound in boards, with muslin back..................... 50 cts.
Cloth, gilt side.. 75 cts.

How Gamblers Win; or, the Secrets of Advantage Playing Exposed. Being a complete and scientific exposé of the manner of playing all the various advantages in Cards. 16mo, paper covers.... 30 cts.
Boards, cloth back... 50 cts.

The Book of Fireside Games. Containing a description of the most Entertaining Games suited to the Family Circle as a Recreation. Large 16mo, paper cover.................................30 cts.
Bound in boards, cloth back .... 50 cts.

The Game of Whist. 16mo, paper cover... 15 cts.

Tambo's End-Men's Minstrel Gags. A collection of Ethiopian Dialogues, Plantation Scenes, Eccentric Doings, Humorous Lectures, Laughable Interludes, End Men's Jokes, Burlesque Speeches, Witticisms, Conundrums, Yarns, Plantation Songs and Dances, &c., &c. This collection embraces all the newest drolleries, End-Men's Gags, comic and sentimental songs and side-splitting acts that are practised by the leading professional minstrel troupes of the present day, and contains sufficient variety for a long series of representations; everything new and rich. 16mo, 144 pages, illuminated paper cover......................30 cts.
16mo, boards...50 cts.

Frost's Proverbs and Charades. Containing a collection of Original Proverbs and Charades, some of which are for Dramatic Performances, and others arranged for Tableaux Vivants. By S. A. Frost. This book comprises a selection of Acting Proverbs and ingenious Charades; a portion of them in the form of short and sprightly comedies, and the remainder arranged to be represented by Tableaux, all the details of which are clearly described. They are all taken from "The Parlor Stage," by the same author. 16mo, illuminated paper cover..30 cts.
16mo, boards...50 cts.

McBride's Humorous Dialogues. Designed for School Exhibitions, Literary Entertainments, and Amateur Theatricals. By H. Elliott McBride. A collection of new and humorous dialogues, full of humor and witty repartee; some of them introducing the inimitable conceits and drolleries of Irish and Yankee Dialect characters. This book thoroughly and completely fulfills its object of affording genuine amusement, being full of droll situations and mirth-provoking eccentricities. 16mo, 192 pages, illuminated paper cover.30 cts.
Boards..50 cts.

McBride's Comic Dialogues for School Exhibitions and Literary Entertainments. A collection of original Humorous Dialogues, especially designed for the development and display of Amateur Dramatic talent, and introducing a variety of sentimental, sprightly, comic, and genuine Yankee characters. By H. Elliott McBride. 16mo, illuminated paper cover.....................................30 cts.
Bound in boards..50 cts.

McBride's All Kinds of Dialogues. A collection of original Humorous and Dramatic Dialogues, introducing Yankee, French, Irish, Dutch and other characters, excellently adapted for Amateur Performance at Evening Entertainments and School Exhibitions. By H. Elliott McBride, 16mo, illuminated paper cover...30 cts.
16mo, boards...50 cts.

Hudson's Private Theatricals for Home Performance. A collection of Humorous Plays suitable for an amateur entertainment, with directions how to carry out a performance successfully. Some of the pieces are for performers of one sex only, and all of them are in one act and one scene. Large 16mo, 180 pages, paper cover...30 cts.
Bound in boards, with cloth back...50 cts.

Brudder Bones' Book of Stump Speeches and Burlesque Orations. Also containing Humorous Lectures, Ethiopian Dialogues, Plantation Scenes, Negro Farces and Burlesques. Compiled and edited by John F. Scott. 188 pages, 16mo, paper cover...30 cts.
Bound in boards, illuminated...50 cts.

Frost's Humorous and Exhibition Dialogues. This is a collection of sprightly original Dialogues, in prose and verse, intended to be spoken at School Exhibitions. Large 16mo, 180 pages, paper cover...30 cts.
Boards..50 cts.

The French Wine and Liquor Manufacturer. A Practical Guide and Private Receipt Book for the American Liquor Merchant. By John Rack, Practical Wine and Liquor Manufacturer. Illustrated with descriptive diagrams, tables and engravings. 12mo, cloth...................................$3 00

Fontaine's Golden Wheel Dream Book and Fortune Teller. Containing 144 pages, illustrated with numerous engravings and a large colored lithographic chart of the Golden Wheel. 16mo, bound in boards, with cloth back..35 cts.

North's Book of Love Letters. With directions how to write and when to use them, and 120 specimen Letters, suitable for Lovers of any age and condition, and under all circumstances. By Ingoldsby North. 16mo, bound in cloth..75 cts.
Boards..50 cts.

The Egyptian Dream Book and Fortune Teller. Containing an Alphabetical list of Dreams with their signification and their lucky numbers. Illustrated with explanatory diagrams. 16mo, boards, cloth back...35 cts.

The Parlor Magician; or, One Hundred Tricks for the Drawing-Room. Illustrated and clearly explained, with 121 engravings. Large 16mo, paper cover..30 cts.
Bound in boards, cloth back...50 cts.

The Book of 500 Curious Puzzles. Containing all kinds of entertaining Paradoxes. Illustrated with numerous engravings. Large 16mo, paper..30 cts.
Bound in boards, cloth back...50 cts.

How to Amuse an Evening Party. A complete collection of Comic Diversions, Scientific Recreations and Evening Amusements. Profusely Illustrated with nearly 200 fine wood cuts. Large 16mo, paper, 30 cts.
Bound in boards, cloth back...50 cts.

The Play Ground; or, Out-Door Games for Boys. A book of healthy recreation for youth. Containing over 100 Amusements. Illustrated with 124 fine wood cuts. Large 16mo, bound in boards........50 cts.
Bound in cloth, gilt side..75 cts.

How to Speak in Public; or, the Art of Extempore Oratory. A valuable manual for those who desire to become ready, off-hand speakers. 16mo, paper cover..25 cts.

Dick's Recitations and Readings. Exclusively designed for Recitation and Reading. Comprising a carefully compiled selection of Humorous, Pathetic, Eloquent, Patriotic and Sentimental Pieces in Poetry and Prose.
No. 1, No. 2. No. 3, No. 4, No. 5, No. 6, No. 7, No. 8, No. 9, No. 10, No. 11, No. 12, No. 13, No. 14,
ARE NOW READY.
This series, uniform in size and style, will include everything that is fresh and popular, introducing also some of the older gems of the English language that are always in demand, but excluding everything that is not eminently appropriate, either for declamation or public reading. Each number contains about 180 pages. Paper cover.. 30 cts.
Bound in cloth... 50 cts.
The fourteen numbers, bound in cloth, uniform, are put up in neat boxes, and will be sold together or separately.

The Debater, Chairman's Assistant, and Rules of Order. A manual for Instruction and Reference in all matters pertaining to the Management of Public Meetings according to Parliamentary usages. It comprises: How to Form and Conduct all kinds of Associations and Clubs; How to Organize and Arrange Public Meetings, Celebrations, Dinners, Pic-nics and Conventions; Forms for Constitutions of Lyceums or Institutes, Literary and other Societies; the Power and Duties of Officers, with Forms for Treasurers', Secretaries', and other Official Reports; the Formation and Duties of Committees; Rules of Order, and Order of Business, with Mode of Procedure in all Cases; How to Draft Resolutions and other Written Business; A Model Debate, introducing the greatest possible variety of points of order, with correct decisions by the Chairman; the Rules of Order, in Tabular Form, for instant reference in all Cases of Doubt that may arise, enabling a Chairman to decide on all points at a glance. The work is divided into different Sections, for the purpose of Consecutive Instruction as well as Ready Reference, and includes all Decisions and Rulings up to the present day. Paper covers..30 cts.
Bound in boards, cloth back... 50 cts.

Worcester's Letter-Writer and Book of Business Forms for Ladies and Gentlemen. Containing Accurate Directions for Conducting Epistolary Correspondence, with 270 Specimen Letters, adapted to every Age and Situation in Life, and to Business Pursuits in General; with an Appendix comprising Forms for Wills, Petitions, Bills, Receipts, Drafts, Bills of Exchange, Promissory Notes, Executors' and Administrators' Accounts, etc., etc. This work is divided into two parts, the portion applicable to Ladies being kept distinct from the rest of the book, in order to provide better facilities for ready reference. The Orthography of the entire work is based on Worcester's method, which is coming more and more into general use, from the fact that it presents less ambiguity in spelling. 216 pages. Bound in boards, cloth back... 50 cts.

Barber's American Book of Ready-Made Speeches. Containing 159 original examples of humorous and serious speeches, suitable for the following occasions: Presentation Speeches; Convivial Speeches; Festival Speeches; Addresses of Welcome; Addresses of Congratulation and Compliment; Political Speeches; Dinner and Supper Speeches for Clubs, Associations, &c.; Trade Banquets, &c.; Off-hand Speeches on a variety of subjects; together with appropriate replies to each. To which are added Resolutions of Compliment, Congratulation and Condolence, and a variety of Toasts and Sentiments for Public and Private Entertainments. 16mo, paper cover... 50 cts.
Bound in boards, cloth back... 75 cts.

Dick's Quadrille Call-Book and Ball-Room Prompter. Containing clear directions how to call out the figures of every dance, with the quantity of music necessary for each figure, and simple explanations of all the figures and steps which occur in Plain and Fancy Quadrilles. Also, a plain analysis and description of all the steps employed in the favorites round adnces, and over One Hundred figures for the "German"; to which is added a Sensible Guide to Etiquette and Proper Deportment in the Ball and Assembly Room, besides seventy pages of dance music for the piano. Paper covers... 50 cts.
Bound in boards... 75 cts.

Burton's Amateur Actor. A complete guide to Private Theatricals; giving plain directions for arranging, decorating, and lighting the Stage and its appurtenances; with rules and suggestions for mounting, rehearsing and performing all kinds of Plays, Parlor Pantomimes and Shadow Pantomimes. Illustrated with numerous engravings, and including a selection of original plays, with Prologues, Epilogues, &c. By C. E. Burton. 16 mo, illuminated paper cover.. 30 cts.
Bound in boards... 50 cts.

Book of Wonders, Mysteries and Disclosures. A complete hand-book of useful information. Giving a large number of Receipts for the manufacture of valuable articles of every-day use, and of great value to manufacturers, store-keepers, druggists, peddlers, and families generally. To which is added, Taxidermy, and Traps and Trapping. 16mo. Paper.. 25 cts.

Howard's Book of Drawing-Room Theatricals. A collection of short and amusing Plays in one act and one scene, specially adapted for private performances, with practical directions for their preparation and management. Some of the plays are adapted for performers of one sex only. 180 pages, paper cover... 30 cts.
Bound in boards, with cloth back... 50 cts.

Hillgrove's Ball-Room Guide and Complete Dancing Master. Illustrated with 176 descriptive engravings and diagrams. By Thos. Hillgrove, Professor of dancing. 16mo, bound in boards, cloth back 75 cts.
Bound in cloth, gilt side.. $1.00

Parlor Theatricals; or Winter Evenings' Entertainment. A collection of Dramatic Amusements and Comic Plays. Illustrated with cuts and diagrams. Large 16 mo, paper cover.........................30 cts.
Bound in boards, cloth back... 50 cts.

One Hundred Tricks With Cards. By J. H. Green, the Reformed Gambler. 16mo, paper cover...30 cts.
Boards, cloth back... 50 cts.

The Dictionary of Love. Containing a Definition of all the Terms used in the History of the Tender Passion, with Rare Quotations from the Ancient and Modern Poets of all Nations, together with specimens of Curious Model Love Letters, and many other interesting matters appertaining to Love, never before published; the whole forming a remarkable Text-Book for all Lovers. This work is really what it pretends to be—a Dictionary of Love. Every phase of the tender passion is defined and explained, and then illustrated by the rarest poetical quotations from ancient and modern poets of all nations. As a book of poetical quotations, it is the best collection ever made. It is emphatically a book for everybody. 276 pages, paper cover... 50 cts.
Bound in boards... 75 cts.

Dick's Irish Dialect Recitations. A carefully compiled Collection of Rare Irish Stories, Comic, Poetical and Prose Recitations, Humorous Letters and Funny Recitals, all told with the irresistible Humor of the Irish Dialect. This collection contains, in addition to new and original pieces, all the very best Recitations in the Irish Dialect that can be gathered from a whole library of "Recitation" books. It is full of the sparkling witticisms and queer conceits of the wittiest nation on earth; and, apart from its special object, it furnishes a fund of the most entertaining matter for perusal in leisure moments. 170 pages, paper cover.. 30 cts.
Bound in boards, cloth back... 50 cts.

Dick's Dutch, French and Yankee Dialect Recitations. An unsurpassed Collection of Droll Dutch Blunders, Frenchmen's Funny Mistakes, and Ludicrous and Extravagant Yankee Yarns, each Recitation being in its own peculiar dialect. To those who make Dialect Recitations a speciality this Collection will be of particular service, as it contains all the best pieces that are incidently scattered through a large number of volumes of "Recitations and Readings," besides several new and excellent sketches never before published. 170 pages, paper cover... 30 cts.
Bound in boards.. 50 cts.

Day's American Ready Reckoner. Containing Tables for rapid calculation of aggregate value, wages, salaries, board, interest money, etc., etc., Also tables of timber, plank board, and log measurements, with full explanations how to measure them, either by the square foot (board measure), or cubic foot (timber measure). All the Tables are original and reliable. 16mo, bound in boards........................ 50 cts.
Bound in cloth, gilt side and back... 75 cts.
Bound in leather tucks (pocket-book style).. $1 00

The Bar-Tender's Guide; or, How to Mix All Kinds of Fancy Drinks. Containing clear and reliable directions for mixing all the beverages used in the United States. Embracing Punches, Juleps, Cobblers, Cocktails, etc., etc., in endless variety. By Jerry Thomas. With plain directions for making Syrups, Bitters, Cordials and Liquors, with the various harmless flavoring and coloring substances used in their preparation, and complete instructions for Distilling, Filtering and Clarifying them. 16mo, illuminated paper cover... 50 cts.
16mo, cloth... 75 cts.

Athletic Sports for Boys. A Repository of Graceful Recreations for Youth. Containing Complete Instructions in Gymnastic and Limb Exercises, Skating, Swimming, Rowing, Sailing, Riding, Driving, Angling, Fencing and Broadsword Exercise. The whole illustrated with 194 fine wood cuts and diagrams. 16mo, bound in boards.. 75 cts.
Bound in cloth, gilt side.. $ 1 00

The Art and Etiquette of Making Love. A Manual of Love, Courtship and Matrimony. Containing sensible advice in relation to all the circumstances incidental to the tender passion, from the commencement of a courtship until after marriage; with the duties and the points of etiquette to be observed by bridesmaids and groomsmen; and all other details of the wedding ceremony. Large 16mo, 176 pages, paper cover 30 cts.
Bound in boards, cloth back... $1 00

Spencer's Book of Comic Speeches and Humorous Recitations. A Collection of Comic Speeches and Dialogues, Humorous Prose and Poetical Recitations. Laughable Dramatic Scenes and Burlesques. Suitable for School Exhibitions and Evening Entertainments. Edited by Albert J. Spencer. 192 pages, 16mo, paper.. 30 cts.
Bound in boards, cloth back... 50 cts.

Barton's Comic Recitations and Humorous Dialogues. Containing a variety of Comic Recitations in Prose and Poetry, Amusing Dialogues, Burlesque Scenes, Stump Speeches and Laughable Farces, designed for School Commencements and Amateur Theatricals. Edited by Jerome Barton. 188 pages, 16mo, paper.. 30 cts.
Boards... 50 cts.

The Independent Liquorist; or, The Art of Manufacturing all kinds of Syrups, Bitters, Cordials, Champagne, Wine, Lager Beer, Ale, Porter, Beer, Punches, Tinctures, Extracts, Brandy, Gin, Essences, Flavorings, Colorings, Sauces, Catsups, Pickles, Preserves, etc. By L. Monzert. 12mo, cloth......$3 00

Howard's Book of Conundrums and Riddles. Containing over 1,200 of the best Conundrums, Riddles, Enigmas, Ingenious Catches, and Amusing Sells ever invented. 16mo, paper cover................ 30 cts.
Bound in boards, cloth back... 50 cts.

The Secret Out; or One Thousand Tricks With Cards. A book which explains all the Tricks and Deceptions with playing cards ever known or invented. Illustrated with over 300 engravings. 398 pages, 12mo, cloth, gilt side...$1 50

Brisbane's Golden Ready Reckoner; or Lightning Calculator. A valuable assistant to Farmers, Traders and Housekeepers in buying or selling all kinds of commodities. 18mo, bound in boards...... 35 cts.

Arts of Beauty; or, Secrets of a Lady's Toilet. With Hints to Gentlemen on the Art of Fascinating. By Madame Lola Montez, Countess of Landsfeldt. 16mo... 25 cts.

Boxing Made Easy; or, The Complete Manual of Self Defense. Clearly explained and illustrated. 12mo..15 cts.

Tony Denier's Secret of Performing Shadow Pantomimes. Showing how to get them up and how to act in them; with full and concise instructions and numerous illustrations. Also full and complete descriptions of properties and costumes. It contains: Introduction; Shadow Bluff, or, Who's Who? Tooth Drawing Extraordinary; Amputation like Winking; The Haunted House; We Won't go Home till Morning; Jocko; or the Mischievous Monkey; The Madcap Barber; Cribbage, or, The Devil among the Cards; The Lover's Stratagem; The Game of Base Ball; Regular Hash, or, The Boarding House Conspiracy; The Mechanical Statue; The African Serenaders; The Model Prize Fight; The Magic Cask, or, The Industrious and Idle Apprentice; The Tragical Duel, or, The Comical Rivals; Old Dame Trot and her Comical Cat. Price..........25 cts.

The American Trapper and Trap-Maker's Guide. A complete and carefully prepared treatise on the art of Trapping, Snaring and Netting; containing plain directions for constructing the most approved Traps, Snares, Nets, and Dead-Falls; the best methods of applying them to their various purposes; and the most successful Baits for attracting all kinds of Animals, Birds, etc., with their special uses in each case; introducing, also, practical receipts for preparing Skins and Furs for Market, and for Tanning them for future use; with concise but comprehensive instructions for Preserving and Stuffing specimens of Birds and Animals in the most natural and durable manner. The entire work is based on the experience of the most successful Trappers, and on information derived from other authentic professional sources. By Stanley Harding. This comprehensive work is embellished with fifty well drawn and engraved illustrations. 16mo, paper cover..50 cts.
Bound in boards, cloth back..75 cts.

Dick's One Hundred Amusements for Evening Parties, Picnics, and Social Gatherings. This book is full of Original Novelties. It contains: New and Attractive Games, clearly illustrated by means of Witty Examples, showing how each may be most successfully played. Surprising Tricks, easy of performance, Musical and other innocent sells. A variety of new and ingenious Puzzles, Comical Illusions, fully described. These surprising and grotesque illusions are very startling in their effects and present little or no difficulty in their preparation. Also an entirely new version of the celebrated "Mrs. Jarley's Wax Works." Illustrated and explained by sixty fine wood engravings. Illuminated paper covers ....30 cts.
Bound in Boards, with cloth back..50 cts.

Dick's Ethiopian Scenes, Variety Sketches and Stump Speeches. Containing Endmen's Jokes, Negro Interludes and Farces, Fresh Dialogues for Interlocutor and Banjo, New Stump Speeches, Humorous Lectures, Dialect Sketches and Eccentricities, Dialogues and Repartee for Interlocutor and Bones, Quaint Burlesque Sermons, Jokes, Quips and Gags. It includes a number of Amusing Scenes and Negro Acts, and is full of the side-splitting vagaries of the best Minstrel Troupes in existence, besides a number of Original Recitations and Sketches in the Negro Dialect. 178 pages, paper covers........................30 cts.
Bound in boards, cloth back ....50 cts.

The Fireside Magician; or, the Art of Natural Magic Made Easy. Being a familiar and scientific explanation of Legerdemain, Physical Amusement, Recreative Chemistry, Diversion with Cards, and of all the minor mysteries of Mechanical Magic, with feats as performed in public by Herr Alexander, Robert Houdin, "The Wizard of the North," and distinguished conjurors of all ages and nations—comprising over one thousand mental and physical recreations, with explanatory engravings—compiled from original sources. By Paul Preston. 132 pages, 16mo, illuminated paper cover....................30 cts.
Bound in Boards, cloth back..50 cts.

How to Join a Circus. This contains all the practical information necessary for the guidance of those who desire to qualify themselves for the Circus or Gymnasium; with hints to Amateurs and advice to Professional Performers; affording thorough instruction in all branches of the business. Profusely illustrated, and including a review of the Circus Business from 1780 to the present time. By the celebrated Tony Denier. By carefully following the advice and instructions contained in this book, any person with a moderate degree of perseverance can become proficient in all the startling acts on the horizontal bar, fly-trapeze and other evolutions that challenge the admiration of all who behold them. 12mo, pages....25 cts.

The Sociable; or, One Thousand and One Home Amusements. Containing Acting Proverbs, Charades, Musical Burlesques, Tableaux Vivants, Parlor Games, Forfeits, Parlor Magic, and a choice collection of curious mental and mechanical puzzles, &c. Illustrated with engravings and diagrams. 12mo, gilt side stamp..$1 50

The Magician's Own Book. Containing several hundred amusing Slight-of-hand and Card Tricks, Perplexing Puzzles, Entertaining Tricks, and Secret Writing Explained. Illustrated with over 500 wood engravings. 12mo, cloth, gilt side and back stamp..$1 50

Tony Denier's Parlor Tableaux of Living Pictures. Containing about eighty popular subjects, with plain and explicit directions for arranging the stage, dressing-rooms, lights, full descriptions of costumes, duties of stage manager, properties and scenery required, and all the necessary directions for getting them up. Price...25 cts.

Amateur Theatricals and Fairy-Tale Dramas. A collection of Original Plays, expressly designed for Drawing-room performance. By Miss S. A. Frost. 16mo, 180 pages, paper cover......30 cts.
Boards, cloth back ....50 cts.

Parlor Tricks With Cards. Containing explanations of all the Deceptions with Playing Cards ever invented. The whole illustrated and made easy with 70 engravings. Large 16mo, paper cover......30 cts.
Bound in Boards, cloth back ....50 cts.

NEW AND POPULAR BOOKS SENT FREE OF POSTAGE AT THE PRICES ANNEXED.

BURDETT'S
Heroic Recitations and Readings.

A carefully compiled collection of original extracts in Prose and Poetry, for the use of Schools, Colleges, and Public Readers.

CONTENTS.

Ballad of Roland Clare, The.
Battle of Fontenoy, The.
Battle of Ivry, The.
Battle of Mongarten, The.
Beau.
Beth Gelert.
Bill Gibbon's Deliverance.
Bill Mason's Bride.
Caldwell of Springfield.
Charge of the Light Brigade, The.
Christian Maiden and the Lion, The.
Cowardly Jim.
Curfew must not Ring To-night.
Death of "Old Braze."
Defence of Lucknow, The.
Diver, The.
Downfall of Poland, The.
Execution of Montrose, The.
Execution of Queen Mary.

Father John.
Fireman, The.
Glove and the Lions, The.
Henry of Navarre before Paris.
Heroism.
Hervé Riel.
How he Saved St. Michael's.
How Jane Conquest Rang the Bell.
In the Tunnel.
Jim Bludsoe.
John Bartholomew's Ride.
John Maynard.
Kate Maloney.
Karl the Martyr.
Last Redoubt, The.
Leaguer of Lucknow, The.
Leap of Roushan Beg, The.
Little Hero, The.

Lochinvar.
Main Truck, The ; or, A Leap for Life.
Marco Bozzaris.
Martyrs of Sandomir, The.
O'Murtogh.
Phil Blood's Leap.
Polish Boy, The.
Ride of Jennie McNeal, The.
Sergeant's Story, The, of the Light Brigade.
Seventh Fusileers, The
Ship on Fire, The.
Spanish Armada, The.
Spanish Mother, The.
Supporting the Guns.
Tom.
Trooper's Story, The.
True Hero, A.

Bound in Illustrated Paper Cover. Price 25 Cents.

Wilson's Ball-Room Guide;
OR,
DANCING SELF-TAUGHT.

The latest and most complete of any publication of its kind out, embracing not only the whole theory and practice of Terpsichorean Art, but full and requisite information for the giving of RECEPTIONS, PARTIES, BALLS, etc., from the commencement to the ending, with clear directions for CALLING OUT THE FIGURES OF EVERY DANCE, and a host of other matters, all expressed in plain language, added to which are clear and practical instruction diagrams of marches, forms of invitations, programmes, etc., together with thirty-eight pages of the latest and most fashionable COPYRIGHT music, never before issued in book form, making this book the most thorough and complete publication on dancing ever issued.

Containing nearly One Hundred Figures for the " German."

Bound in Illuminated Board Cover, with Cloth back................Price 75 cents.
"   "   Paper   "   .... " 50 "

For sale by all Booksellers or will be sent postpaid on receipt of price.

NEW AND POPULAR BOOKS SENT FREE OF POSTAGE AT THE PRICES ANNEXED.

Art of Training Animals.—A complete guide for amateur or professional trainers, giving all the secrets and mysteries of the craft, and showing how all circus tricks, and all feats of all performing animals—from elephants to fleas—are accomplished. It also has an improved system of horse and colt breaking, breaking and training sporting dogs, care and tuition of song, talking, and performing birds, snake charming, bee taming, and many other things, making a large, handsome volume of over 200 pages and 60 illustrations. It would take a page of this catalogue merely to mention what the book contains. As the New England *Farmer* says, "A large variety of information, truly, to be embodied in a single book at so small a price." "A more complete manual of the art of animal training than this would be difficult to imagine," says the N. Y. *Express.* Every farmer and animal-owner will find this book valuable, and every boy who has dogs or other pets will find it a source of endless amusement. One gentleman writes us that his boys have organized quite a circus with their pets, who have been taught amusing and wonderful tricks from our book, and he proposes getting them a little tent. Remember this book at the holidays. It is a good present..50 cts.
(An edition embracing also The Horseshoer's Manual and Youatt's Treatise on Diseases of the Horse's Foot, in one handsome cloth-bound volume, at $1.00.)

Art of Wood Engraving.—A practical instructor by which any one can learn a good trade. Many young ladies have had gratifying success, and executed very creditable and profitable work after a few months' practice. Profusely illustrated..25 cts.

Artist's Manual.—A practical guide to Oil and Water-Color Painting, Crayon Drawing, etc. By JAMES BEARD and other eminent artists. Now that so many are taking up art studies, this book meets a want which can be filled by no other single volume. It is very clear, full, and explicit, and teaches the best methods. Mr. Beard is widely and favorably known as an artist and writer, and his book may therefore be relied upon. It gives the able and conscientious aid of an expert, hence is peculiarly helpful. Illustrated.50 cts.

Bad Memory Made Good, and Good Made Better.—Shows how a wonderful power of memory may be acquired by a simple art, readily, and enables its possessor to achieve feats incomprehensible to those ignorant of the secret. For instance, how to remember any number of words after one reading, how to remember a series of words from different pages of a book, so as to be able to name the page, how to remember figures, dates, historical, geographical, and all other facts, how to repeat a hundred random figures after hearing them once, how to remember a speech or sermon; stage memory; impaired memory, causes and cure. etc. Not difficult to master. It will be of great assistance to teachers, pupils, and professional men generally. Clergymen and speakers will save much time by its chapter on Speaking without Notes; students preparing for examination will be greatly aided..15 cts.

Baker's Manual.—This is a practical instructor in all branches of the business, including American, French, and German styles of work, pastry, cake, and various kinds of bread, biscuit, etc. It gives many novelties whose recipes are sold at high prices, and any baker will find it pay him to get this book. To any one starting in the business it will prove a storehouse of information and a reliable guide upon all points. A good idea of the real value of this book is given by the fact that the only similar work, scarcely as large, has been selling to the trade for $5 a copy. Any intelligent cook can make the most palatable and attractive articles with the aid of our plain and simple directions. Special attention is directed to the line of fashionable cakes and pastries. The breadmaking instruction is also very reliable and covers every variety.........................50 cts.

Barkeeper's Manual.—Only professional book of the kind and the recognized standard with New York barkeepers. It gives all plain and fancy mixed drinks, and the popular beverages of all sections. It is designed for hotels, steamers, restaurants, club houses, saloons, and wherever a reliable guide of this kind is required. It also gives chapters on preparation of wines, cordials, liquors, bitters, syrups, aerated summer beverages, artificial champagne, cider, and numerous useful recipes and practical suggestions to the profession. As the New York *Clipper* says, "with this book before him every man can be his own barkeeper." 50 cts.

Black-Board in the Sunday-School.—A practical guide for Superintendents and Teachers. By FRANK BEARD. With numerous illustrations. Just the thing wanted, giving just the information needed to enable any superintendent or teacher to use the Black-board in the work of the Sunday-School, including instructions for plain and colored drawings and every branch of the subject. Cloth, gold and black stamping......................$1.50

Book of Scrolls and Ornaments.—For Car, Carriage, Fresco, and other Painters. This book is now used in many prominent car shops, and for ornamental work generally. Mr. J. H. Loudolphe gives the best ideas and his work herein maintains the reputation his work in the shop gave him. It is principally devoted to *flat* ornamentation. The work is a favorite with the profession, and is a storehouse of valuable designs for a great variety of purposes..$1.00

Book of Alphabets.—For Painters, Draughtsmen, Designers, etc. Including all standard styles and many new and popular ones. Among others, German, French, Old English, etc...........50 cts.

Book of Japanese Ornamentation.—A collection of designs adapted to the use of decorators, designers, sign painters, silversmiths, and others. It meets the want created by the prevailing fashion for "Jap," and will be found highly useful for a variety of purposes. The designs are all *practical*, and range from the simplest styles to the most elaborate work. "This collection will be found useful to the sign painter, designer, decorator, and others for whom it is intended."—*Painter's Magazine.* "Deserves study by all painters interested in decoration."—*Hub*....................................$2.00

Books of Advertised Wonders.—This is a collection of the secrets, money-making recipes, wonders, and various things advertised by circulars and newspapers to catch curious people. Some are good, some bad, some indifferent. $250 were spent to collect them, and here you have them for 50 cents, with our comments as to the humbugs when they are such. There are enough good things to pay almost any one for the outlay of fifty cents, and many persons will avoid paying much higher prices for some by getting this book. It gives the famous $5 art of making vinegar in ten days from cider, sorghum, molasses, etc., without machinery, drugs, or chemicals; Ale without malt or hops; Cure for asthma; Imitation cognac brandy equal to finest French genuine; Chinese art of dwarfing trees; Chemical paint, durable and odorless, of any color, without oil; Nickel plating without a battery; Art of saw-filing; "Mad-stones," how to find, how to prepare, and how to use the great natural remedy for bites of poisonous or rabid animals; Excelsior axle grease; Art of sharpening saws; Magical British washing powder; Preserving grapes in their natural condition all winter; How to make brandy from shavings; Apple butter without apples; Old orchards made new; Kainite, or tree medicine; 100 pounds of soap for one dollar; How to keep apples fresh and sound all winter; How to make honey from tomatoes; Chinese art of catching fish; Infallible remedy for potato rot, Barrel of soft soap for 75 cts,; Rat killing without traps or poison; Maple sugar without maple trees;

NEW AND POPULAR BOOKS SENT FREE OF POSTAGE AT THE PRICES ANNEXED.

Fifty methods of making money; How to add 50 per cent to yield of grain at trifling labor and expense; Hardening gloss for printer's inks; Beautiful art of transferring any kind of pictures to glass; Great American washing fluid; Liebig's great fertilizer; Water witching, or the art of finding hidden water, oil, or other valuable fluids beneath the ground, with the forked switch; Yeast from grape leaves; How to soften hard water; Butter without milk or cream—artificial butter which cannot be told from genuine; Artificial fruit-syrups for soda water, and a secret for adding largely to profits; Meat preserving in hot weather; Bordeaux wine imitation; Art of waterproofing cloth; Psychrometric fascination, or art of soul charming; Colored fire for theatrical and other purposes; Boiler incrustation preventive; Egg preserving secret; Laundry secrets; Art of pickling meat in one day, and others too numerous to mention..................................50 cts.

Candy Maker.—A complete guide for making all plain and fancy candies, bonbons, etc. It tells exactly how to boil the sugar or molasses successfully for every kind of candy, how to color, flavor, and every operation. This is a good trade in every city, town, and village, and is easily learned. Fresh candies of all fashionable kinds sell readily at immense profits, and will build up a trade in any community now using the factory kinds. Any grocer or baker could add largely to his profit in a small place by introducing a few of these specialties. The book also gives a full line of syrups for soda water, recipes for many popular styles of ice cream, and other information. Illustrated..50 cts.

Carpenter's Manual.—Instructs in the use of tools and the various operations of the trade, including drawing for carpenters, forms of contracts, specifications, etc., with plain instructions for beginners, and full glossary of terms used in the trade. Also gives plans and specifications for building a number of frame houses. Illustrated...50 cts.

Detectives' Club.—A most interesting book of detective life and adventure. Curious, amusing, and thrilling. Large illustrated volume......25 cts.

Diseases of Dogs.—Their pathology, diagnosis, and treatment, to which is added a complete dictionary of canine materia medica. A practical guide for every dog owner. Tells how to prevent as well as to cure diseases, and gives much information on care and management of dogs. If you have a valuable sporting or watch dog, or a pet dog of any kind, you should get this book for its valuable suggestions on care of dogs, and for handy reference in any emergency. It is thoroughly reliable, and simple and explicit in its language......25 cts.

Dog Training.—Chapters on dog training from the "Art of Training Animals." The following briefly gives an idea of its contents: Watch dogs, their selection and value, shepherd's dogs, different kinds and their respective merits and defects, their rearing and training. Varieties and merits of sporting dogs; preliminary training, lessons in the field; water dogs. *Performing dogs.*—Simple tricks and training, to teach him his name, to leap, to walk erect, to dance, to jump rope, to sit and lie down at command, to beg, to give his paw, to sneeze, to speak for it, to fetch and carry, to bring you his tail in his mouth, to stand on a ball and roll it up and down a plank, to walk on stilts, to go up and down a ladder, to stand on his head, and walk on fore legs, to "sing," lump of sugar trick, to feign death. *Wonderful Feats of Dogs.*—Celebrated canine performers of the world; to teach dogs the alphabet; to select from a number of articles any article called for; to place any article in any place directed, or to give it to any designated person; to eat any article of food and leave any other as he may be ordered; to play dominoes; "Munito" and "Mlle. Bianca," their wonderful performances, and how they were really achieved..............................25 cts.

Dyer and Scourer.—A complete practical guide, designed especially for the use of job dyers. It includes dyeing silk, stuff or mixed goods, cotton, raw wool scouring, scouring for job dyers, and job dyeing in all its branches..............50 cts.

Employment Seeker's Guide.—Gives advantages and objections of different trades and professions; how to succeed in business; how to get good situations, new openings, and much valuable practical information. Boys and young men will get useful hints from its pages that may assist them throughout their business career. Parents would find it a good book, interesting as well as helpful, to place in the hands of sons or daughters, as the employments of woman are also treated...25 cts.

Exhibition Dialogues.—A collection of dialogues varied in character to suit different varieties and degrees of ability and preferences of teachers. Well suited to meet the wants of school exhibitions...............................25 cts.

Fun Everlasting.—A large collection of choice humorous stories, jests, puns, witticisms, etc., which will afford hearty laughter, the whole illustrated by numerous comic engravings. You can invest a dime with certainty of being well pleased, to say nothing of giving your whole family something to amuse them into the bargain. It is one of the best-selling funny books, and it pleases every time......................................10 cts.

Furniture and Cabinet Finisher.—A guide to polishing, staining, dyeing, and other preparations of hard and soft woods, including the various imitations of costly woods, and a multitude of trade recipes, and secrets of the trade............50 cts.

Gilder's Manual.—A practical guide to Gilding in all its branches as used in the several trades, such as interior decoration, picture and looking-glass frames, oil and water gilding, regilding, gilding signs. glass, china, pottery, etc., gilding on muslin, silk, etc., gilding on metals, imitation gilding, gilding for printers, silvering, silver electroplating, silvering looking-glasses, etc., etc...50 cts.

Guide to Authorship.—A practical instructor in all kinds of literary work, and all business connected therewith. Useful to professionals and invaluable to inexperienced writers desiring to get into print. Also includes editing, proofreading, copyrights, value and disposal of MSS., etc. It is just the book needed by all who write for the press, and as the New York *Evening Mail* says, "will save them asking a great many questions or making a great many blunders." *Godey's Lady's Book* says that it " will be of great service to those who contemplate a trial of the pleasures and pains of a literary life." The Philadelphia *City Item* says: "Those who read it will never regret those who do not will be compelled some day to acknowledge they have neglected an interesting and valuable work." Many teachers and others are doing well by writing during leisure hours. Though not a "school" book, it will be useful to pupils preparing "compositions," essays, valedictories, etc..........................50 cts.

Gunsmith's Manual.—A complete handbook for the American gunsmith, being a practical guide to all branches of the trade. This book is designed to furnish such information as shall be of most use in the actual every-day work of the shop, and for such demands or emergencies as are liable to challenge the knowledge or skill of the workman. It is manifestly not the province of such a book to assume to guide a manufacturer in the conduct of a great factory. Were such a work at all feasible, it could not also properly meet the wants of the ordinary gunsmith, and the scope of his little shop. He is the man whose needs have been kept steadily in view, and no pains have been spared to make every detail full, explicit, and reliable, and to give the best methods. The work covers descriptions of guns and pistols, fitting up a shop, general gunsmithing, taking apart, cleaning, and putting together; tools required; how to make tools; the work-bench: working in iron, steel, copper, brass, silver, and wood; gun-stocks, gun-barrels, tools for breeching guns, tools for chambering breech-loading barrels. gun ribs, thimbles, rifling guns, gun locks, fitting gun hammers, nipples, or cones, springs, rods, bullet molds, screw-making tools; nomenclature; browning and recipes for browning; miscellaneous recipes too numerous to mention; powder and shot; judging the quality of guns; using the rifle, using the shot-gun, using the pistol; vocabulary of mechanical terms used by gun-makers; vocabulary of chemicals and substances used in varnishes, etc.; calibers of guns; rifling, twist of rifles, etc.; directions for taking apart and assembling guns, rifles, and pistols. A handsome volume of nearly 400 large pages, with numerous engravings, diagrams, and plates. Cloth..................$2.00

Hand-book of Dominoes.—Giving all popular and new games to be played with dominoes. ....15 cts.

Hand-book of Ventriloquism.—A practical self-instructor, with examples for practice and exhibition. This book is the best for learning the art. Many boys have done so from its instruction, and have exhibited to us specimens of their accomplishments. Any boy can learn by intelligent practice with its aid. No one can become a ventriloquist by merely reading. It tells also how to make the "magic whistle," for imitating birds, animals, insects, etc..................15 cts.

Haney's Readings and Recitations.—For professional and amateur readers and reciters, and for school practice and exhibition. Large size, and large, legible type. Choicest standard and new pieces in prose and verse, dramatic, heroic, pathetic, humorous, and dialect. Fifteen books now ready, all different; any one of them will suit you. [Contents of each book mailed on application.] Price of each..................25 cts.

Haney's Fancy Alphabets.—For sign painters. This work meets a want. It gives the fashionable styles of the day, and original designs of great beauty and utility. Sign painters who want the novelties of New York experts should get this work; it will help you to keep customers and get new ones..................50 cts.

Home Recreations; *or, How to Amuse the Young Folks.*—Designed to afford fresh and agreeable entertainment for juvenile parties, holidays, and the home circle. It will give many pleasant hours and keep young folks out of mischief, and make them find enjoyment in their home circle contentedly. Parents, get a copy by all means. Illustrated..................25 cts.

Horse-Shoer's Manual.—Includes preparation of foot, choice of shoes and their preparation, fitting, filing, nails and nailing, shoeing with leather, cutting, removing, etc. Also, Youatt's Treatise on Diseases of Horses' Feet. Bonner's famous horse, Dexter, owed much of his value to good shoeing, and with all horses it is of grave importance. This book should be in the hands of every professional horse-shoer, and every horse owner..................25 cts.

Houdin the Conjurer.—This life of the famous French Conjurer is full of interesting adventures, "more fascinating than fiction." Illustrated with numerous engravings..................50 cts.

How I Became a Ventriloquist.—Describing the methods by which the author acquired the amusing art, and also his diverting experience therewith..................10 cts.

How to Make Up for the Stage.—A practical illustrated guide for amateur theatricals, charades, tableaux, etc. This is invaluable to any one getting up or participating in any of these entertainments..................15 cts.

Humors of Ventriloquism.—Full of the most entertaining and laughable scenes, etc. 10 cts.

Hunters and Trappers' Practical Guide.—This little book has immense sale, and gives satisfaction every time. It is a practical guide to gunning and rifle shooting, tells how to choose arms and ammunition, about different kinds of game, making and using traps, snares, and nets, baits and baiting, trailing game, preserving, dressing, tanning, and dyeing skins and furs; season for trapping, hints to trappers, fire hunting, pigeon catching, camping out; sporting vocabulary, recipes for sportsmen, secret of successful fishing, and, in a word, a perfect mine of interesting and valuable information for the sportsman. Boys, this is the book you want and no mistake. Every boy in the country will find this book a treasure. It has more information than books costing $1 to $2, and must not be confounded with any catchpenny. It has fifty engravings..................20 cts.

Impromptu Speaker.—This is not a collection of set speeches, but guides the speaker in making his own. While there are several works on the principles of oratory, and *collections* of speeches innumerable, it is believed that the specialty selected as the subject of the present work has been but barely, if at all, touched upon elsewhere. There are few of us who are not at some time called on to say a few words in public; these demands may come when least expected. To be unable to say anything under such circumstances is not only humiliating to the individual himself, but may seem discourteous to those who have honored him by the call. There are many having all natural qualifications demanded, who fail for the want of a few hints and helps. The difficulties experienced are often of an imaginary character, or of such trifling nature that an experienced speaker would have little comprehension of their crushing effect upon the novice. To point out the requirements of all ordinary occasions of impromptu speech-making, and to afford such aid as may be useful, are the aims of this little treatise. While avoiding formal rules and elaborate disquisitions, care will be taken to show clearly the things to avoid, as well as the things to strive for, in both the matter and the manner of the speech, and the particular points of etiquette to be observed. 25 cts.

Infant Star Speaker.—A collection of choicest pieces for little speakers, adapted to different styles and abilities. A valuable feature of this book is the instruction on training and managing the little speakers, and how to make the most effective appearance at school receptions and exhibitions..................25 cts.

Joe Green's Trip to New York.—A highly diverting account of a stranger's amusing haps and mishaps in the metropolis. Illustrated..10 cts.

Lessons in Horse Judging.—A practical guide for dealers and buyers, by which any intelligent person may become a good judge of horses, their adaptability for particular uses, and the points which go to determine their serviceability and value. Illustrated with numerous engravings and diagrams. Every farmer and every boy in the country should secure this book. There are many chances to make a profitable trade if you know how, and this book gives points that it pays to know..................50 cts.

NEW AND POPULAR BOOKS SENT FREE OF POSTAGE AT THE PRICES ANNEXED.

Manual of Hair Ornaments.—For jewelry or souvenirs. A guide for a tasteful recreation for leisure hours, and a source of profitable employment for jewelers and others. This book gives full directions whereby any one can acquire the art. The book is illustrated with over eighty explanatory engravings and beautiful designs for work. 50 cts.

Marine and Landscape Painting in Oil.—A practical guide, fully illustrated.........50 cts.

Marine and Landscape Painting in Water-Colors. — A practical guide, fully illustrated...50 cts.

Marvels and Mysteries of Detective Adventure.—A collection of thrilling and interesting stories of the detectives, full of daring adventure and curious episodes. It is one of the most attractive works of the kind ever issued. Illustrated. 25 cts.

Mind Reading.—A practical explanation of the curious phenomena exhibited by "Brown, the Mind Reader," enabling any one to perform the experiments. It will furnish a fund of amusement and wonder for an evening party or a public entertainment. Many persons with a little practice have given very successful tests of "reading a person's thoughts." Illustrated..............15 cts.

Nightside of New York.—This book is a vivid and truthful portrayal of the great city after the gas is lighted. It presents high and low life as they actually are; the fashionable life and the life in the slums; it tells about the peculiar characters and scenes which go to make up life in the metropolis, the rogues of various degrees, the snares of various kinds, and in a word all that so many are curious to know about, and often learn by experience at heavy cost. It does not seek sensationalism, nor to draw on fancy for its matter. "Truth is stronger than fiction." Illustrated........25 cts.

Painter's Manual.—A complete practical guide to house and sign painting, graining, varnishing, polishing, kalsomining, papering, lettering, staining, gilding, glazing, silvering, analysis of colors, harmony, contrast, philosophy, theory and practice of color, principles of glass-staining, etc. Including a new and valuable treatise on How to Mix Paints. This book is the best general treatise on the painter's trade yet written, and gives the information really wanted. Experienced painters have repeatedly borne witness to its value, and have found hints and helps which they had not happened to learn with years of practice. To the learner the book is simply indispensable.....50 cts.

Phonographic Hand-book.—For self instruction in the modern improved system, used by practical reporters in the courts of law and on the newspapers. It unites simplicity with thoroughness, and is the best work for beginners..... 25 cts.

Rapid Reckoning.—System of the famous "Lightning Calculator," whose exhibitions seemed almost miraculous; any one can learn and apply; valuable to clerks, book-keepers, teachers, and business men. "This is not a gift, but a scientific process. * * * It will be of immense advantage in trade, commerce, and science, and revolutionize the tedious mode of addition throughout the world."—*N. Y. Tribune* It is not a "table-book," but the art of performing arithmetical calculations with almost instantaneous speed by processes fully taught and easily learned by this book ..... 25 cts.

Rogues and Rogueries of New York.—Exposes all frauds and swindles of the great cities, from confidence operators to quack doctors, and swindles and humbugs by mail. Nearly 100,000 copies have been sold, and it has broken up many swindles. There are plenty yet operating, and this book has been repeatedly enlarged to cover new schemes as they arise. It is highly interesting, as well as valuable. If you haven't read it don't fail to do so. Illustrated...........:..............25 cts.

Royal Society Drawing Book.—This book took the prize offered for the *best* by the London Society of Arts. It advances the learner rapidly, at the same time making him thorough in all he learns. It is adapted to self-instruction or use in classes. It has the quickest and best methods, clearly presented. Its instructions are exact and always to the point, and so clear that the learner cannot go astray. It is profusely illustrated, covering the whole ground of Free-hand Outline from Outline or from the Flat, Free-hand Outline from Objects or from the Round, and Practice of Free-hand Outline from Solids and Real Objects. If you want to learn drawing understandingly and correctly as well as rapidly, this is the proper guide...................... ....50 cts.

Scene Painting and Painting in Distemper.—This work gives not only full instructions in the preparation of the colors, drawing for scene painters, stage settings, but also useful information regarding stage appliances and effects. It has numerous illustrative diagrams and engravings.. ....$1.00

Secrets Worth Knowing.—A guide to the manufacture of hundreds of useful and salable articles, including patent medicines, perfumery, toilet and dental articles, and many others easily made at trifling cost; selling readily at large profit. A single article may afford livelihood to person making and introducing to the public; storekeepers, agents, and others can make a line of salable goods and make money in any community. This is no imagination or guess work; it has been done and is being done. If you are looking out for something, this is worth trying..............25 cts.

Second Sight.—A guide to performing this famous feat as practised by Heller and other Conjurers, adapted to parlor or school exhibition, with a *new* method of performing never before published, far more easy of performance and bewildering in its effect upon an audience......15 cts

Self Cure of Debility.—*Including Consumption, Dyspepsia, Nervousness, etc.* Advertises no doctor or medicine, but gives full and plain instructions for self cure by simple means within reach of all, which will cost *nothing*, and are the surest, safe, and quickest methods of cure. Dangers of advertised modes of treatment, quack nostrums, etc., are pointed out. This is a *good* book, designed to aid in the best way any needing its help. It is not designed to pander to merely idle curiosity. It is a work which has been much needed, and it fully answers all requirements, being prepared with remarkable ability and evidently with the most conscientious aim on the part of the author to guard and save the inexperienced, for whose special benefit are several chapters of vital moment, which every young man will find it a profitable monitor regarding his health and physical welfare. It will do more than anything else to break up quackery, for it tells the truth, and quackery thrives on falsehood.... 75 cts.

Self Cure of Liquor and Opium Habits.—This book exposes dangers and fallacies of advertised modes of treatment and quack nostrums, and gives the best and most successful treatment known. This book gives recipes for preparations which can be given in tea, coffee, or other fluid unknown to the drinker, to cure the liquor habit. These preparations are advertised and sold at high prices................... ....75 cts.

NEW AND POPULAR BOOKS SENT FREE OF POSTAGE AT THE PRICES ANNEXED.

Self Cure of Stammering.—The most approved and successful methods of Self Treatment, with exposures of empirical and dangerous devices. By aid of this book many sufferers have overcome embarrassing impediments, and its information is the stock in trade of several "schools" and "professors," who are doing a lucrative business. Every parent having a child affected with any impediment or imperfection of speech should get this book, and by its suggestions save the child from possible life-long affliction. Every teacher should have this book to correct faults in pupils' articulation..25 cts.

Sign, Carriage, and Decorative Painting—This book is the combined work of several prominent painters, and is full of valuable points upon the several branches of the trade, very complete. It includes Fresco and Car painting, and other useful matters...50 cts.

Sign Writing and Glass Embossing.—This standard work, so widely and favorably known, is now issued in new edition, with newly engraved illustrations, and at a greatly reduced price. This work is too well known to the trade to need eulogy at our hands. It has been long regarded as a standard work and invaluable to every one interested in its line...75 cts.

Slow Horses Made Fast, and Fast Horses Made Faster.—System of increasing speed practised by the most famous and successful horsemen. Endorsed by Robert Bonner, Esq. Illustrated...50 cts.

Sketching from Nature in Pencil and Water-Colors.—This is an excellent work for young art students; full of practical information, which they will find clearly presented. Illustrated.50 cts.

Snares of New York.—The most complete exposure of the perils and pitfalls of this city, the clever devices of wily men and women to entrap the innocent or the stranger, and the traps of swindledom high and low. A mammoth double-column volume of nearly 200 pages, profusely illustrated, which, besides being invaluable as a protection against all forms of roguery, it is "more fascinating than fiction."..................................50 cts.

Soap-Maker's Manual.—Plain and practical guide for the manufacture of plain and fancy soaps, washing fluids, medicinal soaps, toilet preparations, shaving soaps and creams, soap powders, etc., for families and manufacturers. Has best American, English, French, and German formulas. Any family in the country can make good soap at trifling cost. It will pay by the improvement on one batch to get this book................25 cts.

Spirit Mysteries Exposed.—A complete exposition of all the marvelous feats of the "spirit rappers" and "mediums," Davenports, Hume, etc., so fully laid bare that any one can perform. The young folks can astonish and amuse their companions and friends by exhibitions of these mysterious doings, doing the wonders seen at private and public seances. Illustrated...................15 cts.

Standard Sign Writer, The.—This book is very generally recognized as the *standard* work on the subject. Its instructions are clear, precise, and practical, and cover just the ground desired by most of the profession. Its merits will be at once apparent to any intelligent painter who examines its scope and character. It is divided into two parts, the first giving detailed instructions for the different styles of lettering according to the practices most approved by the best practical signwriters. The second part consists of a variety of large engraved plates, designed especially for this work, and giving some of the best styles of lettering, model alphabets, designs for signs, and other things of interest to the profession. It is well named "Standard," for the trade at large recognize it as a standard authority and a reliable guide...$2.00

Standard Scroll Book, The.—This is a collection of upward of *two hundred* designs suitable for painters, jewelers, designers, decorators, draughtsmen, and almost every branch requiring ornamental scroll work. It is thoroughly practical, aiming to meet the wants of practical men, rather than to merely present a "pretty book." It is the result of many months' labor, and we feel we are not exaggerating in saying that it is a perfect treasury of useful designs. It must be seen to be appreciated, and we hope every painter will examine it—all we want is to have it examined—it will sell itself. Prominent features in this book are the *Shaded scrolls* and the designs for *Signs, Wagons,* and *Omnibuses.*...........................$1.00

Standard Irish Readings.—Gives choicest selections in prose and verse, many rare ones, suited to recitation or public reading. While specially interesting to Irish people, many of the pieces are well adapted to general use, being very fine..25 cts.

Taxidermist's Manual.—This is the only complete and practical work giving full and plain instructions for collecting, preparing, preserving, stuffing, and mounting all birds, animals, and insects. It is written in popular language, so that any intelligent boy can understand and apply its instructions. It is not, however, an amateur's guide; it is a standard with professional taxidermists, and gives all the secrets and processes of the profession. It is illustrated with many fine engravings and descriptive diagrams.......... 50 cts.

Tricks on Travelers.—A little work exposing frauds practised on travelers, and other information useful to strangers in great cities. Illustrated..15 cts.

Uncle Si's Black Jokes.—This is one of the funniest books you ever saw. It is quaint and curious, and real darkey humor. Illustrated.10 cts.

Use of Colors.—A valuable treatise on the properties of different pigments and their suitableness to uses of artists and students. Full of useful information. This book will be of great assistance to every artist and art student in aiding him in the proper selection and most efficient use of the several pigments, and also guidance in the proper combination of different coloring matters, to secure the best effects and avoid the injury often resulting from chemical changes produced by improper commingling........ ....25 cts.

Watch and How to Repair It, The.—By Seconds, Practical Watchmaker. This is the experience and instruction of an expert in this line, who has been regarded in the trade as a first-class authority. He tells all about it in simple, straightforward style, for practical men. Every watch repairer should have this book, and to every young man learning the trade it is simply invaluable. New, revised, and enlarged American copyright edition. Cloth...............................$1.00

Watchmaker's and Jeweler's Manual—Gives latest and most approved secrets of the trade, embracing watch and clock cleaning and repairing, tempering in all its grades, making tools, compounding metals, alloys, plating, etc., with plain instructions for beginners. Greatly enlarged edition...................................50cts.

NEW AND POPULAR BOOKS SENT FREE OF POSTAGE AT THE PRICES ANNEXED.

BURDETT'S
IRISH DIALECT RECITATIONS AND READINGS.

This new collection of rare Irish sketches in prose and verse, arranged for public representation, embraces the most sparkling Irish wit, set forth with the irresistible humor of Irish brogue. Besides the new and original pieces never before published in book form, this volume brings together all of the most popular Irish dialect readings and recitations of the time. It contains the gleanings from the whole field of Irish drollery. No other book of the kind equals it for brilliancy and fun.

CONTENTS.

The "Ager."
The Battle of Limerick.
Biddy McGinnis on the Phonograph.
Biddy McGinnis at the Photographer's.
Biddy's Trials among the Yankees.
Biddy's Troubles.
The Birth of St. Patrick.
The Donkey.
Don't be Tazing Me.
The Emigrants.
How Pat Saved His Bacon.
Irish Coquetry.
An Irish Letter.
The Irish Philosopher.
The Irish Schoolmaster.
The Irish Traveller.
An Irishman's Letter.
The Irishman's Panorama
Jimmy McBride's Letter.
Katie's Answer.
Larrie O'Dee.
Larry's on the Force.
Love in the Kitchen.
Make it Four Yer Honor.
The Man He Was Waiting to See.

Mike's Confession.
Miss Maloney on the Chinese Question.
Miss Maloney Goes to the Dentist.
Modern Astronomy and Philosophy.
Mr. Moloney's Account of the Ball.
Norah Murphy and the Spirits.
The O'Nayle who had Lost the Big "O."
O'Reilly's Nightmare.
O'Thello.
Paddy Blake's Echo.
Paddy's Courting.
Paddy's Dream.
Paddy the Piper.
Paddy O'Rafther.
Paddy's Reflections on Cleopathra's Needle.
Pat's Criticism.
Pat's Letter.
Pat and His Musket.
Pat and the Oysters.
Patrick O'Rouke and the Frogs.
Paudeen O'Rafferty's Say Voyage.
Peter Mulrooney and the Black Filly
Tim Murphy's Irish Stew.
The Wake of Tim O'Hara.
The Widow Cummiskey.

PRICE, - - - 25 Cents.

BURDETT'S
New Comic Recitations and Humorous Readings.

A new volume of comic and humorous selections, compiled by the celebrated humorist, James S. Burdett, many of which have never before been published in book form. In addition to the new and original pieces here contained, this book has the advantage of *bringing together into one volume* all of the very best selections of a comic nature which have hitherto attained a wide popularity through the public representations of the most renowned humorists of the day. It is the newest, handsomest, and choicest book of its kind.

CONTENTS.

Add Ryman's Fourth of July Oration.
The Aged Stranger.
A Baby's Soliloquy.
Be-Yu-Ti-Ful Snow.
The Blue Bottle Fly.
The Book Agent Beats the Bandit.
The Brakeman at Church.
Brigg's Rash Bet.
Buck Fanshawe's Funeral.
Butterwick's Little Gas Bill.
The Captain's Speech to the Montgomery Guards.
The Car Conductor's Mistake.
The Case of Young Bangs.
Confessing their Faults.
Faithless Sally Brown.
Fast Freight.
The Frenchman and the Flea Powder.
Darius Green and His Flying Machine.
He had been to Candahar.
How "Ruby" Played.
How She Managed It.
How they Play the Piano in New Orleans.
How to Manage Carpets.
How Tom Sawyer Got His Fence White-washed.
How we Hunted a Mouse.
An Idyl of the Period.
The Irrepressible Boy.
Jim Wolfe and the Cats.
John Spiner's Shirt.
Love in Oyster Bay

Maiden's, Beware!
Mr. Ephraim Muggins on Oilymargarine.
Mr. Potts' Story.
A New Primer.
Nobody's Mule.
One of those Awful Children.
Only a Pin.
The Parent with the Hoof.
A Plea for the Opera.
The Presentation of the Trumpet.
The Puzzled Census Taker.
Pyrotechnic Polyglot.
A Receipt for Actors.
She Meant Business.
She was too Fastidious.
A Similar Case.
The Simple Story of G. Washington.
A Speech which Every Congressman Could Understand.
Spoopendyke's Suspenders.
A Struggle with a Stove Pipe.
That Bad Boy Again.
That Emerson Boy.
That Hired Girl.
"Toujours Jamais."
Travelling in a Mixed Train.
The Two Boot Blacks.
The Villian Still Pursued Her.
The Wrong Ashes.
The Yarn of the "Nancy Bell."

PRICE, - - - 25 Cents.

Any of the above Books sent postpaid to any address on receipt of price.

NEW AND POPULAR BOOKS SENT FREE OF POSTAGE AT THE PRICES ANNEXED.

EXCELSIOR
RECITATIONS AND READINGS.

Being a new and carefully compiled selection of HUMOR-
OUS, DRAMATIC, SENTIMENTAL, PATRIOTIC,
ELOQUENT, PATHETIC, and DIALECT
PIECES, in Prose and Poetry.

DESIGNED AND ARRANGED FOR PUBLIC AND PARLOR
RECITATION AND READING.

CONTENTS OF NO. 1.

Bachelor's Dream, The..*Thos. Hood*	Marriage Tour, A...*S. J. Pardessus*
Before and After Taking...........	Mary's Lamb......................
Boy's Essay on Girls, A...........	Miner's Protege, The.............
Border Funeral, A.................	Modern Sermon, A.................
Brother Bill........*Geo. Thatcher*	Music Grinders, The..............
Brother Gardner on Liars.........	*Oliver Wendell Holmes*
Detroit Free Press	Ninety-eight......*Dr. Campion*
Cane-Bottomed Chair....*Thackeray*	No. 5 Collect St....*S. J. Pardessus*
Countryman at the Show, The.....	Not Opposed to Matrimony........
Clown's Baby, The.................	Old Actor's Story, The...........
Margaret Vandegrift	*George R. Sims*
Cow, The. A Boy's Composition..	Old Sergeant, The................
J. P. Durfee, Jr.	*Forceythe Willson*
De Cake Walk......*Wade Whipple*	On the Other Train...............
Death-Bed of Benedict Arnold.....	Oratory and the Press............
Geo. Lippard	*Daniel Dougherty*
Drummer's Bride, The.............	Original Love Story, An..........
Engineers Making Love...........	Our First Cigars.....*P. H. Bowne*
R. J. Burdette	Paddy's Lament...................
Erin's Flag...........*Father Ryan*	Parson Snow's Broad Hint........
Essay on the Elephant............	*Parmenas Mix*
Father Prout's Sermon............	Philip Barton, Engineer..........
J. S. Mackenzie	Photograph Album, The..........
Fireman's Story, The..............	*Ella Bevier*
Fisher's Wife, The.............*Swiz*	Railway Matinee, A.*R. J. Burdette*
Free Seat, A......................	Religious Card Player............
Freckled-Faced Girl, The.........	Robert Emmet.....*L. G. Goulding*
Boston Globe	Romance of a Hammock..........
Frenchman's Version of Young	Shoemaker's Daughter, The......
Norval........*P. H. Bowne*	*Thomas Dunn English*
Froward Duster, The.*R.J.Burdette*	Smiting the Rock............*By M.*
Grannie's Picture.................	Solomonism......*R. J. Burdette*
Mrs. M. E. Sniffen	S'posin'...........................
He Understood It..................	Stage Driver's Story, The........
Arkansaw Traveller	*Bernard Bigsby*
Horse or Husband.................	Supper of St. Gregory, The......
How We Fought the Fire.........	Tale of the Tenth Hussars........
Will Carleton	*F. C. Burnand*
In Der Shweed Long Ago..........	Test, A.........*Drake's Magazine*
Oofty Gooft	That Queen.......................
Intensely Utter..*Rockland Courier*	Trying to Lick the Teacher.......
Inventor's Wife, The..*E. T. Corbett*	*Eugene T. Hall*
Irrepressible Yankee, The.........	Unknown Dead..........*L. D. M.*
Jim's Kids...........*Eugene Field*	Widder, The....*Hawley Chapman*
Little Meg and I.....*C. T. Murphy*	Widow's Son, The................
Lost Grave, The...*Walter Pelham*	Woman at Poker........*Si Slokum*

Bound in illuminated paper cover. Price.................25 cts.
Nos. 2 and 3 ready, to be followed by other numbers in rapid succession.
Each number is complete in itself. Nothing is repeated.

PAYNE'S
Business Letter Writer and Book of Commercial Forms, Etc.

Containing specimen Letters on all possible business topics, with appropriate answers. There is scarcely a business transaction that can happen to an ordinary person in the course of his life-time that is not covered by the Letters and Replies contained in this work. If you want to hire help, find a situation, inquire about prices of goods, buy anything, from a paper of pins to a house and lot, borrow or lend money, or anything at all, you will find the plainest and most business-like methods of expressing your objects and desires, besides being able to reply in a suitable manner to the offers and inquiries of others. Many a good and profitable business transaction has fallen through for want of being expressed in plain, clear, and indisputable language.
Added to this are a great number of Forms for Business Papers and Documents, such as **Agreements, Promissory Notes, Bonds, Leases, Mortgages, Receipts,** and a host of other Forms, which require to be correctly worded to be binding and of legal force. This is the best Letter Writer for those who are thoroughly versed in business matters, and cannot express themselves plainly in writing, and it proves of valuable assistance to those who are well informed, as a handy book of reference on doubtful matters of Expression or Form, to which is added a comprehensive dictionary of synonyms and abbreviations, also a glossary of Commercial terms.

Bound in boards, with cloth backs.....................................Price 50 cents.

Any of the above Books sent Postpaid to any address on Receipt of Price.

NEW AND POPULAR BOOKS SENT FREE OF POSTAGE AT THE PRICES ANNEXED.

DUNBAR'S COMPLETE HANDBOOK OF ETIQUETTE.

This work presents, in a clear and intelligible manner, the whole art and Philosophy of Etiquette. As its name implies, it is a COMPLETE HANDBOOK on all matters relating to ETIQUETTE and usages of society. Among the contents are:

BODILY DEPORTMENT—
Position of the Body,
The Head,
The Tongue,
The Hand.

CONVERSATION—
The Manner of Speaking,
Speak Grammatically,
Egotism,
Memory,
Truth,
The Splendid Speaker,
Self-Respect,
Modesty,
Boldness,
Forwardness,
Diffidence,
Civility,
Attention,
Large Talk and Small Talk,
Anecdote,
Punning,
Laughter,
Table-Talk,
After Dinner,
Accomplishments,
Pedantry,
Social Characters,
The Ladies,
How to Dress,
Dancing,
The Etiquette of Conversation,
Prudence in Conversation,
Useful Hints for Conversation,
Good Taste,
The Topics of Conversation,
Letters of Introduction,
Dinner Parties,
Visiting,
Traveling,
Bridal Etiquette.

Bound in boards, with cloth back.
Price 50 cents.

HOW TO DRAW AND PAINT.

A complete Handbook on the whole art of Drawing and Painting, containing concise instructions in

OUTLINE, LIGHT AND SHADE, PERSPECTIVE, SKETCHING FROM NATURE; FIGURE DRAWING, ARTISTIC ANATOMY, LANDSCAPE, MARINE, AND PORTRAIT PAINTING;

the principles of Colors applied to Paintings, etc., etc., with over 100 Illustrations.

12mo, boards, with cloth back. Price 50 cents.

It must be of great service to all teachers and students of drawing and painting.—*Davenport (Iowa) Daily Gazette.*

It certainly seems to us the best work of the kind we have met with.—*The Connecticut Farmer*, Hartford.

HOW TO DRAW AND PAINT, a neat elementary manual. The little work is illustrated with over one hundred engravings, combining accuracy of detail and excellence of execution. The value of the instructions lies in their simplicity, and the object of the author is well carried out; to afford the beginners such plain directions as may be at once most serviceable, suggestive, and trustworthy. —*New York Star.*

An excellent text-book, containing instruction in outline, light and shade, perspective, sketching, figure drawing, artistic anatomy, landscape, marine, and portrait painting, etc. It also contains over one hundred illustrations.—*The Golden Rule*, Boston, Mass.

GERMAN AT A GLANCE.

A new system, on the most simple principles, for Universal Self-Tuition, with English pronunciation of every word. By this system any person can become proficient in the German language in a very short time. It is the most complete and easy method ever published. By Franz Thimm. (Revised Edition.)

Bound in paper cover, - - - price 25c.
Bound in boards, cloth back, - - price 35c.

FRENCH AT A GLANCE.

Uniform and arranged the same as "German at a Glance," being the most thorough and easy system for Self-Tuition. (Revised Edition.)

Bound in paper cover, - - - price 25c.
Bound in boards, cloth back, - - price 35c.

SPANISH AT A GLANCE.

A new system for Self-Tuition, arranged the same as French and German, being the easiest method of acquiring a thorough knowledge of the Spanish language. (Revised Edition.)

Bound in paper cover, - - - price 25c.
Bound in boards, cloth back, - - price 35c.

ITALIAN AT A GLANCE,

Uniform in size and style with German, French, and Spanish, being the most simple method of learning the Italian language. (Revised Edition.)

Bound in paper cover, - - - price 25c.
Bound in boards, cloth back, - - price 35c.

ALL THE ABOVE BOOKS SENT POSTPAID ON RECEIPT OF PRICE.

NEW AND POPULAR BOOKS SENT FREE OF POSTAGE AT THE PRICES ANNEXED.

THE MODERN BARTENDER'S GUIDE.

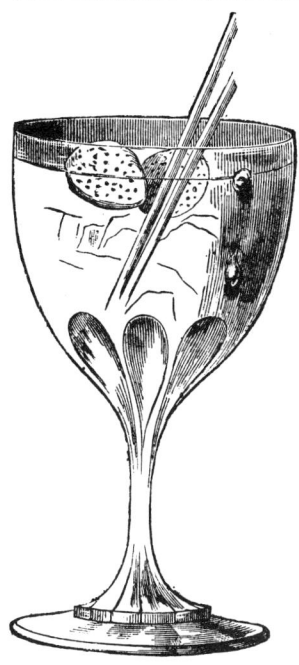

A new and thoroughly reliable work on the correct method of mixing fancy drinks, as they are served to-day at the principal Bar Rooms of New York, and other leading cities of the Union. This is not a rehash of all the fancy drinks of the last generation, but a modern work on modern mixtures. It contains all the Punches, Slings, Fizzes, etc., which form the specialties of the leading Bartenders, besides all the favorite drinks which are in demand everywhere.

With this work any Bartender can become an expert in a very short time.

To which is added receipts for making all kinds of

BITTERS, CORDIALS AND SYRUPS, CONCENTRATED FRUIT SYRUPS, FRUIT BRANDIES, FRUIT WINES, LIQUEURS, MINERAL WATERS, TABLE BEERS, CIDERS, BRANDIES, TEMPERANCE DRINKS, Etc., Etc.

A Handsome Illustrated Cover. Price   - -   50 cts.
Bound in Full Cloth, Gilt. Price - - - - 75 cts.

BURDETT'S DUTCH DIALECT RECITATIONS AND READINGS.

Being No. 1 of the Burdett Series of Recitations and Readings. This collection of amusing and laughable Recitations embraces all the newest and most successful pieces, original and selected, with which the celebrated reader, Jas. S. Burdett, invariably "brings down the house," besides a host of other Dialect Selections in general use by other leading Public Readers of the present day.

CONTENTS.

Barbara Frietchie.................
Betsey und I Hafe Bust Ub.............
Charge of de "Dutch Brigade," The............
Deitsche Advertisement................
Dem Old Dimes Habbiness and dem New........
Der Baby.................
Der Dog und der Lobster....................
Der Drummer..................
Der Good Lookin' Shnow...................
Der Moon....................
Der Mule Shtood on der Steamboat Deck.........
Der Nighd Pehind Gristmas...................
Der Schleighride.....................
Der Wreck of der Hezberus...................
Dhree Skaders....................
Don'd Feel Too Big..................
Dot Funny Leetle Baby................
Dot Lambs vot Mary Haf Got............
Dot Leedle Loweeza................
Dot Loaf of Bread..............
Dot Shly Leedle Raskel..............
Dot Surprise Party...................
Dot Young Viddow Clara..................
Dutchman's Experience...................
Dutchman's Dolly Varden, A..................
Dutchman's Telephone, A.................
Dutchman's Testimony in a Steamboat Case, A...
Dutchman and the Raven, The................
Dutch Recruiting Officer, A..................
Dutch Sermon, A..................
Dutchman's Serenade, The................
Dutchman's Snake, The..................
Dutchman and the Yankee................
Dyin' Vords of Isaac....................
Ein Deutsches Lied.................
Fine Old Dutch Gentleman, The..............
Fritz und I.................
German Speech of Herr Hans Yager, The......
Go Vay, Becky Miller, Go Vay.............
Gosling's Wife Snores................
Hans Breitman and the Turners................
Hans and Fritz..................
Hans in a Fix.................
Han's Midnight Excuses...................
Hans Sourcrout on Signs and Omens..............
Home Again...................
How a Dutchman was Done................
How Hans Yager Enjoyed the Opera.............

How Jake Schneider Went Blind..............
How "Sockery" Set a Hen...............
How the Dutchman Killed the Woodchuck........
Initiated as a Member of the United Order of Half-Shells................
Isaac Rosenthal on the Chinese Question........
I Vash So Glad I Vash Here...............
Jew's Troubles, A.................
Katrina Likes Me Poody Well................
Katrina's Visit to New York...............
Life, Liberty, and Lager..................
Lookout Mountain, 1863—Beutelshbach, 1880....
Little Yawcob Strauss..................
Maud Muller.................
Marriage Ceremony, The.................
Mine Katrine.................
Mine Shildren..................
Mr. Schmidt's Mistake...............
Mygel Snyder's Barty...................
Oration on the "Labor" Question...............
Overcoat He Got, The................
Pretzel's Speech Before the Illinois Assembly....
Romeo and Juliet..................
Schlausheimer's Alarming-Clock................
Schlausheimer Don't Gonciliate................
Schlosser's Ride...................
Schneider's Ride...................
Schnitzel's Philosopede.................
Schneider Sees Leah.................
Schneider's Tomatoes.................
Shake's Telephone..................
Shoo Flies..................
Shonny, Don'd You Hear Me?..............
Shonny Schwartz....................
Snyder's Nose....................
Sockery Kadacut's Kat.................
Teaching Him the Business................
Temperance Speech..................
Tiamonds on der Prain..................
To a Friend Studying German................
Touching Appeal, A.................
"Two Tollar".............
Vas Bender Henshpecked................
Yawcob's Losing Deal..................
Yankee and the Dutchman's Dog, The........
Yoppy Varder unt Hees Droubles................
Zwei Larger................

In a handsome Illustrated cover. Price 25 cents.

Any of the above Books sent Postpaid to any address on Receipt of Price.

NEW AND POPULAR BOOKS SENT FREE OF POSTAGE AT THE PRICES ANNEXED.

BRUDDER GARDNER'S
STUMP SPEECHES
AND
Comic Lectures,
CONTAINING

some of the Best Hits of the Leading Negro Delineators of the Present Day, Comprising the Most Amusing and Side-Splitting Contribution of Oratorical Effusions which has ever been Produced to the Public.

A SURE CURE FOR THE BLUES.

Bound in Illustrated Paper Cover,

Price 25 cents.

THE COMPLETE DEBATER.
CONTAINING
DEBATES, OUTLINES OF DEBATES, AND QUESTIONS FOR DISCUSSION, TO WHICH IS ADDED AN ORIGINAL AND COMPLETE DEBATE ON FREE TRADE.

In addition to these are a large collection of debatable questions. The authorities to be referred to for information being given at the close of every debate throughout the work, making it the most complete work on the subject ever published. Containing the following complete Debates:
1. Is the Protection afforded to American industry by duties on Imports beneficial to the American people?—2. Which is of the greatest Benefit to his Country, the Warrior, the Statesman, or the Poet?—3. Are the Mental Capacities of the Sexes equal?—4. Is Capital Punishment justifiable?—5. Does Morality increase with Civilization?—6. Has the Stage a Moral Tendency?—7. Which was the greater Poet, Shakespeare or Milton?—8. Which has done the greater Service to Mankind, the Printing Press or the Steam Engine?—9. Which does the most to make the Orator—Knowledge, Nature, or Art?

Bound in boards, with cloth back, containing over 200 pages..........................Price 50 cents.

THE STANDARD AUTHORITY.

BYRNE'S LUMBER AND LOG BOOK,
READY-RECKONER AND PRICE BOOK.

By OLIVER BYRNE, Civil, Military, and Mechanical Engineer.

"BYRNE'S READY-RECKONER" is the most concise, complete, and correct work ever issued. Among its contents will be found Tables arranged to show values from one-sixteenth of a cent each upwards; Tables of Board, Scantling, and Plank Measure; Logs reduced to Board Measure; Round Timber when Squared; also Spars and other Timber; Wages and Board by the Week; Interest Tables at .06 and .07 per cent from $1.00 to $30,000; Compound Interest Tables from 1 to 25 years; Standard Weights and Measures; Gold and Silver Coins of the United States; Value of Foreign Coins as fixed by the Laws of the United States; Foreign measures of Length compared with American; "How Interest Eats"; Laws of each State and Territory regarding Rates of Interest and Penalties for Usury; Statutes of Limitations in the several States and Territories, etc., etc.

All Comprised in one volume 18mo, of 180 pages, bound in illustrated board covers, extra cloth back, title in gold.   Price 35 cents.

MADAME ZADKIEL'S
PERFECT FORTUNE TELLER,
CONTAINING

Answers, Alectromancy, Astragalomancy, Augury by Dice, Calender of Fate, Cauls, Candle Omens, Charm of the Rose, of Affection, of the Dove, of the Myrtle, of the Candles, of the Ribbon, concerning Birth of Children, Fortune Telling with Dominoes, Cards and Dice; Dreams and full explanations; Palmistry, Napoleon's Oraculum, Physiognomy, the Abracadabra Amulet, the Events of Life, The Egyptian Circle, the Mystic Spell, etc., etc. With Illustrations, and a double-page Chart printed in Colors. 156 pages, 16 mo. Bound in handsomely illuminated board covers. Price 35 cents.

Napoleon's Oraculum; or, Book of Fate.

Including the true Interpretation of Dreams, Visions, and Omens of the Wedding Day. By the Countess of Blessington. The Egyptian Circle; or, Ancient Wheel of Fortune. Illustrated, etc., etc. 48 pages 16mo, paper covers. Price 10 cents.

Madame De Stael's Dream Book and Fortune Teller

With Illustrated Charts. Also, the Signification of Dreams, expressed in numbers; Physiognomy, Signs and Auguries, etc., etc. 48 pages 16mo, paper covers. Price 10 cents.

Any of the above Books sent Postpaid to any address on Receipt of Price.

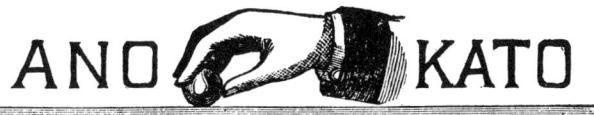

THE NEW ELECTRIC TOY.
ANO KATO.

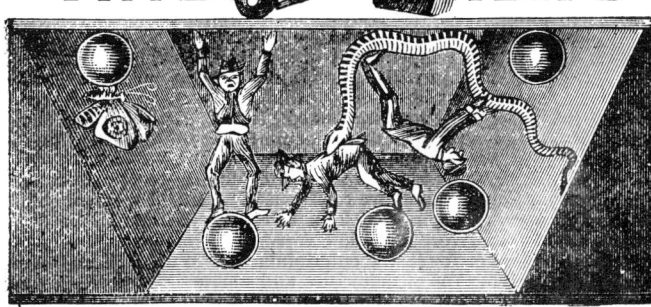

The best recent novelty in the toy line. Useful to the student in electricity, and a source of never-ending entertainment to the young and old. The annexed cut represents the toy in operation. The figures are jointed, and men, snake, butterfly and balls, move rapidly up and down, and form curious attitudes and combinations. It cannot get out of order, and will last for years. It is enclosed in a neat wood box with a sliding cover. It can be sent by mail or express, price, each 75c. We will not be responsible for the safe deliverance if sent by mail.

THE AMERICAN SAFETY RAZOR.

For the past half-century the most celebrated cutlers of the world have occupied themselves with the task of discovering a razor which would dispense with a loss of at least one hour daily in badly ventilated barber-shops, and with which invalids, aged and extremely nervous men could shave themselves with positive safety and comfort.

DIRECTIONS FOR USE.—The new Safety Razor consists of a short blade of the finest tempered steel, cased in a nickel-plated metal safety-visor. When shaving, the visor rests upon the surface to be shaved, while the blade is drawn easily and leisurely over it. As the soap accumulates during the operation it is removed by dipping the entire instrument into water, instead of wiping on paper, as in the old method. To sharpen the blade remove it from the safety-visor, and place it in the socket with handle, which accompanies each razor.

If we could not recommend this article we would not offer it. Samples boxed, by mail, postage paid, $1.00.

LANTERN CHARM.

If any of our customers are not satisfied with this Watch after one month's trial, we will exchange it for any other goods that we advertise. We guarantee it to give satisfaction.

Price of Watch in Box, as above...$3 50
" Nickel-plated Steel Chain..25
" Gold-plated Lantern Charm, with Red, White or Blue Glass...............25
Cost of Postage and Registering...30
We will send all complete for...4 00

Exact Size.

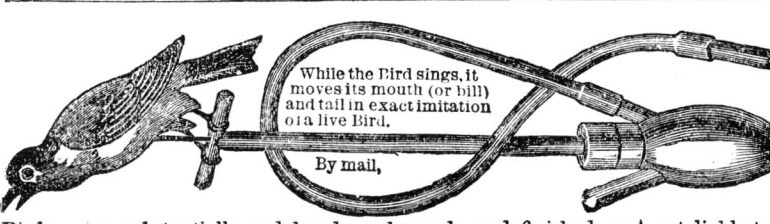

While the Bird sings, it moves its mouth (or bill) and tail in exact imitation of a live Bird.

By mail.

THE AMERICAN SONGSTER.

The greatest novelty and wonder of the day. They are painted in a variety of bright colors, in almost perfect imitation of life. They sing as clear and liquid as the best Song Birds. Are substantially and handsomely made and finished, and not liable to get out of order. It is highly appreciated by Ladies, who use it to teach birds to sing. It supersedes the Bird Organ, and when used near a bird it will induce it to start up its best notes immediately. Each Bird is made life size. Packed in a neat box with full directions sent by mail for 75 cents.

KICKING MULE.

The Mule and Rider being brought into position, a slight touch on a knob at the base causes the mule to kick and throw the rider over his head. One of the best toys ever placed on the American market. Price, each, $1.00.

[N. B.—Prices in this Catalogue cancel all others previously issued by us.]

THE SENSITIVE MERMAID.

A truly wonderful article. This genuine curiosity is very amusing and instructive. If you lay it on the palm of your hand it will begin to squirm and wriggle, continually rolling over and over and curling in all manner of shapes, its antics depending upon the temperament of the person. It won't keep quiet, and pleases alike both young and old.

"If you wish to know the temperament of a person, lay the mermaid in the palm of his left hand, and you will be delighted to see it move of itself. If a person is of a sanguine temperament, it rolls itself quickly up and falls from the hand; if he is of a choleric temperament it rolls itself up and runs towards the arm; if he is of a phlegmatic temperament, it rolls itself up and remains lying; but if he is of a sanguine-choleric temperament, it seldom moves.

Our illustration is a correct representation of this amusing and instructive novelty. The upper portion of the figure represents a beautiful woman. The lower part of the figure represents a fish. This novelty is pleasing to the eye, and with it one is enabled to divert a whole company its impartial judgment always giving sufficient matter for jocose entertainment. With each mermaid we send a printed sheet giving the peculiarities and characteristics of persons of different temperaments. These explanations of different temperaments in connection with the antics of the mermaid, will prove very entertaining and instructive at evening parties and social entertainments. Send for one, and amuse yourself and friends.

Price, only 10c.; 3 for 25c.; one dozen, 75c., by mail, post-paid.

THE LIGHTNING SAUSAGE, OR THE MAGIC BOLOGNA.

If the stories of some people are true, the history of the sausage would form the basis of a genuine dime novel story. Perhaps many thousand dogs have been butchered, and untold millions of cats slaughtered to satisfy the sausage fiend. But we doubt this, and our respect for the bologna is so great that we have prepared an imitation sausage, which is the greatest joke out. Apparently, it is simply a small package, about two inches square. Hand it to a friend to open, saying it is something nice, and on his complying, a huge bologna, ten times the size of the package, springs out like lightning, causing intense astonishment on all sides. This "sausage" will not spoil by keeping, and will create fun for a lifetime. If you want to try the nerves of a friend, and enjoy a good laugh at the same time, send for the "Lightning Sausage."

Price 15c.; 2 for 25c.

THE SURPRISE CIGAR CASE.

Just out, and the best practical joke of the season. It is to all appearance an ordinary cigar-case made of handsome imitation pebbled leather and is of proper size for carrying in the pocket. Double gilt bands and the word "Segars" ornament the top of the case, and there is nothing suspicious-looking about it, but the joke is hidden inside. Ask your friend to have a segar, at the same time handing him the case. As he attempts to open it an ugly looking gorilla six inches in height suddenly pops up and confronts the astonished victim. It is a capital joke and will be fully appreciated by any one upon whom it has been perpetrated. Agents can make money rapidly selling them; in fact they sell themselves, as any one who has been caught by this cunning device is sure to want one for use among his friends. Price, 25c.; 3 for 60c.; one dozen, $2.00, by mail, post-paid; three dozen, by express, $5.00; six dozen, $9.50; twelve dozen, $18.00.

THE BEST POCKET COAT AND HAT RACK.

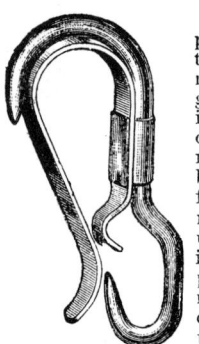

The device represented in this circular, and the purposes for which it is intended, are so well illustrated that little need be said on the subject of its merit. If this does not strike the beholder at a glance, he will learn nothing from a long study of it. Everybody who has travelled in railroad cars, or who has visited theatres, or other places of public resort, has realized that in such places, except possibly in parlor cars, there are no facilities provided for disposing of the overcoat and hat. There are many of projections, but no hooks or pegs that may be utilized for this purpose. The Coat and Hat Rack is intended to act as the connecting link between these projections and the overcoat, when the heated atmosphere renders it burdensome, and the hat, which custom demands shall be lifted from the head in all places of public resort, and personal comfort requires removal when traveling. When not in use, it may be folded into compact form, and carried, without inconvenience, in the vest pocket.

FOLDED. OPEN FOR USE.

For convenience of handling and also of affording a ready means of display, the Racks are arranged on cards 7x9 inches, illustrated with a cut showing the device in action, and the title. One dozen are securely fastened to each card.   Sample Rack by mail, 15 cents. Per dozen, $1.00.

"The Waterbury."

HOW THE WATERBURY WATCH IS REGARDED.

The inventor has given several years of constant toil to perfecting this Watch. It is made on scientific principles, which have been thoroughly tested. Letters patent have been granted in ten foreign countries. We know of leading business men of large wealth, who own watches that cost from one to three hundred dollars, who now carry a Waterbury Watch. These gentlemen take pride in showing their friends the result that has been achieved by skill and fine machinery in producing a Watch for $4 00 that will keep nearly as correct time as a Watch that costs almost one hundred times as much.

How the Watches are Tested at the Factory.—When the Watches are finished they are taking to the Testing Room. Here are a large number of adjustable racks, each having 144 apartments. The Watches having been wound and set are placed in the apartments of these racks. The inspector then places a cover over the rack, so that it is impossible for the watches to fall out. For **six days** these watches are wound each night and morning, and are made to run in different positions. The rack swings on pivots, so that the watches are run in a perpendicular position, at an angle, then on their faces, and last on their backs. They are inspected each day. Any watch not coming up to the inspector's standard is returned to the work-room again.

In this new, **solid plate** movement the position of the regulator has been changed; it will be found projecting beyond the plate, immediately under the bezel holding the glass. The danger of injuring the hair-spring in regulating is hereby obviated, which is a most desirable feature in this full dial watch.

All watches are cased in cases made of an entirely new **metal** called Nickel-Silver. For the purpose, this metal is the nearest to silver yet attained, will wear white, and, although more expensive than the one abandoned, we shall make no change in the price of the watch.

Each watch will be put up in our handsome new improved spring-box, satin-lined, which will carry the watch safely through the mails. Price, complete in box, $3.50.

Protection Against SUN, WIND, DUST, AND HEAT.

SCHWEIZER'S ENGLISH EYE PROTECTORS.

Indispensable for Drivers, Farmers, Workmen, Fishermen, Bicyclists, Boatmen, Yachting, Lawn Tennis, Tourists, and Sporting-men in general, are made of White, Blue, Green and London Smoke-colored glass, each pair is put up in a neat tin box.

Per pair, by mail.................................20 cts.
3 pair.......................................50 cts.
1 dozen pair................................$1 50

THE BLISS TELEPHONE.
CHEAP ENOUGH FOR A TOY AND GOOD ENOUGH FOR PRACTICAL USE.

This simple little instrument is sure to meet a general want in supplying the place of Speaking Tubes and Electric Bells at less than one-quarter of the cost. While it may safely be warranted to work a mile, its principal recommendation lies in the readiness with which it may be put to practical use in connecting separate rooms in the same or adjoining building, such as Manufactories, Shops, Stores, Dwellings, Offices, &c., &c.

It has been thoroughly tested, and its satisfactory working—together with the low price at which it is offered, must insure its general use.

Complete directions for setting up, also **100 feet of composition wire accompany** each Telephone. Additional wire will be furnished by us at the rate of twenty-five cents per hundred feet.

Price complete, $1.00.

USEFUL AND AMUSING NOVELTIES FOR THE CITY, COUNTRY AND FARMERS' FIRESIDE.

Buttons can be Attached Instantly, Without Sewing.

FOR BOOTS, SHOES AND CLOTHING.

THE PERFECT BUTTON FASTENER.—Every person who wears a button shoe, knows that the buttons are often insecurely fastened, and that they fly off at the slightest provocation. When one button gives way the whole row frequently follows, and nothing looks more slovenly and awkward than a shoe partially buttoned. These button fasteners will be hailed with delight by all wearers of button shoes; the buttons can be attached instantly without sewing. By their use the buttons will never come off, stretch out, or look untidy as when sewed on. Another advantage of these fasteners is that they can easily be removed from one pair of shoes to another, and can also be used for clothing, saving the time of sewing on buttons. They are warranted not to hurt the foot, injure the stocking, or the finest dress upon which they may be placed When once used in the family they will never do without them. Willie's or Mary's shoes can be fixed in an instant, thus doing away with the bother of sewing on the buttons. Each box contains 36 fasteners, 36 shoe buttons and 1 handsome new style nickel shoe-buttoner. Sample box 25 cts.; 3 boxes 60 cts.; one dozen boxes $1 75. By mail, post-paid.

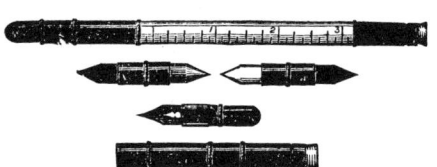

COMBINATION PENCIL AND PEN-HOLDER.—

The latest Parisian novelty. Eight articles in one. This is a most ingenious and useful novelty, containing a Penholder and Pen, 1 Lead Pencil, 1 Slate Pencil, 1 Blue Crayon, 1 Red Crayon, 1 Ink Eraser, 1 Three-inch Measure, being divided into halves, quarters, eighths and sixteenths of an inch, so that it is possible to measure the smallest spaces; and 1 Metre or French Measure. It thus combines eight different articles for different uses, and will prove most handy and convenient to clerks, bookkeepers, school-children, travellers, workingmen, the housewife and all who desire to carry in small compass and ready at a moment's notice the instruments necessary to produce accurate ruling, shading, spacing, drawing and erasures in combination with the ever indispensable pen and pencil. The different articles all fit neatly into the handsome metal holder, and may thus be safely carried about in the pocket and cannot get lost or broken.

Our illustrations show the combination open and closed. When closed it occupies no more space than an ordinary lead pencil. The changes from one article to another can be made instantly, all of them fitting closely into the case.

Combinations inferior to this one retail for 25 cents. We have placed this one at the low price of 15 cents, and we expect to sell 100,000 of them during the next six months. Agents can sell them as fast as they can hand them out, as every man, woman or child in the land needs one. Price, all complete, only 15 cents; 2 for 25 cents; one dozen, $1 00, by mail, post-paid; one gross by express $9 00.

ELECTRIC SLEEVE-BUTTONS.

These beautiful goods are perfect gems, and create a sensation wherever they are shown. They are constructed upon a very novel principle. The figures, as shown in the cut, represent ballet girls, who go through every movement known to the finished danseuse. The ballet-girls are continually in motion, and the sleeve-buttons cannot be held so steady but what these lively dancers will be making some graceful or laughable movement. While the slightest motion of the hand will send them off on a lively gallop, waltz or jig. With a very little practice the wearer can cause them to perform a variety of amusing terpsichorean feats. They are the **cutest** sleeve-buttons ever invented. Everybody is anxious to get them at any price. You can have any amount of solid fun with these electric figures; their actions are life-like, and it is almost as good as going to theatre to see them dance. The buttons are very handsome, gold finished, and the figures are covered with glass. If you want the **tallest** sleeve-button out. send for the electric ballet-girls. Price, 50 cents per pair.

UNIVERSAL POCKET PUZZLE.

This puzzle is made of elegant silver-nickel wire, bent in an endless spiral form. Linked in this wire is a little ring, and the question is, how to get it off. You can do it as quick as a flip; if you only know how· but if you don't —well, the best you can do is to send for one and learn.

Price 15 cents each.

NOVELTIES IN HEAVY GILT AND BEST ROLLED HEAVY GOLD PLATE JEWELRY.

Having had continual inquiries for Jewelry from our patrons for the past several years, we have now concluded to keep a small line of such as we think will meet the wishes of the majority of them. They will all be of the latest and most approved styles; they are made of the best metals, heavy electro gilt, and will wear for years without tarnishing. In looks it is almost impossible to detect them from solid gold jewelry, and in price they are about one-twentieth cheaper. They are excellent goods for Weddings, Birthdays, Christmas, New Year, Philopene, or suitable presents for any occasion or season of the year. If we find these goods are satisfactory to our patrons, we will continually add to our stock new styles as they come out, and will advertise them in our catalogue that follows. The Chains we keep are all full sizes in length and well finished.

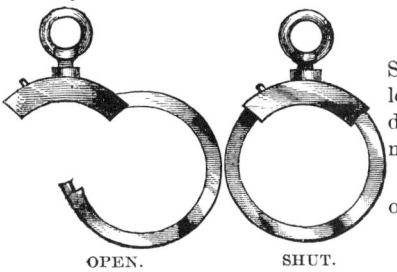

OPEN.   SHUT.

Something entirely new and very desirable, the Patent Security Ring for Watch Chains in place of the ordinary Bar, locking the Chain fast to the button hole, thereby prevent dropping the Watch or its being taken by pick-pockets. We furnish this Patent Ring on all our Watch Chains.

One illustration shows the Ring closed as on vest, the other open ready to attach.

New, useful and showy articles for men, in the way of Cigar Clippers and Watch Charms combined. They are made of Heavy Rolled Gold Plate, each with a fine steel knife for clipping the ends of Cigars and work with perfect ease.

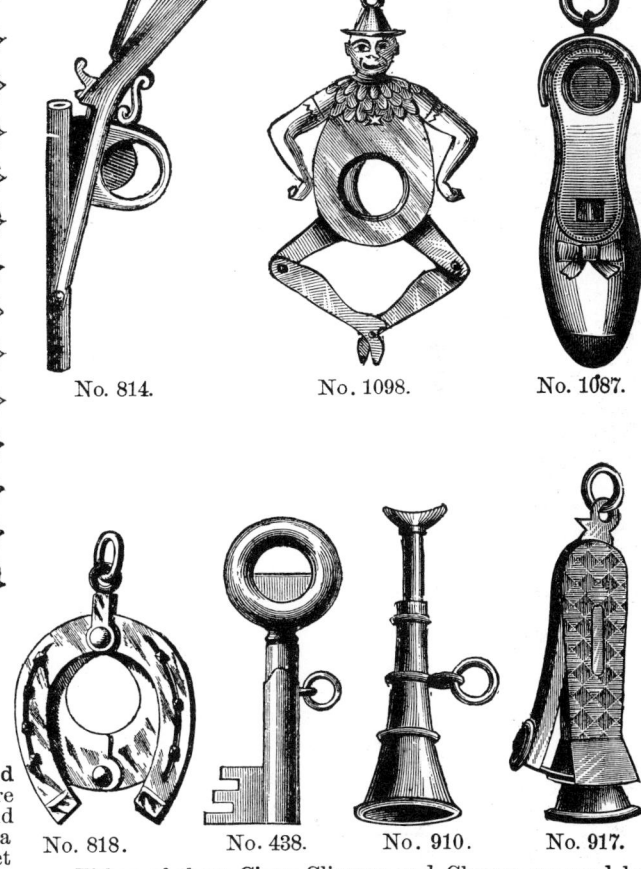

No. 814.   No. 1098.   No. 1087.

No. 1000.—**Ladies' Neck Chain and Charm.**—The best Gold Plate, Fire Gilt Finish and warranted to stand Acid, and wear for years. We have a variety of different patterns. Each set is packed in a neat box lined with satin.
3 for $3.75.   Each, by mail, $1.50

No. 818.   No. 438.   No. 910.   No. 917.

Either of these Cigar Clippers and Charms we send by mail postage paid for 50 cents each.

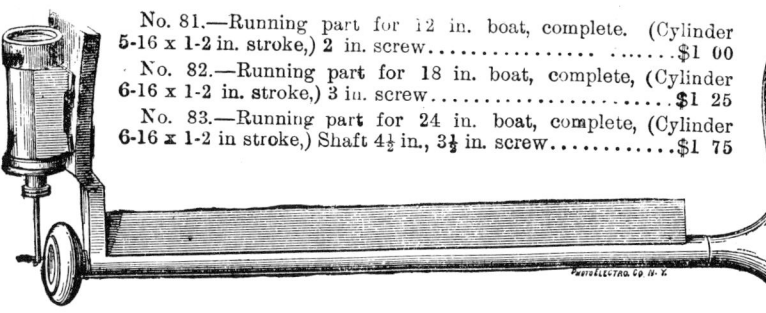

This cut represents our **RUNNING PARTS FOR PROPELLERS** (Steam Chest, Cylinder, Shaft, Screw.) Prepaid, by mail, in paper box.

No. 81.—Running part for 12 in. boat, complete. (Cylinder 5-16 x 1-2 in. stroke,) 2 in. screw.................$1 00
No. 82.—Running part for 18 in. boat, complete, (Cylinder 6-16 x 1-2 in. stroke,) 3 in. screw.................$1 25
No. 83.—Running part for 24 in. boat, complete, (Cylinder 6-16 x 1-2 in stroke,) Shaft 4½ in., 3½ in. screw.............$1 75

No. 84.—Running part for 30 in. boat, complete, (Cylinder 6-16 x 1-2 in. stroke,) Shaft 5 in. 3½ in. screw.............................$2 00
No. 85.—Running part for 36 in. boat, complete, (Cylinder 1-2 x 1-2 in. stroke,) Shaft 6 in. 4 in. Screw..............................$2 50

Boilers of all the goods we make also made to order. Any other parts of our goods at proportionate prices.

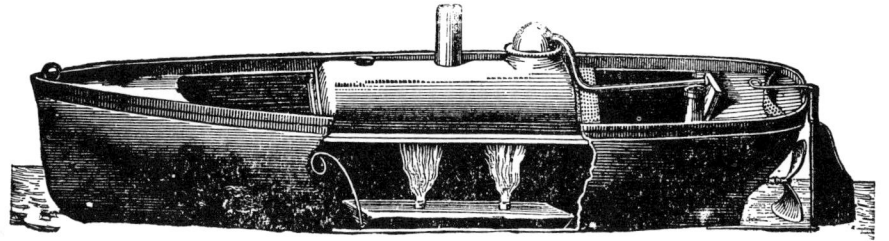

This sectional cut shows the mechanical arrangements in all of the propellers.

No. 50.   No. 57.

No. 50. **The Little Pet.**—Thirteen inches long. Boiler, stack and hull of bright brass. Engine 5-16 bore x ¼ inch stroke; very fast; will run about twenty minutes. In wood box, by mail,........Each $3 25

The following propellers are 26 inches long; hull of heavy brass, handsomely painted; copper boilers, with flue · are very fast and will run about one hour.

No. 57. Plain deck, very fine..........each, $15 00 | No. 59. Very high finish and extra painting,
" 58. Plain deck, tub, boiler........ "   18 00 | Each...................... $20 00

We also make them to order up to 40 inches long and of any finish desired.

No. 52.—**STEAM YACHTS, &c.**

Without Express Charges

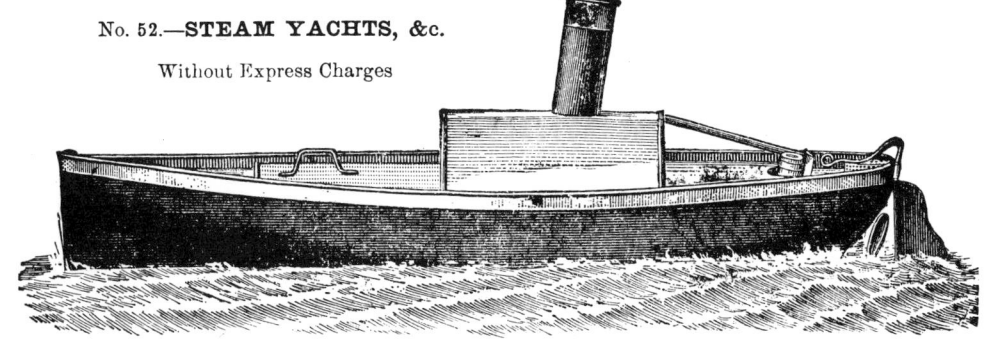

No. 52. 19 inch hull, plain, low deck, will run 30 minutes.............................Each, $4 50
" 53.   "   "   "   "   larger, will run 35 minutes........................... "   5 00
" 54.   "   hull, fancy deck, will run 45 minutes................................. "   6 00
" 55.   "   "   "   flue and tubular boiler, very fast, will run 45 minutes.... "   7 00
" 55 A. Flue and tubular boiler, fancy ornamented, will run 45 minutes.............. "   8 00

The decks 54, 55 and 55 A are of the same style as on cut above, representing Nos. 57 to 59.

MINIATURE STEAM LOCOMOTIVE AND RAILWAY.
ONE OF THE LATEST AND BEST NOVELTIES.

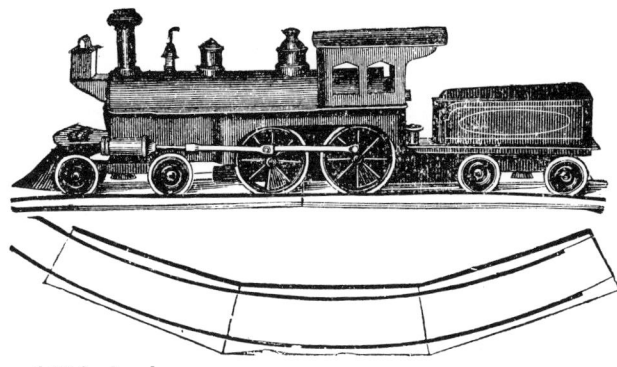

A practical toy, and perfectly safe. Cannot explode. So simple that a child 10 years of age can run one and keep it in working order by following the printed directions. Amusing and instructive to the whole family. Made in the most careful manner. Every Engine thoroughly tested with steam, and in good running order before leaving the Factory. A great attraction for store windows. Will run from twenty to thirty minutes, the driving wheels making from ten to fifteen revolutions per second, the exhaust steam escaping from the smoke-stack. Will draw a train of cars, giving it the exact appearance of a train on a large road. Engine and track may be packed in a space 5x7 inches, and 25 inches long.

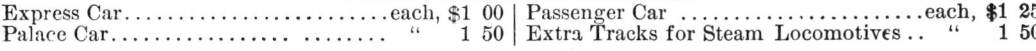

4 wheel Locomotive with Circular Track..Price complete,	$6 00
Full Nickel-plated 4 wheel Locomotive with Circular Track.................... " "	9 00

Tracks 4 feet 4 inches in diameter.

Express Car......................each,	$1 00	Passenger Car ....each,	$1 25
Palace Car.................. .... "	1 50	Extra Tracks for Steam Locomotives.. "	1 50

No. 19-0.—FINE MECHANICAL LOCOMOTIVES.

Length, 8¼ inches; height, 5¼ inches. The above cut of our Mechanical Locomotive, which the trade will pronounce to be the most perfect toy of the kind ever offered at so low a price. It is neatly and strongly made, and works perfectly well. Each one in a neat box.................Price, $1 00.

No. 19-1.—Length, 9½ inches; height, 7 inches. Each one in a neat box.
Price, $1 75

No. 19-3.—Large Fine Locomotive, length, 11¼ inches; height, 8½ inches. Each one in a neat box...................Price, $3 00

19-2—WHISTLING LOCOMOTIVES.

These locomotives are the same sizes as those mentioned above and are provided with our *patent whistling arrangement,* so that when running they give forth a sharp, shrill, rapid whistle, making them among the most attractive and salable toys ever put upon the market. (See cut.)......Price, each, $3 00

No. 19-4.—Whistler, length, 11¼ inches; height, 8½ inches. Each one in a neat box.
Price, $3 50

IRON FREIGHT TRAIN, "BIG 6," (24 inches long.)

This train is strongly made and neatly painted, and consists of a locomotive, tender, and two cars. Made entirely of iron. A very salable toy. Each train in a strong wood box.   Price, each, $1 00
N. B.—We carry a full stock of Imported Model Steam Locomotives. Price, $5 00 to $75 00 each.

MODEL MACHINE SHOPS. Boxes made of Stained Wood, Varnished, Slide Front and Top, sent only by Express.

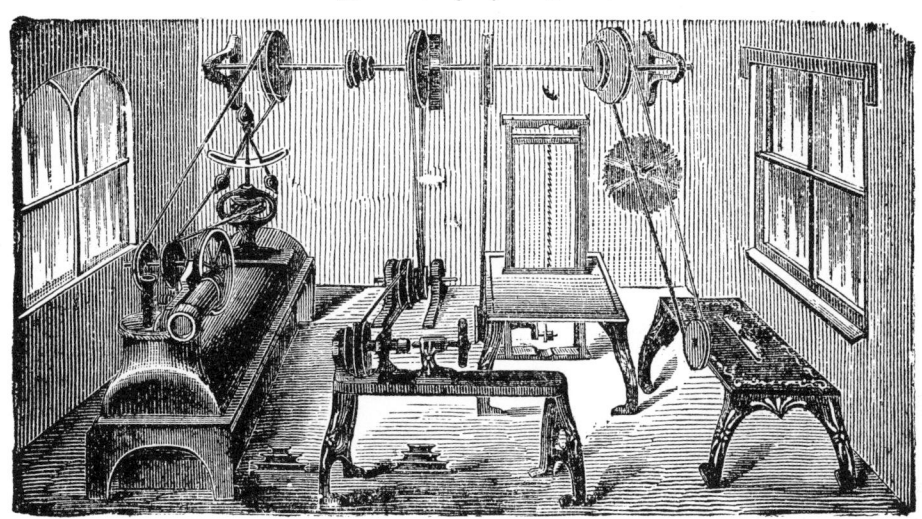

This cut represents a miniature factory or shop. No more practical mode of instruction can possibly be imagined, showing at a glance how machinery is adjusted, and why it runs at different speeds from one shaft.

Machine Shops by Express.

20.—16 in. long, No. 4 Engine, Shaft, Hangers, Lathe......................................$ 4 00 each.
22.—16 in. long, No. 4 Engine, Shaft, Hangers, Lathe, Saw, Grindstone.................... 5 50 "
24.—22 in. long, No. 5 Engine, Shaft, Hangers, Lathe, Saw, Grindstone, Planer............ 7 00 "
26.—26 in. long, No. 7 Engine, Shaft, Hangers, Lathe, 2 Saws, Grindstone, Planer, Governor..... 10 00 "
And made to order in all styles and sizes to 40 inches.

MACHINERY, Prepaid by Mail.

Governor, run by belt..............50 cents each.	Governor, run by gear..............60 cents each.
Circular Saw and Table.............50 " "	Turning Lathe....................75 " "
Metal Planer....................75 " "	Grindstone.....................40 " "
Cone Pully to connect with Lathe....20 " "	Hangers for Shafting...............10 " "
Pulleys, $\frac{1}{2}$ inch to $2\frac{1}{2}$ inches, from 2 to 5 " "	

This Cut represents our single pump, No. 16, it is 5 inches long and $4\frac{3}{4}$ inches high, made of metal, takes water by suction, and will throw from 10 to 20 feet. Can be run by any Engine by belt. Packed complete in wood box, $1.50.

This Cut represents our Fire Engines No. 30 to 36. The Boiler is made of copper, with flue, highly polished, and fire box attached. Engine working direct over Pump, takes water by suction through hose, and throws it from nozzle, from 10 to 20 feet. It is $10\frac{5}{8}$ inches long and $8\frac{3}{4}$ inches high. Packed complete in wood box.

No. 30. Single Pump, Furnace, wheels and frame nicely painted, **$5.00**
" 32. " " of Bright Brass, wheels &c., " 6.00
" 34. Double Pump " " " " " " 7.00
" 36. " " " " with doors, " 8.00

PECK & SNYDER'S PERFECT MODEL AND SAFETY WORKING ENGINES.

No. 3.

No. 1.

No. 1. The Wonder, is a model Steam Engine, with solid brass boiler, plated fly wheel and cylinder, and metal pulley wheel for connecting and running small machinery, such as a circular saw, lathe, planer, etc. This little engine will run with great speed for one-half hour at one filling of the boiler. With proper care it will last a life time. It is perfectly safe for any child to handle; the self-acting safety valve renders explosion impossible. By mail, each, 50 cents.

No. 3. **The Small Horizontal.** Length, 6 inches; height, 4½ inches weight, 21 ounces; heavy brass boiler (no unsoldering), regular Safety Valve, Brass Pipe, connecting Boiler and Steam Chest, 1 inch stroke, cross head running on steel ways; more than 1,000 revolutions per minute; has eight times the power of our famous little Half Dollar Engine. Packed in a box complete, with lamp, funnel, &c.

Price, each, by express, $2.50; by mail, post-paid, $2.75;

No. 5. **The Popular Walking Beam Engine** is 7 inches long by 7 inches high, with 4 inch fly-wheel and 4½ inch walking beam. Heavy Riveted Copper Boiler, with Safety Valve. Packed complete, in **box,** with lamp, funnel, &c.

Price, each, by Express, **$5.00**.

No. 5.

NOTE.—This line of Engines are all manufactured by an experienced machinist, and we can safely warrant them to be perfect running models. Full printed directions, accompanies each engine.

PECK & SNYDER'S PERFECT MODEL & SAFETY WORKING ENGINES.

No. 6. **The Holly Steam Engine.** A very skillful manufacturer is now making for us the Holly Steam Engines, which are strong, safe, and easily managed. No engines of the same capacity and finish have been sold for less than $15. The Holly Engine has a strong cast-iron frame on which rests the brass boiler. This is surrounded by a sheet-iron jacket, with brass bands, the same as a locomotive engine. This is a perfect-working steam engine in all its parts. It is just the engine for parents to purchase who wish to interest their children in mechanics. A boy can make a good-sized toy saw-mill, grist-mill or machine-shop, and the Holly Engine will run the machinery with ease, but not for practical use. It is especially adapted for the use of High Schools and Academies, when teaching the principles of the steam engine. It cannot explode, as it has perfect-acting safety valves.

No. 6. (This Cut is less then ¼ size.)

Description—Brass Boiler, 7¼x3¼; Outside Jacket, 8¼x4¼; Fly Wheel, 5¼ diameter; Cylinder, ⅝; Stroke, 1⅜.

Price, by express, **$10.00**.

No. 4. (This Cut less then ¼ size.)

No. 4. The Large Horizontal is 7 inches long by 4 inches high; with 4½ inch fly-wheel; weight 4 lbs. Heavy Riveted Copper Boiler, with Safety Valve. Packed complete, in box, with lamp, funnel, &c.

Price each, by express, **$3.50**; by mail, post-paid, **$4.00**.

No. 2. (Cut ⅛ size.)

No. 2. **The Eclipse Engine.** Points of superiority: Large boiler, running parts best proportioned to get the most work from it; improved lamp, filled without removing wick, 2 "speed" to belt pulley, thus better adapting it for running model (or toy) machinery; boiler held more securely on the stand, and feet of stand have holes in for fastening down. Packed in box, with **lamp**, wicks, &c., By mail, each, **$1.00**.

WORKING MODELS OF STEAM ENGINES AND SEPARATE PARTS.
For description see following pages.

No. 425.   No. 1.   No. 2.

No. 8.

No. 3.

No. 415.

No. 9.

No. 4.

No. 5.   No. 6.   No. 7.

No. 2. Single Action Oscillating Cylinders.

No.		Each.	No.		Each.
1.	$\frac{3}{8}$ inch Bore, 1 inch Stroke	$0 85	3.	$\frac{1}{2}$ inch Bore, $1\frac{1}{2}$ inch Stroke	$1 25
2.	$\frac{3}{8}$ " $1\frac{1}{4}$ "	1 00			

No. 3. Double Action Oscillating Cylinders, with Steam Block and Pivot.

No.		Each.	No.		Each.
1.	$\frac{3}{8}$ inch Bore, 1 inch Stroke	$1 50	7.	$1\frac{1}{4}$ inch Bore, $2\frac{1}{2}$ inch Stroke	6 50
2	$\frac{1}{2}$ " 1 "	2 00	8.	$1\frac{1}{2}$ " 3 "	9 00
3.	$\frac{5}{8}$ " $1\frac{1}{4}$ "	2 50	9.	$1\frac{3}{4}$ " $3\frac{1}{2}$ "	11 25
4.	$\frac{3}{4}$ " $1\frac{1}{2}$ "	2 75	10.	2 " 4 "	14 00
5.	$\frac{3}{4}$ " $1\frac{3}{4}$ "	3 25	11.	3 " 5 "	16 00
6.	1 " 2 "	4 25			

No. 7. Double Action Slide Valve Cylinders.

No.		Each.	No.		Each.
1.	$\frac{3}{8}$ inch Bore, 1 inch Stroke	$2 50	6.	1 " 2 "	4 75
2.	$\frac{1}{2}$ " 1 "	3 00	7.	$1\frac{1}{4}$ inch Bore, $2\frac{1}{2}$ inch Stroke	6 75
3.	$\frac{5}{8}$ " $1\frac{1}{4}$ "	3 25	8.	$1\frac{1}{2}$ " 3 "	9 00
4.	$\frac{3}{4}$ " $1\frac{1}{2}$ "	3 75	9.	$1\frac{3}{4}$ " $3\frac{1}{2}$ "	10 50
5.	$\frac{3}{4}$ " $1\frac{7}{8}$ "	4 25	10.	2 " 4 "	14 00

No. 50. Horizontal Slide Valve Cylinders, lagged with Mahogany.

No.		Each.	No.		Each.
1.	$\frac{3}{4}$ inch Bore, 1 inch Stroke	$6 25	2.	1 inch Bore, 2 inch Stroke	8 00

No. 51. Beautifully Finished Horizontal Slide Valve Cylinders with Cross Heads, Connecting Rod, Parallel Guides and Rollers, on Card—ready for fixing together.

No.		Per Set.	No,		Per Set.
1.	$\frac{3}{4}$ inch Bore, 1 inch Stroke	$8 00	2.	1 inch Bore, 2 inch Stroke	10 50

No. 6. Slide Valve Cylinders for Beam Engines.

No.			No.		
1.	$\frac{3}{4}$ inch Bore, $1\frac{1}{2}$ inch Stroke	$3 25	3.	$1\frac{1}{2}$ inch Bore, 3 inch Stroke	4 50
2.	1 " 2 "	4 00			

No. 52. Beautifully Finished Double Action Slide Valve Cylinders in Gun-metal, Turned and Lacquered.

No.		Each.	No.		Each.
1.	$\frac{1}{2}$ inch Bore, $1\frac{1}{2}$ inch Stroke	$4 50	3.	1 inch Bore, 2 inch Stroke	7 50
2.	$\frac{3}{4}$ " $1\frac{1}{2}$ "	6 25			

No. 5. Double Action Slide Valve Cylinders, with Glass Barrel to Cylinder and Glass Cover to Slide Valve Box.

No.		Each.	No.		Each.
1.	$\frac{1}{2}$ inch Bore, 1 inch Stroke	$4 75	2.	$\frac{3}{4}$ inch Bore, $1\frac{1}{2}$ inch Stroke	5 75

No.	Each.	No.	Each.
No. 8.—1. Connecting Forks	$0 75	No. 8.—3. Connecting Forks	1 15
2. "	1 00	4. "	1 25

No. 10. Eccentric, with Band and Rod.

No.		Each.
1.	For No. 1 Slide Valve Cylinder	$0 60
2.	" 2 "	0 75
3	" 3 "	0 85
4.	" 4 "	1 00
5.	" 5 "	1 25
6.	" 6 "	1 50

No. 18. Pulley Wheels.

No.		Each.
1.	Pulley Wheels	$0 25
2.	"	0 30
3.	"	0 45
4.	"	0 55
5.	"	0 75
6.	"	1 00

No. 9. Spring Safety Valves.

No.	Each.
1.	$0 25
2.	0 35
3.	0 45
4.	0 65
5.	0 75
6.	1 00

No. 12. Turned Iron Shaft and Crank.

For No.		Each.
1.	Cylinder	$0 45
2.	"	0 55
3.	"	0 80
4.	"	1 20

No. 14. Glass Water Gauge.

No.		Each.	No.		Each.
1.	Without Taps	$1 25	3.	With three Taps	$2 75
2.	"	1 50	4.	" "	3 50

No. 11. Model Force Pumps, with Eccentrics.

Nos	1	2	3	4
Price, each	$3 50	4 00	4 50	5 00

No. 17. Governors.

Nos	1	2	3	4
Price, each	$2 25	2 75	4 00	5 25

No. 15. Spring Lever Safety Valve.

Nos	1	2	3	4
Price, each	$2 00	3 00	3 25	4 50

No. 22. Straight Water Taps.

Nos	1	2	3	4
Price, each, seconds.	$0 25	0 30	0 40	0 50
Price, each, best	$0 35	0 40	0 50	0 60

No. 21. Bent Water Taps.

Nos	1	2	3	4
Price, each, seconds.	$0 25	0 30	0 40	0 50
Price, each, best	$0 40	0 45	0 55	0 65

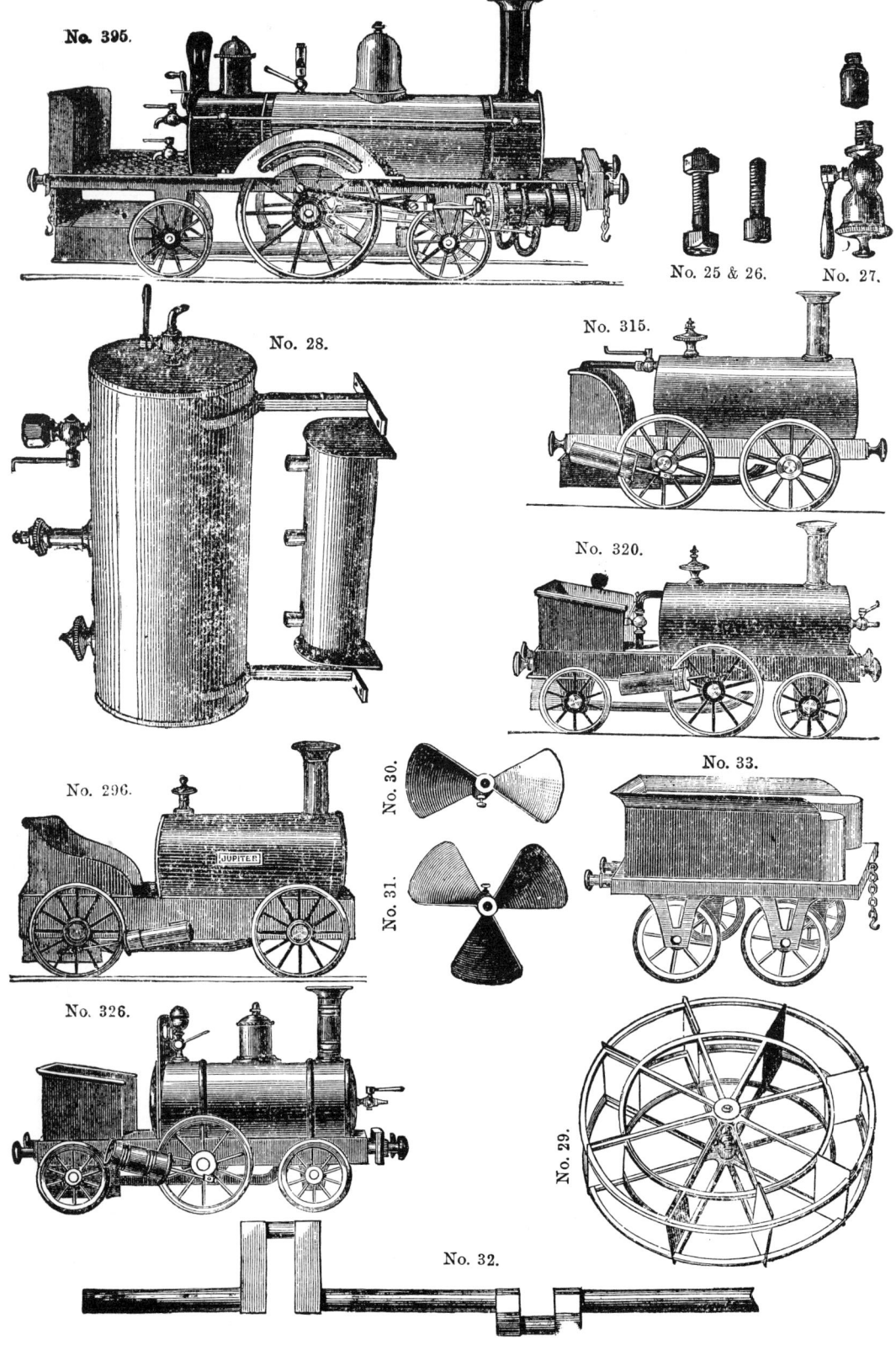

PRICES OF LOCOMOTIVES, TENDERS, BOILERS AND PARTS OF ENGINES.

For illustrations see opposite page.

No. 296.—**Large Size Green Japanned Locomotive,** on 4 brass flanged wheels, 2 brass cylinders, safety valve, and steam tap ....each, $3 00

" 315. Locomotives, all bright brass, with spring safety valve and steam tap........ " 7 00

" 320. " bright Brass Boiler, 2 in. diameter, 4 in. long, on japanned bed plate with tender, 2 cylinders, 6 brass flanged wheels, steam tap, water tap, and safety valve, complete, with lamp........each, 8 00

" 326. Locomotive copper boiler, with bright brass bands, 4 in. long, 2½ in. diameter, with steam dome, safety valve, whistle, water tap and steam tap, on bright brass bed-plate, 2 cylinders, 6 brass-flanged wheels, buffers and spirit lamp........each 10 50

" 395. **Locomotive Engine,** on 6 brass wheels, boiler, 2½ in. diameter, 8½ in, long, fitted with starting lever, 2 gauge taps, wind guard, 2 steam domes, safety valve, whistle, cylinders, ⅝-inch bore, 1¼-inch stroke, 2 eccentrics, waste steam to blow through funnel, entire length, 14-inch, to run either backwards or forwards........each 28 00

" 415. **Screw Engine,** bright copper boiler, 5 in. long, 3¾ in. wide, 3 in. deep, safety valve, pair of double action oscillating cylinders, ½ in. bore, 1 in. stroke, steel crank, water and steam taps, steam pipes, with screw and all necessary fittings, on mahogany stand........each, 28 00

" 425. **Superior Screw Engine,** with one slide valve cylinder, 1 in. bore, 1¼ in. stroke, with quadrant and reversing lever, heavy driving wheel, bright copper boiler, 7 in. long, 5 in. wide, 4½ in. deep, with steam dome, steam tap, safety valve, man-hole, and two gauge taps, with 3 inch screw propeller and spirit lamp, on mahogany stand, each, 40 00

No. 33. Locomotive Tenders.

Beautifully Japanned and shaped, on four brass flanged wheels, with brass buffers.

No.				Each.
1.	4½ inches long,	3½ inches wide,	on 1¾ inch diameter wheels........	$3 00
2.	6 "	4 "	2 "	4 75
3.	7½ "	4½ "	2½ "	6 00

PECK & SNYDER, 126, 128 & 130 Nassau Street, New York.

Importers and Dealers in English Toy Locomotive Engines and Parts.

No. 25. Nuts and Bolts........No. 1, $1.60, No. 2, $2.00, No. 3, $2 50, per dozen.

No. 26. Machine Screws, assorted sizes........per dozen, $0 20

A Plate with five Holes and Taps for Cutting Threads........$1.75 each.

No. 27. Lubricators.

Nos.	00	0	1	2	3	4	5	6
Price each........	12c.	15c.	18c.	20c.	25c.	30c.	35c.	85c.

No. 28. Boilers for Engines.

Brass Boiler with stop cock, steam pipe, safety valve, and spirit lamp on brass supports.

No.		Each.	No.		Each
1.	1 inch diameter, 4 inch long........	$2 25	3.	2½ inch diameter, inch long........	$4 25
2.	2¼ " 5½ "	3 25			

Brass Boiler with 2 gauge taps, stop cock, manhole, lever safety valve, steam pipe, and spirit lamp.

No.		Each.	No.		Each.
4.	3 inch diameter, 9½ inch long........	$6 75	6.	4 inch diameter, 12 inch long........	$12 00
5.	3½ " 11 "	9 00	7.	5 " 14 "	18 00

No. 29. Paddle Wheels.

Nos........	1	2	3	4	5	6
Inches........	2¼	2¾	3¼	4½	5	5¾
Price, per pair........	$2 00	2 50	3 50	3 75	4 25	5 00

No. 30. Two-Bladed Screw Propellers.

Nos........	1	2	3	4	5	6	7	8
Inches........	1½	2	2½	3	3½	4	4½	6
Price, each........	20c.	35c.	50c.	65c.	80c.	$1 00	$1 25	$1 50

No. 31. Three-Bladed Screw Propellers.

Nos........	1	2	3	4	5	6	7	8
Inches........	2	2½	3	3½	4	4½	5	6
Price, each........	45c.	65c.	80c.	$1 15	1 40	1 55	1 75	2 00

No. 32. Forged and Turned Iron Cranks (Double).

No.		Each.
1.	½ inch throw for Pair 1 inch stroke cylinders........	$3 00
2.	⅝ " 1¼ "	3 50
3.	¾ " 1½ "	3 75
4.	⅞ " 1¾ "	4 25
5.	1 " 2 "	4 75
6.	1¼ " 2½ "	5 25

No. 34. Forged and Turned Iron Cranks.

No.		Each.	No.		Each.
1.	½ inch throw for 1 inch stroke cylinder..	$0 45	4.	⅞ inch throw for 1¾ inch stroke cylinder.	$1 25
2.	⅝ " 1¼ " ..	0 55	5.	1 " 2 " ..	1 75
3	¾ " 1½ " ..	0 75	6.	1¼ " 2½ " ..	2 25

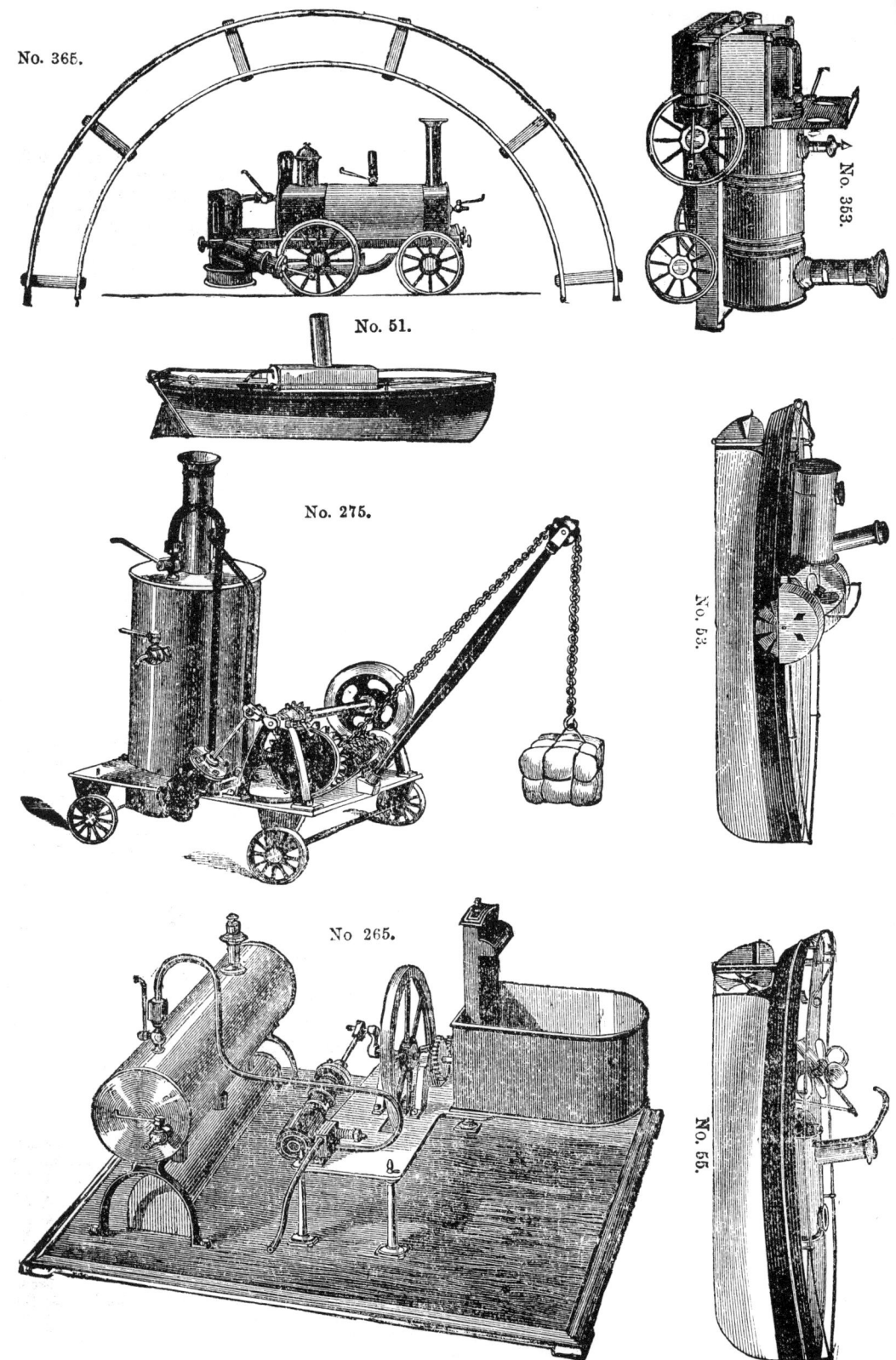

No. 19. BRASS SPIRIT LEVEL.—Very substantially made and very accurate, each one in a strong Tin case.

Diameter	3 inch.	4 inch.	5 inch.	6 inch.
Each	$0 75	1 00	1 25	1 50

No. 20. BOAT COMPASS.—In strong brass case, with slip cover, jeweled, and floating dial.

Diameter	2½ inches.
Each	5 50

No. 23. GOGGLES.—Very useful in driving or on the Plains, Glasses, White, Blue, Green and Smoke....Price, 25 cents.

No. 22. LEATHER COVERED OPERA GLASSES, (all in cases).

Black Leather, good Lenses, medium size.... $3 50
Very best Lenses, medium size, Crescent.... 7 50
" " Fancy trimmings, Gilt Sides.... 9 00
We sell none but fully reliable makes.
Opera and Field Glasses combined (see cut No. 21).... 14 00
" " large size, very fine article.... 23 00
Field or Marine Glasses, medium size, good Lenses.... 9 00
" " " fine ".... 14 00
Field or Marine Glasses, large, size 8 x 5 inches, adopted as the best glass by the U. S. Army and Navy Signal Service.... 30 00
Very long Field Glasses, slender faames, with hinge in centre for adjustment to variation of distances between the pupils of the eye. Extra high power, and very easily carried, being light and of small bulk, though 12 inches long.... 50 00

No. 27. Compound Microscope, of brass, in black walnut case, 6½ inches high, 3 lenses and condensers, jointed rack and pinion adjustment iron stand....each, 6 50

No. 265. **Centrifugal Pump,** connected with Horizontal Engine, brass boiler, fly-wheel, safety valve, taps, oscillating cylinder, cogwheels, &c., on mahogany stand....each, $17 00

No. 275. **Model Crane Engine,** with vertical brass boiler, 2½ in. diameter by 4½ in. high, double action oscillating cylinder, ½-in. bore, 1-in. stroke, cog wheels, fly wheel, brake and starting lever, brass gib, safety valve, and brass chain, with spirit lamp. Each.... 21 00

No. 353. **Bright Copper Locomotive** on bright brass bed plate, on 4 brass flanged wheels, bronzed ends to boiler, bright bed plate, with whistle, safety valve, steam and water taps, complete, with spirit lamp to run in a circle....each, 5 00

No. 365. **Small Brass Locomotive,** with one cylinder, fitted with steam tap, safety valve, whistle and water tap, with 2 foot circular rails, complete....each, 8 00

No. 51. Mechanism Extraordinary.

No.		Each.
1.	The Smallest Size Steamboat, in neat box, with printed directions	$0 40
2.	Superior finished, with Deck and Wire Gunwale	0 50
3.	Superior finished, 9 in. long	0 75
4.	Superior finished, 10½ inch long	$1 00
5.	" 14 "	1 25
6.	" 17 "	2 00
7.	" 20 "	3 00
8.	" 27 "	4 50

No. 53. The "Nautilus" Paddle Steamboat.

No. 1.	12 inch long, in deal box, with directions complete.	each,	1 50
" 2.	20 "	"	3 25
" 3.	27 "	"	6 75

No. 55. The "Achilles" Screw Steamboat.

No. 1.	10 nch long, in deal box, with directions complete	each,	1 50
" 2	20 "	"	3 25
" 3.	27 "	"	6 75

No. 13. Stop Cocks, or Steam Taps.

Nos	1	2	3	4
Price, each, seconds.	$0 35	0 40	0 45	0 50

Nos	1	2	3	4
Price, each, best	$0 45	0 50	0 55	0 60

No. 23. Steam Whistles.

Nos	1	2	3	4	5	6
Price, each	$0 50	0 55	0 60	1 00	1 25	1 75

No. 20. Lever Safety Valves.

Nos	1	2	3	4	5	6
Price, each	$0 85	1 00	1 50	2 00	2 75	3 50

No. 35. Turned Brass Fly Wheels.

Nos	1	2	3	4	5
Inches	2¾	3	3¼	4	4½
Each	$0 35	0 40	0 50	0 80	1 00

Nos	6	7	8	9	10
Inches	5	6	7	8	9
Each	$1 50	1 75	2 00	2 50	[illegible]

No. 19. Flanged Locomotive Wheels.

Nos	1	2	3	4
Inches, diameter	1½	2	2½	3
Per pair	$0 50	0 65	0 75	1 00

No. 16. Standards for Engines.

Nos	1	2	3	4	5	6	7	8
Inches high	3½	4½	5½	6½	8	10	12	14
Per pair	$1 25	1 75	3 00	3 50	5 00	7 00	11 00	13 00

No. 24. Capped Bearings.

Suitable to use with No. 1 cylinder	$0 45
" " 2 "	9 50
Suitable to use with No. 3 cylinder	$0 75

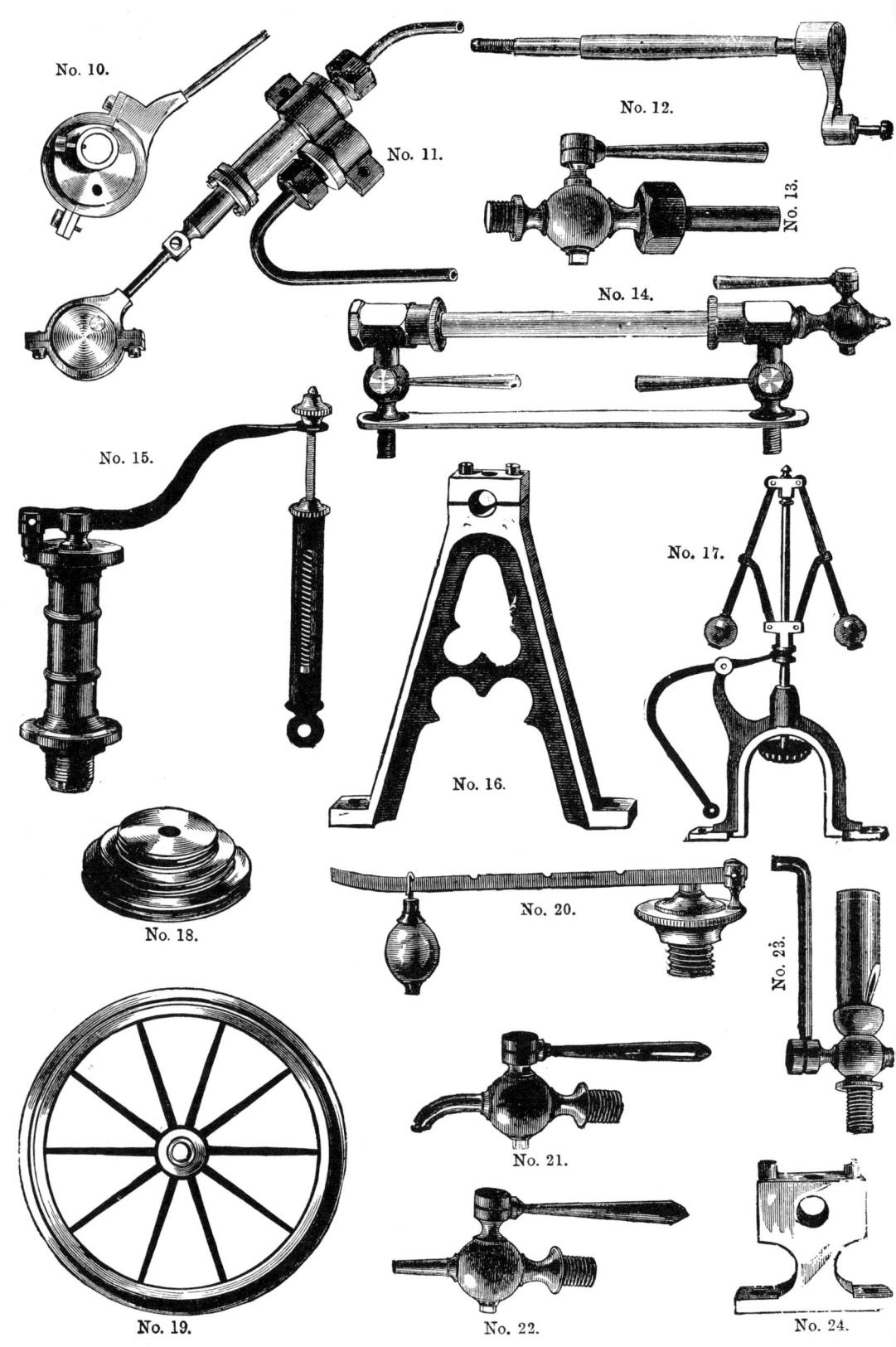

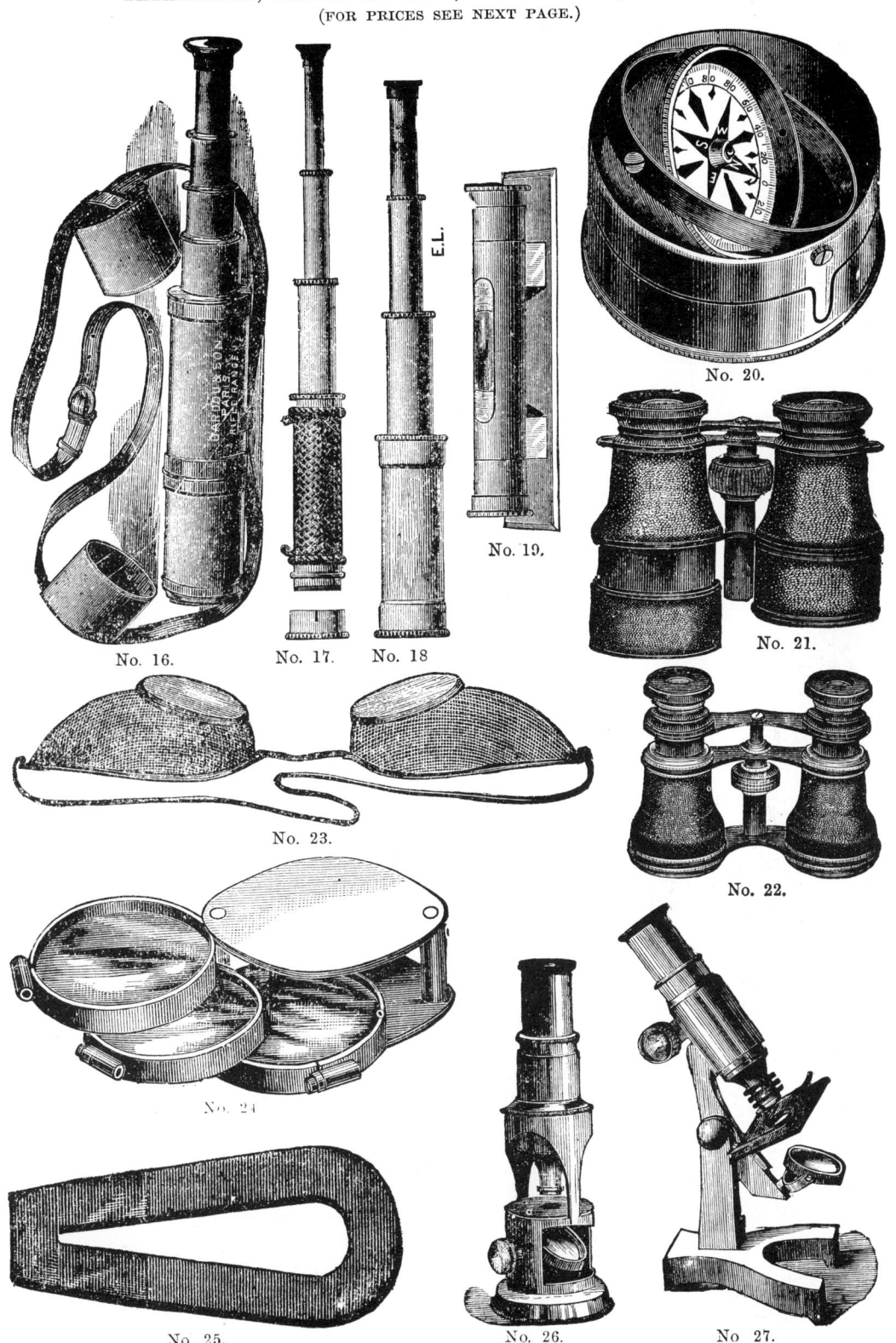

MICROSCOPES, POCKET LAMPS, BURNING GLASSES, &c.   For prices, &c., see next page.

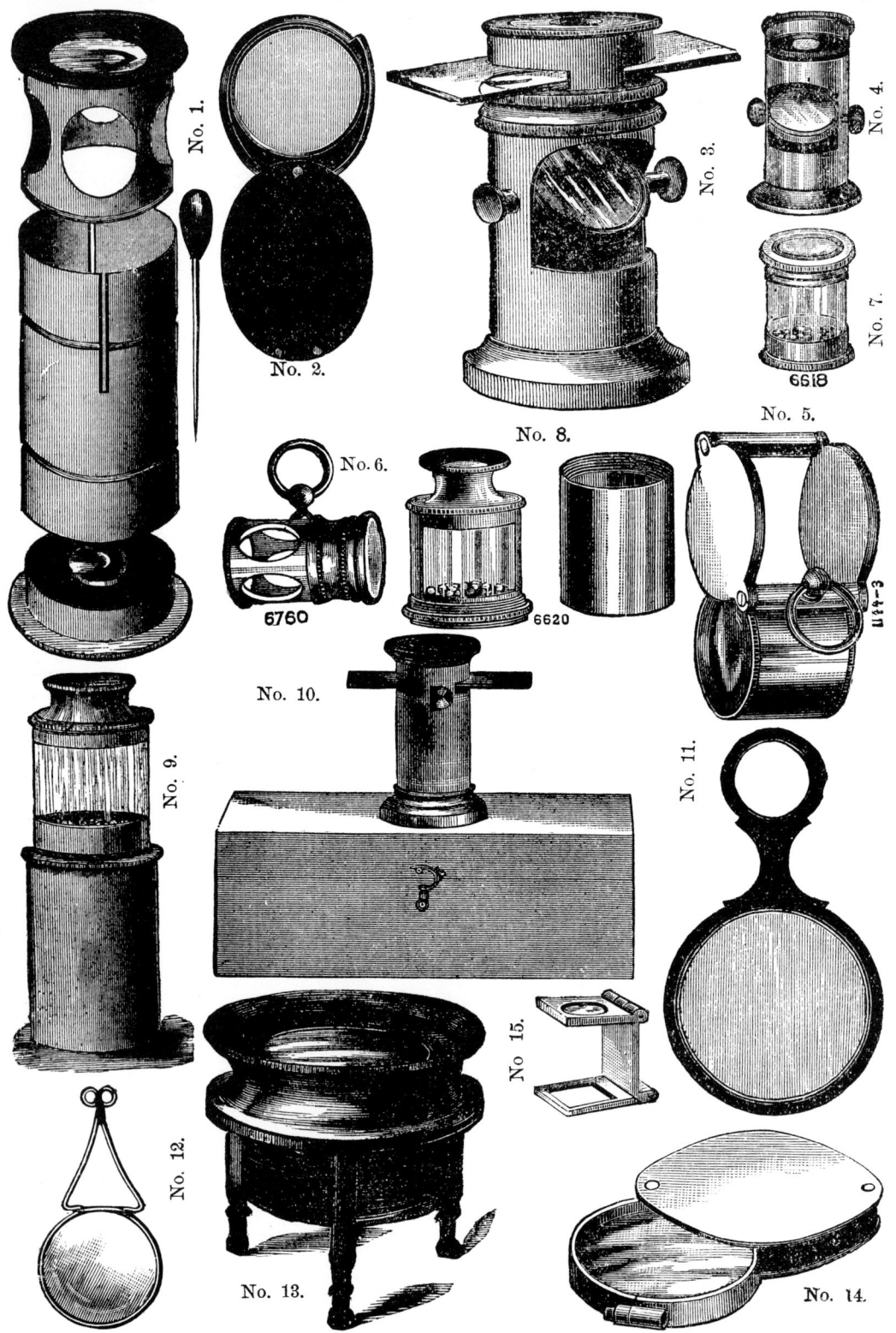

MICROSCOPES, TELESCOPES, SPY GLASSES, &c. (For prices see opposite page.)

No. 11. Reading Glasses, Rubber Frames,

Diameter of glasses, inches	1½	2	2½	3	3½	4
Each	50c	75	$1 00	$1 25	1 50	2 00

No. 5. Coddington Folding Loupes, German silver frames, very strong lens, with ring. Each, $1 25, 1 50, 1 75, 2 00, 2 50.

No. 1. Combination Microscope or Floroscope, 2 inches long, has, in addition to a powerful microscopic lens, a mineral glass for examining plants, minerals, bugs, seeds, flowers, &c... Each, 50c.

No. 4. Microscope, 2 inches high with mirror, (article to be placed upon the lens)..... " 50c.

No. 6, Charm Microscope, 1 inch long, very powerful, nickel-plated or gilt .... " 25c.

No. 10. Home and School Microscope, 2¼ inches long, has 6 prepared and 6 plain sides, with spring to hold them, (see cut), magnifying power 50 times; the light is received through a hole in the base. All complete, in neat wood box.......... ....Each, $1 50

No. 7. Seed Microscope, brass stand, 1¼ inch high .... " 35c.

No. 8. " " when covered with protecting cap, 2½ inches long, full length, 5 inches.......... " 75c.

No. 9. Seed Microscope, brass stand 3 inches high.......... 25c.

No. 26. Compound Microscope, of brass, in black walnut, case, 6 inches high, 1 lens with tweezers, and 3 object slides..........Each, $2 50

Nos. 2, 14, 24. POCKET FOLDING LOUPS.—German Silver of very strong construction. Lenses very powerful. Size of lenses 1 inch diameter.

Single Lens, price each	$0 75	Rubber, 1½ inch diameter, single, price each	$1 00
Double " "	1 00	" 1½ " double, "	1 50
Triple " "	1 50	" 2 " single, "	1 50
Rubber, 1 inch diameter, single price each	0 60	" 2 " double, "	2 50
" 1 " double, "	1 00		

No. 3. Brass Microscope with Reflector, (cut exact size) to hold the rays of light beneath the object Lens. Has three glass slides for holding water and substances, and has a magnifying power of 500 times. This is no toy. For its size, 2¼ x 1¼ it is the best Microscope made. Price, each, $1 25

Microscopes, 6 inches high.................$2 75 | Microscopes, with 3 object lenses......... 4 00

No. 25. MAGNETS.

Price, each	15c.	25	30	35	40	50	75	$1 00	1 25	1 50
Inches	2½ in.	3	3½	4	4½	5	6	7	8	9

No. 5.—CODDINGTON MICROSCOPE.—Extra thick glasses, the strongest pocket Microscope in use. Nickel plated.

Size when closed 1x1, price	$2 75	Size when closed ¾x½, price	$2 25
" " ¾x¾, "	2 50	" " ½x½, "	2 00

No. 12. Burning Glasses in Cases.—2 inch glass.......... ...Price, 20 cents.

No. 13. Three Leg Microscope.—Very powerful Lenses for examining Seeds, Flowers, &c., the light strikes the object from all sides. Size when smallest 2 inches x 2¼. Price, each, 75c.

No 15. Brass Linen Tester to Count the Threads.—Folds into very convenient form for carrying in the pocket.. ....Price, 50 cents.

No. 16. Bardou Rifle Range Telescope, kid covering and caps, oxydized brass slides and shades, very substantially made, full length 38½ inches. Magnifying power, thirty-three times.......... ....each, 25 00

No. 17. Achromatic Telescope, corded cover to body, polished brass slides and ends, with caps and sliding eye-piece cover.

Length.	Draw.	Full length.	Magnifying power.	Diam. of object glass.	Diam. of Body.	
5¼ inch.	3	14½ inch	10 times.	10 lignes.	1 inch	$2 75
6 "	3	16½ "	13 "	12 "	1 3/16 "	3 00
7 "	3	18 "	15 "	14 "	1⅜ "	3 50
8½ "	3	24 "	20 "	16 "	1⅝ "	5 00
10 "	3	29¼ "	25 "	19 "	1⅞ "	7 00

No. 18. Boys' Perspective Telescope, strong brass frame, body painted to imitate rosewood; in cases.

Length.	Draw.	Full length.	Diam. of object glass.	Magnifying power.	Each.
3¼ inches	1	5½ inches.	1¼ inches.	2½ times	$0 75
3¼ "	2	7½ "	1¼ "	4½ "	1 00
4¼ "	3	9 "	1¼ "	5½ "	1 25
3¼ "	4	11 "	1¼ "	6½ "	1 50
4 "	3	12 "	1½ "	7 "	1 75
5 "	2	11 "	1¼ "	8 "	2 00

No. 565. Fine wood body, French polish, 7 inches long, 1 drawer, Spy Glass.......... 0 75

No. 566. Fine wood body, French polish, 7 inches long, 2 drawers, Spy Glass 1 25

No. 567. Fine wood body, French polish, 13 inches long, 3 drawers, Spy Glass.......... 1 50

No. 568. Fine Rosewood body, French polished, fine lens, 5½ inches long, 1 drawer, Spy Glass.. 0 75

No 569. Fine Rosewood body, French polished, fine lens, 7¾ inches long, 2 drawers, Spy Glass. 1 00

No 570. Fine Rosewood body, French polished, fine lens, 10 inches long, 3 drawers, Spy Glass. 1 50

No. 571. Tourists' and Sportsmen's Telescopes, 3 drawers, fine, a chromatic lens, brass caps, top and bottom, length, 16½ inches.......... ..each, 4 50

No. 573. Very fine Telescope, 3 drawers, a chromatic lens, brass caps, etc., length, 23 inches... 7 00

No. 576. Fine Telescope, 3 drawers, fine chromatic lens, brass cap top and bottom, with extra dark glass to be attached for looking at the sun. Length, 17 inches. With this you can see a distance of 2 miles very distinctly..........Price, 5 00

SMALL FONTS OF TYPE

With Quads and Spaces, put up in Wood Cases with Slide Lid Cover.

FIGURES GO WITH EACH FONT WHERE THEY ARE SHOWN.

No. 50.	5 A.	$0.60.
BEAUTIFUL DREAMER WE ARE OUT ON THE HIGH 123

No. 51.	2 A. 5 a.	$0.80.
HAND STAMPS for Marking Clothing 1234567

No. 52.	5 A.	$0.60.
CABINETS FOR THE SHORT-TYPE 123

No. 53.	5 A.	$0.75.
AMERICAN EXCHANGE 123

No. 54.	5 A.	$0.85.
AN UNITED NATION 123

No. 55.	2 A. 5 a.	$0.80.
Romantic Loves of Abelard and Helouise 12

No. 56.	5 A.	$0.60.
IMPORTANT NEWS FROM ENGLAND 456

No. 57.	5 A.	$0.85.
TIME IS MONEY 23890

No. 58.	5 A.	$0.75.
BI-CENTENNIAL 1266

No. 59.	5 A.	$0.85
NORTH AMERICAN 123

No. 60.	3 A.	$1.00.
GOULD MINES 12

No. 61.	4 A.	$1.00.
HARD TIMES 13

No. 62.	2 A. 5 a.	$1.05.
Philadelphia Wilmington and Baltimore 123

No. 63.	2 A. 5 a.	$1.10.
Beautifully Designed Card 12345

No. 64.	2 A. 5 a.	$1.10.
Grand Annual Reception 1234

No. 65.	2 A. 5 a.	$1.25.
Myrtle's 16th Anniversary

No. 66.	2 A. 3 a.	$1.20.
Ninth Annual Reception 12

No. 67.	2 A. 5 a.	$1.05.
BEST Star Printing Press 12

No. 68.	2 A. 5 a.	$1.00.
PEACHES AND CREAM 1234

No. 69.	2 A. 5 a.	$0.95.
General George Washington. 130

No. 70.	2 A. 5 a.	$1.05.
Boommerang Conventionalisms

No. 71.	2 A. 5 a.	$1.00.
Pauline M. Richardson. 10

No. 72.	2 A. 5 a.	$1.50.
Washington's Tomahawk

No. 73.	2 A. 3 a.	$1.75.
Dumplings of Mankattan

No. 74.	2 A. 3 a.	$2.00.
Waltz by my Turtle

No. 75.	2 A. 5 a.	$0.95.
The Grand Adventure of an Albino

No. 76.	2 A. 5 a.	$1.00.
Annie M. Barrington.

No. 77.	2 A. 5 a.	$1.50.
Wamma Gamma Damma

No. 78.	2 A. 3 a.	$1.75.
Manganasian Agan

No. 79.	2 A. 3 a.	$2.00.
Radaman Freaks

The Victor Card Press, No. 1.—Same Press as No 2, but with less fixtures, &c. The outfit consists of Victor Card Press, No. 1, Composition Roller, Can best Card ink, Package of Cards, Gold Bronze, Set of Furniture, Spaces, and Quads, and a 5 A Font of Type..........Price, complete, $1 75

No. 2.—Victor Printing Press, and Complete Outfit together with a Cabinet, as shown in the above cut, with everything requisite to print neatly; will do as good work as can be done on any press. Size of chase, $3\frac{1}{2}$ x 2 inches.

The Victor Printing Press, mounted on a Cabinet, with two type cases and a drawer, Composition roller, pack of Cards, Set of Furniture, Can Best Card Ink, Full Font of Fancy Card Type with Spaces and Quads. Price, all complete, $3.00. Short or long type may be used on the "Victor."

With this press and full outfit, a boy can start business for himself, print business cards for storekeepers, or visiting cards for ladies and gents. Labels for Drug Stores, small hand bills for Concerts, Balls, &c. He can do any kind of small work that is done on any printing press. Send and get one for your boy. Fixtures for Victor Presses, by mail, extra roller 15c., roller handle 15c., can of ink 15c., font of type, figures, &c. 60c., gauge with grippers 15c., gold bronze 15c. Printing material, stock, &c. supplied at lowest cash prices. The types used on these presses are the same as used by regular printers. Liberal discount to the trade.

Short Type to be used with Pallet only. Price of Pallet 25 cents, will fit all of these styles. Postage and Pallet, 10 cents.

The names printed below show the style the Type prints.

No. 1. Engravers. 75 cents per Box, Postage paid.

Beautiful Visiting Card Type.

No. 2. Prints 3 styles, 75 cents per Box, Postage paid.

NORTH AMERICA. UNITED NATIONS. RUBBER STAMPS. 1874.

No. 3. Prints two styles, 75 cents per Box, Postage paid.

GOLD MINE. Time is Money. 1875.

2A 3a FONT OF GT. PRIMER SCRIPT. No. 187, with figures

Grand Reception and Ball. 1876.

This Type $1.45 per Box, Postage paid.

Box of figures, three of each, from 1 to 0, to fit all the above styles. By mail, 30 cents.

Extra Roller, by mail $0 15	Box Gold Bronze.................................$0 15
" Roller and Handles............ 25	Can Red Ink................................. 20
Can Black Card Ink.................. ... 15	

MULTUM IN PARVO SKATE, KNIFE AND SCISSORS SHARPENER.

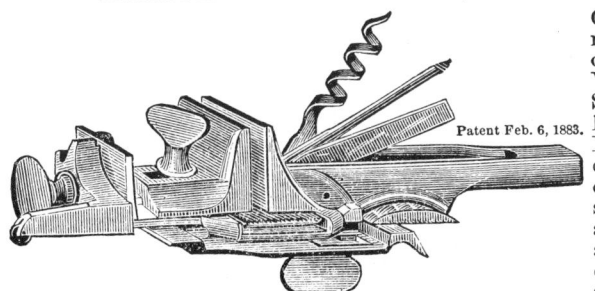

Patent Feb. 6, 1883.

Combines twelve practical and useful tools, needed in every household and by every mechanic, viz.: Saw Jointer, Saw Set, Hand Vice, Glass Cutter, Skate Sharpener, Scissors Sharpener, Knife Sharpener, Gimlet, Screw Driver, Corkscrew, Bit Stock and Wrench. Every part is made of steel, is strong and durable, easily adjusted, and cannot get out of order. Will sharpen both groove and flat skates; is easily adjusted to fit any runner, and will do the work complete without the aid of a vise. Every part is a practical tool of itself, and it only needs to be seen to be appreciated. Price, complete, 1.25.

THE MARYLAND PRESS.

Will Print a Card 1½x3 inches.

THE MARYLAND PRESS is an improvement on the usual made hand inking presses of this size. It is made for practical use, and not simply to sell cheap. It is beautifully japanned. Every press is tried, and none sent out but what we can warrant as perfect.

Price of Press with Roller, - - - - - - - $1.50.
With outfit including 1 font of No. 52 Type, 50 Blank Cards, Ink and Furniture in a box, $2.50.

Weight of Press and Outfit Boxed, 7½ pounds.

BALTIMOREAN No. 1.

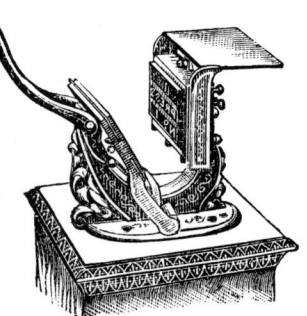

Hand-Inking.   Will print a card 2½x4.

This is the most complete hand-inking press made, beautifully designed, elegantly constructed, and tastefully finished. This press is capable of doing a great variety of small Printing, such as, Cards, Envelopes, &c.

Price of Press and Roller, boxed, - - - $3.75.
With Office of one Font of No. 71 Type, 50 Blank Cards, Ink and Furniture in a Box, - - - - - - $5.00.

Weight of Press and Outfit Boxed, 14 pounds.

BALTIMOREAN No. 1.

The Little Beauty.

Self-inking.   Will print a Card 2½x4

This size is especially adapted for printing small jobs, such as Cards, Envelopes, &c. It carries one or two rollers; has grippers; the handle and roller holders are Nickel Plated, and it is in every way a complete Self-inking Press.

Price of press with one roller, - - $6.25.
With outfit of Type, No. 71, 50 Blank Cards, Ink and Furniture - - - - - $7.50.
Price of Press, extra finished, with TWO ROLLERS - - - - - $8.00.
With outfit of Two Fonts of Nos. 50 and 64 Type, 50 Blank Cards, Ink and Furniture in a Box - - - - - $10.00.

Weight of Press and Outfit Boxed, 20 pounds.

The handles of all the above presses are beautifully Nickel Plated.

Baltimorean Nos. 2 & 3.

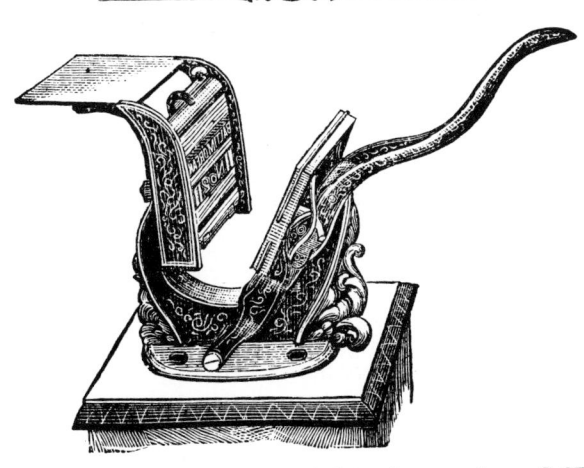

No. 2 Hand-Inker, Size of Chase 4x6, (weight of press boxed 67 lbs.) Price, $10 00
With outfit of 4 fonts of Type, Nos. 51, 56, 57 and 71 with Composing
    Stick, Planer, Furniture, Leads, Ink, Cases, &c.   -   -   -   15 00
No. 3 Hand-Inker, Size of Chase, 5½x8, (weight of press boxed 109 lbs.)   14 00
With outfit of 5 fonts Type, Nos. 51, 56, 57, 61 and 71 with Composing
    Stick, Planer, Furniture, Leads, Ink, Cases, &c.   -   -   20 00

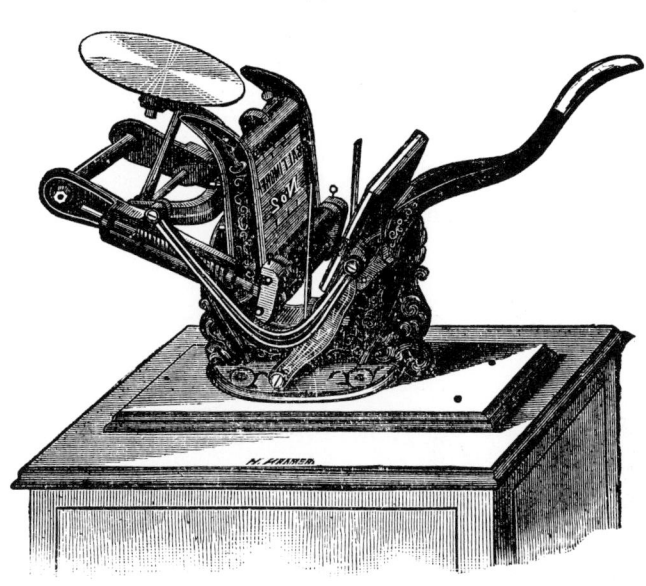

No. 2 Self-Inker, Size of Chase, 4¼x6¼ (weight of press boxed 80 lbs.) Price, $16 00
With Office of 4 Fonts of Type, Nos. 51, 56, 57 and 71, with Composing
    Stick, Planer, Furniture, Leads, Ink, Cases, &c.   -   -   - $21 00
No. 3 Self-Inker, size of Chase, 5½x8, (weight of press boxed 125 lbs.)   25 00
With outfit of 5 Fonts Type, Nos. 51, 56, 57, 61 and 71, with Composing
    Stick, Planer, Furniture, Leads, Ink, Cases, &c.   -   -   - $31 00

BOXWOOD AND IVORY POCKET RULES, TRY SQUARES AND PLANES FOR FRET AND SCROLL SAWING AND PRACTICAL USE. For prices see next page.

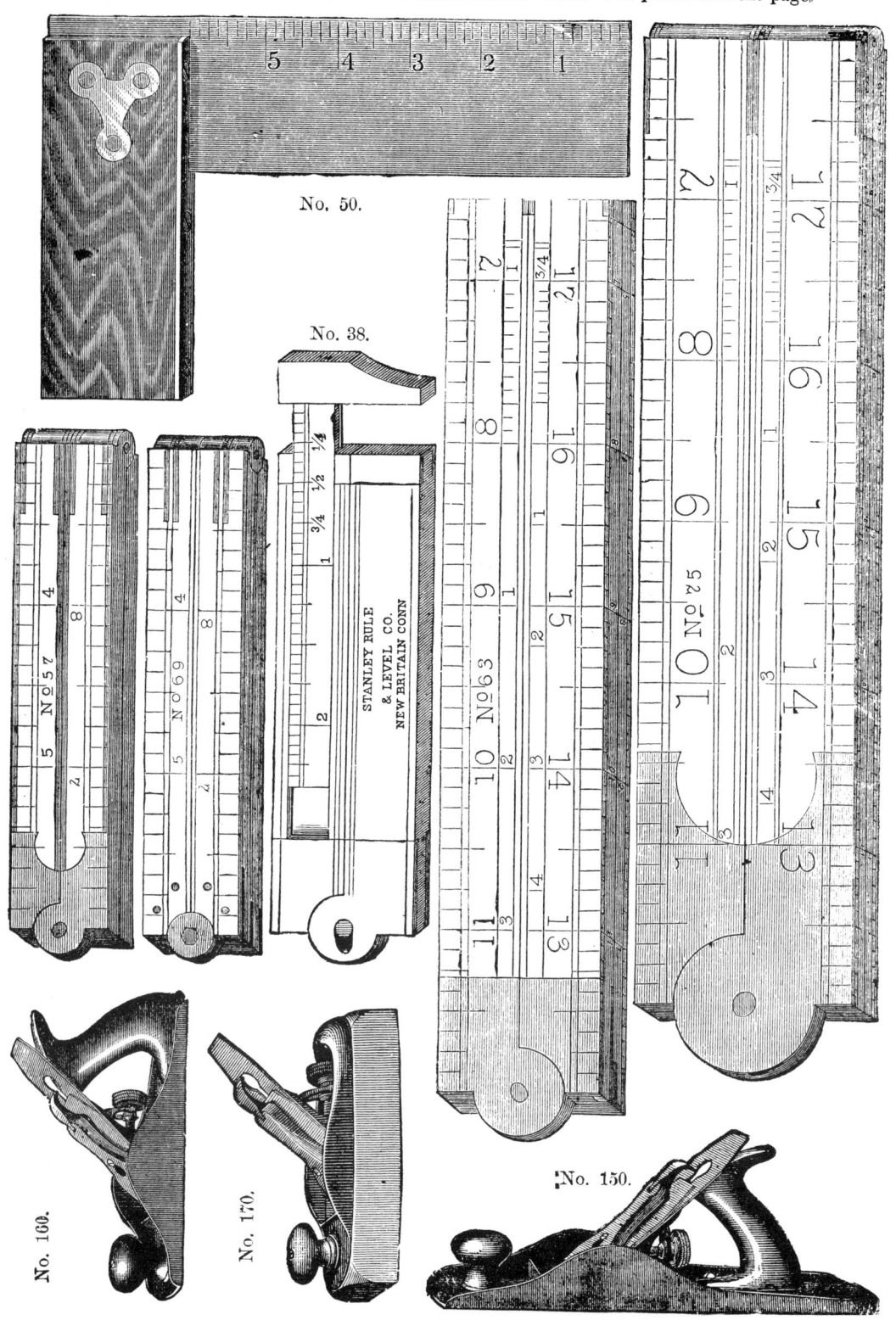

USEFUL TOOLS FOR GENERAL AND PRACTICAL USE.

No. 50. Iron Bound Try Squares, graduated steel blades

Inches, blade	3	$4\frac{1}{2}$	6	$7\frac{1}{2}$	9	10	12	15	18
Each	25c.	35	50	60	70	75	85	1 15	1 40

Boxwood and Ivory Rules, 1 and 2 feet long, 4 folds.

No. 69. Round joint middle plates, 8ths and 16ths inches, $\frac{5}{8}$ inch wide....................each, $0 25
No. 69x. Round joint brass middle plates, 8ths and 16ths inches, ivory.................. " 0 90
No. 57. Arch joint bound, 8ths and 16ths of inches, $\frac{5}{8}$ inch wide.................. " 1 00
No 68. Round joint middle plate, &c., 1 inch wide, 2 feet long.................. " 0 35
Ivory rules, bound with German silver, 1 foot long, $2 25; 2 foot long.................. " 5 00
No 38 Boxwood caliper rules, 6 inches, 50 cents; 12 inches.................. " 0 75
No. 39 Ivory caliper rules, 6 inches, $1 25; 12 inches.................. " 2 50
No. 63. Square joint, edge plates, 8ths, 10ths, 12ths and 16ths of inches, drafting scales, 1 inch wide.................. " 0 65
No. 75. Arch joints, edge plates, 8ths, 10ths and 16ths of inches, drafting scales, $1\frac{3}{8}$ inches wide.................. " 1 00

Bailey's Patent Iron Planes.

These planes meet with universal approbation from the best mechanics, as their extensive sale abundantly testifies. For beauty of style and finish, they are uneqaled and the superior methods for adjusting them readily in all their parts, render them economical to the owner.

No. 160 Smooth Plane, $5\frac{1}{2}$ inches in length, $1\frac{1}{4}$ inch Cutter.................. each, $2 25
Smooth Plane, 7 inches in length, $1\frac{5}{8}$ inch Cutter.................. " 2 75
Smooth Plane, 8 inches in length, $1\frac{3}{4}$ inch Cutter.................. " 3 00
Smooth Plane, 9 inches in length, 2 inch Cutter.................. " 3 25
No. 150. Jack Plane 14 inches in length, 2 inch Cutter.................. " 3 75
Fore Plane 18 inches in length, $2\frac{3}{8}$ inch Cutter.................. " 4 75
Jointer Plane, 22 inches in length, $2\frac{3}{8}$ inch Cutter.................. " 5 50
Jointer Plane, 24 inches in length, $2\frac{5}{8}$ inch Cutter.................. " 6 50
Block Plane, 10 inches in length, 2 inch Cutter.................. " 6 50
Carriage Makers' Rabbet Plane, 14 inches in length, $2\frac{1}{8}$ inch Cutter.................. " 4 50
Belt Makers' Plane, $2\frac{5}{8}$ inch Cutter.................. " 3 00
No. 170. Wood Smooth Plane, 7 inches in length, $1\frac{3}{4}$ inch Cutter.................. " 2 00
Wood Smooth Plane, 8 inches in length, $1\frac{3}{4}$ inch Cutter.................. " 2 00
Wood Smooth Plane, 9 inches in length, $1\frac{3}{4}$ inch Cutter.................. " 2 00
Wood Smooth Plane, 8 inches in length, 2 inch Cutter.................. " 2 00
Wood Block Plane, $9\frac{1}{2}$ inches in length, $1\frac{3}{4}$ inch Cutter.................. " 2 00

OLMSTED'S IMPROVED MITRE BOX.

The above engraving is an exact representation of Olmsted's Improved Miter Box.

The frame is made of hard wood, of the best quality selected for the purpose, and made from boards one inch thick, and consists of two upright pieces which are fastened rigidly to the edges of a bottom board.

Upon the upper edges of these two uprights are fastened irons, made the exact angle to form a Mitre, and serve as a guide for the saw.

The two centre irons are fastened firmly, and are not movable; the four other irons slotted where the screws pass through them, and can be moved up to and from the fixed irons, thereby adjusting the space between the irons to fit any thickness of saw blade.

These Mitre Boxes are of the best workmanship, and are nicely finished; the iron work is painted and varnished, the frames are finished in oil varnish, making them impervious to the action of the atmosphere.

With No. 1, a moulding 3 by $1\frac{1}{2}$ inches can be sawed in them.................. Price, $1 50
" " 2, " 4 by $2\frac{1}{2}$ " " " " .... " 2 00

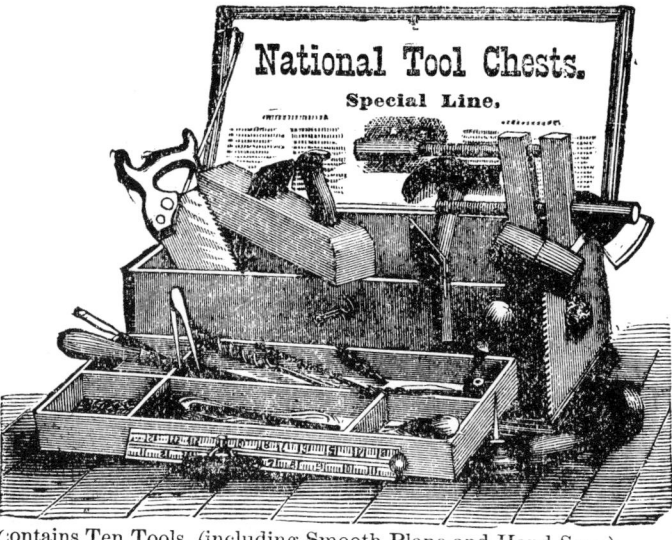

BOYS' NATIONAL TOOL CHESTS.

(All Sizes given are inside measure.)

No. 28.—Pine Box, Slide Cover, size 7¾ x 4 x 1¾, Locked Corners, and contains Nine Articles.
Per Chest, 10c.

No. 30.—Pine Box, Slide Cover, Size 9 x 4 x 2, Locked Corners, and contains Fourteen Articles.
Per Chest, 20c.

No. 40.—Basswood Box, Slide Cover, Size 9x4x2¼, Locked Corners, and contains Ten Tools, (including Hand Saw.) Per Chest, 25c.

No. 45.—(New,) Chestnut Box, Size 9 x 4 x 2½, Locked Corners, Hinged Cover, Walnut Mouldings, Varnished Finish, and contains Ten Tools, (including Hand Saw.)
Per Chest, 35c.

No. 60.—Chestnut Box, Size 11x 5x3, Varnished, with Till, Trimmed with Black Walnut Mouldings, Locked Corners, Hinged Cover, and contains Ten Tools, (including Smooth Plane and Hand Saw.)
Per Chest, 50c.

No. 80.—Chestnut Box, Size, 12x5½x3½, Varnished, with till, Trimmed with Black Walnut Mouldings, Locked Corners, Hinged Cover, and contains Fourteen Tools, (including Plane, Hand Saw and Hatchet.)
Per Chest, 75 cts.

No. 600.—Chestnut Box, Size, 14x6¾x5¾, Varnished, Movable Tray, Locked Corners, Hinged Cover, Trimmed with Black Walnut Mouldings, and contains Eighteen Tools, (including Plane and Hand Saw.)
Per Chest, $1.00.

No. 700.—Chestnut Box, Size 15½x7½x5¾, Varnished, Movable Tray, Locked Corners, Hinged Cover, Trimmed with Black Walnut Mouldings, and contains Twenty-three Tools.   Per Chest, $1.00.

No. 725.—(New,) Box same as No. 700, but with different tools and more of them, including Ball Brace and Brace Bit, very useful tools. Box well finished and contains Twenty-four tools.
Per Chest, $1.25.

No. 750.—(New,) Chestnut Box, Size 16¼x7¾x5¾, Varnished, Movable Tray. Locked Corners, Hinged Cover, Trimmed with Black Walnut Mouldings, and Bronze Handles, and contains Twenty-five Tools (including Pincers, Pliers, &c.)
Per Chest, $1.50.

No. 800.—Chestnut Box, Size 17x8x6, Varnished, Movable Tray, Locked Corners, Hinged Cover, Trimmed with Black Walnut Mouldings, and Bronze Handles, and contains Twenty-six well made Tools.
Per Chest, $2.00.

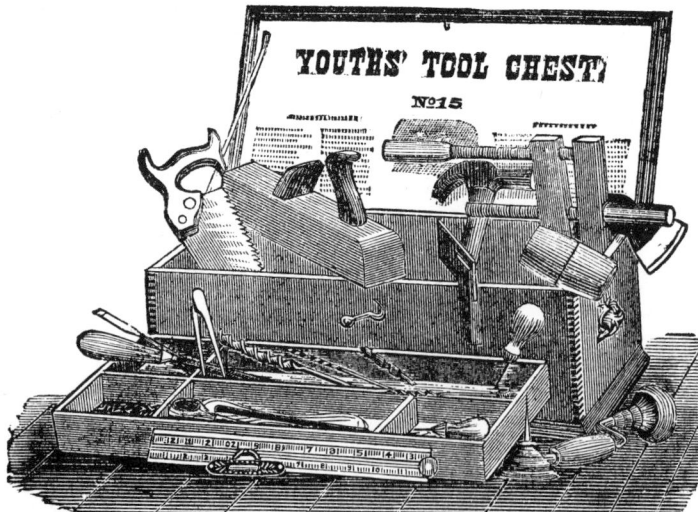

YOUTHS' SUPERIOR TOOL CHESTS.

(All Sizes given are inside measure.)

No. 12.—Size 15¼ inches long, 7½ inches wide, and 5⅝ inches deep. Chestnut Box, Black Walnut Moulding, Bronze Handles, and contains Twenty-four Superior Tools. Per Chest, $3.75

No. 13.—Size 17 inches long, 8 inches wide, and 6 inches deep. Finished same as No. 12, and contains Twenty-nine Tools.
Per Chest, $5.00

No. 14.—Size 18 inches long, 8½ inches wide, and 6¼ inches deep. Finished same as No. 12, and contains Thirty-four Tools.
Per Chest, $7.00

No. 15.—Size 19 inches long, 9 inches wide, and 6¾ inches deep. Finished same as No. 12, and contains Forty-one Tools.
Per Chest, $9.00

No. 16.—Size 20 inches long, 9½ inches wide, and 7½ inches deep. Finished same as No. 12, and contains Forty-five Tools.
Per Chest, $11.00

Liberal discount to the Trade and Sunday Schools allowed from above prices.

GENTLEMEN'S EXCELSIOR TOOL CHESTS.

All Sizes given are inside measure.

These **Tool Chests are** made of Selected Chestnut Stock, Heavy Black Walnut Mouldings, Large Drawer, fitted with Lock and Key, and Bronze Handles.

No. 20.—Size 14 inches long, 6½ inches wide, and 5 inches deep. Contains Twenty Tools.
Per Chest, $5.00

No. 21.—Size 16 inches long, 7¼ inches wide, and 5¼ inches deep. Contains Twenty-five Tools.
Per Chest, $7.00

No. 22.—Size 18 inches long, 8¼ inches wide, and 6¼ inches deep. Contains Thirty-four Tools.
Per Chest, $9.00

No. 23—Size 19¼ inches long, 9½ inches wide, and 7¼ inches deep. Contains Forty-six Tools.
Per Chest, $12.00

No. 24.—Size 21 inches long, 10¼ inches wide, and 8¼ inches deep. Contains Sixty-one Tools.
Per Chest, $16.50

No. 25.—Size 25 inches long, 12¼ inches wide, and 9 inches deep. Contains Seventy-two Tools.
Per Chest, $24.00

GRIFFIN'S PATENT HACK SAWS.

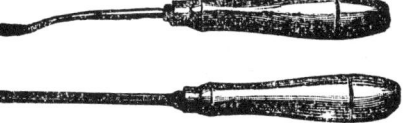

For Sawing Brass, Iron, Steel, Lead Pipe, and Metals of all kinds. An invaluable Tool for the home, the Farm and the Workshop.

The Best Hack Saw Made.
FULLY WARRANTED.

An improvement over all others in that it performs the same work with a great saving of expense, time, and annoyance. As shown in cut, the blade is secured in place by two pins, and may be readily detached. The tension is regulated by a lever in the open handle. The blades are very highly tempered, and require no filing. As the cost is far less than was formerly paid for filing alone, they may be thrown away when dull. Price each, $1.00.
By Mail, Postage Paid, $1.25.

CARVING TOOLS. Gouge, Chisel and **Parting** Tools, &c.

These tools are put up six in a box, with Beachwood handles, and nicely fitted for use. They are equal to imported tools, and sell at a lower price.
Per set of six, $1 00

No. O.	Table Vise	....	$1 00
" A.	Spring "	....	0 75
" B.	" "	....	1 00
" C.	" "	....	1 50

COMPANION SLIDE VICE.

This Vice has a clamp by which it can be attached to a table, and can be removed at pleasure by turning a thumb screw.

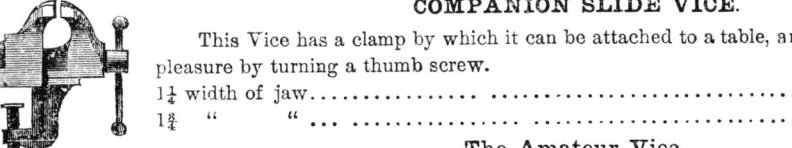

1¼ width of jaw...$2 00
1¾ " " 2 25

The Amateur Vice.

Jaws 1½, opens 2 inches.. 1 10

IRON LOCOMOTIVES, Without Movements, to Draw with a String.

These are the best cheap Toy Locomotives yet offered to the public. Made entirely of Iron, and handsomely painted. They are good models of large locomotives.
No. 66-3 Locomotive only, 7 inches long.. Price $0 85
" 66-4 " 9½ " .... " 1 25
" 66-5 " with Tender, 10¼ inches long... " 1 00
" 66-6 " 13 inches long, with Tender, (see cut)... " 1 50

No. 19 10.—MECHANICAL IRON LOCOMOTIVE, WITH TENDER.

One of the best and cheapest toys yet made. A good imitation of a large locomotive; they are very strong, and work perfectly, either in a straight line or a circle Each one in a strong wood box.

Ten inches long, with tender. Each one in a strong wood box.................Price, complete, $1 50
No. 19-9.—Locomotive 7 inches long, otherwise same as 19-10, but without tender.......Price, $1 25
No. 19-11—9½ inches long, without tender......................................Price, $1 50
No. 19-12—13¾ inches long, with tender. Same as No. 19-11, with the addition of a tender, and a more powerful movement. Each one in a strong wood box........................Price, complete, $2 25

LADD'S PARLOR SEE-SAW OR TEETER.

No. 2. Suitable for Children from 5 to 8 years of age, $1 75.
No. 3. Suitable for Children from 8 to 12 years of age, $2.25.
No. 4. Suitable for Children from 12 to 16 years of age, $2.50.

Solves the problem, how to make home pleasant for Children, particularly during inclement weather. It affords more amusement and pleasure than any other pastime. The propensity to "Seesaw" is inborn, and Children never tire of it.

It is nicely and strongly made, the smallest size being sufficiently strong to support the weight of 500 pounds or more, and is practically indestructible. Requires no adjustment for balancing, operating equally as well when used by a heavy person on one end and a lighter person on the other. When folded it occupies but little room. Weight 10 to 15 pounds.

SOLID BRASS FIXTURES FOR TOY YACHTS, BOATS, &c.

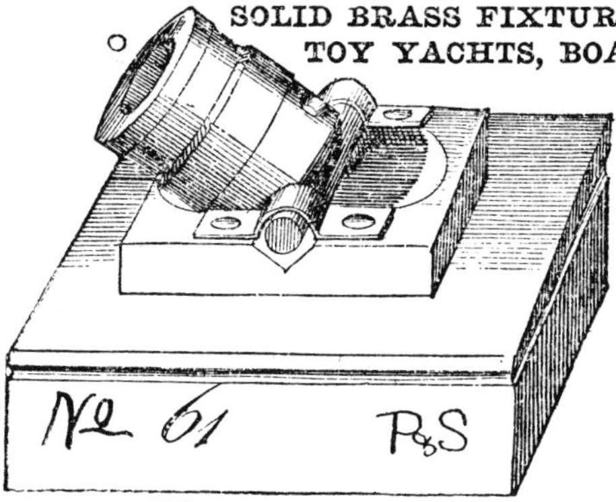

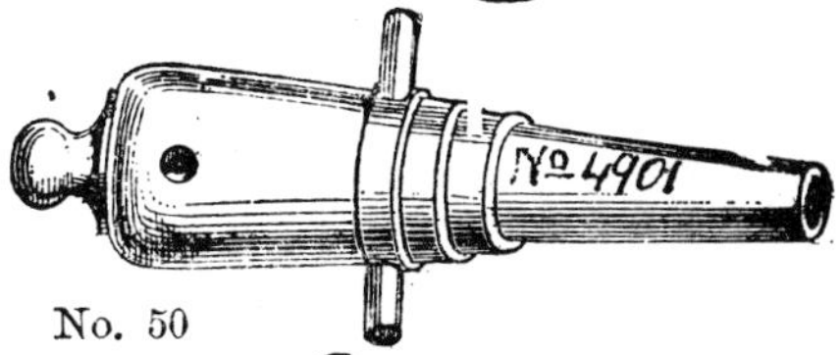

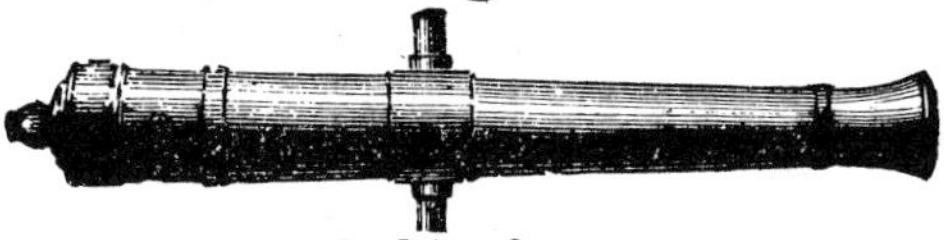

No. 50. Solid Brass Cannon Barrels, for Toy Yachts, &c.

Nos.	1	2	3	4	5	6	7	8	9	10	11	12	13	14
Size, inches	$1\frac{1}{4}$	$1\frac{1}{2}$	$1\frac{3}{4}$	$2\frac{1}{8}$	$2\frac{1}{4}$	$2\frac{3}{8}$	$2\frac{7}{8}$	$3\frac{1}{8}$	$3\frac{3}{8}$	$3\frac{5}{8}$	$3\frac{7}{8}$	$4\frac{1}{4}$	5	$5\frac{1}{2}$
Each	5c.	6	8	10	12	15	18	20	25	30	35	40	50	75

No. 131. Solid Cannons Mounted on Brass Carriage.

Nos.	1	2	3	4	5	6	7	8	9	10	11	12	13	14
Size, inches	$1\frac{3}{8}$	$2\frac{1}{8}$	$2\frac{1}{2}$	3	$3\frac{1}{4}$	$3\frac{1}{2}$	4	$4\frac{1}{2}$	$5\frac{1}{8}$	$5\frac{1}{2}$	6	7	$7\frac{1}{2}$	$8\frac{1}{4}$
Each	15c.	20	25	30	35	40	50	60	65	75	85	$1 00	1 25	1 50

Solid Brass Barrels on Wood Blocks with Brass Wheel Chains, &c.

Nos.	1	2	3	4	5	6	7	8	9
Size, inches	2	3	$3\frac{1}{2}$	$3\frac{3}{4}$	$4\frac{1}{4}$	5	$5\frac{1}{4}$	$5\frac{3}{4}$	$6\frac{3}{8}$
Each	30c.	40	45	50	65	75	$1 00	1 25	1 75

No. 4901.—Solid Brass Cannon Barrels, 81 Ton Model.

Nos.	1	2	3	4	5	6	7	8	9
Size, inches	$1\frac{1}{4}$	$1\frac{1}{2}$	$1\frac{3}{4}$	2	$2\frac{3}{8}$	$2\frac{5}{8}$	$3\frac{3}{8}$	4	$4\frac{1}{2}$
Each	8c.	10	15	20	25	30	40	50	65

Solid Brass Mortars on Wood Blocks.

Nos.	61	62	63	64	65
Size, inches	1	$1\frac{1}{4}$	$1\frac{3}{8}$	$1\frac{1}{2}$	$1\frac{3}{4}$
Each	50c.	65c.	75	$1 00	1 25

Solid Brass Anchors for Toy Yachts and Boats.

Nos.	1	2	3	4	5	6	7	8
Size, inches	$1\frac{1}{4}$	$1\frac{1}{2}$	2	$2\frac{3}{8}$	3	$3\frac{1}{2}$	$4\frac{1}{8}$	$4\frac{1}{2}$
Each	6c.	8	10	12	15	25	30	40

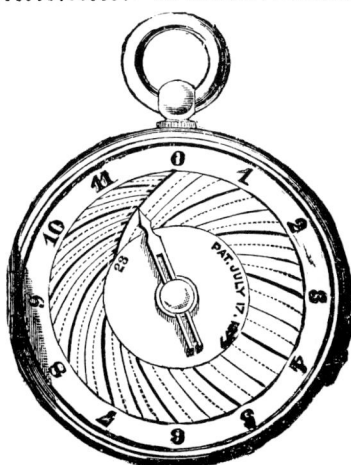

THE AMERICAN PEDOMETER. Cut exact size.

English and French Pedometers have been in existence many years, but owing to the delicate machinery required, the difficulty of adjusting them to the length of step, their inaccuracy, their liability to get out of order, and the high price asked for them, they have not met with a ready sale, nor are they generally known in this market.

The American Pedometer is a simple piece of mechanism, easily adjusted to any length of step from 23 to 35 inches, cannot easily get out of order, measures accurately, is the size of an ordinary watch, in a nickel-plated case, can be carried in the vest pocket.

Its Utility.—It will measure the exact distance you walk, enable you to ascertain the shortest route between any given points, and the speed with which you walk. It is a true indicator of the amount of exercise taken in and out of doors. It is useful to Ladies, Professional and Business Men, Surveyors, Farmers, Pedestrians, Tourists, Passengers at Sea, Students, Sportsmen, Trainers and their Pupils. Invalids will find it invaluable in regulating their exercise. Full directions together with ready reference table accompanies each one. Price, $4.00

A COMPLETE ASSORTMENT OF
FRET OR SCROLL SAWS CONSTANTLY ON HAND,
ALSO,
SAW BLADES,
FANCY WOODS,

PLANES,

DRILLS.

VICES,

TOOL HOLDERS,

WRENCHES,

AND ALL FIXTURES.

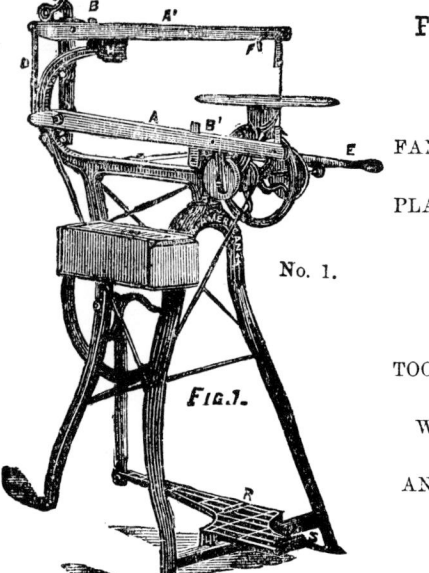

BEACH'S NEW IMPROVED AMERICAN COMBINATION FRET SAW. (See cut No. 1).

Handsome in Design, and claimed to be the Lightest Running and the Best Made Tool in the World for the price; and unequaled for Cheapness, Simplicty, Speed and Efficiency Several engravings and much space would be required to explain all its parts, and its working, ingenious improvements, etc. Is built almost wholly of iron and steel; stands firmly without fastening down. Will cut Horn, Ivory, Pearl, Shell, Brass, and all kinds of Wood up to 1½ inch thick, Saw runs straight up and down. Has a tilting table to cut at angles. Has 20 inches swing, for largest Brackets Has Drill Attachment always ready for use. Also Turning Lathe for work 12 inches long, and 4 inches diameter, with speed of 1,500 revolutions per minute. Also set of Steel Turning Chisels, made from *Jessup's Best Improved* English Steel.

Price complete, including *Lathe* and *Drilling Attachment*, one Morse Flint Drill, Wrench, Oil Can, Screwdriver, six Improved Fret Saws, and one large Saw, 3-16 inch wide, for cutting up timber. Also one set of Turning Chisels, boxed tight and all complete for $8 00
Or as per above cut, all complete, except turning lathe............ ....$6. 00

NEW FOLDING FRET SAW. (See cut No. 2).

Every Home, however humble or magnificent, is more beautiful if adorned with brackets and other homes hands. Hundreds of thousands of such homes work produced by now exist, where only the slow and tedious hand frame fret saws have been available. More recently the foot-pedal and multiplying wheels have come into use, and the increasing demand has tended to cheapness and improvement. We are now happy to announce another *large advance in Perfection, Cheapness, and Portability, by which are secured stronger, better working machines; a material reduction in price, and a great saving in cost of carriage or delivery, as well as in storage room when not in use, with sundry other improvements and advantages: All the above are secured in this new saw.* By a simple arrangement the table is lowered to a convenient working height for a boy of 5 or 6, or raised high enough for the tallest man, and at every heighth it stands *firmly* and, when not in use, it can be folded up and put away It has a *tilting* table, and will execute fine scroll-work or inlaid work, Though as strong and durable as any one could desire, the weight is only 15 pounds.   Price complete and in crate, $2.00.

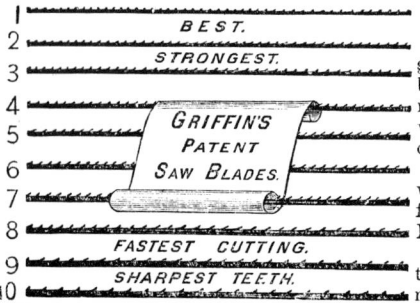

GRIFFIN'S PATENT SAW BLADES.

We feel a just pride in announcing that American skill an ingenuity has at last produced a blade which is far superior in durability in cutting quality to those imported from France and Germany. We have put these blades to the severest tests; both in wood and metal, and the result is they cut faster and longer than other blades.

We are the Agents for these blades in the United States. We will send them to you at the following prices, postage paid: Sizes from No. 1 to 6 inclusive, 15 cents per dozen, or $1 25 per gross. No. 7 to 12 inclusive, 20 cents per dozen, or $1 50 per gross.

We guarantee that one Griffin's Patent Saw Blade will outwear two of the best French or German Blades. At least one-third more work can be done in one day with the Griffin Blade than with any other Blade ever sold in the United States.

PRICE LIST OF FANCY WOODS.

PLANED TO THE FOLLOWING THICKNESS.		⅛-inch.	3-16-inch.	¼-inch.
Black Walnut............per foot...		9c	10c	11c
White Holly............................	"	9	10	11
Poplar..................................	"	5	6	7
Plain White Maple.....................	"	7	8	9
Oak.....................................	"	8	9	11
Cherry.................................	"	8	9	10
Red Cedar.............................	"	12	14	16
Spanish Cedar.........................	"	10	12	14
Mahogany..............................	"	10	12	15
Bird's eye Maple......................	"	12	15	16
Corcobola.............................	"	16	18	20
Rosewood..............................	"	16	20	25
Amaranth..............................	"	16	20	25
Satin Wood............................	"	20	25	30
Hungarian Ash........................	"	30	40	50
Tulip..................................	"	30	40	50
Ebony.................................	"	40	50	60

IRON PLANES AND FIXTURES FOR PRACTICAL USE.

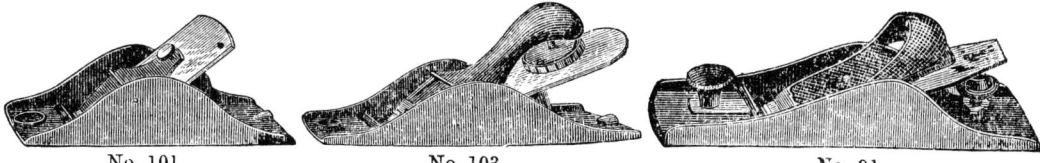

No. 101.   No. 103.   No. 9¼.

These planes were first introduced as convenient tools for amateurs and others, who work with scroll saws, picture framing, &c. They have proved so valuable to mechanics in all the lighter kinds of wood working, and so useful about offices, stores and dwellings, for making slight repairs of windows, doors, furniture, etc., that they seem likely to be wanted in every household.

No. 101. Block Plane, 3½ inches in length, 1 inch cutter...........................each, $0 25
" 102.   "   5½   "   "   1¼   "   .... " 0 50
" 103. Adjustable Block Plane, 5¼ inches in length, 1¼ inch cutter.................. " 0 75
" 9¼. Excelsior Block Plane, 6 inches in length, 1¾ inch cutter..................... " 1 50
" 15.   "   "   "   7   "   "   1¾   "   .... " 1 75

Cast Steel Cutters furnished for the above Planes, extra from 10 to 20 cents each.
No. 80. Rabbet Plane, skew, 9 inches in length, 1¼ inch cutter...................... 1 10
No. 90. Rabbet Plane, skew, 9 inches in length, with spur........................... 1 25

A full line of Boxwood and Ivory Rules, all styles and sizes always on hand. Prices each, 25c to $3 00.

BULL NOSE RABBET PLANE.

No. 75.—This will be found a very useful tool by all wood workers, enabling the owner to work close up into the corners, where it is found necessary to do so. The mouth of the Plane can readily be made open or close by means of the screw on the top which passes through a slot in the upper section of the stock. Iron Stock 4 inches in length, 1 inch. Cutter.

Each, 50 cents.

HAND DRILL.

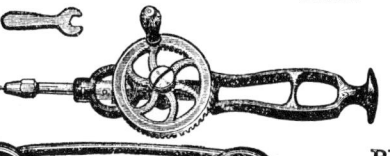

These Drill Stocks are made of Malleable iron, with steel spindle and jaws, and rosewood head and handle. It will hold any size drill from 1-64 to ⅛ inch in diameter. Six Drill Points and Wrench are sold with each stock. Price, by mail, pre-paid, $1 00

PECK & SNYDER'S NEW BRACKET SAW.

Consisting of one Saw Frame in neat pasteboard box, 15 Designs for sawing Brackets, Card Receivers, Vases, &c., ½ dozen Extra Saw Blades, one Brad Awl, one piece Sand Paper.

PECK & SNYDER'S Multum in Parvo Scroll Saw will saw through steel, iron, wood or any article, and is well adapted for Jewelers, Machinists, Lapidaries, Tinsmiths, &c.

It is well adapted to any kind of fret or scroll wood sawing. Size of blade four inches, full size of saw, eight and a half inches. Price, by mail, 25 cents.

SMALL NICKEL-PLATED WRENCH

Price, 50 cents.

MODEL FITTINGS OF WOOD & BRASS FOR TOY YACHTS, SHIPS, STEAMBOATS, &C.

We keep constantly on hand every description of fittings for model rigging to be had. In ordering fittings, it would be best to send the length, beam and depth of Vessel.

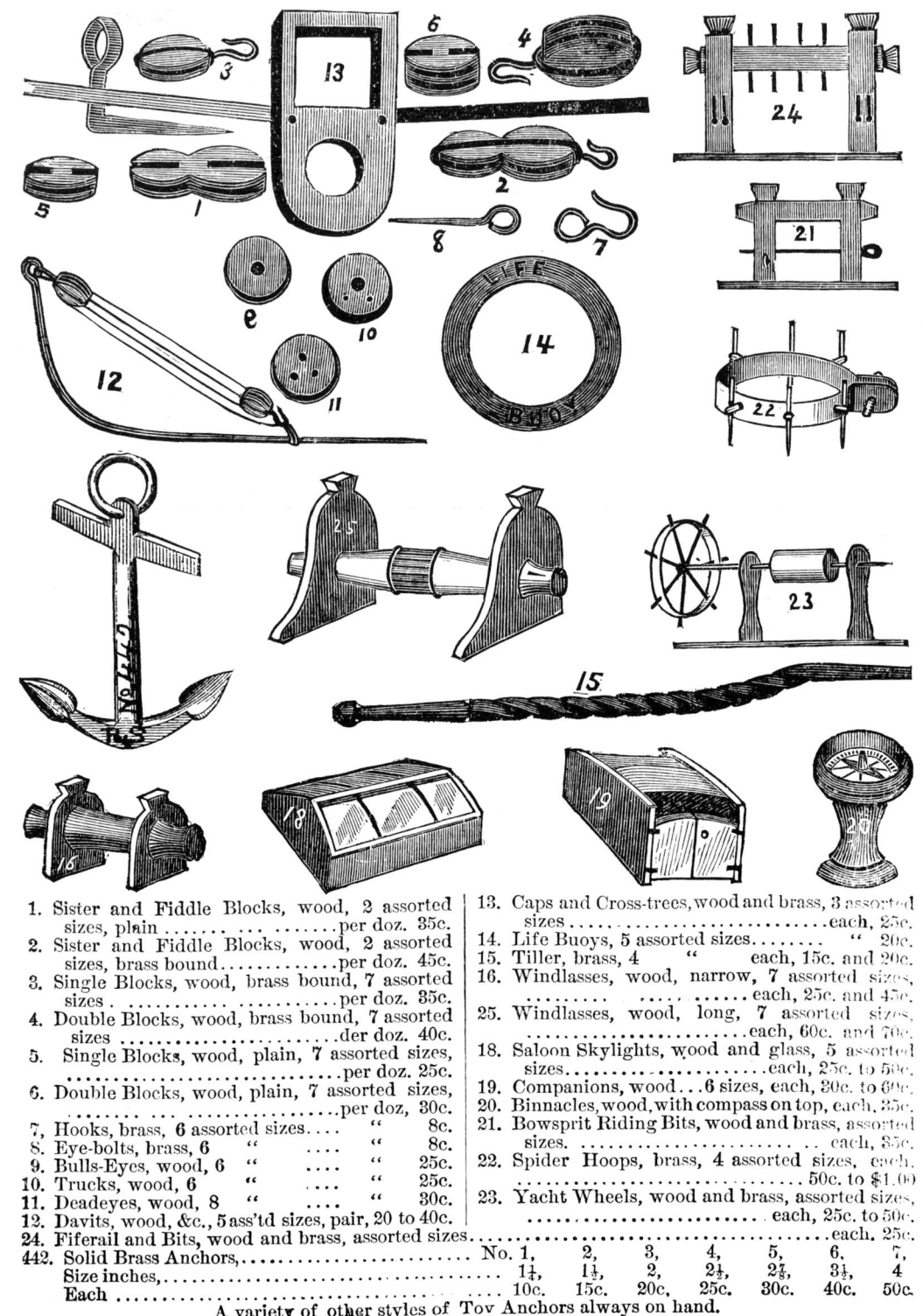

1. Sister and Fiddle Blocks, wood, 2 assorted sizes, plain ....per doz. 35c.
2. Sister and Fiddle Blocks, wood, 2 assorted sizes, brass bound...............per doz. 45c.
3. Single Blocks, wood, brass bound, 7 assorted sizes. ....per doz. 35c.
4. Double Blocks, wood, brass bound, 7 assorted sizes ....per doz. 40c.
5. Single Blocks, wood, plain, 7 assorted sizes, ...per doz. 25c.
6. Double Blocks, wood, plain, 7 assorted sizes, ...per doz. 30c.
7. Hooks, brass, 6 assorted sizes.... " 8c.
8. Eye-bolts, brass, 6 " " 8c.
9. Bulls-Eyes, wood, 6 " " 25c.
10. Trucks, wood, 6 " " 25c.
11. Deadeyes, wood, 8 " " 30c.
12. Davits, wood, &c., 5 ass'td sizes, pair, 20 to 40c.
24. Fiferail and Bits, wood and brass, assorted sizes.
442. Solid Brass Anchors,.......................
    Size inches,.......................
    Each ....

13. Caps and Cross-trees, wood and brass, 3 assorted sizes ....each, 25c.
14. Life Buoys, 5 assorted sizes........ " 20c.
15. Tiller, brass, 4 " each, 15c. and 20c.
16. Windlasses, wood, narrow, 7 assorted sizes, ...each, 25c. and 45c.
25. Windlasses, wood, long, 7 assorted sizes, ...each, 60c. and 70c.
18. Saloon Skylights, wood and glass, 5 assorted sizes.......................each, 25c. to 50c.
19. Companions, wood...6 sizes, each, 30c. to 60c.
20. Binnacles, wood, with compass on top, each, 35c.
21. Bowsprit Riding Bits, wood and brass, assorted sizes. ....each, 35c.
22. Spider Hoops, brass, 4 assorted sizes, each, ...50c. to $1.00
23. Yacht Wheels, wood and brass, assorted sizes, ...each, 25c. to 50c.
    ....each. 25c.

No.	1	2	3	4	5	6	7
Size inches	1¼	1½	2	2¼	2⅝	3½	4
Each	10c.	15c.	20c.	25c.	30c.	40c.	50c.

A variety of other styles of Toy Anchors always on hand.

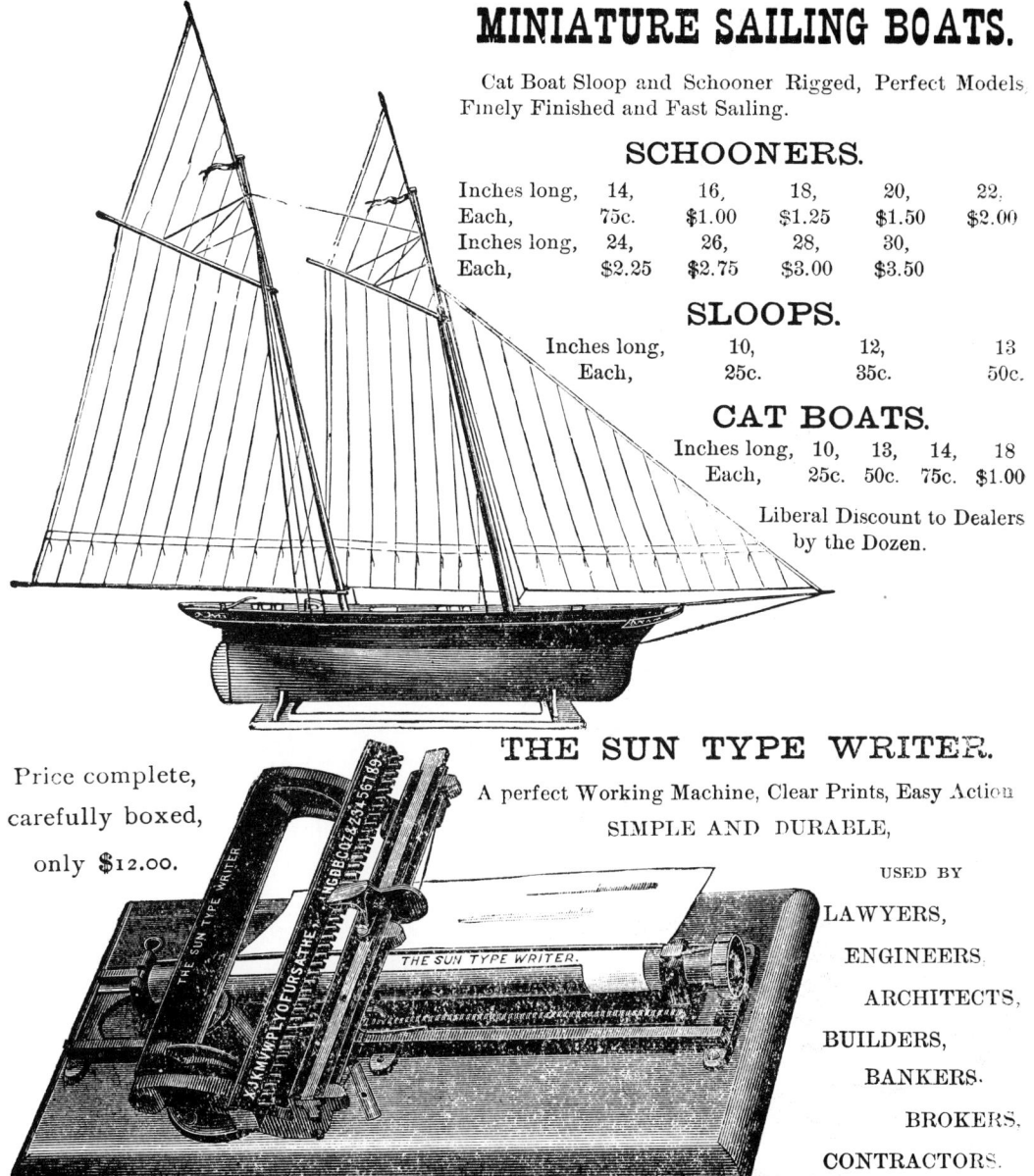

MINIATURE SAILING BOATS.

Cat Boat Sloop and Schooner Rigged, Perfect Models Finely Finished and Fast Sailing.

SCHOONERS.

Inches long,	14,	16,	18,	20,	22,
Each,	75c.	$1.00	$1.25	$1.50	$2.00
Inches long,	24,	26,	28,	30,	
Each,	$2.25	$2.75	$3.00	$3.50	

SLOOPS.

Inches long,	10,	12,	13
Each,	25c.	35c.	50c.

CAT BOATS.

Inches long,	10,	13,	14,	18
Each,	25c.	50c.	75c.	$1.00

Liberal Discount to Dealers by the Dozen.

THE SUN TYPE WRITER.

Price complete, carefully boxed, only $12.00.

A perfect Working Machine, Clear Prints, Easy Action

SIMPLE AND DURABLE,

USED BY

LAWYERS,

ENGINEERS,

ARCHITECTS,

BUILDERS,

BANKERS,

BROKERS,

CONTRACTORS.

The Sun Type Writer meets the popular demand for a low-priced Type Writing Machine which will do perfect work rapidly and easily.

Any one can write with it without practice and do perfect work. Its action is easy and rapid. With a few hours' practice rapidity can be attained. Can be used by the hour without tiring the operator. It is very simple and strong in construction, and cannot get out of order or break. It is small and light, occupying a space twelve inches long, eight inches wide and three and a-half inches high, and weighs but four and a-half pounds. Any one can use it. It is suitable for use in the Office for business purposes, or at Home for private letter writing. Paper of any size can be used up to eight and a-half inches in width. Envelopes addressed and Postal Cards written. Its print is clear and perfect. The impression is made direct from the type. No inking ribbon is used.

THIS IS THE STYLE OF TYPE USED ON THE SUN TYPE WRITER.

THE COLOR OF INK IS BLACK, WHICH COPIES PURPLE.

This Machine is the latest design in the way of a Type Writer, and its simplicity of construction and manipulation are wonderful. Its action is easy, and simply consists in placing the "Stylus" point in front of the letter desired to be printed, and depressing slightly. The rest of the action is automatic. Familiarity with the position of the letters is all that is necessary to produce rapid work.

For making manifold copies it has no superior. Hektograph ink can be used, and one hundred copies taken from Hektograph Pad. Directions for using with every machine.

936 THE IMPROVED PANTOGRAPH.

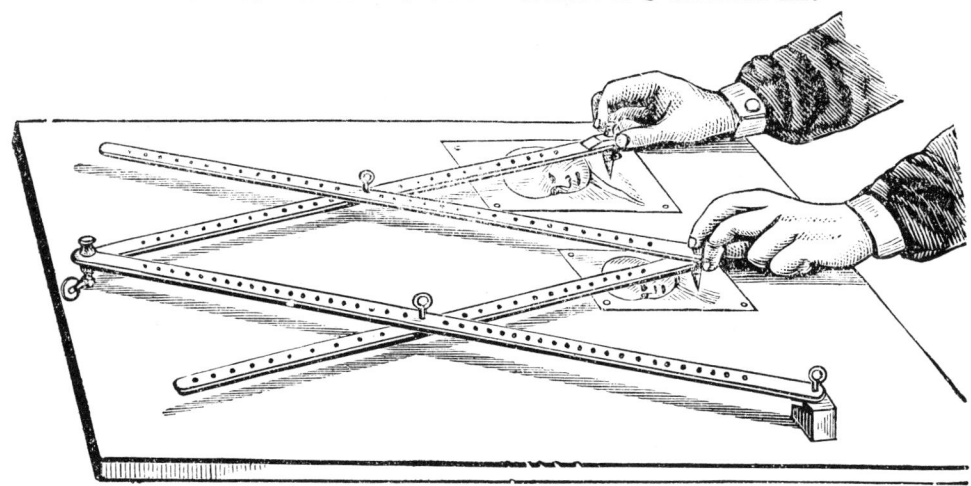

This Instrument ENLARGES or REDUCES all kinds of Drawings, Portraits, Landscapes, Machinery, etc. Its accuracy in working, and its finish, is superior to any instrument selling for double its price. It combines four arms. Attached to one of them is a block that fastens to the Drawing Board or Table, and remains stationary. The four arms have the same number of holes (49), which are the same distance apart, and are numbered from 1 to 49. Besides this, the holes have a graduated scale, showing in what proportion to change or reduce. The scale is marked from $\frac{1}{8}$ of a size to seven sizes (or eight times larger). When you wish to enlarge, look on the scale for figures denoting the required enlargement, and the number opposite, then adjust the four arms together, ALL AT THE SAME NUMBER, by shifting the two steel screws.

Drawings are reduced in the same manner with the exception of changing the tracing or pencil points. The Instrument closes at one size added to the drawing (or making it twice as large), the numbers on all the four arms at the centre pivots being twenty-six. It is a most valuable article for persons owning Scroll or Bracket Saws.

The above Pantograph is made of polished wood, with brass trimmings, and will make a picture 6 feet or 2 inches large, packed in a neat paste board box and sent by mail, postage paid, for..... **$2.50.**

937 THE SCHOLAR'S PANTOGRAPH.

It is used for the same purpose as No. 936, is made of Black Walnut. with steel trimmings, and will make a picture very near as large.

Sent by mail, postage paid .... 25 cts.

The Combination and Adjustable Tool Holder.

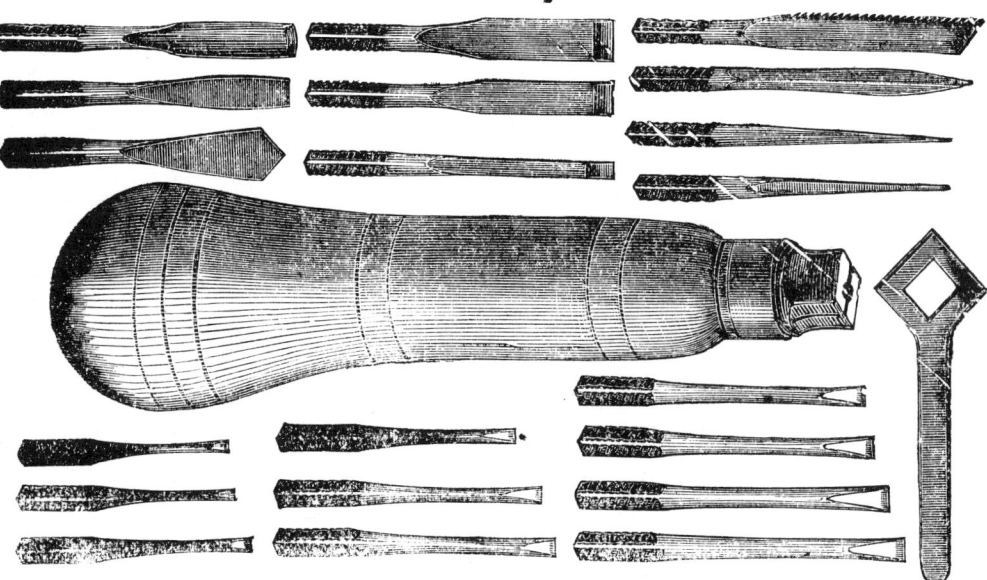

Contains 20 Cast Steel Tools, each the size of above cut, and when not in use, can be inclosed in handle. Sent by mail for .... **$1.00.**

THE ELECTRO RADIANT No. 2.
The Most Popular Magic Lantern Ever Introduced.

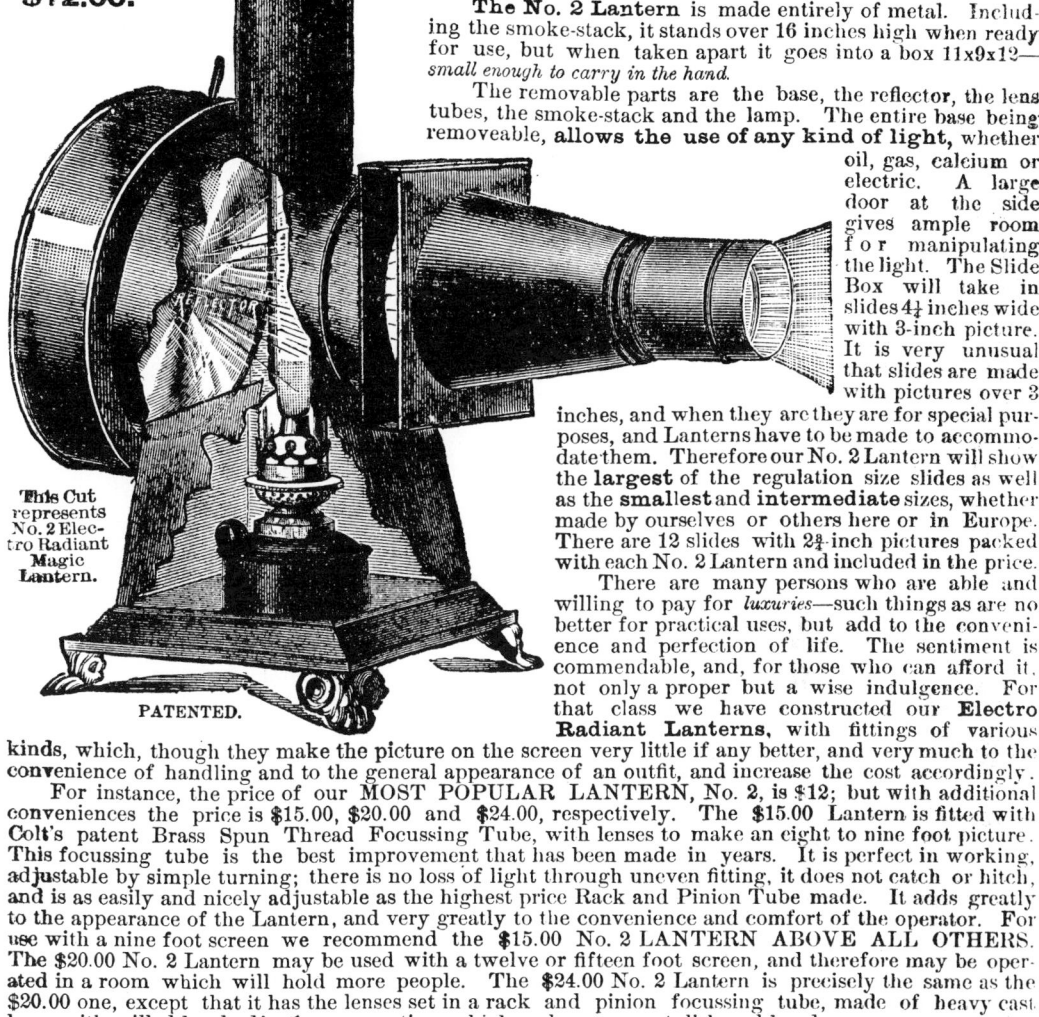

$25.00 Lantern for $12.00.

This Cut represents No. 2 Electro Radiant Magic Lantern.

PATENTED.

The body of the **ELECTRO RADIANT** is a cone-shaped reflector which gathers each divergent ray of light and concentrates them all on the main reflector, whence the whole mass of brilliancy illuminates and projects the picture with startling clearness. No combination of lenses, however ingenious, has ever been known to produce equal effects with the light used.

The **ELECTRO RADIANT No. 2 projects on screen a picture 8 feet in diameter.**

The No. 2 Lantern is made entirely of metal. Including the smoke-stack, it stands over 16 inches high when ready for use, but when taken apart it goes into a box 11x9x12—*small enough to carry in the hand.*

The removable parts are the base, the reflector, the lens tubes, the smoke-stack and the lamp. The entire base being removeable, **allows the use of any kind of light,** whether oil, gas, calcium or electric. A large door at the side gives ample room for manipulating the light. The Slide Box will take in slides 4¼ inches wide with 3-inch picture. It is very unusual that slides are made with pictures over 3 inches, and when they are they are for special purposes, and Lanterns have to be made to accommodate them. Therefore our No. 2 Lantern will show the **largest** of the regulation size slides as well as the **smallest** and **intermediate** sizes, whether made by ourselves or others here or in Europe. There are 12 slides with 2¾-inch pictures packed with each No. 2 Lantern and included in the price.

There are many persons who are able and willing to pay for *luxuries*—such things as are no better for practical uses, but add to the convenience and perfection of life. The sentiment is commendable, and, for those who can afford it, not only a proper but a wise indulgence. For that class we have constructed our **Electro Radiant Lanterns,** with fittings of various kinds, which, though they make the picture on the screen very little if any better, and very much to the convenience of handling and to the general appearance of an outfit, and increase the cost accordingly. For instance, the price of our MOST POPULAR LANTERN, No. 2, is $12; but with additional conveniences the price is $15.00, $20.00 and $24.00, respectively. The $15.00 Lantern is fitted with Colt's patent Brass Spun Thread Focussing Tube, with lenses to make an eight to nine foot picture. This focussing tube is the best improvement that has been made in years. It is perfect in working, adjustable by simple turning; there is no loss of light through uneven fitting, it does not catch or hitch, and is as easily and nicely adjustable as the highest price Rack and Pinion Tube made. It adds greatly to the appearance of the Lantern, and very greatly to the convenience and comfort of the operator. For use with a nine foot screen we recommend the **$15.00 No. 2 LANTERN ABOVE ALL OTHERS.** The $20.00 No. 2 Lantern may be used with a twelve or fifteen foot screen, and therefore may be operated in a room which will hold more people. The $24.00 No. 2 Lantern is precisely the same as the $20.00 one, except that it has the lenses set in a rack and pinion focussing tube, made of heavy cast brass with milled head adjusting connection, which makes a very stylish and handsome appearance.

Price List of No. 2 Electro Radiant Magic Lanterns.

No. 2. With Piano Convex Lenses........$12.00	No. 2B, Double Achromatic Lenses in Colt's Pat. Spun thread tube..........$20.00
No. 2A. " " " " in Colt's Pat Spun thread focussing tube........$15 00	No. 2C. Double Achromatic Lenses in heavy brass rack and pinion focussing tube. $24.00

12 slides are packed with each No. 2 lantern.

PECK & SNYDER,
126, 128 & 130 NASSAU STREET, NEW YORK.

Importers and Dealers in English, French and German Magic Lanterns, at prices from $2.00 to $50.00 each, also in those of the best American make, prices $5.00 to 75.00 each.

THE ELECTRO RADIANT MEGASCOPE,

For projecting on the Screen reflections of opaque objects, and enlarging them to four and six feet, and even more in some instances. For instance, the works of a watch in motion may be enlarged to three or four feet, while the head and bust of the human figure may be enlarged six feet or more. The size of the enlarged picture may be regulated to suit different purposes. If it is desired to throw on the screen a fac-simile of a portrait for the purpose of sketching, it would not be needed any larger than life size; but if it was wanted to show to an audience of several, it might be desirable to throw it up as large as possible. This can be regulated by the distance of the Lantern from the screen.

The Megascope differs from the Magic Lantern in that it will show only opaque objects, while the Magic or Direct Acting Lantern will show only transparent pictures or objects.

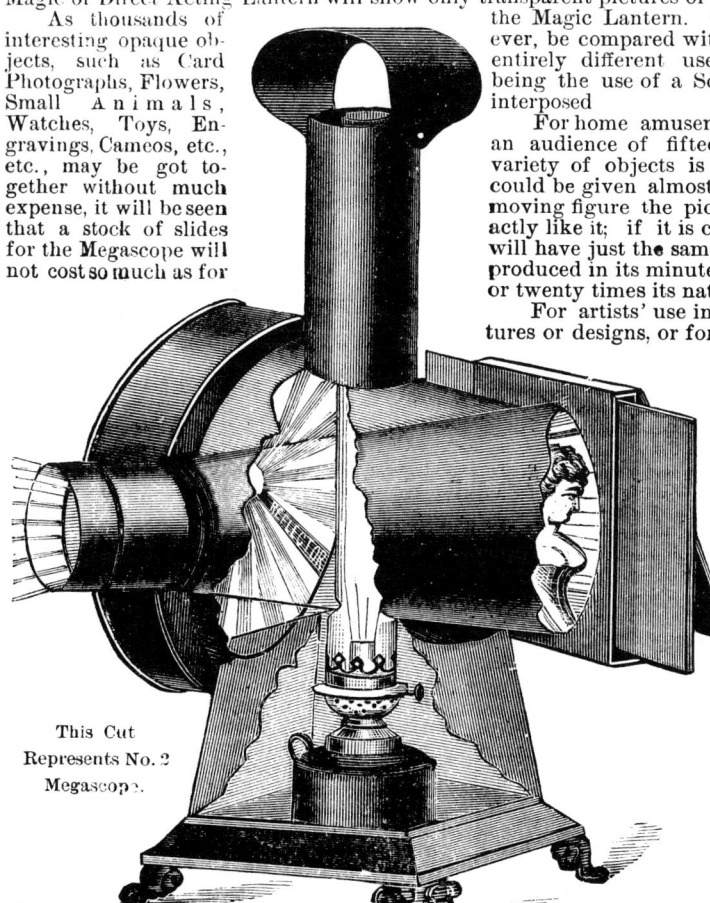

This Cut Represents No. 2 Megascope.

PATENTED.

As thousands of interesting opaque objects, such as Card Photographs, Flowers, Small Animals, Watches, Toys, Engravings, Cameos, etc., etc., may be got together without much expense, it will be seen that a stock of slides for the Megascope will not cost so much as for the Magic Lantern. The Megascope must not, however, be compared with the Magic Lantern. It is for entirely different uses, the only thing in common being the use of a Screen before a light with Lenses interposed

For home amusement the Megascope will delight an audience of fifteen or twenty persons, and the variety of objects is so great that a fresh exhibition could be given almost every night. If the object is a moving figure the picture on the screen will move exactly like it; if it is colored, the picture on the screen will have just the same colors; in fact, the object is reproduced in its minutest detail and enlarged five, ten or twenty times its natural size.

For artists' use in enlarging and transferring pictures or designs, or for manufacturers' use for enlarging delicate parts so that they may be examined more readily, the Megascope is invaluable.

In the manufacture of the Megascope we have utilized the principles covered by patents the same as in our Electro Radiant Magic Lanterns, and have spared no pains in making a substantial and attractive article. The body of the Megascope is made of Japanned and decorated metal, with proper openings for ventilation and convenience of operating. It has a Lamp with Argand Burner and Chimney, or it may be used over an Argand Gas Burner. It is the most satisfactory Lantern in every way ever made to show opaque objects, and does not get out of order easily.

PRICES.

No. 2. Electro Radiant Megascope, with 100 assorted pictures and objects. Brass Lamp and Argand Oil Burner........ ...Each, $15 00
Same as above, but fitted with our New Automatic Adjustable Lens Tube.....Each, 18 00
Fitted with Argand Gas Burner and six feet of rubber tubing........ ...Extra—Each, 5 00
No. 1. Imperial E. R. Megascope, in which Cabinet or Imperial Photographs can be used ; also any picture or object not larger than 4x8 inches ; Extra Lenses, Brass Rack and Pinion Adjustable Lens Tube, Parabolic Reflector and Argand Oil Burner ; handsomely japanned and decorated body, about 8x11x14 inches ; very elegant instrument...................... Each, $60 00

$50.00 OUTFIT—Electro Radiant Magic Lantern No. 2. Screen 9x9 feet, First Quality.

12 Colored Slides, 4¼x3¼..	12	views
7 Gem Slides, Set No. 10, American Civil War..................................	21	"
3 " " 12 Comics..	9	"
4 " " 18 Pilgrim's Progress............................	12	"
12 3¼x4¼, Foreign Views...	12	"
12 Slip Slides...	12	"
3 Lever "	6	"
1 Chromatrope Slide	1	"
Total...	85	views

The construction of this Lantern is such as to especially commend it to Exhibitors.

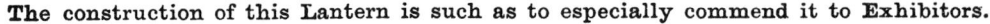

Electro Radiant Lantern, No. 10.

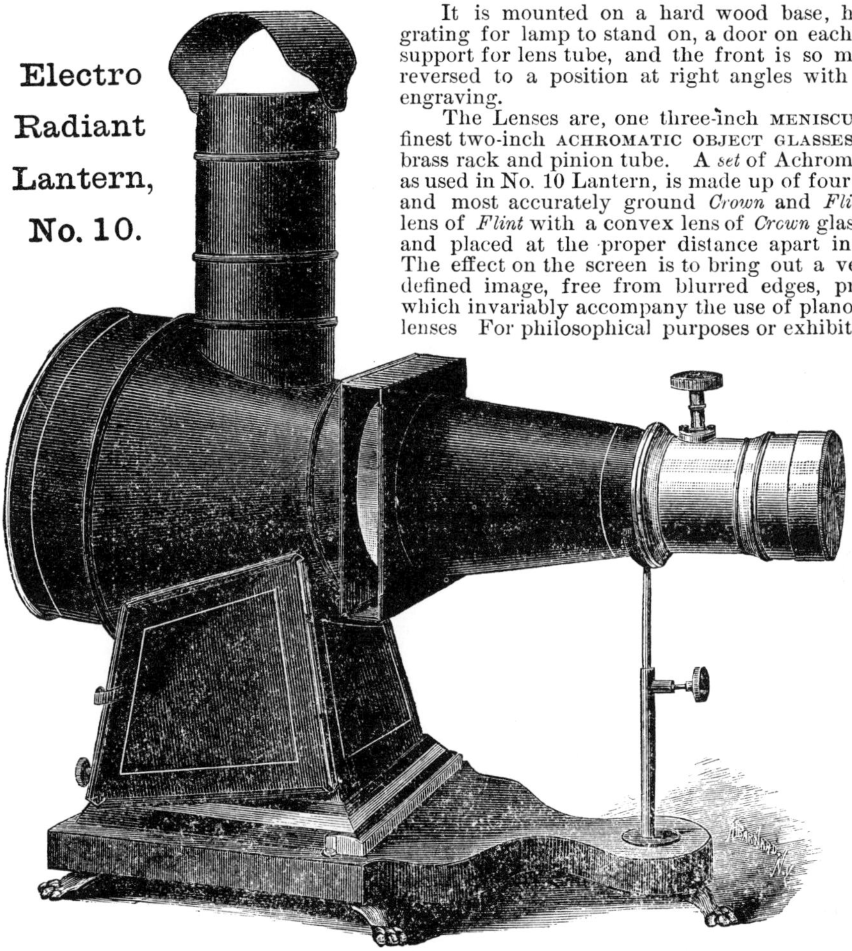

It is mounted on a hard wood base, having a perforated grating for lamp to stand on, a door on each side, an adjustable support for lens tube, and the front is so made that it may be reversed to a position at right angles with that shown in the engraving.

The Lenses are, one three-inch MENISCUS and a set of the finest two-inch ACHROMATIC OBJECT GLASSES mounted in heavy brass rack and pinion tube. A *set* of Achromatic Object Glasses, as used in No. 10 Lantern, is made up of four Lenses of the finest and most accurately ground *Crown* and *Flint Glasses*, a *concave* lens of *Flint* with a convex lens of *Crown* glass are paired in cells and placed at the proper distance apart in the focusing tube. The effect on the screen is to bring out a very sharp and well-defined image, free from blurred edges, prismatic color, etc., which invariably accompany the use of plano, or concavo-convex lenses For philosophical purposes or exhibitions before an audience of considerable numbers *Achromatic Lenses* are indispensable. For clearness of definition according to the light used, for ease of adjustment, and general convenience in working, this Lantern has no equal at the price. It accommodates slides of all makes now in vogue and is thoroughly well adapted for dissolving effects.

The Brass Lamp for this Lantern has an ARGAND BURNER of ten candle power (Photometic test United States Light House Department), giving a clear steady light when the best kerosene oil is used.

Price of Electro Radiant Lantern No. 10, without views................................. $26 00
Price of pair of No. 10 Lanterns, with Dissolver 5 80

For the best effects obtainable short of lime or electric light, the two following illuminators have been arranged for us in the Electro Radiant Lanterns Nos. 2 and 10, viz.:
Extra fine 23 candle power kerosene burner and large glass fount on adjustable stand........... $6 00
Argand gas burner; adjustable, with eight feet of rubber tubing............................... 6 00

Artists can save many hours of work and attain great accuracy of expression by using in connection with our Sketching Lantern a photograph negative of the subject to be produced. An adjustable support on the Lantern enables the artist to arrange his negative or positive, if he prefers to use the latter, at any height or angle, and the picture may be thrown on to the paper or canvas, anywhere from miniature to twice life size, for any part of the negative which will come within a three-inch circle. Not only the outlines of a picture may be quickly sketched but indications of the proper shading may be marked in the right places, thus saving much labor in the working up of a subject. The room in which the work is done need not be so dark as for lantern exhibition purposes, as a sufficiently clear outline to work may be had in a moderately dark room. The engraving represents our Sketching Lantern, with Colt's patent focusing tube, having $\frac{1}{4}$ size achromatic glasses.

The price of this Lantern is $20.00, being the lowest price by far for which Lanterns of similar power have been sold.

We also apply to the same body Plano Convex Lenses in Slip Focusing Tube at $12.00 each.

A lamp with Argand Burner using best kerosene oil is supplied with the Lantern, though an Argand Burner and common gas may be used if more convenient. Each Lantern is packed in a neat box and is light and portable.

By the use of this Lantern the sketching may be done by a boy or girl, saving the artist's time and talent for shading and finishing touches. If an artist is not a photographer, an arrangement can generally be made with some photographer to furnish at a low figure a negative plate for use with the Electro Radiant Sketching Lantern.

Sketching Lantern, with Achromatic Lenses, in Colt's Patent Focusing Tube............ $20 00 | Sketching Lantern, with Plano Convex Lenses, in Slip Focusing Tube $12 00

ELECTRO RADIANT MAGIC LANTERN NO. 3.

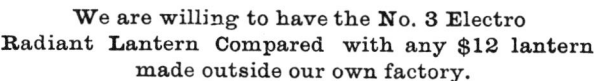

This Lantern was designed Especially for Youths, not only for its remarkable effects on the screen, but also for its limited effect on the pocket.

Most boys can raise $8.00 without much trouble, and if they invest it in a No. 3 lantern, they will have a foundation for pleasure or profit that is seldom, if ever covered by so small an outlay.

It will enlarge a 2 inch picture to **four feet**, is suitable for showing the "Gem" and "Chromatype" slides in this list, as well as slides of any make not over 3 inches wide, and ½ inch thick. The lantern is handsomely japanned, has Colt's Patent focussing lens tube, removable "front" and smokestack, brass lamp with "argand" burner, and round chimney, and the whole, including 12 views and complete directions, is packed, in neat hinged cover box.

We are willing to have the **No. 3 Electro Radiant Lantern Compared** with any $12 lantern made outside our own factory.

With a No. 3 Lantern a boy may amuse a party of friends, or he may, by charging a small admission fee, earn considerable for any object he may set his heart upon. There is as much pleasure for the operator as for the audience. An ingenious boy will have tickets of admission, programmes, music of some sort and numberless little devices to heighten the theatrical, magical and mysterious effect, whether he charges one pin or a dime for admission. All devices he will execute himself, filling leisure hours in writing out his tickets and programmes and making other arrangements to make his exhibition a success. This is not an amusement for one day only, but comes up time and time again with increasing interest even for years. Parents and friends should not ignore the instruction and other beneficial effects, and should by all means make their young people owners of a Lantern.

PRICE OF ELECTRO RADIANT MAGIC LANTERN No. 3, WITH TWELVE VIEWS, ONLY $8.00.

ELECTRO RADIANT MAGIC LANTERN No. 4.

This Lantern is the same as No. 3, except that it has no smokestack and the lamp has a no-chimney burner. For equal distinctness therefore, the effects must be confined to a smaller circle on the screen.

PRICE OF No. 4 LANTERN, WITH TWELVE VIEWS, $6.00.

SCREENS.

We furnish screens made of best quality material, with loops around the four sides of the screen. By these loops the Screen can be attached to a wooden Frame, though the most convenient plan is to dispense with a frame and to screw two small screw rings into the wall, or window frame, one on each side of the hall, near the ceiling; then pass a stout cord or rope through the loops on the upper edge of the screen, and through the rings, bringing the ends of the cords down and securing them. By the loops on the sides and lower edge, the screen can be held firmly in position by cords attached to screw rings on the floor.

Prices of Screens.

7½ feet square	$2.50	12 feet square	$ 7.00	18 feet square	$12.00
9 feet square	4.00	15 feet square	10.00	24 feet square	18.00

$13.00 OUTFIT—The Electro Radiant Magic Lantern No. 3.

12 Colored Slides, Nos. 531 to 537 and 571 to 575	12	views
12 Chromatype Slides	12	"
12 French Slides 2½ x 8	50	"
2 Gem Slides, Visit of Santa Claus	6	"
Total	80	views

$25.00 OUTFIT—The Electro Radiant Magic Lantern No. 2.

12 Colored Slides, 3¼ x 4¼	12	views
8 Gem Slides, Nos. 1, 2, 15, 16, 17, 18, 19 and 20, 2½ x 8	24	"
3 Slips " " " " 4¼ x 7	3	"
3 Lever " " " " 4¼ x 7	3	"
1 Chromatrope Slide " " " 4¼ x 6	1	"
Total	43	views

OUTFITS.—For the convenience of purchasers and to save detail, we have arranged to pack the above combinations or *outfits*. They will be found to comprise a good assortment suitable for home and public exhibitions at a less cost than the same assortment if ordered separately. *As a present*, or for a beginner wishing to start economically, these outfits are just the thing.

GEM SLIDES.

The Gem Views enumerated in this list are all choice Photographic Transparencies. In quality, uniformity of tone and finish, they are equal to the best Foreign and American Slides now made, and are superior to most. Every Slide has a protecting glass, insuring it from damage by scratching. They consist of **Views from Nature, Old and New Testament, Temperance, Statuary, Natural Phenomena, Comic Scenes, U. S. History,** and **Miscellaneous Subjects.**

The Gem Slides are eight inches long, and each Slide has three views two inches in diameter. Printed Lectures are furnished **free** with Sets Nos. 2, 3, 4 and 5 when the set is ordered.

Imagine the effect on an audience when pictures like the following are enlarged three to eight feet in diameter, with every line and feature clearly shown.

POOR DONKEY.

[From Slide No. 90.]

POOR CHILDREN.

Gem Slides. Set No. 1. Views from Nature. 14 Slides. 42 Pictures.

SLIDE NO.
1. AMERICA.—Niagara Falls. Mirror Lake, Yosemite. The Pool, White Mountains, N. H.
2. ENGLAND.—House of Parliament. Windsor Castle. Waterloo Bridge.
3. VENICE.—Grand Canal. Bridge of Sighs. The Rialto.
4. IRELAND.—Giant's Causeway. Queenstown. Holy Cross Abbey.
5. SWITZERLAND—Sea of Ice. Castle Chillon. Falls of Staubach.
6. CONSTANTINOPLE.—Palace of the Sultan. Fountain of St. Sophia. Mosque of Mahomet.
7. EGYPT.—The Nile Boat. Pyramids and Sphynx. Statues at Thebes.
8. JERUSALEM —Mosque of Omar. Church of the Holy Sepulchre. Damascus Gate.
9. GERMANY—St. Goar on the Rhine. Castle Ehrenfels. City of Cologne.
10. RUSSIA, Moscow.—The Kremlin. The Great Bell. Church of St. Brazile.
11. SCOTLAND.—Melrose Abbey. Balmoral Castle. Calton Hill, Edinburgh.
12. ROME.—St. Peter's Church, exterior. St. Peter's Church, interior. View of Rome from St. Peter's.
13. ROME —The Colosseum, exterior. The Colosseum, interior. Dying Gladiator.
14. PARIS.—Panorama of Paris. Notre Dame. The Louvre.

Price 75c. each Slide, or $10.50 for the Set.

Gem Slides. Set No. 2. Scripture. 6 Slides. 18 Pictures.

SLIDE NO.
15. Joseph Sold. Joseph's Bloody Coat. Joseph Meeting His Father.
16. Rebecca at the Well. Eliezer at the House of Bethuel. Arrival of Rebecca.
17. Moses Saved. Moses Assisting the Daughters of Jethro. Destruction of Pharaoh's Host.
18. The Annunciation. Wise Men Guided by the Star. Birth of Christ.

SET No. 2, Continued.
SLIDE NO.
19. Baptism of Christ. Christ's Entry into Jerusalem. Sermon on the Mount.
20. Last Supper. Christ Rejected. The Crucifixion.

Price of Set No. 2, $4.50.

Gem Slides. Set No. 3. Temperance. Drunkard's Progress. 4 Slides. 12 Pictures.

SLIDE NO.
21. Domestic Happiness—the Greatest of Earthly Blessings. The Temptation. Introduction of Sorrow—A Loving Heart Made Sad.
22. The Rum Hole, a Substitute for Home. Rum Instead of Reason. Degraded Humanity.
23. The Cold Shoulder by Old Friends. Rumseller's Gratitude. Rejection Instead of Injection. Poverty and Want.
24. Robbery and Murder the result of drunkenness. Mania-á-Potu, the Horror of Horrors. The Death that Precedes Eternal Death.

Price of Set No. 3, $3.00.

Gem Slides. Set No. 4. The Bottle. 3 Slides. 9 Pictures.

SLIDE NO.
25. The Bottle is brought out for the first time. Discharged for drunkenness. Execution sweeps off the furniture.
26. Unable to obtain employment. Cold, misery and want. Fearful quarrels.
27. The husband kills his wife. The bottle has done its work. Delirium tremens.

Price of Set No. 4, $2.25.

Gem Slides. Set No. 5. Ten Nights in a Bar Room. 4 Slides. 12 Pictures.

SLIDE NO.
28. Arrival at the "Sickle and Sheaf." Joe Morgan's little Mary begs him to go home. Slade throws a glass at Joe Morgan and hits Mary.
29. Joe Morgan suffering the horrors of delirium tremens. Death of Joe Morgan's little Mary. Frank Slade and Tom Wilkins riding off on a spree.

30. Willie Hammond is induced by Harvey Green to gamble. Harvey Green stabs Willie Hammond to death. Quarrel between Slade and his son Frank.
31. Frank Slade kills his father with a bottle. Meeting of the citizens in the bar-room, The departure from the "Sickle and Sheaf."
Price of Set No. 5, $3.00.

Gem Slides. Set No. 6. Statuary—Rogers' Groups, etc. 9 Slides. 27 Views.
SLIDE NO.
32. Rip Van Winkle at home. Rip Van Winkle on the mountains. Rip Van Winkle returned.
33. Thorwaldsen's Gems—Spring. Summer. Autumn.
34. Thorwaldsen's Gems—Winter. Night. Morning.
35. Parting Promise. Courtship in Sleepy Hollow. Coming to the Parson.
36. Mail Day. Town Pump. Village Schoolmaster.
37. The Bushwhacker. The Sharpshooter. Wounded Scout.
38. We Boys. Uncle Ned's School. Country Post Office.
39. Eve Before the Fall. Bird Family Monument. Simply to Thy Cross I Cling.
40. The Serenade. The Courtship. Ariadne and the Tiger.
Price of Set No. 6, $6.75, or 75c. per Slide.

Gem Slides. Set No. 7. Miscellaneous. 19 Slides. 57 Pictures.
SLIDE NO.
41. The Ill-fated Ship. The Ship sailing with a fair wind. Height of the storm. The Ship on fire.
42. Fate of the Steamship. Leaving Port. Mid-Ocean. The Wreck.
43. Fort Sumter in peace—Daylight. Fort Sumter in peace—Moonlight. Fort Sumter on fire during the bombardment.
44. Bay of Naples and Mount Vesuvius—Day. Bay of Naples—Night. Bay of Naples—Eruption of Mount Vesuvius.
45. Courtship for the second wife. Ghost of the first appears—and creates the utmost consternation.
46. The First Meeting; Five minutes after. Declaration; Five years after. Consequences.
47. Frigid Zone Temperate Zone. Torrid Zone.
48. Steamboat race on the Mississippi. Wooding up. The explosion.
49. Sick Monkey. Monkey duel. Darwinian.
50. Moving day. Life boat. Protection.
51. Mud Pies. Washing day. Playing at doctor.
52. Whitewashing the Negro. Flaw in the Title. Oh, Fitzgerald.
53. Ecce Homo. Mater Dolorosa. Prayer.
54. Jerusalem in her grandeur. Jerusalem in her fall (Selons). Garden of Gethsemane.
55. To the rescue. Saved. Jack in office.
56. Temperance meeting. The friendly meal. The horse fair.
57. The Prodigal Son—The Carousal. Swineherd. The return.
58. Rock of Ages; Sea. Cross in Sea. Figure clinging to rock.
51. The Lake. The Glacier. Near the Falls.
Price of Set No. 7, $14.25, or 75c. per Slide.

Gem Slides. Set No. 8. Comic. 6 Slides. 18 Pictures.
SLIDE NO.
60. Romance. Reality. Injured Innocence.
61. Bull-Dozing. Picturesque Africa. Hold on to suffin', its goin' off dis time.
62. Dey say I can't—but I'se gone done it. Platonic love.
63. Nip and Tuck. Battle for Doll, both victorious. We met by chance.
64. Come into the garden, Maud. I will not ask to press that cheek. Take back the heart thou gavest.
65. 'Twere vain to tell thee all I feel. Darling, I am growing old. 'Twas a calm, still night.
Price of Set No. 8, $4.50, or 75c per Slide.

Gem Slides. Set No. 9. United States History, etc. 5 Slides. 15 Pictures.
SLIDE NO.
66. Landing of Columbus, 1492. Marriage of Pocahontas, 1613. Landing of the Pilgrims, 1620.
67. Penn's Treaty with the Indians. 1682. Battle of Bunker Hill. 1775. Washington Crossing the Delaware, 1776.
68. Declaration of Independence, 1776. Washington at Valley Forge, 1777. Indian Massacre at Wyoming, 1778.
69. Capture of Major Andre. 1780. Surrender of Cornwallis, 1781. Commodore Perry at Lake Erie, 1813.
70. "Old Abe After the Battle." "Yankee Doodle." Goddess of Liberty.
Price of Set No. 9, $3.75, or 75c. per Slide.

Gem Slides. Set No. 10. American Civil War. 7 Slides. 21 Views.
SLIDE NO.
71. Bombardment of Fort Sumter. Battle of Bull Run. Battle of Wilson's Creek.
72. Battle of Roanoke Island. Capture of Fort Donelson. Battle of Pittsburg Landing.
73. Capture of New Orleans. Battle of Fair Oaks. Battle of Antietam.
74. Attack on Fredericksburg. Siege of Vicksburg. Battle of Gettysburg.
75. Battle of Chickamauga. Battle of Lookout Mountain. Battle of the Wilderness.
76. Attack on Fort Wagner. Capture of Petersburg. Naval combat between Monitor and Merrimac.
77. Naval combat between Kearsarge and Alabama. Sherman's march through Georgia. Surrender of General Lee.
Price of Set No. 10, $5.25, or 75c. per Slide.

Gem Slides. Set No. 11. American Scenery. 11 Slides. 33 Views.
SLIDE NO.
78. NEW YORK.—Central Park. Post Office. Stewart's Store.
79. NEW YORK—City Hall. East River Bridge. Elevated Railroad.
80. NEW YORK.—Shipping. East River. The Tombs. Trinity Church.
81. WASHINGTON.—Capitol. White House. War Department.
82. WASHINGTON.—Smithsonian Institute. Patent Office. Treasury Building.
83. BOSTON.—Faneuil Hall. Bunker Hill Monument. Old South Church.
84. PHILADELPHIA.—Independence Hall. Girard College. Masonic Hall.
85. Harbor of San Francisco. Capitol—Sacramento. Salt Lake City.
86. SAN FRANCISCO.—Palace Hotel. Chinese Joss House, exterior. Chinese Joss House, interior.
97.—YOSEMITE.—Cathedral Rock. Yosemite Falls. YELLOWSTONE—Bee Hive Geyser.
88. SALT LAKE CITY.—Brigham Young's House. Mormon Temple, exterior. Mormon Temple, interior.
Price of Set No. 11, $8.25, or 75c. per Slide.

Gem Slides. Set No. 12. Comic. 3 Slides. 9 Views.

SLIDE NO,
89. Another Negro Rising. Same. Pleasure before business.
90. Poor Donkey. Poor Children. That husband of mine:
91. The Three Graces. Great Expectations. A pleasure party.
Price of Set No. 12, $2.25, or 75c. per Slide.

Gem Slides. Set No. 13. Anatomy. 4 Slides. 12 Views.

SLIDE NO.
92. Human Skeleton. Anatomy of the Ear. Diagram of the Eye.
93. Muscles—Front View. Muscles—Back View. Muscles of the Head, Neck and Face.
94. Heart and Lungs, Stomach, Liver and Pancreas. Digestive Organs in Place.
95. Nerves—General View. Nerves—Fifth Pair. Nerves—Facial.
Price of Set No. 13, $3,00, or 75c. per Slide.

Gem Slides. Set No. 14. Microscopic Objects. 4 Slides. 12 Views.

SLIDE NO.
96. Sheep Tick. Human Head Louse. Dog Flea.
97. Leg of Blow Fly. Eye of House Fly. Proboscis of House Fly.
98. Scales from Wing of Moth. Section of Wheat Straw. Heliopelta.
99. Saws of Saw Fly. Foot of Spider. Sting of Bee.
Price of Set No. 14, $3.00, or 75c. per Slide.

Gem Slides. Set No. 15. Rip Van Winkle. 2 Slides. 6 Views.

SLIDE NO.
100. Rip Van Winkle Playing with the Children. Rip Van Winkle at the Village Inn. His Scolding Wife.
101. Rip Van Winkle on the mountains. Rip Van Winkle returns after a nap of twenty years. Relating his story.
Price of Set No. 15, $1.50, or 75c. per Slide.

Gem Slides. Set No. 16. Drunkard's Daughter. 2 Slides. 6 Views.

SLIDE NO.
102. Her Mother Dying. She is left alone in the world. She endeavors to support herself by sewing shirts. Payment for her work is refused for alleged imperfections.
103. Unable to pay rent, she is turned into the street. In a moment of despair she plunges into eternity. Take her up tenderly, lift her with care.
Price of Set. No, 16, $1.50, or 75c. per Slide.

Gem Slides. Set 17. Uncle Tom's Cabin. 4 Slides. 12 Views.

SLIDE NO.
104. George Harris takes leave of his wife. An evening in Uncle Tom's cabin. Escape of Eliza and child on the ice.
105. Uncle Tom sold and leaving his family. Eva St. Clair makes a friend of Uncle Tom. Uncle Tom saves Eva from drowning.
106. George Harris resisting the slave hunters. Eva and Topsy. Eva reading to Uncle Tom.
107. Eva's dying farewell. Legree's cruelty to Uncle Tom. Death of Uncle Tom.
Price of Set No. 17, $3.00, or 75c. per Slide.

Gem Slides. Set No. 18. Pilgrim's Progress. 4 Slides. 12 Views.

SLIDE NO,
108. Pilgrim and his burden. The Shining Light. The Slough of Despond.
109. Pilgrim at the Gate. Christian and the Three Shining Ones. Pilgrim and the lions.
110. Christian armed. The fight with Appollyon. Vanity Fair.
111. The Pilgrims found sleeping. The Pilgrims and the shepherds. Passing through the Waters.
Price of Set. No. 18, $3.00, or 75c. per Slide.

Gem Slides. Set No. 19. Scripture. 6 Slides. 18 Views.

SLIDE NO.
112. Creation of Light. Adam and Eve expelled from Garden of Eden. The Deluge.
113. Saul and the Witch of Endor. David in camp of Saul. Daniel in the lion's den.
114. Flight into Egypt. Shadow of the Cross. Return to Nazareth.
115. Christ and the Samaritan Woman. Christ healing the sick. Christ raising the daughter of Jairus.
116. Christ preaching on the sea. Christ tempted. Sermon on the mount.
117. Saul on the way to Damascus. Death on the pale horse. Angel shows Jerusalem to John.
Price of Set No. 19, $4.50, or 75c. per Slde.

The foregoing GEM SLIDES are suitable for any lantern, from a toy to the most powerful limelight Stereopticon. They are on glass, eight inches long by two-and-a-half inches wide, the view being two inches in diameter. They are equal to the best Foreign or American Slide, and far better than most, no pains having been spared by our photographers in making them perfect. The above list of subjects, if ordered in the old style of one view on a Slide, would cost $178.50, while we furnish the same number of views in just as fine quality, and only a little smaller, for $80.25. The Electro Radiant Magic Lantern No. 4 will enlarge the Gem Views to three feet, while the No. 2 Lantern will run them up from five to six feet in diameter.

Printed Lectures are furnished with some of the Sets, and are sent FREE when an unbroken set is ordered.

The subjects enumerated in the List of Gem Slides, as well as many other subjects, will be furnished on 4x3¼ Slide, one 3 inch view to the Slide, at $6.00 per dozen for plain photographs, or at $18.00 per dozen beautifully colored.

Gem Slides, artistically colored to order, 75c. each, extra.

SLIDES TO ORDER.

Though the list of subjects prepared and carried in stock by ourselves and other makers are counted by the thousands, and though we are prepared to furnish any slide of any make at makers prices, it often happens that special views for special purposes are wanted. As illustrations of some of the various needs in this respect we give the three following instances of late experience:

For a party in Boston Mass., we furnished from his originals a set of views of the "Gay Head" disaster—Wreck of Steamer Columbus.

For a Western branch of a United Brotherhood, a set of views copied from their chart.

For a Texas doctor. Several views of persons in different stages of convalescence and after they were cured. Also nimself surrounded by revolving colors. Also of several bits of Texas scenery, as well as a number of lettered slides for advertising his various cures and medicines.

CHROMATYPE SLIDES.

These Slides are 4x3 inches, having a transparent view two inches in diameter. They are the most effective cheap slides ever produced, and are made only by the manufacturers of the Electro Radiant Magic Lanterns. The colors are brilliant, and are distinctly defined on the screen.

The subjects selected up to this time are more for amusement than instruction, and will keep an audience laughing constantly. No exhibition should be given without using a number of these Chromatype Slides, as they keep an audience, whether composed of young or old people, in thoroughly good humor. Each slide is numbered to correspond with this list.

533b.

The Cromatype Slides are suitable for any Lantern. Where letters follow the numbers on this list, it indicates several illustrations of the same subject.

547d.

Price, $2.00 Per Dozen.

501a. Watermelon Market—Steady.
502b. Watermelon Market—Rising.
503a. Dey say I can't.
504b. But I'se gone and done it.
505a. Alpine Travel—Bottom out.
506b. Alpine Travel—The fall.
507a. Cutting a swell on ice.
508b. Making a dive under it.
509. Winter scene in Maine.
510. Mill in winter time.
511. Steamer homeward bound.
512. Yacht under full sail.
513. A Winter scene.
514. Chinese punishment.
515. The two jolly frogs.
516. The serenade.
517. Coming through the rye.
518. The little gymnast.
519. Little Miss Muffett, etc.
520. As I went over the water, etc.
521. Hey diddle, de diddle, etc.
522. Tom, Tom, the Piper's Son, etc.
523. Boy on a pig.
524. Neptune rising from the sea.
525. A stormy day.
526. I aint seen nuffin' of your chickens.
527. Biddy and the baby.
528. The art critic.
529. Humpty Dumpty as a policeman.
530. Two souls with but a single thought.
531. Between two fires.
532a. Uncle Bumberton Green visits the city, to hear the sounds and see the sights.
533b. This is the first sound he hears, and it nearly upsets him.
534c. A pack of fire crackers go off, much to his astonishment.
535d. He discovers fire, and runs for the engine.
536e. The boys set fire to his rockets, but he holds on to them.
537f. Finally reaches his cousin's house by way of the chimney.

538. The shooting season has begun.
539a. Ah! Ha! Gold!
540b. Ha! Ha! Sold!
541. Turn about is fair play. Hand over that gun, sir.
542a. A tight fitting boot.
543b. Which comes off rather suddenly.
544a. Four and twenty blackbirds baked in a pie.
545b. The King was in his counting house, etc.
546c. The Queen was in the parlor, etc.
547d. The maid was in the garden.
548. The clarionet player.
549. The clown.
550a. The danger.
551b. The rescue.
552. Darkey and child.
553. The fantastic basso player.
554a. Profit and loss—Golly, what luck!
555b. Profit and loss—Whar's dem eels!
556. Fatherless.
557. Pleasure before business.
558a. So near, and yet so far.
559b. Too near for comfort.
560a. Mischievous Tom.
561b. Mischievous Tom.
562a. By Shiminy, I dinks dot bavements will stand on my head.
563b. Don't I told you so.
564. Rabbit transit.
565. Getting lots of bites.
566. The Monk.
567. A bear majority.
568. An absent-minded tourist.
569. Making a trade.
570. The jolly tar.
571a. ⎧ The invitation. ⎫
572b. ⎪ The mount. ⎪
573c. ⎨ The start. ⎬ Mrs. Simpson's ride.
574d. ⎪ The journey through the air. ⎪
575e. ⎩ The arrival on the ground. ⎭

SCREENS.

We furnish screens made of the best material, with Loops around the four sides of the Screen. By these loops the Screen can be attached to a wooden Frame, though the most convenient plan is to dispense with a Frame and to screw two small screw rings into the wall (or window frame), one on each side of the hall, near the ceiling; then pass a stout cord or rope through the Loops on the upper edge of the Screen, and through the rings, bringing the ends of the cords down and securing them. By the Loops on the sides and lower edge, the Screen can be held firmly in position by cords attached to screw rings on the floor.

Prices of Screens.

7½ feet square............$2 50	12 feet square............$7 00	18 feet square............$12 00
9 feet square............ 4 00	15 feet square............ 10 00	24 feet square............ 18 00

COMIC SLIP SLIDES.

Size 4 1-2x7 inches.

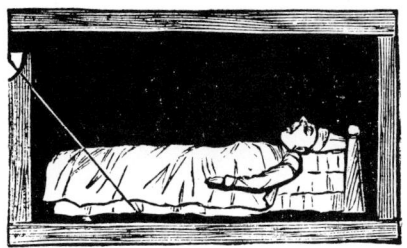 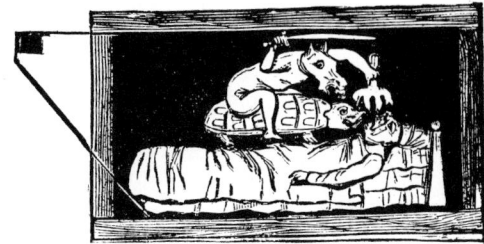

FIRST VIEW   Slide No. 1.   SECOND VIEW.

These Slides are so constructed that two effects are shown on the screen without removing the slide from the lantern. Part of the picture is painted on one glass and the other part on another glass. The two are arranged in a frame so that one glass slips over the other, and very comical effects are produced. It is a great mystery to the uninitiated, and they cannot understand how the transformations are made. The subjects are all comic, so that laughter and good humor are always produced in the audience. The No. 2 Electro Radiant Magic Lantern will reproduce these pictures 8 to 12 feet in diameter.

Price of Comic Slip Slides, 75 Cents Each.

SLIDE NO.

1. DREAM OF A DYSPEPTIC.—A high liver asleep, and some of the horrible objects which appear in his dreams.
2. A PLEA FOR TEMPERANCE.—The lecturer's arguments are supplemented by the stronger one of the sudden appearance on the scene of a poor fellow in the last stages of drunkenness.
3. DRAWING TEETH EXTRAORDINARY.—With old-fashioned forceps a dentist is tugging away at a refractory tooth in the jaw of a patient and it comes out with a jerk.
4. GROWING FAT ON WATER.—A man at the fountain continues drinking until he is as broad as he is long.
5. FIRST-CLASS SHAVE.—Tonsorial artist at work on a stout customer with heavy beard.
6. BOOTS.—Boy tugging at his master's boots, finally starts them and—himself at the same time.
7. FAMILY JARS.—As illustrated by scolding wife and a meek husband.
8. A WINDY DAY.—A gaily dressed lady finds the wind too much for her, It sets her bonnet and false hair flying.
9. OLD LADY AND PET MONKEY.—A pet monkey is perched on the back of an arm-chair in which an old lady is taking a comfortable snooze. The monkey seizes the old lady's cap, wig and all waking her unceremoniously.
10. HIGHLAND FLING.—A fine Scotch laddie in full Highland costume is having a "Fling" all to himself.
11. THE HAPPY PAIR.—A luscious pear suddenly changes to a jolly old couple.
12. FARMER AND PIG.—The farmer, having bought a good-sized pig, thinks he will ride him home. to which plan the pig objects, and with a grunt and a jump sends Mr. farmer in the air.
13. OPENING ROSE—A tiny rosebud gradually developes into a full-blown rose.
14. THE SLEEPING RAT-EATER.—A bearded Russian is sleeping when a rat crawls over the bed and jumps into the sleeper's open mouth, when, instead of waking, he gently chews, as if eating a delicious morsel.
15. THE HAPPY BLACKSMITH.—Never so happy as when at work. Is hammering at his anvil and making the sparks fly.
16. PARSON AND THE PIG.—A jolly fat parson is just putting his knife into a succulent little roast pig, which lies on a platter before him, but piggy is not ready to be eaten yet, and shows his disapproval by leaping from the dish and catching the parson by the nose.
17. WHO GOES THERE?—Two rats are nibbling at a cut cheese on a shelf in happy contentment, when the cat steps in and they leave in a hurry. The sudden disappearance of the rats and comical movements of the cat's eyes are ludicrous in the extreme.
18. THE FISHERMAN AND THE BULL.—A lover of fishing stands on the bank of a river waiting for a bite, all unconscious of danger, when an infuriated bull sends him flying.
19. WITH A GROWING FAMILY.—How a city man provides a play-ground for his children. His nose grows with each new comer, providing ample room.
20. GOOD-NIGHT.—Punch, in full costume, with cap, bells and enormous hump, placard in one hand and club in the other, gently hints it is time to go. This is a good slide with which to close an exhibition.
21. STEALING APPLES.—As the boy who has been stealing apples descends the tree a gentle bull-dog appears and helps him down from behind.
22. AFTER THE CIRCUS.—Animals dancing on the breast of the man who went to the circus, and then went to bed to dream of them.
23. HINDOO AND IDOL.—A devout Hindoo prostrates himself before an idol only to be mocked by it.
24. THE DYNAMITER.—In an unlucky moment the bomb explodes and carries the poor fellow's head high in the air
25. BIRD NESTING.—A boy stealing eggs from a bird's nest gets his deserts, as the old bird flies at him and twists his nose with vengeance.
26. MONKEY DIPPING CAT.—A mischievous monkey holds a cat by the tail over a tub, and gives her an occasional dip in the water.

PECK & SNYDER, 126, 128 & 130 Nassau Street, New York.
IMPORTERS AND DEALERS IN MAGIC LANTERNS AND SLIDES.

CHROMATROPES.

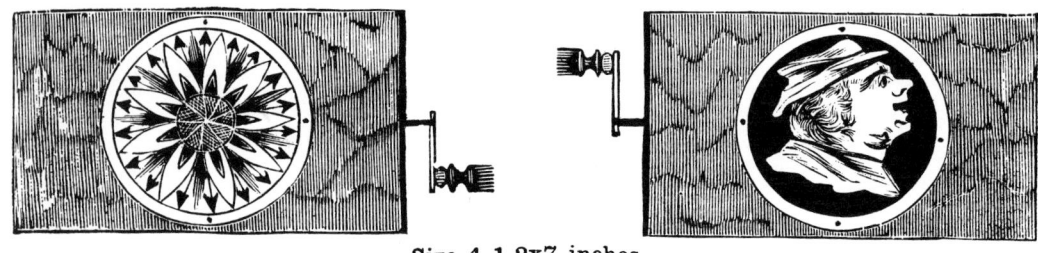

Size 4 1-2x7 inches.

These are handsomely painted geometrical or other figures on two glasses, which, by an ingenious arrangement of crank-pinion and gear wheels, are made to revolve in opposite directions, producing an endless variety of changes, almost equal to a grand display of fire-works. Heretofore "Chromatropes" have been very expensive, on account of the hand-work on the metal parts. We have, at large expense, completed machinery for the production of the metal work, which will reduce the cost about one-half.

The Electro Radiant Magic Lantern enlarges these views to eight and twelve feet in diameter, according to size of your screen.

Prices—three-inch Double Glass.

FINE GEOMETRICAL PATTERNS, with brilliant chromatic effects............Each, $1 50
CHANGEABLE HEADS.—(3-inch single glasses) 1 50
GOOD-NIGHT CHROMATROPE.—The words "Good Night" in a handsome design, around which revolve a display of brilliant colors, very effective in closing an exhibition ....Each, 2 50
LANDSCAPE CHROMATROPE.—A landscape finely painted is shown, with mill and revolving water-wheel, or like effect...Each, 3 00
CAUDLE LECTURES.—Mr. and Mrs. Caudle sitting in bed, the changing expressions of their faces as the curtain lecture proceeds is very comical and suggestive......Each, 3 00
CHANGEABLE FEATURE CHROMATROPE.— View of a head, or of rocks or shrubbery. When revolved changes into quite another picture...................Each, $3 00
INTERCHANGEABLE CHROMATROPES.— We have arranged a Chromatrope Frame in such a manner that the colored views may be easily removed and changed. Price of Frame, each, $1.50. Price of Views, each 75c................Per pair, 1 50
TOO MANY COOKS.—A large pot is standing over a fire and a number (which seems endless) of cooks are cast into the pot and are apparently boiled into soup, or they may be ejected from the pot, as if they were boiling over........................Each, 3 00
RAT EATING EXTRAORDINARY.—Rat after rat crawls up the bed clothes, and running along the bed disappears into the open mouth of a heavy sleeper..........Each, 3 00

DIORAMIC SLIDES.

Size 4 1-2x12 to 14 inches.

These Slides are exceedingly beautiful. The painting is artistic and elaborate, and the wonder is they can be sold so cheaply. A scene is painted on a fixed glass, and over this is made to pass a long procession of figures—soldiers, vessels, trains of cars, caravans, as the case may be—with the most pleasing and wonderful effects.

The list comprises such subjects as Israelites Crossing the Red Sea, Noah Entering the Ark, Cars crossing New Canti-lever Bridge over Niagara River, with Falls in the distance, Seventh Regiment National Guard passing Fifth Avenue Hotel, New York City, and many others, any one of which is valuable in a Lantern outfit.

Price of Dioramic Slides, $3 00 each.

DISSOLVING VIEW APPARATUS.

The most beautiful effects that can possibly be produced are made by using two lanterns at once. Placed side by side at such an angle that the light from both strikes exactly in the same circle on the screen, it is evident that with a slide in each lantern that both pictures will be projected exactly in the same place ; so that if the light is intercepted at one lantern, only one picture will appear on the screen. By a simple mechanical arrangement operating in front of the lanterns, one picture is made to gradually disappear or dissolve, while at the very same moment the other picture just as gradually makes its appearance, the one seeming to be evolved out of the other. The effect is indescribably impressive.

PRICES WITHOUT VIEWS.

Pair No. 3, Electro Radiant Magic Lanterns..$15 00
Pair No. 2, Electro Radiant Magic Lanterns... 24 00
Pair No. 2A. E. R. Lanterns, with Colt's patent focusing tubes 30 00
Pair No. 2B. E. R. Lanterns, with Colt's patent focusing tubes.................... 40 00
Pair No. 2C. E. R. Lanterns, with rack and pinion focusing tubes.................. 50 00
Pair No. 10. E. R. Lanterns, " " " " 58 00

We challenge competition with Lanterns of American or foreign make at double the prices of ours. Simple, complete, plain directions, as well as list of views, packed with each Lantern.

PECK & SNYDER 126, 128 & 130 Nassau Street, New York.
IMPORTERS AND DEALERS IN MAGIC LANTERNS AND SLIDES.

LEVER SLIDES.

Cut No. 1.   Size, 4 1-2 x 7 inches.   Cut No. 2.

The moving effects produced on the screen by lever slides are very life-like. The picture is painted part on one glass and part on another. One glass is fixed in a wood and the other in a metal frame; the latter is placed over the stationary part in such a manner that it may be moved by the handle or lever attached. In cut No. 1 (shown above) the horse is put in motion by the lever, and appears to be cantering. In No. 2, the children go up and down as natural as can be, and the audience can hardly believe that they are not alive. The No. 2 Electro Radiant Magic Lantern reproduces these pictures 8 to 12 feet in diameter. We consider the Lever one of the very best mechanical effects.

Price of Lever Slides, $1.75 Each.

200. SEE SAW.—See Cut No. 2.
201. BOY BEATING DONKEY.—Cruel blows descend on poor donkey's head.
202. LADY RIDING.—See Cut No. 1.
203. GABRIEL GRUBB AND THE HOB GOBLIN.—See Sawing on Tombstone, keeping poor Grubb in a terrible fright.
204. DONKEY RUNNING AWAY.—With buxom country lass.
205. CITY MAID AND THE COW.—

The city maid wandered in the sweet green fields
  Until tired and weary, to repose she yields,
  Her lovely form reclines with grace,
  And dimples and smiles surround her face.

As she dreams, a gentle faced cow comes passing by,
  The city maid flees with a wild, woful cry,
While the cow remains in a contemplative state
  To demolish the parasol left to its fate.

206. JUDY AND THE BABY.—Judy appears at the window with the baby, which she tosses up and down, much to baby's delight.
207. SAM WELLER BLACKING BOOTS.—Sam brushes away, but with no thought of the approaching searchers for " Jingle " and the lady.
208. FREE LUNCH.—Man at an American lunch counter, raises the dainty morsel on his fork.
209. MENDICANT AT COTTAGE DOOR.—A half frozen beggar lifts his hat in appeal to the sturdy woman at a cottage door.
210. AMERICAN GENTLEMAN.—A portly, well-to-do gentleman gracefully raises his hat. A good slide with which to open an exhibition.
211. CAMEL DRINKING.—A camel with oriental rider on its back, stops at a desert well, and lowers his head to drink.
212. DENTIST AND PATIENT.—To draw a refractory tooth, dentist and patient brace themselves for a heavy pull, but to the dentist's horror, his patient's HEAD as well as his tooth comes out.
213. CAVALIER.—A soldier sitting at table, raises glass of wine to his lips.
214. BEGGAR AND CHILD.—A street beggar bows, asking alms from a child.
215. WOMAN BATHING.—

She daintily crawls by the life-line extended
  Hoping nothing will grab her poor feet undefended.
A saucy big wave carries her far from the shore
  And she helplessly rolls amid old ocean's roar.

216. THE PRINCE OF BORNEO AND THE ALLIGATOR.—The frightened prince feeling discretion to be the better part of valor, hastily climbs the nearest tree shaking with fear, while the alligator snaps his mighty jaws in close proximity.
217. HOW DO YOU LIKE IT YOURSELF ?—A cat after a rat runs into an open wire trap and is caught, while the rat sits on its haunches and raises paws to nose.
218. THE HYPOCRITE.—An old woman, who with her eyes turned upward looks pious, but when she casts them down and her jaw drops, looks a veritable old hag.
219. THE COQUETTE.—A sweet maid of fifty or thereabouts, turns her head this way and that with very comical effect.
220. —DEFIANCE.—A fierce-looking woman with her arms akimbo, shakes her head defiantly.
221. —THE SHOEMAKER.—An industrious Cobbler hammers at the leather on his lap-stone.
222. THE SLEEPY DEACON.—The deacon stands with folded hands, apparently listening, but in reality fast asleep, nodding.
223. SAMBO WITH BANJO.—Moves hand and arm very naturally.
224. SAMBO WITH CYMBALS.—Playing vigorously.
225. WITH THE MAJOR'S COMPLIMENTS.—A bouquet of flowers being delivered with profuse bows of the messenger.
226. GIRL AND KITTEN.—A pretty little maid stands tossing a kitten.
227. PORKER, THE COOK.—A Pig in Cook's costume, stands before the kitchen range and tastes the savory dishes before him.

SLIDES TO ORDER.

The above illustrations will perhaps show the range of possibilities, and while we would have to make special estimates in some cases, we can give the following prices as a groundwork, viz :

3¼x4¼ Photographs, 2¼ to 3 inch Picture, uncolored .... $1 50 each.
"   "   "   "   "   colored .... 2 50   "
Mechanical Effects, "   "   "   .... $3 00 to 15 00   "
Lettered Advertisers, "   "   "   black letters .... 75c.   "
   Above cannot be used in smaller lanterns than our Electro Radiant No. 2.

COMIC SLIDES, COLORED, FOR Nos. 1, 2, 3, 4, 5, 6 & 8 MAGIC LANTERNS.

	Per doz.
6 inch paper edges, in box	$2 25
8 " " " "	2 75
8 " mahogany frames "	4 25
10 " " " "	5 50
12 " " " "	7 50
13 " " " "	9 00
14 " " " "	12 00

NATURAL HISTORY SLIDES, Colored, for Nos. 1, 2, 3, 4, 5, 6 & 8 MAGIC LANTERNS.

	Per doz.
6 in. paper edges, in box	$2 75
8 " " " "	3 50
8 " mahogany frames "	5 00
10 " " " "	7 50
12 " " " "	10 50
13 " " " "	12 00
14 " " " "	15 00

NURSERY TALE SLIDES, Colored, for Nos. 1, 2, 3, 4, 5, 6 & 8 MAGIC LANTERNS.

	Per doz.
6 in. paper edges, in box	$2 25
8 " " " "	2 75
8 mahogany frames "	4 25
10 " " " "	5 50
12 " " " "	7 50
13 " " " "	9 00
14 " " " "	14 50

Astronomy Slides.

	Per doz.
6 in. paper edges, in box	$2 50
8 " " " "	3 00
8 " mahogany frames "	5 75
10 " " " "	8 25
12 " " " "	11 25
14 " " " "	15 00

Colored Scripture Slides,	Inches,	6	8	8	10	12	13	14
	Per doz.	2 25	2 75	4 25	5 50	7 50	9 00	12 00
Colored Landscape View Slides,	Inches,	6	8	8	10	12	13	14
	Per doz.	2 25	2 75	4 25	5 50	7 50	9 00	12 00

The above slides have from 3 to 5 pictures on.

Comic Changing Slides.	Lever Action Slides.	Chromatrope Slides
Per doz.	Per doz.	Per doz.
For No. 1 and 2 Lanterns, $2 75	For No. 1 and 2 Lanterns, $3 50	For No. 1 and 2 Lanterns, $8 50
" " 3 " 4 " 3 25	" " 3 " 4 " 4 75	" " 3 " 4 " 10 75

Revolving Wind and Water Mills, for Nos. 1 and 2 Lanterns....................Per doz., $8 50
" " " " for " 3 " 4 " .... " 10 75
" Rat-eater, Bee Hive, and Fish Globe, for Nos. 1 and 2 Lanterns.......... " 9 50
" " " " " " for " 3 " 4 " .... " 12 00

PANORAMAS
with moving Ships, Figures, &c.

Slide 14 in. long, for Nos. 6 and 8 Lanterns........each, $4 50
Slide 12 in. long, for Nos. 4 and 5 Lanterns..........each, $3 25

VIEWS
with moving Figures, Ships, &c.

Slides 14 in. long, for Nos. 3 and 8 Lanterns..each, $2 75
Slides 12 in. long, for Nos. 4 and 5 Lanterns..each, $2 25

Mottoes, &c., on blue ground and mounted, in mahogany frames, for Nos. 6 & 8 Magic Lanterns, each, $1 00
Comic Mottoes, mounted in mahogany frames, for Nos. 6 and 8 Lanterns....................each, $1 50
Moving Waters, &c., with rippling effect, mounted, in mahogany frames, for Nos. 6 and 8 Lanterns,
each, $1 50...For Nos. 4 and 5 Lanterns, each, $1 00
Illustrated Jokes, mounted in mahogany frames, for Nos. 6 and 8 Lanterns.............Per doz., $10 75
Natural History Subjects, mounted, in mah'ny frames, &c., colored, for Nos. 6 & 8 Lanterns, per doz., $10 75

CHANGING COMIC SLIDES.   CONUNDRUMS.

Changing Comic Slides, in mahogany frames, for Nos. 6 and 8 Lanterns.................Per doz., $7 25
"   "   "   "   "   " Nos. 4 and 5 " .... "   5 75
Conundrum "   "   "   "   " Nos. 6 and 8 " .... "   6 00

LEVER ACTION SLIDES.

In mahogany frames, for No. 6 and 8 Lanterns....each $1.75
In mahogany frames, for No. 4 and 5 Lanterns....each $1.25
Of superior quality and Novel movements, for 6 and 8 Lanterns.................$2.25

CHROMATROPE.   RACKWORK.

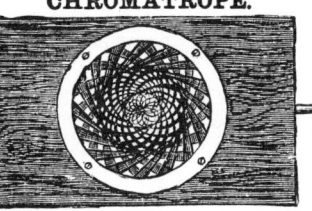

Assortment on these and the above slides from 100 to 650 different kinds.

Chromatrope, 2 in. diameter, in mahogany frames, for Nos. 6 and 8 Lanterns.................each, $2 75
"   2½ "   "   "   "   " Nos. 6 and 8 " .... "   3 50
"   3 "   "   " with portraits, motto verses, &c., in centre .... "   4 50
Rackwork, Fountain, Aquarium with Fishes, Knife-grinder and Rat-eater, for Nos. 6 and 8 Lanterns, ea. 5 00
" Wind and Water Mills, Vesuvius, and Donkey's Head, for Nos. 6 and 8 Lanterns, each...... 4 25
Mechanical Slides, Curtains to roll up, Snow Storms, Gymnastics, Hair Brushing, &c. Various prices.

THE "DISSOLVING" CARRIERS.

For holding the square glass views in a Dissolving-View Apparatus or Stereopticon, causing the views to "register" accurately upon the screen, and thus adding greatly to the beauty of an exhibition. Price per pair..$1.50

COMBINATION CARRIER.

Those using the unmounted Square Glass Views, have been heretofore subjected to much inconvenience for the want of some suitable contrivance to support the views in the proper position in front of the Condensing Lenses, and cause them to succeed each other without any interruption; besides the great risk of breaking the Views. Combination Carrier effectually overcomes all the difficulties, and enables the unmounted views to be used with facility and safety. The Carrier is designed to hold and center either of the Standard sizes of square views. *Stop No. 1,* will center those of the usual English pattern, (3¼x3¼ inches). *Stop No. 2,* is adapted for those of the French pattern (3¼x4 inches), and *Stop No. 3,* is adjusted for views on glass 3¼x4¼ inches......................50c.

Small Lots of Lantern Slides by Mail. Glass is now mailable at Merchandise rate (One cent per ounce) when forwarded in Patent Metallic Cases, several sizes of which have been made expressly for our use. Cannot mail slides of larger sizes than 4x7 inches.

THE "NEW IMPROVED DUPLEX" MAGIC LANTERN.

The rapid increase in the sale of this lantern since its introduction is, for us, the best proof of having met a long-felt want for a parlor lantern, and that its merits as such are being duly recognized by the public.

The "New Improved Duplex" is of our own manufacture, and *superior to any lantern of the same price in the market*, and, comparing it with the different styles, with due consideration of their respective merits, is *the cheapest Lantern made*.

The optical part, dimensions and general appearance, combine to make it most desirable for use, not only in the parlor, but also for the Sunday-school and lodge room, and we can warmly recommend it to the beginner who, having embraced the vocation of an exhibitor, wishes to begin his career in the country.

The size of the condensing lens, three and a-half inches in diameter, permits the use of all slides of the *standard size*, colored and uncolored; and the powerful light produced by the "Duplex Lamp," which is turned to full account by a highly polished nickel-plated reflector, four and a-half inches in diameter, will enlarge them to any desired size up to five or six feet in diameter, perfectly illuminated and preserving all detail in the picture.

The body of our *Improved Duplex Magic Lantern* is made of tin, 6x8 inches square, japanned in and outside, and is mounted on a solid walnut base.

We furnish with the above twelve choice colored slides, making a collection of about fifty pictures, a tin slide carrier, and twelve entertainment tickets. The whole is packed in a strong, neat box, with hinged cover, with full directions for operating pasted on inside. Price, complete, $12.

AROUND THE WORLD IN EIGHTY DAYS.

1 set of 12 slides, with about 70 pictures, illustrating the principal scenes in the above narrative. Size of slides, 4 x 12 inches. Each set put up in a fancy wood box, sliding top. Price, complete, $4 50

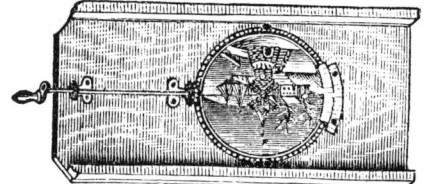
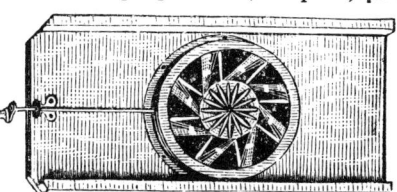

NEW CHROMATROPE SLIDES.

A selection of about 12 different designs on hand; frames 4 inches wide. *Specially adapted to the* Improved Duplex Magic Lantern. Each, $1 75

Chromatropes, movable pictures and Bible views of various sizes, to fit lanterns Nos. 8 to 40, kept in stock.

Nos. 8, 10, 12, 14, 16, 18 and 20 MAGIC LANTERN.

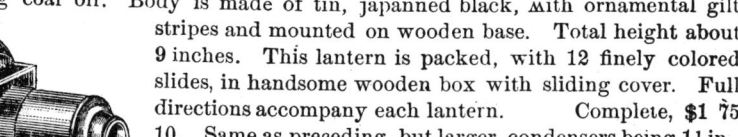

No. 8. A good magic lantern, having condensers 1¼ inches in diameter, and burning coal oil. Body is made of tin, japanned black, with ornamental gilt stripes and mounted on wooden base. Total height about 9 inches. This lantern is packed, with 12 finely colored slides, in handsome wooden box with sliding cover. Full directions accompany each lantern. Complete, $1 75

10. Same as preceding, but larger, condensers being 1½ in. and total height 10 inches. Complete, $2 25
12. Same as above, condensers 1⅝ in., height 10¼ in., $2 50
14. " " " 1¾ " " 11½ " 3 50
16. " " " 2 " " 12½ " 4 00
18. " " " 2¼ " " 14 " 5 00
20. " " " 2½ " " 15 " 6 00

PECK & SNYDER, 126, 128 & 130 Nassau Street, New York.
Importers and Dealers of MAGIC LANTERNS, SLIDES AND ALL FIXTURES.

WRENCH'S CELEBRATED LONDON MAKE MAGIC LANTERNS.

These Lanterns are considered the best and cheapest of any make in the world, see prices as follows:

PECK & SNYDER, SOLE AGENTS.

No.	Lantern only in Wooden Box	Diameter of Condenser.	Width of Slides adapted for the Lantern	Distance to be placed from Screen.	Size of Disc. shown on screen.
	$	in.	in.	ft.	ft.
1 With Lamp, Reflector, &c....	2 00	1½	1¾	4	3
2 " " " "	2 50	1¾	2	5	4
3 " " " "	3 00	2	2⅝	6½	5
4 " " " "	5 00	2½	2¾	8	6
5 " " " "	8 00	3	3	10¼	8
6 With Brass Front, double wick Lamp, Reflector, &c.......	12 00	3½	3	10¼	10
8 " " " "	18 00	3½	3	12	10

The Favorite German Lantern for a small Lantern this is one of the best to be had, it is neatly painted and packed in a wooden box complete with Focusing Tube Lamp, to burn Oil, Chimney, Reflector and 12 assorted slipping slides, of 40 pictures, and illustrated book of instructions. Price, **$2.00**

NEW STYLE FRENCH MAGIC LANTERNS.

Made of bronzed tin and very ornamental, (see cut,) and are complete and ready for use. They have Focus Tube, with cap to cover when not in use and keep from breaking, Lamp, Reflector and 12 assorted long slipping slides of Comic, Nursery and Fairy Tales, &c. Each Lantern packed in a wooden box, are complete with directions printed in English, ready for use.

Nos..............	814	815	816	817	818	819
Each, with Slides...	$2.50	$3.00	$3.50	$4.75	$6.00	$7.00
Extra Slides per doz.	$1.25	$1.50	$2.00	$2.50	$3.00	$3.50

Notice the Slides used in these Lanterns and as priced above can be used with any of the English or German Lanterns sold by us, the lowest pricesf or the smallest.

IMPROVED BICHROMATIC BATTERIES.

These batteries are intensely powerful, give off no fumes, are always in working order, and require no attention.

½-pint.	Pint.	Quart.	3 Pints.
$2 00	$3 50	$5 00	$6 00

Wire for Telegraph or Magnetic use.

Cotton covered copper wire, fine, per 100 feet........ .... 50c.
"   "   "   "   medium, per 100 feet................................. 60c.
"   "   "   "   large,   "   "   "   .... 70c.
Gutta Percha covered wire and cotton, extra covered fine, per 100 feet......... 60c.
"   "   "   "   "   "   "   medium, per 100 feet..... 70c.
"   "   "   "   "   "   "   large,   "   "   " 80c
New and improved latest style Printing Telegraph Machine, works perfect.....**$75 00**

A full line of other goods can be seen at our stores.

THE IMPROVED TRIPLEXICON, 100 CANDLE POWER.

PRICE Complete in a Strong Wooden Box, $35.00.

The *body* of the improved Triplexicon is constructed of the best Russia iron, and has been made as small as is consistent with good work and efficient ventilation.

The *light* is produced by a system of *three wicks*, placed parallel with the optical axis of the lantern, and enclosed in a flame chamber also of Russia iron, which connects with a chimney made of the same material.

The *flame chamber* is provided at the rear end with a highly polished nickel-plated reflector, which collects all the rays falling upon it, and concentrates them upon the condensers. The front end, nearest the condensers, is closed by a glass plate, allowing the free passage of the *light*. The reflector is protected from the influence of heat by a sheet of mica, and is pierced in the center, so that the operator may at any moment regulate the light without removing the lamp.

The chimney, which connects with the flame-chamber, is made in two parts, one sliding into the other, telescope fashion.—This allows of the most exact regulation of the current of air supplied to the flame to effect perfect combustion.

The isolation of the lamp from the body of the lantern is so complete that the latter may be handled as comfortably, after being two hours in operation, as at the beginning of the exhibition. The reservoir, which will hold enough oil for two and a-half hours' work, is *completely* out of reach of the heat.

The Improved Triplexicon is furnished with four-inch condenser, consisting of two plano-convex lenses in heavy brass mounting. They can easily be screwed apart for cleaning, etc. *Particular care* has been taken in the mounting of the lenses to allow for their expansion by heat, thus avoiding all liability of breakage from that cause.

The objective consists of a double combination of achromatic lenses, specially ground for projection, and of high power, mounted in finely finished brass tube, with rack and pinion adjustment, and brass cap. It may be changed to low-power by removing the back-combination, and the apparatus used at a longer distance from the screen.

Our new slide-carrier (not in cut) is the most convenient contrivance, and sure to give perfect satisfaction. It does entirely away with the cumbersome tin and wood carriers, and will receive slides of three and a-quarter and four inches width, in succession, without necessitating any change whatever while the spring clips adjust themselves to slides of every thickness, firmly holding them in position before the condensers.

Owing to the great power and whiteness of the light produced by our improved three-wick lamp, the Triplexicon will enlarge the finest photographic slides, both plain and colored, to any size up to twelve feet in diameter, with a brilliancy and clearness of outline to be surpassed only by the best lime-light stereopticons.

The high power of the Triplexicon, combined with its smallness and portability, makes it a most valuable instrument for society and school exhibitions, and it is just the thing for illustrating lectures in small halls and churches, while its perfect safeness makes it a most desirable medium for home entertainments, which, with a well-chosen collection of slides, can be made most delightful and highly instructive.

Nos. 21-32.—MAGIC LANTERN.—A superior magic lantern of the same general description as No. 8, but having a better finish, chimney and lens-tube being of polished brass. Condensers 1¼ inches, total height 9 inches. Securely packed in strong and handsome wooden box, with hinged cover, and furnished with full directions for operating. Twelve finely colored slides accompany each lantern.... $2 00

22. Same as No, 22, condensers 1½ inches, height 10 inches..... 2 50

No. 26. Same as No. 22, condensers 1⅞ in., height 10 in., 3 25
" 30. " " 2¼ " 14 " 5 50
" 32. " " 2½ " 15 " 6 50

PECK & SNYDER, Importers,
126, 128 & 130 NASSAU STREET, N. Y.

THE NEW IMPROVED DUPLEX MAGIC LANTERN, No. 2.

Encouraged by the flattering success of our New Improved Duplex Magic Lantern, and desirous of effecting its introduction into *every* household within our reach, we have concluded to manufacture a *reduced copy* of it, as shown in cut, which we have styled The New Improved Duplex Magic Lantern, No. 2. The only material difference between this and its predecessor lies in the size of condensers, those of No. 2 measuring three inches in diameter, most admirably adapting it for showing the peerless "Gem" and other slides of the same size.

We furnish with the above twelve finely colored slides, making a collection of about fifty pictures and twelve entertainment tickets. Packed together in a strong, snug box, with hinged cover, with full directions for operating pasted on inside. Price, complete, $10.00

Nos. 44, 46 & 48.

44. This is a new pattern of magic lantern of elegant design, japanned tin, with gilt facings, illuminated by coal oil lamp with glass chimney and nickel-plated reflector. Lens-tube and chimney are of brass, highly polished. The lantern is mounted on wooden base 4¾x4 inches, and packed in handsome wooden box, with hinged cover. Twelve superior colored slides, having glass cover to protect pictures from scratching, one chromatrope, one movable scene, and full directions for operating accompany each lantern. Height of lantern, 10½ inches, condenser 1½ inches diameter. Price, complete, $6.00

46. Same as No. 44, but twelve inches high, base 5¼x4⅞ inches, and condensers 1⅝ inches diameter. $7 50

48. Same as preceding, but fourteen inches high, base 6x7 inches, and condensers 1⅞ inches diameter. $11.00

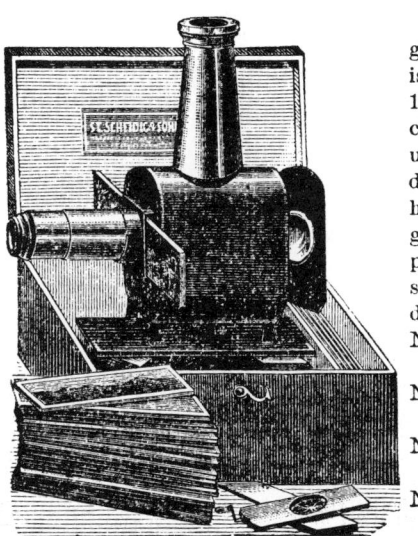

No. 34. This is a very neat and compact magic lantern, and gives surprising results for so small an apparatus. The body is of japanned tin, with ornamental gilt stripes, and stands 10¼ inches high, with chimney. A coal-oil lamp with glass chimney furnishes the light, which is furthermore concentrated upon the lenses by a nickel-plated reflector attached to the door. Chimney and lens-tube are of polished brass. A handle on side of lantern adapts it admirably for Phantasmagoria effects. This lantern has condensers 1½ in. diameter, is packed in elegant wooden box with hinged cover, 12 handsomely colored slides, 1 chromatrope, 1 comic slip slide, and full directions for operating accompany each one. Complete, $3 50

No. 36. Same as No. 34, but 12 inches high, and condensers 1⅝ inches in diameter........ .... $4 50
No. 83. Same as No. 34, but 13 inches high, and condensers 1⅞ inches in diameter........ ..... 6 00
No. 40. Same as No. 34, but 14 inches high, and condensers 2 inches in diameter................ 7 00
No. 42. Same as No. 34, but 15½ inches high, and condensers 2½ inches in diametre............. 8 50

THE POLYOPTICON--A WONDER CAMERA.

This Great American Invention—AN OPTICAL WONDER—is thus described by the *Christian Guide and Home Magazine:* "This is a wonderful invention whereby views from newspapers, magazines and book illustrations, portraits, comic cuts, photographs, chromo cards, IN ALL THEIR COLORS, flowers, etc., can be thrown on a screen in the parlor, enlarged about 400 times. Our little ones are wonderfully delighted with it, and must have it in use every evening. It does more than is claimed for it by the manufacturers."

The Christian Union says: "One is always finding cuts in the magazines or pictures on cards that would make a pretty parlor exhibition, if they could only be thrown upon a sheet by some means that would not be too complicated or costly. Such an apparatus has been now invented. It is known as the Polyopticon. In the magic lantern the display is limited to the glass slides; in the Polyopticon it is practically unlimited, since any small engraving, photograph or drawing may be used. The instrument serves admirably for parlor use, throwing a disk upon the screen of from four to five feet in diameter. It is hard to see how, for the comparatively small price at which the Polyopticon is sold, anything better of the kind could be produced, and it is quite certain that nothing for the money will furnish a more varied and attractive source of entertainments."

USES OF POLYOPTICONS.

The style No. 1, Lamp-shade Polyoption, was the first cheap article of the kind, introduced at the price of $2.50, to take the place of expensive imported wonder cameras, costing from $20 to $60, for artists' use in enlarging portraits, designs, etc., and as a cheap source of home amusement. Its success as a thing of use for artists is attested in the testimonial of Mr. L. Hulstein, of Philadelphia, Pa., who, in acknowledging the receipt of it, writes: "It works very satisfactory for copying portraits—a very economical substitute for the solarscope. Shall recommend it to brother artists."

THE LAMP SHADE POLYOPTICON is made of heavy binder's board, neatly covered with leatherette, and has metal parts as required, including two reflectors. It is made so as to be easily adjusted to all round-wick or argand lamps (those using straight or student's lamp-chimneys), and as these are the best lights for reading they are to be had everywhere. It rests on argand (round-wick) burners in such a way as to permit the regulating of the light below. With a good light it is possible to show a picture on a screen six feet distant, and a circle of light four feet in diameter.

THE COMPLETE (No. 2) POLYOPTICON

The Complete Polyopticon consists mainly of two wooden boxes, with highly polished nickel-plated brass reflector, lamp and burner, chimney, large lens, and a door so swung that the exhibition of pictures, when properly cut and mounted, is very convenient and speedy. The wooden boxes are preferable to metal because they do not become too hot to handle, and there are special means for ventilation and cooling not possessed by any other magic-lantern apparatus (but not required in the No. 1 Polyopticon, where less heat is generated.)

The Complete Polyopticon shows a more brilliant and larger picture than the No. 1 instrument. It also has a picture-window three inches in diameter, while that of the No. 1 Polyopticon is only 2¼ inches.

POLYOPTICON PARTIES

are all the go in social circles from New York to San Francisco. The San Francisco *Morning Call* reports that "Several Polyopticon parties have been arranged for the coming winter, when each guest will bring with him a few of the ordinary picture advertising cards and their photographs, or natural flowers, whereby an entire change of views can be seen every evening, which is impossible to do with the magic-lantern without a great expense in purchasing new slide for each evening."

Over 200 Free Pictures,

Worth $20 if on glass, for use with a magic-lantern, are given with each Polyopticon, thus affording a lot ready for immediate use, including: Around the world, in 80 sights; Bible Pictures—Old and New Testament, Ancient and Modern Statues, Portraits of Prominent Persons, Illustrations from Robinson Crusoe, Illustrations of a temperance lesson; Over 100 comic German figures in procession, and silhouettes.

PRICES.

No. 1, Lamp-shade Polyopticon and Pictures - $2.50
No. 2, Complete   "   "   "   -   5.00

THE POLYOPTICON PICTURE BOOK, No. 2, contains 100 beautiful colored (chromo lithographic) pictures of children's stories and fairy tales; Red Riding Hood, Cinderella, Jack and the Bean-stalk and several others. Price only 50 cts.

POLYOPTICON PICTURE BOOK, No. 3, contains 100 colored pictures of amusing and miscellaneous subjects executed by *Puck's* own publishers. Price only 50 cents. Such an assortment of pictures for ordinary lanterns would cost $100.

The Polyopticons were awarded a MEDAL OF MERIT at the Grand Fair of the New York American Institute for 1883, after practical tests of both instruments in presence of the judges, and abundance of testimonials from purchasers could be offered. Rev. Jesse H. Jones, of Massachusetts, has employed one at home and writes: "The exhibition was a complete success; the inventor has conferred a favor on mankind; its great merit is in taking pictures as they are, and reproducing them enlarged." A gentleman in Jersey City gave a successful Sunday school entertainment to two hundred people, and says, "the expressions of delight were uproarious," but its main usefulness will be in **Making Home Attractive,** and as the *Youth's Companion* says, "a happy home is usually an enduring one."

THE "GEM" MAGIC LANTERN.

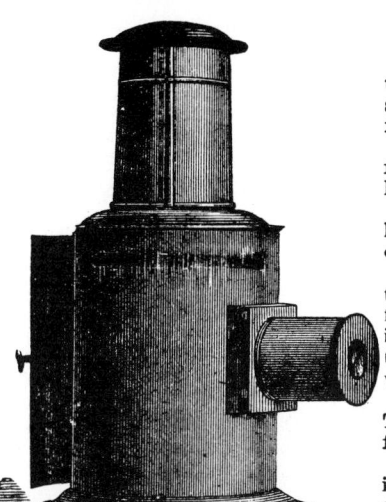

The GEM is a new style of Magic Lantern, designed especially for the amusement and instruction of the young; and intended to supersede the imported "Toy" Magic Lanterns over which it possesses the following advantages:

1.—THE BODY OF THE GEM MAGIC LANTERN, is convenient in form—is substantially made of strong tin, neatly japanned, and will last for years.

2.—THE LENSES OF THE GEM MAGIC LANTERN are of excellent quality, accurately ground and polished, and define the Views clearly upon the Screen.

3.—THE LIGHT OF THE GEM MAGIC LANTERN is obtained by the use of an improved candle in a patented carrier which keeps the flame constantly in the central line of the Lenses, and yields a good illumination. As there is no oil or fluid of any kind, cleanliness is the result, and a child can safely operate The Gem Magic Lantern without difficulty.

4.—THE MAGNIFYING POWER OF THE GEM MAGIC LANTERN is abundant, and the Views can be distinctly enlarged to three feet in diameter, or larger.

The Gem Magic Lantern consists of 24 slides, 2¼ inches wide, 9 inches long, having four or five figures on each side; Screen, 6 feet square with loops by which to suspend it; 12 Gem Candles; all packed in neat Walnut case with lock and key.

The SLIDES are neatly finished and highly colored; illustrating Fairy Tales, Caricatures, Comic Subjects, Popular Nursery Tales, Bible History, etc. This Lantern is of cylindrical shape, 6 inches diameter, 9 inches high, on firm base, with hinged door. The Condensing Lens 2¼ inches diameter. Printed directions furnished with each. The GEM MAGIC LANTERN, HOLIDAY OUTFIT.................................$12 00

THE AMATEURS' AND STUDENTS' CABINET OF GALVANISM AND ELECTRICITY.

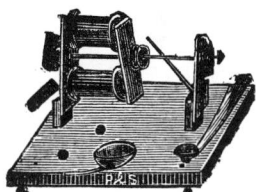  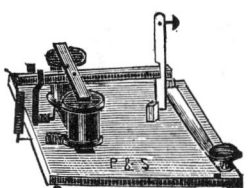

That wonderful and invisible force, known as Galvanic or Voltaic Electricity, has, of late, attracted almost universal attention.

Its phenomena, which border to a certain extent on the marvellous, the wonderful, and almost incredible results that it is capable of producing, and the many useful purposes to which it is being daily applied, have given to it the strongest claims to popular consideration, and have interested many in the study and investigation of the subject. In order to assist those who may desire to obtain a practical knowledge of the science, we have prepared this Cabinet. It is designed to aid the Amateur or Student in obtaining not only a general experimental knowledge of the subject, but also to show them how a practical application of it is made, by enabling them to construct, and to put in actual operation, a number of the most important Electrical instruments, such as are in daily use. Among the Instruments that can be readily made from the different prepared parts of the Cabinet, are:—

A COMPLETE SET OF TELEGRAPH INSTRUMENTS, consisting of a Morse Key, Sounder and Battery.

AN ELECTRO-MAGNETIC ENGINE, that will run small toys, etc., making several thousand revolutions per minute.

AN ELECTRIC CALL BELL, either single stroke or continuous ringing.

AN ELECTRIC BURGLAR ALARM, that can be connected by means of long wires to any door, window, or money drawer.

AN ELECTRIC CLOCK ALARM, that can be connected by means of wires to any clock, and will give the alarm in any part of the house.

AN ELECTRO-MAGNET, for making permanent magnets, etc.

AN INDUCTION COIL, consisting of separable primary and secondary coils, self-acting contact breaker, electrodes and conducting cords, for showing the physiological and other effects of the induced current, giving powerful shocks, etc. It can be used, if desired, for medical purposes.

A POWERFUL CELL OF GALVANIC BATTERY.—This battery is easily managed, emits no fumes or smell, and can be safely used in any part of the house; with it can be performed all the experiments to be found in ordinary text-books, such as effecting chemical decomposition, burning metallic wires, exploding gunpowder, lighting gas, the vapor of alcohol, etc. All the parts are separately numbered to correspond with the printed instructions, and can be easily put together by any one, in a few moments.

Students will find this cabinet of great aid to them, giving them a practical knowledge of the science not to be obtained from books.

Parents can not give their children a more instructive and amusing present; it will give a taste for the study and investigation of the wonders of natural science, and it may help to develop the germ from which will spring the Franklin, Morse or Edison of the future.

No. 1 Cabinet contains everything complete, as above.................................... $5 50
" 2 "   "   all of the above except Induction Coil............................... 4 00

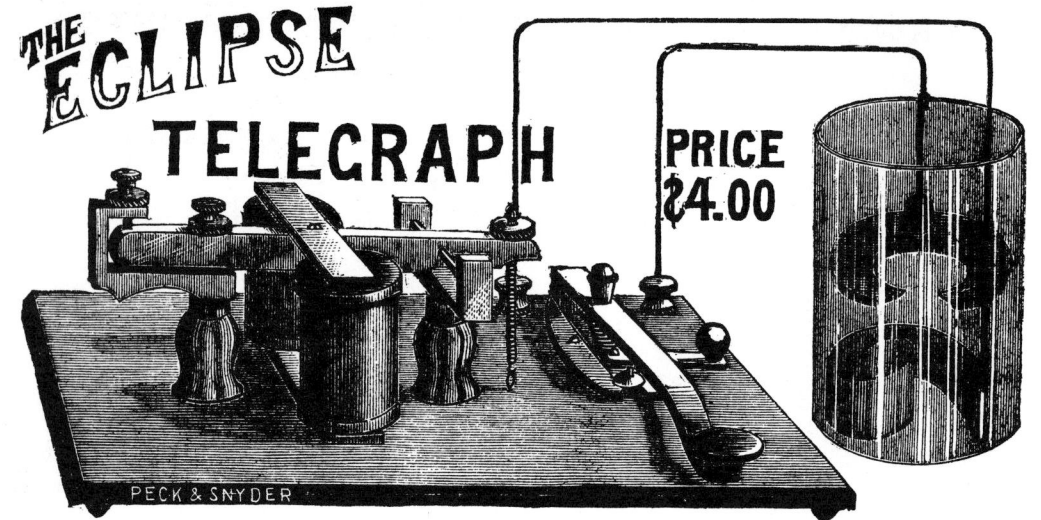

OUR NEW TELEGRAPH OUTFIT.—The only low priced instrument that is made entirely of BRASS, all others are merely cast-iron painted or japanned black. This outfit consists of a full-size Morse Key and Sounder, a cell of Gravity battery, a package of Blue Vitriol, a coil of insulated office wire, and instructions for learners, the whole forming a complete FIRST-CLASS outfit for learners, home practice, or for short-line service. The key is of the latest approved style, with long curved lever, and switch circuit closer.

The Sounder has rubber headed magnets, and perfect adjustments. Both Key and Sounder are made entirely of brass, finished and lacquered, and are mounted on a polished mahogany base.

The whole outfit, complete with battery and 50 feet of insulated wire, is carefully packed in a light
wood box for shipping..By express, $4 00
The Telegraph complete, except battery..By mail, 3 75
Prices of extra parts and fixtures of the Eclipse Telegraph Lightning Arrester............each, 0 75
Battery... 0 50
Insulated Wire, per 100 feet, 50 cents ; extra zinc.. 0 25

Persons when buying the outfit, without Battery, can use any ordinary tumbler.

ELECTRIC BELL OUTFIT.—This outfit consists of an iron frame, nickel-plated electric bell, a bronze press button or signal key, a cell of galvanic battery, 30 feet of insulated copper wire, and full and plain directions for putting up, connecting wires, &c.

There is scarcely a dwelling, store or shop, where an electric bell will not be found of service. They are used for innumerable purposes, as calls for servants or workmen, as door-bells, to connect house and stables, as an alarm to store-doors, &c., &c.

They can be used in or out of doors without regard to distance. Connected with doors, windows or out-buildings, they afford complete protection against burglars. They are quickly and easily put up, and are not apt to get out of order. The battery works from six months to a year without recharging. No acids or chemicals are necessary; nothing but a little common salt and water.

The whole outfit, complete with battery and 50 feet of insulated wire..............By express, $4 00
Price, complete, without Battery..By mail, 3 75
Price, Battery, extra....................50 cents ; Press-button............................. 0 25
Price, Bells, extra..................each, $1 50 ; Insulated Wire, per 100 feet............. 0 50

NEW BOOKS ON PHOTOGRAPHY, JUST PUBLISHED.

Modern Dry Plates or Emulsion Photography, by Dr. J. U. Eder and H. Baden Prichard, F.C.S., late Honorary Secretary of the Photographic Society of Great Britain. This book contains all the latest and best improvements in the manufacture and working of Dry Plates that is in present use, and with receipts for the mixing of different chemicals for general use, both for professional and amateur use. 138 pages...Price, $1 50

Photography with Emulsions, by Capt. Abney, R.E.F.R.S. Contains practical working details of Emulsion Processes in Photography, with theoretical explanations of the phenomena met with in them also a complete treatise on the theory and practical working of the Collodeon and Gelatine Emulsion processes. 284 pages, with illustrations..Price, $1 50

FIREWORKS
OF EVERY DESCRIPTION FOR EXHIBITION AND PRIVATE USE.

A $5 00 Lot contains Fireworks valued.....................................at wholesale prices, $7 00
   10 00   "   "   "   ....   "   "   12 00
   15 00   "   "   "   ....   "   "   18 00
   20 00   "   "   "   ....   "   "   24 00
   25 00   "   "   "   ....   "   "   28 00

Our assortment of the above goods is as large as any dealer's in the country, and for the brilliancy of colors, beauty or design, and durability when under exhibition cannot be surpassed: and we sell at manufacturer's lowest cash prices. Send stamp for full illustrated catalogue.

NEW DOUBLE ACTING ELECTRIC ENGINES.

No. 3.

These Engines are more powerful for their size, easier to manage, cost less to run and are safer to use than any others.

As no Acids, Battery Fluid, or Solutions are employed, there is no danger of injury to clothing or furniture. One charge of this battery will run the Engine at high speed for several days. Not the slightest attention is required until the battery needs recharging, which can be done in a few minutes, when the Engine will start again as powerful as ever. The cost of running is very trifling, a few cents will keep one running steadily for a month.

The power can be doubled or trebled by using additional battery, every extra cell of battery used gives increased power.

They can be used for running Toys, Moving Figures, small Machinery, turn tables for show windows, &c.

Every Engine is furnished complete, with one cell of battery, connecting wires, directions, and materials for charging the battery, everything necessary to start it running at once.

No. 1, Circular Engine, complete with Battery, sent by Express only..................Price, $3 00
" 2, Walking Beam Engine   "   "   "   "   "   "   .... " 3 50
" 3, Horizontal   "   "   "   "   "   "   "   .... " 4 50
Battery extra..Price, each, 50 cts.

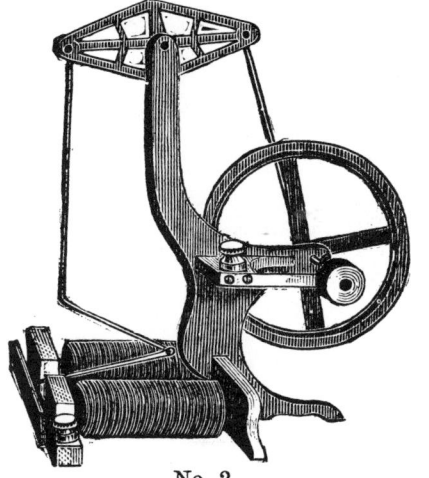

No. 2.

No. 1.

PECK & SNYDER,
126, 128 & 130 NASSAU STREET, NEW YORK.
Manufacturers, Importers and Dealers in Electric Goods.

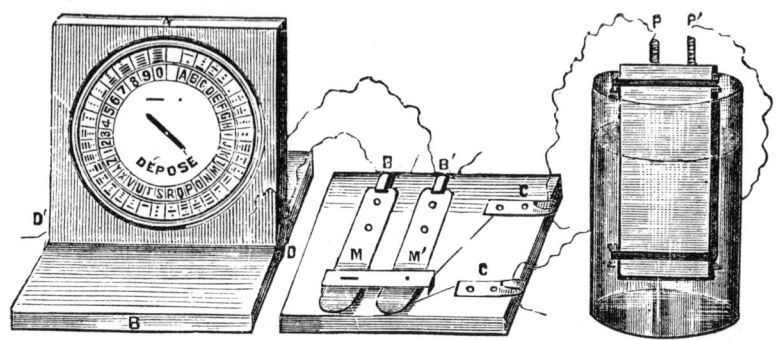

INSTRUCTIVE AND AMUSING.
MINIATURE ELECTRIC TELEGRAPH.

This Telegraph consists of a sending and a receiving instrument, a spool of wire for connecting them together, and the elements of a galvanic battery for working them, the whole contained in a box with directions. The form is that known as the single needle instrument, and is used with the ordinary Morse Alphabet, which is composed of dots and dashes. A movement of the needle, on the dial, to the right indicates a dot, and a movement to the left a dash. It is very simple, and easily arranged, and any child can understand and operate it.
Price each, $1.50, $2.50, $5.00.

HOPE'S MAGNETIC BATTERY.

This is a very convenient, compact and cheap electro-magnetic machine, and by far the most powerful for the price. We have used it and can strongly commend it. It can be operated with the cheapest fluid used, and from which there is no danger. It can be operated with safety by old and young. It is used by many physicians to aid in the relief and cure of rheumatism, diseases of the throat, nervous troubles, debility, colds, earache, toothache, etc. Sufficient material goes with each machine to operate several times. We offer it for sale, postage paid by us, for $4.25   Large Size, complete, $6.00

THE LATEST NOVELTY IN SCARF PINS.

PRICE LIST OF THE PINS COMPLETE AND OF SEPERATE PARTS.

Incandescent Electric Light Scarf Pins,..Each, $5 50
Incandescent Electric Light Hair Pins,... "   5 50
Incandescent Electric Light Breast Pins,.. "   5 50
Illuminated Imitation Gems.—Diamonds, Rubies, Emeralds, Carbuncles, Amethysts... "   9 00
These Goods are nearly as brilliant as the Genuine Stones.
The above prices include any one of the articles with Battery, complete.

We will furnish you the Gems, without Battery at $4.50 each. the Pins and Lamps at $3.50 each. You can thus furnish yourself with a variety of our Incandescent Electric Light Pins or Gems, using the same Battery for any one of them.
In sending Orders, please state whether you wish to carry Battery in the Hip or Vest Pocket, they are very light and weigh but 4 ounces. Price of Battery without Light,......................$3 75
Price of Incandescent Electric Light Lamp, from one to six candle power, $1.50 each, or $12.00 per Dozen.

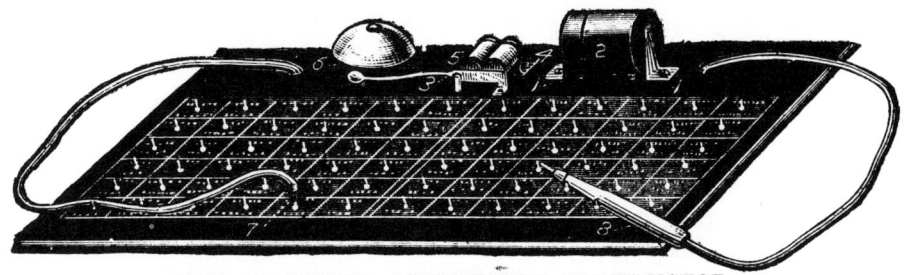

THE ELECTRIC AUTOMATIC INSTRUCTOR.

One of the most wonderful inventions of modern times! Something every family in the land should have! More knowledge and information can be obtained than from hundreds of dollars' worth of books! The Electric Automatic Instructor, while being the best Educator for children or grown persons, is also most valuable for the amusement and entertainment it affords. Young and old equally interested. A whole evening's entertainment for family and friends. The Electric Automatic Instructor is intelligent, and in its electric way talks to you.

"Its working is simple and novel." "It acts both as teacher and scholar" "Very valuable for Kindergarten Schools." Questions on all subjects are answered by the "Electric Instructor." The following are a few:

No. 1. Alphabetical Questions ⎫
" 2. Arithmetical Questions ⎬ Designed for Children.
" 3. " " ⎪
" 4. " " ⎪
" 5. " " ⎪
" 6. " " ⎭
" 7. Nicknames of different States.
" 8. Biblical Questions.
" 9. Geographical Questions.
" 10. Latitude, Longitude and Astronomical.
" 11. Conundrums. (Very interesting.)
" 12. Capitals of every State.
" 13. " foreign countries.
" 14. Time required to digest meats, fish, vegetables, etc.
No 15. Biblical Questions.
" 16. Distance from New York to all important cities.
" 17. Distance from New York (by water) to foreign countries.
" 18. Interesting statistical card.
" 19. " conundrums.
" 20. " questions about the War, important battles, etc.
' 21. Astronomical Questions.
" 22. Important events of the 19th century.
" 23. Names of all the Presidents and other important U. S. Officers.
" 24. Important events in New York State and elsewhere.

New subjects and cards being introduced each week and month.
To avoid mistakes, always mention *number* as well as *name* of card.
These cards are sent by mail to any address in the United States and Canada. Price, 10 cents each, or $1 per dozen. Postage 4 cents per dozen, (always add postage in ordering cards.)
The whole complete with cards, Battery, Bell, Solution Powder, etc., in a neat box, **$5.00**.

THE ELECTRO-MAGNETIC AND AMERICAN ELECTRIZER MACHINE.

This is a very convenient, compact and cheap electro-magnetic machine, and by far the most powerful for the price. We have used it and can strongly commend it. It can be operated with the cheapest fluid used, and from which there is no danger. It can be operated with safety by old and young. It is used by many physicians to aid in the relief and cure of rheumatism, disease of the throat, disease of the nerves, neuralgia, paralysis, debility, colds, headache, earache, toothache. The most compact, convenient and cheapest medical battery in the world, and by far the most powerful for the money. Every family ought to have one. Sufficient material with each machine to operate several times. We offer it for sale, postage paid by us, for $4.25.

By express, large size, complete, $6.00
The annexed cut represents the Electrizer in use as a Medical Benefactor.

THE POCKET TELEGRAPH. (Cut exact size.)

No battery, acid, or wire needed for operating this little wonder. With this little instrument any person can learn the art of Telegraphing, and messages may be sent and received after a few hours' practice. The instrument, blued steel, with Morse's Alphabet and full instructions, will be mailed. Blued steel, 25 cents. Nickel plated, 50 cents.

We are Agents in the United States for the sale of William E. Statham's and the Scientific Novelty Company's Goods, (London.)

CHEMICAL MAGIC SCIENTIFIC AMUSEMENTS,
PHOTOGRAPHIC AND ELECTRICAL APPARATUS, &c.

Statham's Boxes of Chemical Magic have been prepared to meet the demand for inexpensive, instructive and amusing experiments, free from danger. Each box contains chemical reagents, apparatus, and full instructions for performing a series of experiments, expressly arranged for beginners, and as they can be sent by post to all parts of the globe with safety, they cannot fail to afford a world-wide source of instruction and amusement.

" B.	"	"	30	"	0 50
" 1.	"	"	50	"	0 75
" 2.	"	"	1 00	"	1 25

STATHAM'S YOUTHS' CHEMICAL CABINET.

Contains sixty chemical tests and apparatus without strong acids or other dangerous articles; they are perfectly safe in the hands of youth, and are admirably adapted as presents, prizes, &c.

No. 1.—In fancy case, paste board, with book of experiments,..... $4 00
" 2.—Cedar case, with book of experiments................... 5 00
Size of case closed, 7 x 5 x 5 inches.
" " open, 12 x 4 x 5 "

STATHAM'S BOYS' OWN LABORATORY.

Contains 54 chemical preparations, and 30 pieces of apparatus for performing.

Endless experiments in chemical magic free from danger.

Price with book, $10.

Size closed 10¾ x 8 x 3 inches.

STATHAM'S STUDENTS' CHEMICAL CABINET

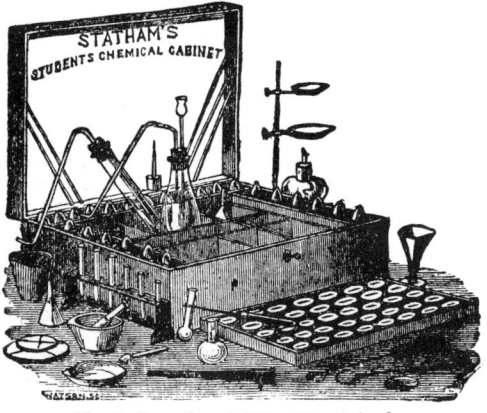

No. 3, Size closed, 15 x 10 x 5 inches.

No. 1 contains 36 boxes and 12 bottles filled with chemicals and a large assortment of apparatus of a practically useful size, arranged in a polished mahogany Cabinet, with lock and key $15 00
No. 2, a handsome polished mahogany Cabinet, fitted with 12 stoppered bottles and 48 turned wood boxes, filled with chemical tests, etc., and 36 pieces of apparatus and materials, in all 96 articles. Size, closed, 14 by 11 by 7½ inches........................$20 00
No. 3 contains 65 chemical preparations and reagents, in corked and stoppered bottles, and turned wood boxes, and a large assortment of useful apparatus, in handsome French polished mahogany case, with tray for boxes, and partitions for apparatus, in all 112 articles. Size, closed, 15 by 10 by 5 inches.......$25 00
No. 4 will be found a good useful working Chest; it contains 66 chemical preparations and re-agents in turned wood boxes, and large-size stoppered and plain bottles, with green-varnished labels; and is fitted with a very large assortment of apparatus of superior size—comprising the articles necessary for manipulation with the gases, in all 130 articles; the whole carefully arranged in bottle racks, tray, and appropriate partitions, in a very superior French polished mahogany Cabinet, with brass name plate, lock, &c. Size, closed, 17 by 11 by 6 inches... ....$35 00

Statham's First Steps in Chemistry. A series of 145 select and amusing chemical experiments, which may be performed with perfect eas and security by youth of both sexes, intended as a companion to Youths' Chemical Cabinets..$0 25

The Young Experimental Chemist, containing complete apparatus and chemicals for performing more than 100 experiments; harmless, instructive and amusing.................................$1 00
The Boy's Chemical Chest, for performing upwards of 40 brilliant experiments............ 0 50
Bidlake's Text Book of Elementary Chemistry.—In cloth, full of illustrations.......... 1 25
The Marvels of Optical and Chemical Magic 50

PECK & SNYDER, SOLE AGENTS FOR THE SALE OF JUDSON'S ENGLISH DYES, AND THEIR HOUSEHOLD NOVELTIES.

Judson's Gold and Silver Imitation Inks.—This elegant preparation is used with an ordinary quill pen. The writing is clear and brilliant, and the effect most attractive. For complimentary correspondence Judson's Gold and Silver Ink is unrivalled. For writing dates and names in photographic albums and on cartes. For imitating gold jewelry in photographic painting. For illuminating texts and artistic lettering. For reviving jewelry and picture frames. By mail, per bottle, each, 25c.

Judson's Paris Polish for Furniture.—This preparation has the properties of both cleaning and polishing furniture with a very small amount of labor. It is not sticky, and a brilliant polished surface may be obtained in ten minutes. Per bottle, by mail, 35c.

Judson's A 1 Marking Ink, warranted. Put up in neat bottles and boxwood boxes. By mail, 25c.

Judson's Crystal Glycerine, warranted pure, for external and internal use. Per bottle, by mail, 30c.

Judson's Gold Paint.—1 bottle gold powder, 1 bottle mixing liquid, 1 cut glass mixing bowl, 1 fine hair brush. For regilding picture and glass frames, for gilding lamp stands and gas fittings, for renewing ormolu ornaments, for illuminating on paper, silk or leather, for artistic cabinet work, and for a thousand useful and domestic purposes. All put in a neat box, with full directions. By mail, 75c.

Judson's Bronzonette.—The application of this most elegant preparation is extremely simple, while its effect upon the articles enumerated below is almost magical, imparting to them a glazed bronze surface of great beauty. IRON.—Fenders, stoves, gas-fittings, ornaments, &c. FENDERS AND STOVES painted with Bronzonette look very handsome, and the trouble of frequently black-leading is dispensed with. PLASTER BUSTS and ORNAMENTS (that have been previously painted or waxed) look like *real bronzes*. LEAVES (real)—Ivy, laurel, holly, &c.—" Effect most charming." Per bottle, by mail, 50c.

JUDSON'S GENUINE ENGLISH DYES.—Ribbons, Wool, Silk, Feathers, completely Dyed in Ten Minutes, without soiling the hands. Full Instructions Supplied.

Dyeing at Home.—**Judson's Simple Dyes** are most useful and effectual. Ribbons, silks, feathers, scarfs, lace, braid, veils, handkerchiefs, clouds, bernouses, Shetland Shawls, or any small article of dress can easily be dyed in a few minutes without soiling the hands; also, carpet rags, carpets, druggets, Easter eggs, confectionary, church decorations, unbroken rice, magenta, violet, crimson, mauve, purple, pink, ponceau, claret, &c.

Photographic Paper Positives or Photo-Prints should be dipped in hot water, then submitted to a hot bath of **Judson's Dyes**. Beautiful effects are thus produced in green, pink, brown and many other beautiful colors. Use **Judson's Dyes** for general tinting.

French Grasses, Flowers and Seaweeds may be dyed most exquisite colors, green, crimson, purple, scarlet, etc., by simply dipping them in a solution of **Judson's Dyes**. Charming bouquets may be composed.

Ink—Ink—Ink.—A bottle of **Judson's Dyes**, violet, read, or Magenta, will make half a pint of brilliant writing Ink in one minute by simply adding hot water.

For Coloring Architectural Plans, etc , much trouble may be saved in grinding up colors to a uniform tint. They may be used either with a brush or pen. Rose, Pink, Purple, Canary, Crimson, Orange, Green, Blue, Magenta, and twelve other shades,

For Staining Wood, diluted with water, they sink deeply into the fibre and will not rub off. They form the most economical stain on record. Light Brown or Mahogany color is excellent; No. 2 for Walnut; Canary for Satin; also Black. Lavender, Magenta, and many other colors.

Thirty-two different colors. Price, per bottle, by mail, 25 cents.

Judson's Mahogany Stain.—By simply adding boiling water a splended Stain is produced, which will not rub off. A bottle makes one quart of Mahogany Stain. Judson's Mahogany Stain serves as a very economical stain for wood, for bed-room floors, &c., or for church decoration, thus saving many a yard of cloth. A rich brown stain is produced. Price, per bottle, 25 cents.

Judson's Black-All, an Enamel Varnish for Stoves. &c.—Imparts a brilliant and lasting polished surface to Stoves, Fenders, Fireirons, and all kinds of Iron Work, resembling polished black marble. Dries quickly. "Black-All" should be applied with a small painter's brush or paste-brush. 25c and 50c per bottle.

Judson's Artist's Black.—This is another useful speciality for various purposes, amongst which may be mentioned,—renewing ebonized cabinets, desks, workboxes, &c.; painting picture frames; reviving plates, knobs, locks, &c ; renewing carriage lamps. A good effect is produced by painting the beading of doors, panels, skirtings, &c., this mode of room decoration being very fashionable. When used in conjunction with Judson's Gold Paint, the effect is very charming and artistic. Judson's A B, supplied in bottles with brush included, will preserve its efficacy for a long time. Price, per bottle, 50 cents.

Judson's Silverine.—For Re-plating Harness Ornaments, Coach and Carriage Fittings and Door Handles, Lamps, Whips, &c., &c. Copper or Brass will plate equally well. Publicans' Fittings may be re-plated. Shake the bottle, then, with a damp rag apply some of the Silverine by rubbing it briskly upon the article, when a complete coating of "real silver" will quickly appear. Polish with dry wash leather. Finally wash in cold water. Price, per bottle. 50 cents.

THE PATENT IMPROVED TIDY FASTENER.

In a moment's time, with a few turns of the fingers, the little spiral is driven through the tidy placed upon the back of the upholstered Sofas, Lounges, Chairs, etc., into the upholstery; there it remains fast, holding the tidy always in place.

The Tidy Fastener never pulls out and never tears the furniture as do pins when used for this purpose, and, besides, adds greatly to the appearance of the tidy. It can be used with equal facility to fasten tidies to cane-back furniture.

The Tidy Fasteners are made in all colors, and can be used to match the tidy or not, as the taste may dictate. The principal colors demanded are white, green, scarlet, cherry, maroon, brown, blue, and black. When ordering goods please state what colors and how many of each you wish.

The Tidy Fasteners is a great ornament to the tidy and to the furniture, and those who have tried it say they would sooner part with tidy than the fastener.

Eight Samples by Mail, postage paid, $0 25 6 doz. " " " " $1 60
1 dozen samples by mail, postage paid, $0 35 12 " " " " $3 00

PECK & SNYDER'S POPULAR AMATEUR PHOTOGRAPH CAMERAS.

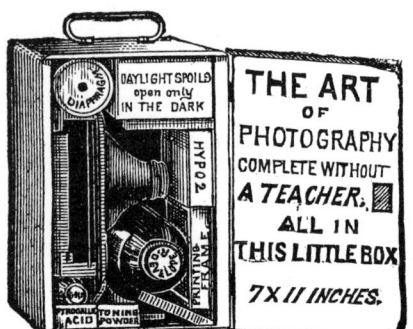

The American Gem.—This is the first complete instrument offered for sale to the public direct. It is made for the purpose of *teaching Photography in a short and concise manner*. To perfect this the author has devoted ten years to unremitting study and experiments. The handbook gives all necessary instruction in such a simple manner that any one possessing ordinary common sense cannot fail to grasp its full meaning. It is the most practical camera ever made, for the purposes for which it is intended, and it is furnished at a price which defies competition.

N. B.—These instruments can be used with any kind of process.

The design of case and tripod, shows the complete packing of one camera with plate holder, printing-frame, cloth and all chemicals for taking negatives and printing on photographic principles.

This apparatus can be used by a regular photographer, amateurs, painters of sketches, mechanics for models, doctors, for slides and magic lantern use, also for all purposes where it is necessary to take pictures. Any one can operate it with perfect success. The most instructive and useful invention of the age. Will make any picture, views, portraits, and pictures for magic lanterns, ferreotype pictures, &c. These Cameras are reconstructed on an entirely "New" plan, with an ingenious mechanical contrivance, by which the most sensitive plate can be exposed without the least danger of getting "light struck," a great advantage over all other Cameras. The chemicals, prepared "dry plates," sensitive paper, &c., &c., are all put up ready to be used, without difficult peparations, and everything is labelled correctly, so as to enable young folks as well as old to operate the instruments successfully and produce the best results.

Full and Complete printed Instructions accompany each outfit. These Cameras are unsurpassed as a travelling companion, and are very useful and amusing. It can be worked inside as well as outside of the house. Anything and everything may be photographed with it, houses, sceneries, portraits, samples, models, machinery, etc. The directions are so clear and concise that any person of ordinary intelligence can, easily take Photographs, from the very beginning and either enjoy his leisure time or earn a living with it. *It is not a toy, but a practical instrument,* not cheaply or roughly made, but substantially gotten up. The Camera rests on a Tripod, which can be adjusted towards any desired direction, and be folded to a straight solid body, which can be carried instead of a cane.

Of these improved Apparatus' we make the different sizes, as follows:

No 0. Apparatus consists of Camera, complete Lens, (mounted in brass Tube) Tripod, Dry Plates, Prepared Paper, all Chemicals and materials to produce Photographs. Size of picture, 2x2¼ inches.

All complete for $6.00.

No. 1. Apparatus consists of Camera complete, size of picture, 3¼x4¼ inches, 1-9 size "Achromatic" View Lens 1 inch in diameter, Tripod, Dry Plates, Prepared Paper, Developer, Toning and Fixing material. Printing Frame. This instrument is made of Black Walnut with Nickel Plated body and Tube.

Price, complete, $12.00.

No. 3½.—**American Gem, for Travelers' Use.** This apparatus is the same as No. 3, only more compact. The camera has an Acromatic Lens including *Three Patent Double Dry Plate Holders, which are fitted to the Carrying Case in regular compartments.* The Operator can easily fill the Plate Holder with Plates in the evening at home, and is then ready the next day to take Pictures all complete with Chemicals, Plates and Tripod.—

Price, $24.00.

No. 3.—**American Gem, for Family Use.**—This Camera is made of Polished Mahogany, with Nickel Plated body and handsomely finished. It has a double 3¼x4¼ inch Patent Dry-Plate holder to admit two Prepared Plates at one time, and also an Achromatic Lens for producing a more perfect picture. Apparatus complete, with all the Chemicals and Plates with a book of Instruction.

Price, $18.00.

PECK & SNYDER, 126, 128 & 130 Nassau Street, New York.

No. 4.—American Gem, for Photographers, Amateurs, Artists, Draughtsmen and Household use,

Is of larger dimensions, has an extra fine combination of double achromatic (Darlot, Paris,) Lens, the tube is with rack and pinion movement for producing the desired focus conveniently, has also an extra focus regulator for long ranges. Focus of Lens, 5½ inches.

The Camera has a double dry plate-holder and will admit plates either horizontally or perpendicularly of following sizes: 4 x 5 inches and 3¼ x 4¼ inches; the latter size is inserted in a kid frame, furnished with the patent double dry plate-holder.

The Camera is made of mahogany, finely polished and finished, has a polished carrying case with handle, lock and hinges, also drawers for the Chemicals and prepared plates, rack for Lens, a compartment for printing-frame and Camera; can be used for photographing portraits, views and sketches for Photographers, Artists and Amateurs. Price, complete, $30 00.

No. 5.—**American Gem.**—This apparatus is the same as No. 4, but larger. It has a Patent Double Dry-Plate Holder which will use either a 3¼ x 4¼ inch, 4 x 5 inch, or 5 x 7 inch Plate; the one Plate-Holder serving for all, and taking Portraits, Views, Etc., either perpendicular or diagontally. The Camera is all complete with Chemicals and Plates for each size Picture.

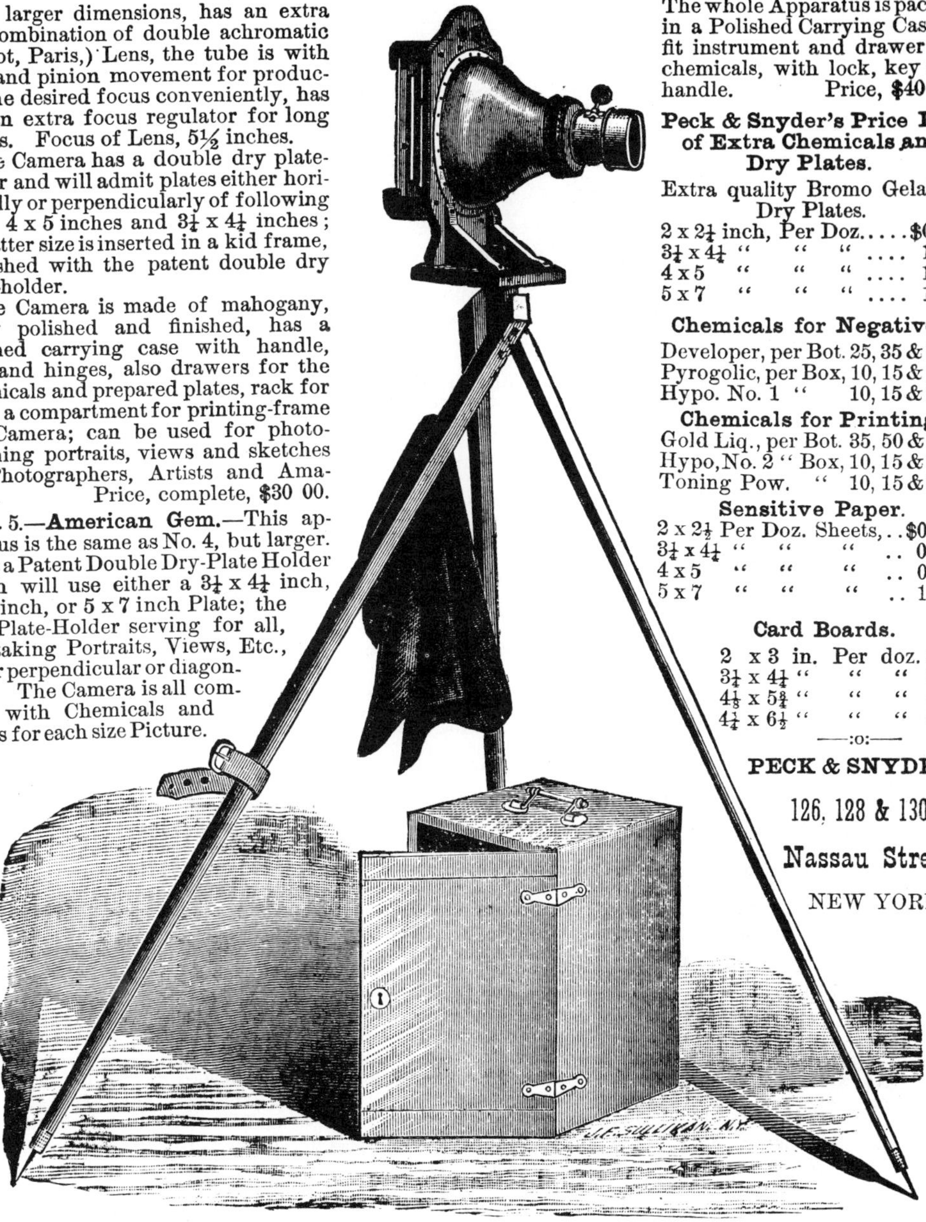

The whole Apparatus is packed in a Polished Carrying Case to fit instrument and drawer for chemicals, with lock, key and handle. Price, $40 00.

Peck & Snyder's Price List of Extra Chemicals and Dry Plates.

Extra quality Bromo Gelatine Dry Plates.

2 x 2¼ inch,	Per Doz.	$0 75
3¼ x 4¼	" "	1 00
4 x 5	" "	1 25
5 x 7	" "	1 75

Chemicals for Negatives.

Developer, per Bot. 25, 35 & 50c.
Pyrogolic, per Box, 10, 15 & 25c.
Hypo. No. 1 " 10, 15 & 25c.

Chemicals for Printing.

Gold Liq., per Bot. 35, 50 & 65c.
Hypo, No. 2 " Box, 10, 15 & 25c.
Toning Pow. " 10, 15 & 20c.

Sensitive Paper.

2 x 2½	Per Doz. Sheets,	$0 30.
3¼ x 4¼	" " "	0 40.
4 x 5	" " "	0 65.
5 x 7	" " "	1 00.

Card Boards.

2 x 3 in.	Per doz.	20c.
3¼ x 4¼	" "	30c.
4⅛ x 5¾	" "	40c.
4¼ x 6½	" "	50c.

—:o:—

PECK & SNYDER,

126, 128 & 130

Nassau Street,

NEW YORK.

Fig 2 PLATEHOLDER.

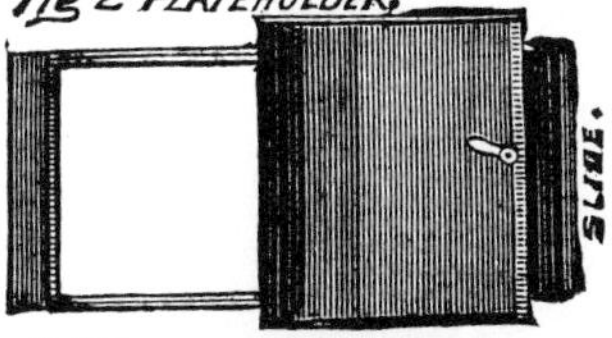

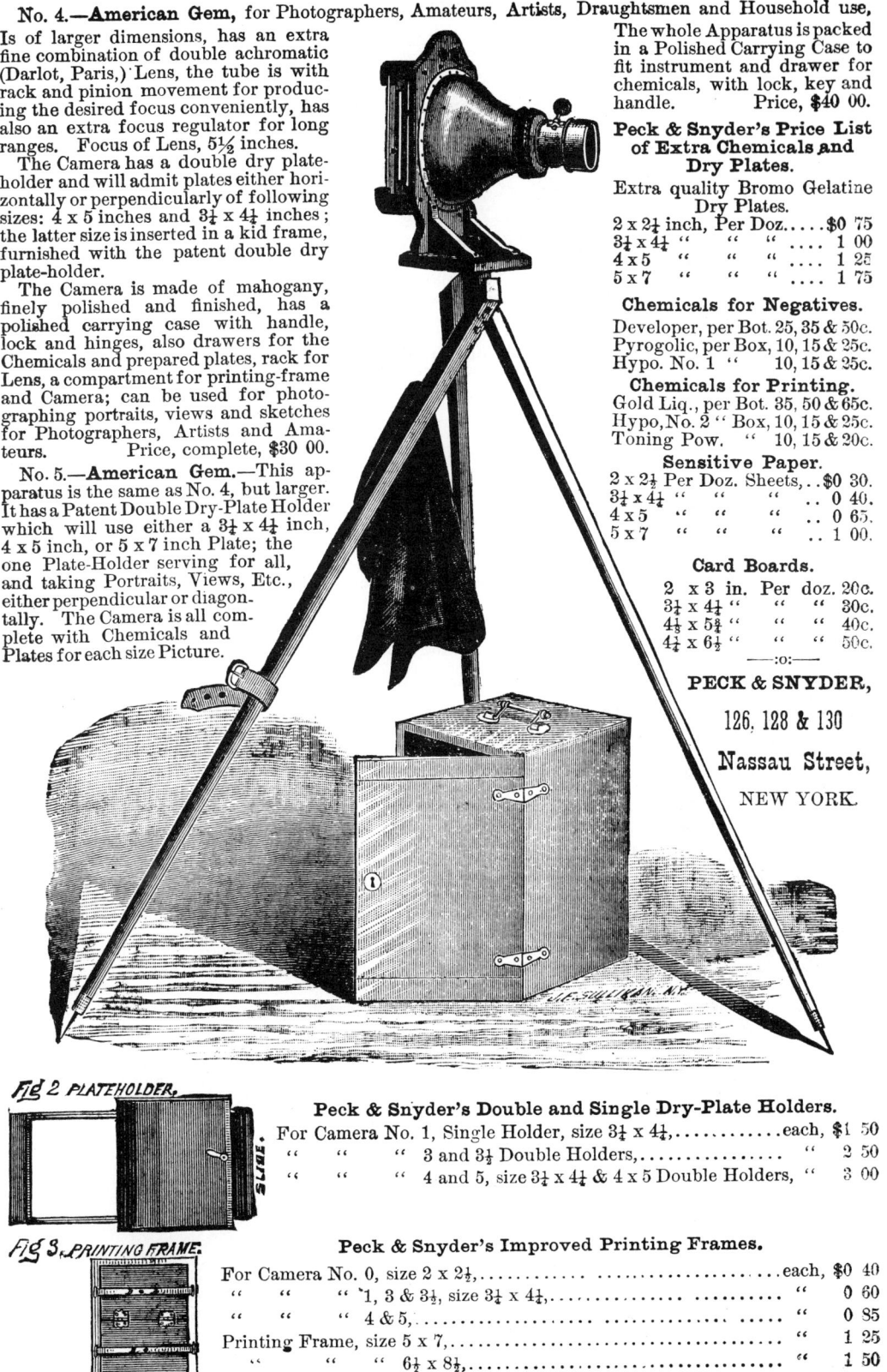

Peck & Snyder's Double and Single Dry-Plate Holders.

For Camera No. 1, Single Holder, size 3¼ x 4¼,	each,	$1 50
" " " 3 and 3½ Double Holders,	"	2 50
" " " 4 and 5, size 3¼ x 4¼ & 4 x 5 Double Holders,	"	3 00

Fig 3. PRINTING FRAME.

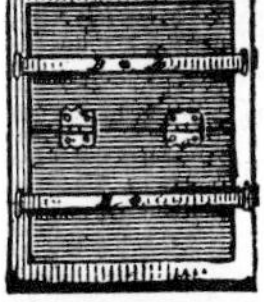

Peck & Snyder's Improved Printing Frames.

For Camera No. 0, size 2 x 2½,	each,	$0 40
" " " 1, 3 & 3½, size 3¼ x 4¼,	"	0 60
" " " 4 & 5,	"	0 85
Printing Frame, size 5 x 7,	"	1 25
" " " 6½ x 8½,	"	1 50

THE IMPROVED PATENT RUBBER TARGET GUN.

The latest and best. An entirely new principle. For Target Practice and Hunting. Shoots Arrows, Bullets or Shot. Shoots almost as straight as a Rifle. Entire length, 39 inches. Its power and accuracy are surprising. Makes no report and does not alarm the game. Has no recoil. Will carry 600 feet. Thousands of them are in use, and never fail to give satisfaction. With every gun are included five Metallic Pointed Arrows, two Targets, and Globe Sight. This Gun will throw an arrow or bullet with nearly double the force of any other similar gun. The arrows are made of hickory, with solid steel points. The Shot Attachment is entirely new, and increases the efficiency of the gun for shooting small game. Price of gun, **$1 00.** Postage, if sent by mail, extra, 25 cents.

Price List of Extras: Hardwood Arrows, with Turned Metal Points, per dozen, by mail, 35c. Shot and Bullet Attachment. This is a very valuable addition to the gun, especially for hunting. With it shot and bullets can be shot with great force.

VENTILATED LUNCH SATCHELS.
Patented in U. S. Sept. 13th, 1881.

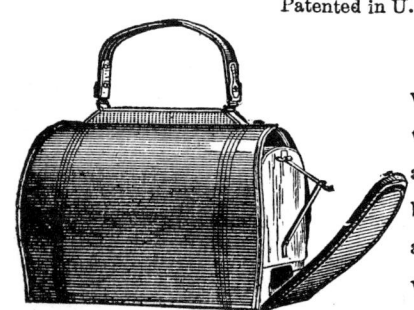

A most Valuable Invention securing every working man and woman a Healthy, Cheap, Palatable, and Hot Dinner in an Attractive and Convenient Shape.

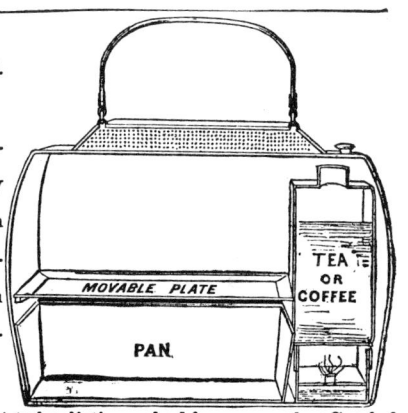

The Ventilated Lunch Satchel in outward appearance not to be distinguished from any other Satchel for the use of workingmen and workingwomen, bookkeepers, clerks, engineers, conductors, drivers, schoolteachers, dressmakers, seamstresses, excursionists, and all such persons, whose business requires their absence from home during the dinner hour.

The Ventilated Lunch Satchel will hold a sufficient quantity of meat, vegetables, bread and pie, coffee, tea or milk for one person's dinner, properly secured in their places, without napkin or paper, perfectly ventilated, and with an independent arrangement for heating them.

The Ventilated Lunch Satchel is manufactured of the finest materials, by competent workmen, and made to last for many years. It will secure its owner a good, healthy, cheap, hot dinner. It will pay for itself in less than two weeks. It will prevent many from becoming dyspeptics. It will do away with unsightly tin cans, lunch baskets, paper parcels, for the Ventilated Lunch Satchel is an article of so elegant shape and appearance, that no gentleman or lady can possibly object to carry it. It is destined to be the working people's vade mecum.

Reasons why every workingman and working woman should procure a Ventilated Lunch Satchel: 1. It enables them to have every day a wholesome, fresh, hot dinner; 2. Its use is conducive to health; 3. It is cheap, substantial, clean and pretty; 4. It is true economy to buy it; 5. It will last for years.

Styles and prices of the Ventilated Lunch Satchel:

Large size, covered with English cambric..... $1 75	Small size, covered with leather, waterproof .. $1 50
" " leather, waterproof... 2 00	Large size painted to imitate leather 1 25
Small size, covered with English Cambric..... 1 25	All sent by mail, postage paid, on receipt of price.

WORKING MODELS FOR WINDOW SHOW.

No. 30, Clock Combination. Fine Figures on Walnut board, 30 inches long, run by an eight day clock movement. More easily managed than a Steam Engine. Will run from one to two hours, and will double the sale of Hot Air Toys. Packed in a wood box, complete, **$4.00.**

THE GREAT EGYPTIAN MYSTERY.

This is undoubtedly the jolliest 'Mystery' ever solved. There is no end to the fun the boys or girls or older people can have with it. In fact it is a startling surprise to any one that attempts to unravel the mystery. It works upon an entirely new principle, and so sudden and complete is the surprise, that the bravest will be frightened. The cadaverous looking genius, who creates all the fun is confined in a handsome little box, about 2¾ inches square, ½ inch in depth and labelled "The Great Egyptian Mystery." When the hook is slipped out of the staple, the "Mystery" like a flash of lightning springs two or three feet into the air, oftentimes into the face of the person who has been so curious to find out what the neat little box contained. This ghostly personage when released from his casket, stands 6½ inches high in his night dress; or more than ten times his height when confined in the box. The "Mystery" alone will frighten a nervous person, but when he makes his sudden leap into the air, the surprise is complete and any one upon whom the joke has been perpetrated is sure to want one for use among his friends. There is nothing suspicious looking about the box, and nine persons out of every ten, to whom you hand it, will instantly open it. But a moment is required to replace the figure and set the box ready for the next victim. Our "Mystery" is always a great success, creating more fun and frolic at a trifling outlay than many mechanical or automatic contrivances of far heavier calibre, higher price, and more pretension. It is light and portable and can be carried in the pocket, occupying no more room than an ordinary tobacco box. We warrant it to cure the worst case of blues or melancholy on record. Price 18 cents, or six 3-cent stamps; 3 for 45 cents; 1 dozen, $1.50, by mail, post paid. One gross by express, $13.50.

PECK & SNYDER'S POCKET PIN CASE.

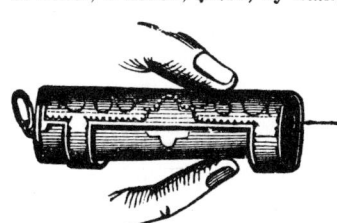

A new and neat invention for carrying pins in the pocket without danger. It is the only thing ever made at all convenient for holding pins, and is something no lady or gentleman should be without. The case is highly ornamental, and makes a beautiful charm to be worn on the watch chain or elsewhere. Each case will hold from twenty-five to thirty pins, and is always ready for use.

DIRECTIONS.—A gentle pressure with the thumb and forefinger will bring the pins as fast as you can count them. To re-fill always put the pins in point first.

Don't fill your clothing with pins when a beautiful Charm and Pin Case can be had for a trifle.

Sample, 25c., by mail, postpaid, or $2 00 per dozen.

THE POLICE CLUB FAN.

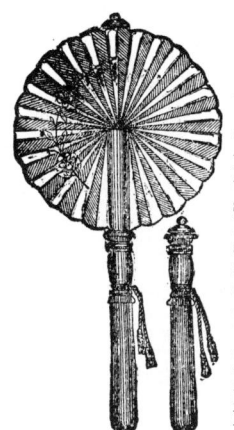

This is an article that will at once attract the attention of both ladies and gentlemen. It is an exact copy of the police club, which is held so much in awe by law-breakers and offenders in general, and is carried so gracefully by our blue-coated protectors as they pose upon the street corners and other conspicuous places. It is very appropriate as a present in the "German;" it is quite a feature at any evening entertainment. A lady may use it as a weapon of defense, should any of her admirers prove too bold, by giving him a thump over the knuckles; or she may arm one of her beaux with it and tie a blue ribbon on his arm, which will clothe him with authority, and tell him to arrest any offender against whom she may have a charge. The fan is constructed on precisely the same principle as the Pencil Fan. It is of the same dimensions and opens and closes in like manner. It is concealed entirely within the handle of the club. The club is made of highly-polished cherry, neatly turned. A handsome silk cord with tassels, in red, white and blue colors, is attached to the smaller end. This piece of decided originality is quite an additional ornament to a lady's costume, suspended in the manner they usually wear a fan. As it is entirely new, we anticipate a large sale. Price 35 cents; three (with red, white and blue tassels if desired) for 90 cents; one dozen, $3 25, by mail, post-paid.

EUREKA POCKET MAGNIFYING GLASS.

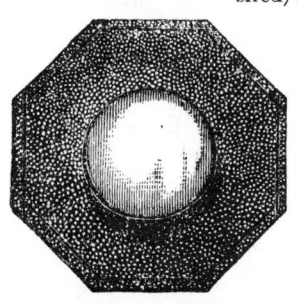

Has great magnifying power. Used for detecting counterfeit money, shoddy in cloth, foreign substances in the eye, in wounds, etc., and to examine insects, flowers and plants; to detect flaws in metals, fineness of wood-grain; to decipher writing otherwise illegible, and for the inspection of grain, tobacco, etc. Useful for everybody. It has a double convex lens, one and a half inches in diameter. Mounted in leather, and can be carried in the vest pocket. It can also be used as a reading glass, the smallest type appearing large and clear. Price reduced to 30c.; two for 50c.; one dozen for $2 25, by mail, postpaid.

SPECIE POCKET CASE.

1 doz. by mail post paid...$1 50

SOMETHING ATTRACTIVE AND SALEABLE.

Beautiful in Design, Simple in Construction and Perfect in its Operation.

Holds all denominations of coins to the amount of Six Dollars.

Every business man will buy it, every conductor will carry it, and every family man will adopt it for his change; and more than all, it sells at a price that no one can resist.

Price by mail, each, 20c.

COMPOUND MICROSCOPE.—The Latest Parisian Wonder!—Magnifies 1,000 Times.—This is the latest and most important discovery in optical science. It unfolds the mysteries of nature. Looking through its powerful lenses, under which one can see the animalculæ in a drop of water, the corpuscle in the blood, insects in old cheese, ever particle of dust on the wing of a butterfly in the form of a feather, a fly as large as an elephant, its trunk and the sponges on its feet being shown, the peculiar construction of a flea and the scales on its body. In fact, any imaginable minute object can be examined with as much accuracy and satisfaction as under any $100 instrument, and without the waste of time and skill used in mounting the object.

The Compound Microscope is constructed of a peculiar grade of pebble-lenses, being a recent discovery, and a secret, and is contrived so simply that any child can use it. It therefore will, no doubt, interfere with the sale of high-priced Microscopes, and take their place. One gross, by express, $20.00; 1 dozen, $2.00.

Samples by mail, prepaid, 25 cts.

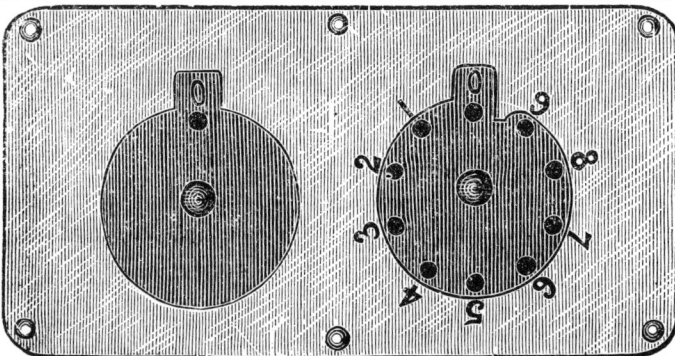

EUREKA MULTUM IN PARVO. (Cut exact size).

An Adding Machine for Adding Figures by Machinery. It is the greatest invention of the age in the mathematical line, adding figures without headwork, proving your trial balance, and carrying on a conversation at the same time. So simple, a child can use it.

This little machine is not intended to supersede headwork, but is intended for a proof or test. It is invaluable to the merchant when taking an inventory, and to the mechanic in proving and testing his accounts. There are but few people who do not get muddled on figures. This little machine is a safe refuge in such cases. It is a mathematical wonder and curiosity. It will teach a child more about multiplication and addition in one week than it can learn in six weeks at school. It is made of brass, heavy nickel plated, made flat, is not liable to get out of order, weighs 2¼ ounces. It is equal to those that sell for three times the value. Sent by mail for $1.50.

AMERICAN STANDARD SHAWL STRAPS.—Warranted Sole Leather Cross Bands.

No. 6.

No. 8.

No. 6. Solid metal, cast in one piece, malleable, full nickel plated, heavy russet straps.
                         3 straps, $1 00 ; 2 straps, each, $0 75
" 8. Solid metal handle, full nickel plated, sole leather cross bands. 3 straps, $1 00 ; 2 straps, 0 75
" 3. Metal handle, nickel plated ends, trimmed with fancy stitched leather. 3 straps, 50c. 2 straps 0 40
" 76 Leather handle, round or flat cross bands.   2 straps, each, 0 25

THE SWISS WARBLER'S BIRD OR ANIMAL CALL.

The only original Bird Call and Prairie Whistle. The only Genuine and Scientific Instrument.

For the use of the hunter they are invaluable, as any animal or bird can be so nearly imitated as to call them at once within range. All the various songs of the Mocking Bird, Canary, and other choice singers, can be given so naturally that the most expert listener cannot detect the difference.

All the astonishing feats of the most expert ventriloquist can be performed by means of the Whistle by a child ten years of age. We recently saw the utmost astonishment created in a large company assembled in a private parlor, by what appeared to be the terrific barking of a dog in the adjoining room. The room was searched, but no dog could be found. Then suddenly a cat commenced an unearthly squall in a closet which had not been opened for more than three months. Then a child cried out in great agony from the interior of a large book-case, and a beautiful bird commenced singing in the corner of the room. Astonishment turned to fear, until a boy, who had been sitting quietly reading all this time, found that his pranks were becoming serious and owned up to having one of the Whistles.

This wonderful instrument can be sent by mail, with full directions, which will enable any person to use it
Price, Three for 25 cts.   75 cts. per dozen.   Each, 10 cts.

THE NASAL HORN BLOWER.

A cheap and striking novelty. It consists of a pocket handkerchief with Trumpet or "Horn" attached thereto. This article is not only good as a toy, but is a first-rate joke, and highly appreciated as such, wherever shown.

Place the largest end of the Trumpetor or "Horn" in the mouth, cover the nose with the handkerchief, being careful not to cover up the lower end of the "Horn" then blow, the result will be startling to those about you, all sorts of remedies will be recommended by those who fear you are in a decline. When the joke is explained it will be appreciated by all.

1 doz. Handkerchiefs and Horns, complete, by mail.................. ...85 cents.
½ "   "   "   "   " ....50 "
1 Hankerchief and Horn, by mail........................... .... 15 "

YOUNG AMERICA'S FIRST SEGAR.

This has been a very bad boy. Against his parent's wishes, has indulged in smoking, and as a natural effect he has become very sick by it. The boy is made of metal, very fancy painted, 4 inches high and packed in box, with one dozen pellets or pills, with full directions, &c.

Sent by mail for..25 cents.
Extra boxes of Pellets, each........ ....10 cents.

A GENUINE STYLOGRAPHIC PEN.

The Manufacturers claim, it is Durable and Simple in Construction. It will never get out of order. It is neat in appearance, at one-sixth the price of others.

Most people are now familiar with the merits of the Stylographic Pen, but it has not been adapted for common use outside of large cities owing to its high price, never having been sold for less than **$1 50 and up to $5 00.** Gollner's Stylographic Pen is everyway equal to the best gold pencil, as it writes with ink. **It is a Reservoir Pen,** which, when once filled with ink, will write for days without refilling, can be carried in the pocket like a pencil, and is always ready for use.

THIS PEN is constructed of a drawn glass tube, **which will never corrode,** that contains the ink, one end of which is brought to a smooth point for writing, with an aperture finer than the point of a needle, through which the ink always flows freely, this being packed with filtering cotton to prevent stopping up the point, while the other end is fitted with a rubber air valve and a caison, giving it the elasticity of a gold pen. This tube is fitted by means of a telescopic screw in a beautiful **POLISHED NICKEL CASE,** from which the pen point protrudes, and when not in use the point is protected by a nickel cap, as shown in the cut. But if by accident the **point** should break, it can be **replaced** the same as any ordinary pen.
One dozen by mail, $2.00. Sample by mail, prepaid, 25cts.

SPORTING CHARMS AND SCARF PINS. (Cuts exact size of Article.)

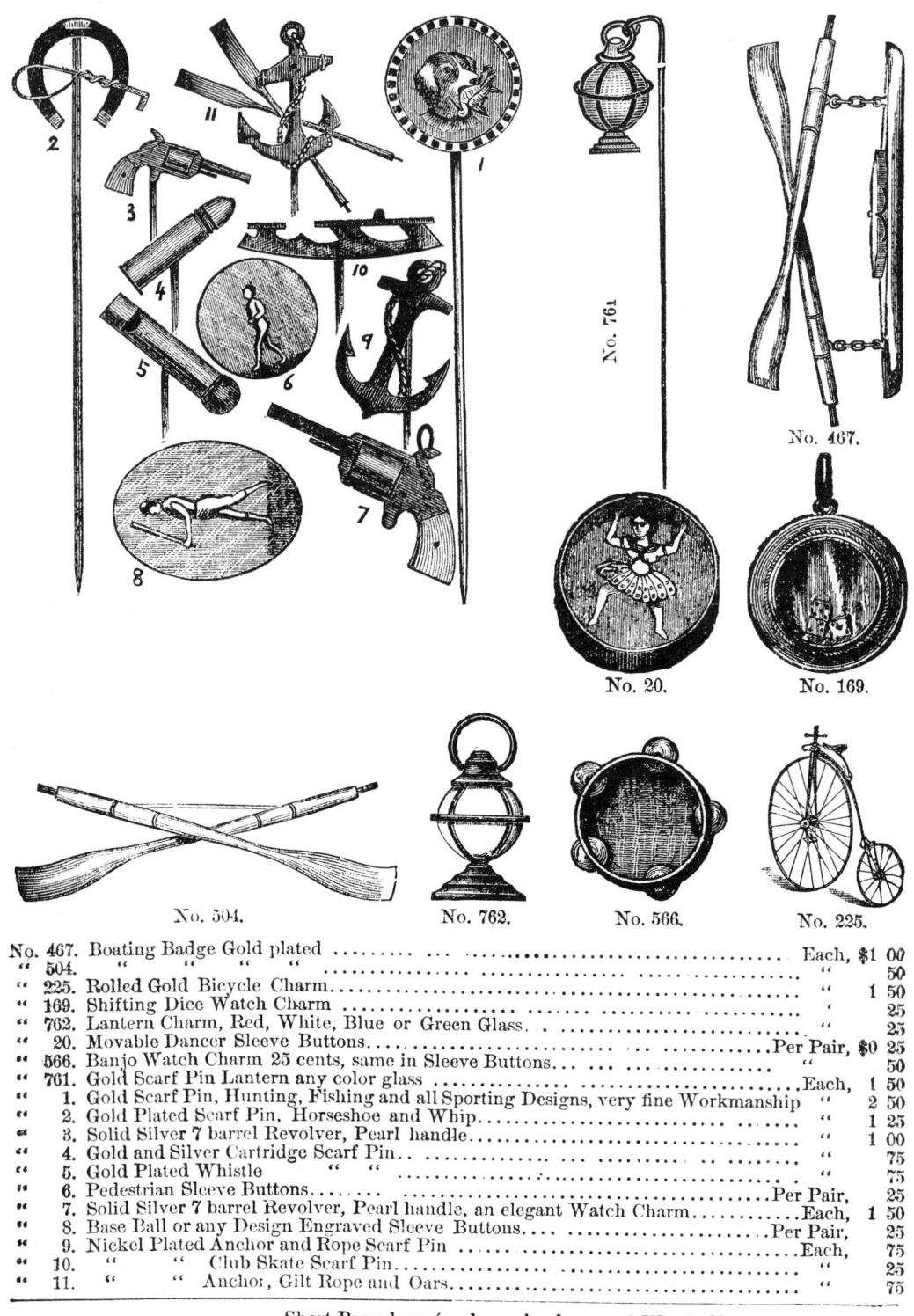

No. 467.	Boating Badge Gold plated	Each, $1 00
" 504.	" " " "	" 50
" 225.	Rolled Gold Bicycle Charm	" 1 50
" 169.	Shifting Dice Watch Charm	" 25
" 762.	Lantern Charm, Red, White, Blue or Green Glass	" 25
" 20.	Movable Dancer Sleeve Buttons	Per Pair, $0 25
" 566.	Banjo Watch Charm 25 cents, same in Sleeve Buttons	" 50
" 761.	Gold Scarf Pin Lantern any color glass	Each, 1 50
" 1.	Gold Scarf Pin, Hunting, Fishing and all Sporting Designs, very fine Workmanship	" 2 50
" 2.	Gold Plated Scarf Pin, Horseshoe and Whip	" 1 25
" 3.	Solid Silver 7 barrel Revolver, Pearl handle	" 1 00
" 4.	Gold and Silver Cartridge Scarf Pin	" 75
" 5.	Gold Plated Whistle " "	" 75
" 6.	Pedestrian Sleeve Buttons	Per Pair, 25
" 7.	Solid Silver 7 barrel Revolver, Pearl handle, an elegant Watch Charm	Each, 1 50
" 8.	Base Ball or any Design Engraved Sleeve Buttons	Per Pair, 25
" 9.	Nickel Plated Anchor and Rope Scarf Pin	Each, 75
" 10.	" " " Club Skate Scarf Pin	" 25
" 11.	" " " Anchor, Gilt Rope and Oars	" 75

Short Brass keys (as shown in above cut) Watch Charm .... 25 cts.
Heavy rolled gold plate keys $1.00
Any of the above by mail on receipt of price.

HINTS TO AMATEURS AND CONJURORS.

A few useful hints given at the commencement tend to make the study of this difficult art tolerably easy to all, by enabling the beginner to overcome those difficulties which beset his path at the outset.

In the first place let the learner study and practice well the instructions given him, and always rehearse privately any trick that he may intend exhibiting to his friends. He must practice talking a good deal, by the way of apparently explaining his tricks, but in reality to confuse the audience. Let him be as funny as he can. He must always keep cool.

When he makes a mistake, or meets with an accident, he must, instead of being unnerved by it, pretend that it was just what he intended, and so turn it to his advantage.

He must keep his audience at a respectful distance.

He must never hurry over anything, but MAKE HASTE SLOWLY.

A trick, however successfully performed, should never be repeated before the same audience.

We are continually receiving and inventing New Tricks, and it is impossible to keep a Catalogue complete to the last novelty, but we will at various seasons publish Supplementary Sheets giving descriptions of New Novelties.

Full and simple instructions sent with every Trick, when possible, and every purchaser taught to perform whatever Tricks he may buy, in the best and newest method, so that he may exhibit them with ease and without fear of detection, and no trouble is spared in order to make him perfect in what he purchases.

We beg to inform our patrons that *the Conjuring Tricks and Magical Apparatus sold by us* for beauty of workmanship and mechanical skill, have never been equaled in the world. They are so handsomely finished that they are an ornament in any drawing-room, although, when used for performing they will cause both astonishment and admiration.

No Trick can on any account be exchanged; if the purchaser does not quite understand the way to work it he will with pleasure be shown again and can have it once more fully explained, but it cannot be exchanged when once the secret has been shown or it leaves our store.

On all orders for goods to be sent by mail the money must be sent with the order. One-quarter the amount of bill must be sent with all orders for goods to be sent by express C. O. D. All magical apparatus, sent by express, we inclose in a wooden box, free of charge for boxing, but in all cases the purchaser pays express charges.

N. B.—We would advise our patrons against buying cheap and very inferior grades of goods, of which the market is flooded. The prices are but a little lower than our own; and will not work perfectly after a few times using. Our goods are of English, French and German make, and are selected by our Mr. Peck, who visits Europe every year to purchase New Goods, Novelties, &c.

THE MAGIC ROSE.

For the opening of a programme of magical illusions, whether public or private, this is admirably adapted. The performer takes his wand in hand as if about to commence, when casting his eyes upon his coat, he exclaims: "I declare, there was a pretty rose handed me by a lady as I came in, and I placed it in the button hole of my coat, but it seems to have flown. Perhaps I can induce it to return." After waiting a sufficient time for all to see that rose is not visible, he waves his hand or his wand over the lappel of his coat and instantly a large fine rose appears there and remains during the performance. It will last for years. Price, 35 cts.

No. 2.—THE WONDERFUL BRASS BALL AND FIVE CLOTH BALLS.

The performer having borrowed an empty hat, is going to perform a trick with it, but, to his surprise, finds that something has appeared in it, and takes out, one after the other, five fancy cloth balls, and lastly, a beautiful brass ball.
Complete, $3

No. 3.—THE MARVELOUS BIRD CAGES.
(THE GREATEST HAT TRICK EVER INVENTED).

The performer borrows a gentleman's hat, and in one instant he takes from the hat (one after the other) three large handsome cages, each containing a canary. This beautiful trick can be performed in the drawing-room, or upon the stage with the greatest ease. The effect of this trick is really astounding, as the cages are all exactly of one size and each cage being as high as the hat itself. Per set of three, $6.00

No. 4.—THE BOTTLE ILLUSION.

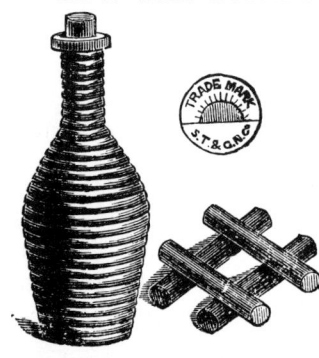

Four pieces of wood, colored respectively black, red, blue and yellow, are supplied with the trick. On one of them being placed secretly in the box, and the lid put on, so that it is utterly impossible to see within, the performer can easily divine which colored stick is within. A very remarkable illusion.
Price, $1.25 & $2.50

THE ENCHANTED COIN DRAWER.

No. 5.

A neat little mahogany case, with drawer, which is given for examination, and shut up perfectly empty. The performer takes a penny, and commands it to pass into the drawer, and upon opening it there it is; he then shuts it up with the penny in it, and commands it to multiply, and upon being again opened two pennies are found in the drawer. Any piece of money can be used. Price, $2.50

BALL OF WOOL TRICK.

No. 6.

A marked coin passes from any object into a ball of wool, from which, on the performer unraveling it, the coin drops into the glass. Price, 50 cts.

No. 7.—THE ELECTRIC RAINBOW CORDS.

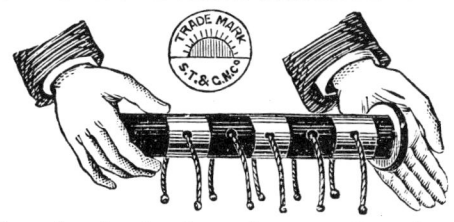

Several cords, of various colours, run through an ornamental wood column. The performer now asks one of the audience to hold it, as shown in the engraving and then he pulls the cords through the holes ; each cord changes colour instantly it is pulled, and while the person who holds it is deeply interested the performer pulls the middle cord, with startling effect. A joke!
Price, 50 cts.

No. 8.—THE MAGIC WINDMILL.

A capital joke and harmless. You take this in your hand, and putting the main shaft in your mouth, prove to your friend that a powder-mill may be blown up with safety. So your friend says 'Oh, that's nothing wonderful!' and taking it, blows in the same way, when an explosion of dust and ashes follows, that causes his whiskers, face and the parts adjacent, to appear as though a charcoal jar had been upset thereabouts.
Price, 50 cts

No. 9.—THE PISTOL TUBE.

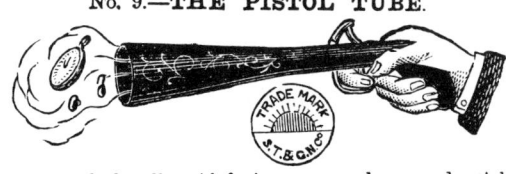

A watch, handkerchief, rings, or any borrowed article is placed in the tube, a pistol is loaded, and the tube fitted on the barrel of it; the performer then fires it off, and the article placed in it is found in the place at which the pistol was fired. Price, with pistol complete, $2.50

No. 10.—THE MAGIC PILL BOX.

A coin is placed in an ordinary pill box, which is placed in a handsome pedestal, and covered over with a lid; on removing the lid, and again opening the pill box, the coin is discovered to have vanished. The pill box is again replaced in the pedestal, and on re-opening it, lo! the coin appears again, at times, when the coin disappears the box is found full of sweets, etc., which can be distributed to the audience. Made of brass, ornamented.
Price, each, $2.50, $3.00 and $4.00

No. 11.—THE ENCHANTED BALL THAT CHANGES TO A ROSE.

A solid ebony ball is shown, and placed in the vase, which is then closed. The performer then places his hand under the table and produces the ball, and on opening the box, in its place is found a beautiful rose.
Price, $3

No. 12.—THE WONDERFUL VASE TO MAKE HOT COFFEE.

A NEW WAY TO MAKE HOT COFFEE FROM WOOL.

The performer shows a pretty metal "vase" which the company can freely examine, the "vase" is filled with real wool, then before the eyes of the company the wool is changed to smoking hot coffee, which is poured from the "vase" into cups for the company to drink. This is a most original "trick" and will give great satisfaction.
Price, each, $3.00 and $5.00

No. 13.—THE DOVE AND BOTTLE TRICK.

An ordinary wine bottle, from which several glasses of wine are poured; the performer then takes the bottle and knocks it with his wand, and breaks it in two, and takes out from it a live dove, perfectly dry and uninjured. This trick may be repeated any number of times. Price, $3. The same trick but the bottle constructed to pour out two different wines. Price, $4

No. 14.—THE PASSE-PASSE TRICK.

A wine-glass is shown, and filled with wine. It is then covered over with a handsome brass cover, which has previously been given for examination; when the cover is taken off the glass of wine has disappeared, and in the place of it is a wine bottle, which is lifted up to show there is nothing under it; the bottle is then covered over, and changes back to the glass of wine.
Per Pair, Price, $2.50 and $3.50

No. 15.—THE WATCH MORTAR.

A watch is borrowed, and placed in the mortar, and a poker is then taken, and the watch smashed up, pieces of the works being shown; the mortar is then covered over, and upon the cover being taken off, the watch has vanished, and is found in the centre of a loaf, or elsewhere uninjured.
Price, $1.50

No. 16.—THE CRYSTAL CASE AND MAGIC BALL.

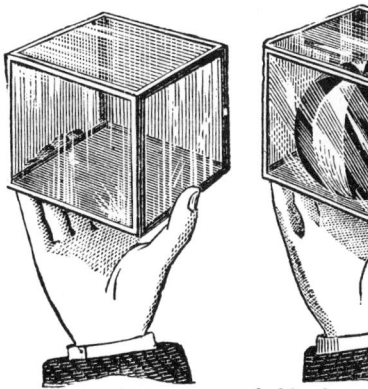

This marvelous and remarkably elegant illusion consists of a pretty case, with glass front and sides, and which the performer proves to be perfectly empty by placing his wand inside, and which the audience can see through the glass front and sides, being inserted to the very back of the box. Nevertheless, on exclaiming Heigh! Presto! the performer makes a large ball appear inside to the great astonishment of the audience. To increase the effect, the casket can be tightly corded, thus proving that the ball which is discovered within could not have been passed through any aperture.
Price of casket with ball, by express, only $1.50

No. 17.—TWO DOZEN GOBLETS

for producing from an empty hat. This is a most extraordinary performance, as the performer produces two dozen large tin goblets from a perfectly empty hat with astonishing effect.

Price, $3

No. 18.—THE MARVELOUS TRICK OF GLASS BOWLS OF WATER AND GOLD FISH.

A borrowed handkerchief or shawl is freely examined, and from it is instantly produced three glass bowls full of water and gold fish; by Express only. The set of three, price $10.00; single bowls, with cover,

Price, $3.50.

No. 19.—THE MAGIC BOTTLE IMP.

The bottle which the old veteran conjuror is bringing to you is a curiosity and a brain puzzler. It will stand up as persistently as a flag-staff, and no one of your friends can make it lay on its side. But as soon as you take it in hand, it will be very obliging, down it will go, and lay as quiet as a sleepy kitten. It causes heaps of fun and wagon loads of merriment. Any one can perform this simple trick, but the way it is done is not easily seen. The bottle can be handed to any one for examination. Price, 10c. Large 15c. Extra large, 40c.

No. 20.—THE INDIAN PUZZLE BALL.

This superb article is a perfectly round ebony ball from three to four inches in diameter, and though it seems no more possible to open than a croquet ball, it can, nevertheless, be open and disclose an interior box capable of holding fifty dollars in gold. Coins or rings can be put in it and heard to rattle, yet an offer might safely be made to give the contents to any person who will get them out, for it is to all appearance a solid ball, with no clue to an opening visible.

Price, $1.50

No. 22.—EGGS OF PHARAOH'S SERPENTS.

Upon igniting one of these eggs, an object having the appearance of a serpent gradually extends itself to a length of two or three feet.

Small size, 12 in a box......25 cts.
Large size, 12 in a box......35 cts.

No. 21.—THE ENCHANTED TEA CHEST;

OR 100 RINGS OF PERFUME FROM AN EMPTY BOX.

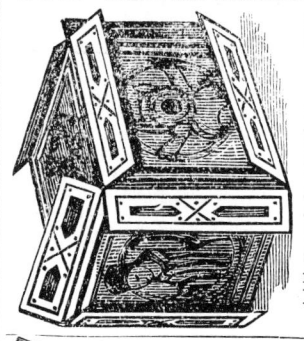

Unique, puzzling and attractive. A perfume casket and puzzle combined. The chest can be easily taken apart and put together by any one who knows how; but one who has never seen it put together might work on it for hours without success.

Price, 25cts.

No. 23. THE MAGIC EGG BAG.

It beats the Patent Yankee Hen's Nest out and out. The operator produces from a common empty calico bag a dozen or more real eggs, which appear one at a time as called for, in a netting corner, and may be examined before being removed from the bag, as well as afterwards. The operator may perform the trick equally well without coat and with his sleeves rolled up.   Price, $1.00.

No. 24.—THE MAGIC RING AND PILLAR AND MYSTIC BARRELS.

This capital trick consists in trying to remove the ring from the pillar and barrels. It is a first-class puzzle, and very deceptive.   Price. 75c.

No. 25. THE MAGIC WRIST OR HAND KNIFE.

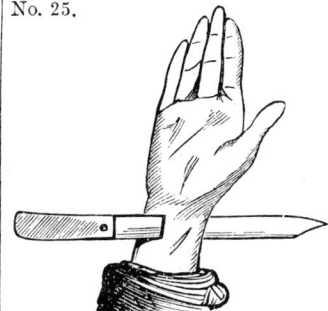

A knife that, after being examined, is plunged through the hand, as seen in the above cut. A wonderful surgical operation that produces neither pain nor injury.

Price, $1.

No. 26.—THE DISSOLVING COIN OR ENCHANTED TUMBLER.

A transparent glass is exhibited and handed for examination. A little water is poured into it, and the glass placed upon the table, a handkerchief and a half dollar borrowed. The coin is then placed under the handkerchief, and held over the glass. At the word of command it is dropped, and heard to fall into the glass; the handkerchief is removed, but, lo! the glass is empty, and the coin is produced from anywhere desired.

Price, 75 cts.

No. 27.—The **NAIL THROUGH** the **FINGER.**
A CLEVER ILLUSION.

An ordinary wrought iron nail is given for examination, then instantly thrust through the fingers, to the horror of the beholder.
Price;　　　　30c.

No. 28.—**THE WONDERFUL MALLET AND BALL TRICK.**

A neat boxwood-mallet, that will strike a ball through the box and table with a single blow.　Price, $1.50 and $2.00

No. 29—**THE MYSTERIOUS CARD TRIPOD.**

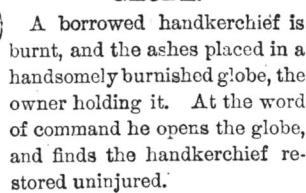

A card is selected from the pack and placed on the tripod, where the performer sets light to it, and burns it entirely *leaving only the ashes.* The performer afterwards commands the card to be restored from its ashes, and it is found again as perfect as when selected from the pack. This is a very useful stage trick.　Price with Cards $2.50

No. 30.—**THE WIZARD'S MAGICAL BURNING GLOBE.**

A borrowed handkerchief is burnt, and the ashes placed in a handsomely burnished globe, the owner holding it. At the word of command he opens the globe, and finds the handkerchief restored uninjured.
Two sizes, Price, each, $2.50 and $3.50.　Extra large $5.00

No. 31.—**MAGIC WHISTLE.—A CAPITAL JOKE.**

The performer can play on the whistle with impunity, but when anybody unacquainted with the trick attempts to play on it powdered charcoal decorates his lips. This is a capital trick for playing upon those young gentlemen—of whom all Conjurors have had experience at one or another, who are always so knowing in their assertions as to their knowledge of the mode of performing the tricks, and sometimes causing annoyance to the performer and the audience by their conceit.　Price, 15 cts.

No. 32.—**THE WIZARD'S BIRD CAGE; OR, THE MAGIC INCUBATOR.**

A handsome circular bird cage, in which the performer places an egg, and borrowing a handkerchief from one of the company, carelessly throws it over the cage; instantly removing the handkerchief the egg is gone, and in its place is found a live bird, greatly to the surprise of all beholders.
Price, by express, $5.00
Extra quality $10.00.

No. 33.—**FAIRY BOX AND BIRD CAGE.**

The performer opens the box and empties out a lot of flowers or bon-bons; he then, having shown it to be perfectly empty, places inside it an egg, and closes the lid, commanding a change to take place; he then opens the box, the egg has vanished, and in place of it is a cage, with a live bird in it, which may be examined. N. B.—The cage which is a very pretty and ornamental one is just the same size as the inside of the box, and completely fills it.
Price, $2.50 and $3.50.

No. 34—**THE CHINESE LINKING RINGS.**

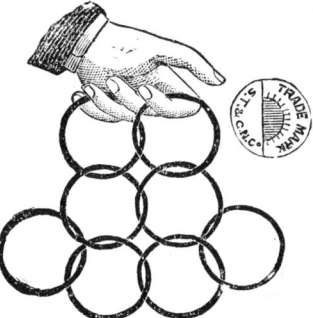

Eight polished steel rings are given for examination, and then the performer, taking two of them and holding one in each hand, places them against one another, and they are instantly joined, then taking them one after another they join together and form a variety of beautiful devices, yet, at the word of command they immediately fall apart.　Per set, $3, nickel plated $5.

No. 35.
THE MAGIC FUSEE BOX.

A First-Rate Puzzle.

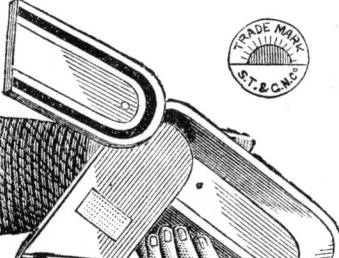

Having lighted your cigar, hand the box to a friend who can neither open the box nor obtain a light.
Polished oak, each, 50 cts. of brass, $1.

No. 37—**THE BOX AND THE MAGIC CORKS.**

Four corks are placed in a card-board box, which is then closed by one of the company; the box is opened, and is found to contain eight corks, which may again be made to disappear at will.
Price, 50 cts.

No. 36.

THE THREE MAGIC BABIES.

A NEW TRICK FOR THE LADIES.

A lady having placed three coins in the little boxwood well, which she holds in the palm of her hand, it is covered for a moment. On moving the cover, the coins are found to be changed to three charming little babies

Price, 75 cts.

No. 38.—THE MARBLE PEDESTAL.

The marble is placed in the pedestal and covered over, it instantly passes through the table and then back again into the box. Price, 30 cts.

No. 39.—THE WEDDING RING BOX PUZZLE.

A neat little box, wood box apparently, without any opening, and yet something is heard to rattle inside, this is a wedding ring, and any lady who can succeed in abstracting it may keep it; but great as her desire will be, she will find all her endeavors useless, and yet the performer takes it out in a second. Price, 50 cts.

No. 40.—THE NEW PERSIAN PUZZLE.

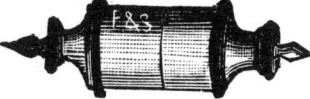

This box will contain rings, etc. The rod runs right through the centre of it, and each part will move seperate from the other, and yet all are bound together in the securest manner. Price, 50 cts.

No. 41.—THE CANNON PUZZLE.

A boxwood cannon, inside which a marble is heard to rattle, an can be seen through the small hole in the muzzle; will bear the strictest examination, the key to the secret being really concealed in the puzzle itself Very ingenious. Price, 50 cts.

No. 42.—THE ASIATIC CABINET PUZZLE.

This puzzle is very ingenious. The lid will unwind continually but will not come off; those in the secret can undo it immediately. The cabinet is very prettily turned in polished box-wood, and forms an interesting ornament for chimney-piece, or a useful receptacle for rings, studs, &c., on the dressing-table. Price, 50cts.

No. 43.—THE BALL BOX.

The ball is taken out of the box, and the box closed, the ball is then passed into the box again, and then through the table, and the box once more shown empty. Small size, 30c. larger, 50c. Extra size $1.00.

No. 44.—The ECCENTRIC BARREL PUZZLE.

A beautifully made barrel is shewn containing a large ball. The puzzle is to let the ball out; but the only opening is at the top, where a little roller passes into the hand and moves the ball about. This opening is only a quarter the size of the imprisoned ball, so the problem takes a deal of solving.

Price 50 cts.

No. 45.—THE TURKISH NUT PUZZLE.

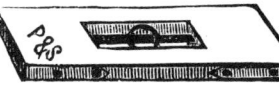

Just out. An extraordinary novelty. The puzzle is to get the ring off the bar which is fast in the wood at both ends, and it seems an impossibility to get it off; yet it can be removed instantly by anyone possessing the secret. The best and most ingenious puzzle ever introduced. Will be the hit of the season. Price, 25 cts.

No. 46.—THE EGG BOX.

In which is shown a real egg, and then the lid is put on, and one of the audience is requested to open his mouth wide, and behold, he has swallowed the egg and the box is empty; but on his blowing on the box the egg reappears in it. Price, $1. Same as above with golden egg, $1.25.

No. 47. THE SECRET BOX.

A beautifully made boxwood box, in which a dime is placed and the box closed; when it is opened again the dime is found to have changed to a quarte of a dollar, which changes back to the dime once more.

Price, 75 cts. & $1.50.

No. 48.—THE NOSE TRICK.

A brad-awl is given for examination, and the piece of wood as shown in drawing is placed on the nose in order to make the operation less painful, the bradawl is then slowly bored right through till the cord comes out the other side, the bradawl is then withdrawn freely backwards and forwards through the nose. Perfectly harmless. Price, complete, 50 cts.

No. 49.—THE BARLEY BOX.

This is a capital trick where there are children present. A showily, japanned tin box is opened carefully and shown to be full of barley, or any seed; it is then closed, but on being opened again, in exactly the same place, the barley has changed to sweets or flowers, which may be emptied out, and distributed among the children. Price $1 and $1.50.

No. 50.—THE SEXAGON EXPERIMENT.

This trick consits of the little box on the sexagon, and twelve ivory counters, numbered 10, 20, 30, up to 120; any one of them may be chosen, placed in the sexagon, and covered over; it is now given to the performer, who immediately divides the number that has been concealed in it. Price, $1.25.

No. 51.—THE ELECTRIC FUSEE BOX.

"SILVER PLATED" AND BEAUTIFULLY MADE.

The Electric "Fusee Box" will be found VERY USEFUL AS WELL AS AMUSING. They can be carried in the waistcoat pocket. You ask a friend if he requires a "Fusee" to light his pipe or cigar. WHEN HE RECEIVES THE "BOX" AND TRIES TO OPEN IT HE RECEIVES AN "ELECTRIC SHOCK," WHICH WILL CAUSE SHOUTS OF LAUGHTER, although the owner of the "Box" can open and and close it with the greatest ease.

Price, each, and $1.00

N.B.—The "Electric Fusee Box" is highly recommended, as they are manufactured in a very superior manner.

No. 52.—THE CUPS AND BALLS TRICK.

Three tin cups, which are given for examination, and three little balls, one of the balls is then taken, and it having first been shown that there is nothing under the cup, it is passed under that and then to the other, then the three balls are made all to appear under one cup; in fact they change, multiply and disappear in a most perplexing manner. Price. $1.00; large size, $2.00

No. 53.—THE MYSTIC EGG VASE.

A beautiful finished brass vase and cover, which is shown full of rice and then covered over, when the rice instantly vanishes, and in the place appears a real egg, which is taken out of the vase, and it is then quite empty. This trick may be varied in many ways. Each $1.50, 2.50, 3.50

No. 54.—THE GREAT SLATE TRICK.

As performed in spiritualistic circles. A common slate is shown, and cleaned on both sides to prove there is no preparation upon it; it is then laid upon the table, a small piece of pencil under it, the hands of the spectators are placed on it, and in a few seconds sounds of writng are heard, and upon lifting up the slate a long message is found, completely covering the underneath side of the slate, it writes answers to questions. Defies detection, yet perfectly simple of performance in any drawing-room. Price, 75 cents.

No. 55.—THE CANISTER TRICK.

A handsomely japanned tin canister is shown to be empty, a lady's handkerchief is borrowed and placed in it, and set light to. The canister is then covered over, and when again open the hankercheif is found perfectly uninjured; or the canister may be shown full of bran, rice, etc., and then change to sweets or flowers. Price, $1.50.

No. 56.—THE NEST OF SIX MAGIC BOXES.

This is a most startling illusion, but the effect is greatly increased by using it in conjunction with another trick. A dime is borrowed and marked by the owner, to enable it to be recognised again. The performer then places it in the brass money box, described elsewhere, or any other receptacle, which he gives to the audience to hold. He now produces a box, and asks one of the audience to take off the lid, which discloses another box inside; this, on being opened, exposes another, and so on until *six* boxes have been opened, and in the sixth and smallest box, the identical coin is found. The extraordinary part of the performance is that to open all these boxes takes quite five minutes, whereas the marked *coin passes there instantly*, and the brass money box is found empty.

Small size, per set, $2.50. Large size, per set, $5.00

No. 59.—THE INEXHAUSTIBLE BOTTLE.

An ordinary bottle is shown, and on the cork being taken out, the performer says he is thirsty and pours out of it a glass of water. He then asks one of the audience whether they would like a glass of water, or would they prefer wine, and ask them to name the kind they prefer, port, sherry, claret, madeira, and he pours out in succession the different kinds as they are ask for.

Price, for two wines, $1.50; three wines, $2.00; four wines, $3.50.

No. 57.—**THE MYSTERIOUS BRAN AND GLASS**.

A glass is shown full of bran, some of which is taken out; it is then covered over with a handsome brass cover, and the bran is commanded to change, and when the cover is taken off the bran has vanished and the glass is full of flowers, bonbons, sweets, etc. By express. Price, $1.50; larger size, $3.50 & $5.

No. 58.—**THE WELSH RABBIT.**

The various ingredients are placed in the saucepan, and a hat and handkerchief are borrowed. The handkerchief is then placed in the hat and set light to and the saucepan held over the flames to cook the ingredients. On opening the saucepan, out jumps a live rabbit, and the hat and handkerchief are restored uninjured. A very effective finishing trick. By express. Price, $2 00

No. 60.—**THE CAPTIVE RING PUZZLE.**

A small black ring moves freely on a pillar, but is prevented from coming off by a large ball securely fixed on each end. The puzzle is to get the ring off, and those in the secret can easily do this, but the uninitiated will give it up in despair. Each 75c

No. 61.—**THE MYSTERIOUS CANDLE.**

The performer extinguishes one of the lighted candles on his operating table, and covers it over with an ornamental case. Upon raising the case immediately afterwards the candle has vanished, an in its place is found a lady's handkerchief, which had been previously borrowed and placed elsewhere. Complete, 75c.

No. 62.—**THE CANNON BALL TRICK.**

The performer borrows a hat, which he shows quite empty and then immediately produces from it a large cannon ball, exactly fitting inside the hat; he again shows it empty, and then produces one dozen beautiful parti-colored cloth balls, some flowers, sweets, toys, etc., the whole forming a splendid display.
Price, complete, with balls, $5; ball only, $2.25

No. 63.—**THE MARKED BULLETS TRICK.**

The performer first gives his pistol for examination; he then asks a gentleman to load it before the audience, and they see the powder, etc., put in; he now takes two leaden bullets, and handing them to the audience asks that they may be marked so as to be known again, and then given to the gentleman who is loading the pistol, who drops them into the barrel, and rams them tightly down; the performer has not touched the pistol at all. A cap having been put on, the performer asks the gentleman to fire the pistol right at him. The explosion is heard, and when the smoke clears away, the performer is seen uninjured and smiling, holding the marked bullet in his hand. Very effective and astonishing. Apparatus complete, price, $15.00.

No. 64.—**THE MAGIC BOTTLE OF WINE AND GROWTH OF FLOWERS.**

The performer commences the trick by pouring wine out of the bottle into some glasses, which he hands to the company; he then gives a paper cover for inspection, and this being proved empty, he places it over the bottle. The performer now commands the bottle to fly, and upon the cover taken off, the bottle has vanished, as it were by magic, and charmed to a white pot filled with flowers, and the cover shown empty once more. $3.50

No. 65.—**The MYSTIC HANDKERCHIEF BOX.**

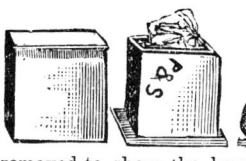

A lady's handkerchief is borrowed and placed in the box, and the mahogany cover is put on; an orange is now brought forward and given to a lady to hold, the cover is removed to show the handkerchief is still in the box, which one of the audience is asked to hold; at the word of command they open it, and find the handkerchief has vanished, and on breaking the orange in two it is found in the centre. Price, $5.00.

No. 66.—**VASE OF INK WHICH CHANGES TO CLEAR WATER AND GOLD FISH.**

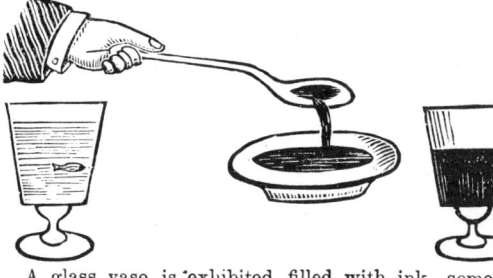

A glass vase is exhibited filled with ink, some of which is taken from it with a ladle and poured into a plate, to prove there is no deception in the contents; on a borrowed handkerchief being thrown over the vase of ink, it is found transformed on its removal, into clear water, forming a remarkably effective trick with ladle.
Price, complete, $3.50. ladle, separate, each, $1.50 & $2

No. 67.—CAP AND SIX CENTS.

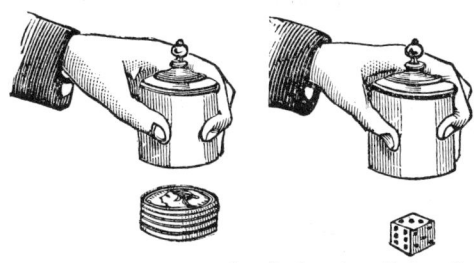

Six cents are borrowed and place in a little pile on the table; a plain leather cover is placed over them, and on removing the cover the coins are found to have vanished, and are discovered under the table or any locality you chose, and their place is occupied by a little ivory dice. This is one of the neatest and cleverest tricks ever invented; cannot possibly be detected, and yet remarkably simple and easy of performance. The cover has no mechanism whatever within it, and can be handed around for examination. For a small pocket trick, which can be introduced on any occasion, it is unrivaled, and always causes intense astonishment. Full instructions for performing are sent with this remarkable trick. Price, 75 cts.

No. 68.—THE DEMON PUNCH BOWL.

A beautiful silverplated punch bowl is shown perfectly empty, and to prove that is so the performer turns it upside down; he now borrows a lady's handkerchief and covers it over; calling for a ladle and some glasses he removes the handkerchief and the bowl is full of hot punch, which he ladles out and offers to the company, but as fast as he takes it out it fills again, till the supply appears inexhaustible.

Price, by express, $4.00, $5.00 and $6.00.

No. 69.—THE BARBER'S POLE AND THE WIZARD'S SUPPER.

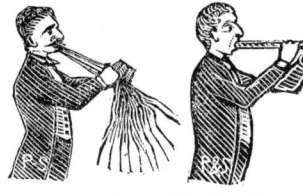

The performer first eats a quantity of paper shavings, but being afraid they would disagree with him, he takes hold of the last piece. He then draws out of his mouth many yards of various colored ribbon, and finally a long barber's pole. Price, 75 cts.

No. 70.—THE WONDERFUL ZULU BOX.

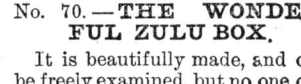

It is beautifully made, and can be freely examined, but no one can open it that is not in the secret, it seems quite an impossibility, still, in an instant it is opened with ease. The mechanism of the Zulu box will cause great admiration.

Price, 50c.

No. 71.—THE CHINESE LANTERNS.

The performer borrows an empty hat, and places it on the table, and immediately proceeds to take from it, one after the other, six beautiful Chinese lanterns, each with a light in it. The six lanterns, when out, are six times as long as the hat. This forms a very beautiful and effective trick $2.50 set of 6, New and large size, Set $3.50.

No. 72.—THE INEXHAUSTIBLE BOX.

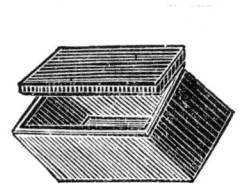 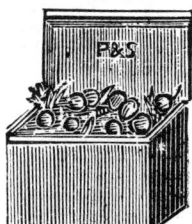

A very handsome box, which, to prove it is empty, the performer lays it on its side and holds open the lid so that all the audience may see that there is nothing in it; but immediately he has stood it up again he proceeds to take from it a glass full of water, flowers, toys, bon-bons, etc., and at any moment the audience may desire he will show it empty or lift it up to show that there is nothing underneath it. Very useful for distributing toys, etc. Price, ebonized wood, inlaid, by express, $10.00.

No. 73.—THE ENCHANTED BOOK.

By blowing on this book and manipulating the pages according to the instructions supplied with it, the most extraordinary effects are produced. The contents of each page change in most surprising style; thus on first looking through it, every page appears to contain a large colored plate of a beautiful lady, but on closing the book and reopening it, the beautiful lady has disappeared, and each page contains a large rose; this again changes to upwards of eight other various designs; and, finally, on opening the book, the pages are discovered to be merely WHITE PAPER, and PERFECTLY BLANK. Price each $1.50

No. 74.—THE PHANTOM ROSE TREE AND THE THREE MYSTERIOUS CARDS,

A PRETTY AND EFFECTIVE TRICK.—The performer introduces to the company a handsome rose tree in a pretty painted pot, *three* cards are also chosen from a pack, torn up and placed in a pistol, which are fired at the rose tree, when instantly the *three* cards appear on top of the tree.

N.B. The three cards can be taken off and handed to the company. Price, $15.00

No. 75.—THE VASE OF FLOWERS AND THE PHANTOM CAGE.

The performer introduces to the company a skeleton vase, filled with pretty and various flowers, some of which are taken out and presented to the ladies, proving that they are real flowers. The performer then places the vase on the table and borrows a pocket handkerchief, which he throws over the vase; he then states to the company that the handkerchief has a charm about it; he then is about to hand the handkerchief back, when to the great astonishment of the company, the performer has hanging on his finger a bird cage and two real birds in it, with perch, &c.

N. B.—The extraordinary mechanism of this trick is something wonderful and highly recommended either for the drawing room or stage, and is the greatest cage trick ever invented, *the vase being no more than 2 inches deep, and the cage which is round, stands 11 inches high.*
Price, $25 00

No. 76.—THE PHANTOM AVIARY.

The performer introduces *a large handkerchief or a shawl* which is shown to the company and examined. The performer then in a extraordinary manner produces a large solid and handsome aviary of birds with perch, &c. This aviary can be produced and used in a variety of ways from a portfolio or scrap-book, &c., with wonderful effect. Price, $6.00, 8.00, 13.00

No. 77.—THE INVISIBLE GIFT PUZZLE.

A piece of money is concealed in the box somewhere, and anyone who can extract it may keep it, but if they cannot succeed within a certain time, they must give you a piece of the same value. A most ingeniously constructed box.
50 cts.

No. 78. THE VANISHING OR CHANGING COVER.

To make any article, oranges, lemons, handkerchiefs, etc., disappear from the table, and make other things appear in their places. Made of brass and ornamented.
Price, $3 00; superior quality, $4.00

No. 79.—THE PEDESTAL TRICK.

The pedestal cover and ball are first given for examination, the little ball is then placed on the top of the pedestal, and the cover put over it; you place your hand under the table and "pass!"—the ball falls into it, and on lifting up the cover it is shown to have vanished from the pedestal, and all is once more given for examination. Prettily japanned. Price, 50 cts.

No. 80.—THE FLORAL WONDER; OR, THE LADIES' DELIGHT.

A small pot, filled with moss, is shown to the audience. Some magic seed is now sprinkled over it, and a handsomely japanned cover is then placed over it for a few seconds, to allow the seed to grow; when the cover is taken off a beautiful rose tree in full bloom is found to have grown.
Price, $1.25; large size, $2.00

No. 81.—THE VANISHING COIN.

A two cent piece is borrowed and marked by one of the audience; the box is given for examination; the coin is then placed in the box, and on the performer blowing on the enclosed box, the coin is seen to fall from the bottom, and yet both the coin and the box may be again examined. Price, boxwood, 35 cts; brass, 75 cts.

No. 82.—THE MYSTERIOUS CONE.

A solid boxwood cone is given for examination and placed under a hat; a paper cover is then shown, which is placed over a ball on the top of the hat. They are then commanded to change places, which is instantly accomplished, the cone appearing on the top and the ball underneath the hat.
Prices, 50, 75 cts. and $1.50

No. 83.—THE FAIRY COLUMNS AND VANISHING BALLS.

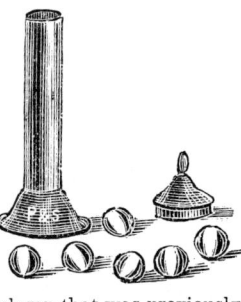

Two beautiful brass columns are shown, into one of which are placed six particolored cloth balls, the other column is left empty; they are then placed at opposite sides of the table, the performer makes a pass with his wand, and commands a change to take place. On examining the columns the six balls have vanished from the one in which they were placed, and are found in the column that was previously empty. Per pair, $12.00

No. 84.—IS YOUR WATCH A REPEATER?

The performer borrows a watch to perform a trick with, and after admiring, remarks that it is a repeater; the owner says he was not aware of it, but the watch immediately strikes the hour, and then, at the command of the performer, answers questions, counts, tells any one's age, or strikes any given number of times. Price, $10.

No. 85.—A COIN CHANGED TO A LIVE BIRD: A STARTLING ILLUSION.

A polished brass box, in which you place half a dollar, which instantly changes to a live bird, mouse or sweets. $2.00.

No. 86.—NOSE AMPUTATING KNIFE.

With this magical piece of cutlery one-half of your friend's nose may be cut off, and it then falls to the floor. Mark, we do not say whether it is the nose or the knife that falls; you must try the knife to know that. We will say, however, that your friend will not suffer any during the operation. Price per pair, $1.

No. 87.—THE WATCH BOX.

A lady's watch is borrowed and placed in a neat mahogany box, and the box is locked and the key retained by one of the audience. The performer now brings forward a loaf of bread, which he places on the table, and commands the watch to leave the box and appear in the centre of the loaf, which he breaks open, and shows the watch embedded in the middle; and on the lady unlocking the box, it is perfectly empty, and bears the strictest examination.

Price, $3.50; extra finish, $4.00 and $5.00

No. 88. Superior, beautifully inlaid, with mechanical arrangements that at any time the watch can be distinctly heard ticking. This is a grand improvement, and entirely a new invention. Price, $10 and $12.

No. 90.—THE MYSTIC VASE, AND GINGER-BEER BOTTLE AND SWEETS.

An empty vase is given for examination, a ginger-beer bottle is introduced and some ginger-beer poured from the bottle; the bottle is then placed in the vase and covered over; on removing the cover the bottle has vanished and the vase is found full of sweets, toys, etc. Price, $4.00.

No. 89.—THE MAGIC CASK.

This is a beautifully finished cask, 5 inches long, resting upon a cross-barred frame, as here shown. The performer, or any one of the audience, pours water into it through the tunnel at the top, when there immediately flows from the faucet wine, beer, milk, tea or coffee, the water having been magically transferred into one of those liquids. As long as water is poured into the cask it will continue to flow from the faucet in its strangely changed condition. This is a strictly scientific operation, and a perfect marvel. It is positively proof against detection, even the owner of the cask not knowing how it is done. Each, $1.25.

No. 91.—The Great JAPANESE BALL TRICK.

This extraordinary trick was performed at the Crystal Palace by the celebrated "Japanese Troupe," and caused the greatest astonishment.—The performer shows a large solid black ball (with a hole running right through it), and a common piece of string; the performer passes the string through the ball, and holds with his foot one end of the string, and with his thumb and finger the other end, the string being held in a perpendicular position to allow the ball to run down the string with the greatest freedom. The performer changes the ends of the string, and again the ball runs down as many times as desired, *but at the command of the performer the ball will remain suspended upon any part of the string mentioned by the company.*

Price, each, 50 cents, 75 cents and $1.50.

No. 92.—THE CHILD FOUND IN A BORROWED HAT.

A CLEVER AND LAUGHABLE TRICK.

The performer borrows a hat (*which is shown quite empty*) and instantly produces from the Hat a "Child" three quarters-of-a-yard long; the "child" is nicely dressed, with cap trimmed with lace and ribbands, a bib, &c.

This "Trick" is not only very astonishing, but always creates shouts of laughter; very easy to perform in a drawing-room or theater. Price each, $10.00.

No. 93.—THE DESTRUCTIVE FINGER.

Borrow a gentleman's hat (if a new one so much the better), telling him you wish to use it in your next trick; now suddenly slip, and in making an afford to save your balance, your finger apparently passes right through the crown. The horrified expression on the owner's face can be more easily imagined than discribed. The finger sent with this trick is beautifully modelled, and moves about through the hat so naturally, that no one has the slightest doubt about the genuineness of it; therefore, when the hat is returned without damage the astonishment is very great.   25 cts.

No. 94.—THE PAIR OF ENCHANTED FLOWER POTS.

A BEAUTIFUL AND EFFECTIVE TRICK.

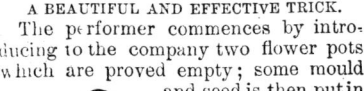

The performer commences by introducing to the company two flower pots which are proved empty; some mould and seed is then put in and the pots are then placed on a chair or a table. The performer borrows a handkerchief and places over the pots and commands the seeds to grow! when upon removing the handkerchief to the great wonder and surprise of the company, both pots will be found full of beautiful flowers! The effect is most miraculous, and far excelling anything of its kind known. This is an entire new experiment and is highly recommended, and suitable for the drawing room or stage, as it is a good opening trick and an ornament throughout the rest of the performance.   Price, complete, $15.00.

No. 95.—THE MAGICIAN'S CIGAR CASE.

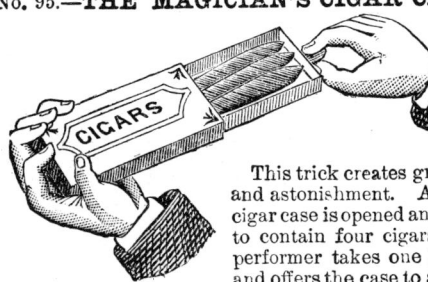

This trick creates great fun and astonishment. A pretty cigar case is opened and found to contain four cigars. The performer takes one himself and offers the case to a friend to help himself. To the friend's surprise, however, when he opens the case it is quite empty, yet the performer opens the case again and finds the cigar.—Superior make, suitable for carrying in the pocket. Complete, 50c. & 75c.

No. 96.—MAGIC TEA CADDY.

A neatly made mahogany tea caddy, with three divisions, the lids are taken off, and it is proved to be quite empty; a lady's handkerchief is borrowed, and placed in one of the divisions; at the word of command it disappears, and the divisions are shown each to be full of flowers, bonbons, or sweets. Very useful, and may be worked in many different ways.   Each, $10 and $12.

No. 97.—Santa Claus' Magical Christmas Box.

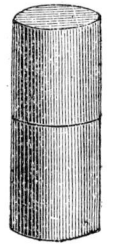 

Into this box all are permitted to look and see that it is empty. Each child then writes his wish on a piece of paper and puts it in the box—or if he cannot write he places his lips to the box and whispers it. The top being on and immediately taken off, a dish full of candies, nuts, raisins, toys, etc., is poured out, astonishing everyone. This box can be used in a variety of ways and is quite useful for amateur magicians.   Price 30 cts.

No. 98.—THE NEW MIRACULOUS CASKET.

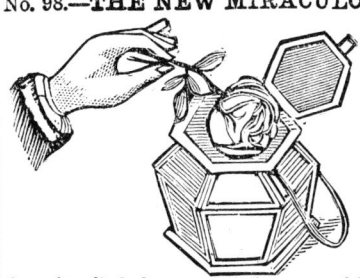

The performer borrows a gentleman's hat, and having shown it to be perfectly empty, he immediately produces from it a beautiful solid hexagon shaped casket, which he opens, and takes out from it a little bouquet of flowers, which he gives to a lady, and then immediately another one, and another, until he has produced six, from each of which he takes a bouquet. Two of the caskets are equal in size to a hat; they are handsomely decorated, and form a great addition to the inexhaustible hat trick.   Each, $1.00.

No. 99.—THE PEPPER BOX.

A marked coin is place in the box, which is then shut; the money is heard to rattle inside. At the word of command, Pass! it is gone, the box is shaken, but there is no sound, and it is shown to be quite empty while the coin that was marked is found elsewhere. Made of tin.

Price, 35 cts.

No. 101.
THE MELTING POT.

A dime is put in the box, and a lady is asked to touch the box with her hand; when opening it again the dime is found to be melted and quite soft still; a gentleman is then asked to touch the box and the money is restored to its proper form.

Price, 50 cts.

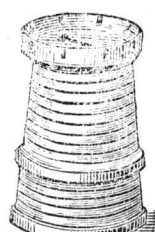

No. 100. THE CASTLE MONEY BOX PUZZLE.

Beautifully made in boxwood. The money can only be extracted by the initiated; very ingenious, yet perfectly simple. Price, 35 cts

No. 102.—THE MYSTERIOUS KEY.

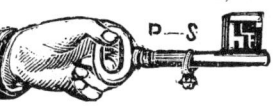

This key can be given to any one for examination, after which a ring is borrowed and put upon it in a mysterious manner. Then the key, with the ring upon it, as above shown, is given to any one, with a request to take the ring from the key. This feat they find it impossible to accomplish, and return it to the performer, who instantly and easily removes it. Price, $1.00

No 103.—THE CHARMED DICE VASE.

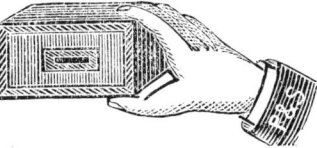

A neat little boxwood vase, in which one of the audience is asked to throw two dice, and shake them well up; the performer now, without touching the vase tells the number thrown by each die, and upon opening it he is proved to be correct. May be repeated as often as desired. Price, $1.00 & $1.50

No. 104.—THE MAGIC "CHEST."

A strongly made little 'Chest" which opens upon a novel and extraordinary principle. Very interesting experiment. Price, 75 cts.

No. 105.—THE MYSTIC BOWL OF FIRE.

The performer borrows a lady's shawl, and standing right in the midst of the audience shows it to be perfectly empty, and asks one of the audience to feel that he has not anything concealed about him; he then waves the shawl gently, and throwing it over his arm, produces instantly a beautiful brass bowl, flaming with fire. The effect is beautiful, and it is perfectly free from danger. Price, $5.00

No. 106. THE GLASS BOTTLE AND FAIRY RIBBONS.

An ordinary glass bottle, from which the performer pours several glasses of water; he then draws out from the bottle several yards of various colored silk ribbons, then pours out more glasses of wine, next more ribbons, and so on till the supply of each appears to never end. Price, $5.

No. 107.—MAGIC RING BOX.

A beautiful made little box, finely inlaid, with looking glass in the lid, is given for examination. A lady's ring is borrowed and place in it; the lady locks the box and retains the key; the ring is heard to rattle in the box, but at the word of command leaves it, appears in any given place. and upon opening the box it is quite empty. French make. Price, $3.50 and $4.50.

No. 108.—THE "WONDROUS PISTOL WAND,"

In varous tricks a pistol is required to be used, but in many instances it is objected to by ladies and young children. To get over this difficulty Mr. Bland highly recommends the "Wonderful Pistol Wand." It is beautifully and strongly made, not in any way larger than the Wands in general use; can be used as a wand the whole evening. and when required can be fired as a pistol, the report as loud as a pistol, or the report not loud enought to frighten a little child. This can be arranged at the desire of the performer, and at once proves that a very great acquistion the "Pistol Wand" must be all magical performances, both to the "amateur" or professor in the private "drawing-room" or public "stage."

The "Wands" are made in Polished Black "Metal' with Ivory Ends.
Price, 10.00.

No. 109.—THE MYSTERIOUS "JAPANESE BALL,"

The "Ball" and string can be examined, afterwards the string is passed through the centre of the "ball" and the "ball" will stop upon any part of the string desired by the performer without being touched in any way, but no other person in the company can make the "ball" stop upon the the string but the performer.
Large size, each, $2.50

No. 110.—THE MAGIC DAVENPORT CABINET.

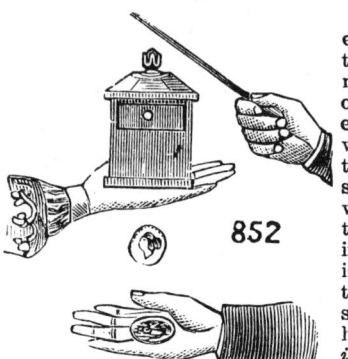

The little cabinet is given freely to be examined; a marked coin, a ring or a watch is placed in the cabinet, which is held on the palm of a person's hand; at the word of command the article placed in the cabinet vanishes, and passes through the person's hand who holds it; *the cabinet is again examined and found empty*, and the article found in any place the performer wishes. Price, $3.00 and $4.00.

No. 111.—THE JOKER'S BOND.

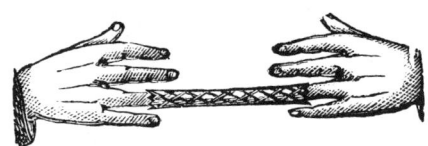

Perfectly harmless, and inevitably successful on those who have never seen it. Hand one to a young lady and gentleman, and, if they follow the directions, they will find themselves united, if not for life, at least until some one in the secret severs the bond. A Joker's Bond in your pocket at a party insures a good time, and as an inciter of uproarious laughter, it beats everything that has appeared since Methuselah was a boy, and Cain and Abel had the measles. Price, 25 cts.

No. 112.—HOUDIN'S VASE OF ENCHANTMENT.

The vase is first shown entirely empty. Two or three handkerchiefs are now borrowed, placed in it, and covered over; when the cover is again taken off, the handkerchiefs have vanished, and from the vase you produce a distribution of bon bons, sweets, toys, etc. Price, $4.00

No. 113.—THE HANDKERCHIEF CASE.

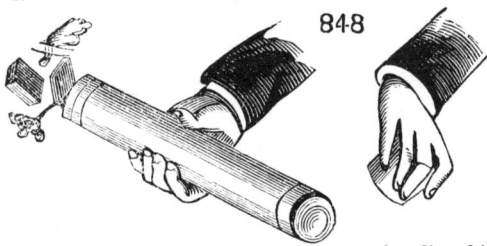

This is first shown to be quite empty; a handkerchief is then borrowed and placed in it, and the lid put on When it is again opened the handkerchief has vanished and the case is full of flowers or bon bons. Price, 75 cts

No. 114.—MECHANICAL MULTIPLYING BALLS.

A hat is borrowed and immediately an immense number of balls appear in it, completely filling it, and when taken out covering the table. They are beautifully made, in parti-colored cloth, and two dozen may, with the greatest ease, be brought from a hat. Price, per dozen, $3.

No. 115.—THE WONDERFUL FRUIT KNIFE

This is very useful for all money tricks. By merely cutting an apple or orange, a marked coin can be found in the centre of the fruit, which can be any one piece of fruit selected from the dish by one of the company, no previous preparation being necessary. This forms a most startling finish to all tricks in which coins are used, and is valued accordingly by the professional or amateur conjuror. Price per pair, $1.50.

No. 116.—BELL AND BUSHEL AND MAGIC SEED BARRELS.

A barrel is shown full of seed; but on being covered by the bell, which has been proved to be quite empty the seed vanished from the barrel, and is found in the bell. Price, $1.00.

No. 117.—THE CARD IN THE BOTTLE.

A card is chosen from the pack by one of the audience, and a common glass bottle is given for examination; the performer takes the card and places it on the top of the neck of the bottle and covers both with a handkerchief; when this is removed the card is seen inside the bottle, which must be broken in order to get it out. Price Card only, 75c.

No. 119.—THE ROD AND THE BALL.
An extraordinary and quite new illusion.

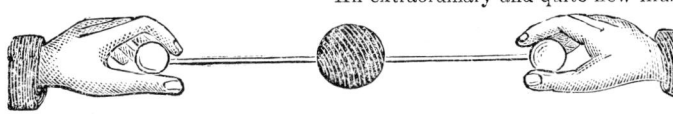

A brass rod with a knob at each end, and a solid ebony ball, with a hole through its centre, are given to the audience for examination; when returned one knob is unscrewed, and the ball is placed on the centre of the rod, and the knob screwed on again; one of the company then holds the rod, one hand at each end, and the ball is covered with a handkerchief; nevertheless, on four rings, being borrowed, placed in a pistol and fired at the handkerchief they instantly appear on the rod, in place of the ball, which is found elsewhere. Complete, with brass rod, ball and knobs, $3 00 and $5.00.

No. 118.—FIRE HANDKERCHIEF.

These handkerchiefs are very useful for conjuring. They are chemically prepared, and when ignited vanish in a brilliant flash of light, the effect being very surprising. They may be worked with great effect in conjunction with any handkerchief trick. Price, 50 cts.

No. 120.—THE FLOATING WAND.
(A STARTLING EXPERIMENT.)

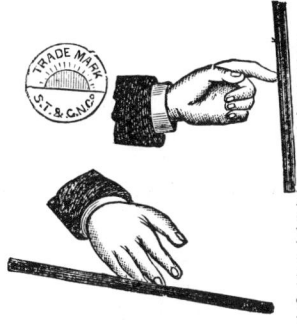

The performer taking in his hands a round black wand such as is used during the performance, about two feet long makes it go through the most extraordinary performance. First he places the bar in the palm of his hand, and holding his hand up in perpendicular position the bar is seen suspending without any support The performer now places the bar to the extreme points of his fingers and holds his arm in a horizontal position, when the bar is again seen suspended without any support in that most difficult position.

To prove this wonderful performance is done without the aid of invisible silk, wire, wax, or mechanism, the operator places the bar against the *back of his hand,* and once more it is seen suspended in mid-air, while he takes it quite close to the company for inspection. Price, $2.00

No. 122.—THE NOT FOR JOSEPH SNUFF OR FUSEE BOX.

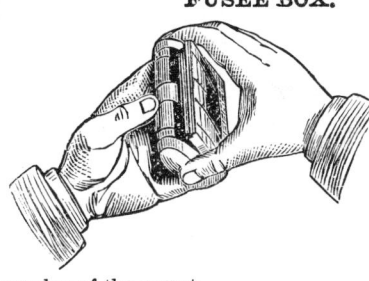

A neat and strongly made box, from which you take a match or pinch of snuff and then hand it to your friend, who is unable to open it nor can he find the slightest clue of the secret. Price, 50 cts.

No. 124.—THE MYSTERIOUS CARD LADLE.

A beautiful japanned ladle is shown, and a piece of paper is given to one of the audience, and he is asked to write his name on it; it is then placed in the ladle and burnt, the ashes being carefully kept in the ladle, but at the word of command the ashes vanish, and the piece of paper with the name on is found perfectly uninjured. Price, $2.50

No. 121.—THE MAGIC PUMP.

You appear before the audience with a handsome pump. On the table you have two tumblers, one half full of water, the other empty. Calling up any person, you in a doctor-like fashion put a teaspoonful of water into his mouth. Then, asking him to hold the empty tumbler, you place the lower end of the pump in his vest pocket, and working the pump, fill the glass he holds with water. This is one of the best tricks, and completely astonishes the audience. With this pump a tumblerful of water may be drawn from a lady's portemonnaie, from a lady's thimble, or a gentleman's cigar case.
Price, $1.00

No. 123.—THE MYSTERIOUS HAT DIE.

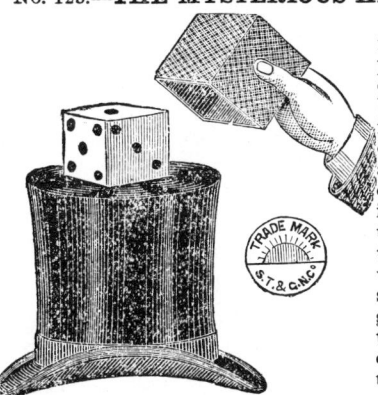

A solid die is shown and placed on the crown of a borrowed hat, it is then covered over, and at the word of command it passes through on to the table without in the slightest degree injuring the hat. An excellent trick.

Price, 35 cts.; larger size, 75 cts.; monster size, $1.25

No. 128.—A Pack of Cards which Change to Sweets.

A pack of cards is exhibited to the audience, and instantly changes to sweets at word of command. Price, 75 cts.

No. 125.—The Wonderful Destroyed Card Trick.

A card is selected from the pack by one of the audience and given to the performer, who tears it in several pieces, and burns them. The ashes are then placed in a box. The box is opened soon after, and the card is found perfectly restored, with the exception of one corner, which is missing. The performer searches the floor and finds the missing corner; then, holding the imperfect card in the left hand, he throws the corner piece at it with the right hand *and instantaneously the card becomes perfect*. This is a beautiful trick for the drawing-room, and causes great astonishment; the performer holding the card fully in view of the audience, and at arm's length, the restoration of the missing piece remains the mystery of the evening. The restored card box is recommended with this trick. Also the magician's pack, which is supplied to match this trick.
Price, 75 cts.

No. 126.—THE MARVELOUS CARD BOOK.

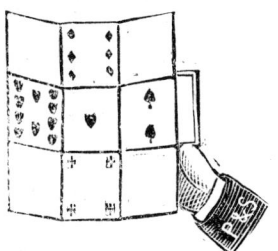

The book is opened out as shown in drawing, and the centre card is under a glass frame; a lady is then asked which of the other cards she would like to take the place of it; the book is then closed, and when again opened the desired change is found to have taken place.
Price, 25 cts.

No. 127.—THE CARD AND ROSE TRICK.

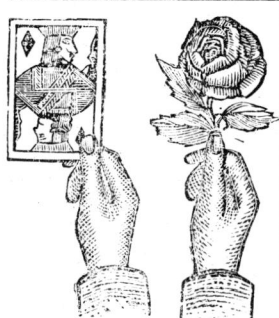

A card is taken from the pack, and simply by breathing on it the card completely vanishes and in its place appears a beautiful rose; this trick can be performed with the sleeves turned up. A very beautiful illusion.
Price, 75 cts.

No. 131.—VANISHING CARD CASE.

A nicely finished cardboard case, which is first shown empty, and then a pack of cards is placed in it, which completely fills it, it is then shut up, but upon opening it again the cards have vanished, and in place of them is found a handkerchief, sweets, or bon-bons. Price, $1.

No. 129.—The Wonderful Sword,

Which catches a chosen card on its point. One of the audience selects a card which is replaced in the pack; the performer scatters the cards by jerking the pack up into the air and catches the chosen card on the point of the sword.
Price, $6 and $10.

No. 130.—The Enchanted Card Frame.

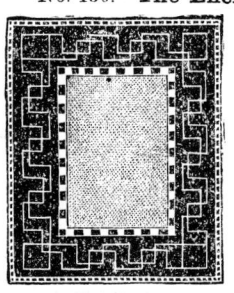
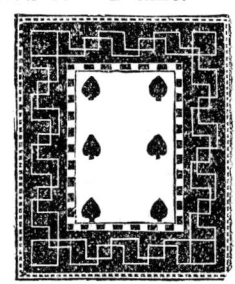

This frame is first shown to be empty, back, front, sides, every part of it is shown; then a card, which has been chosen from the pack, is commanded to appear in it, and instantly does so, without removing it from sight of the audience. The card may then be taking out, the back of the frame removed, and they can then see right through the glass. It will disappear again if desired. A carte-de-visite, photograph, or picture, may be made to appear, instead of a card, if wished. Price, $2.

No. 132.—The Restoring Card Coffre.

A lady is asked to chose a card from the pack and tear it in pieces, placing all except one piece in the coffre (a handsome box of fancy wood which has been previously examined,) she is now requested to lock it and retain possession both of it and the key; the conjuror without going near it or touching it commands the card to be restored; the lady now unlocks it and there is the card perfect, with the exception of the piece kept out, which will be found to fit it exactly.
Price, $8.

No. 134.—The Diminishing Pack of Cards.

The performer takes a pack of cards in his hands and opens them out. He then rubs his fingers over them and they gradually diminish, until they are only half the original size. He then takes them again, and they gradually get smaller and smaller till they are not much larger than a dime, and finally they vanish altogether. Improved principle, very superior quality, French make.
Per set $3.

No. 133.—THE "FLYING CARDS" AND MAGIC BOX,

Three cards are selected from a pack of cards by the company, the cards returned to the pack and the pack shuffled, then placed in the "magic box." The performer asks the company to name the cards they selected, and as they are named THEY FLY OUT OF THE BOX FROM THE PACK, THE CARDS ARE THEN EXAMINED AND FOUND TO BE SAME AS WHERE SELECTED. A very astonishing "trick," highly recommended. Price, complete 3.50.

No. 135.—THE MARVELLOUS "STICKING" PACK OF CARDS.

Three cards are selected from a pack by the company, then returned to the pack and shuffled; The performer now takes the pack of cards in his hands, and with one blow sticks the entire pack against the wall, he then asks the person who selected the cards to name them, and as they are name the cards are named the cards rise, one after the other, up from the pack, and as the cards rise the performer takes them from the pack, one at a time and shows them to the company. A pretty and effective "trick"
Price, complete pack, 2.00.

No. 136.—THE ENCHANTED "AERIAL FLOWERS,"

A New and Charming Hat Trick, the Flowers are Extra Large and Very Handsome.

The performer borrows a gentleman's Hat, and *instantaneously shows the Hat full of pretty flowers*; then the performer takes the flowers, one by one, from the Hat, and, as he throws them up in the air, WHEN THEY ARE SEEN TO FALL TO THE GROUND, FIXING THEMSELVES UPRIGHT IN A NATURAL POSITION, UNTIL THE GROUND LOOKS LIKE A FLOWER GARDEN.

NOTE.—The "Flowers" will fix themselves on a carpet or upon a boarded floor with the greatest certainty, WITHOUT SLIGHTEST INJURY TO "CARPET" OR "FLOOR," AS THE "FLOWERS" ARE FIXED UPON NEEDLE POINTS.
Price, per set of twelve—$3,00 & $5,00.

No. 137.—THE WAND TO PRODUCE SWEETS.

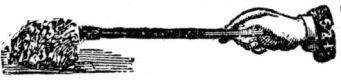

This trick possesses great interest for the juveniles. The wand, although apparently solid, is beautifully turned in fancy wood. It can thus be filled with small sweets, the mechanical ends being fitted so accurately that the wand may be freely given for examination. The sweets can be produced at any moment from a boy's pocket or a lady's handkerchief. Each, $2 00.

No. 138.—The "Enchanted Head of Mystery,"

A "Demon's Head," beautifully modelled, and fixed upon a very handsome stand, is placed upon the table. The performer borrows a gentleman's watch, and asks the company to select cards from a peck. He then places the borrowed watch and the three select cards into a pistol AND FIRES AT THE "ENCHANTED HEAD," WHEN INSTANTANEOUSLY THE BORROWED WATCH APPEARS IN THE "DEMON'S" MOUTH, AND THE THREE SELECT CARDS ON THE TOP OF HIS HEAD. THEN THE "BORROWED WATCH" IS TAKEN FROM THE MOUTH, AND THE THREE CARDS FROM THE "HEAD" THE "WATCH" AND CARDS BEING RETURNED TO THE COMPANY. THE THREE CARDS AND "BORROWED WATCH" APPEAR LIKE A FLASH OF LIGHTNING.
Price, $25.00.

No. 139.—The Magician's Pack of Cards.

Very Superior Make and Finish. Highly Recommended. Will be found very useful for amateurs and others, enabling them to perform many interesting card Tricks with ease, without understanding "sleight of hand."
Price, complete pack, 50 & 75 cts.

No. 140.—THE ANIMATED CARD WITH THE WALKING PIP.

The performer shows the back, the front, the sides, the bottom of card, then commands one of the pips upon the face of the card, to to walk from one end of the card to the other, AND THEN IS DISTINCTSY SEEN THE PIP MOVING ACROSS THE CARD, AND BACK TO ITS PLACE. The experiment can be repeated as many times as desired, and the cards is only held by the tips of the performer's fingers. Price, each, 75 cts.

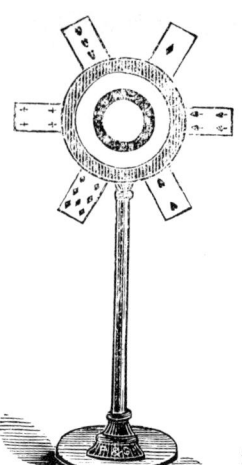

No. 141.—The Demon Target

Several cards are selected from a pack, and a watch is borrowed also from the audience. These are then placed in a pistol, and a target having been placed on the table, the performer takes aim and fires. Immediately the watch is seen in the centre of the target, and the chosen cards are suspended round the outside.

Price, $15.00; with bottle in place of stand, $18.00.

No. 142.—The Electrical Pack of Cards.

The performer takes an ordinary pack of cards in his hands and shuffles them, then commences by making the cards run from one hand to the other several inches at a time, till he elongates them two or three feet. The performer can repeat this wonderful trick as many times as he likes. He then takes the cards in the palm of his left hand and with his right hand runs the cards from the palm of the left hand right up to the shoulders, the cards laying on the arm one by one in the most beautiful order, and then, in an instant, the cards run down the arm and are caught in the palm of the hand. Other wonderful effects can be produced. This beautiful arrangement will be found a good introduction to all card tricks, as it can be exhibited in any room, with the greatest ease, by the amateur as well as a professional, and has the appearance of pure sleight of hand. Price per pack, $2.50.

No. 143.—THE WIZARD'S BOAST.

The performer borrows a gentleman's hat, and noticing it is rather heavy, he looks inside and instantly he produces from it a large ornamental box. This takes place the very moment he receives the hat from the owner. The performer now asks permission to turn up the lining of the hat, and then he continues to produce *eleven more large and beautifully ornamented boxes*, sufficient to cover an ordinary drawing-room table—the performer even turning up his sleeves to prove the boxes really come from the hat.

Per set of 12, by mail, $2.00, $6.00 and $8.00

No. 144.—The Magic Court Card.

The performer holds a cards (say the King of Diamonds) by the tips of his finger and thumb, and at command the "King of Diamonds" becomes the "King of Clubs," again the "King of Clubs" becomes the "King of Diamonds," without its leaving the sight of the audience.

This wonderful change can be repeated as many times as desired by the performer. The above card is highly recommended, as it will be found very useful for many tricks. A full assortment of all the Court cards.

Price, 75 cts.

No. 145.—The Mysterious Sphynx.

The Great Wonder of Ancient Egypt. Will answer Questions in a seemingly Miraculous Manner. An endless source of Entertainment and Surprise. Price, 15c.

No. 146.—THE ASTOUNDING CHANGING CARD.

The performer takes two cards of different suits, and holds them by the tips of the fingers, one in each hand; then, while the eyes of the audience are fixed upon them, he instantly causes them to change places, the left hand card going to the right hand, and the right hand card to the left hand. This change is accomplished instantaneously, and as many times as desired. This trick can be performed with one card, in which case two cards are drawn from the pack by the audience, and produced by the performer, who changes the first card into the second by merely blowing on it. Beautiful designs. Three different styles. Price, per pair, 75c.

No. 147. THE DISAPPEARING SPOT CARDS.

Four cards are either all blank, 4 deuces, or 1 deuce and 3 tens. Price, per set, 20 cts.

No. 148.—THE MAGIC CARD AND BOX.

A neat box is shown perfectly empty and is given to one of the audience to hold, a card is then selected from and returned to the pack and shuffled yet it vanishes from the pack and is found in the box although the box was in the posession of the audience the whole time. Price, 25 cts., extra make, 50 cts.

No. 151.—THE GREAT SPIRITUALISTIC TRICK.

A large sack is produced, and the performer requests two gentlemen from the company to securely fasten him in the sack, and then to guide him outside the room. Two gentlemen having volunteered, they tie the performer securely in the sack, and return again to their friends. Hardly have they got through the door, however, when, to their intense surprise, they *find the performer following them, with the identical sack over his arm, and the string still unbroken.* The sack may be thoroughly examined, and fastened with seals over the string, yet the result will be the same. The performer can always escape from the sack in one minute, however securely he may be fastened. Sack complete with directions by mail. Price, complete, $2.00.

The Performer securely tied in. Immediate re-appearance with sack securely fastened.

No. 149.—Rag Babies from a Man's Hat.

From a modest young man in your audience, or from an old batchelor whom everybody knows, borrow a hat. As you pass with it to your table, suddenly turn and ask the owner "what in the name of nature" he's got in the hat, causing it to be so heavy. Of course he will say, "there's nothing in it." This naturally excites you, and emphatically declare "there certainly is." Then thrust in your hand and draw out a full dress baby and place it on your table; then another, and yet another, until six, eight or a dozen of them are paraded in front of the audience. By this time the audience are convulsed with laughter, and you return the hat with a quotation from some ancient author. Price, each, 50 and 75 cts.

No. 150.—The Magic Coffre the Fairy Bird, and the Enchanted Card.

(A very Handsome and Beautifully Finished Box made in various Coloured Woods, Richly Polished.)

The Coffre is first examined and found perfectly empty: a card, selected by the company, is taken from a pack, and placed in the empty Coffre, WHICH IS HELD IN THE HAND OF ONE OF THE COMPANY, who on opening the Coffre finds in place of the card A LIVE BIRD, which is taken from the Coffre, and the card produced anywhere the performer wishes.
Each, Price, 5.00 extra finished 8.00.

No. A.—THE PUZZLE BRAIN LINKS. (new)

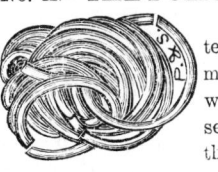

Consists of 11 steel links, interwoven together, and in such a mechanical way that a person who does not understand the secret it would take weeks to get them apart. Each, by mail, 25c.

No. 152.—FAUST'S DECANTERS.

The ornamental glass decanters are exhibited, one filled with stout and the other with whiskey. The performer then places a silk handkerchief over each, partly covering the contents. He now commands the liquids to change places, and instantly *the stout appears in the whiskey decanter and the whiskey in the stout decanter*, even while the eyes of the audience are fixed upon them. The decanters may be placed on separate tables to prove their is no connection between them. Each trick consists of two decanters, silk handkerchiefs and the apparatus. By express only. Price complete $2.00

No. 153.—AERIAL TREASURY.

This trick causes most profound astonishment, and is not known to the amateur, being one of the latest conceptions of a very clever prestidigitator. The performer remarks that he is never short of money, as he has a method of his own which puts even the alchemists in the shade, for they only produce gold, while he in a few moments can produce half dollars from space, sufficient to fill his hat. Then, borrowing a hat, he turns up his sleeves, showing his hands empty, then, *suddenly clutching at the air, he catches a half dollar between his thumb and finger*, which he hands round for examination, to prove it is genuine. Then he continues to catch half dollars until the hat is sufficiently full to allow the glittering contents to be exhibited on a large dish.
Price complete by mail, $2.00

No. 155.—The Magic Multiplying China Plate.

This trick consists of a real china plate of ordinary make. the performer commences by borrowing eight dimes. These are placed in the plate by the audience, and counted one by one, yet when the money is poured into a borrowed hat the *eight dimes have, by some mysterious means, multiplied to twelve dimes.* The hat and plate will bear strict examination. Very useful with all coin tricks. Price complete, $2.25

No. 154.—The Dissolving Coins and Bottle of Beer.

The performer shows a small box, and asks the audience to fill it with coins, which they are to mark, to recognize again. The box, which holds about four coins, is now placed on the table, and the performer requests the audience to observe that he does not remove the box from their sight for one instant. He now fetches a bottle of stout, and commands the money to pass from the box into the bottle of stout. The cork is now drawn, and the money is heard distinctly to rattle inside the bottle, and the box, on being opened, is found empty, although it has remained on the table the whole time. The performer now takes a hammer and breaks the beer bottle, as it is impossible to get the money out without, the neck being too small to allow even a dime to pass inside, and the coins which fall from the bottle are recognized as the same by the marks on them. This is a wonderful illusion, and quite new.

By mail, price complete, $2.25

No. 156—THE "MAGIC COIN" THROUGH THE HAT.

The performer borrows a "hat" and also borrows a "50c. piece," then before the eyes of the company he passes the "coin" through the crown of the borrowed hat, and the "coin" is seen moving outside the crown of the hat, the performer then takes the "coin" from the crown of the hat and passes the "coin" through the side of the hat, where it is also seen moving; the "coin" is then taken from the borrowed hat and returned to the owner. This extraordinary experiment is very easy to perform, and can be performed as many times, and with as many "borrowed hats" and borrowed "coin," as desired, causing the greatest astonishment. Sent, complete, by mail, for $1.00

No. 157. MAGIC BRAD AWL.

What makes this "brad-awl" superior in every way to all others, is that it can be freely examined before and after the trick, and the "brad-awl" is not changed in any way. A hat is borrowed, and the brad-awl is seen to go right through the crown of the hat, down to the handle of the brad-awl, through the hand, or through any article handy by. This is repeated as many times as desired, and causes great laughter. Price, 25 cts.

No. 158.—THE ZAZEL PUZZLE.

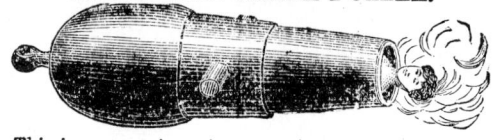

This is a very ingenious puzzle on a new principle. Zazel is in the gun, and the object is to extricate her. The opening is very small, only allowing room for the head to come through; yet those in the secret can release the young lady from her awkward position.

Complete by mail, $1.50

No. 159.—THE SPIRITUALISTIC PILLAR.

An ornamental boxwood pillar is handed round for examination to prove it is perfectly solid. The performer then takes it in his left hand, *leaving the top of the pillar fully exposed to the audience.* He then commences rubbing the pillar between his hands, and, to the amazement of all, the pillar *gradually vanishes*, and is found elsewhere. The performer turns up his coat sleeves before commencing this trick, so that the secret of its disappearance remains an inexplicable mystery.

By mail, 75 cents.

No. 160.—The Chamelion Billiard Ball.

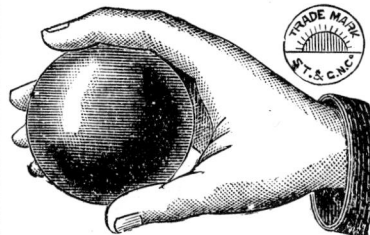

A *red* billiard ball is handed round for examination. The performer then takes it in his *right hand*, which he holds extended, and rubs it with his left hand; and, removed from although it is the view of the audience, it instantly changes from red to black. The performer then asks the color of the ball, and directly the audience reply, black, the performer says, I think you have made a mistake, and instantly they see the ball is *green;* yet when they acknowledge it is green, they find it is *yellow*. This is a most effective and startling trick.

Complete by mail, $2.25

No. 161.—MAGICAL "POUCH."

A great novelty, impossible to open the pouch by any person *not in the secret*.

Strongly made in leather 50c.; cloth 25c.

No. 164.—THE BALLOT PUZZLE.

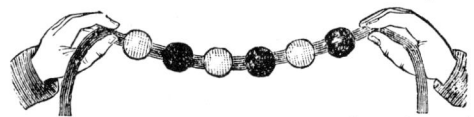

This is a capital puzzle, and causes universal surprise. Three red balls and three black ones are threaded on string, and the ends of the string are given to one of the company to hold. The performer then asks which they will have, the red or black, and whichever they select he instantly extracts from the string, and then hands the balls round for examination to prove they are solid.

Price, 50c

No. 162.—MAGIC "PICCOLO."

A clever and laughable experiment; the owner can blow with impunity upon the piccolo, but upon any other person trying to do so for their trouble they will have a nice moustache, black or white, as desired by the performer, The piccolo is beautifully made.

By mail, price 75c.

No. 163.—**The Dissolving Flag and Candle.**

This is a startling trick, consisting of a series of surprises. The performer first shows a beautiful silk flag, which he rubs in his hands, and commands to pass into a lighted candle, standing on the table. The flag is then seen slowly to melt away, the performer showing both hands empty. He then takes the lighted candle, and extinguishes it by wrapping it in a piece of news-paper, which he screws up very tight, until it breaks with the twisting, when, instead of the remains of the candle, the silk flag is discovered tightly twisted in the paper, and the candle has entirely disappeared. This is one of the most effective tricks ever invented, and is quite new.

Price complete by mail, $2.00

No. 165.—**The Dissolving Handkerchief.**

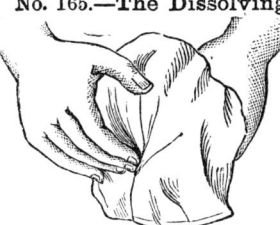

The performer borrows a lady's handkerchief, then turns up his coat and shirt sleeves to the elbow. He now places the borrowed handkerchief in the palms of his hands, and commences rubbing them. The handkerchief yields to the magic influence, and gradually gets smaller and smaller before the eyes of the audience, *until it has entirely vanished.* The performer shows both his hands empty, and then a small speck of white is observed, which gradually gets larger and larger, until the handkerchief is restored to its original size and substance. This is a wonderful trick, because the handkerchief is borrowed from the audience, and the arms being bare, it is impossible to secrete it about the person, and the performer does not turn his back for an instant.

By mail complete, $2.00

No. 166.—**THE COMFORTABLE CANDLE.**

This candle makes itself comfortable anywhere. The performer borrows a hat, and thrusts it over the candle, which comes through the top, where it is lighted by the performer. The hat is afterwards restored uninjured.

Price, 75 cts.

No. 167—**THE LITTLE VANISHING MAN.**

A VERY CLEVER ILLUSION.

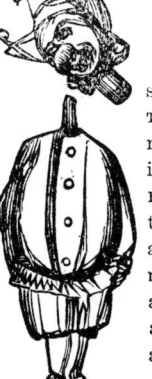

A little grotesque figure of a man is shown, also a little "cloak," WHICH IS TURNER INSIDE OUT to show there is nothing concealed in it; the little man is placed inside the "cloak" WITH HIS HEAD THROUGH THE TOP, at command the little man vanishes, the "cloak", again turned inside out to show he is not in, when "presto" the little man again appears. This can be repeated as many times as desired, and the trick always causes great laughter.

By mail, 50c.

No. 168.—**GRANDFATHER'S PURSE.**

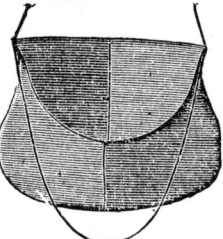

This purse is made of several pieces of cloth of various brilliant colors. There is apparently no opening, but those in the secret can instantly place their money inside, and need have no fear of having any of it abstracted. A very useful purse for careless people, and a capital puzzle.

Price, 50c.

No. 169. **THE MYSTERIOUS HANDKERCHIEF.**

From which innumerable and queer things are brought forth. Eggs, beans, seeds, marbles, &c.

Price, 50 cts.

No. 171. **MY GRANDMOTHER'S NECKLACE.**

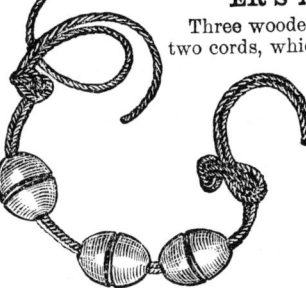

Three wooden beads are strung on two cords, which are tied firmly and held on each end by some of the audience. They are covered with a handkerchief and the beads remove from the strings without cutting them or using any force. This is an excellent trick and the apparatus admits of full examination.

Price, 25 cts.

No. 172.—**MAGNESIUM RIBBON.**

This has been very appropriately called captive sunshine, as it burns with a brilliancy that rivals the sun's rays. Its effect is very startling and beautiful in a room full of company, especially if lit as a surprise. The light is so dazzling that a room brilliantly illuminated with gas seems in darkness after this light.

Per package, 25 cts.

No. 170.—The Magic Wonderscope.

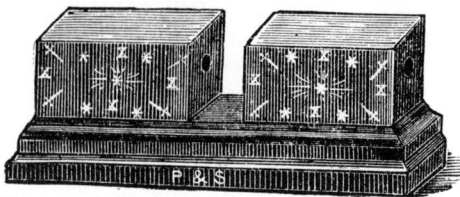

This remarkably curious optical instrument consists of two sections, resting, with an intervening space, on a black walnut base. On placing the eye at one of the holes any person can look directly through and see objects beyond. A solid block of wood is placed between the two sections, completely obstructing the line of vision, as is evident when, upon placing the eye at the aperture, nothing can be seen—all is darkness. Without removing the block of wood, the performer waves his magic wand over the instrument and causes the solid block to become transparent. Upon now applying the eye to the hole, though the solid block is still there, any one can see as plainly through it as though it were not. Then the block is removed and nothing can be seen; an evidence, so says the performer, that it is easier to look through the block than it is to see through the lines of holes. The operation of this instrument is very easily managed, and defies detection. Price, $1.50

No. 173.—DRAWING-ROOM LIGHTNING FLASHES.

Each box contains several dozen flashes in various vivid colors. When lit they should be thrown quickly across the room; the effect is then very beautiful, lighting up the whole place, yet instantly vanishing, and leaving no trace behind. Per package, 25 cts.

No. 174.—THE FAIRY PALM TREES OR FAIRY FERNS.

This is a wonderful chemical discovery. A piece of prepared paper is placed on the table and ignited, and instantly rows of beautiful miniature palms start into life, waving their crested heads, and curling their leaves as if fanned by the agency of a gentle breeze.
Per package, 25 cts.

No. 175.—Parlor Amusements, or the Art of Entertaining.

Being a volume intended to amuse everybody, and enabling all to amuse everybody else. Home amusements; instructions in acting proverbs, charades, tableaux, parlor games, forfeits, burlesques, riddles, puzzles, tricks, slight-of-hand, card tricks, scientific recreations, parlor magic—in fact, a regular encyclopedia of social evening entertainment. By Frank Bellew. Bound in cloth, 216 pages, 134 illustrated. Price, 75 cts.

No. 176.—The Fairy Rose. A Novel and Charming Trick with a "Rose" and a "Lady's borrowed Ring."

THE "ROSE" CLOSED.   THE "ROSE" OPENING AND SHOWING THE BORROWED RING IN IT.

A beautiful large rose is shown to the company with the rose not yet budded; a lady's ring is borrowed and locked in a small box, the box being held in the hand of one of the company. At the command of the performer the ring leaves the locked box (which is found empty), and instantly appears in the centre of the rose, which opens and shows the borrowed Ring embedded in the centre of the leaves. The ring is then taken from the rose and given to the lady. The effect of the move-ment of the Rose while opening will cause great admiration. Price, each, 1.50 2.00 & 3.50

No. 177.—Japanese Drawing-Room Fireworks.

Highly recommended. Can be used by a child with the greatest safety. The "fireworks" are of the most beautiful and brilliant description, and are expressly imported by us. 30 in a box, with directions, post free. 25 cts.

No. 178.—THE PROFANE PUZZLE.—A JOKE.

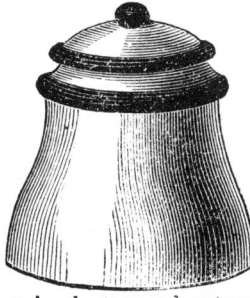

This little box is beautifully turned and polished boxwood, and has a lid which revolves freely, but will not unscrew. The puzzle is to get the lid off. Members of parliament, officers in the army, clergymen's son's, and even bishops have attempted to unravel the mystery, with a smile upon their face, but, somehow, just when they fancy they have succeeded, they utter an involuntary and extremely unparliamentary expression, which, from its very sameness, and repetition, has compelled us to call this the profane puzzle. N. B.—This puzzle will open, but everyone tries the wrong way. Price 75c.

Nos. 179 & 180.—THE FOUNTAIN ROSE AND FOUNTAIN RING.

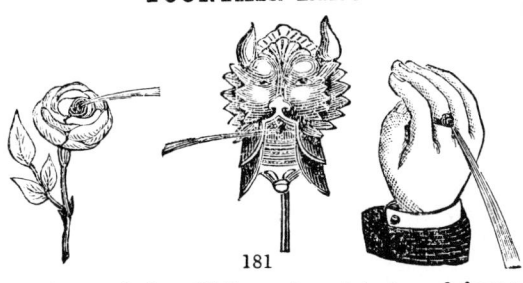

181

This rose is beautifully made, and is formed from a composition exactly resembling the living flower, that it cannot be recognized as artificial except by the touch. It is, therefore admirably suited for a gentleman's coat or lady's hair, and at the will of the wearer a spray of perfume issues from its petals. The spray, although issuing with great force, is so minute that the person on whom it is directed is unable to discover its source, and always suspects an innocent individual, causing much laughter. The ring acts in the same manner, and is of chaste design. Both rose and ring can be instantly replenished. Put up in neat boxes. Each, 50c.

No. 181.—THE MAGIC SCARF PIN.

More fun can be obtained with this pin in five minutes than ordinary mortals can expect in a life-time. The pin is worn in the scarf and connected with an india-rubber ball in the pocket by a very thin india-rubber tubing, made expressly for the purpose. The ball can be filled with water or scent, and when slighty pressed a very fine jet comes through the mouth of the pin with great force. Of course, the person you practice upon never thinks it is you, because pour hands are in your pockets, but any poor wretch who is standing near, and happens to be rubbing his eyes or chin, or moving his hands in any way, is immediately accused and sacrificed. The above demon head is our own design, and beautifully finished, being a work of art worth double the money as a scarf pin alone. Each, 50 cts

No. 182.—THE DISSOLVING HANDKERCHIEF AND EGG BEWITCHED.

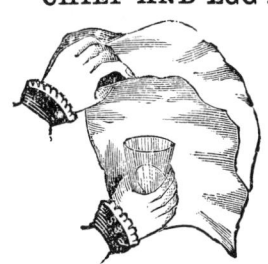 

The performer borrows a white pocket handkerchief from a lady; he then fetches an ordinary tumbler and an egg, and asks the lady to hold the tumbler at arm's length and having placed the *egg inside the tumbler*, he covers it over with the lady's handkerchief. The performer now proceeds to the further extremity of the room, and taking a red silk handkerchief in his hands, he commences gently rubbing them together. This process has an immediate effect upon the silk handkerchief, as it is seen to *gradually melt away and entirely vanish.* But before the audience even have time to realize its entire disappearance. The egg that was placed in the tumbler *is seen to appear in his hand.* The tumbler is now uncovered, and instead of the egg, the red silk handkerchief is found inside. Price, complete, by mail, $2.25.

No. 183.—Glass of Water Illusion.

The performer takes a handkerchief and waves it in the air. Immediately afterwards he produces a tumbler *filled to the brim with water.* He now borrows a handkerchief from the company to show the trick requires no preparation, and immediately a second tumbler of water is produced. He then covers the tumbler with the handkerchief, and throws the tumbler, handkerchief and all at the audience. This, however, does no harm, as only the handkerchief falls, the tumbler of water having disappeared. The performer then requests permission to place the handkerchief over an old gentleman's head, and immediately he lifts from the gentleman's head a glass of water. He afterwards produces several others from equally strange places.
Price, complete, $2.25.

No. 184.—The Great Demon Sand Trick.

This extraordinary trick was first introduced into this country by the Indian jugglers, and has remained a mystery until quite recently. The performer brings forward a quantity of fine dry sand in a bag, and a large basin of water. He then throws several handfuls of sand into the water, and stirs it round with a stick. He then asks the audience whether he shall bring the sand out of the water wet or dry, and they, of course, answer "dry" Immediately he plunges his open hand into the water, and brings out the sand perfectly dry. Any one else attempting to do so signally fails. By mail, 75 cts.

No. 185.—The Mysterious Dissolving Coins.

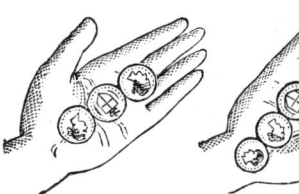

The performer borrows three pennies, and places them in the palm of his hand; he then pulls up his sleeves. and, having shown his other hand empty, he passes it over the coins, and *instantly they have changed to four pennies;* again he waves his hand, and they change back to three; in fact, they seem to multiply and decrease, also, change from heads to tails at will, to the wonder of all.
Complete, $1.

No. 186.—Great Tobacco Smoke Illusion.

Two glasses are shown perfectly empty and clean. The performer then inverts one over on the other, and covers them with a handkerchief. A cigar or pipe is now lighted by the performer, who has proceeded to the furthest extremity of the room, and he puffs a few mouthfulls of smoke towards the glasses, which are now separated, and found full of smoke. The smoke can even be sent invisibly from another room. Complete, $1.25.

No. 187.—THE MOUCHIOR DU DIABLE.

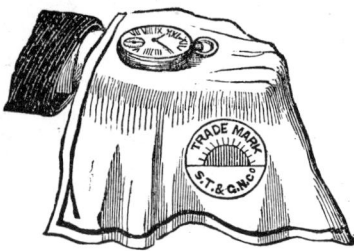

This handkerchief possesses the peculiar and oftentimes convenient property of making everything disappear that is placed beneath it—watches, rings, eggs, or money, if only covered by it for an instant, vanish entirely. The handkerchief can also be used very advantageously with other tricks, such as the rattling money or drawbox, in which case the vanished articles can be immediately found elsewhere. Price, $1.

No. 188.—THE ORDER OF STUPIDS.

The medal should be worn only by those who fail to unravel our mysteries. Their capacity is best tested with the medal itself, the object being to get the ring off. Whoever succeeds in this can unite for our next test. Price, 25c.

No. 189.—THE MAGIC MOUSE.

By means of a mechanical appliance, which is quite invisible, the mouse is made to run over the hands and up the arms, the movements being so natural as to exactly resemble the living mouse, and great fun is caused by its sudden disappearance, which generally causes a stampede amongst the ladies. Each, 15c.; 2 for 25c.

No. 190.

A few grains of powder are sprinkled upon a basin of water, the most gorgeous vegetation starts into life. Millions of long delicate roots shoot down in all directions, and beautiful miniature foilage resembling water lilies grows over the surface, glistening in all the colors of the rainbow. A tiny glass wand is now dipped into the bottle of liquid electricity, and the point of the wand is then brought into contact with the foliage on the surface of the water; the effect is instantaneous and beautiful in the extreme. The entire vegetation springs away in all directions. The roots quiver as if in agony of terror, and also make for the sides of the vessel, and the water which a moment before was teeming with life and color remains deserted as long as the hateful rod is in contact with it. New, complete, 75 cts.

No. 196.—The Seven Racers.

A Perfectly Perplexing Puzzle, or Solitaire Game, of new and original construction. With key, showing how it is done. Price, 20 cts.

No. 191.—DR. BAUTIER'S MARVELLOUS ILLUSIONS, THE FLYING CAGE.

This beautiful mechanical trick is unravelled for effect either on the professional or drawing-room stage. The performer appears before the audience with a full-size cage and containing a live or artificial bird, then, after exhibiting it, he holds it at arm's length and commands the bird and cage to fly away; instantly it vanishes while the eyes of the audience are fixed upon it, leaving no trace behind! Price $8.00 and $6.00. Extra Quality, $15.00.

No. 192.—The Dragon Snake.

The Latest Scientific Novelty.

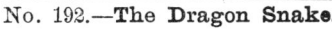

On setting fire to the dragon at first, a firey tongue will consume the snake, and when it reaches the head of the dragon a flame will envelope the whole, and ashes will ascend baloon like in the air, in a compact form, coming down in fantastic shapes resembling the consumed dragon.

Price per pack, 25 cts.

No. 193.—Clairvoyance or Second Sight.

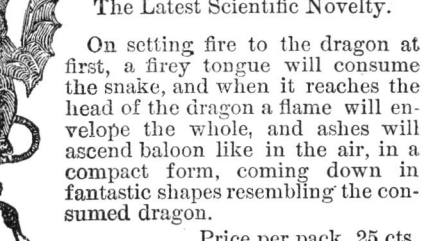

The performer gives a small box to the audience and requests them to place coins, rings, or other trinkets inside, and although the lid is securely fastened, he will devine the contents. He then gives the box to another of the company to hold, having first covered it with a handkerchief, calling out the contents of the box *naming each article singly, also giving the dates on the coins*, to the great astonishment of the various owners. Having named all the articles, the performer takes hold of the corner of the handkerchief, and tells the person who is holding the box to let go when the box vanishes entirely from his hand, and the articles, box and all, are found in a loaf or a gentleman's pocket in another part of the room.

Complete, $2.00.

No. 194.—Which is the Largest?

An Optical Puzzle. This curious contrivance will puzzle the eyes of all, both old and young. It presents a problem in Optics which the most experienced will find difficult to solve, and will be found to be an object which, whenever introduced, will interest, astonish, and amuse every one. Price, 15 cts.

No. 195.—Magic Picture Puzzle Cards.

New, Unique, Curious, Puzzling and Amusing; each Picture disclosing, upon close examination, much more than is at first seen; the set consisting of five pictures, each printed on white cards $2\frac{3}{4}$ by $4\frac{1}{4}$ inches. The whole accompanied with an explanatory key. Price, per set, 25c.

No. 200.—The Enchanted Egg.
A New and Startling Trick.

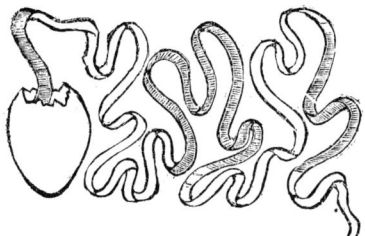

The performer takes from a plate a real egg and gives it for examination. And then in full view of the audience he breaks it open and takes out about fifty yards of Ribbons. It can be performed in the middle of the audience and with the sleeves rolled up. No sleight of hand used. This is one of the finest egg tricks ever produced.

Price Each Egg 30 cts.   Large Goose Egg 80 cts.

No. 201.—THE EXTRAORDINARY DIVINING BOX.

The performer shows a nicely made little Box, and seven Tablets, upon which are the Seven Days of the Week. The performer asks some one in the company to take possession of all the "Tablets," and secrete one of them in the Box, placing the lid securely over the "Tablet." Now the performer (without seeing in any way the other tablets) takes the Box in his hand, and by merely looking at it instantly divines the "Tablet" placed inside the Box, by mentioning the Day of the Week upon the "Tablet," and in the same way the performer divines every "Tablet" with the day of the week upon it secretly placed in the Box.   Price, $2.50

No. 202.—THE MIRACULOUS GLASS CASKET, A SEEMING IMPOSSIBILITY.

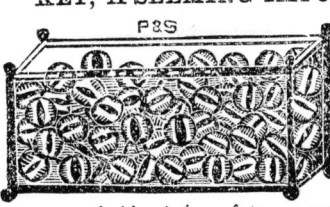

A very handsome Transparent Glass Casket is shown to prove it is quite empty. The Company can see right through, and every part of the "glass Casket," the top, bottom, and sides being of transparent glass. The performer holds the "Casket" in front of him, and commands the empty "Casket" to become full of colored cloth "Balls," presto! instantly before the eyes of the audience, the Casket is seen to be full of balls, the effect being truly marvelous, as the Casket is not covered in any way, or placed upon a table, the performer holding the "Casket" right in front of himself, so that the company can see all round, and every part of the casket during the entire "trick." One instant, the "Casket" being seen to be perfectly empty, and the next instant, seen full of Balls will cause great amusement, as the wonderful change takes place right in front of the company, without the performer turning his back in any way.
Price each, $25.00 & $30.00.

No. 203.—THE WONDERFUL SECRET BALL.

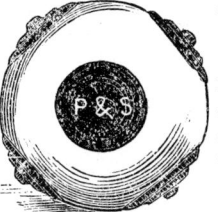

The "ball" is beautifully made, in polished boxwood, with ebony ornaments. The secret of opening the ball will cause very great astonishment combined with amusement.
Price each, $1.00.

No. 204—The FAIRY BIRD THAT VANISHES FROM THE HAND.
THE HAND WITH THE BIRD IN IT.

The performer holds in his hand a beautiful canary bird—Head, Tail, and Body moving while in the hand; by simply placing one hand over the other, the bird vanishes, and the hands seen empty. "Presto," again the bird re-appears in the hand as before. This is done as many times as the performer wishes, right before the eyes of the company, and without the performer turning his back in any way.

This extraordinary trick is performed without the aid of coat sleeves or any part of the performer's dress, table, chair, or any other assistance. It is very easy to perform, and will be found very useful and effective with other tricks. Bird complete, by mail in box. Price, $2.50

No. 205.—THE MARVELLOUS PLUMES.
ROBERT HOUDIN'S CELEBRATED TRICK.

The performer borrows a handkerchief or shawl, turns it inside out to show it is quite empty, then instantly produces from it 6 or 12 handsome plumes with extraordinary effect. The plumes are in various colors. *This is a very beautiful Trick for the drawing room, and very easy to perform;* always causing great admiration and astonishment.

Note.—The "Plumes" are taken to the Ladies in the Company for their inspection.
Price each, $2.00.

No. 206.—THE MARVELLOUS HAT BRUSH.
A GREAT NOVELTY.

The performer borrows a gentleman's hat, shows that it is quite empty, then after making various remarks about the "Hat" being rough, calls for a "Hat Brush," with which the performer brushes the Hat, then as he goes to return it he finds in the "Hat" various articles, which, as he takes out, causes great wonderment.

This beautiful "Hat Brush" is made with real hair and wood, and can be used under the very eyes of the company, defying detection, the novel mechanism will cause the greatest admiration. The "Hat Brush" can be used with the greatest ease for a number of clever tricks for filling a borrowed Hat, thus doing away with the aid of "tables" or confederates. During the performance the performer never turns his back or goes near a table.
Price each, $8.00.

No. 207.—THE SEVEN ENCHANTED LOCKED BOXES.

THE BOXES ARE BEAUTIFULLY MADE AND FINISHED.

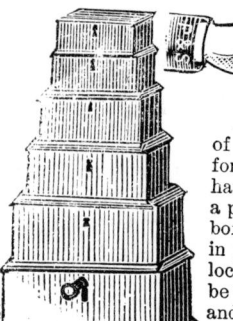

A locked box is held by one of the company, then the performer borrows a watch and a handkerchief, which he places in a pistol, and fires at the box, the box is unlocked and opened, and in it are found six more boxes locked, but all the six boxes must be unlocked to get to the seventh and smallest box, which, upon being opened, is found to contain the borrowed watch and handkerchief. *The trick is performed instantaneously with great effect, although seven boxes must be opened to get the borrowed articles out.* The Boxes can be used for many Tricks with great effect.

Price each, $12.00 & $15.00.

No. 208.—THE MIRACULOUS GLASS BOWL OF FISH AND WATER UPON A SILVER TRIPOD.

AN EXTRAORDINARY NOVELTY.

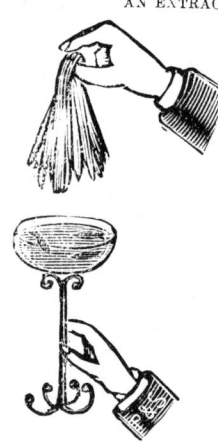

The performer *stands in front of the company*, he takes a small thin cloth, (which is freely examined to prove it is quite empty) and in one instant the performer, without turning his back in any way, produces from the empty cloth a large transparent "Glass Bowl," full of Water and Gold Fish, and attached to the "Glass Bowl" is a large and massive silver plated "Tripod," which the performer gives to the company to examine, to prove the " silver plated Tripod" is solid, "made of metal," and not in any way mechanical; thus proving this wonderful trick to be one of the most extraordinary ever seen in this or any other country, *although it can be performed with ease in the "Drawing Room" or upon the stage.*

Price each, $15.00.

No. 209.—THE WONDERFUL DISSOLVING CONE AND MYSTIC BALL.

AN EXTRAORDINARY NOVELTY, MADE IN POLISHED BOXWOOD.

The performer shows a large solid cone with a black ball on the top, he borrows a hat and covers the "cone" and mystic ball with the hat, then the performer takes a sheet of paper and places it on the top of the hat, now a wondrous change takes place, the "cone and ball" passes from under the hat, and is found on the top of the hat, under the sheet of paper, the hat lifted up to prove the "cone and ball" is not under the hat, then another wonderful change takes place, the cone passing from the crown to underneath the hat, where it is again found. The "cone and ball" is seven inches in height, and is highly recommended.

Price each, $4.00 & $8.00.

No. 210.—THE MIRACULOUS CRYSTAL CASKET.

A NOVELTY OF THE MOST WONDERFUL KIND.

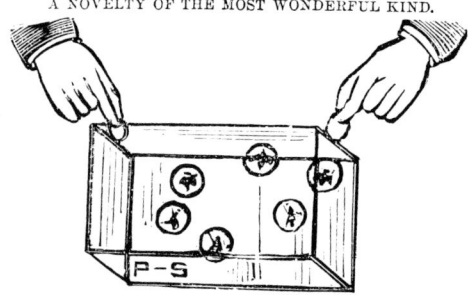

A white "transparent glass casket" is shown to the company to prove it is perfectly empty. The performer asks one of the company to hold the "casket" up in front of him, so the company may see right through, and all parts of the "glass casket" while being held up.

The performer now borrows six pieces of money of any kind, and also borrows a pocket handkerchief; he wraps the coins in the borrowed handkerchief, and remarks to the company that he will strike the handkerchief with the money in it against the outside of the "glass casket," and the six pieces of money shall pass from the handkerchief and instantly fall into the "casket" before the eyes of the company; the performer then standing at the side of the person holding the "casket" strikes the handkerchief against the glass, when instantly the six pieces of money are seen to fall into the empty "glass casket." Then the "casket" is opened by some one in the company who takes from it the money, *and the handkerchief is examined and found quite empty.*

N.B.—The "Miraculous Crystal Casket" can be shown to the company before and after the Trick, and all sides of it are tightly closed during the performance of the Trick, although the company can see through every part of the "Casket," and from the time one of the company holds the "Casket" in his hands, the performer does not go near it.

Price each, $25.00 & $30.00.

No. 211.—THE MAGIC INCUBATOR AND THE FAIRY BIRDS.

The performer shows a very handsome "Incubator," bound with gilt bands, the lid is taken off and the "Incubator" is found full of beautiful flowers, to prove there is nothing but flowers in the "Incubator," the performer turns all the flowers out before the company, and then shows the "Incubator" quite empty, he returns the flowers to it, and places in it (with the flowers) three real eggs, then covering the "Incubator" with the lid, the performer asks one of the company to hold the "Incubator," and then commands all the flowers, with the three eggs, to vanish from the "Incubator," and in their place to appear a large handsome bird cage, with a live bird in. *The bird and cage are given to the company for examination.* The effect of producing the bird and cage from the "Incubator," which one instant before was full of flowers, is truly miraculous, as the cage is nearly the size of the "Incubator," itself.

Price each, $25.00.

No. 212.—The Enchanted Negro's Head.

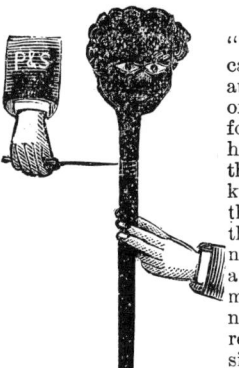

The performer shows a "Negro's Head," beautifully carved and polished in ebony, and FIRMLY FIXED upon the top of an ebony wand. The performer takes a small knife in his hand and says he will cut the head off, by passing the knife right through the neck, then he several times passes the knife clean through the neck of the Head, but without any result, as the head still remains firmly fixed upon the neck. The experiment can be repeated as many times as desired, AND ALWAYS DEFIES DETECTION. N.B.—*The Enchanted Negro's Head can be fixed to the top of a "Walking Stick" or "Umbrella," and will form a great curiosity.*

Price, each, **$5.00**

No. 213.—"The Demon Target."

An Extraordinary Novelty. Different in every way to all other Target Tricks.

The performer borrows a lady's or a gentleman's watch, which he places in a pistol, the pistol (with the borrowed watch in it) being held by a gentleman in the company, the performer holding by the tips of his fingers, a small Black and White Target, "only six inches square," asks the gentleman holding the Pistol to fire at the "Target," when instantaneously with the firing of the Pistol, the borrowed Watch appears upon the centre of the "Target," then the watch is taken from the "Target," and returned to the owner.

Price, 4.00

No. 214.—Magic Barrel and Seed.

A barrel is shown, and also a bag of seed. The barrel is then filled with seed, and covered over with a gentleman's hat. The performer then orders the seed to leave the barrel and pass again into the bag. When the hat is raised the barrel is found empty, and the bag (which may be placed a long distance away) is again full.

Price, 50c.

No. 215.—The Novel and Extraordinary Conjuring Table.

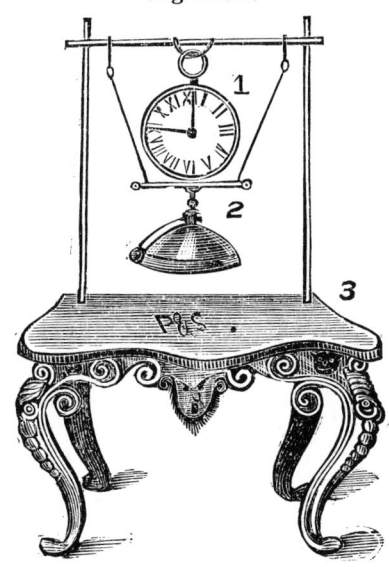

We beg to state that these beautiful tables are constructed upon an entirely new principle never before seen in this country. They are very handsome, fit for a gentleman's private drawing-room or the theatre; can be taken to pieces (for travelling), and placed together again in a few minutes; they are fitted, among other novelties, with a wonderful double-changing trap, one of the most beautiful pieces of mechanism ever seen. But the principal novelty that causes these tables to surpass all others is, that they are fitted with beautiful electrical mechanism, which enables the performer to exhibit every trick (worked by electricity) with the greatest ease. The tricks work from the top of the table (as seen in the engraving); the batteries generally in use caused very great inconvenience, both in the time they took in preparation and the noxious smell from the acids; all this is now done away with, there being no smell, dirt, or any other inconvenience, as the battery will only take two minutes in preparing, and when once prepared will last for months, and is always ready for use, one liquid only being employed, although the battery is strong enough to peform every electrical trick known in the magic art.

The table can be used without the electrical apparatus, as it is full of traps, pistons, etc., to enable the operator to perform all the modern tricks with it, both in the private drawing-room or theatre, thus combining two superior conjuring tables in one. Price, $150.00 and $200.00
Electric Clock, No. 1................Price, $75 00
Electric Bell, No. 2................. "   30 00
Tables without the Electrical appliances from $50 to $100.

No. 216.—The Fire Eater.

The performer after going through various evolutions and astonishing everybody, increases the wonder and astonishment of the lookers on by suddenly ejecting from his mouth thousands of brilliant sparks. This is done with perfect safety and so simple that any one can easily perform the trick   Price 30 cts.

Extra quality 50 cts.

No. 220.—The Magic Card Box.

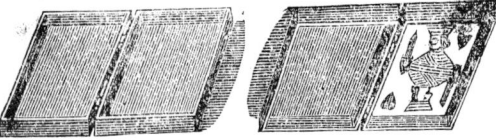

A neat box is shown perfectly empty and is given to one of the audience to hold, a card is then selected from and returned to the pack and well shuffled, yet it vanishes from the pack and is found in the box although the box was in the possession of the audience the whole time. Price 25c. Extra make 50c.

No. 197.—THE TWIN PILLARS.

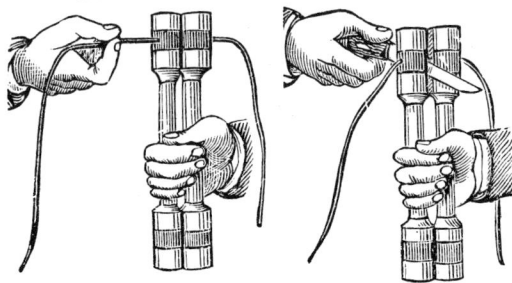

Two pillars of fancy turned wood are shown, and attention is drawn to the string running through. The performer requests the audience to pull the string themselves backward, and forward, to prove there is no join, and then to cut the string between the pillars, as shown in the engraving. The performer now separates the pillars to show the string is cut through, and then informs the audience he will join the string again. Instantly the string is joined, but there is no trace of the join visible. Price, 25 cts.

No. 198.—The Magic "Champagne Bottle."

A perfect model of a "champagne bottle" with a cork in it, and unlike all other "bottles" it can be freely examined; it will LAY DOWN OR STAND UP at the will of the performer, but no other person will be able to make the bottle lay down. This clever trick will cause endless laughter and amusement.
Price, each, 50 cts.

No. 199.—The Animated Pump.

The performer hands an ornamental funnel round for examination, and then asks one of the audience to drink a glass of wine. He then holds the funnel to the person's elbow, and commences moving the other arm up and down very quickly like a pump-handle. In a few seconds *the wine which was drank is seen to come through the funnel at the elbow*, and is caught in a glass underneath— causing great merriment.
Price, 75c. and $1.25.

No. 217.—THE ENCHANTED PYMARIDS

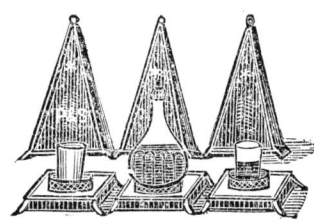

This superbly elegant trick is accompanied with very showy apparatus. It is easily performed, without the aid of confederates, and without leaving the table upon which it is exhibited. It is adapted for professional public exhibitions, as well as for amateur private entertainments. Three elegant stands are placed at equal distances apart. On the centre stand is placed a decanter of wine and water, and on each of the others is an empty goblet. The performer states that he proposes to cause the mixture of wine and water to separate and leave the decanter, the wine to appear in one of the goblets and the water in the other, and it is for the audience to say in which shall be the wine and in which the water. This being determined upon, the performer places over each a handsome pyramidal case, and waves his wand gracefully above the three. He then removes the pyramids from the goblets and exhibits them filled as desired. He then removes the one from the decanter and it is seen that it is empty. This trick can be varied by using milk instead of wine, and making it an amusing feat by proposing to test the honesty of the milkman by an analysis of the article. After it has been performed it is evident that the decanter of milk was one-half water. Price, $15.00. Extra finish, $25.00.

No. 218.—The Enchanted Nest and Fairy Egg.
(Made in Polished Brass, Richly Decorated.)

THE "EGG" IN THE NEST.   THE "EGG" CHANGED TO A BIRD.

A pretty brass vase with cover is shown, in the vase is a bird's nest with egg. The vase is covered, and given to a lady to hold. Now the performer commands the nest and egg to vanish, and in their place a live canary to appear. Then the lady herself takes the cover off the vase and finds, instead of the nest and egg, a live canary bird which she takes from the vase.

N. B.—The above beautiful "vase" can be used in conjunction with many tricks.
Price, each, $2.00 & $2.50.

No. 219.—The Phonoscope.

By merely speaking into this wonderful instrument, the most marvelous effects are produced upon a sensitive transparent diaphragm, and the eye is delighted with millions of lovely figures and devices of indescribable beauty and variety of color. Each note of the human voice producing its distinct forms, thus rendering sound visible. Price, $1.50.

No. 221.—THE WONDERFUL BOX THAT BREAKS TO PIECES, AND THE MYSTIC CHINESE RIBBONS.

THIS EXTRAORDINARY "MECHANICAL BOX" IS MADE IN VARIOUS FANCY WOODS, RICHLY POLISHED

A beautiful box is shown empty, then closed, and on being opened again is found full of bon-bons, flowers, &c.; these being distributed, *the performer proves there is nothing more in the box, by breaking it to pieces;* then putting it together again, one of the company takes possession of the box and on opening it finds it full of pieces of different colored ribbon; these the performer places in a borrowed hat, and although the ribbons where in pieces when placed in the hat, he produc s from it 50 yards of silk ribbons all joined together; the effect of taking the joined ribbons from the hat is very astonishing. We highly recommend the above beautiful box, (with its wonderful mechanism) as a perfect work of art. Price, $12.00 and $15.00

No. 223.—The Money Bottle of Midas.

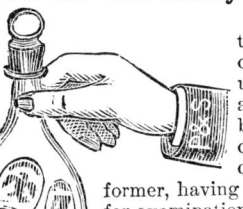

An appeal is made to the audience for the loan of four half dollars, which, upon being obtained, are put into a box and the box handed to one of the company, who retain it during the trick. The performer, having passed out a glass bottle for examination, takes it and holds it as shown in the cut. A word from him and the half dollars that were put in the box are seen, as in the engraving, to fall in the bottle, though the head of the bottle is too small to allow a coin of one-half their size to pass it. At this the surprise of the audience is very great, as the bottle during the performance is not concealed in any way.
Price, $10.00.

No. 224—The Half Dollar Wonder Wand.

What appears as merely a small round stick, in the hands of the magician, changes to an object of wonder when, thrusting it at a man's nose, he picks a real half dollar therefrom, hands it to the astonished victim and tells him to put it in his pocket. While all are expressing their surprise at this, another coin is taken from the top of a lady's head, and yet another from a boy's eye. All this and much more can be done with this wonderful wand, which is only about one-half inch in diameter. Ten or a dozen real half dollars may be produced, one by one, seen on the end of the wand, and taken off and handed to the audience. Price, each, $6.00 and $8.00.

No. 225.—THE TROJAN CORD.

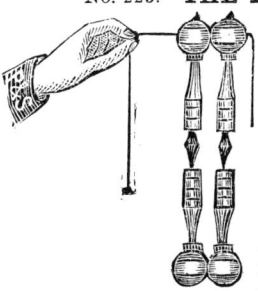

Two elegant finished boxwood columns that can be easily held in the hand are shown to the company. A silk cord passing directly through the ends of these columns is drawn back and forth, as shown in the first of the above engravings. A knife is taken by any one and forced between the columns, completely severing the cord. Each of the columns is then taken, and, as shown in the second engraving, wholly disunited from the other, the ends of the cord being seen where they were cut. The columns are then placed together, and instantly the ends become united, and the cord is drawn smoothly through as at first. Price $2.50

No. 226.—The Marvellous "Tablet" for changing Money.
A New and Beautiful Experiment.

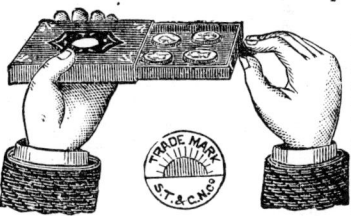

With this Clever little piece of Apparatus, Four Marked Coins can be changed under the very eyes of the Company without fear of detection. Amateurs and Professors will find the "Tablet" exceedingly useful, as the coins are changed while the Tablet is held in the hands of one of the company Price, each, 75c.

No. 227.—THE FAIRY FLOWER STAND.

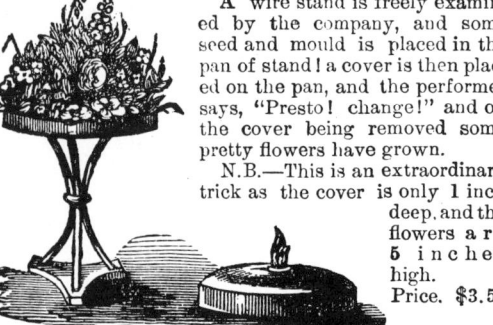

A wire stand is freely examined by the company, and some seed and mould is placed in the pan of stand! a cover is then placed on the pan, and the performer says, "Presto! change!" and on the cover being removed some pretty flowers have grown.

N.B.—This is an extraordinary trick as the cover is only 1 inch deep, and the flowers are 5 inches high.
Price. $3.50

No. 228.—The Wondrous "Drawer-Box.
BEAUTIFULLY MADE AND HIGHLY POLISHED.

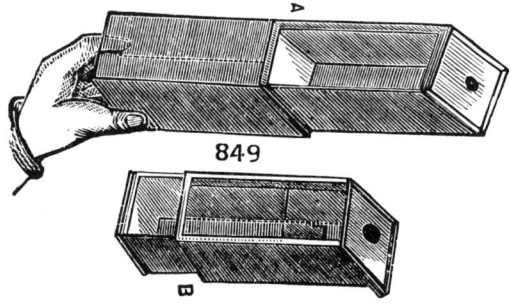

The performer shows the "Drawer Box" to the Company, and, to prove the "Drawer" is perfectly empty, PULLS THE DRAWER OUT FROM THE BOX. Then, closing the "Drawer," the performer asks one of the company to hold the box. Now the performer commands the drawer to appear full of various articles. THEN, UPON ONE OF THE COMPANY TAKING OUT THE DRAWER, IT IS FOUND FULL OF FLOWERS, BON-BONS, OR A LADY'S BORROWED HANDKERCHIEF, &C.

Note.—The "Wondrous Drawer-Box" will be found very useful for many tricks, as borrowed articles can be made to appear and disappear at pleasure.
Price, each, $5.00, $6.00, $8.00

No. 229.—The Magic Trick Box.

A finely finished wooden box with side cover, apparently perfectly plain and solid inside, and the closest examination will not discover any chance for deception. Ask one of the company to drop a marked penny into the box, and immediately close the same. The penny will be distinctly heard to rattle within, but when the box is opened it will be found *empty*, and the penny in your mouth, or some other odd place, into which you have opportunity to transfer it. Price, 50 cts.

No. 230.—Chiromagica,
is a scientific amusement consisting of a magnetic hand, arranged in a cherry box, twelve inches square, and a series of rings and disks containing geographical, historical and nonsensical questions and answers. When properly adjusted, the hand will move round with life-like intelligence, and point out the correct answer to the question asked.
Price, $2.00.

No. 231.—The "Enchanted Chest of Drawers."
A charming Experiment with Cards.

The performer shows to the company a handsome secretary "Chest of Drawers," containing five drawers, each of the five drawers being show separately to prove they are all empty. The performer asks one of the company to keep the "Chest of Drawers" in their possesion, then four cards are selected from the pack of cards by the audience, each card being placed separately in one of the empty drawers; the performer now commands the four cards to leave the four drawers, one by one, and to appear altogether in the fifth drawer, which was just shown perfectly empty, then the performer shows the four drawers (in which the four selected cards were placed) to be now quite empty, and the fifth drawer (which was empty) to contain the four selected cards, which are giving to the company for examination.
Price, each, $15.00

No. 232.—The Rattling Money Box.

This is a very good trick, and can be used in almost every illusion in which money takes part. A wooden box is shown perfectly empty; a coin is placed inside, and the box is then handed to one of the company to open. The money is heard to rattle inside the box after leaving the hands of the performer, yet when opened the box is found empty. The money having secretly passed into the performer's hand, can be found in any place desired. Price, 75c.

No. 233.—THE JAPANESE FAN TRICK.

THE FAN BROKEN.   THE FAN PERFECT.

Note.—The Fans are beautifully and strongly made, and can be used in the house or at the opera.

The performer hands to the ladies in the company the "Enchanted Fan"—they can freely examine and Fan themselves with it. Then the performer takes the Fan in his hands, but upon his doing so THE FAN FALLS INTO PIECES. Again the Fan is made perfect, but at desire once more is broken. This is repeated as many times as desired, AND WILL CAUSE VERY GREAT ASTONISHMENT.
Price, each, $1.00. Extra finish, each, $1.50.

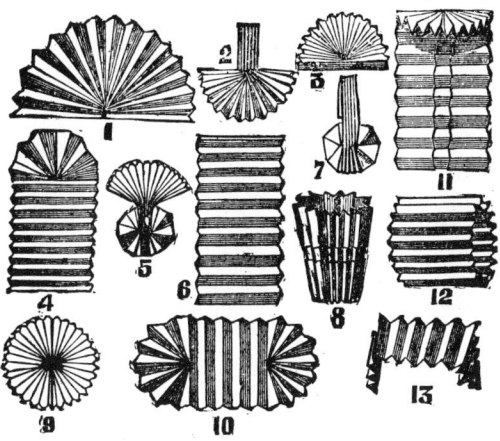

No. 234.—THE MAGIC FAN.

This Wonderful Fan can be made to represent One Hundred Different Objects, of which the following are the most interesting:
1. The Fan. 2. Chopping-Knife. 3. Paper of Pins. 4. Jagging-Iron to cut out Cakes. 5. Cut-Glass Tumbler. 6. Rosette for Ladies' Dressing-Table. 7. Table Mat. 8. Door. 9. Water-Wheel for a Mill. 10. Cradle. 11. Tack-Hammer. 12. Currycomb. 13. Tin Dipper. 14. Mushroom. 15. Target. 16. "Gypsey" Bonnet. 17. Ornamental Headdress. 18. Wineglass. 19. Pancake Turner. 20. Toilet-Box, with cover. 21. Quart Measure. 22. Coffee-Roaster. 23. Cake in a Pan. 24. Tailor's "Goose." 25. Dumb-Bells. 26. Seat in Garden, with top for shade. 27. Stew-Pan. 28. Contribution-Box. 29. Boy's Cap. 30. Wood Sleigh. 31. Floating Dry-Dock, for vessels. 32. Straw Hat. 33. Lantern. 34. Steamboat Wheels. 35. Entrance to Cathedral. 36. Mississippi Scow, or Flat-Boat. 37. Cutter, for sleigh-riding. 38. Hat and Cloak Rack. 39. Fruit Dish. 40. Decanter, with large stopple. 41. Pig-Trough. 42. Cup and Saucer. 43. Hotel and Dining-Room Table. 44. Centre-Table. 45. Knife-Tray. 46. Wheel for Chain Pump. 47. Common Flower-Pot. 48. Hay-Rack, for horse. 49. Carpenter's Plane. 50. Corn Mill. 51. Ruffled Shirt-Bosom. 52. Jelly Mould. 53. Lady's Cuff. 54. Old-fashioned High Back Chair. 55. Reflector for Lamp. 56. Sugar-Scoop. 57. Ornamental Chair. 58. Hyacinth-Glass. 59. Shaker Bonnet. 60. Flower Vase. 61. Mantel Ornament. 62. Buttrice, for paring the hoofs of horses.

FULL DIRECTIONS ACCOMPANY EACH FAN, illustrated with an engraving of each article, and the manner in which each is made. No more pleasant entertainment for an evening can be produced than with one of these Fans in the hands of man, woman or child. One Fan is enough, in the hands of an experienced performer, to give a whole evening's entertainment. Price, complete, in a neat box, by mail........................50 cts.

No. 235.—The Ticking Watch Box.

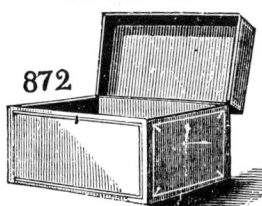

A watch is borrowed by the performer from some of the audience. This box is then produced and the watch taken and placed within it, and the box locked, the key given to one of the audience, and the watch can be distinctly heard ticking in the box. Upon reopening it, it is found empty, and the watch, after considerable of a search, is found in any place the operator may have previously selected. Superior make, and beautifully inlaid.
Price complete, $10. and $12.

No. 236 —The Magic Wonder Books.

A series of Pictures with Life-like Motions. This Scientific Novelty is the adaptation of a celebrated German toy to the form of a book. By holding the book in the left hand, and holding the top with the thumb and forefinger of the right, allowing the leaves to spring rapidly from beneath the thumb, every picture seems alive. In one a Shoemaker stitches away "like all possessed"; in another, a Windmill is in motion, grinding forty millions bushels of imaginary corn; another represents Children Tilting; while another a grim visitor,—a sort of BONY PART,—pops up and down like a dolphin. No. 1, The Shoemaker, 15 cts.; No. 2, The Tilting, 15 cts.; No. 3, The Windmill, 15 cts., No. 4, The Skeleton, 15 cts. The whole set, 50 cts.

No. 237 —The Mysterious Sphynx.

The Great Wonder of Ancient Egypt. Will answer Questions in a seemingly Miraculous Manner. An endless source of Entertainment and Surprise.
Price, 15 cts.

No. 238 —Labyrinthian Puzzles.

A series of Three Intricate Journeys. By A. Maze. Printed on three cards, red, green, and yellow, 4½ by 7, all enclosed in an envelope, 5 by 8¼. Price, per set, 25 cts.

No. 239.—Magic Ladle.

With this ladle, black or any other ink can be dipped from a man's hat or from an empty jar, box, plate or goblet, and can be used with many other tricks.
Price each, $1 50.

No. 240.—LUMINOUS PAINT OR CAPTIVE DAYLIGHT.

This marvellous chemical compound possesses the remarkable property of absorbing daylight or sunlight in such quantities that it is really stored up until darkness sets in when it is again emitted only to be again absorbed and bottled up as it were, immediately the sun peeps over the horizon, and this property continues day after day and year after year, for experiment has proved that neither fire or water affect the chemical properties of the powder.

The Luminous Paint now in such demand is prepared by an eminent french chemist who has brought it to a state of perfection after many years patient experiment, and the preparation is applied to a variety of useful purposes that were not invented when the first Luminous Paint was discovered. Watch dials will now show the time in the dark, and railway carriages diffuse a soft light when running through tunnels. Divers coat their dresses with it and can be seen on the surface of the water when at a great depth themselves. Powder Magazines are lit up without fear of explosion by carrying large sheets of card board into daylight for a few minutes and than hanging them on the walls of the vaults. Life buoys when thrown into the water to rescue some drowning sailor, now shine brilliantly, and names of streets and numbers on doors can be seen at a distance even on a dark night. Boys also now design skeletons on the walls of bedrooms, paint luminous babies in maiden aunts beds, and produce other comical and spectral effects. Put up complete in box containing one bottle of powder, a heavy cut glass for mixing the powder and a small fancy box for distributing. Price, 50c.

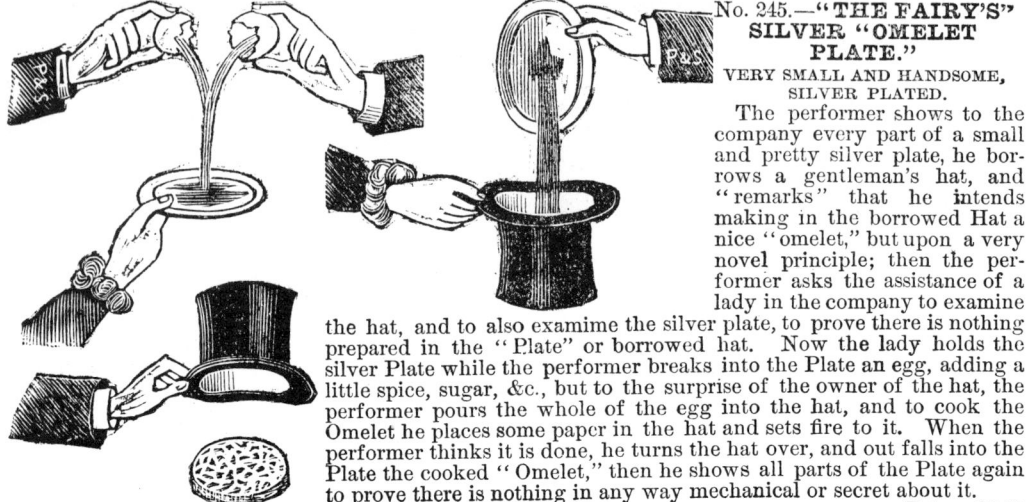

No. 245.—"THE FAIRY'S" SILVER "OMELET PLATE."

VERY SMALL AND HANDSOME, SILVER PLATED.

The performer shows to the company every part of a small and pretty silver plate, he borrows a gentleman's hat, and "remarks" that he intends making in the borrowed Hat a nice "omelet," but upon a very novel principle; then the performer asks the assistance of a lady in the company to examine the hat, and to also examime the silver plate, to prove there is nothing prepared in the "Plate" or borrowed hat. Now the lady holds the silver Plate while the performer breaks into the Plate an egg, adding a little spice, sugar, &c., but to the surprise of the owner of the hat, the performer pours the whole of the egg into the hat, and to cook the Omelet he places some paper in the hat and sets fire to it. When the performer thinks it is done, he turns the hat over, and out falls into the Plate the cooked "Omelet," then he shows all parts of the Plate again to prove there is nothing in any way mechanical or secret about it.

Price, $3.50

No. 246.—THE "ENCHANTED GLASS CASKET" and the TWO WONDERFUL BALLS.

A NEW AND CHARMING EXPERIMENT.

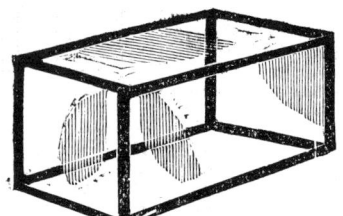

The performer shows a very pretty "Glass Casket," perfectly empty, then without covering the Glass Casket in any way, and while standing right in front of the company, the performer commands two large Balls to appear inside the empty casket. Now, to the wonderment of everyone two large Balls are instantly seen to appear inside the Casket. The Balls are taken out and shown to the company.

Price, $3.50

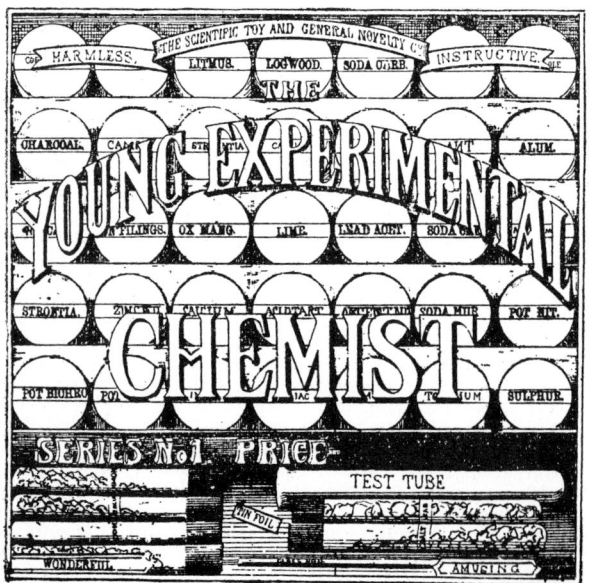

No. 247.—This box, as its name implies, is devoted to chemistry, and every boy who examines the list of experiments will be surprised at the wonderful things he can perform. Parents should encourage children to employ their time with scientific toys of this description, which elevate the mind, and form a source of delightful occupation during the winter evenings.

Price, $1.00 each.

N. B.—We are Agents for Statham's (of London,) Students' Chemical Cabinets and Boy's own Laboratory, prices, $4.00 $5.00, $10.00, $15.00, $20.00 $25.00 and $35 00 each. Also a full line of Books on Chemistry and Electricity.

No. 248.—The "Miraculous Box."

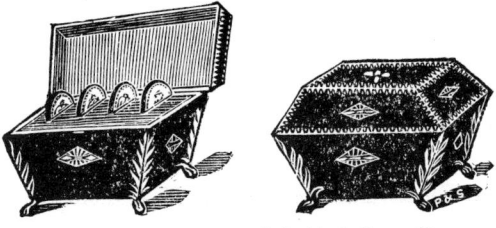

To make four borrowed half dollars disappear from the "box," one at a time, while the box is held upon the hand of one of the company.

NOTE.—The "Miraculous Box" is very handsome, being richly made in silk velvet, or leather, with gilt ornaments.

The performer borrows from the company four half dollars, which are placed in the "Miraculous Box," and to prove the extraordinary nature of the trick, the performer asks one of the company to hold the box upon the palm of their hand during the entire experiment, then the performer, without touching the "box" in any way, commands one coin to disappear from the "box." The "box" is opened, and only three coins found in it; the "box" closed and opened, and only two coins remain; once more the "box" is closed and opened, and only one coin is seen; then for the last time the "box" is closed and opened, when it is found perfectly empty, and the "box" is turned upside down to prove all the coins have disappeared from it.

N. B.—This beautiful "trick" can be performed with the greatest ease by the amateur or professor.

NOTE.—The "half dollar wand," can be had to be used in conjunction with the miraculous "box," and which together forms a very beautiful and finished trick, the coins disappearing from the "box," one by one, and appearing upon the top of the "wand," one by one. Price of box, $10.00

No. 249.—The Fairy Bird Cage and Magic Flowers.

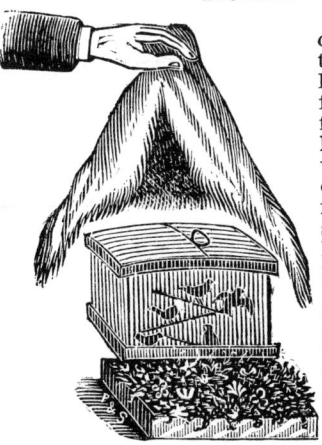

The performer commences the trick by showing a handsome flat box full of beautiful flowers, he takes a handkerchief, which he throws over the box of flowers, in one instant he lifts up the handkerchief, and then is seen a very large solid wire cage (richly decorated) standing upon the top of the flowers. The cage being four times as big as the box; the cage has a perch, and contains live birds. This will be found a very charming illusion, "birds and flowers," and will delight every one who sees it, as the size, construction, and mechanism of this extraordinary cage will cause great astonishment; it can be examined by the company.

NOTE.—This beautiful experiment can be performed by a lady holding the flower box in her hands. Price, $20.00

No. 250.—The Enchanted Portfolio.

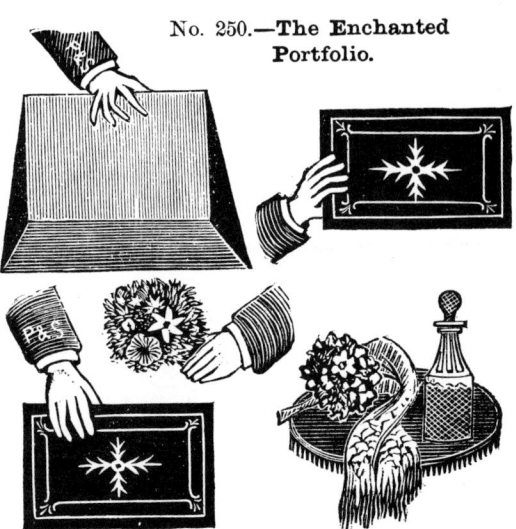

The performer shows every part (both inside and out) of the "Portfolio," to the company, he then closes it *quite flat*, thus proving there is nothing concealed or mechanical about the "Portfolio"; still, in one instant, the performer takes from the "Portfolio" enough objects to cover the top of a table, then again the portfolio is shown perfectly flat and every part examined Still, once more the Portfolio is found full of various articles.

This beautiful trick is highly recommended for the "Drawing Room" or "Stage." Price, $7.00

No. 251.—The Two "Enchanted Vases" and Mysterious Balls.

The "Vases" are very handsome and richly polished.

The performer commences this beautiful "trick" by giving the two "vases" and two balls to be freely examined by the company, he then places in one "vase" a *solid white ball*, and in the other "vase" a *solid red ball*, the performer placing the covers over the "vases," commands the white and red balls to change places in the "vases," then upon lifting up the cover, the company see a wondrous change, for in the "vase" that contained the white ball, the red ball appears, and in the "vase" that contained the red ball, a white ball appears, once more the two balls are commanded to change places and return to their original "vases," when the company see the white and red balls appear in the "vases" they were first placed in. Then, to make the illusion more extraordinary, only white balls appear, one in each "vase." Again, another change, only red balls appear, one in each "vase." Presto! The performer commands the white and red Balls to return to the "vases" they were first placed in, and there they are found, and the company (at the finish as at the commencement) freely examine both balls and "vases." Price, $3.50

No. 252.—The Demon's "Billiard Ball."
A NOVEL AND WONDERFUL TRICK.

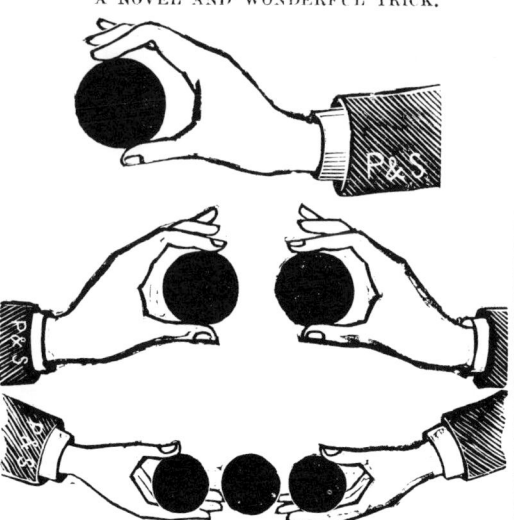

The performer commences the trick by *turning up the sleeves of his coat, and shows the back and front of his hands to prove there is nothing concealed about him,* he then takes in his hands a solid black billiard ball, and holds it up between his thumb and fingers, and waving the billiard ball to and fro—*instantaneously* two "billiard balls" appear in the performer's hands, then the two "billiard balls" are waved to and fro, when, to every one's astonishment, three billiard balls appear. The performer remarks that as he has made the billiard balls appear in a very mysterious manner, he will make them disappear in the same way. Presto! the three balls are rubbed together when only two balls are seen; then the two balls are rubbed together, when the original solid black billiard ball is seen once more between the performer's fingers. During the entire trick the performer stands right in front of the company. Price, $3.50.

No. 253.—The "Headless Man."
A STARTLING NOVELTY.

The performer shows a nicely dressed figure to the company, he then takes the "head" off from the neck of the figure and gives the head to be examined by the audience. The performer borrows a lady's handkerchief, which he throws over the headless body and the head is placed in his pocket. Now the performer, standing a long way from the figure, commands the "head" to leave his pocket and return to its original place on the neck of the figure, then one of the company takes off the handkerchief from the figure, when "lo," the "head" is found firmly fixed upon the neck of the "figure," which is taken to the company for examination, the effect of the "head" being found again upon the neck of the "figure" is truly marvelous, and will cause great astonishment. Price, $7.00.

No. 254.—The Demon Candle & Mystic Coins.

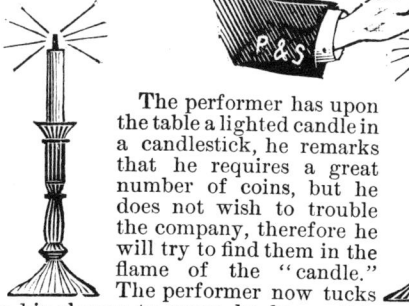

The performer has upon the table a lighted candle in a candlestick, he remarks that he requires a great number of coins, but he does not wish to trouble the company, therefore he will try to find them in the flame of the "candle." The performer now tucks up his sleeves to prove he has nothing concealed about him and holding the candle and candle-stick in one hand (right away from the table) with the other hand takes from the flame of the candle as many real coins as he requires. The money is taken from the flame of the candle, one by one, and as they are taken, the money is given to be examined, to prove they are real coins. This wonderful trick, although easy to perform, is of the most extraordinary description. Price, $3.00.

No. 255.—The Red and White Rose of Enchantment.

A gentleman takes in his hand a beautiful white rose, asks a lady to breathe upon it, then, before the eyes of all the company, the white rose instantaneously changes its color and becomes red. The effect is most charming, and will delight every lady in the company. Price, $3.00.

There are two things a boy is sure to possess before he is six years of age—a whistle and a magnet. The whistle he prizes because it is an annoyance to everybody, and the magnet because it is a puzzle to everybody. He knows the latter will lift a key, and make iron filings run across the table, but when he asks his mother why it does so, she tells him because it does. Thus, being a mystery, it possesses a certain charm for him, and will therefore be found within the inmost recesses of his trousers' pocket for many years. Now, as mothers and magnets have little in common, we have decided to come to the boy's assistance, and in the above box we give a book of experiments performed with the magnet, and many wonderful things can now be accomplished which would never otherwise be thought of. The box also contains a beautiful brass compass, with inner glass dial and brass lid, also two magnets, induction rod, teetotum, metal filings, spangles, and metal fish, combining delightful amusement and instruction for the young of both sexes. Price, 50 cents each.

No. 259.

This extraordinary compound was discovered by Sir Humphrey Davy. When a small piece is thrown into water, it forms a beautiful silver ball, and rushes about all over the surface of the water as if alive, enveloped in a beautiful film of violet-colored flame. If the tears are wrapped in thin paper and thrown into water they catch fire instantly. Price, 50c. each.

No, 260.—The "Wondrous Card in the Light."

A NOVEL AND EXTRAORDINARY EXPERIMENT.

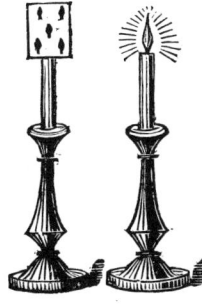

The company select a card from a pack; the card is torn up, and the pieces placed in a pistol. The performer places upon the table a lighted candle in a brass candlestick, one of the company takes the pistol, (with the pieces of card in it), and at the word of command fires at the lighted candle, when instantly the selected card appears right upon the top of the lighted candle, in place of the flame of the candle,

NOTE.—The effect of this wonderful experiment must be seen, for the beautiful mechanism to be appreciated. Can be performed with the greatest ease upon any table, or the performer can hold the candlestick in his hand and show the front, back, and all parts of it to the company, to prove there is no card concealed, thus demonstrating the extraordinary nature of the trick.

Price, Complete with Pack of Cards, $10.00

No. 279—THE ENCHANTED MIRROR.

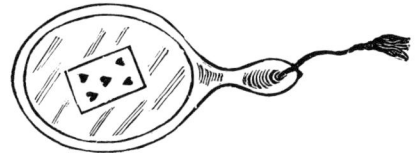

Several cards are chosen from a pack which are put back and shuffled by one of the audience. The cards are then one by one thrown against the mirror. The cards fall to the ground, but the chosen ones are found fastened to the glass. The cards and glass can be examined freely.

Price complete with cards, $6.00

No. 280—The Magician's Scarf Pin.

Every performer should have one, it moves its eyes and tongue very comical. Price, each, $1.50

No. 281—The Vanishing & Reappearing Glass

The performer comes forward holding a very large, ornamentally engraved glass in his outstretched hand. Covering his hand for a moment with a borrowed handkerchief, the glass is found to have vanished when the former is removed. Waving the handkerchief in the air the glass is reproduced at once again, which proceeding may be repeated any number of times. The performer concludes by filling the glass with wine which he drinks to the health of the audience.

This very fine illusion is performed on an entirely new principle. The hands never approach the body of the performer, and the handkerchief is not prepared in any way.

Price, each, $3.50

No. 261.—The Wonderful "Plateau" and the Enchanted "Brass Box."

The performer asks the company to *secretly mark* two or three coins *of any kind*, which the company themselves place in the wondrous brass box, and keep possession of the box during the entire trick. The performer shows the company a very handsome "plateau" (or tray); upon the "plateau" he places a small transparent white glass, and holding the "plateau" at arm's length, commands the marked coins to leave the "brass box" (still in possession of the company) and to fall into the glass upon the "plateau," which the performer holds in his hand, then the marked money is seen and heard to fall into the glass upon the "plateau," and the "brass box" (still retained by the company) found perfectly empty, *the marked coins are taken by the owners from the glass*, thus demonstrating the extraordinary character of the experiment.
Complete, $18.00

NOTE.—With the Wonderful "Plateau," we also send the wondrous "Brass Box," No. 85, without extra charge, which makes the beautiful trick complete.

No. 262.—The "Enchanted" Drawing-Room Bird Cage.

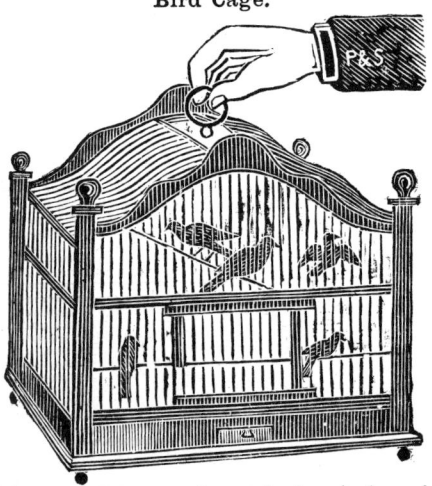

This beautiful cage is made in nicely painted wires, and decorated sides, and in appearance, and construction, the same as would be seen in any drawing-room. The performer freely shows every part of the cage to the company to prove it is perfectly empty, he asks a lady to hold the cage, and then simply passing a handkerchief over it, "Presto!" in an instant the cage is found full of beautiful birds, to the wonderment of every one, and then again the cage can be freely examined.

NOTE.—*The cage can be used by itself*, or in conjunction with other bird tricks. The construction and mechanism of the cage will cause the greatest admiration.
Price, $20.00

No. 263.—The Corpse Candle, or Sepulchral Light.

This wonderful light is made entirely of metal burning ordinary gas, and fits any burner. It retains its properties upwards of twenty years, and instantaneously changes the living into the dead. For evening parties and harmless drawing-room amusement.
Complete, 75 cents.

No. 264.—The Miraculous Swallowing Wand.

A NOVELTY OF THE MOST EXRAORDINARY DESCRIPTION.

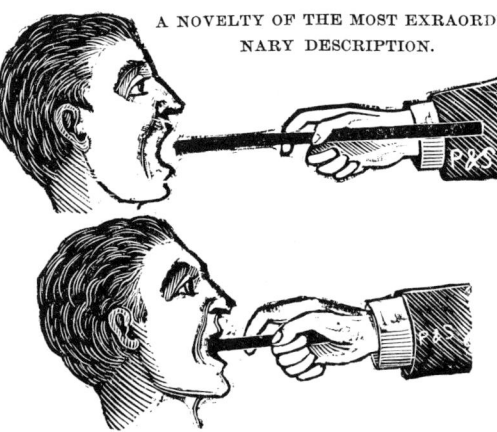

The performer commences by giving his wand to be minutely examined by the company, then he asks a gentleman to oblige him by assisting him in the experiment, first asking him to freely examine in every way the wand. The performer now places the point of the wand in the gentleman's mouth, and to the wonderment of everyone the wand is seen slowly to pass down the gentleman's throat to the other end of the "wand" in the performer's hand, then the performer slowly brings back the "wand" from the gentleman's mouth, and as the wand returns it is placed in the gentleman's hands to once more minutely examine it, thus proving the extraordinary wonderment of the trick. The "wand" is made of ebony polished wood, with silver-plated ends.
Price, $3.00

NOTE.—The "wand," with which the trick is performed, is of solid wood without springs or any other mechanism, and defies detection.

No. 265.—**The Bewitched Pack of Cards.**

A VERY CLEVER "TRICK."

Two pieces of money are borrowed, marked, and locked in a box, The performer takes a pack of cards and places them upon an ordinary drinking glass, covering both cards and glass with a lady's borrowed handkerchief, he then commands the marked money to leave the box and pass through the pack of cards and fall into the glass. When the money is distinctly heard to fall into the glass, then one of the audience takes from the glass the money. To prove it is the same that was marked, the top, bottom, and sides of the pack of cards can be shown to the company to prove the wonderful character of the trick. Price, $5.00

No. 266.—**The Multiplying Eggs and Handkerchief.**

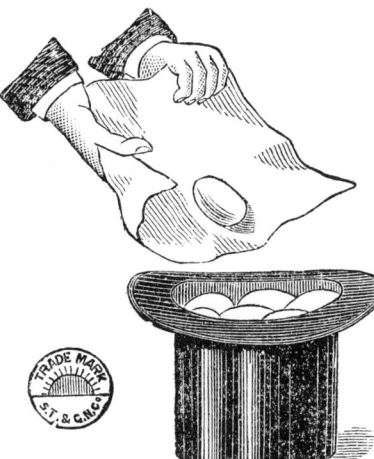

The performer shows an ordinary silk handkerchiefs and request, the audience to satisfy themselves there is no preparation about it. He then takes the handkerchief by the corners, and shakes it gently, and instantly something is seen suspended in the center of it, although it has just been examined by the company. The handkerchief is opened and is found to contain a real egg, which is placed in a borrowed hat. Again the performer shakes the handkerchief, and immediately a second egg appears, and this continues until the hat is full of eggs, although where they come from remains a mystery. Price, $2.00

No. 267.—**Is your Watch a Stem-Winder?**

Can also be used in connection with a Watch Repeater.

A lady's or gentleman's stem-winding watch is borrowed by the performer and held in the hand; he then asks the person of whom he borrowed it whether they have wound it up, at the same time he commences to wind it, when a loud noise is heard as if he is winding up a clock. With a surprised look, he hands it back and exclaims, that will not do; he borrows another, and does the same thing.
Price, by mail, 50 cents.

No. 268.—**CONJURING WAND.**

Very superior and beautifully made in Satin Wood, with polished ebony ends. The "Wands" are to hold in the hand during a magical performance, and will be found very useful. Each $1.00.

Conjuring Wands, for same use as No. 268, but more beautiful every way; is made of ebony, with ivory trimmings. Each, $2.00

No. 269.—**The Vanishing Glass Bowl of Fish.**

The performer borrows a lady's shawl, turns it inside out, allows it to be examined by the company to prove that there is nothing in the shawl. Then taking it in his hands, he instantly produces from it a transparent glass bowl of water and fish. Now, to make this trick more extraordinary, the performer covers the bowl of water and fish with the shawl, and instantaneously causes "glass bowl," "water," and "fish" to vanish in the most mysterious manner, and again gives the shawl to be examined by the company, as before. Price complete, $5.00

No. 270.—**The Magic "Ribbands;" 100 yards found in a Borrowed Hat.**

The Ribbands are beautifully made, and are a very great "novelty."

The performer borrows a gentleman's hat, and instantly produces from it *over one hundred yards of strong paper "ribbands," in various beautiful colors.* The performer holds the borrowed "hat" right in front of him, and continues taking the ribbands from the "hat" till the table, floor, &c., is covered with them, the supply of "ribbands" appearing endless. The trick is performed without the aid of "table" or confederate.

N. B.—The ribbands can always be used again as many times as required, as they are strongly made, and over an inch in width. Each, 75 cents.

FIRST POSITION.

SECOND POSITION.

NATURAL.

No. 271.—**The Magic Mirror.**—The most wonderful and surprising novelty of the day. It consists of a handsome *convex* mirror, which fits closely into a neat case of a proper size to carry in the side pocket. Upon looking in the mirror when held in an upright position, a person's face appears five times its real length, the features being contracted or drawn out, as it were, to a frightful extent, a most ludicrous appearance. The teeth, if shown, resemble, in length and shape, a picket fence, while the general make up of the face is laughable in the extreme. Upon reversing the mirror, holding it in a horizontal position, the opposite effect is produced. Instead of being drawn out, the features are flattened, the forehead and chin extending back, the nose protruding forward, and the person transformed into a being of such immense proportions that Barnum's fat woman would be nowhere by comparison. In either position the features and outlines of the face are preserved, so that anyone would at once recognize the person, notwithstanding the wonderful transformation. One look in the Magic Glass cures melancholy, peevishness, ill-nature, and a host of ills arising from keeping late hours and bad digestion. If your mother-in-law is ugly, or your girl proud and conceited, the Magic Glass will at once reduce them to a state of docility and meekness by showing them their *great* imperfections. Samples mailed postpaid, on receipt of 25 cts. Per doz., $1.75.

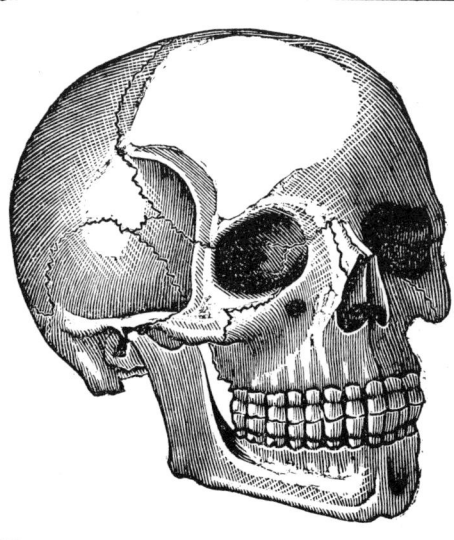

No. 272.—**THE MESMERIZED SKULL.**—This marvelous and mystifying illusion has been performed with the greatest effect and has defied detection. The performance commences by the Magician bringing forward two ordinary chairs and placing them about three feet apart, in the centre of the room or stage. On the top of the backs of these he lays a piece of ordinary window glass about twelve inches wide, which may be examined. He now shows to the audience a beautifully modeled skull, which he also passes round for examination. When it is returned to him he places it on the glass shelf, and goes some distance away from it. The company may now ask any questions, which the skull will answer by shaking its head for "No," or nodding for "Yes," or count any number by a succession of nods. At any time the skull may be taken up and examined. Or finally, to make the illusion more extraordinary still, an ordinary glass shade may be placed completely over the skull, and yet it will continue to answer questions with the same correctness as before. $6 and $15 each.

FIGURES FOR VENTRILOQUISM.

All these figures are beautifully made and dressed. They are of superior make and finish, are artistically modelled and painted in oil colors. They are made very strong; the movements being so arranged as to be very convenient for working, and are not liable to get out of order.

No. 1 Knee figure, mouth made to move and head to turn, $14.00
No. 2, " " arm and mouth made to move, 15.00
No. 3, " " eyes, arm and mouth made to move, 20.00
No. 4, " " " " mouth and head " " 25.00

PECK & SNYDER, 126, 128 & 130 Nassau Street, N. Y.
IMPORTERS AND DEALERS IN TRICKS, NOVELTIES, MAGIC, &c., &c.

No. 273.—THE "DEMON HAND" SHAKING.

An astounding trick, which will cause shouts of laughter and wonderment in the private drawing-room or theatre.

The performer asks some gentleman to shake hands with him, which a gentleman does most cordially, but suddenly he is seen "to start," "to jump," and then to make some extraordinary grimaces, "dance and caper" about all over the room; no matter how strong the person may be who shakes hands with the performer, he is held as in a vise, and finds it impossible to get away, although only held by one hand of the operator. Now the performer leaves the gentleman's hand free, and thanks him for his kind assistance, and the gentleman retires amidst roars of laughter.
Price, with Complete Apparatus, $25.00

No. 274.—THE MYSTIC CONE AND GROWTH OF FLOWERS.

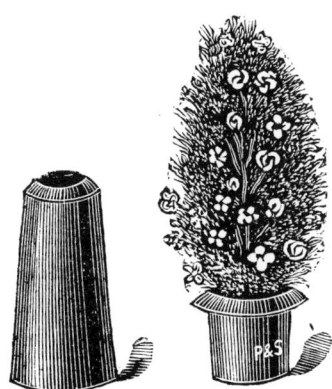

The performer first shows the Cone, which is made of metal, beautifully japanned, and he puts his arm right through it, to prove there is nothing concealed inside, simply a thin metal cone, without any top to it. He now takes a common flower pot and asks one of the audience to fill it with mould; he then places the cone on the top of the flower pot, and taking great quantities of various kinds of seeds, he pours them inside the cone, until the interior is full; now making some passes with his wand, he commands the seeds to grow, and removing the cone, reveals a beautiful bouquet of flowers, much higher than the cone, and the seeds have all vanished. The cone stands 13 inches high, and the bouquet of flowers 18 inches high. Performed by Dr. Holden before Her Majesty the Queen, at Balmoral, Scotland.
Price, $25.00

No. 275.—The Blood Writing on the Arm.

Full apparatus and instructions for performing this most marvellous and effective Trick, on the most approved principle. Equally adapted to Professional or Amateur.
Price, $1.00

No. 276.—The Electrical Skull Scarf Pin.

The latest sensation in Scarf Pins. Can be freely examined. It is made of the finest Gold, and enameled with Diamond Eyes. Moves its jaws and eyes. Can be made to work any number of times, and to stop or work as the performer wishes. This is a very fine piece of work, and makes an elegant scarf pin.

Price of Skull complete.................$65 00
2 Skull with Jocky Cap on..............100 00
3 Monkey Head, moves Eyes and Mouth..85.00

These are all worked with a small Battery that can be carried in the vest pocket.

No. 277.—The Charmed Plate and Four Magic Cards.

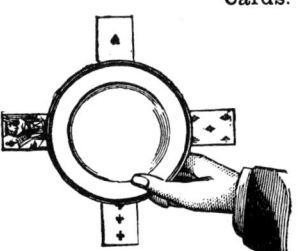

The performer allows four cards to be drawn from a pack by the audience, they are then placed in a pistol which is fired at the plate, when the four cards will be seen sticking to the plate. They are then taken off and examined by the audience. This is a new and very effective card trick.
Price complete with cards, $6.00

No. 278.—The Snake and Handkerchief Illusion.

The performer brings forward for inspection, two silk handkerchiefs on a plate, a green and a yellow one, by twisting them together he at once produces a large snake with protuding tongue. With handkerchiefs complete.
Price, $3 50

PUNCH AND JUDY FIGURES, &c.

The most pleasing and attractive draw to a Magical Exhibition is the introduction of the side-splitting freaks of Mr. Punch and the comicalities of his numerous family. As it is very essential that the figures and all apparatus should be perfect and complete, Peck & Snyder call attention to the fact that they manufacture and finish in the most approved style the following

Best Dressed Figures, With Solid Wooden Heads

	EACH		EACH
Punch	$1 50	Crocodile	$2 00
Judy	1 50	Stage Bedstead	2 00
Pretty Poll	1 50	Bed and Pillow	75
Doctor	1 50	Punch's $25,000 Box	2 25
Policeman	1 50	Skeleton Mouth, mov'le	2 25
Clown	1 50	Ghost	1 50
Jack Ketch	1 50	Gallows	1 25
Old Nick	1 50	Coffin	1 26
Scaramouch	1 50	Snake	1 50
Opera Singer	1 50	Servant's Bell	75
Darkie	1 50	Baby	75
Irishman	1 50	Squeakers	15
Dutchman	1 50	Punch's Club	20
Punch's Dog	1 75	Book of Dialogues	25
Horse	1 75		

The above described are made large and strong for showmen's use.

MADE OF PAPER MACHE.

No. 595.	Per set of 6 Figures	$3 00
No. 596.	" " 6 "	4 50
No. 597.	" " 6 "	5 00

We also keep on hand Punch and Judy Shows, Complete with 6 Figures.

No. 0.	Height 24 inches, width 13 inches, 6 Figures, each	$ 3 75
No. 1.	" 26½ " " 13 " 6 "	4 25
No. 2.	" 28½ " " 13 " 6 "	5 00
No. 4.	" 36 " " 18 " 6 "	8 00
No. 29.	" 63 " " 30 " 6 "	13 00
No. 31.	" 66 " " 22 " 6 "	17 00

Ventriloquist Figures Dressed.

		EACH.
No. 1.	Full Length Boy Figure, Eyes, Arms, Mouth and Head, to move, Price	$24 00
No. 2.	Eyes, Arm and Mouth made to move	20 00
No. 3.	Arm and Mouth made to move	15 00
No. 4.	Mouth made to move and Head to turn	14 00

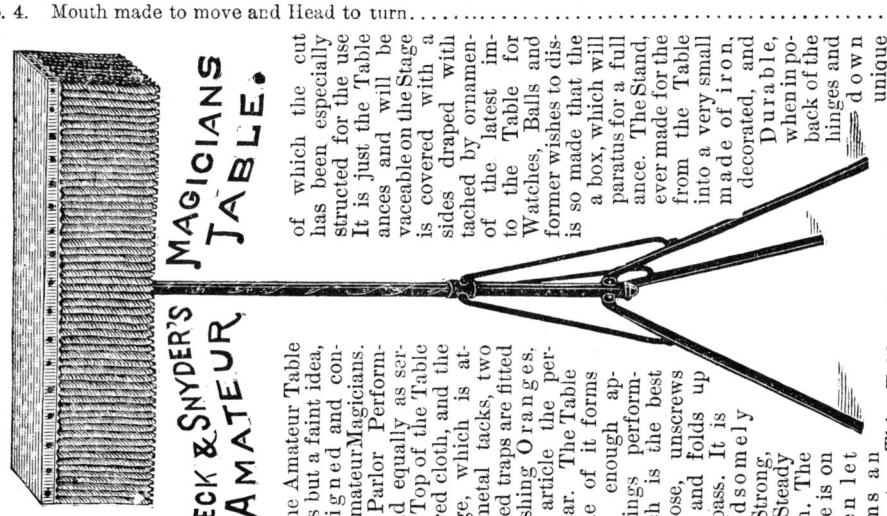

PECK & SNYDER'S AMATEUR MAGICIANS TABLE.

The Amateur Table gives but a faint idea, designed and constructed for the use of Amateur Magicians. for Parlor Performances and will be found equally as serviceable on the Stage. The Top of the Table is covered with a figured cloth, and the fringe, which is attached by ornamental metal tacks, two proved traps are fitted of the latest improved traps to dis- vanishing Oranges. appear. The Table for any article the per- Watches, Balls and inside of it forms former wishes to dis- hold enough ap- is so made that the paratus for a full box, which will evenings perform- ance. The Stand, which is the best ever made for the purpose, unscrews from the Table Top and folds up into a very small compass. It is made of iron, handsomely decorated, and is Strong, Durable, and Steady po- when in po- sition. The sition of the Table is on back of the when let hinges and forms an down Servante. This unique Table will undoubtedly become a favorite with the Amateur world. It is the cheapest ever offered for sale. Price, $15.00. Extra finished and decorated, $20.00.

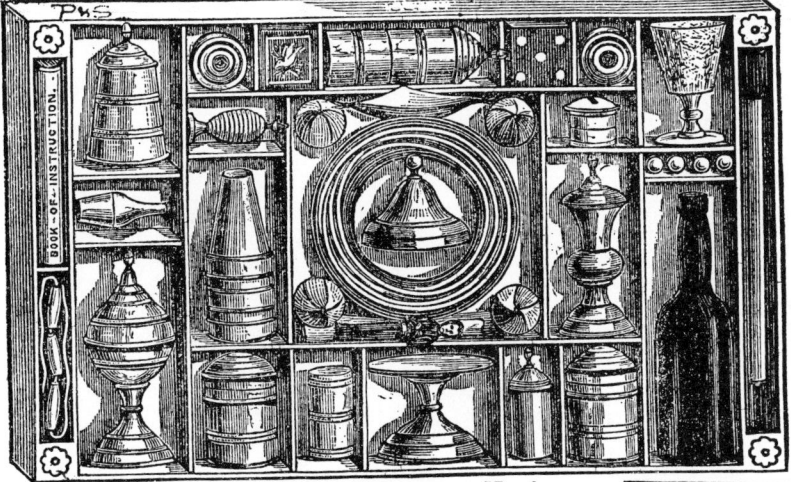

No. 6.

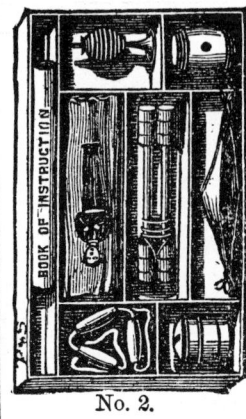

No. 2.

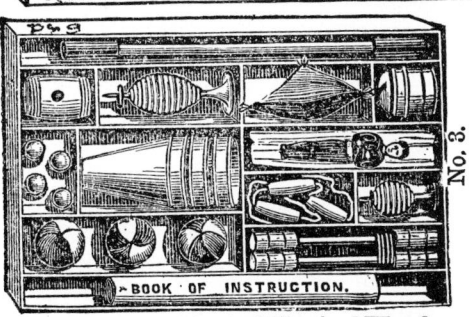

No. 1.—A Cabinet of Magical Wonders.—This box of clever tricks will give great satisfaction. It contains a variety of amusing tricks, which we can highly recommend. Price, per box, by mail, 75 cents.

Peck & Snyder's Box of Conjuring Tricks, No. 2.—This box contains a collection of amusing tricks, well made, and is certain to please a juvenile.

CONTENTS.—The little vanishing man, the seed barrel, the secret purse, the magic pillars of Solomon, the secret money-box, my grandmother's beads, the magic ball box, and a book of instructions.
Price, $2 50

Peck & Snyder's Box of Conjuring Tricks, No. 3.—This box contains a larger assortment of conjuring tricks than No. 1, and will give every satisfaction.

CONTENTS.—The three cups and balls, three solid cloth balls, the egg-cup with three changes, the little vanishing man, the magic ball-box, the magic seed barrel, Solomon's Pillars, my grandmother's beads, the secret money-box, the magic cloth purse, a nicely made polished wand, and a book of instructions.
Price, $5 00

Peck & Snyder's Box of Conjuring Tricks, No. 4.—This box contains a large and beautiful assortment of conjuring tricks, many of them being made in polished brass, suitable for a youth.

CONTENTS.—The magical birth of flowers, the Chinese linking rings, the three cups and balls, the four solid cloth balls, the magic vanishing dice, a nicely made polished wand, the twin vanishing boxes, the vanishing man, the secret money-box, the magic seed barrel, the magic ball box, the secret cloth purse, my grandmother's beads, and a book of instructions.
Price, $8 00

Peck & Snyder's Box of Conjuring Tricks, No. 5.—This box contains a complete set of beautiful apparatus of a very superior description; many of the tricks being made in polished brass, and richly decorated.

CONTENTS.—The magic bird's nest, the magical growth of flowers, the Chinese linking rings, the wonderful flageolet, the magic vanishing dice, the secret purse, the enchanted money cover, the magical coin box, the three cups and balls, the twin vanishing boxes, the four solid cloth balls, the vanishing man, my grandmother's necklace, Solomon's wonderful pillars, a nicely made satin wood wand, and a book of instructions.
Price, $11 00

Peck & Snyder's Box of Conjuring Tricks, No. 6.—This box contains a complete set of beautiful apparatus, and is very highly recommended as being suitable for an adult. The tricks and apparatus are of a large size and of a superior description. Very handsome, and are so well finished that they will last for years.

CONTENTS.—The burning globe, for borrowed handkerchief, a pair of magical coffee and rice vases, the magic card tripod, the magic glass vase and mystic bran, the wonderful three-egg cup, four solid cloth balls, magical coin box, magic vanishing dice, the inexhaustible bottle, the magic purse, the extraordinary brass changing vase, the Chinese linking rings, the magical growth of flowers, the three cups and balls, the twin vanishing boxes, the magic bottle and four colors, the money box the vanishing man, my grandmother's beads, a nicely made wand in polished satin wood, and a book of instructions.
Price, $25 00

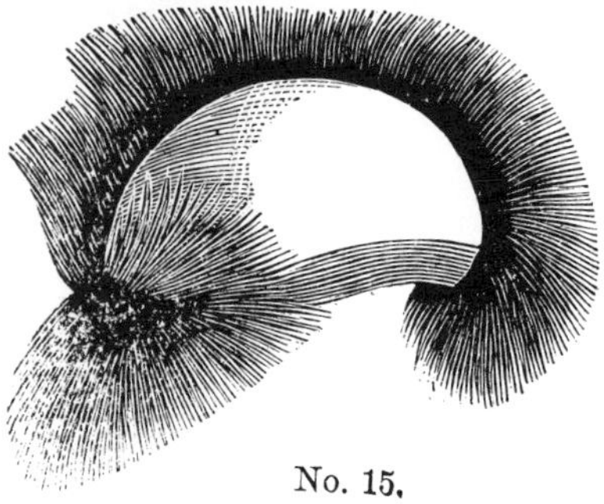

No. 15.

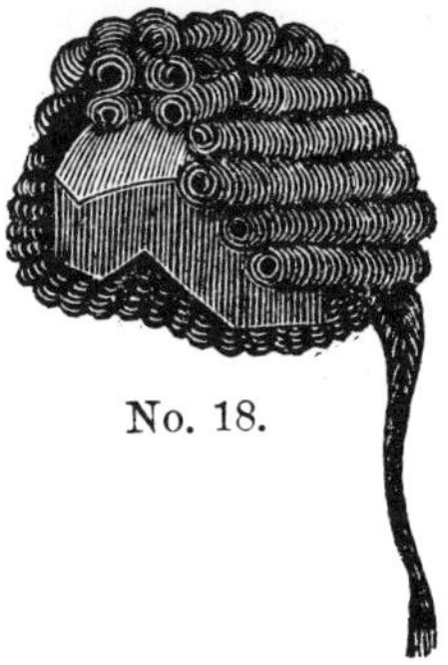

No. 18.

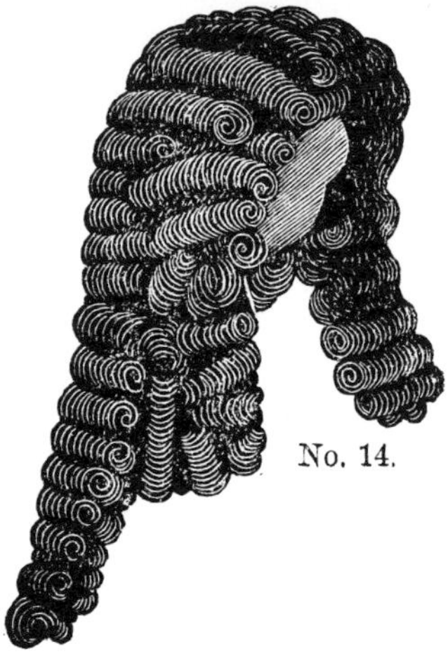

No. 14.

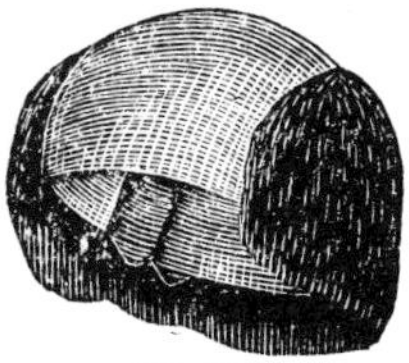

No. 17.

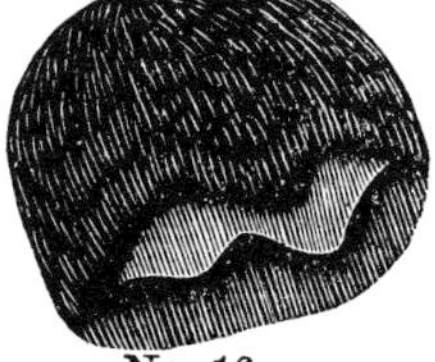

No. 16.

Ladies' Wig in curls or in long hair, so it can be made up in any style, see cut No. 14...Each, $10 00
Gent's Comic Character Bald Wig, any color, see cut No. 15.......................... " 4 50
Gent's Dutch Crop Wig for German character, " " 16........................... " 4 50
Gent's Bald Wig for old man character, grey or white, see cut No. 17.................. " 4 50
Gent's Court Wig with bag or tie, see cut No. 18...................................... " 4 00

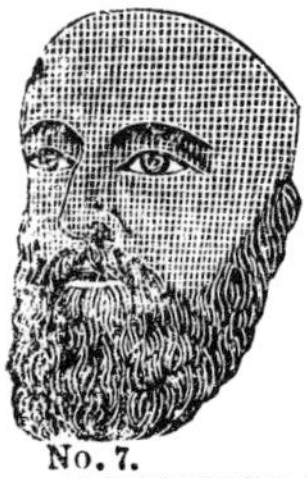

No. 7.

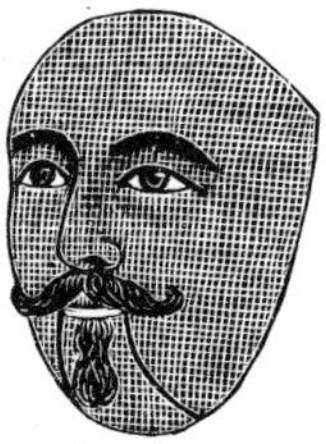

No. 5.

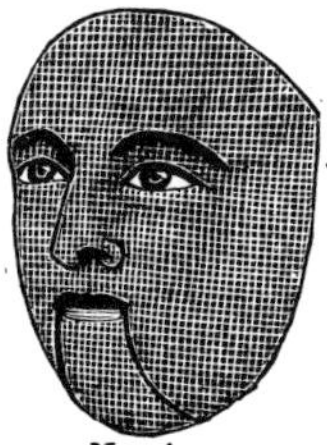

No. 4.

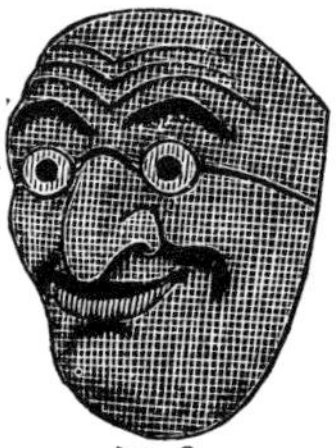

No. 3.

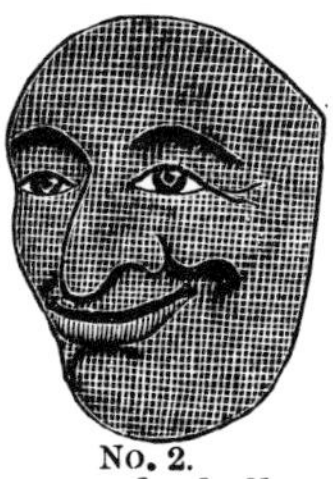

No. 2.

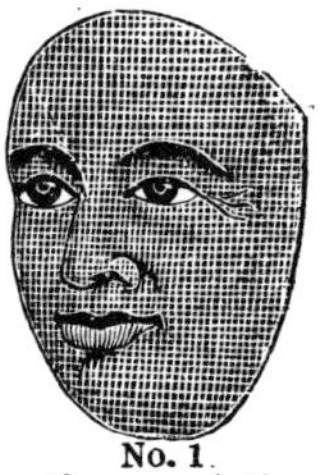

No. 1.

FRENCH WIRE MASKS.—Flesh color, (imported), for masquerade balls, parties, societies, either for Ladies' or Gentlemen's use, are very light, neat and effective, and a person with one on could not be recognized by their most intimate friends.

Nos. 1 and 4 are more for ladies and beardless men and youths.

No. 1. Plain Mask, colored to represent nature..each, $0 50
No. 2. Same as No. 1, but with colored eye-brows and moustache.......................... " 0 65
No. 3. Painted to represent Indians, Clowns, Devils, Negroes, Sports, &c..................... " 0 75
No. 4. Same as No. 1, but with mouth to open and shut..................................... " 0 75
No. 5. Same as No. 4, but with hair, moustache and goatee.................................. " 1 00
No. 6 Neatly painted, with full beard as cut No. 7, or side whiskers and moustache, or any style whisker required, assorted color hair .... " 1 25
No. 7. Same as No. 6, but with movable mouth.. " 1 50

A complete illustrated price-list of other masks will be issued in October. Send stamp.

NO 23

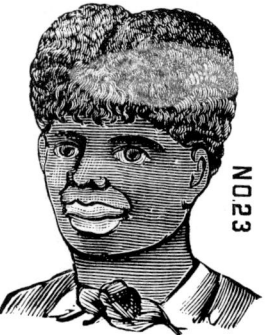

NEGRO FEMALE WENCH SCALP ATTACHMENT.

It can be put on any negro wig and will answer same as a wench's wig.

To change from a plain negro wig to a female wig, it can be put on and taken off instantly, without leaving the stage.

Price, each scalp..$1 25.

PECK & SNYDER'S PROFESSIONAL BANJOS.

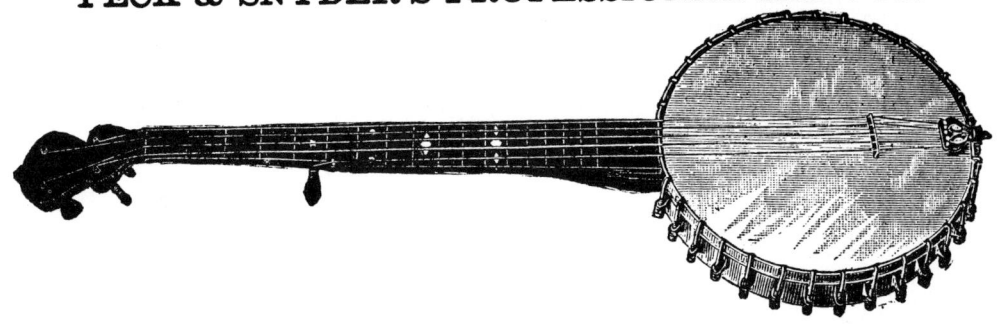

The following styles of Banjos are made by the best class of workmen in this line, only the very best materials are used in their manufacture, such as Strings, Pegs, Calf Heads, and other trimmings. All necks are made of selected Black Walnut with Scroll heads, and the finger board is either Rosewood or Ebony Veneered, with raised G. S. Frets; Hoops are grooved and are furnished with the patent Metal tailpiece. Every Banjo is thoroughly tested before leaving the factory, and guaranteed *Correct.*

No. 1. 11 inch. Rosewood Veneered Rim, Scroll Walnut Neck, R. W. Veneered finger board, with raised G. S. Frets. 20 Nickel Globe Brackets. $8.00

No. 2. 11 inch. Nickel Rim, Wire top and bottom, Plain Walnut Neck, R. W. Veneered finger board, with raised Frets, Nickel Hoop and 20 Nickel oblong Brackets. $11.00

No. 3. 11 inch. Nickel Rim, Wire top and bottom, Scroll Walnut Neck, R. W. Veneered finger board, raised Frets and Single Positions at the 5th, 7th, 9th and 12th Fret, 22 oblong Nickel Brackets, Nickel grooved hoop and Nickel tailpiece. $14.00

No. 4. 11 inch. Nickel Rim, Wire top and bottom, Scroll Walnut Neck, Ebony Veneered finger board, G. S. raised Frets with Single Positions marked at 5th, 7th, 9th and 12th Frets. Grooved Nickel hoop, 24 small oblong Nickel Brackets, with the Hexagon Safety nuts and Nickel tailpiece. $15.00

No. 5. 11 inch. Same as No. 4, but with 38 small Globe Nickel Brackets, with the Hexagon Safety nut. $16.00

No. 6. 11 inch. Nickel Rim, Wire top and bottom, Scroll Walnut Neck, Ebonized finger board, raised Frets, with Double positions marked; grooved Nickel hoop, 24 Nickeled Oblong Brackets. Nickel tailpiece, Ebony pegs and all trimmings Nickel plated both inside and outside. $17.00

The following Three Styles are only made to order, are 11 inch, and have double wired edges to rims.

No. 7. 11 inch. German Silver Rim, Fancy Scroll Walnut Neck, highly polished Ebony finger board, with raised Frets, Pearl Positions, Ebony Pegs. Selected Heads, grooved hoop, 24 oblong Brackets and Metal tailpiece. All trimmings Nickel-plated inside and outside. $20.00

No. 8. German Silver Rim, Solid Rosewood Neck, highly polished; with fancy Scroll top, Ebony finger board, with raised Frets and Pearl Positions; Ebony inlaid Pegs. Selected heads, grooved hoops, 24 Oblong Brackets and Metal tailpiece. All trimmings Nickel-plated inside and outside. $30.00

No. 9. German Silver Rim, Solid Ebony Neck (dead finish), fancy Scroll top, flush Ivory or raised Frets, inlaid fancy Pearl Positions, Ivory pegs, extra selected heads. Grooved hoops, 24 Oblong Brackets and Metal tailpiece. All trimmings nickel-plated inside and outside. $40.00

No. 10. **Lady's Banjo.**—This Banjo is made specially for ladies' use, with best selected head, and six strings. It has a scroll walnut neck, ebony veneered finger board, raised G. S. Frets, and double positions, marked at the 5th, 7th, 9th, 12th frets, also a grooved nickel hoop, 24 small hexagon safety nuts and Nickel tailpiece, $15.00

Baize Banjo Bags..Each $1.75
Leather   "   .... " 5.00
Paste-board Banjo Bags .... " 1.50

SAMBO AND DINAH.

These lively "cullud people" are exceedingly popular wherever introduced, both with young and old. They are each eleven inches high, and are dressed in bright southern costumes of the old plantation style. Their movements are so natural that one is inclined to think them endowed with real life. They will dance, to music bow, fall down, rise up, &c., without the manager being anywhere near them, and the secret of their movements can be discovered only by the closest examination.

During the short time which has elapsed since we introduced these figures. the sale has numbered many thousands, and we have yet to hear the first complaint from our patrons who have purchased them. Sambo and Dinah are intensely funny creatures, their comical antics and queer motions making them jolly company for a winter's evening, especially to those who enjoy a hearty laugh.

By mail, post paid, price 15 cents each, both for 25 cents.

Beards, Whiskers, Moustaches, Wigs, &c., for Theatrical and Amateur use, Detectives, Fancy Dress Balls, &c.

The Wigs are made with either a tape or spring at the back, by which means they can be regulated to any size. The colors kept in most of the following goods are Black, White, Grey, Light Brown, Dark Brown, Fair, Red, and Ginger Red. No wigs lent out on hire. Any wig can be made to order.

White Old Man	$4.50
Iron Grey	4.50
Yankee	4.50
Irish (see cut No. 9)	4.50
Crop (all colors)	4.50
Fright	5.00
Negro (see cut No. 1)	1.25
" (white old man)	1.50
" (grey old man) see cut No. 3	1.50
" (with top knot)	1.50
" (wench)	5.00
Sir Peter Teazle	5.00
Shylock	4.50
Court Wig with Bag	3.50
Court Wig with Tie	3.50
Paul Pry	4.50
Dundreary	5.50
Light Dress Wig, with parting (see cut No. 13)	5.50
Rough Irishman	4.00
Flaxen Country Boy	4.00
Physician or Lawyer (White)	5.00
Gentlemanly Irish, with parting	5.00
Bald Wigs, Grey or White	4.00
Rip Van Winkle	4.50
Grey Dress Wig, with parting	4.50
White Dress Wig, with parting	4.50
Clowns, in colors	4.00
Pantaloon, Wig and Beard	5.00
Robinson Crusoe	4.50
Monk	4.00
Box and Cox, 2 Wigs, each Wig	3.50
Chinaman, with Pigtail	5.00

LADIES.

Court Wig	$6.50
Grand Duchess	6.50
Lady Teazle	7.00
Marie Antoinette	7.50
Mother-in-Law	5.50
Female, plain, Long Hair, so that a lady can do up as she wishes; a really fine Wig	10.00
Ladies' Wigs, Blonde, Light and Dark Brown and Black, made up in present fashion	5.50

BEARDS, WHISKERS, MOUSTACHES, &c.

Side Whiskers and Moustache on Wire, No. 8	1.50
Side Whiskers and Moustache, on Wire, superior	1.75
Side Whiskers, no Moustache, Wire	1.00
Side Whiskers and Moustache, Gauze	2.00
Side Whiskers and Moustache, on Gauze, superior	2.25
Side Whiskers, without Moustache on Gauze	1.50
Side Whiskers, without Moustache on Gauze, superior	1.75
Full Beard on Wire, No. 6	1.75
Full Beard, superior, on Wire	2.00
Full Beard, without Moustache (see cut No. 10)	1.50
Full Beard no Moustache, superior	1.75
Moustache on Wire (see cut No. 2)	0.25
Imperials (see cut No. 7)	0.30
Chin Beard and Whiskers, combined, for Irish characters (see cut No. 12). Price	1.00 each.
Moustaches on Wire, No. 4	0.40
Moustaches on Gauze, No. 5	0.40
Moustaches on Gauze, superior	0.50

Crape Hair.—For making False Whiskers, Moustaches, &c.
Colors: Black, White, Light Brown, Dark Brown, Iron Grey and Red. Price, per yard.........$0.30

Just published, "*Stage Costume;*" Practical hints on the above, including instructions and illustrated patterns for making Hats, Boots, Sword Belts, Lace Ornaments, Ballet Shirts, and other necessary articles of costume required by Actors. A most valuable work for amateurs and professionals. Written by Cyril Bowen. Price 40 cents.

The Carnival of Authors, containing full directions for producing this magnificent entertainment in all its details of organization, with description of the main Stage, the eight Booths, the Grand Entree, the Fan Drill, the Minuet, and over 112 scenes from the works of the principal authors of the world. All of which can be used separately or together, for hall and parlor performances, as full particulars of costume, position, and grouping are given by a manager of long and varied experience, who has selected them from the best Carnivals and from his original novelties. Price 25 cents.

Peck & Snyder's Popular Make-up Boxes.—By the introduction of Grease Pains, the art of "Making-up" has been very much simplified, and rendered more effective.

A further important advantage is, that being of a greasy nature, they are to a great extent impervious to perspiration.

They are made in various colors, viz: Light Flesh, Dark Flesh, Brown, Blue, Black and White. Ladies, too, will find this an invaluable addition to their dressing-case. Sold in neat cases, with full instructions, and containing the above colors. Price 75 cents per box. Chrome and red are also kept in stock. Single sticks of above, 15 cents. Large box, each, $1.25.

Make-up Book.—How to "Make-up." A practical guide for Amateurs, &c., showing, by a series of Novel Illustrations, the manner in which the face may be "Made-up" to represent the different stages of Life, viz: Youth, Manhood, Maturity, Old Age, &c., with Twenty-three Colored Illustrations, 50 cents.

Make-up Box for Professionals.—Contains everything necessary for making up the face, viz.: Rouge, Pearl Powder, Whiting, Mongolian, Ruddy Rouge, Powdered Antimony, Joining Paste, Violet Powder, Box and Puff; Crome, Blue, Burnt Cork, Pencils for the Eyelids, Spirit Gum, Indian Ink, Burnt Umber, Camel Hair Brushes, Hares' Foot, Wool, Crape Hair, Cold Cream, Paint Saucer, Miniature Puffs, Scissors and Looking Glass. Each article is of the best quality. Packed neatly in a Strong, Cloth-covered Box, $4.00: Elegant Tin Case, $5.00. We can strongly recommend the Tin Cases as being very durable. The above articles to be had separately.

As amateurs do not, as a general thing, know how to get the different articles needed in giving their performances, or even what those accessories are, we have decided to keep a stock of the best of their several kinds, which are all perfectly harmless, and offer them as below—

Tableaux Lights.—These are always used to heighten the effect of a scene, and anyone who has witnessed any spectacular play knows that they are indispensable. Our Tableaux Lights are very easily used and are of the best manufacture. They are not liable to spontaneous combustion, and are expressly made for amateurs. They only require to be ignited in an ordinary flower-pot saucer. Plainest directions accompany each. We have the following colors: red, green, blue. All Colors, prices each 25 cents.

We particularly recommend the Red and Green, as they burn entirely without smoke or fumes. Blue cannot be made without a little sulphur. Our lights are dazzling in their brilliancy, requiring no reflectors.

Colored Fire in Bulk.—Put up in half-pound packages. Not less than half a pound of each color is sold in *Bulk*.
Price per pound $1.75. Per half pound $1.00

Magnesium Tableaux Lights.—A metal capable of being ignited by a common match, and burning with great brilliancy, producing a light that can be seen thirty miles. Unequalled in beauty and brilliancy. This is the best light for moonlight and statuary. It is so intense that it causes gas-light to cast a shadow. To light it, undo half an inch of the metal and hold it well in the flame.
Price each package 25 cents, per dozen $2.50

Blue.—For unshaven Faces. This is very necessary in low comedy characters. Per box 30 cents.

Prepared Burnt Cork.—For Negro Minstrels. This article we can recommend as it can be taken off as easily as put on, in which it differs from most all others manufactured. In tin boxes enough for 25 performances. Price per box 40 cents. Per pound $1.50. Per half pound $1.00.

Carmine.—For the face and to heighten the effect of the Burnt Cork in Negro characters. A most brilliant color. Price per packet 30 cents.

Chrome.—For sallow complexions, also for lightening the eyebrows, moustaches, &c, Price per box 25 cents.

Prepared Dutch Pink.—For pale, sallow, and wan complexions. Price per box 25 cents.

Email Noir.—To stop out teeth for old men characters, witches, &c. *See Make-up Book. Cannot be sent by mail.* 40 cents.

Prepared Fuller's Earth.—To powder the face before "making-up." In elegant box 30 cents.

Joining Paste.—For joining bald fronts of wigs to the forehead. Price per stick 15 cents.

Lightning for Private Theatricals.—Package containing the necessary material and full instructions for producing the same without danger.
Per package 25 cents.

Lining Color.—For wrinkling the face. This being a liquid, obviates the necessity of mixing color for this purpose. The bottle to be well shaken. Brown or Black. *Cannot be sent by mail.*
Small bottle 15 cents, large 25 cents.

Mascaro or Water Cosmetique.—For darkening the eyebrows and moustaches without greasing them and making them prominent. A most useful article. In neat case with looking-glass and ebony brush complete. It can be applied by wetting in cold or warm water Brown or black. 60 cents.

Miniature Puffs.—For applying powders to the delicate parts of the face. Per pair 25 cents.

Mongolian.—For Indians, Mulattoes, &c.
Price per box 30 cents

Beards, Wigs, Whiskers, Moustaches. Negro Wigs, small Mutton Chop Side Whiskers on Wire, &c., &c., for Theatricals, Detectives, Street Parades, Home Amusements and all purposes.

The Wigs are made with either a tape or spring at the back, by which means they can be regulated to any size. **To get an exact fit send size of Hat worn.** The colors kept in most of the above goods are Black, White, Grey, Light Brown, Dark Brown, Fair, Red, and Ginger Red.

For a more complete description of above goods, see next page. Send for complete illustrated price list of all hair goods, also Grease Paints, Burnt Cork, Colored Fires, Make up Boxes, Clogs, Shoes, Uniforms, Magic and Sleight of Hand Tricks, Musical Instruments, &c. Sent by mail for 10 cents.

THEATRICAL AND FANCY COSTUME WIGS.

(For Illustrations of all these goods, see next page.)

NOTICE.—In ordering Wigs, Beards, etc., be particular to mention the Color desired. The size of a hat worn by a gentleman will usually indicate the proper size of Wig, but if a more exact or nice fit is desired, measure the head with a tape measure as follows:

No. 1.—Around the head, beginning at edge of hair in middle of forehead, then to top of base of right ear, then around base of skull, touching top of base of left ear to point of beginning.

No. 2.—From same point of starting, measure over the top of the head to middle of nape of neck.

No. 3.—Across over top of head from ear to ear.

No. 4.—Around back of head from temple to temple, (edge of hair.) We make our Wigs either with a tape or spring at the back, by which means they can be regulated almost to any size. The Colors we keep mostly on hand are Black, White, Grey, Light Brown, Dark Brown, Fair and Red. We can make up any Wig to order.

BEARDS, WHISKERS AND MOUSTACHES OF EXCELLENT QUALITY.

These are of two kinds, viz.: Mounted on Wire and Mounted on Gauze, the latter being much the best. We can furnish any desired color. Be sure in ordering to mention the color desired.

Cut No. A.—Represents a gentleman with Dress Wig and smooth face.
Price of Wig, any Color, $5 00 each.

Cut No. B.—Represents a gentleman with Moustache.
Price on Gauze .... 40 Cents.   Of Superior Make .... 50 Cents.
No. 2, on Wire .... 25 "   No. 4, on Wire, Superior Make .... 40 "

Cut No. C.—Represents a gentleman with Moustache and Goatee on Gauze.
Price of Moustache and Goatee .... 70 cts.   Price of Goatee separate .... 30 cts.

Cut No. D.—Represents a gentleman with Side Whiskers.
Price on Gauze .... $1 50 Each.   Side Whiskers on Wire $1 00
Of Superior Make .... 1 75 "   Small Mutton Chop Side Whiskers on Wire, 50 cts. Per Set.

Cut No. E.—Represents gentleman with Lord Dundreary Side Whiskers and Moustache Combined.
Price on Wire.... $1 50 Each.   On Wire, Superior.... $1 75 Each.   Made on Gauze, $2 00 Each.

Cut No. F.—Represents a gentleman with Full Beard. Made on Gauze..........each, $4 00
Price on Wire..... $1 75 Each.   On Wire of Superior Make .... $2 00 Each.

Cut No. G.—Represents the Chin Beard and Whiskers Combined and is used for Irish Characters. Made on Wire only, and made of any color hair.   Price, $1 00 Each.

Cut No. H.—Represents gentlemen with the Long Hair Wig, used for Cow Boy, Yankee or Buffalo Bill characters.   Price, $4 50 to $6 00 Each.

Cut No. I.—Represents Ladies' Circassian Wig, made up of best quality hair in light or dark colors.   Price, $7.00 each.

CRAPE HAIR.—An excellent imitation of Natural Hair, used for making Beards, Whiskers and Moustaches. We can furnish any color.   Price per yard, 30 cts.

NEGRO MINSTREL WIGS OF THE BEST QUALITY AND MAKE.

		Each.
No. 19.	Negro Fright Wig, with mechanical contrivance for making the hair stand on end	$4 00
" 20.	Old Man's Negro Wig, either white or gray, with bald top	1 50
	With eyebrows and whiskers to match	2 50
" 21.	Negro End Men's Wig, with top-knot	1 50
" 22.	Negro Stump Speech and Comic Wig, for comic business	3 00
Plain Black Negro Wig for first part use		1 25
Short Crop Plush Negro Wigs		1 50
Negro Wench Wigs, with curls		5 00
Burnt Cork to black up with	per pound,	1 50
Burnt Cork to black up with	per half pound,	1 00
Burnt Cork, for ten performances	per box,	40
Rouge, for use on the lips, to make a large mouth	"	30
Mongolian, for Chinese and Indian Character	"	40
Whiting, for Clown Face and Pantomine	"	40

DANCING CLOGS, SONG AND DANCE SHOES, WOODEN SHOES, &c.

No. A

Dancing Clogs, Song and Dance Shoes, Sandals and Rattles.

Red, Black or Blue Morocco Clogs, fancy stitched, wood soles, all in one piece, See cut A...Per pair, $3 00
Brass Jingles, plain round, with hole and screws
    Per set, of four, 25

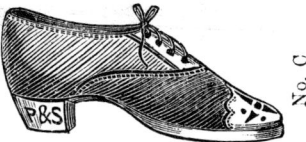

No. B   **Silver and Gold Leather Clogs.**   No. C

Fancy stiched with silk Gold or Silver, (See cut B).........................Per pair, $5 00
Fine kip Dancing Clogs... " 3 00
" " " extra Tips. (See cut C)......................... " 3 50
Brass Heels extra.. " 25
" with Rattles. Extra... " 50

No. D   No. E   No. H

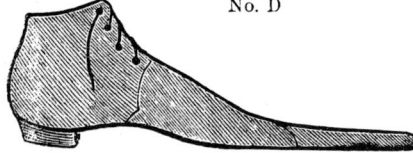
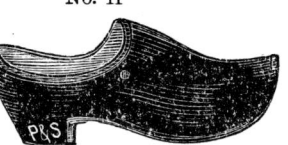

Song and Dance Shoes. (See cut D. 12, 14, 16, 18 and 20 inches long................Pair pair, $5 50
Dutch Clogs. (See cut E).. " 3 50
Wooden Shoes for Dutch Comedians, and also used extensively in Dyeing Establishments, Hotel Kitchens, Laundries, Wine Cellars, Farm Dairies, etc. (See cut H.)......................Per pair, $2 00
Clogs, Song and Dance Shoes, etc., sent by mail upon receipt of 25 cents extra.

No. F   No. G

Spring Clogs with Rattles, (See cut F) Per pair $6 00

Roman Sandals of any Fancy Colored Leather. (See cut G,).......................Per pair $6 00

Roman Sandals of Gold or Silver Leather " 7 00

EASY METHOD OF CLOG DANCING.

By WILLIAM F. BACON, Teacher to the Profession.

Containing instructions especially adapted to those not within the reach of a teacher. The steps in this edition are for beginners. An inexperienced person needs very easy steps to commence with, and then gradually advances to more difficult ones. This method is the plan of the author, and he assures all that any one with practice, and his rules, can become proficient.
    Price 25 cents.

NEGRO, IRISH AND DUTCH ONE ACT SKETCH BOOK.

As the name indicates, this is a book composed of One Act Sketches, the very book so many amateurs want; supplying the need of Clubs and Parties giving performances. This book contains twenty-one Sketches, all one act, and with from two to six characters.
    Price, 10 cents.

MUSICAL INSTRUMENTS,
A complete and full line kept constantly on hand.

VIOLINS.—NO BOWS.

No.	Description	Price
No. 2	Red shaded, Common	Each $ 1 50
" 3	" good shape	" 1 80
" 6	" " better, etc	" 2 25
" 8	Imitation Flamed Wood, Lion Head	" 3 00
" 9	" " neatly made, good	" 3 50
" 15	Brown, highly polished, good	" 4 00
" 17	" well formed, neatly made	" 5 25
" 21	Plain, neatly made, dark	" 6 00
" 80	Brown, STAINER, Swell Top and Back	" 5 50
" 23	Plain, well made, reddish Brown, Ebony Trimmings	" 7 00
" 81	GLASS, deep brown, STAINER Model	" 9 50
" 84	" shaded " oil finish	" 12 00
" 91	SCHWEIZER, shaded brown, neat	" 9 00
" 92	GUARNERIUS, nut brown, fine smooth finish	" 15 00
" 98	STAINER Model, highly polished, light shade	" 10 00
" 99	" " "	" 12 50
" 131	" " " brown	" 13 00
" 132	" " " selected wood, etc., fine	" 18 00
" 94	" handsome Bird Eye Maple Sides, Back and Neck	" 20 00
" 91	STRADUARIUS, oil varnished, very fine imitation of old violin	" 25 00

VIOLIN BOWS.
FULL LENGTH.—BEECH WOOD.

No.	Description	Price
No. 10	Black Stick, Bone Frog, Black Slide, Round Bone Button and Tip	Each $ 75
" 11	Red " Ebony " White " " " " "	" 60
" 12	" " " " " Octagon " " "	" 70
" 18	Imitation Snakewood, Ebony Frog, White Slide, Round Bone Button and Tip	" 65
" 22	Red Stick, Good Ebony Frog, Pearl Slide, Octagon Bone Button and Tip	" 75
" 25	Imitation Snakewood " " " German Silver " " "	" 1 00
" 30	Red Stick, " " " " " " "	" 1 25
" 36	Imitation Snakewood, " " " " " " "	" 1 50

VIOLIN STRINGS.

No.	Description	Price
No. 9	Violin E, 4 lengths, Silk, superfine quality	Each 25 cts.
" 8	" E, 4 " " extra "	" 20 "
" 4	" E, 3 " " " "	" 15 "
" 20	" E, 4 " Italian ⎰ Not Transparent. ⎱	" 25 "
" 20	" A, 2½ " " ⎱ For Artists only. ⎰	" 20 "
" 20	" D, 2½ " "	" 30 "
" 40	" E, 4 " German ⎰ Unfinished, ⎱	" 20 "
" 40	" A, 2½ " " ⎱ Transparent, ⎰	" 20 "
" 40	" D, 2½ " " ⎰ Durable. ⎱	" 25 "
" 15	" E, 2½ lengths, German, white, good quality	" 10 "
" 33	" A, 2½ " French, " "	" 10 "
" 35	" D, 2½ " " " "	" 10 "
" 32	" G, 1 length, American, Pure Silver, not coiled	" 75 "
" 33	" G, 1 " " Silvered Wire, "	" 20 "
" 34	" G, 1 " " Best Quuality, coiled	" 15 "
" 35	" G, 1 " " Red Silk Ends, good quality. coiled	" 10 "

STEEL VIOLIN STRINGS.

No.	Description	Price
No. 60	Violin E, 1 length, Steel, with Knots	Each 10 cts.
" 65	" A. " " " "	" 10 "
" 75	" D, 1 " Covered, with Steel Wire Centre	" 10 "
" 80	" G, 1 " " " " "	" 10 "

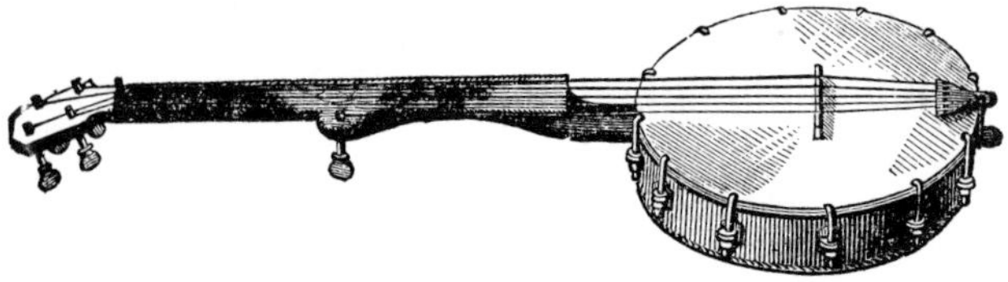

BANJOS.

A LARGE AND COMPLETE ASSORTMENT.

No. 0	8 inch, Sheepskin, Tack Head Maple Rim	Each	$ 1 70
" 1¼	10 " " " "	"	2 00
" 1	12 " " " "	"	2 25
" C	8 " " Brass Rim, 4 Brackets	"	2 25
" 2¼	10 " " 4 Brackets, No. 0, Maple Rim	"	2 50
" 2	12 " " 6 " " 0, "	"	3 20

CALF SKIN HEAD, STAGE SIZE 11 INCH, WITH FRETS.

No. 20	Maple, Walnut Neck, 6 Brackets, No. 5	Each	$ 4 50
" 4½	Brown, " 8 " " 1	"	5 60
" 25	Maple, " 12 " " 5	"	6 00
" 5½	Brown, White Wood Neck, 16 Brackets, No. 0	"	6 50
" 6	" " " 24 " " 0	"	8 00
" 9½	Rosewood, Walnut Neck, 12 " " 5	"	10 00
" 12½	" " 20 " " 8	"	12 00
" 14	Maple, " 12 " " 5, Patent Head	"	10 00
" 10¾	Rosewood, " 16 " " 8, "	"	15 00
" 93	Ebonized Rim and Neck, 10 Brass Brackets, No. 5	"	7 00
" 94	" " " 12 Nickel Brackets, No. 8½	"	11 00
" 95	" " " 24 " " 8½	"	17 00
" 96	" " " 16 " " 19½	"	18 00
" 97	" " " 24 " " 19½	"	22 00
" 98	" " " 20 " " 19½, German Silver Finger Board	"	25 00

BANJO TRIMMINGS. (Brackets).

No. 0	Brass Cast Shield, with Hook and Nuts	Dozen	$1 70
" 1	" " Eagle, " "	"	2 00
" 2	" Heavy Shield, " "	"	2 50
" 2½	The same, Nickel Plated, " "	"	4 00
" 4	Brass, large Spread Eagle, " "	"	2 50
" 5	Brass, Oblong, " "	"	2 50
" 5½	The same, Nickel Plated, " "	"	4 00
" 8	Brass, Globe, " "	"	2 50
" 8½	The same, Nickel Plated, " "	"	4 00

BANJO CASES.

No. 8	Pasteboard, good quality	Each	$1 50
" 12	Wood, Hook and Lock, for 11 inch Banjo	"	5 00

BANJO WRENCHES.

No. 8	Brass, Shape of Key	Each	25 cts.

BANJO THIMBLES.

No. 9	German Silver	Each	20 cts.

BANJO TAILPIECES.

No. 4	Small, Black, plain	Each	10 cts.
" 6	" Ebony, " extra	"	15 "
" 8	" Black Pearl, Inlaid	"	15 "
" 15	" Ebony, " "	"	50 "
" 18	" " " "	"	75 "
" 28	Nickel Plated, Extra, New Style	"	40 "

BANJO BRIDGES.

No. 2	Whitewood, Cedar, etc., assorted	Each	10 cts.
" 4	Black, Rosewood, etc., "	"	10 "
" 8	Ebony, assorted Patterns	"	10 "
" 10	" Pearl Inlaid	"	25 "
" 12	Ivory, Plain	"	75 "

BANJO STRINGS.

No. 1	Gut, 1st String, 2 length, very thin	Each	15 cts.
" 2	" 2d " same as Violin E	"	15 "
" 3	" 3d " " " A	"	15 "
" 6	Covered 4th String, on finest white Silk, American	"	15 "
" 9	" 4th " " Best Gut, American	"	15 "
" 1½	Steel Wire, 1st String	Pr. Doz.	$ 50
" 2½	" 2d "	"	50
" 3½	" 3d "	"	50
" 4½	" 4th " Covered	"	1 00

CONCERTINAS.

No.	Keys	Description	Price
1	10 Keys,	Imitation Rosewood Concertina	$1 80
2	20 "	" " "	2 00
33	20 "	Mahogany, good "	5 00
36	20 "	Rosewood, Leather Bellows, Anglo-German, Broad Reeds	10 50
38	20 "	Mahogany, " " " " "	11 00

20 Keys, with 2 Sets Reeds, Organ or Celestial.

No.	Description	Price
3	Imitation Rosewood.....Each	$3 25
12¼	Rosewood, German Silver Edges, Double Bellows...... "	5 00
15¼	" " " Inlaid, Double Bellows...... "	5 50
18¼	" " " Trumpets, Double Bellows...... "	6 00
21	" " " " "	7 00
25	" " " " "	8 00
27	" " " " "	10 00
28	" " " " "	10 00
29	" " " " "	12 00
30	" " " " "	14 00
39	Anglo-German, Rosewood........ "	6 00
50	" " Leather Bellows, fine........ "	12 00
50¼	Same as No. in Wood Case........ "	13 00
55	AnglGerman, Mahogany, Leather Bellows, fine........ "	13 00
55¼	Same as No 55, in Wood Case........ "	15 00
70	Anglo-German, Mahogany, very fine........ "	20 00
70¼	Same as No. 70, in Wood Case........ "	22 00

Nos. 50, 55 and 70, have Broad Reeds.

FIFES.

No.	Description	Price
5	B or C. Maple, no Rings......Each	$ 35
7	B or C, Maple Black, German Silver Rings........ "	50
8	B or C, Rosewood, Brass Rings........ "	60
9	B or C, Cocoa, Brass Rings........ "	85
10	B or C, Cocoa, German Silver Rings........ "	1 00
10½	B or C, Cocoa, G. S. Rings, G. S. Mouthpiece........ "	1 75
11	B or C, Ebony, German Silver Rings........ "	1 25
12	B or C, Ebony, G. S. Rings, G. S. Mouthpiece........ "	2 00
21	B or C, German Silver, Raised Holes........ "	2 50

Also, Fancy Ebony Fifes.

Tin Fifes, 10 to 14 inches long........Each 15c. to 30c.

Flute Mouthpieces, Britannia, best........Each 50 cts.
Fife "   " Brass Screw........ " 35 "

FLAGEOLETS.

No.	Description	Price
64 B	1 Key, Boxwood, Black........Each	$2 50
64 C	1 " " " .... "	2 25
65 B	1 " " " Bone Rings........ "	3 00
65 C	1 " " " " " .... "	2 50
61 B	1 " Cocoa, German Silver Rings........ "	4 50
61 C	1 " " " " " .... "	4 00
80 C	4 " " " " " .... "	5 00
86 C	6 " " " " " .... "	6 00

FLAGEOLET FLUTE.

No.	Description	Price
3	Boxwood, One Key, Bone Rings........Each	$4 00
90	Cocoa, " German Silver Rings........ "	6 00

FLAGEOLETS WITH PICCOLO.

No.	Description	Price
70	Boxwood, 1 German Silver Key, Tipped, in box........Each	$4 00
72	" 5 " " " " " .... "	6 00
75	Cocoa, 4 " " " " " .... "	6 00
76	" 6 " " " " " .... "	7 00

FLUTES WITH 1 KEY, IN BOXES.

No. 2 D Maple, Black, Bone Rings..	Each	$1 50
" 3 D Boxwood, " " "	"	2 50
" 9 D or G Cocoa, German Silver Tipped—American...............	"	3 50
" 12 D Cocoa, " " " " with Slide....................	"	5 00
" 3 F or G Boxwood, Black Bone Rings...................................	"	2 00
" 9 F Cocoawood, German Silver Tipped—American..............	"	3 50
" 12 F " " " " with Slide............................	"	4 50

FLUTES WITH 4 KEYS, IN BOXES.

No. 15 D or F Boxwood, German Silver Tipped with Slide.........	Each	$5 50
" 24 D or F Cocoawood, " " " "	"	6 50
" 24½ D Cocoa, " " " Slide, Cork Joints, &c........	"	7 00

FLUTES WITH 6 KEYS, IN BOXES.

No. 18 D or F Boxwood, German Silver Tipped, with Slide.......	Each	$7 50
" 26 F Cocoawood, " " " " with Cork Joints, &c......	"	7 50

WITH 8 KEYS, IN PASTEBOARD BOXES.

No. 28 D Grenadilla, Slide, German Silver Tipped....................	Each	$12 00
" 28¼ D " " " Cork Joints, &c..................	"	13 00
" 28½ D " " " Embouchure........................	"	15 00
" 28¾ D " " " Head and Slide Joint............	"	20 00
" 29 D " " Ivory Head, Cork Joints, &c...................	"	32 00

SHEEP AND CALF SKIN HEADS.

12 inch Sheepskins for 10 inch Tambourine, Drum or Banjo................	Each	$	30
14 "	"	12 "	"	"	35
16 "	"	14 "	Drum...................................	"	50
20 "	"	16 "	"	"	75
22 "	"	17 "	"	"	1 00
28 "	"	24 "	Brass Drum	"	1 80
30 "	"	26 "	"	"	2 00
32 "	"	28 "	"	"	2 00
34 "	"	30 "	"	"	2 00
36 "	"	32 "	"	"	2 50
12 " Calfskin for 10 inch Tambourine, Drum or Banjo................	"	40
14 "	"	12 "	"	"	75
16 "	"	14 "	Drum...................................	"	1 00
20 "	"	16 "	"	"	1 75
22 "	"	17 "	"	"	2 00
28 "	"	24 "	Brass Drum	"	3 80
30 "	"	26 "	"	"	4 50
32 "	"	28 "	"	"	5 60
34 "	"	30 "	"	"	6 00
36 "	"	32 "	"	"	7 20
38 "	"	34 "	"	"	8 00
40 "	"	36 "	"	"	8 50

Prices of above subject to Change.

BUGLES

of Brass, Copper and German Silver for Officers, &c., each, $4.50 to $12.00.

AMERICAN ZITHER.

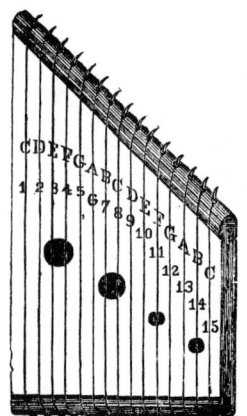

The most popular String Instrument ever invented. Just out and creates great excitement.

The great American Zither is something similar to a harp in construction, and played in a like manner to a Guitar. The music it produces is very sweet and effective, and as an accompaniment to other instruments, and for singing, it excels anything of the kind ever introduced. The strings are all numbered, and we have prepared Sheet Music to accompany each instrument, which enables ANYONE to perform upon it AT ONCE.

Price, 10 Strings, with Instructor and five tunes, $1.00; 15 Strings, with Instructor and eight tunes, $1.50. Carefully packed and sent to any address on receipt of price.

INSTRUCTION BOOKS FOR MUSICAL INSTRUMENTS.

Winner's New Primer for German Accordeon, Banjo, Concertina, Clarionet, Flute, Guitar, Piano, Violin...	each	$0 50
Bertini's Piano—Complete Edition...	"	2 50
Moralt Zither Instructor in German...	"	2 25
" " " English...	"	2 80
Ryan's Tune Instructor for German Accordeon, German Concertina, Banjo, Bugle, Cabinet Organ, Cornet, Clarionet, Drum, Fife, Flageolet, Flute, Guitar, Piano, Violin, Violoncello...................	"	50

TAMBOURINES.

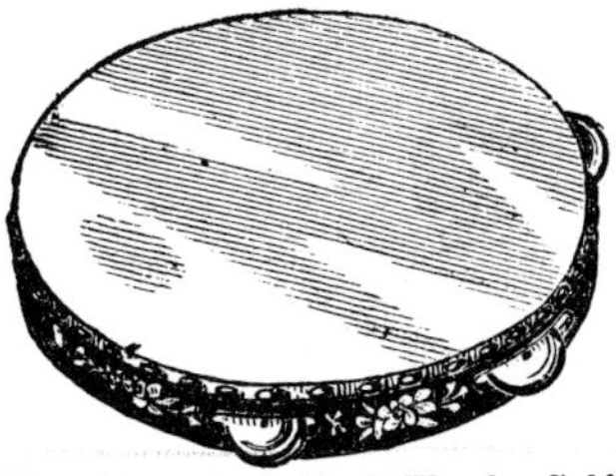

No.							
0	8 inch Tack-Head—Sheepskin, 3 sets Brass Jingles					Each	$ 75
2	12 "	"	"	3 "	"	"	1 00
4	10 "	"	"	4 "	" Fancy Painted.	"	1 50
5	10 "	Screw-Head	"	3 "	"	"	1 75
6	12 "	"	"	4 "	"	"	2 00
7	10 "	"	Calfskin	3 "	"	"	2 25
9	10 "	"	"	3 "	" fine, fancy	"	2 50
10	12 "	"	"	4 "	" " "	"	3 00
14	12 "	Tack-head	"	6 "	" " "	"	2 35
No. 19	10 inch Tack Head—Calfskin, 6 sets German Silver Jingles, German Silver Rim					"	5 50
" 20	10 "	"	" 5 "	"	" Rosewood Venered	"	3 00
" 21	12 "	"	" 6 "	"	" "	"	3 25
" 2	Tambourine Jingles—Brass					Per Doz.	25
" 3	German Silver Tambourine Jingles					"	1 00
" 2	Tambourine Screws, Brass, with Trimming					"	2 00

TRIANGLES.

No. 4	Steel, Heavy,	4 inch	with Handles		Each	$0 75
" 5	" "	5 "	"		"	0 85
" 6	" "	6 "	"		"	1 00
" 7	" "	7 "	"		"	1 25
" 8	" "	8 "	"		"	1 35
" 10	" "	10 "	"		"	2 00
" 12	" "	12 "	"		"	2 50

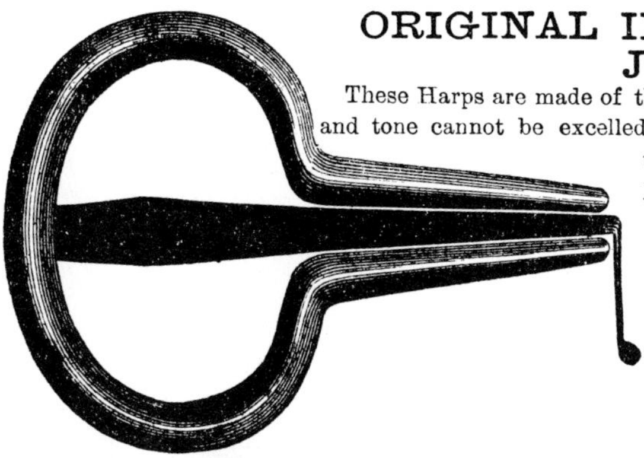

ORIGINAL IMPROVED T. P. P. IRISH JEWS' HARP.

These Harps are made of the very best silvered steel, and for beauty of finish and tone cannot be excelled; the frames are nickle plated, with brass tipped tongues.

No. 2	Size, 2½x1⅝ in., by mail, post-paid		each	20c.
" 3	" 2¾x2	" " "	"	25c.
" 4	" 3 x2¼	" " "	"	30c.
" 5	" 3¼x2¼	" " "	"	40c.
" 6	" 4 x3	" " "	"	55c.
" 7	" 4½x3¼	" " "	"	85c.

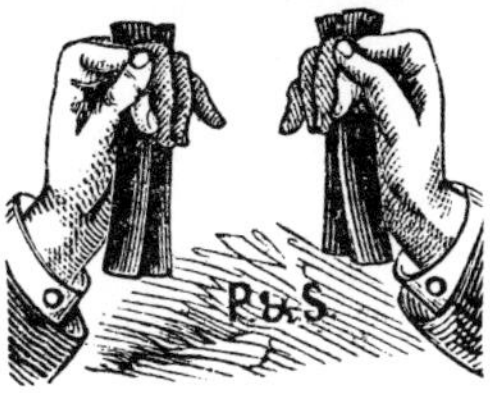

CLAPPERS, OF EBONY OR ROSEWOOD.

Ebony, 7 or 8 inches long, 1¼ inch long, 1¼ inch wide, set of 4, by mail	$1 00
Rosewood, 7 or 8 inches long, 1¼ inch wide, set of 4	75
Rosewood, 5½ inches long, 1 inch wide, set of 4	40
Black Walnut, 7 inches long, wide, patent, set of 4	40
Violet Wood, perfumed, 5 inches long by 1 inch wide, set of 4	30

MUSICAL BOXES.

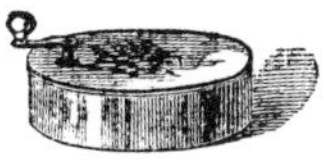

No. 1

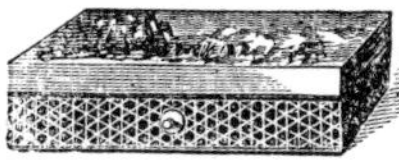

No. 2

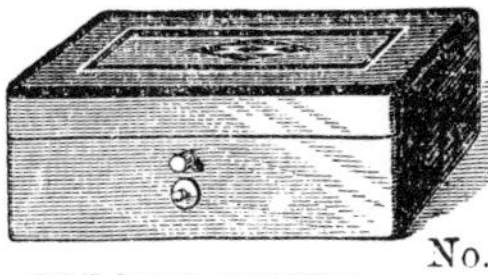

No. 5

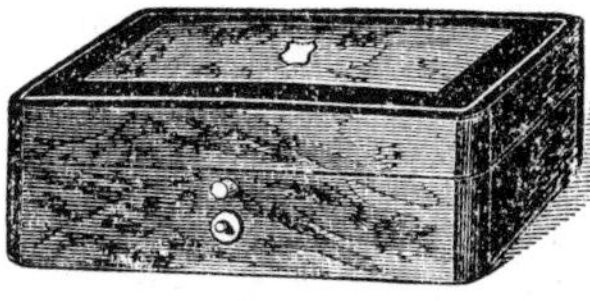

No. 11

SMALL SIZES.

No. 1	Tin, Round, with Crank, 1 Air, large size	Each	$ 2 [illegible]
" 2	" Oblong, " Spring, 2 " 2½ inch barrel	"	7 00
" 3	" " " " 3 " 2¾ " "	"	10 00

WITH GLASS COVER INSIDE.

No. 5	Wood, Inlaid, with Spring, 3 Airs, 2⅞ Inch Barrel	Each	$12 00
" 8	" " " " 4 " 2⅞ " "	"	15 00
" 11	" " " " 6 " 3½ " "	"	25 00

The above are Staple Styles. A variety of other Patterns in stock, with spring movements, inside glass cover, prices, each, $30 00 to $75 00.

GUITARS—Imported. Maple, Red and Shaded.

No.			
2	Peg Head, Polished Sound Board, good quality	Each	$ 5 00

WITH PATENT HEAD.

No.			
3¼	Polished Sound Board, good quality	Each	$ 7 00
6	Imitation Rosewood, White Edges, etc.	"	8 00
9	Red, Pearl Inlaid Sound Hole	"	9 00
12	" " " better	"	12 00
12½	" " " " New Style Metal Peg	"	14 00
14	Imitation Rosewood, plain, good	"	12 00
16	" " Pearl Sound Hole	"	12 00
17	" " " etc.	"	13 50
19	" " " " better	"	14 50
20	" " " " "	"	15 00
21	" " " " "	"	16 00
28	Bird Eye Maple, Red " " "	"	17 00
30	Ebonized Inlaid Back, Inlaid Sound Hole	"	19 00
33	Maple, Flamed Wood, Red Pearl " etc.	"	15 00

GUITAR STRINGS.

No.						
50	E or 1st String, finest English Steel Wire, Brass Knot				Each	5 cts.
51	B or 2d	"	"	"	"	5 "
52	G or 3d	"	"	"	"	5 "
61	E or 1st	"	"	" on spools	"	25 "
62	B or 2d	"	"	"	"	25 "
63	G or 3d	"	"	"	"	20 "
38	D or 4th	"	Covered, BRUNO, finest white silk		"	10 "
38	A or 5th	"	"	"	"	15 "
38	E or 6th	"	"	"	"	15 "
48	G or 3d	"	"	Steel Wire Centre	"	10 "
48	D or 4th	"	"	"	"	15 "
48	A or 5th	"	"	"	"	15 "
48	E or 6th	"	"	"	"	20 "
58	D or 4th	"	"	Fancy Silk Knot Ends	"	15 "
58	A or 5th	"	"	"	"	15 "
58	E or 6th	"	"	"	"	20 "

CASTANETTS—Spanish.

No.			
3	Ebony, large size, French	Per Set	$1 60
4	" small size, "	"	1 30
5	Boxwood, large size, "	"	1 20
6	" small size, "	"	1 00

ROSIN.

No.				
3	Small Cakes, Paper Wrappers		Each	5 cts.
6	Large " " Boxes		"	5 "
9	Small " Pasteboard Boxes		"	5 "
12	Large " " " oblong		"	10 "
14	" " " "		"	10 "
15	" " " " square		"	10 "
16	" " " "		"	15 "
18	Lipinski, large, square		"	10 "
23	French G. & B. Superior to Viliaume		"	50 "
60	For Double Bass Bows, square		"	30 "
70	" " " " French, round		"	40 "
25	For Violoncello Bows, square		"	15 "

THE OCARINA,

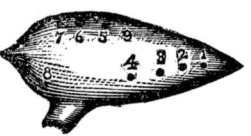

As played at Drury Lane Crystal Palace, London. Can be learned in half-an-hour. This original musical instrument is unequalled for the beauty and voice-like quality of its tone and the ease with which it can be acquired—a very little practice enabling the performer to play operatic or other melodies. It has a complete chromatic scale. A charming accompaniment to the pianoforte.

Ocarinas of Italian Clay, 9 Holes, by mail, with Music and Instructions.................Each $1 50

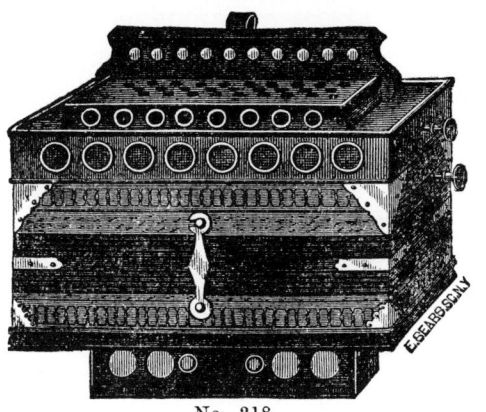

No. 218.

No. 18.

BEST GERMAN MAKE ACCORDEONS.

No.	17	6 Keys, Imitation Rosewood, with Bass Keys	Each	$1	50
"	18	8 " " " " (see cut)	"	1	80
"	19	10 " " " "	"	2	15

With Black Moulding Frame. Silver Stamped Top. Leather Cloth Bellows Folds.

No.	928	8 Keys, Imitation Rosewood, 2 Sets Reeds, 1 Stop	Each	$3	70
"	929	10 " " " 2 " " 1 "	"	4	30
"	928¼	8 " " " 1 " " 1 " 1 Bell	"	4	30
"	929¼	10 " " " 1 " " 1 " " "	"	4	90
"	928C	8 " with Nickel Plated Corners and Clasps	"	4	00
"	929C	10 " " " " "	"	4	60
"	928¼C	8 " " " " 1 Bell	"	4	60
"	929¼C	10 " " " " 1 "	"	5	20

With Black Moulding Frame. Large Size. Leather Cloth Bellows Folds.

No.	727	10 Keys, Assorted Colors, 2 Sets Reeds, 1 Stop	Each	$5	00
"	727¼	10 " " " 1 " 1 Bell	"	5	60
"	727C	10 " with Nickel Plated Corners and Clasps	"	5	30
"	727¼C	10 " " " " 1 Bell	"	5	90

With Broad Moulding Frame. Ne Plus Ultra Reeds. Double Bellows. Corners and Clasps. Large Trumpets. Mirror Back.

No.	210	10 Keys, 2 Sets Reeds, 1 Stops, Single Bellows	Each	$9	00
"	212	12 " 2 " " 1 " " "	"	10	50
"	216	10 " 2 " " 1 " Double Bellows	"	9	50
"	218	10 " 2 " " 2 " " " Italian Tremolo, (see cut No. 218)	"	11	00
"	222	10 " 3 " " 2 " " "	"	11	50

Ebonized Moulding and Top. Silver Stamped. Double Bellows. New Design Corners and Clasps.

No.	305	10 Keys, 2 Sets Reeds, 1 Stop	Each	$8	00
"	305¼	10 " 2 " " 1 " 1 Bell	"	8	60

No. 972.

Black Moulding. Silver Stamped Top. Double Bellows. With Corners and Clasps. Two Rows Keys and Four Bass Keys.

Each.

No.	970	17 Keys, 4 Sets Reeds, 2 Stops,	$15	00
"	971	19 " 4 " " 2 "	16	50
"	972	21 " 4 " " 2 " (cut 972,)	18	00

Mahogany. Rococo Covered Moulding. Heavy Corners and Clasps. Knee Rests. Two Rows Long Ivory Keys. Six Upright Bass Keys. Double Bellows.

Each.

No.	981	21 Keys, 2 Sets Reeds, 4 Stops,	$30	00
"	982	21 " 2 " " 4 " Extra Fine Leather and Gilt Bellows	33	00

Accordeon Trimmings of all kinds kept on hand.

HARMONICAS OR MOUTH ORGANS.

No. 5, 16 holes,

No. 90.

No.												
"	5	8	Holes,	Single,	Fancy and Lacquered Tin Covers (In Boxes)						Each	25 cts.
"	5	12	"	"	"	"	"	"	"			"	30 "
"	5	16	"	"	"	"	"	"	"	(see cut No. 5)		"	40 "
"	5	20	"	"	"	"	"	"	"			"	50 "
"	8	16	"	"	Brass Covers, Black Wood, Extended Ends (Zinc Plate						"	50 "
"	8	20	"	"	"	"	"	"	"			"	60 "

4 SIDE HARMONICAS. (Richter's)

No.	47	40	Holes, 4 Sides, German Silver Covers, Brass Plates			Each	$3 20
"	90	40	" 4 " Engraved German Silver Covers, Brass Plates, (see cut No. 90)			"	3 50
"	90	48	" 4 " " " " " "			"	4 20
"	90	72	" 6 " " " " " "			"	6 30
"	210	48	" 4 " " " " " Double Reed			"	6 00
"	210	72	" 6 " " " " " "			"	9 00

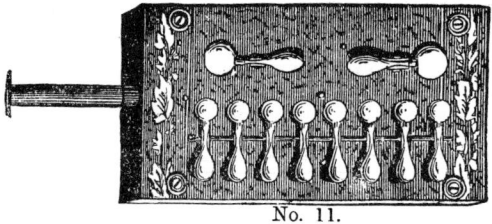
No. 11.

FLUTE HARMONICAS.

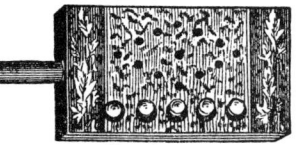
No. 3.

No.	3	5 Keys, Tin, Painted, (see cut No. 3)		Each	$ 1 25
"	6	7 " " " "		"	2 00
"	9	7 " German Silver		"	3 00
"	10	7 " " Tremolo		"	4 00
"	11	7 " and 2 Bass Keys, Tin, Painted, (see cut No. 11)		"	3 00
"	12	7 " " 2 " German Silver		"	4 20
"	12¼	7 " " 2 " and Bell		"	5 00
"	36	12 " Tin, Painted		"	4 00
"	39	12 " German Silver		"	6 00
"	52	12 " and 2 Bass Keys, German Silver		"	6 50
"	60	7 " " 4 " "		"	6 00
"	65	17 " " 4 " "		"	10 00

RICHTER CONCERTS.

No.	19	10 Holes, Single, Engraved German Silver Covers, Brass Plates		Each	$ 50
"	19	12 " " " " " "		"	65
"	100	10 " " " " " "		"	60
"	100	12 " " " " " "		"	75
"	100	20 " " " " " "		"	1 25
"	100	24 " " " " " "		"	1 50

No. 21,

CONCERT HARMONICAS.--Double Reed.

No.	21	20 Holes, Double, Engraved, German Silver Covers, Brass Plates, (see cut No. 21)		Each	$1 50
"	21	24 " " " " " "		"	1 85
"	21	32 " " " " " "		"	2 50
"	8	24 " " Brass Covers, Black Wood, Extended Ends (Zinc Plate)		"	75
"	8	32 " " " " " "		"	1 00
"	8	40 " " " " " "		"	1 25
"	5	20 " " Fancy and Lacquered Tin Covers (In Boxes)		"	50
"	5	24 " " " " " "		"	60
"	5	32 " " " " " "		"	75
"	5	40 " " " " " "		"	1 00

HALF CONCERT. LANGHAMER PATTERN.

No	285	20 Holes, Double, German Silver Covers, Wood Ends, Brass Plates		Each	$1 00
"	285	24 " " " " " "		"	1 25

LIST OF PLAYS
FOR SALE BY
PECK & SNYDER.

Suited for Amateur Performance, with the Number of Male and Female Characters in each.

PRICE, 15 CENTS EACH.

* In these pieces the Lady assumes Male attire.   (c) Means costume or powder pieces.   For One Male Character, and for pieces without Female Characters, see pages 4 and 5.

One Female Character.—A Night of Suspense.

Two Females.—A Fair Encounter.

Two Characters.—One Male and One Female.

After the Party.	Haunted Mill, operetta.	Love and Rain.	* Rifle Volunteer.
* Antony and Cleopatra.	Household Fairy.	Man that follows the Ladies.	Ring and the Keeper, operetta.
Bumble's Courtship.	Husband in Clover.	Morning Call.	Sympathy.
Conjugal Lesson.	I Love You.	One in Hand, etc.	Twenty Minutes under an Umbrella.
Forty Winks.	Locked in with a Lady.	* Pair of Pigeons.	
For Better for Worse.	Locked Out.	Peace at any Price.	
Happy Pair, A.	Love Test.	Personation.	

Three Characters.—Two Males and One Female.

Angel of the Attic (c).	Cut off with a Shilling.	Our Bitterest Foe.	Uncle's Will, Is.
Book III., Chapter I.; or, The Subterfuge.	Delicate Ground (c).	Queen of Hearts (operetta).	Unprotected Female.
Box and Cox.	* Devilish Good Joke (c).	Ruth's Romance.	Victor Vanquished (c).
Brown, the Martyr.	Jeannette's Wedding Day (c).	Silent Woman, A.	Wanted a Young Lady.
Change of System.	My Wife's Diary.	Six Months Ago.	Which shall I Marry ?
		State Prisoner (c).	

Two Females and One Male.

Fair Rosamond's Bower, burlesque.	Lady and Gent in a Perplexing Predicament.	Speak out Boldly.	Two Flats and a Sharp.
Incompatibility of Temper.	Opposite Neighbors.	Two to One.	Winning a Wife.

Four Characters.—Two Males and Two Females.

An Optical Delusion.	Cozy Couple.	* My Wife's Out.	Under the Rose.
Best Way, The.	Doubtful Victory, A.	One of You must Marry.	Who Killed Cock Robin ?
Betsy Baker.	Found in a Four-wheeler.	Only a Halfpenny.	Woman that was a Cat, The (c).
Bilious Attack, A.	Give a Dog a Bad Name.	Sweethearts, 2.	* Young Widow.
Bonnie Fish Wife.	Kiss in the Dark, A.	Terrible Secret, A.	
Comedy and Tragedy.	Mr. Joffin's Latchkey.		

One Male and Three Females.

Follow the Leader.   Extremes Meet.   Not False, but Fickle.

Three Males and One Female.

Ample Apology, An.	Dentist's Clerk.	Our New Man.	Romance under Difficulties.
Billy Doo.	* Faint Heart *did* win Fair Lady (c).	Patient Penelope, musical extravaganza (c).	Was I to Blame ?
Comical Countess } from (c). } same	Intrigue.	Villikins and Dinah, burlesque (c).	Wooing in Jest.
Lucky Hit, A (c). } original.	Matrimony (c).		Woman's the Devil.

Five Characters.—Three Males and Two Females.

Absent Man.	Cousin Peter (c).	Mistress of the } translations Mill. } from same	Storm in a Tea Cup.
Affair of Honor, An.	Day after the Wedding.	Windmill (c).	To oblige Benson.
Aged 40.	Decided Case, A.	My First Fit of the Gout.	Turn Him Out.
Area Belle.	Desperate Game, A.	My Very Last Proposal.	Tweedleton's Tail Coat.
As Like as Two Peas.	Done on Both Sides.	Nabob for an Hour.	Ugly Customer, An.
A. S. S.	Don't Judge by Appearances.	On the Sly.	Very Serious Affair, A.
Aunt Charlotte's Maid.	False and Constant.	Perfection.	We all have our Little Faults.
Borrowed Feathers.	Good for Evil, serio-comic, 2.	Philippe (c).	Whitebait at Greenwich.
Borrowed Plumes.	Keep your Eye on Her.	Poetic Proposal.	Winning Hazard, A.
Cantab, The.	Lad from the Country.	Rights and Wrongs of Women.	Who Speaks First ?
Capital Match, A.	Ladies' Battle, 3.	Sea Gulls.	Who is Who ?
Caught in his own Trap.	Larkin's Love Letters.	Silent Protector, A.	Your Vote and Interest.
Chiselling.	Lottery Ticket.	Somebody Else (c).	You Can't Marry your Grandmother.
Cool as a Cucumber.	Model of a Wife, A.		

Four Males and One Female.

Blue Devils.	His Own Enemy, drama.	Only a Clod.	State Prisoner, drama, 1.
Caught by the Cuff.	I've Eaten My Friend.	Only a Penny-a-Liner, comedietta.	Ticket of Leave.
Cup of Tea.	Keeper of the Seals.	Paul Pry Married.	Two Heads Better than One.
Curious Case, A.	Match-Making.	Sentinel.	Wilful Ward.
Family Failing (c). [Dials.	Monsieur Jaques. [ness.		
Fearful Tragedy in Seven	Mrs. Green's Snug Little Business.		

Two Males and Three Females.

Box and Cox Married.	Maid of Honor (c).	Obliging a Friend.	Pretty Piece of Business, A.
Christmas Boxes.	Mr. Scroggins.	Phantom Breakfast (c).	Twice-told Tale, A.
In for a Holiday.	My Husband's Secr.	Poor Pillicoddy.	Widow Bewitched.
Jessamy's Courtship.			

(1)

Three Males and Five Females.

Last of the Pigtails. Who's to Win Him? Pampered Menials.

Six Males and Two Females.

Bachelor Arts, 2.
Cabinet Question.
Crimeless Criminal.
Dead Shot.
Doing Banting.
Faint Heart never won Fair Lady (c).
Fighting by Proxy.
Fitzsmythe, of Fitzsmythe Hall.

Floating Beacon, 2 (c).
Follies of a Night, 2 (c).
Frederick of Prussia (c).
Jocrisse the Juggler, 3.
King Rene's Daughter (c).
Ladies of St. Cyr, 3 (c).
Last Life, 3.
Married Bachelor.
Midnight.
Midnight Watch (c).

Mummy.
My Daughter's Debut.
My Wife's Husband.
On Guard, 3.
Our Wife, 2 (c).
Porter's Knot, 2.
Review.
Rival Valets.
She Would and He Wouldn't, 2 (c).

Sink or Swim, 2.
Time Tries All, 2.
Uncle Zachary, 2.
Up for the Cattle Show.
Village Nightingale.
Weathercock.
Where there's a Will there's a Way (c).
Who Stole the Clock, musical farce.

Six Characters.—Two Males and Four Females.

Home of One's Own. | Chopsticks and Spikins. | Popping the Question. | Three Furies.

Three Males and Three Females.

Always Intended.
Anything for a Change.
Awaking.
Bobby A 1.
Bought, 3.
Doing my Uncle.
Dowager (c).
Dying for Love.
Fast Coach.
Flies in the Web, 3.

Give Me My Wife.
Goose with the Golden Eggs.
Handsome Husband, A.
House or the Home, 2..
Jacobite, 2 (c).
Lesson in Love, 3.
Little Toddlekins.
Lodgings for Single Gentlemen.
Love's Telegraph, 3 (c).

Man Proposes.
Mistaken Story, A.
More Precious than Gold.
Mrs. White.
My Dress Boots.
Observation and Flirtation.
Orange Blossoms.
Pretty Predicaments.
Sarah's Young Man.
Short and Sweet.

Silent System.
Sunshine through Clouds.
The William Simpson.
Trying It On.
Two Bonnycastles.
Two Puddifoots.
Vandyke Brown.
Very Suspicious.
Your Life's in Danger (c).
Which is Which?

Four Males and Two Females.

Alone, 3.
B. B.
Behind Time.
Blue Beard (c), oriental romance, by B. Heber.
Captain of the Watch (c).
Charles II. (c).
Daddy Hardacre, 2.
Dandelion's Dodges.

Double-bedded Room.
Fascinating Individual.
Founded on Facts.
Four Sisters.
Grimshaw, Bagshaw, and Bradshaw.
He Lies like Truth.
Irish Tutor.
I've Written to Brown.

John Wopps.
Leave it to Me.
Little Savage.
Lucky Sixpence.
Match in the Dark.
Model Husband.
New Footman.
Nursey Chiokweed.
Old Gooseberry.

One too many.
Petticoat Government.
Phenomenon in Smock Frock
Real and Ideal.
Rough Diamond.
Secret.
Siamese Twins.
Station House.
Withered Leaves.

Five Males and One Female.

Blow in the Dark.
Cherry Bounce.
Chesterfield Thinskin.

Done Brown.
Good for Nothing.
Lucky Hit (c).

Practical Man.
Retained for the Defence.

Unlucky Friday.
Wicked Wife, A (c).

Seven Characters.—Four Males and Three Females.

Bowled Out.
Brother Bill and Me.
Chapter of Accidents.
Clockmaker's Hat.
Cure for the Fidgets.
Dearest Mamma.
Did I Dream It?
Englishman's House is his Castle.

Green-Eyed Monster, 2.
Hold your Tongue.
Husband to Order, 2 (c).
If I had a £1000 a year.
John Smith.
Mad as a Hatter.
My Turn Next.
My Wife's Dentist.
My Wife's Second Floor.

Nice Quiet Day, A.
Nine Points of the Law.
Object of Interest.
Old Trusty.
Peace and Quiet.
Railroad Station.
Rifle and How to Use it.
Samuel in Search of Himself.
Second Love, 3.

Shadows of the Past.
Splendid Investment.
Spring and Autumn, 3.
Ticklish Times (c).
Urgent Private Affairs.
Wandering Minstrel.
William Thompson.
Woodcock's Little Game, 2.

Two Males and Five Females.

Birds in the Little Nest Agree. | Cruel to be Kind. | I Couldn't Help It.

Five Males and Two Females.

Better Half.
Chimney Corner, 2.
Dreams of Delusion.
Duchess of Nothing (c).
First Night.
Fish out of Water.
Irish Tiger.
Jeweller of St James's, 3 (c).

Lady and the Devil (c).
Lend Me Five Shillings.
Loan of a Lover (c).
Make Your Wills.
Nothing Venture, etc., 2 (c).
Old Honesty, 2.
Old Phil's Birthday, 2 (c).
*Out of the Frying Pan.

Plots for Petticoats.
Separate Maintenance.
Shadows (c), drama, 4.
Slasher and Crasher.
Spectre Bridegroom.
State Secrets (c).
Suit of Tweeds.
Up in the World.

Village Lawyer.
Wedding Day.
Wilful Murder.
Your Vote and Interest (c), farce.

Three Males and Four Females.

Allow Me to Apologize.
Domestic Economy.

Everybody's Friend, 3.
Hard Struggle.

Ici on parle Français.
Laurence's Love Suit, 2.

My Sister from India.
Simpson & Co.

Six Males and One Female.

Caught by the Ears.
Diamond Cut Diamond.

Hunting a Turtle.
Thrice Married.

Turned Head.

Turkish Bath.

Eight Characters.—Two Males and Six Females.—How's your Uncle?

Four Males and Four Females.

Boots at the Swan.
Deaf as a Post.
Family Pictures.

How will they get out of it? comedy, 3.

Love in Livery.
Noemie, drama, 2.

Plague of my Life, farce, 1 act.
Quiet Family, farce.

Five Males and Three Females.

Bachelor's Buttons.
Balance of Comfort.
Bathing.
Cavalier, drama, 3 (c).
Census.
False Alarm.
Goose with the Golden Eggs.
If the Cap Fits.

Jacket of Blue.
Loan of a Wife.
Lost Diamond, drama, 2 (c).
Loving Cup, 2.
Love Wins, comedy, 3.
Neighbors, 2.
Old Sailors, 3.
Old Man, An, 2.

O'or Geordie.
Pipkin's Rustic Retreat.
Post Boy, 2.
P. P.
Quiet Day, A.
Rendezvous.
Roland for an Oliver, 2.
Sergeant's Wedding (c).

Stage Struck.
Sudden Thoughts.
Twice Killed.
Waltz by Arditi.
Who's my Husband?
Wonderful Woman, 2 (c).
Young England.

Seven Males and One Female.

Harvest Storm, drama.
Lancers.
Payable on Demand.

Spanking Legacy (c). } translation from
Thumping Legacy (c). } same original.
The Galley Slaves, drama, 2.

Nine Characters.—Three Males and Six Females.—Court of Oberon (c).

Four Males and Five Females.

From Village to Court, 2 (c).   Mischief Making (c).

Five Males and Four Females.

Agnes de Vere, 3.
Appearances.

Crossing the Line (c).
Omnibus.

Pygmalion and Galatea, 3 (c).
War to the Knife, 3.

Six Males and Three Females.

An Appeal to the Feelings.
Bamboozling.
Birthplace of Podgers.
Champagne.
Faces in the Fire, 3.
Fortune's Frolic.
Friend in Need, 2.

Honesty best Policy, drama, 2 (c).
Hush Money.
Hans Von Stein, drama, 2.
Irish Doctor.
Irishman in London, farce.

Irish Post, farce.
Maud's Peril, drama, 4.
Mendicant, drama, 2.
Midnight Hour, 2 (c).
My Heart's Idol, 2.
Old Soldiers, 3.

Old Score, 3.
Our Pet, 3.
Sleeping Hare, 2.
Shipmates, 3.
Tit for Tat, 2.
Veteran of 102 (c).

Seven Males and Two Females.

Amateurs and Actors.
Artful Dodge.
Blue Beard, Byron (c).

Charles XII., 2 (c).
Debt, 2 (c).
Dodge for a Dinner.
Illustrious Stranger (c).

Innkeeper of Abbeville, melodrama, 2 (c).
Lion in Bay, drama.
Next of Kin.

Paul Pry, 2.
Raising theWind.
Review.
St. Patrick's Day.

Eight Males and One Female.

'Twould Puzzle a Conjuror (c).   To Paris and Back for £5.

Ten Characters.—Four Males and Six Females.—Adonis Vanquished, 2 (c).

Five Males and Five Females.

Everybody's Husband.
My Preserver.

Old Story, 2.
Playing with Fire, 3.

Six Males and Four Females.

Adopted Child, drama, 2 (c).
Broken Ties, 2.
Fame, 3.

Glass of Water, 2 (c).
Mary Edmonstone, 2.
Our Boys, 3.

Our Nelly, 2.
Ready Money, drama, 4.
Regular Fix, A.

Rely on my Discretion.
Therese, drama, 3 (c).

Seven Males and Three Females.

Aggravating Sam.
Broken Sword, drama, 2 (c).
Cæsar the Watch Dog, drama, 2.
Chain of Guilt, 3 (c).

Does he Love me? 3 (c).
In the Clouds, extravaganza, 1.
Lucky Stars, (c).

Master's Rival, 2.
Mistletoe Bough (c), melodrama, 2.

Muleteer of Toledo (c).
Steeplechase.
Tradesman's Son, drama.

Eight Males and Two Females.

All at Coventry.
Comfortable Lodgings.
Cramond Brig (c).

Don Cæsar de Bazan, 3 (c).
Man with the Carpet Bag.
Point of Honor (c).

Robert Macaire, 2 (c).
Self Accusation, drama, 2 (c).

Still Waters Run Deep.
Unfinished Gentleman.

Eleven Characters.—Five Males and Six Females.—Christening.

Six Males and Five Females.

Delicate Attention.   Love Knot.   Return Ticket.

Seven Males and Four Females.

Blow for Blow, drama, 3.
Charcoal Burner, drama, 3 (c).

Don't Lend your Umbrella, 2.
High Life Below Stairs.

His First Champagne.

Sister and I.

Eight Males and Three Females.

Barark Johnson, drama.
Death Token, drama, 3 (c).
Father and Son, drama, 2 (c).

Frank Fox Phipps, Esq. (c), farce.
Haunted Inn, farce, 2.

Heir at Law (c), 3.
Married in Haste, 4.
Miss Chester, drama, 3.

Old Offender, 2 (c).
Plot and Counterplot (c).
Roll of the Drum, drama, 3 (c).

Four Males and Seven Females.

Milliner's Holiday.   Too Much for Good Nature.

NEW PLAYS JUST PUBLISHED.

Title	M.	F.
Bow Bells, comedy, 3	3	4
*Caste, comedy, 3	5	3
Daniel Druce, drama, 3	8	1
Daniel Rochat, comedy, 5	15	5
*David Garrick, comedy, 3	9	3
Did you ever send your Wife to Camberwell? farce, 1	2	2
Engaged, comedy, 3	5	5
Enoch Arden, drama, 5	13	3
Freezing a Mother-in-Law, farce, 1	3	2
For Her Child's Sake, comedy, 1	3	1
Funnibone's Fix, farce, 1	6	2
*Home, comedy, 3	4	3

Title	M.	F.
Infatuation, drama, 4	7	4
Married for Money, comedy, 3	4	3
Broken Hearts, fairy play, 3 (c.)	2	4
Childhood's Dreams, comedy, 1	2	2
George Geith, drama, 4	6	5
Second Thoughts, comedietta, 1	1	2
Two Roses, comedy, 3	4	5
Wild Flowers, comedietta, 1	2	3
May; or, Dolly's Delusion, drama, 3	7	3
My Awful Dad, comedy, 2	8	5
Never too Late to Mend, drama, 4	12	2
On Bail, comedy, 3	9	7

Title	M.	F.
Our Relatives, comedietta, 1	3	2
*Ours, comedy, 3	6	3
Out in the Streets, temperance drama, 3		6
Platter vs. Clatter, farce, 1	5	2
Pinafore, opera		5
Plot for Plot, comedietta, 1	1	1
*School, comedy, 4	5	3
That Dreadful Doctor, comedietta, 1	2	1
Tom Cobb, comedy, 3	6	4
Wicked World, fairy comedy, 3 (c)	3	6

*By T. W. Robertson, Esq. Only correct edition published, being printed from his private manuscripts.

(3)

TEMPERANCE PLAYS.

Price 15 cents each.

Title	SCENE	M	F
Aunt Dinah's Pledge, drama	2	6	3
Bottle, drama	2	11	6
Drunkard; or, The Fallen Saved, drama	5	12	5
Drunkard's Children, drama	2	15	6
Drunkard's Doom, romantic drama	3	15	3
Drunkard's Warning, (c.) drama	3	6	3
Fatal Glass, drama	3	11	9
Fifteen Years of a Drunkard's Life, melodrama	2	10	4
Fruits of the Wine-cup, drama	3	6	3
Temperate Doctor, drama	2	10	4
Ten Nights in a Bar-room, drama	5	11	5

Just Published, the Great Moral, Sensational, Temperance Drama, entitled

THE SOCIAL GLASS.
Price, 15 cents.

Six Male and Three Female Characters. It is easy to get up, and can be played in any Lodge-room or Temperance Hall. Pronounced by Pulpit and Press as being the *Best Temperance Play ever Written.*

IRISH PLAYS.

Price, 15 cents each.

A list of Plays in which the Irish Character is prominent.

Title	SCENE	M	F
Aline, drama	3	9	5
Andy Blake, comedy	2	4	3
Barney the Baron, farce	1	7	3
Born to Good Luck, farce	2	10	3
Brian Boroihme, drama	3	7	2
Brian O'Linn, farce	2	7	4
Colleen Bawn Settled, farce	1	5	2
Don Paddy de Bazan, farce	1	4	1
Eily O'Connor, drama	2	8	4
Gentleman from Ireland, comedy	2	6	2
Green Bushes, drama	3	12	8
Grin Bushes, burlesque	1	5	4
Handy Andy, drama	2	10	3
Happy Man, farce	1	5	2
His Last Legs, farce	2	4	3
How to Pay the Rent, farce	1	9	3
I'm not Mesilf at All, farce	1	3	2
Invincibles, farce	2	9	6
Ireland as it Was, drama	2	8	3
Ireland and America, drama	2	7	5
Irish Ambassador, comedy	1	7	2
Irish Assurance, farce	1	4	3
Irish Attorney, farce	2	8	2
Irish Broom-maker, farce	1	7	3
Irish Doctor, farce	1	8	3
Irish Emigrant (Temptation), drama	2	6	3
Irish Lion, farce	1	8	3
Irishman in London, farce	2	6	3
Irishman's Manœuvre, comedy	2	1	4
Irish Post, drama	2	6	3
Irish Tiger, farce	1	5	2
Irish Tutor, farce	1	4	2
Irish Widow, farce	2	6	1
Irish Yankee, drama	3	15	3
Kathleen Mavourneen, drama	4	11	4
Katty O'Sheal, farce	2	8	4
King O'Toole, extravaganza	1	10	10
Knight of Arva, drama	2	7	2
Last Life (The), drama	3	8	2
Limerick Boy (Paddy Miles), farce	1	5	2
MacCarthy More, drama	2	6	6
Miss Eily O'Connor, burlesque		6	3
More Blunders than One, farce	1	4	5
Norah Creina, drama	1	5	2
O'Flanagan and Fairies, drama	1	7	4
Omnibus, farce	1	4	4
O'Neal the Great, drama	3	18	2
Othello Travestie, burlesque		8	2
Paddy Carey, farce	1	10	3
Paddy Miles (Limerick Boy), farce	1	5	2
Paddy the Piper, comic drama	1	10	3
Peep O'Day, drama	4	19	7
Perfection, farce	1	4	2
Pyke O'Callaghan, drama	2	7	3
Review, musical farce	2	8	4
Robber's Wife, drama	2	11	1
Robert Emmet, drama	3	11	2
Rory O'More, drama	3	6	7
St. Patrick's Day, farce	1	8	2
St. Patrick's Eve, drama	3	11	4
Servants by Legacy, farce	1	5	2
Shandy Maguire, drama	2	11	6
Siamese Twins, farce	1	4	2
Teddy Roe, farce	1	4	2
Teddy the Tiler, farce	1	10	5
That Rascal Pat, farce	1	3	2
West End; or, The Irish Heiress, comedy	5	7	3
White Horse of the Peppers, drama	2	8	2
Wild Irish Girl, drama	3	9	6

ETHIOPIAN DRAMAS.

Price, 15 cents each. Sent by mail on receipt of price.

Title	SCENE	M	F
Academy of Stars	2	5	1
Actor and Singer	1	4	0
Arrival of Dickens	2	5	0
Black Crook	2	7	2
Black Mail	1	3	0
Black Ole Bull	1	4	0
Black Shoemaker	1	4	2
Black Statue	1	4	2
Blackest Tragedy of All	1	7	1
Blinks and Jinks	1	3	1
Boarding School	1	5	0
Bone Squash, 2 acts	8	9	3
Box and Cox	1	2	1
Camille	1	1	1
Challenge Dance	1	3	0
Comedy of Errors	4	4	2
Coopers	1	6	1
Corsican Twins	1	7	1
Cousin Joe's Visits	1	2	1
Dar's-de-Money	1	1	1
Dead Alive	1	3	0
Deaf as a Post	1	2	0
Deaf in a Horn	1	2	0
Deserts	1	4	0
De Trouble begins at 9	1	2	0
Echo Band	1	3	0
Feast	1	5	1
Fenian Spy	1	2	1
Fighting for the Union	3	4	2
Great Arrival	1	3	0
Hamlet the Dainty	3	6	1
Handy Andy	1	2	0
Haunted House	1	2	0
Highest Price for Ole Clothes	1	3	0
Hop of Fashion	2	5	0
Hypochondriac	2	2	0
Intelligence Office	1	2	1
Jack's the Lad	6	7	2
Jeemes the Poet	1	4	0
Jolly Millers	1	3	1
Les Misérables	1	3	0
Lucky Number	1	3	0
Magic Penny	3	6	1
Mazeppa, 2 acts	5	7	2
Mischievous Nigger	1	4	2
Mystic Spell	7	7	0

ETHIOPIAN DRAMAS.—Continued.

	SCENE.	M.	F.
New Year's Calls	5	6	2
Night at a New Hotel	1	3	0
Nobody's Son	1	2	0
No Cure no Pay	1	3	1
No Tater or Man Fish	7	5	1
Oh, Hush	3	4	1
Old Dad's Cabin	1	2	2
Old Hunks	1	3	0
Othello	4	4	1
Owl Train	1	2	0
Portrait Painter	1	4	1
Quack Doctor	1	5	1
Quarrelsome Servant	1	3	0
Railroad Explosion and Echo	2	4	2
Railway Scare	1	2	0
Rip Van Winkle	2	3	1
Rival Lovers	1	4	2
Robert Make Airs	9	9	3
Rooms to Let	1	2	1
Rose Dale	2	4	1
Running the Blockade	1	3	0
Scenes in a Studio	1	3	0
Sham Doctor	3	4	2
Shylock	4	5	2
Sixteen Thousand Years Ago	1	3	0
Somebody's Coat	1	3	1

	SCENE.	M.	F.
Spirits	1	2	0
Sports on a Lark	1	3	0
Sports with a Sportsman	1	2	0
Stage Struck Darky	1	2	1
Stocks Up, Stocks Down	1	2	0
Ten Days in the Tombs	1	3	0
Thieves at the Mill	4	4	2
Three Blacksmiths	1	3	0
Ticket Taker	2	8	1
Tom and Jerry	1	3	0
Trip to Paris	1	5	1
Troublesome Servant	1	2	0
Turkeys in Season	2	3	0
Two Pompeys	1	4	0
That Wife of Mine	1	2	0
The Thumping Process	1	4	0
Uncle Jeff	5	5	2
Unhappy Pair	1	3	0
United States Mail	1	2	2
Upper Ten Thousand	1	3	2
Villikins and his Dinah	1	4	1
Virginian Mummy	2	6	1
Who Stole the Chickens?	1	2	0
Wig Makers	1	3	0
William Tell	1	4	5
Wreck, The	1	4	3

DARKY DRAMA.

Price, 40 cents each Part.

A COLLECTION OF APPROVED ETHIOPIAN ACTS, SCENES, INTERLUDES, Etc.

The figures denote the number of characters required for each piece.

PART I.—The Echo, 1; Deaf—in a Horn, 2; Railroad Explosion, act in 2 scenes, for company; Dar's-de-Money (Othello burlesque), 2; Tinpanonion, musical act for principals and company; Stocks Up, Stocks Down, 2 principals and instrumental quartette; Challenge Dance; De Trouble Begins at Nine, 2; Scenes in the Studio, 3; 16,000 Years Ago, 3.

PART II.—Virginia Mummy, farce, 7; Mischievous Nigger, 6; Jolly Millers, 4; Sham Doctor, 6; The Coopers, 7.

PART III.—Quack Doctor, 6; Oh, Hush; or, The Virginny Cupids, 4; The Troublesome Servant, an Ethiopian interlude, 2; Rooms to Let without Board, an Ethiopian farce, 3; The Black Shoemaker, a negro farce, 6. Uncle Jeff, 7.

PART IV.—An Unhappy Pair, an Ethiopian farce, 3; Sport with a Sportsman, an Ethiopian extravaganza, 2; Three Blacksmiths, an original Ethiopian eccentricity, 3; A Night in the New Hotel, an original African fancy, 3; The Great Arrival, an Ethiopian scene, 3; The Hop of Fashion, a negro farce, 12.

PART V.—The Magic Penny, a nigger melodrama, 8; Fetterlane to Gravesend; or, a Dark Romance, from the "Railway Library," 3; Tailors' Strike; or, Highest Price for Left-off Clothes, an original darky drama, 3; Old Hunks, an original sketch, 3; Handy Andy, a darky sketch, 2 Villikins and Dinah, a negro farce, 5.

PART VI.—Box and Cox, a nigger farce, 3; Othello, Ethiopian Burlesque, 5; No Cure, no Pay, Ethiopian farce, 4; Black Mail, negro comicality, 3; Nobody's Son, Ethiopian act, 2; Hypochondriac, negro farce, 2.

PART VII.—Quarrelsome Servants, Ethiopian interlude, 3; Camille, negro interlude, 2; Les Misérables, negro farce, 3; Sports on a Lark, negro interlude, 3; Comedy of Errors, an uproarious burlesque, 9; Black Statue, Ethiopian farce, 6.

PART VIII.—Stage-struck Darky, an interlude, 3; Rival Lovers, negro farce, 6; Haunted House, Ethiopian sketch, 2; Old Dad's Cabin, negro farce, 4; Portrait Painter, pantomime farce, 5; Thieves at the Mill, Ethiopian drama, 6.

PART IX.—Bone Squash, a comic opera, 12; William Tell, an Ethiopian interlude, 4; The Fenian Spy; or, John Bull in America, 3; Hamlet the Dainty, an Ethiopian burlesque, 7; United States Mail, a farce, 4.

PART X.—Wig Makers, 3; Black Crook, 9; Corsican Twins, 8; Mazeppa, 9; Shylock, 7; Robert Make-airs, 12.

NIGGER JOKES AND STUMP SPEECHES.

Being a collection of approved Nigger Jokes, Stump Speeches, Conundrums, and the Essence of Minstrelsy. Parts I. and II. are now ready. **Price, 25 cents each.**

MAKE-UP BOOK. HOW TO MAKE-UP.

A PRACTICAL GUIDE FOR AMATEURS, Etc.

Showing, by a series of novel illustrations, the manner in which the face may be "made-up" to represent the different stages of life, viz.: Youth, Manhood, Maturity, Old Age, etc., with twenty-three colored illustrations. **Price, 50 cents.**

TABLEAUX VIVANTS.

Arranged for Private Representation. By J. V. PRITCHARD.

Containing 80 selected Tableaux, with instructions how to get them up, cast of characters, costumes required, and full description of each picture. Also information respecting the use of the Tableaux lights and other effects, and describing the music required for each representation. **Price, 25 cents.**

Mrs. Jarley's Far-Famed Waxworks.
In Two Parts. Price, 25 cents each.

A new and unique entertainment, which affords a fund of amusement for all ages. Very popular to raise funds for Schools, Churches, Societies, etc., etc.

The impersonators have to dress up in imitation of the waxwork figures, and are exhibited by one who assumes Mrs. Jarley.

PART I.—Mrs. Jarley—Little Nell—John and Peter—The Chinese Giant—Mrs. Jack Sprat—Two headed Girl—Lord Byron—Sewing Woman—Childe Harold—Mrs. Winslow—The Live Yankee—Captain Kidd—The Old-fashioned Sewing Machine—Victim—The Cannibal—The Mermaid—The Bachelor—The Maniac—His Lady Love—The Siamese Twins—Mother Goose—The Boy that Stood on the Burning Deck—Little Bo-Peep—The Giggler—The Dwarf—Old King Cole—Blue Beard—The Contraband—Signorina Squallini—Babes in the Wood—Jack Sprat—Little Red Riding Hood—Fair One with Golden Locks. *The Antique Chamber* (lately added)—Models represented : Jupiter—Juno—Bacchus—Minerva—Apollo—Hebe—Mars—Cupid.

PART II.—*Chamber of Beauty*—Opening Speech of Mrs. Jarley—Sleeping Beauty and the Prince—Queen Eleanor and Fair Rosamond—John Alden and Priscilla—Rebecca and Rowena—Alonzo the Brave and Fair Imogene—The Gracchi—Beatrice Cenci. *Chamber of Horrors*: Mrs. Jarley's Speech—Medusa—Violante—Vampire—Father Time—Savage and His Flying Victim—Ruffian Disarmed by a Smile—Spoiled Child—Bearded Woman—Man Monkey. *Historical Chamber*: Mrs. Jarley's Speech—Joan of Arc—Robin Hood—Alexander the Great—Robinson Crusoe—King Alfred—Diogenes—Man with the Iron Mask—Nero—King Cophetua and the Beggar Maid. *Shakesperian Chamber*: Mrs. Jarley's Speech—Lady Macbeth—Titania—Ophelia—Juliet—King Lear—Hermione—Richard III.

A MOCK TRIAL
FOR BREACH OF PROMISE OF MARRIAGE.

Arranged for public or parlor entertainment, and equally adapted to amateur or professional ability. It has been produced with marked success. There are 24 male and 3 female characters. The trial throughout is very funny, and the jury is composed of an Irishman, German, Frenchman, Negro, Chinaman, and Yankee. We recommend this as being a very amusing entertainment.

Price, 15 cents.

GUIDE TO SELECTING PLAYS;
Or, MANAGER'S COMPANION.

Showing how to select Farces, Comedies, Dramas, Tragedies, Burlesques, Operas, Charades, Ladies Plays, Plays for Male Characters, Plays with a French Character, Plays for Children, Plays suitable for Club, Private or Public Performance ; giving the number of characters, class of play, how many acts, the author's name, the scenery, costumes, time in representation, the style of characters, and the plot or advice, connected with 1500 pieces, and arranged according to the requirement of any company.

Price, 25 cents.

CABMAN'S STORY,
AND OTHER READINGS IN PROSE AND VERSE.

By RE HENRY. With an Introduction by Mrs. Stirling, and read in public by her, Miss Cowen, Marlande Clarke and others.

Price, 25 cents.

STAGE COSTUME.

Practical Hints on the above, including Instructions and Illustrated Patterns for making Hats, Boots, Sword Belts, Lace Ornaments, Ballet Shirts, and other necessary Articles of Costume required by Actors. A most valuable work for Amateurs and Professionals. Written by CYRIL BOWEN.

Price, 40 cents.

THE CARNIVAL OF AUTHORS.

Containing full directions for producing this magnificent entertainment in all its details of organization, with description of the Main Stage, the eight Booths, the Grand Entrée, the Fan Drill, the Minuet, and over 112 scenes from the works of the principal authors of the world. All of which can be used separately or together, for hall and parlor performances, as full particulars of costume, position, and grouping are given by a manager of long and varied experience, who has selected them from the best Carnivals and from his original novelties.

Price, 25 cents.

SCENERY.

WITH a view to obviate the great difficulty experienced by Amateurs (particularly in country houses) in obtaining Scenery, etc., to fix in a Drawing-Room, and then only by considerable outlay for hire and great damage caused to walls, we have decided to keep a series of Scenes, etc., colored on strong paper, which can be joined together or pasted on canvas or wood, according to requirement. Full directions, with diagrams showing exact size of Back-Scenes, Borders, and Wings, can be had free on application. The following four Scenes each consists of thirty sheets of paper :

GARDEN.

The above is an illustration of this Scene. It is kept in two sizes. The small size would extend to 15 feet wide and 8 feet high, and the large size to 20 feet long and 11½ feet high. It is not necessary to have the Scene the height of the room, as blue paper to represent sky is usually hung at the top. Small size, with Wings and Border complete, $7.50 ; large size, with Wings and Border complete, $10.

WOOD.

This is similar in style to the above, only a Wood-Scene is introduced in the centre. It is kept in two sizes, as the previous Scene, and blue paper can be introduced as before indicated. Small size, with Wings and Border complete, $7.50 ; large size, with Wings and Border complete, $10.

FOLIAGE.—This is a sheet of paper on which Foliage is drawn, which can be repeated and cut in any shape required. Small size, 30 inches by 20 inches, 25 cents per sheet ; large size, 40 inches by 30 inches, 35 cents per sheet.

DRAWING-ROOM.

This Scene is only kept in the large size, to extend to 20 feet long and 11½ feet high. In the centre is a French window, leading down to the ground, which could be made practicable if required. On the left wing is a fireplace with mirror above, and on the right wing is an oil painting. The whole Scene is tastefully ornamented and beautifully colored, forming a most elegant picture. Should a Box Scene be required, extra wings can be had, consisting of doors each side, which could be made practicable. Price, with Border and one set of Wings, $10 ; with Border and two sets of Wings, to form Box Scene, $12.50.

COTTAGE INTERIOR.

This is also kept in the large size only. In the centre is a door leading outside. On the left centre is a rustic fireplace, and the right centre is a window. On the wings are painted shelves, etc., to complete the Scene. A Box Scene can be made by purchasing extra wings, as before described, and forming doors on each side. Price, with Border and one set of Wings, $10 ; with Border and two sets of Wings, to form Box Scene, $12.50.

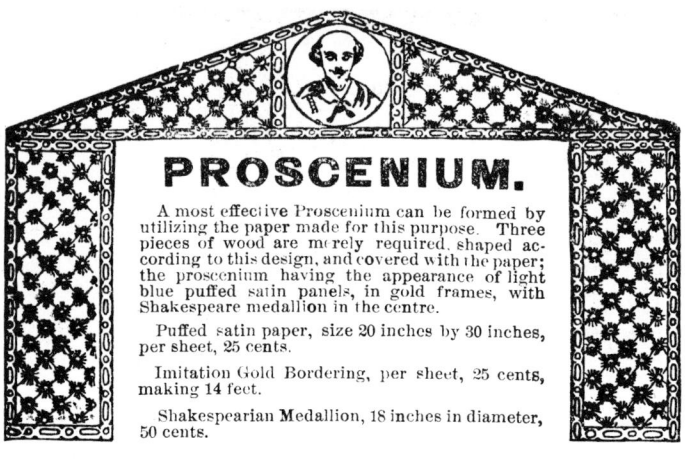

PROSCENIUM.

A most effective Proscenium can be formed by utilizing the paper made for this purpose. Three pieces of wood are merely required, shaped according to this design, and covered with the paper; the proscenium having the appearance of light blue puffed satin panels, in gold frames, with Shakespeare medallion in the centre.

Puffed satin paper, size 20 inches by 30 inches, per sheet, 25 cents.

Imitation Gold Bordering, per sheet, 25 cents, making 14 feet.

Shakespearian Medallion, 18 inches in diameter, 50 cents.

DOORS.—These comprise three sheets of paper each, and can be had either for drawing-room or cottage purposes. Size, 7 feet by 3 feet. Price, complete, $1.25 each.

WINDOW.—This is a parlor window formed with two sheets of paper, and could be made practicable to slide up and down. The introduction of curtains each side would make it very effective. Size, 3 feet by 4½ feet. Price, $1, complete.

FIREPLACE.—This is also made with two sheets of paper. The fire is lighted, but should this not be required a fire-paper can be hung over it. It will be found most useful in many farces wherein a character has to climb up a chimney, and many plays where a fireplace is indispensable. By purchasing a door, window, and fireplace an ordinary room scene could easily be constructed with the addition of some wall-paper. Size, 3 feet by 4½ feet. Price, complete, $1.25.

MAKE-UP BOX.

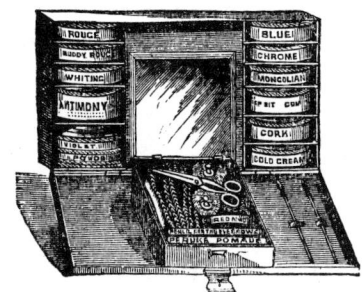

TIN CASE, $5.

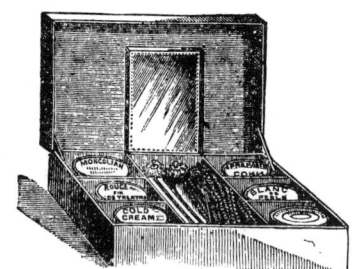

CLOTH BOARD, $4.

Contains everything necessary for making up the face, viz.: Rouge, Pearl Powder, Whiting, Mongolian, Ruddy Rouge, Powdered Antimony, Joining Paste, Violet Powder, Box and Puff, Chrome, Blue, Burnt Cork, Pencils for the Eyelids, Spirit Gum, Indian Ink, Burnt Umber, Camel-hair Brushes, Hares' Foot, Wool, Crape Hair, Cold Cream, Paint Saucer, Miniature Puffs, Scissors and Looking-glass. Each article is of the best quality. Packed neatly in a strong cloth-covered box, $4; elegant tin case, $5. We can strongly recommend the tin cases. They are very durable, and any article can be used without disturbing another, a great advantage in making up.

THE ABOVE ARTICLES TO BE HAD SEPARATELY. SEE PRECEDING PAGE.

WHITTINGTON TRAVELLING CHESS BOARD.

8 inch Slide Lid Bone Chess................ $4 00
(See cut No. 1.)
8 inch Folding Flaps, Bone Chess............ 6 00
(See cut No. 2)

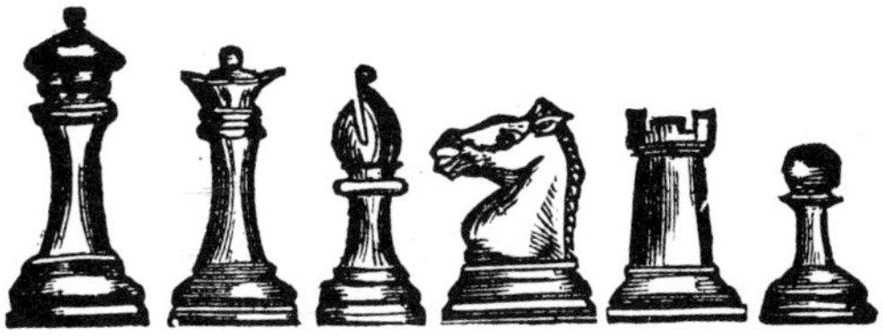

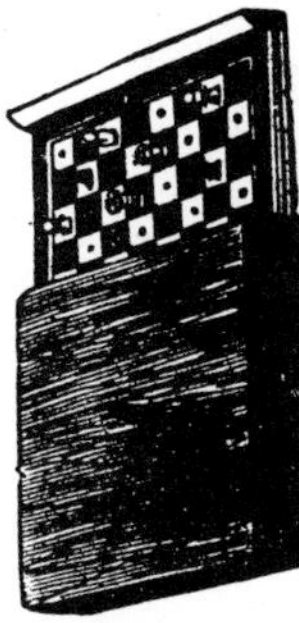

No. 1.

No. 2.

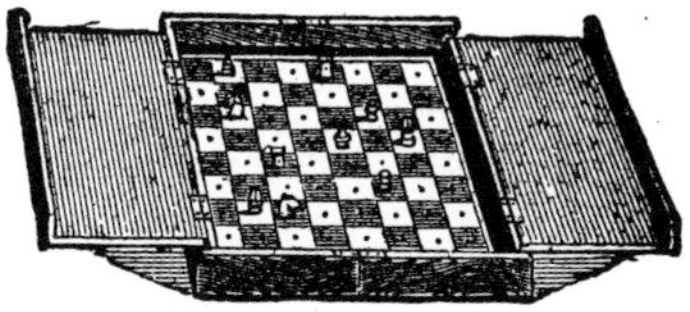

PLAIN FRENCH BOXWOOD CHESS.

Nos........................	313	314	315	316	317	318
Diameter of King at Base...........	¾ inch	⅞ inch	1 inch	1 inch	1 1-16 inch	1⅛ inch.
Per Set........................	75c.	85c.	$1 00	$1 25	$1 50	$1 75

Polished French Boxwood Chess.—Staunton Pattern.

Nos........................	325	326	327	328
Diameter of King at Base...........	1¼ inch	1 5-16 inch	1 7-16 inch	1 9-16 inch.
Per Set........................	$2 00	$2 25	$2 50	$3 00

Fine English Ebony and Boxwood Chess.—Staunton Pattern, in Polished Boxes.

Nos........................	3	4	5	6	7
Diameter of King at Base...........	1¼ inch	1 5-16 inch	1 7-16 inch	1½ inch	1⅝ inch.
Per Set........................	$3 00	$4 00	$5 00	$6 00	$7 00

Fine English Ebony and Boxwood.—Loaded Club Chess Staunton Pattern in Polished Boxes.

Nos..................................	1	2	3
Diameter of King at Base..................	1½ inch	1⅝ inch	1⅞ inch
Per Set	$10 00	$15 00	$20 00

Bone Chess in Polished Boxes.

Nos........................	2	3	4	5	6	7	8
Diameter of King at Base...........	1 in.	1 1-16 in.	1⅛ in.	1 3-16 in.	1¼ in.	1⅜ in.	1½ in.
Per Set........................	$2 00	$2 50	$3 00	$4 00	$5 00	$5 50	$6 50

Fine English Bone Chess.—Staunton Pattern, in Polished Boxes.

Nss........................	1	2	3	4	5
Diameetr of King at Base...........	1⅛ inch	1 3-16 inch	1 5-16 inch	1 7-16 inch	1½ inch.
Per Set........................	$4 00	$4 50	$6 00	$6 50	$8 00

THE PURDY ADJUSTABLE DOUBLE TRACING WHEEL AND COMPASS. (Patented Nov. 7th, 1882.)

For Designing on Paper, Leather, Wood, and other Material. For Tracing, Transferring and cutting Garment Patterns in any form or style. For Copying Singly and in Manifold from other Patterns, or from the Garments themselves. For Dressmakers, Draughtsmen, Surveyors, Civil Engineers, Architects, Pattern Makers, Ornamental Leather Work, Etc.

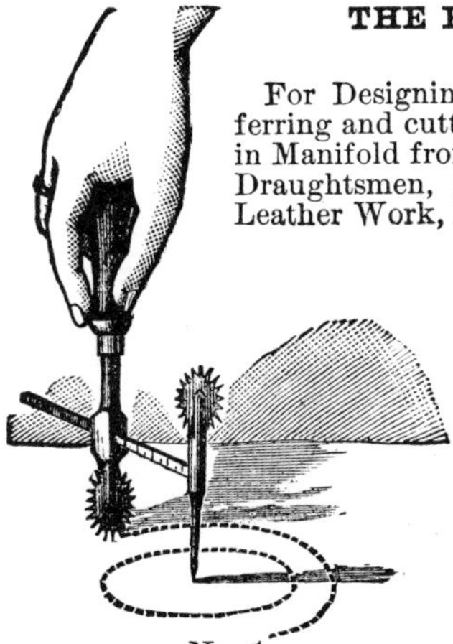

No. 1.

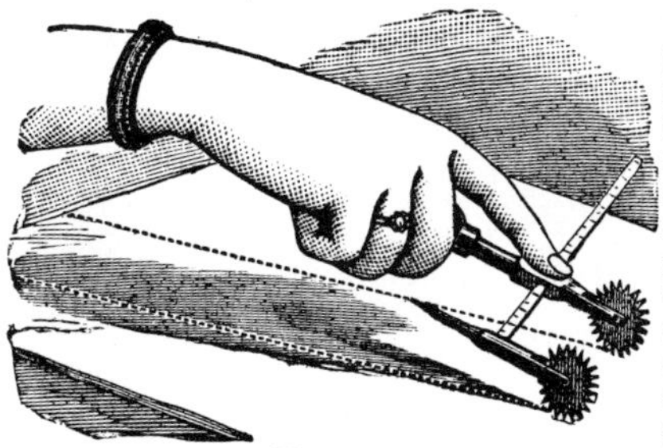

No. 2.

No. 1 shows it as a Compass, by loosening the arm and turning it over, the compass point is brought in front; the ingenious instrument then becomes a compass. with dotting wheel for the use of designers of plans, patterns, etc., and of especial utility and convenience to draughtsmen, surveyors, civil engineers and architects, in describing curved lines, as arcs, circles, single or concentric—in varied ornamental forms.

The dotting wheel here substitutes the troublesome (because always out of place) pencil point used ith the ordinary compass, and is better, because simpler, always in place and instantly adjustable.

No. 2 shows it as a Tracing Wheel. (Used single or double).—To the Dressmaker it is indispensable; especially for tracing two lines at any required distance apart—one to cut by, the other to sew by.

The wheels are of hardened steel, well pointed, so as to pierce and copy at least fifteen pattern folds at a time. Their distance apart is adjusted by sliding the arm, which is gauged to the measure of sixteenths of an inch, and held in place or changed by the slightest turn of the handle, the foot of ich serves as the set screw.

N. B.—For compass use turn to the left. The instrument is nickel-finished, light, simple and strong. It cannot break or bend, and has no loose parts to become lost or get out of order. Every Lady needs one. The Draughtsman must have it. To the Designer it is a Treasure. No Sewing Machine complete without it. It sells at sight. Price, by mail, 75 cents.

   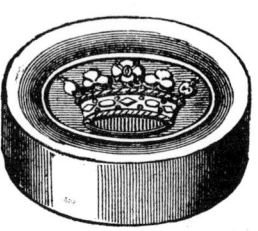

PLAIN STAR CHECKERS.

30 Pieces, made of Hard Woods and packed in Manilla Paper Boxes. ⅞ in. 1 in. 1⅛ in. 1¼ in. Per set, 10c.

Polished Crown Checkers. (See Cut.)

30 Pieces, made of Selected Woods and neatly finished, packed in Wood Boxes covered with Glazed Paper.
1 in. 1⅛ in. 1¼ in. Price per set, 25c.

Enameled Crown Checkers. (See Cut.)

30 Pieces, packed in covered Wood Boxes. These men are enameled by a Patent Process. The enameled is very durable. The device of the Crown is useful in "making Kings," by simply reversing the man.
1 in. 1⅛ in. 1¼ in. Price per set, 35c.

Polished Interlocking Crown Checkers.

With the old style of checkerman you must hold both men to move a king, when one has been placed on top of the other; with these the rings interlock, and they may then be moved as one man, which is a great improvement over the old style. 30 Pieces, packed in covered Wood Boxes, with Engraved Labels.
1 in. 1⅛ in. 1¼ in. Price per set, 25c.

Enameled Interlocking Crown Checkers.

A great improvement upon anything ever made in this line, with the Old Style of Checkerman you must hold both men to move a king, when one has been placed on top of the other; with these the rings interlock, and they may then be moved as one man. 30 Pieces, packed in Covered Wood Boxes, with engraved Labels.
1 in. 1⅛ in. 1¼ in. Price per set, 35c.

English Ebony and Boxwood Stained Checkers.

30 Pieces, packed in Paper Boxes. Price per set, 1 in. 35c., 1¼ in. 40c., 1½ in., 50c.

English Cocus and Boxwood Polished Checkers.

30 Pieces, packed in Paper Boxes. Price per set, 1 in. 40c., 1¼ in. 50c., 1½ in. 65c.

English Ebony and Boxwood Stained Checkers.

30 Pieces, packed in Hard Wood Boxes. Price per set, 1 in. 40c., 1¼ in. 50c., 1½ in. 65c.

English Cocus and Boxwood Polished Checkers.

30 Pieces, packed in Hard Wood Boxes. Price per set, 1 in. 65c., 1¼ in. 75c., 1½ in. 85c.

Fine English Ebony and Boxwood Checkers, (Best.)

Round Edges, French Polished. 30 Pieces, packed in Polished Mahogany Boxes.
Price per set, 1 in. 90c., 1¼ in. $1.00, 1½ in. $1.25

Compressed Ivory Checkers.

Red and White. 30 Pieces, packed in Heavy White Pasteboard Boxes.
Price per set, 1 in. 60c, 1⅛ in. 75c. 1¼ in. $1.00

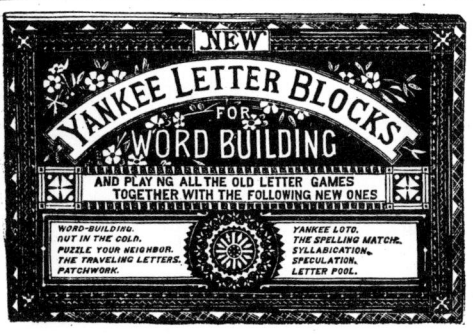 

Yankee Letter Blocks.—Superior to all others for playing Letter Games. They consist of round wooden blocks, with plain Capital letters printed on their faces. Full directions for playing ten *new* Games, of high order. Put up in handsome covered wood boxes.

No. 1 has 150 Letters............Retails, each, $0 50 | No. 3 has 300 Letters..........Retails, each, $1 00
No. 2 " 225 " " " 0 75 |

Loto: New American.—This favorite German game is fast becoming popular with the American people. Our four kinds vary in size, and the variety of their implements, which excel anything heretofore furnished in Loto games.

No. 1.......................Retails, each, $0 50 | No. 3......................Retails, each, $1 00
No. 2....................... " " 0 75 | No. 4...................... " " 1 50

DOMINOES OF WOOD, BONE, IVORY AND PEARL.

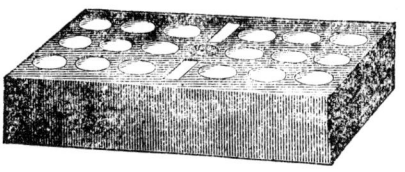 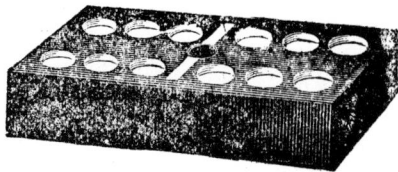

	Per Set
Compressed Wood Dominoes, Black, White Spots, see cut	$ 50
" " " Double Nines, Black, White Spots, see cut	1 50

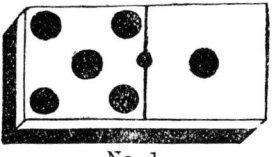 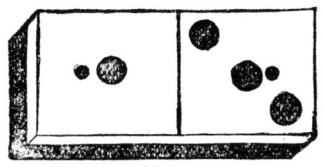 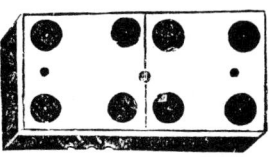

No. 1. No. 2. No. 3.

Per Set.
No. 630, Bone Dominoes, in Wood Boxes, 14 Lines, 1 Pivot.................................$0 50
No. 633,   "   "   "   "   16 "   1 "   65
No. 634,   "   "   "   "   18 "   1 " see cut 1,............................ 85
No. 635,   "   "   "   "   18 "   2 Rivets, see cut 2........................ 1 25
No. 636,   "   "   "   "   18 "   1 Pivot and 2 Rivets, see cut 3........... 1 50
No. 637, Polished Bone Dominoes, in Mahogany Boxes, 22 Lines, 1 Pivot, Beveled Edge... 4 00
No. 638,   "   "   "   "   Wood Boxes, 20 Lines, 1 Pivot, 2 Rivets.............. 2 00
No. 639, Pearl Dominoes, Ebony Back, 1 Centre Rivet, in Fine Inlaid Ebony Box, with Lock and Key, a
         very Fine Set, 22 Lines, 1 Pivot... 20 00
No. 640, Bone Dominoes, in Mahogany Boxes, 22 Lines, 1 Pivot, 2 Rivets.................. 3 50
No. 647, Solid Ivory Dominoes, in Mahogany Boxes, a very Fine Set, 22 Lines, 1 Pivot.... 18 00
No. 648, Bone Dominoes, in Wood Boxes, 18 Lines, 1 Pivot................................ 1 35
No. 641,   "   "   "   "   24 "   1 "   2 Rivets........................... 4 00
No. 649, Double Nines, Bone Dominoes, in Wood Boxes, 22 Lines, 1 Centre Rivet, and 2 Rivets... 4 00
No. 650, Double Nines, Bone Dominoes, in Wood Boxes, 24 Lines, 1 Pivot.................. 5 00

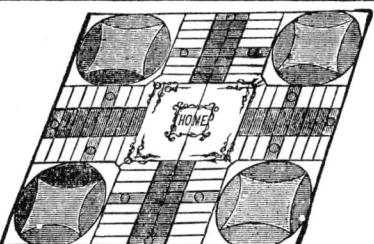

PARCHEESI is designed in such a distinct and attractive manner that it is quickly comprehended by children, putting their wits on the alert at once, and engaging the excited interest of the oldest players for hours. It is published in four styles as follows:

No. 1. Popular Edition, is bound in durable and handsome green paper, (imitation cloth), with scarlet labels printed in best gold bronze. A box containing eight dice, 16 counters of heavy pasteboard, and directions, accompany the board; the whole forming the most complete and attractive dollar game in the market. Each, $1 00

No. 1½. In answer to a demand made by the trade, we are now putting up the popular edition with Brassbound Counters (same as used in No. 2.) instead of pasteboard counters, and 2 dice cups in each box. Each, $1 50

No. 2. Medium Edition, is bound in book muslin, embossed and stamped in gold. The box contains eight dice, four dice cups, sixteen counters, metal rimmed, and directions. This style is very nicely gotten up. Each, $2 00

No. 3. Fine Edition, is bound in morocco cloth, (imitation leather,) embossed with a very handsome gold border. The inside is an elegant lithograph, in eight brilliant colors, of an entirely new design. The box contains eight dice, four dice cups bound in red leather, sixteen ivory counters and directions. The whole forming the finest and most complete game ever published in this country. Each, $3 00

PROF. HELLER'S WONDROUS MAGIC TRICK CARDS.

With full instructions for executing the many astonishing and miraculous feats that can be performed with them, and them only. Price per set, by mail, 20 cents.

Triplicate.

Indicators.

ANDREW DOUGHERTY'S
CELEBRATED
PLAYING CARDS.
A complete and large stock always on hand.
THE TRADE SUPPLIED.

No.		Per dozen.	Per pack.
0.	No. 2 Steamboats, assorted Star, plaid and calico backs, "with Indicators"........	$0 65	$0 10
0.	Steamboats, convex corners, assorted Star, plaid and calico backs, "with Indicators," each pack in a box.................................	1 00	0 15
1.	Steamboats, first quality, assorted Star, plaid and calico backs, "with Indicators"..	1 75	0 20
1.	"Extra" Steamboats, first quality, "convex corners," assorted Star, plaid and calico backs, "with Indicators," each pack in a box.....	2 25	0 25
7.	Great Mogul, fancy backs, "convex corners," "with Indicators," each pack in a box,	2 75	0 30
10.	Triplicate Pure Linen, "Patented" convex corners, each pack in a box..........	2 75	0 30

Enameled Ivory Finished Cards.

9.	Tally-Ho, (convex corners) with Indicators, each pack in a box...	2 00	0 25
9 G	Tally-Ho, Gilt Edges, convex corners, with Indicators, each pack in a box	3 00	0 30
14.	Climax, " " " " " "	3 50	0 35
14 G.	Climax, Gilt Edges, " " " " " "	4 50	0 50
28.	Great Mogul (Euchre) convex corners, 32 cards to the pack.............	4 50	0 50
70.	Ivorettes, Patented, convex corners, each pack in a box.......................	6 50	0 75
60.	American Club, each pack in a box.	6 50	0 75
50.	Indicators, convex corners, each pack in a box..........................	6 50	0 75
50 G.	Indicators, Gilt Edges, convex corners, each pack in a box.................	8 50	1 00

50 and 60, with Indicators, Fancy Backs.

Convex Corners, second quality.................................	3 00	0 35
18. Triplicate, Patented, convex corners, each pack in a box	6 50	0 75
18 H. Triplicate, Patented, convex corners, Dog, Horse and Cat Backs.............	7 50	0 85
18 G. Triplicate, Patented, convex corners, gilt edges, each pack in a box........	8 50	1 00
18 H. G. Triplicate, Patented, convex corners, Horse, Dog and Cat Backs, gilt edges, each pack in a box...........................	9 50	1 10
Marked Back or Advantage Playing Cards, Assorted Backs, with directions.........	12 00	1 25

HOFFMAN'S TRICKS WITH CARDS.

Containing all the modern Tricks, Diversions and Sleight-of-hand Deceptions, with descriptive Diagrams showing how to Make the Pass, to Force a Card, to Make a False Shuffle, to Palm a Card, to Ruffle the Cards, to Change a Card, to Get Sight of a Drawn Card, to Slip a Card, to Draw Back a Card, to Turn Over the Pack, to Spring the Cards from one Hand to the Other, to Throw a Card. Large octavo volume, containing 142 pages, with handsome paper cover.   Price, 50 cents.

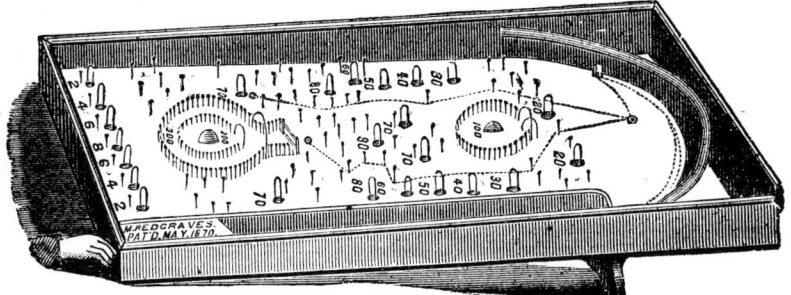

PATENT PARLOR BAGATELLE TABLES, WITH SPRINGS.

No. 1 Table—5 feet long, by 2 feet 6 inches wide, covered with billiard cloth, rich black walnut frame, mounted with one silver and four brass bells, silver plate and screws, and suitable for the most handsomely furnished parlor or drawing-room............. $20 00

No. 2. Table—4 feet long, by 1 foot 8 inches wide, covered with billiard cloth, rich black walnut frame, mounted with one silver and two brass bells, silver plate and screws, This table is particularly adapted for family use.................................... 10 50

No. 3 Table—4 feet long, by 1 foot 8 inches wide, covered with green enameled cloth, black walnut frame, silver plate, one silver and one brass bell and cups, substantially made, and suitable for public or private use. (See Cut)................................. 8 50

No. 4 Table—36 inches long, by 16 inches wide, covered with cloth, rich black walnut frame, silver plate, one silver and one brass bell and cups. This table is quite a favorite 6 50

No. 5 Table—2 feet 4 inches long, by 11 inches wide, black walnut frame, one silver bell. A handsome, cheap and useful toy 2 00

No. 6 Table—1 foot 9 inches long, by 9 inches wide, black walnut frame, one brass bell. An entertaining, cheap and useful toy for the nursery............................. 1 00

The above Tables are complete with marbles and full and easy instructions for playing the games.

THE WONDERFUL CONJUROR'S PACK OF CARDS.

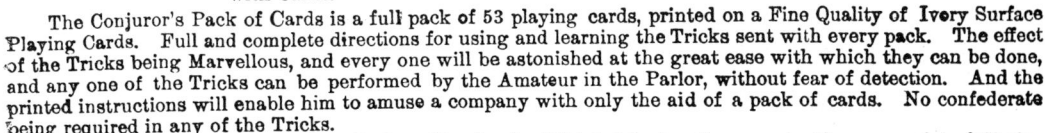

These are the cards used by all Professors of Legerdemain, or the Black Art and with them you can Restore the Torn Card, Burn a Card and afterwards restore it whole and perfect, Cut a Pack and Name the Top Card before the cut is made, Burn a Card, and then Find it in the Pocket of the person who burned it, Burn a Card and afterwards Find it under the Door, To Discover a Card by its Weight or Smell, To Destroy a Card and afterwards Find it in a Hat, To Find a Selected Card with a Sword or Knife, To Send a Selected Card Through a Table into the Table Drawer, To Destroy a Card and Find it in a Locked Box, Under a Chair Cushion, In a Lady's Card Case, In a Clock, In a Book, In a Sealed Envelope, In a Lady's Pocket, In a Gentleman's Pocket, In a Tumbler under a Hat, and Hundreds of other Tricks, of the most Beautiful, Surprising and Delightful, ever performed with Cards.

The Conjuror's Pack of Cards is a full pack of 53 playing cards, printed on a Fine Quality of Ivory Surface Playing Cards. Full and complete directions for using and learning the Tricks sent with every pack. The effect of the Tricks being Marvellous, and every one will be astonished at the great ease with which they can be done, and any one of the Tricks can be performed by the Amateur in the Parlor, without fear of detection. And the printed instructions will enable him to amuse a company with only the aid of a pack of cards. No confederate being required in any of the Tricks.

We send a complete Pack of 53 Cards, with a book of Printed Instructions, postpaid upon receipt of 50 cts.

Parlor Tricks with Cards. Containing explanation of all the Tricks and Deceptions with Playing Cards ever invented, The whole illustrated and made plain and easy with seventy engravings. Paper covers, 30c. Bound in boards, with Cloth back..50c.

French Transparent Playing Cards. Grimaud's genuine French Cards, imported by us direct, full pack, round corners, gilt. (these are not obscene cards). Price, per pack, 75c.

The Changeable Pack of Cards. A most extraodinary trick, but easy to perform. The five eights change to deuces; the deuces change to black cards; the black to red, the red change to two deuces and two eights, and finally they change back to all eights. Price, 75c.

CARD CASES FOR HOLDING FULL PACK OF CARDS.

No. 1, Made of paste-board, cloth covered, to slide, each,....................15c.
" 2, " " " " neck cover " ....20c.
" 3, " " " " with dials " ....25c.
" 4, ". " in Morocco " " " ....60c.
" 5, " " Turkey " " " " ....75c.

THE GREAT WIZARD'S PACK OF CARDS.

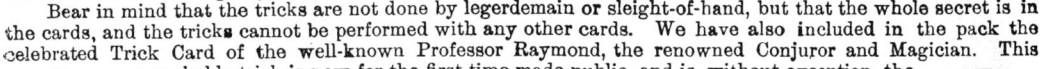

Wonderful! Surprising! Astounding! A full pack of 52 cards, appearing precisely the same as an ordinary pack of Playing Cards; but by the aid of the instructions given, any one can perform some very wonderful and apparently impossible tricks. Some of the feats exhibited are truly marvellous, and will delight, astonish and amuse a whole audience. Some of them may, however, become so puzzled and bewildered at the mysterious and inexplicable character of many of the tricks as to attribute them to the agency of the "Evil One."

Bear in mind that the tricks are not done by legerdemain or sleight-of-hand, but that the whole secret is in the cards, and the tricks cannot be performed with any other cards. We have also included in the pack the celebrated Trick Card of the well-known Professor Raymond, the renowned Conjuror and Magician. This remarkable trick is now for the first time made public, and is, without exception, the most remarkable feat of the day.

As a means of amusement and entertainment, these Cards are unequalled. They are always fresh, interesting and mysterious. The interest in them will never grow old, and the possessor will be a welcome guest to every entertainment or festive occasion. We mail the whole pack of 52 cards and Professor Raymond's Trick Card, making 53 cards altogether, for $1 00.

THE WONDERFUL GYPSY ORACLE FORTUNE TELLING CARDS.

The most truthful and beautiful Fortune-Telling cards ever invented. They are by the greatest of all Fortune-Tellers, the celebrated Mme. Lenormand, who was for so many years famous throughout the civilized world; her who prophesied to the Emperor Napoleon I his greatness and likewise his downfall, and who was so much sought after by kings and princes, who came hundreds of miles and paid fabulous prices for her aid in exposing conspiracies, directing love affairs, and unfolding their whole future life to them with unswerving accuracy and precision; all of which was performed solely with the aid of these selfsame cards, and all of which has been attempted, but without success, by the so-called fortune tellers and fortune-telling cards of a later day. Previous to her death, Mme. Lenormand imparted her secret and cards to her only child, Mlle. Lenormand. The only thing then remaining to be done was to get possession of the original cards, and have the plates engraved and the cards printed a *fac simile* of the original ones once owned by the dead Mme. Lenormand, which we have at last succeeded in doing at an enormous sacrifice of both time and money. But our reward is now certain, as we are selling thousands upon thousands every month. They are printed on very fine transparent card board, done up in a neat case with an eight-page book of directions, explaining the meaning of each card, &c. Per pack 50c.

CRIBBAGE BOARDS & BOXES. Handsomely Inlaid and complete with Pegs.

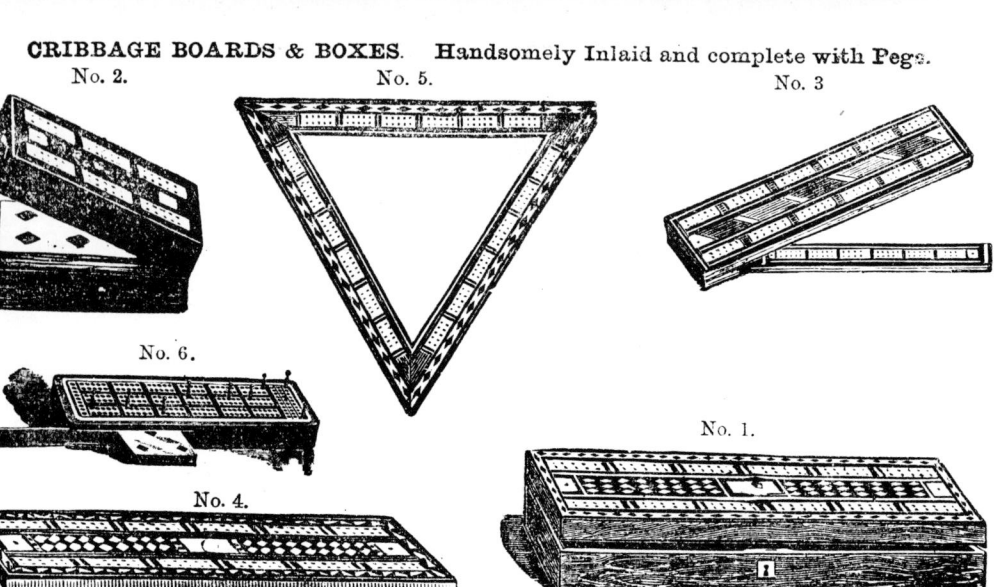

Cribbage Pegs of Bone extra make, Colored Red and White per set of 4 by mail, 10 and 15 cents.

Cribbage Boxes. (For two packs of Cards, see Cut No. 1.)

Nos.	1	2	3	4	5
Each	$1.25	1.50	2.25	3.50	5.00

Cribbage Boxes. (For one pack of Cards, see Cut No. 2.)

Nos.	XX	X	0	1	1½	2
Each	50	65	75	85	90	$1.00
Nos.	2½	3	4	5	6	7	8
Each	$1.25	1.50	1.75	2.00	2.25	2.50	3.00

Cribbage Boards. (For three players, Layout, see Cut No. 3.)

Nos.	1	2	3	4	5	6	7	8
Each	65	85	$1 25	1.50	1.75	2.00	2.50	3.00

Cribbage Boards. (Straight Boards, see Cut No. 4.)

Nos.	X	0	1	2	3	4	5	6	7	8	9
Each	30	35	40	65	75	85	$1.00	1.25	1.50	2.00	2.50

Cribbage Pins, Red and White, Small, per set of four, (see cut No. 7,) .... 10 cents.
" " " Large, " " .... 15 cents.

Triangular Cribbage Boards. (For three Players, see Cut No. 5.)

Nos.	0	1	2	3	4	5
Each	60	75	$1.00	1.25	1.75	2.00

Cribbage Boards.

Handsomely inlaid, for Saloons and Club Rooms, size of board, 14x4½ in.

Nos.	A,	B,	C, for two and four-handed game.
Each	$2.25	2.75	5.50
Nos.	D,	E,	F, for two, three and four-handed game.
Each	$2.75	3.50	6.50

No. 6. The New Patent Cribbage Board will score for two, three or four players, and keep tally for the game. For convenience and neatness it is the best. Has safe compartments for two packs of Cards, and for nine-pins. They are made of Polished Black Walnut, with heavy metal tops, sliding sides for cards, nickel plated, metal pins, (see cut 6,)... Each, $1 50

Compressed Ivory Billiard Balls.

1¾ inch	per set, $4 00	2⅜ inch	per set, $10.00
2 "	" 6 00	2½ "	" 12.00
2¼ "	" 8 00		
2¼ " Fifteen Pool Balls, assorted colors			" 26 00
2⅜ " " " " "			" 30 00

Bagatelle Balls.

1¾ inch............per set, $8 00 | 2 inch............per set, $10 00

The above Balls are of the same weight and elasticity of Ivory, do not get out of round and colors will not fade.

French Cue Tips, best........per doz. $0 30 | Chalk........................per doz. 25c.

CHECKER OR CHESS AND BACKGAMMON BOARDS.

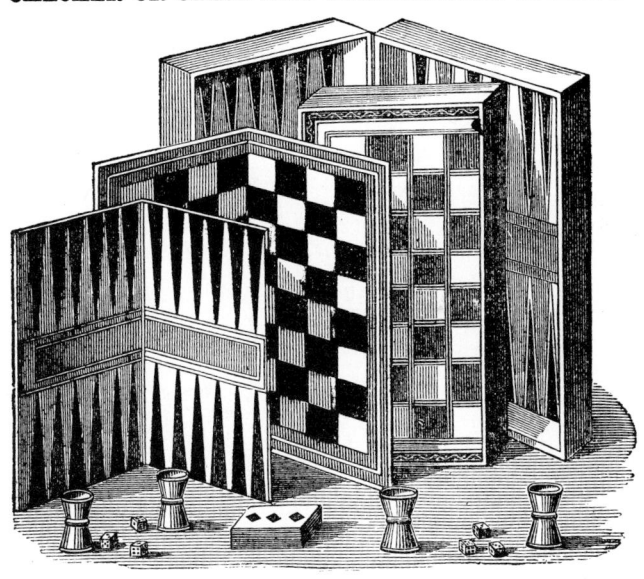

Nos.		Per Board.
111	Paper, Marble Border, Red and Black Squares...............................	14x14..$1 00
112	" " " " " "	17x17.. 1 25
113	Cloth Im. Leather Black Border, Red and Black Squares.....................	14x14.. 2 00
114	" " " " " " "	17x17.. 2 25
115	Leather Outside, Marble Border, Red and White and Black and White Squares...	14x14.. 2 50
116	" " " " " " " " "	17x17.. 3 00
117	Solid Eng. Leath. Ex. Fine, Red and Black, Red and White, and Black and White Squares	.14x14.. 4 00
118	" " " " " " " " " "	.17x17.. 4 50
119	Leatherette " " " "	.14x14.. 2 25
120	" " " Red and Black Squares..................	....17x17.. 2 50

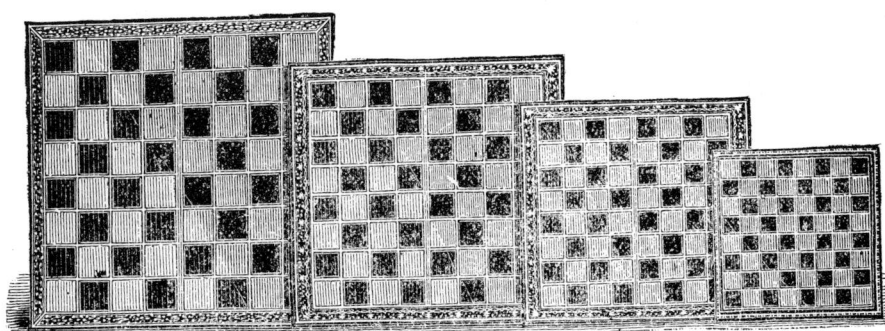

FLAT CHECKER OR CHESS BOARDS.

Nos.		Per Board.
102	Morocco Paper, Gold Stamped Back, Extra Heavy, Red and Black Squares...........	10½x10½....35c.
103	" " " " " " " " "	14 x14 ....50c.
104	" " Backgammon on Back, " " " " "	14 x14 ....60c.
105	Im. Leather Marble Border and Back, Extra Fine, " " " "	14 x14 ....75c.
106	" " " " " " " " "	17 x17 ..$1 00
107	" " " " " " " " "	20 x20 .. 1 50

IMPROVED TABLE CROQUET.

No. 1, Boxwood Set.—Containing eight 1¼ inch Boxwood Balls, finely polishsd and painted. Eight Boxwood Mallets of handsome design, polished and painted. Two Boxwood Stakes, polished, painted and weighted. Ten Weighted Wickets, enameled. Four Screw Clamps, for corners of tables, with fine long Belt. Packed in a blackwalnut box. Per set, complete, $3.50

No. 2, Rock Maple Set.—Containing eight 1¼ inch Maple Balls, finely polished and painted. Eight Maple Mallets, (*new design*) finely polished and painted. Two Weighted Stakes, with Weighted Wickets. Clamps and Belts similar to No. 1. Packed in a neat hinged-lid pine box, varnished
Per set, complete, $2.00

No. 3, The Set for the Million.—Containing eight fine Hard Wood Mallets. Eight 1¼ inch Balls, well painted. Ten Weighted Wickets. Two Painted Stakes. Wire Clamps and Belt, complete. Packed in a slide-cover pine box. Per set, complete, $1.00

THE DIAMOND C ⟨C⟩ HORIZONTAL STEAM ENGINE.

PRICE ONLY $12
For Alcohol or Gas.

CUT ONE-FOURTH ACTUAL SIZE.

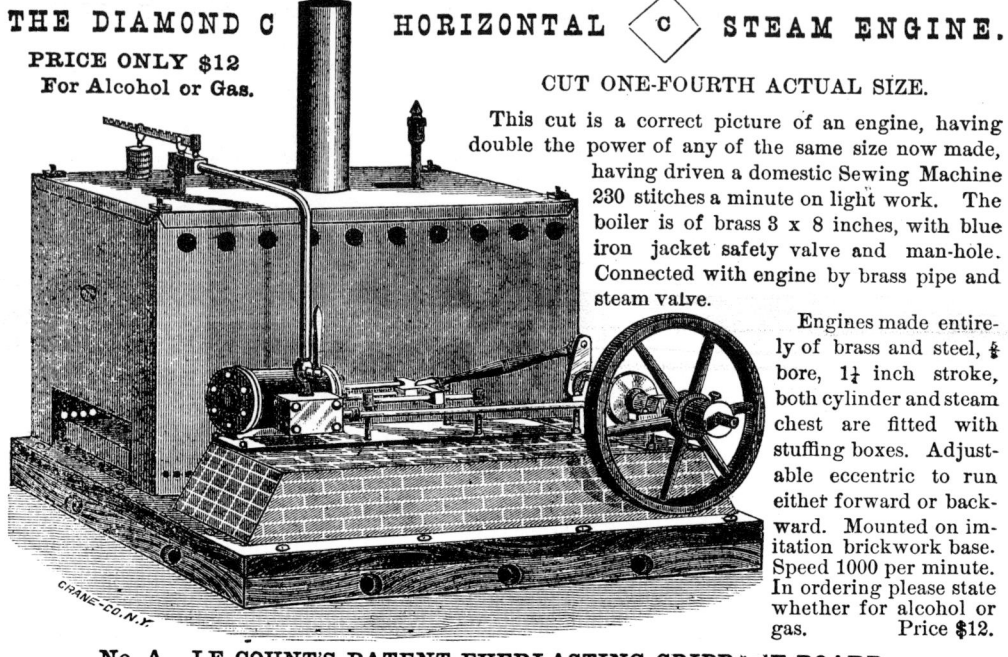

This cut is a correct picture of an engine, having double the power of any of the same size now made, having driven a domestic Sewing Machine 230 stitches a minute on light work. The boiler is of brass 3 x 8 inches, with blue iron jacket safety valve and man-hole. Connected with engine by brass pipe and steam valve.

Engines made entirely of brass and steel, ⅜ bore, 1¼ inch stroke, both cylinder and steam chest are fitted with stuffing boxes. Adjustable eccentric to run either forward or backward. Mounted on imitation brickwork base. Speed 1000 per minute. In ordering please state whether for alcohol or gas.   Price $12.

No. A.—LE COUNT'S PATENT EVERLASTING CRIBBAGE BOARD.

The case is wood, nicely polished. Has a compartment for nine plated brass pins, covered by a nickel slide. No boxes for cards. Will score for three or six players, and keep tally of the games. Has a metal top, polished and nickel plated.
   Price complete .... 75 cents.
   Prepaid by mail $1 00

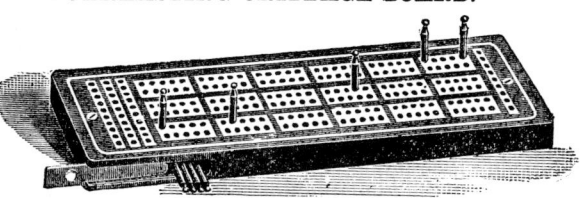

No. B.—LE COUNT'S CLIMAX CRIBBAGE BOARD.

This Board has a safe compartment for one pack of cards, and for six plated brass pins. It will score for two or four players, and keep tally of the games. The case is nicely polished. Has a metal top, polished and nickel plated. The slides of compartments are metel and polished. This board is made of white wood—stained, and is made to fill a demand for something cheaper. It is a very neat article.
   Price complete, $1 00.   Prepaid by mail, $1 25.
An extra set of nine turned and nickel plated pins, 15 cents.

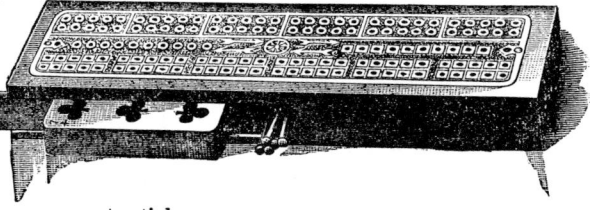

No. C.—LE COUNT'S NEW PATENT CRIBBAGE BOARD.

This Board has safe compartments for two packs of cards, and for nine plated brass pins. It will score for three or six players, and keep tally of the games. The case is made of black walnut, nicely polished. Has a metal top, polished and nickel plated. The slides of compartments are metal and polished.

Price complete, $1.25.   Prepaid by mail, $1.50

GYMNASIUM MATTRESSES.

Made of extra heavy canvas, knotted, leather handles and corners, filled with 2 inch Felt, $12.00, unfilled, $9.00, size, 6 x 5 feet, all hand made.

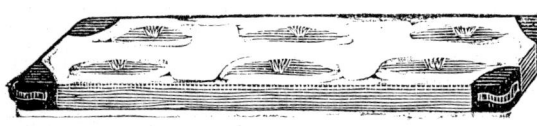

BONE CHIPS. (Round)—Bone Checks and Counters, Assorted Colors, and Finely Finished.

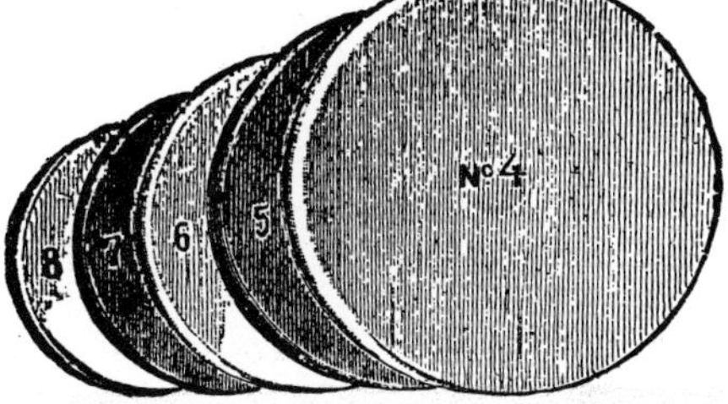

SECOND QUALITY THIN.

No. 667½, 1⅛ inch Red, White or Blue		$0 80
" 669, 1⅜ " " " "		1 25

FIRST QUALITY THICK.

No. 670, 1¼ inch Red, White or Blue	per 100,	$1 50
" 671, 1⅜ " " " "	"	1 65

FIRST QUALITY DOUBLE THICK.

No. 672, 1¼ inch Red, White or Blue	per 100,	$1 75
" 673, 1⅜ " " " "	"	2 00

Dennison's Ivory Finish Game Counters, or Poker Chips.

	Per 100.		Per 100.
No. 1, 1 inch in diameter	$0 50	No. 3, 1½ inch in diameter	$1 00
" 2, 1⅜ " "	0 75		

Waterproof, noiseless, slip easy, and cheap. Put up 100 in fine box (20 blue, 30 red, 50 white).

Compressed Ivory Checks and Whist Counters. Assorted Colors.

	Per 100.		Per 100.
1¼ inch plain	$1 25	1⅜ inch lined	$3 50
1⅜ " "	1 50	1½ " engraved	4 25
1½ " "	1 75		

Fine Morocco Covered Boxes for holding 200 Checks and Two Packs of Cards. Price of Box....$5 00

WITH SPLITS, MARKERS AND COPPERS.

	Per 100.		Per 100.
1¼ inch plain	$2 25	1½ inch lined	$4 25
1⅜ " "	3 25	Put up in Black Walnut Boxes.	

No. 4.

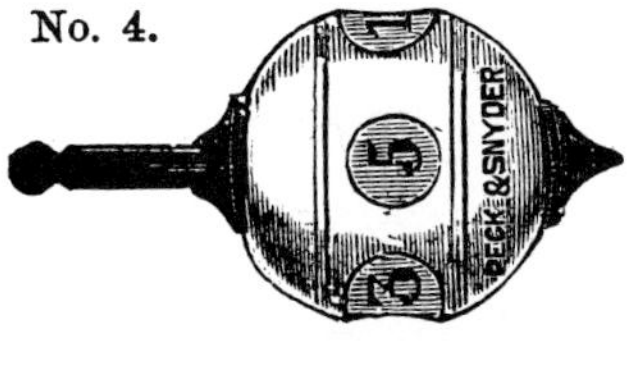

TETOTUMS OR SPINNING DICE.

No. 4. French make, very neat and accurate, made of fine Turkey Boxwood, numbered 1 to 6, and painted red or black, can be set so as to make any number wished to come on top every time, by mail each..........$1 50

Loaded Dice, per Set of Nine.

Three High, Three Low, Three Square..........Per Set, $5 00

Nos.	1	2	3	4	5	6	7	8	9
Diameter	¼ in.	5/16 in.	⅜ in.	13/32 in.	7/16 in.	½ in.	9/16 in.	19/32 in.	⅝ in.
Per Doz.	15c.	20c.	25c.	35c.	40c.	50c.	65c.	85c.	$1 00

DICE, EXACT SIZE, SQUARE CORNERS.

DICE FOR RAFFLING, ROUND CORNERS.

Nos.	1	2	3	4	5	6	7	8	9
Diameter	¼ in.	5/16 in.	⅜ in.	13/32 in	7/16 in.	½ in.	9/16 in.	19/32 in.	⅝ in.
Per Dozen	25c.	30c.	40c.	50c.	60c.	70c.	80c.	$1 00	$1 25

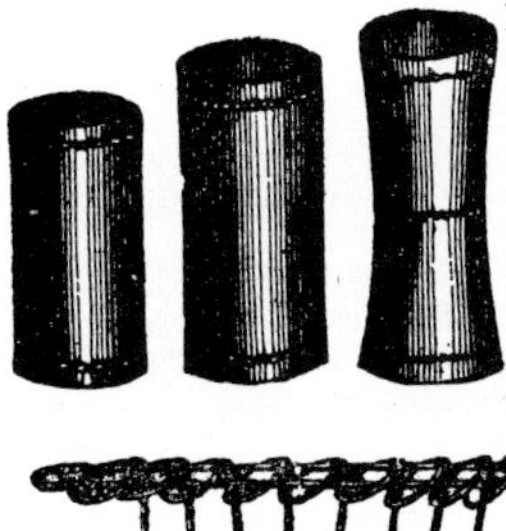

D, Pasteboard Cups, covered with leather,	per pair,	25 cents.
C, " " " " "	"	30 "
B, " " " " "	"	40 "
No. 1, Sole Leather, Small	"	30 "
No. 2, " " Medium	"	40 "
No. 3, " " Large	"	50 "
No. 2, Heavy Sole Leather, Small	"	50 "
No. 3, " " " Medium	"	65 "
No. 4, " " " Large	"	75 "

DICE CUPS of bone, beautifully chased for presents, $2.50 to $5.00 per pair.

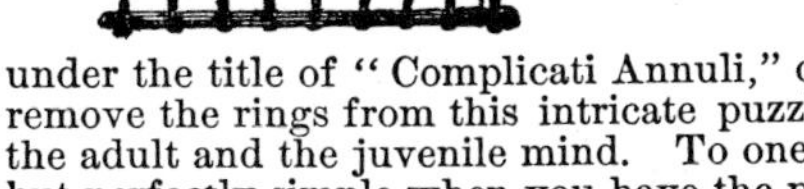

CHINESE PUZZLING RINGS.

This mechanical puzzle engaged the attention of Cardan in the 16th century; and the celebrated philosopher and mathematician, Doctor Wallis, has given a clear and elaborate description of the same in the second volume of his works, under the title of "Complicati Annuli," or Puzzling Rings. It requires from five to eight minutes to remove the rings from this intricate puzzle, after you have solved its solution. It will equally engage the adult and the juvenile mind. To one not in the secret it is next to impossible to disconnect the rings, but perfectly simple when you have the printed instructions which we send with each puzzle.

Price 25 cents. post-paid

SPECIALTIES IN GOOD GAMES,
For Home Amusements and the long Winter Evenings.

FOLDING BOARD GAMES.

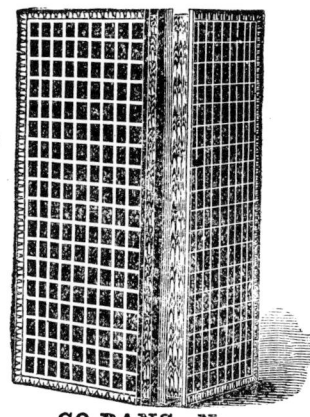

GAME OF LIFE'S MISHAPS.
Domine Rex and Diamonds and Hearts. Three Games in one Board. Complete $1.25.

GO BANG—New.
Russian Tivoli, Fox and Geese, Solitare, and the German Siege Game. Five Games in one Board. Complete $1.25.

THE MONOPOLIST—New.
Ten-Up, and Mariner's Compass. Three Games in One Board. Complete $2.00.
 On this board the great struggle between Capital and Labor can be fought out to the satisfaction of all parties, and, if the players are successful, they can break the Monopolist, and become Monopolists themselves. Ten-Up is named from its ten points to be made, and, like the Mariner's Compass, is fresh from the domain of invention.

THE PILGRIM'S PROGRESS.
Going to Sunday-School, and Tower of Babel. Three Games in One Board. Complete $2.00.
 A triple combination of moral games. The Pilgrim's Progress illustrates Bunyan's great book, The Sunday-School Game, The Temptations of Youth, and The Tower of Babel is based on the biblical accounts of the great tower.

 New Home Games.—These games have been thoroughly revised, and improved, and a new style Double Teetotum added, which is the best substitute for dice yet made. In their new dress, these boards are the best cheap folding games on the market.

QUOITS, TIGHT ROPE DANCING, CROQUET, NAVAL ENGAGEMENT, BEAR HUNT, RABBIT HUNT,
FISHING, THE PEARL DIVERS, FALCONRY, SPIDER AND FLY, LEAP FROG, DUCK SHOOTING.

Each of the above board-games also contains Morrice and Archery, thus having Three Distinct Games at the low price, per set...$0 75

JOHN GILPIN.—Rainbow Backgammon, and the Bewildered Travelers. Three Games in one board.—In the Gilpin Game, the famous order of the great "Train Band Captain" is made a reality—the Inn of the game being as difficult to reach as was the famed Inn at Islington. Rainbow Backgammon excels all other backgammon games, and the Bewildered Travelers is an originality that rarely fails to amuse. Complete, $2 00

Tousel, Checkers and Backgammon.—Three games in one board.................. " 1 25
The Captive Princess, Tournament and Pathfinders.—Three games in one board.... " 1 25
Ambuscade, Bounce and Constellation. Three Games in one board.................. " 1 25
Cats and Mice, Gantlope and Lost Diamond.—Three games in one board......... " 1 25

Picture A B C Blocks, Letters and Pictures.—Three sides contain Letters, and three Pictures. Finely Printed in Colors. Put up in covered wood boxes, handsome varnished label.
No. 1, 12 Cubes..................per Set, $1 00 | No. 3, 30 Cubes..................per Set, $2 50
No. 2, 20 "   ....   "   1 50 |

A B C Blocks, Letters.—Three sides red and three white. Ornamented edges. Plain Black Capital Letters. Put up in covered wood boxes.
No. 4, 12 Cubes...... ....per Set, $0 75 | No. 5, 20 Cubes..................per Set, $1 25

A B C Picture Blocks, Half Cubes.—Pictures and Letters in colors. Put up in covered wood boxes, showy label.
                                    No. 6, 13 Blocks..................per Set, $1 00

JEROME PARK STEEPLE-CHASE GAME.

The Balky Horse and Pool. Three Games in One Board. Complete $2.50.

The great hurdle-race game, whose merits have made it popular on both Continents. Balky Horse and Pool are both lively and fitting companions for it.

VARIETY COB HOUSE BUILDING BLOCKS.

These Blocks, for beauty, perfection and variety, surpass anything of the kind yet designed for our little friends. They will prove a treasure to the whole household. The little baby on the carpet will never weary of the endless ways of building with them. Boys and girls will find continual delight in the puzzles and houses they present, and adults can join with equal pleasure in playing their pretty and instructive games.

Each set contains an assortment of 176 Letters.

Each set will make six different Picture Puzzles, and a row of modern House Puzzles.

Each set will build a Cob House or Log Cabin, and Houses, Towers, Fences, and other structures in great variety.

Each set can be used to play a superior Letter Game, and to form words and sentences.

Each Puzzle House, Game, or use that these Blocks are intended for, is as perfect as though it were made for that special purpose alone. Complete set in box by express, $2 00

PECK & SNYDER'S AMERICAN CLUB ROLLER SKATE.

It is acknowledged by all skaters on ice that the "American" Club Fastening as used upon our popular ice skate for the past ten years is more quickly adjusted, and more secure than any other mode of adjustment ever invented. Roller skating has now become a popular amusement, and the demand for a Skate for experts has warranted us in producing a first-class Roller Skate with the "American Club" fastening. We place this Skate upon the market, believing its merits will at once put it in the front rank among expert Roller Skaters.

Price per pair, full Nickel Plated, with the best Turkey Boxwood Wheels, steel axles. &c.... $5.00

WINSLOW'S ALL CLAMP VINEYARD.
No. A. C.

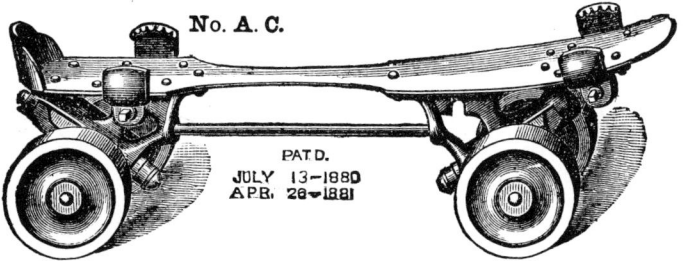

Ladies' Sizes, from 7 inches to 9½ inches. Gents' Sizes, from 10 inches to 11¼ inches.
Price per pair, Nickel-plated, all sizes... $5 00
In oiling, use Castor Oil.

WINSLOW'S HALF CLAMP VINEYARD.
No. S. C.

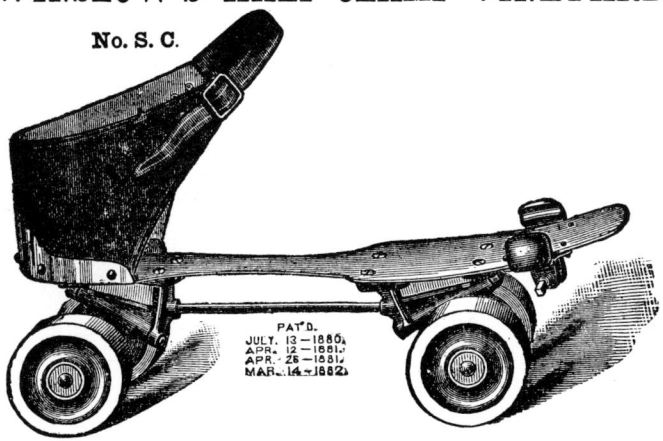

The annexed cut represents the New Half Clamped and Heel Strapped Roller Skate with Steel Top, Nickel-plated Heel Band and Plate. This skate is very much sought for by those having tender feet and requiring a support for the ankle. It is much preferred by expert skaters because of its lightness, and the neat appearance it presents upon the foot. The mechanism of the running parts is the same as that of Vineyard Roller "A," with Clamped Toe and Strapped Heel. This pattern is very much admired by ladies, and its use is becoming very general.

Price per pair, Nickel-plated, Sizes, 6½ to 11½ inches.................................. $5 00

THE RAYMOND "EXTENSION" SKATE.

No. 1. Gents' All-Clamp.

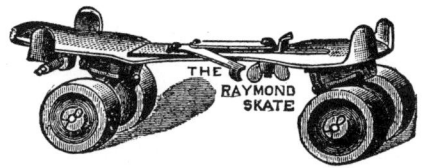

This is the only Adjustable All-Clamp Skate in the world. It is made to fit any size foot, and of the best material that money can buy. Is entirely new, and finely Nickel-Plated.

No. 1. Gent's Full Polished......Per Pair, $5 00
" 1. B. " Half Nickel....... " " 3 75

No. 3. Ladies' All-Clamp.

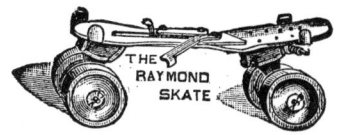

Made same as No. 1, but of lighter material. Can be adjusted to the smallest heel or narrowest toe.

No. 3. Ladies' Full Polished.....Per Pair, $5 00
" 3. Prize Ladies, all clamp .... " " 10 00
" 1. Gents' Racing Skate....... " " 10 00

No. 2. Gents' Half-Clamp.   FIT ANY SIZE FOOT.   No. 4. Ladies' Half-Clamp.

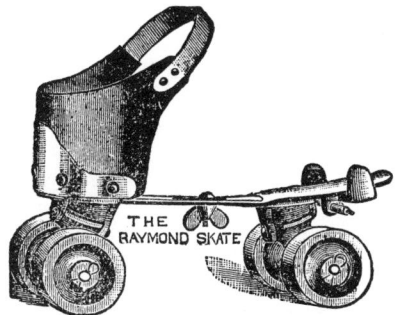

This Skate is made of Steel, finely Nickel-Plated, and adjustable to any size foot. Steel Axles. Turkish Boxwood Wheels, and the only one of the kind in the world.

No. 2. Gents' Full Polished......Per Pair, $5 00
" 2. B " Half Nickel........ " " 3 75

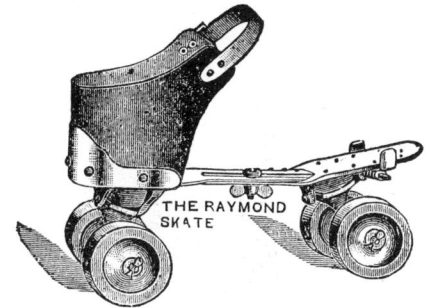

Made same as Gent's Half-Clamp but much lighter Clamps to fit the narrowest toed boots.

No. 4. Ladies' Full Polished......Per Pair, $5 00
" 4. B. " Half Nickel..... " " 3 75
" 5. Children's Full Polished... " " 4 00
" 5. B " Half Nickel .... " " 3 25

No. 4. Ladies' Prize Skate.   USED IN THE BEST RINKS.   No. 6. Rink Skate.

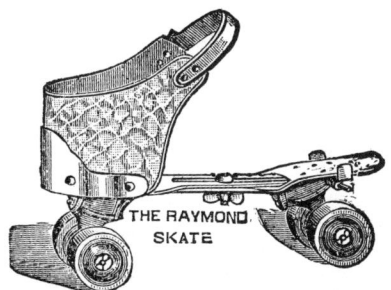

This Skate is handsomely polished and plated—the straps are of genuine Alligator skin of different colors, and the wheels have our patent Oil Guards attached, which is a safe protection from oil, a device fully appreciated by the ladies.

No. 4. Prize Ladies' Half Clamp, Per Pair, $10 00

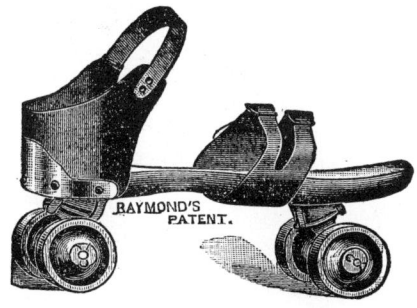

This Skate needs no recommendation, being perfect in every particular. Rock-Maple Woods, Turkish Boxwood Wheels, Steel Axles, and warranted in every respect.

No. 6. Rink Skate........... ....$2 50

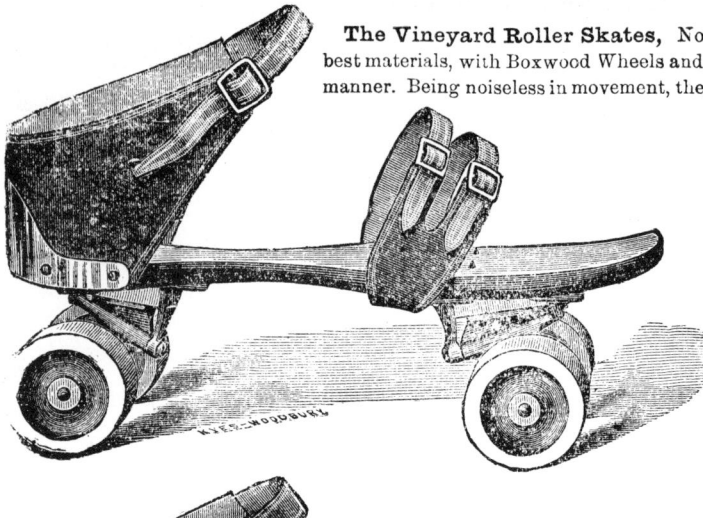

The Vineyard Roller Skates, No. A.—These Skates are made of the best materials, with Boxwood Wheels and Steel Axles, and finished in the best manner. Being noiseless in movement, they are very desirable for use in Rinks. The facility of the action of the circular or lateral mechanism enables the skater to perform all the difficult figures, as in ice skating, with natural ease and grace. Their merits have been thoroughly tested by thousands of skaters during the past season, and they have given complete satisfaction. Lengths, $6\frac{1}{2}$, 7, $7\frac{1}{2}$, 8, $8\frac{1}{2}$, 9, $9\frac{1}{2}$, 10, $10\frac{1}{2}$, 11, $11\frac{1}{2}$, 12, $12\frac{1}{2}$. With Ebonized Wood Tops, strapped complete with Patent Buckles. Price, per pair, $2 50

The Popular Roller Skates, with Four Boxwood Wheels.—They are thoroughly well made and nicely finished. The wheels are so adjusted as to balance the Skater without the danger of falling backward. Beginners can readily learn to skate upon them without fear of falling and hurting themselves. Use castor oil on the bearings. Lengths, 7 to $11\frac{1}{2}$ inches. Price, per pair, $1.00

Sample Pairs of Skates sent by Express on receipt of price, or by registered mail for 50 cents in addition to price for registering and postage.

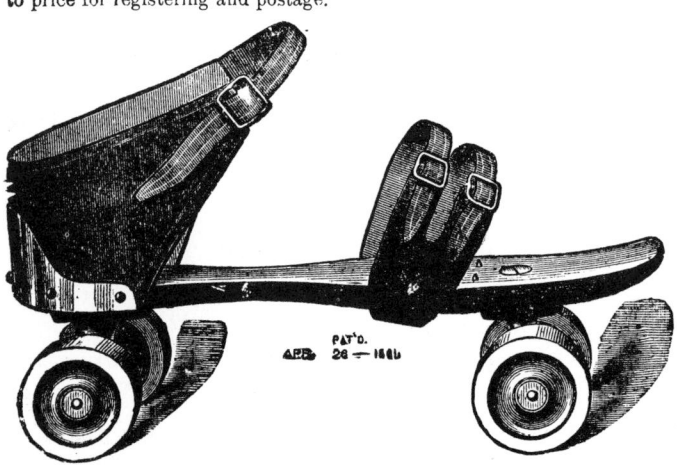

Climax Roller. The Roller Skates represented by the above cut are manufactured of the best materials and nicely finished in Ebonized Wood, with Pat. Buckle Straps Steel Axles and Malleable Iron Castings, having bearings one inch in length, which effectually prevents the wearing out by constant friction, as in the case with other low price Roller Skates. The Axles revolve in the hanger bearings, and the wheels revolve on the Axles, thus doing away with the friction that is common with other Roller Skates. Patent for these Axles and Bearings on Roller Skates was granted April 26, 1881. Sizes of Skates, 7, $7\frac{1}{2}$, 8, $8\frac{1}{2}$, 9, $9\frac{1}{2}$, 10, $10\frac{1}{2}$, 11, $11\frac{1}{2}$ inches.

Price per pair with Ebonized Woods, Boxwood Rolls... .$1.25

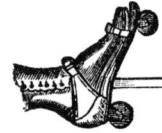

ROLLER SKATE SCARF PIN,
(Nickel Plated.)

This cut is the exact size. By mail, each, 25¢ Six by mail, $1.25. One doz., by mail, $2.00

BAGS AND BOXES FOR ROLLER SKATES.

   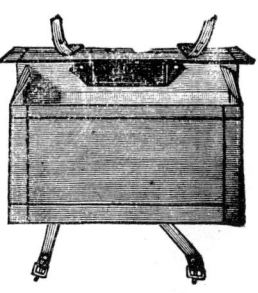

No. G.   No. A.   No. C.   No. H.

Each.
- No. A, Bag made of water-proof Duck, colored, for Clamp Skates, 9 inches and under $0 75
- " B, " " " " " " 9½ " and over 1 00
- " C, " " " " " " for Ladies' or Strap Skates, all sizes 1 25
- " D, " " of Russet Leather, fine finish, Clamp Skates, 9 inches and under 1 25
- " E, " " " " " " 9½ " over................ 1 50
- " F, " " " " " " for Ladies' or Strap Skates, all sizes........... 1 75
- " G, Box, " " " " " Clamp Skates, all sizes 2 50
- " H, " " " " " " for Ladies' or Strap Skates, all sizes............ 3 00
- " K, " Genuine Alligator Leather, Velvet Lined, lock and key for Clamp Skates......... 3 50
- " L, " " " " " " " " for Ladies or Strap Skates. 4 00
- " M, Russet Leather Shoulder Straps, for either of the above....................... 0 25
- " N, " " " " " " " " extra quality and finish........... 0 50

N. B.—All the above bags are of extra make and finish, with Nickel Plated Buckles and Trimmings.

POLO UNIFORMS.

	Each.	Dozen.
Worsted Polo Jerseys, Standing Collar, Plain Colors or Striped.......................	$4 50	$48 00
" " " no Collar " " "	3 75	42 00
" " " Navy Blue 2d quality only,....	2 25	24 00
Initial of Club on Shirt 25 cents extra.		
Complete name 2 inch letter 5 cents each letter.		
Jersey Polo Pants, all colors..Per Pair,	3 00	33 00
" " " Navy Blue only... "	1 50	15 00
Flannel " " All Colors... "	2 50	27 00
" " " White, Navy or Grey.. "	2 25	24 00
Corduroy Polo " All Colors... "	3 50	36 00
" Coats " "	9 00	96 00
" Polo Caps...	1 00	9 00
Flannel " "	0 75	8 00
Regulation " " Cloth, Patent Leather Visor...........................	1 50	15 00
Cotton Ribbed long Stockings, all colors................................Per Pair,	0 50	5 00
Worsted " " " " " " "	1 00	10 00
" Plain " " Navy, Red, Brown and Blue............... " "	0 50	5 00
Caps for Managers of Rinks, Directors, Aides and Ect...............$1 50, $2 00 and	2 50	
Embroidered Silk Initials for front of Shirts, Jerseys and Ect.......................	25	2 50
Low Estimates to Clubs on application, on any desired Uniform.		
Stocking Supporters..25c. and 50c. **Each.**		

FLANNEL POLO CAP.   KNIT POLO CAP.

THE BEST SKATE ROLLER AT A LOW PRICE.

No. 13.—**THE LAMINATE WOOD SKATE ROLLERS,**

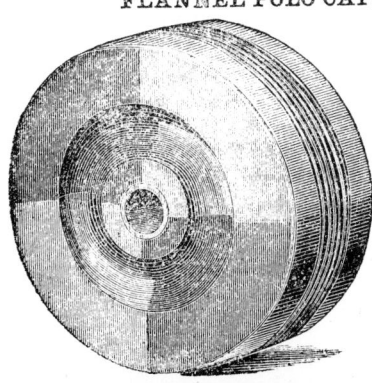

Are superior to Boxwood. Will not split, crack or Chip. **Will** not slip on the floor. They are light, handsome and durable.

They are made of tough hard wood Veneers, so constructed that the wear when in use, comes entirely on the end grain of the wood, causing them to wear exactly round.

They are accurately bushed, and run true and easy.

Each set neatly boxed. In ordering please state size **of spindle** and make of Skate used.

Order a set for trial. Write for price in lots.

Price, per set, 75 cents.

PRICE LIST OF SKATE ROLLERS AND FIXTURES FOR ROLLER SKATES.

When ordering Roller Wheels, or parts, please mention what Skate required for, as the arbor of different makes vary in size, we always keep on hand for the American Club, Raymond and Winslow.

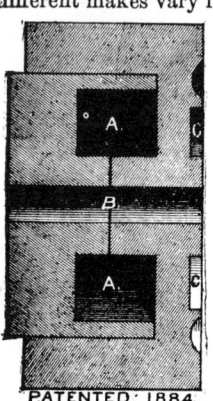

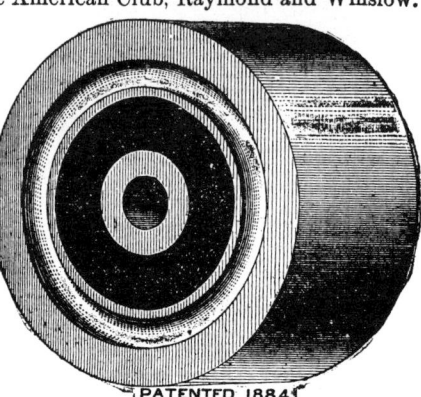

A A—Chamber containing oil sufficient to outwear the roller.

B—Capillary or small hair-line tube through which oil is supplied.

C—Felt absorbent. Prevents clothing and floor becoming soiled.

Ladies take notice, and dispense with your oil cans. Always clean, always oiled and ready for use.

No. 1.
Self Lubricating Skate Roller, always clean, always oiled and ready for use, made of Boxwood, 2 inches diameter.   Per Set of 8, $1.25

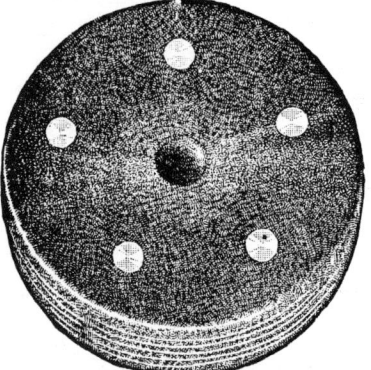

No. 2. **Patent Cork Rollers,** made with two thicknesses of Boxwood outside and one center thickness of Cork two inches diameter....per set $1.00
No. 3. Same as No. 2, but Brass Bushed....... .... " 1.50
No. 4. **Peck & Snyder's New Racing Rollers** made with three thickness of Boxwood and two of Cork, 2¼ inches diameter.............per set $1.50
No. 5. **Peck & Snyder's New Racing Rollers** made from the best selected Boxwood and finely finished, are very durable, were used in the 6 days Race, at Madison Square Garden, March 2–7, 1885, and not one of them was broken or worn out, can be used only upon the American Club Roller, size 2¼ inches diameter..per set, $1.00
No. 6. **Peck & Snyder's New Roller,** made same as No. 5, only smaller size, 2⅛ inches in diameter......................Price, per set, $0 75
No. 7. **Peck & Snyder's New Rollers,** made same as No. 5, only smaller size, 2 inch diameter,................................per set, 60 cts.

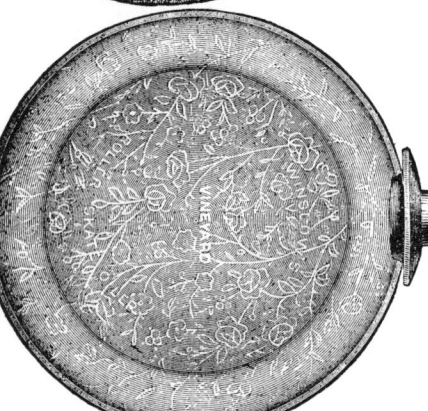

No. 8. **SOLID RAW HIDE SKATE ROLLERS.** We call the attention of manufacturers of Roller Skates, Proprietors of Skating Rinks, Dealers and others, to our Skate Rollers made wholly of Raw Hide.

These Rollers are very durable, comparatively noiseless, need but little oil, do not slip, and cannot break. They have been thoroughly tested and have given perfect satisfaction, they are made extra secure and strong with the improvement of 5 brass screw rivets passing through them. Demand steadily increasing. Orders should state diameter of axle.

Price, diameter 2 inch............................per set $1.50

THE NEW POCKET OILER.

VINE PATTERN.

This Oiler is made of Figured Brass and Finely Nickel-plated, it is an indispensable article for all Skaters,

Bicycle Riders, Sportsmen and Machinists, and is useful in every household.   Nickel, sent by Mail for 15 cents each.
Gold Plated............20 cents "

No. 9—A PERFECT ROLL—THE KEYSTONE RUBBER COMPANY'S PATENT HARD RUBBER COMBINATION ROLLER.

These Rollers are made of the best rubber, and are indorsed and conceded by experts to be the only perfect skate roller made. They are furnished with a metal box or bushing, thus reducing the friction to a minimum. They will not slip. They are practically noiseless. They will not chip. The wear in use is hardly appreciable, and they will outlast three sets of other rollers.   Price per set, $1 25.

No. 10—THE NEW COMPOSITION PATENT AGATINE SKATING WHEELS.

This cut represents the new Jennie Houghton Skate Wheel which is made especially for professionals and persons having their own skates. These wheels are made of the very best materials combined in the most substantial and artistic manner, the journals, spokes and felloes being cast in one piece of the finest composition or gun metal, and the tire or floor contacting surface is made of the new and durable compound called "Agatine," noted as a hard and tough substance, filling all the requirements for a practical Skate Wheel. They are heartily endorsed by all who have tried them for easy running, smooth, and not slipping.   Price per set, $2.50. 10c. extra by mail.

PECK & SNYDER, THE LARGEST DEALERS IN ROLLER SKATES and FIXTURES IN THE TRADE. LIBERAL TERMS TO RINKS AND DEALERS.

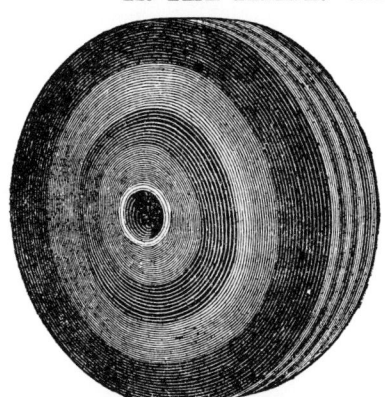

No. 11.—THE "LAMINAR" ROLLER

Is unquestionably the handsomest as well as the best roller in the market, and has many points of superiority over all others, due to its peculiar construction. It is composed of fifteen layers of thin wood, firmly cemented together with the grains running transversely. The great advantages secured by this construction are as follows: It will not split; it will not notch across the tread; it will not slip or slide; the tread will not wear off unevenly, as do many of the boxwood, and can keep going easier because there is less resistance on the floor. They are free from knots and defects. A set of rollers weigh about 3 ounces less than a set of the boxwood, hence they are easier to handle and do not tire the skater so soon. Owing to the tread being narrower our roller presents a much more handsome and graceful appearance than the boxwood. Being finished a rich mahogany color, they do not show the dirt or oil as do the light colored rollers, and on account of its peculiar shape is much more easily cleaned. It is the lightest roller in market.

Price, per set, 2 inch, $1.00 ; 2¼ inch, $1.25

No. 12.—PATENT COMPRESSED FIBRE SKATE ROLLER.

ONE OF THE BEST IN THE WORLD.

Outwear all others   Run easier. Do not slip. Require less oil. Make less noise. Do not chip or break, and are consequently safer and more adapted for fancy skating.

Price per set, $1.75

No. 14.—THE BONTON SKATE ROLL.

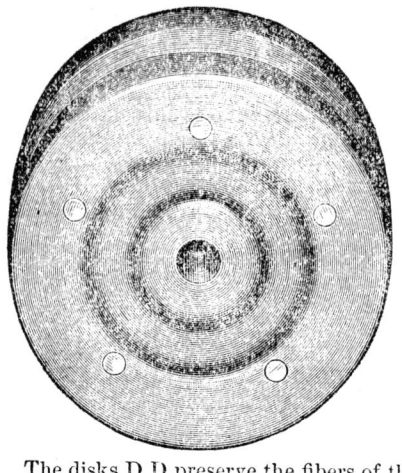
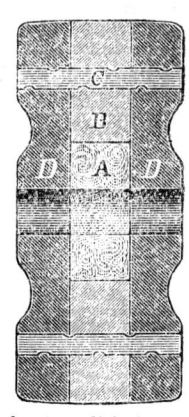

These rolls are made of three or more disks, B. D. D. securely united by screw-threaded wires, C, passing through the entire roll. The centre A is formed of a disk of felt, which once saturated with oil will supply sufficient lubrication for more than a week of constant use. B is an annular disk of leather which is slightly larger than the two inclosing disks of raw hide, or leatheroid, or similar material, bringing the pressure upon the leather disk, and securing that frictional contact of the leather which will afford a "clinging" or slight resistance to SLIDING while it allows the skate to roll freely This peculiar action of the fibrous leather disk on the floor gives a steadiness and accuracy of motion which no skater will fail to notice and appreciate.

The disks D D preserve the fibers of the leather disk from being worn away by abraision, and as they are made of a semi-elastic material they will not mar or injure the floor.

The method of lubrication is an important advantage as the outer surface of the roll and bearing is always clean, and when the roll is in motion the oil is securely held in the interior chamber by centrifugal force and prevented from flying and soiling the clothing of the skater.

Put up one set of 8 rolls in a neat box, per set, $1.75

THE BAY STATE SKATE ROLL.

In introducing the "Bay State" Roll, a want long felt is supplied, in giving a metallic roll, light, handsome, of moderate price, durable and exceedingly easy running. These qualities we claim for the "Bay State." While the rolls have a metallic centre, they also have a bearing or bushing of fibre, on semi-elastic material, thus avoiding the direct contact between the axle and a metal wheel.

A band or tire of the same material precludes the possibility of marring the floor, and at the same time gives a smooth and almost noiseless running roll with all the necessary "clinging" qualities.

It is in the manner of construction that we claim the "Bay State," superior to any other metal roll. While no glue, cement, pin or screw are used, and without even "shrinking" on the band, by our process the roll becomes virtually solid, the bearing being secured in a like way.

Put up one set of 8 rolls in a neat box, per set, $1.75

SKATING POLO SHIN GUARDS.

A new and useful article now extensively used in the game of Roller Skating Polo. Are a great protection to the ankles or shins from accidental hits with the Polo sticks. Made of selected hard wood, painted and varnished, strong straps and buckles...per pair, $0 75

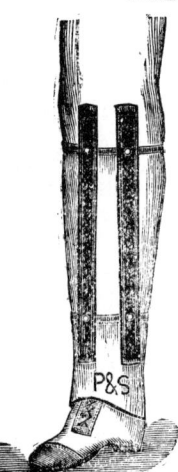
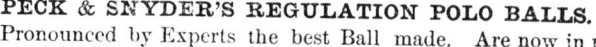

PECK & SNYDER'S REGULATION POLO STICKS.

Made from thoroughly seasoned straight grained wood and well balanced.........................Per Dozen, $5.00. Each, 50 cents.

PECK & SNYDER'S REGULATION POLO BALLS.

Pronounced by Experts the best Ball made. Are now in use throughout all the Rinks in the States and Canada.

Per Dozen, $9.00. Each, $1.00

Goal Posts, per Set of 4..$5.00
" Flags of Bunting, per Set of 4.......................... 2.00
Playing Rules of Rink Polo............................... 0.10

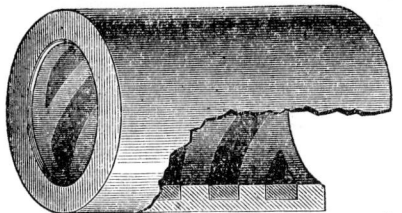

THE PATENT GRAPHITE BUSHING

Is offered to Roller Skaters. One bushing fitted in each roller for the axle to bear on, makes the best lubrication yet offered to skaters.

Bushing is made of closely knit hard brass, filled with graphite composition, the lines in black showing same; the graphite and brass surfaces are flush, wear evenly, and require no refilling.

The kind of Oil.—Use Neats-foot Oil, or Castor Oil thinned with some kerosene. Avoid Sperm Oil or any others tending to make gum. If any gum appears wipe same off or use a little kerosene, which will cut it away. It is advisable to use your own oil for occasionally oil will be found in rinks that works thick and gummy.

Cleanliness of Roller.—These bushings, when oiled before skate is adjusted to foot, can be oiled so sparingly that it will not run on roller; if it does, if wiped clean the roller will be clean for the intervals between oiling.

About Axles—The tests made have shown that much greater service results from skates using perfectly round axles, made of steel and tempered hard.

In connection with the bushing, some of Stubb's English Steel has been cut and tempered and is offered as a superior axle for experts' use.

Advantages of Graphite Bushing.—It runs almost without oil. It is swift and indescribably smooth—no exertion in maintaining motion, thereby lessening fatigue and reducing the tendency to overheating; no jarring sensation under foot; the skating is uniform. The bushing having a round hole and wearing very slowly it remains round; this is a valuable feature, because the constant skating and turning corners in one direction rapidly wears away the hole in roller. The only extra expense is the bushing itself, as the replacing of rollers is a necessary outlay, and this is lessened because only the wear on outside edges must be provided for. This is the only Bushing before the public that can be replaced in roller, other bushings are discarded with the rollers.

Set of bushings, $1.25. Set of rollers fitted with bushings ready for use, $1.75. Set of axles temp. from Stubbs' steel, 60 cents. 2¼ inch Boxwood Racing Wheels with Graphite Bushings, per Set, $2.00.

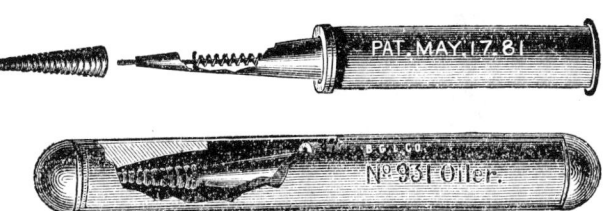

This little oiler is especially adapted to ladies' and gentlemen's use in connection with the bushing. Each oiler enclosed in small wood tube convenient to carry in the pocket.

Pressing the protruding wire plunger releases one drop of oil. This oiler insures freedom from waste, coagulation, or leakage. The sheath is an additional safeguard. Price, each, 25 cents.

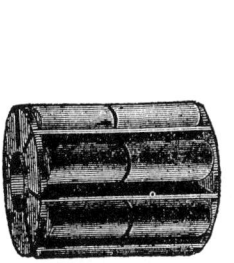

Side View.

ROLL.

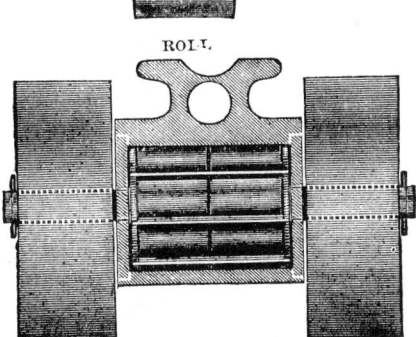

End View.

BARRETT'S ANTI-FRICTION ROLLER BEARING.

The Best yet Produced for Roller Skates. Patented January 13th, 1885.

Among the leading advantages are:

1st. They run twice as easy as the regular Skate.
2d. They require oiling but once a month when in constant use, otherwise once a year.
3d. There is no oil coming out on your clothes, as they are perfectly clean. Any lady or gentleman can wear the finest clothes with safety.
4th. The spindle upon which the wheels are on, passes through a bushing that is as hard as can be made, which is three times the diameter of the spindle, upon which there are 14 hard rolls, ¼ inch in diameter, and are warranted never to wear out or break.
5th. Once tried, you would not be without them. Specially adapted for racing and fancy skating. Any one can put them on to their own skate of any make, but are made more especially for the Winslow and American Club Roller Skate........................Price, Nickel Plated, Per Set, $3.50

PRICES FOR ODD PARTS FOR ROLLER SKATES.

		Each.
No. 1.	Hangers for Sidewalk or Popular Roller	$0 15
" 2.	Axles for Sidewalk or Popular Roller	0 10
" 3.	Wheel Pins or Cutters	0 01
" 4.	Maple Wheels	0 03
" 5.	Boxwood Wheels Vineyard or Climax	0 06
" 6.	Vineyard Hangers, complete	0 50
" 7.	Climax " "	0 20
" 8.	Axle for Vineyard Skates	0 15
" 9.	Rubbers for Vineyard Skates	0 05

CHEAP ROLLER SKATES.

No. 5. SPECIAL.
(See Illustration.)

This is a good reliable Skate, with first-class patent buckle straps........Per Pair, $1 00

No. 6. SIDEWALK.
The same style as No. 5, only with narrow strap in front.
Per Pair...$0 75

No. 7. YOUTHS.
The same style as No. 6, only with narrow straps at both heel and toe, the cheapest Skate in the market.......Per Pair, $0 50

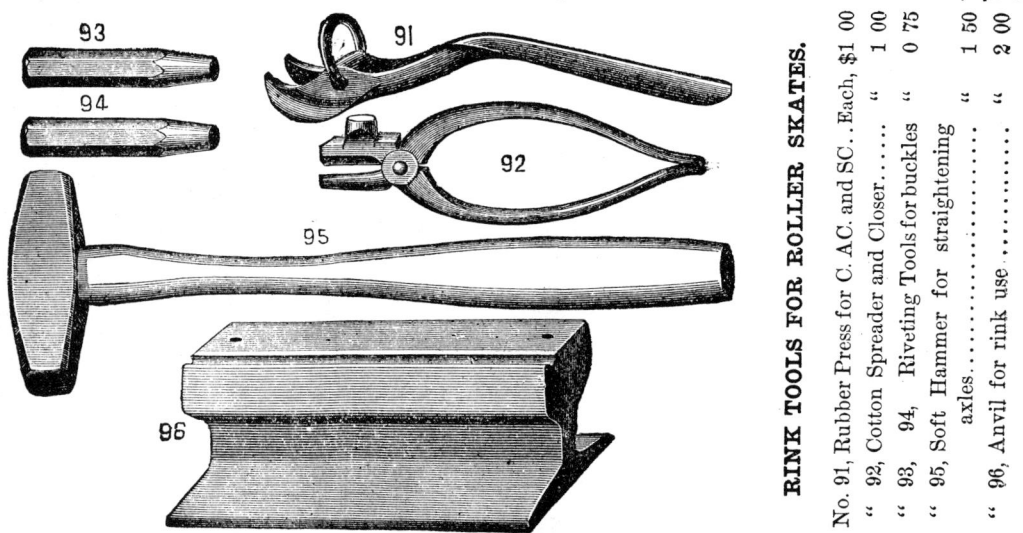

RINK TOOLS FOR ROLLER SKATES.

No. 91, Rubber Press for C. AC. and SC..Each, $1 00
" 92, Cotton Spreader and Closer...... " 1 00
" 93, 94, Riveting Tools for buckles " 0 75
" 95, Soft Hammer for straightening axles............................ " 1 50
" 96, Anvil for rink use.............. " 2 00

RAW HIDE SKATE BOXES FOR ROLLER SKATES.

Something new they are very light and pretty, lined with flannel and are the only water proof boxes made, they are made in two styles, for Ladies' Skates and Club Skates, when ordering please mention size of Skate and if for Club or Ladies' Skates.
Prices, each....................................Ladies' Skates, $2 50, Club Skates, $2 00

No. 2. HOUSEHOLD TOOL.

This new candidate for public patronage unites in one, eight different implements, as follows: Glass Cutter, Wrench, Can Opener, Ice Pick, Knife and Scissors Sharpener, Saw Set, Tack Hammer and Cork-Screw.

Dozen, by mail, $1.25; 100 by express, $6.50; sample, by mail, 25 cents.

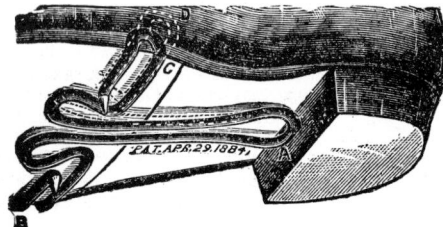

WEST'S PATENT STEEL WIRE ICE CREEPERS.—The only Ice Creeper made requiring no screws or staps to adjust.

Can be put on and taken off instantly and worn with either shoes or rubbers.

Send for a sample pair, and give them a trial, before buying any of the old styles. Every creeper warranted.

Price $2 per dozen   Per pair, 25c.

PECK & SNYDER'S PATENT SELF-ADJUSTING AMERICAN CLUB SKATE.

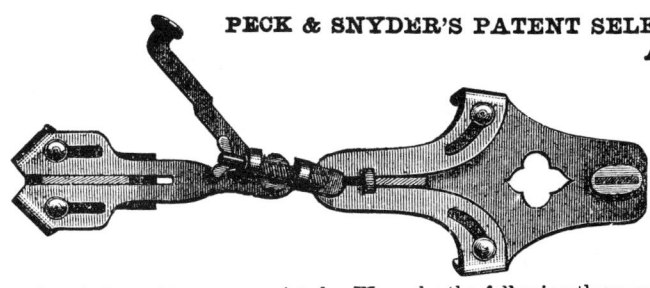

To fasten the American Club Skate to the foot, throw the lever forward and adjust the clamps to the width of the sole and heel by turning the thumb screw. Do not adjust too tight. If you cannot bring the lever in position by a firm pressure of the thumb, you have the adjustment too tight. The increased sale of this popular Skate each year since their introduction, is a sufficient guarantee to us that their merits are appreciated. We make the following three grades of finish:

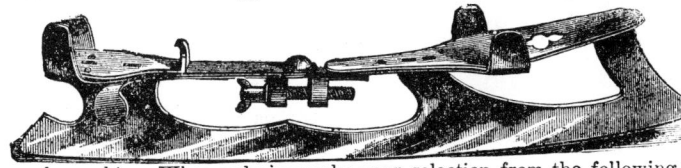

No. 1. This style is of the best quality, with welded, tempered and polished steel blades, and blued steel foot rest and clamps. As we make no second quality of the American Club Skate this number is as good as our No. 4, except in point of finish and workmanship. When ordering make your selection from the following sizes, which must correspond with the length of shoe from heel to toe. Sizes— 8, 8½, 9, 9½, 10, 10½, 11, 11¼ and 12 inches.

Ladies when buying Skating Shoes should select the flat "Common Sense" heel, as no clamp fastening can be secured to a French heel.

Price, per pair, $4.50

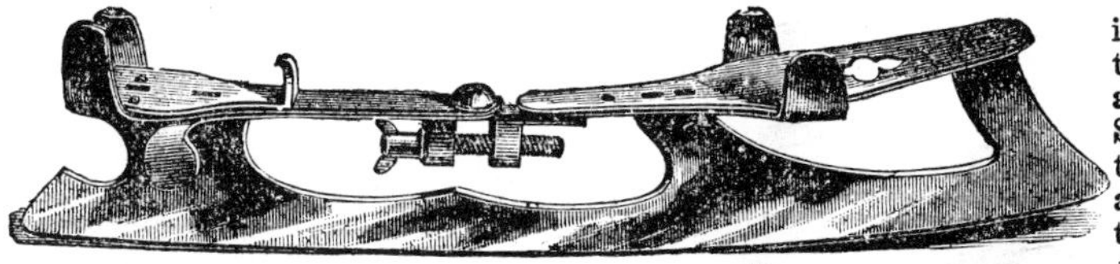

No. 2. The above style in all respects is the same as No. 1, with the exception of the parts instead of being blued are "tumbled" bright, and the entire Skate is then electro-nickel plated. As this process adds very much to the appearance as well as being a preventative against rust, this makes No. 2 the most popular style.

Price, per pair, $5.50

No 4. This is the finest finished Skate in the country, each part before being assembled is highly polished and Nickel Plated. Price, per pair, $7.00
Fancy lined Morocco cases for holding the above. Each, $2.00.

New York Club Skates, No. A. D. —All Steel, in latest design. They are strong and tough, and will not break with hardest wear. Broad Toe Straps, Heel Buttons and Plates. The best article ever made, at smallest cost. Lengths, 7 to 11½ inches.

Price, per pair, 50 cents.

New York Club Skates, No. H. —In new design, all steel, unbreakable in use, with Double Acting Toe Clamps, Japanned Tops, Heel Plates and Buttons. The cheapest Club Skate with Toe Clamps. Recommended for strength and serviceable quality. Lengths, 7½ to 11¼ inches.

Price, per pair, $1.00

All Clamp Club Skates, No. A. X. —Can be instantly adjusted without Straps, without Heel Plates. All Steel Tops and Runners. Perfect working parts. Lengths, 8 to 12 in.

Price, per pair, $1.25

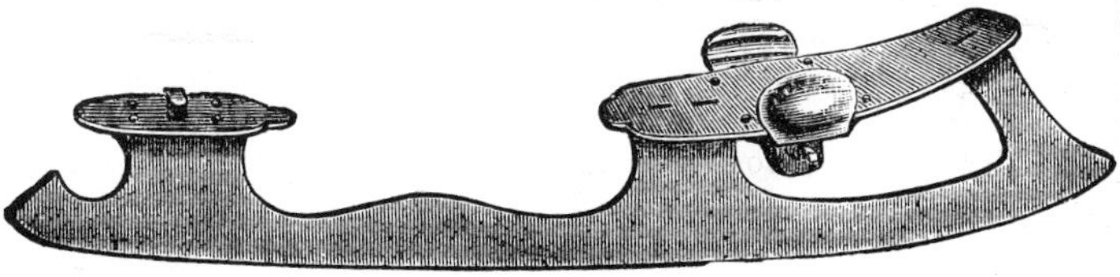

New York Club Skates, No. B. B. —Cast Steel Polished Blades, Blue Steel Tops, Double Acting Toe Clamps, Heel Buttons and Plates. An excellent Skate in graceful design. The very low price at which they are sold has made this style one of the most saleable patterns throughout the United States and Canada. Lengths 8 to 12 in.

Price, per pair, $2.00

THE HALIFAX PATTERN.

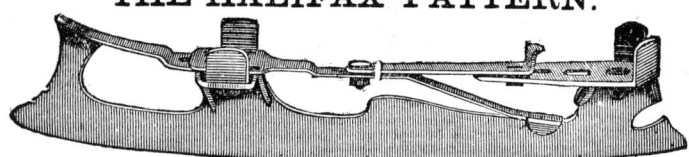

No. 5. Plain finish, Hardened Runners...Per Pair, $1 25
" **6.** Full Nickel Plated... " 2 00

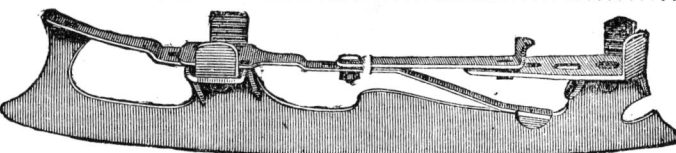

No. 7. Best Steel Runners, Blued, Foot Rests,.................................Per Pair, $3 00
" **10.** Same as No. 7, full Nickel Plated...................................... " $4 00

NOTICE. WHEN ORDERING SKATES PLEASE OBSERVE THE FOLLOWING INSTRUCTIONS.

Scale of Sizes of Ice and Roller Skates as adapted to Shoes worn by Ladies, Children and Men.

No. of Shoe	12 or 12½	13 or 13½	1 or 1½	2 or 2½	3 or 3½	4 or 4½	5	6 or 7	8 or 9	10
No. of Skate	7	7½	8	8½	9	9½	10	10¼	11	11½

No. 348. Blued Tops, Rolled Cast Steel Polished Runners, Black Leather Heel Straps with Brass Heel Bands Patent Buckles, and double acting Toe Clamps.
Price, per pair, $2 75

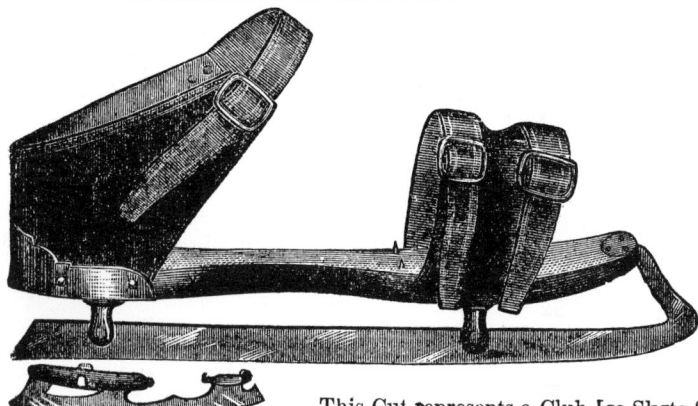

No. 349. Runners Welded Steel Hardened, Nickel-plated and Buffed, Black or White Stitched Leather Heel Straps, Nickel-plated Heel Bands, Patent Buckles, style same as No. 348. Sizes, 8 to 10¼ inches.
Price, per pair, $3 75

No. 286. Nickel-plated Runners, Standards and Heel Bands, Ebony Woods, Black or Russet Leather Trimmings, lined and stitched, Pat. Buckles. Sizes, 7 to 10¼ inches.
Price, per pair, $3 00

This Cut represents a Club Ice Skate Scarf Pin, exact size, it is made of German Silver, Nickel plated, and got up very neatly.
Price by Mail,...25 cents.

STEAM WHISTLE FOR STEAM ENGINES.

Can be attached in a moment to any of our engines. Has a Slide Valve, and can be opened and shut at pleasure. Each, 15 cents.
Steam Whistles, small models, and same as are used on steamboats, engines and locomotives, solid brass, English make, Each, 75 cents; $1 00 and $1 50

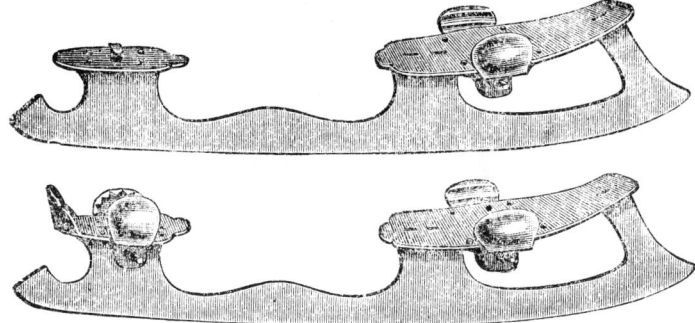

New York Club Skates, No. C. C.—All Nickel Plated, New York Club, Cast Steel Polished Blades, Double Acting Toe Clamps. Not liable to rust, durable and desirable. Lengths 8 to 12 inches.

Price, per pair, $3 00

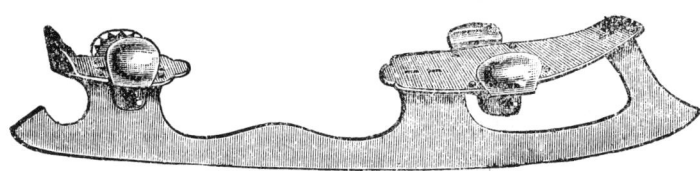

All Clamp Club Skates, No. B X.—All Clamp Club. Cast Steel Runners, Blued Steel Tops. Double Acting Heel and Toe Clamps, working independently of each other, admit of ready adjustment to all forms of soles, and is a most secure fastening. Is in the best style of Double Clamp Skates, thoroughly strong, at moderate cost. Lengths, 8 to 12 inches. Blued Tops, Polished Blades, $2.50

Price, per pair, Nickel-plated $3 50

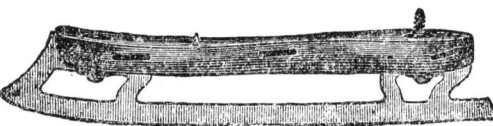

No. A C., the same Style as B X.—The Blades are made of Best Welded Steel face, extra tempered. Blued Steel Tops. Double acting Heel and Toe Clamps. The Nickel Plated Skates are thoroughly plated and buffed in the best manner, making a very durable and ornamental Skate. They are fully warranted. Lengths 8 to 12 inches.
Polished Blades, Blue Tops, Per pair, $3 00
Nickel Plated and Buffed, Per pair, 4 00

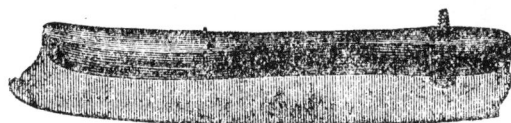

No. 95. Wood Top Skates for Broad Toe Straps and Narrow Heel Straps. The runners are of best steel castings and fastened into the wood with screws and nuts at toe and heel in such a manner that the woods will not split. Has Heel Screws and Toe Points. Sizes, 7 to 11 inches. Price, per pair, without Straps, 75 cents.

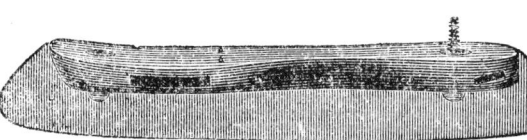

Half Rocker, No. 200.—The Heel Screw passes through a Brass Thimble, which greatly strengthens the Skate, and prevents the wood splitting. Sizes, 7 to 11 inches. Price, per pair, without straps, $1.00

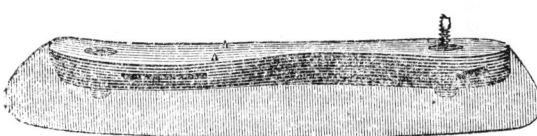

Half Rocker, No. 245.—Varnished Beech Woods, Solid Runners, fastened in a secure manner to the woods by Brass Thimbles—a device which ingeniously and effectually prevents the breaking or the splitting of the woods. With Heel Screws. Sizes, 8 to 11½ inches.

Price, per pair, without Straps, $1 25

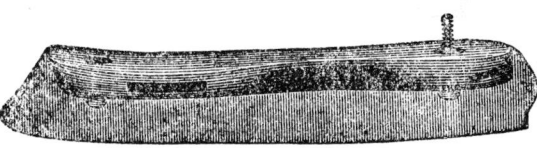

Rocker, No. 250—Varnished Beech Woods, Solid Runners, finished in same manner and fastened with Brass Thimbles, as in No. 245. Sizes, 8 to 11½ in.

Price, per pair, without Straps, $1 25

Half Rocker, No. 295—Solid Cast Steel Blades, French Polished Beech Woods, fastened with Brass Thimbles. Sizes, 8 to 11½ inches.

Price, per pair, without Straps, $1 75.

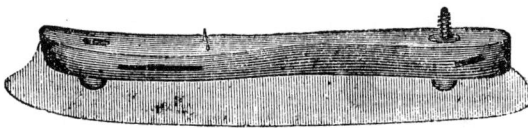

Rocker, No. 300.—Solid Cast Steel Blades, French Polished Beech Woods, fastened with Brass Thimbles. Sizes, 8 to 11½ inches.

Price, per pair, without Straps, $1.75
For Price of Straps see following page.

No. 220. The Wood Tops of these Skates will not split. Have Heel and Toe Spurs. The Runners are of best steel castings fastened into the woods with Screws and Nuts.

They are furnished ready for use with Black or Russet Leather Heel and Broad Toe Straps, Brass Heel Bands. Sizes, 7 to $10\frac{1}{2}$ inches.

Price, per pair, $1 25

No. 270. Runners of best Steel castings, Wood Tops fastened to Runners with Screws and Nuts which effectually prevents splitting or breakage. Black Leather Heel and Broad Toe Straps with Brass Heel Bands. Sizes, 7 to 10 in.

Price, per pair, $1 50

Standard Frame Steel Blades. —**No. 272.** French Polished Beech Woods, Strapped complete, with Brass Heel Bands, Broad Toe straps, Black Leather Trimmings, Buckles with Brass Tags. Sizes, 7 to $10\frac{1}{2}$ in.

Price, per pair, $2 00

Standard Frame Steel Blades. —**No. 280.** French Polished Beech Woods, Strapped complete, with Nickel-plated Heel bands, Broad Toe Straps, Patent Buckles, Black or Russet Leather Trimmings, lined and sfitched. Sizes, 7 to $10\frac{1}{4}$ in.

Price, per pair, $2 5(

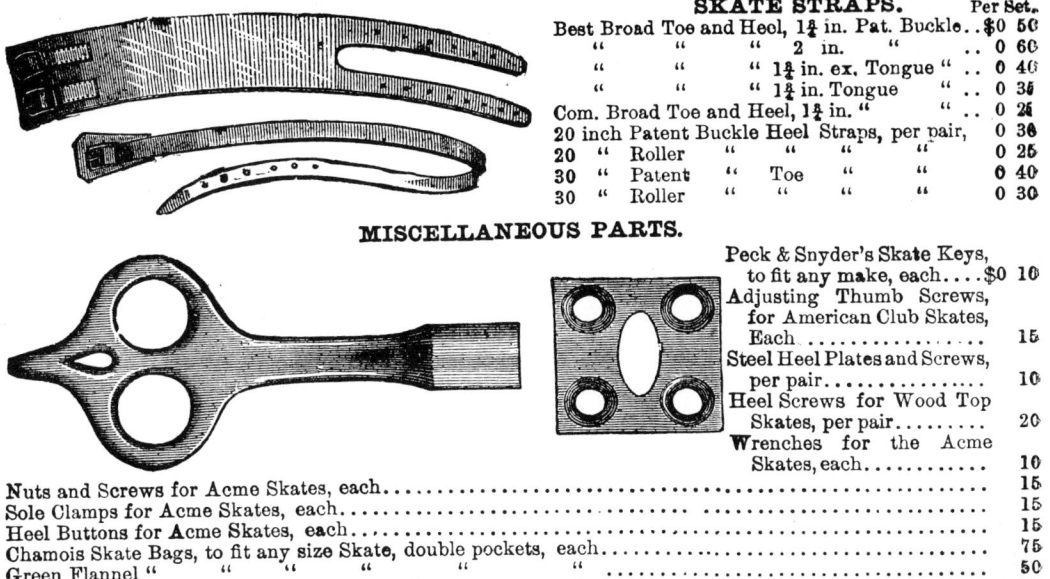

SKATE STRAPS.

	Per Set.
Best Broad Toe and Heel, 1¼ in. Pat. Buckle..	$0 50
" " " " 2 in. " ..	0 60
" " " " 1¼ in. ex. Tongue " ..	0 40
" " " " 1¾ in. Tongue " ..	0 35
Com. Broad Toe and Heel, 1¼ in." ..	0 25
20 inch Patent Buckle Heel Straps, per pair,	0 30
20 " Roller " " " "	0 25
30 " Patent " Toe " "	0 40
30 " Roller " " " "	0 30

MISCELLANEOUS PARTS.

Peck & Snyder's Skate Keys, to fit any make, each....	$0 10
Adjusting Thumb Screws, for American Club Skates, Each	15
Steel Heel Plates and Screws, per pair	10
Heel Screws for Wood Top Skates, per pair	20
Wrenches for the Acme Skates, each	10
Nuts and Screws for Acme Skates, each	15
Sole Clamps for Acme Skates, each	15
Heel Buttons for Acme Skates, each	15
Chamois Skate Bags, to fit any size Skate, double pockets, each	75
Green Flannel " " " " " " "	50
Green Baize Bags, (extra heavy) double pockets, " "	65

Fig. 2.

Fig. 3.

Fig. 2. HEULING'S PATENT FIELD OR ICE SPIKE.

Can be worn both in the street or parlor. No trouble to adjust. No such thing as slipping when these are worn.

Price, per pair, Brass, 75 cents; Iron, 50 cents.

Fig. 3. THE CHICAGO ADJUSTABLE SPIKES.

These Spikes are now considered as the best in the market. The points are of steel, struck from a steel plate, with leather strap extending over the toe, also around the ankle, as shown in the annexed illustration. This is the only spike that can be place on a rubber shoe without defacing it.

Price, per pair, by mail, post-paid, 50 cents.

Fig. 4. ADJUSTABLE ICE CREEPERS. HORSE SHOE PATTERN.

The annexed heel clamp (Fig. 4) is the best heel creeper now in use; it can be put on or taken off in a moment. Send size of heel when ordering.

Price per pair, 25 cents.

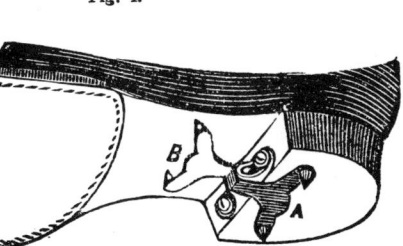

Fig. 4.

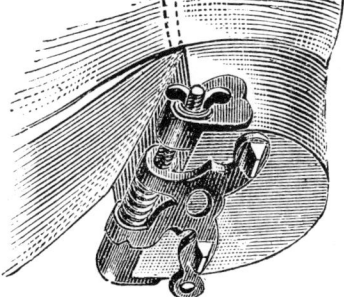

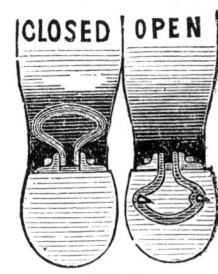

Fig. 6.   Fig. 7.   Fig. 5.

Fig. 5. THE EXCELSIOR FOLDING CREEPER.

The illustration shows the Creeper open on the boot for use, and closed when not required, made of malleable iron, a light serviceable creeper. Per pair, 25 cents.

Fig. 6. "CLIMAX" REVERSIBLE ICE CREEPER.

Patented April 30, 1876. The best made for the price. "A" represents the Creeper ready for use. The dotted line "B" shows the Creeper thrown back entirely out of the way when not in use, or walking in doors.

Price, per pair, by mail, post-paid, 25 cents.

Fig. 7. SCOTT'S ADJUSTABLE CREEPER.

These Creepers as shown in the illustration can be placed on or taken off any sized heel by means of the side adjustable thumb screw. Per pair, 25 cents.

Samples of Ice Creeper, Skate parts and Straps sent by mail post paid on receipt of price.

In all the above goods we keep the largest and most complete assortment of any house in the trade, dealers can always rely on getting goods from us and at the lowest prices. Peck & Snyder, 126, 128 & 130 Nassau St., N.Y.

SLEDS FOR BOYS, GIRLS, MEN AND WOMEN.

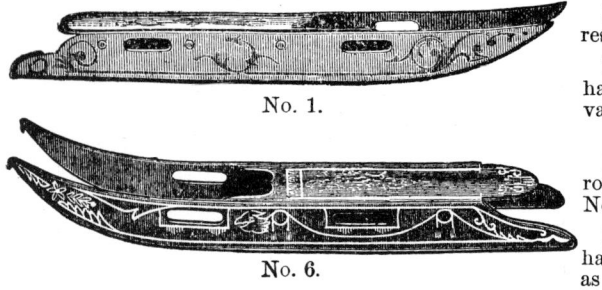

No. 1.—Children's Sleds.—This cut represents our line of low priced clipper sleds.

No. 1. 9 inches wide, 30 inches long; has half oval shoes; hand places cut in the sides; varnished and ornamented on the wood.
Each, 75 cents.

No. 2. 10 inches wide, 33 inches long; has round iron spring shoes. Finished same as No. 1. Each, $1.00

No. 3. 10½ inches wide and 40 inches long; has round iron spring shoes, and finished same as No. 2. Each, $1.25

No. 4. 11¼ inches wide, 46 inches long; has round iron spring shoes of seven-sixteenths iron. Each, $1.75

No. 5 11¼ inches wide, 46 inches long; heavy round iron spring shoes. Painted in vermillion and expensively ornamented. Each, $2.25

No. 6.—Oak Clippers.—This cut represents our best grades of clipper sleds. They are all made of heavy oak timber, and have hand holes nicely cut in the sides.

No. 6. 9½ inches wide, 38 inches long; has polished shoes of three-eighths round iron.
Each, $1.75

No. 7. 10¼ inches wide, 44 inches long; has polished shoes of seven-sixteenths round iron. Each, $2.25
No. 8. 11¼ inches wide and 50 inches long; has polished shoes made of half-inch round iron. Each, $2.75

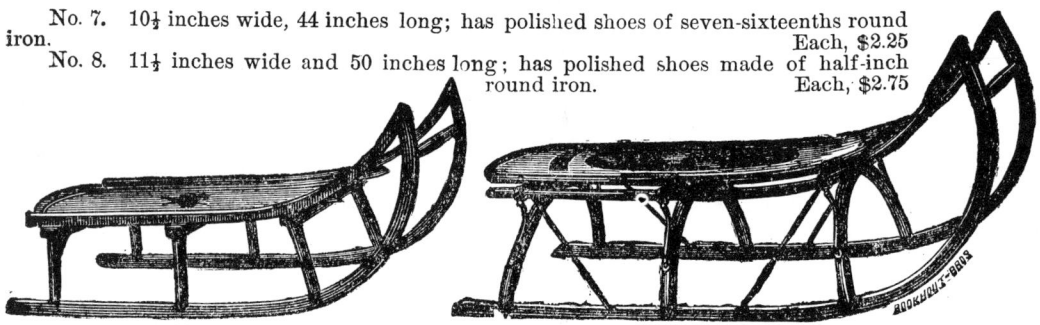

No. 9. Same size as number 7, but with higher finish, and more elaborately ornamented; has highly polished steel shoes, seven-sixteenths in size. Each, $3.25
No. 10. Same size as number 8; finished same as number 9, with one-half inch round steel shoes.
Each, $4.00

No. 13.—Dirigo Clippers. The Boy's Popular Sled.—No. 13. 10½ inches wide, 36 inches long; has polished shoes of three-eighths round iron. Each, $2.00
No. 14. 11¼ in. wide, 42 in. long; has polished shoes of seven-sixteenths round iron. Each, $2.25
No. 15. This number is greatly improved this season, the sides being all made of one piece, cut and bent to the desired form. 12½ inches wide, 48 inches long; has polished shoes of one-half inch iron.
Each, $3.00
No. 16. Same size as number 14; has highly polished shoes of seven-sixteenths round steel, and is either very finely ornamented, or upholstered with tapestry carpet if desired. Each, $4.00
No. 17. Same size as number 15; has highly polished shoes of one-half inch round steel, and finished same as number 16. Each, $4.25

No. 18.—Oak Frame Sleds.—No. 18. 12 in. wide and 26 in. long; has two knees. Each, $1.00
No. 19. 13 inches wide and 30 inches long; has three knees. Each, $1.25
No 20. 14 inches wide and 34 inches long; has four knees. Each, $1.50

No. 21.—Paris Cutter.—This cut represents style and make of Nos. 21 to 25 inclusive. They are made of the best oak timber, varnished on the wood, very nicely finished and ornamented, and have polished shoes.

No. 21. 11 inches wide and 28 inches long. Each, $2.00
No. 22. 12 inches wide and 33 inches long. Each, $2.25
No. 23. 13 inches wide and 40 inches long. Each, $2.50
No. 24. Same size as No. 22; has oval shoes, highly polished, and plated braces. We have spared no pains in finish and paint to make this the most attractive sled in the market. Each, $4.00
No. 25. Same size as No. 23, and finished same as No. 24. Each, $4.50

No. 6.—Baby Box Sleighs.—Are nicely painted, nickel plated arms and dark rails, and very neatly upholstered, with and without reversible handles. Prices, each, $6.50, $8.00 and $10.00

THE NEW WINTER SPORT, TOBOGGANING.

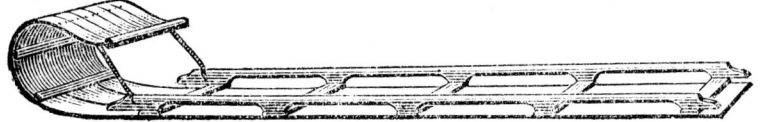

The "Star Patent" Toboggan.—The "Star Patent" is the finest and swiftest Toboggan ever made. The running surface gives much less friction than any other, and so the speed is greatly increased. It is very strongly made, and will outwear the best of any other make. If a slat is in any way broken, it can be very easily replaced. We confidently recommend this Toboggan to those who want the best in style, speed and durability. It is made from the best quality of Hard Maple, or Rock Elm.

Prices, each 5 feet, $5 50; 6 feet, $6 00; 7 feet, $6 50.

The No. 1 New York Toboggan—Is a strictly first-class Toboggan; equal to any other made, except the "Star Patent." It is strong and as finely finished, but has not the curved running surface, which is peculiar to the "Star." Made of Hard Maple, or Rock Elm.

Price, 5 feet, $4 50; 6 feet, $5 00; 7 feet, $5 50.

The No. 2 Expert Toboggan.—Is made to supply the demand for a cheap, but good serviceable Toboggan. Of good material, well finished.

Price, 5 feet, $3 00; 6 feet, $3 50; 7 feet, $4 00.

The "Boy's Own" Toboggan.—Every boy will want one of them at sight. It will be the Christmas present most desired. Made of good material, well finished.

Price, 2½ feet, $1 50; 3 feet, $1 50; 3½ feet, $2 00; 4 feet, $2 00.

Toboggan Cushions.—We furnish an extra quality of Cushions, in Tapestry or in Ingrain, at the following low prices: Tapestry, 5 feet, $4 50; 6 feet, $5 00; Ingrain, 5 feet, $3 50; 6 feet, $4 00.

Toboggan Tuques or Caps—All colors............................$1 25
Extra Heavy and Long Worsted Stockings—All colors............ 1 50
Toboggan Sashes, with Tassels—Red, Blue or White, 2½ yards long.... 1 50
Suits Made of Blanket Cloth—Of an color, to order.
Prices on application.
Lowest estimates to clubs who will order in quantities.

OIL-TANNED MOCCASINS OR PACKS—For Hunting, Fishing, Canoeing, Tobogganing, &c. They are easy to the feet, and very durable.

Per pair, $3 00; by mail, $3 25

INDIAN MOCCASINS—For Hunting, Fishing, Camping, Canoeing, Tobogganing, &c. They are easy to the feet and durable.

Buckskin Moccasins.................... $2 75 per pair; by mail, $3 00
Mooseskin   "   .... 2 50   "   "   2 75
     "   Lined, ... 3 50   "   "   3 75

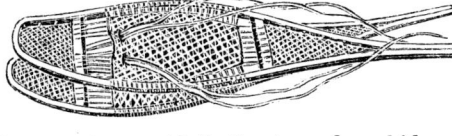

SNOWSHOEING, an old favorite winter sport of Canada, and now becoming popular in our own States, when snow is plenty.

Snowshoes are made as follows: The frame or outside rim, are of well seasoned young hickory, and they are strung with Indian tanned rawhide, cut in narrow strips and netted, as shown in cut.

Men's Walking, medium, per pair........ $3 00; Men's racing, per pair...................... $5 00
  "   "   large,   "   .... 3 50; "   extra racing, per pair................ 6 00
Ladies' "   medium,   "   .... 3 00; Ladies' fancy, extra finish, per pair 4 00
Boys' or Girls' Walking, "   .... 2 50; Men's extra heavy, for lumbering, per pair... 4 00

They run in sizes, 10½ x 36 inches; 11½ x 36 inches; 12 x 42; 10 x 30 inches.

Amusette, or Portable Family Billiards.

Can be attached to any table, as shown in Cut. Can be played all seasons of the year.

This set of billiards consists of 4 clamps or corner posts ; three colored cords (prepared for the purpose) each 18 feet long : 4 Boxwood Balls, colored in imitation of regular billiard balls, and handsomely polished 2 Cues (same as used on large billiard tables, but somewhat smaller) ; 1 Bridge ; 2 Dial Markers for keeping game ; 4 Polished Pins, to represent Pockets. (Does not include Table or Cloth.

The cords will be found equal to the best cushions. It is packed (with the exception of the cues) in a box (8x6 in.) ; is not cumbersome or bulky ; can be adjusted to a table in five minutes, and removed in a short a time, and can also be packed in a trunk and carried when traveling.

Those accustomed to playing billiards can do so at home, upon their own dining or sitting-room tables with as much skill and pleasure as upon a costly billiard table. In consequence, Amusette furnishes an endless fund of amusement for the household circle, as the fascination of billiards is well known. The expense and inconvenience of a table has heretofore been the only restriction to the *growing popularity of this truly and beautiful game.* Complete set, in a neat dove tailed box...$4 00

We can furnish extra parts, and send by mail, postage paid, (except cues which can be sent only by express), for the following prices :

4 Boxwood Balls, handsomely polished and colored, per set..................................	$1 00
4 Clamps or corner posts, " " "	1 75
2 Large cue sticks, " per pair..................................	50
1 Bridge " " " each..................................	25
1 " for cue " "	10
3 Cords, each 18 feet long " " set..................................	50
2 Dial Markers " pair..................................	10
1 piece of chalk..................................	05
4 small Ten Pins, polished per set..................................	15

Prices of Compressed Ivory Billiard Balls.

(These Balls are of the same weight and elasticity of Ivory, do not get out of round, and colors will not fade.

1¾ inch., per set of 4.................................$2.00	2⅜ inch., per set of 4..........................$8.00
2 " " " " "............................ 4.00	2½ " " " " "............................10.00
2¼ " " " " "............................ 6.00	

As it is rather difficult to procure a cheap cloth suitable for the "Amusette, or Family Billiards", by most of our Patrons, we now inform all who may be in want of the same, that we have had made Clothes that may be suitable to all both in quality and price.

1st quality, Color Green, width 1½ yard..Price per yard, $1 25

PECK & SNYDER, 126 Nassau St., N. Y., Manufacturers & Sole Owners of the above Patent

STRONG IRON SAVINGS BANKS FOR CHILDREN.

No. 200. Height, 8 in. Length, 7½ in. Width, 3 in.
Price,.................................$1 00

No. 265. Height, 8¼ in. Length, 7¾ in. Width, 3½.
Price,.................................$1 00

No. 285. Height, 6½ in. Width, 5¼ in. Depth, 5½ in.
Price,.................................$1 00

No. 275. Length, 4¼ in. Height, 3⅝ in. Width, 3 in.
Price,.................................50 cts.

No. 120. Height, 6¾ in. Width, 4⅞ in. Depth, 4⅞ in.
Price,.................................$1 00

No. 111. Height, 3 in. Diameter, 4 in.
Price,.................................50 cts.

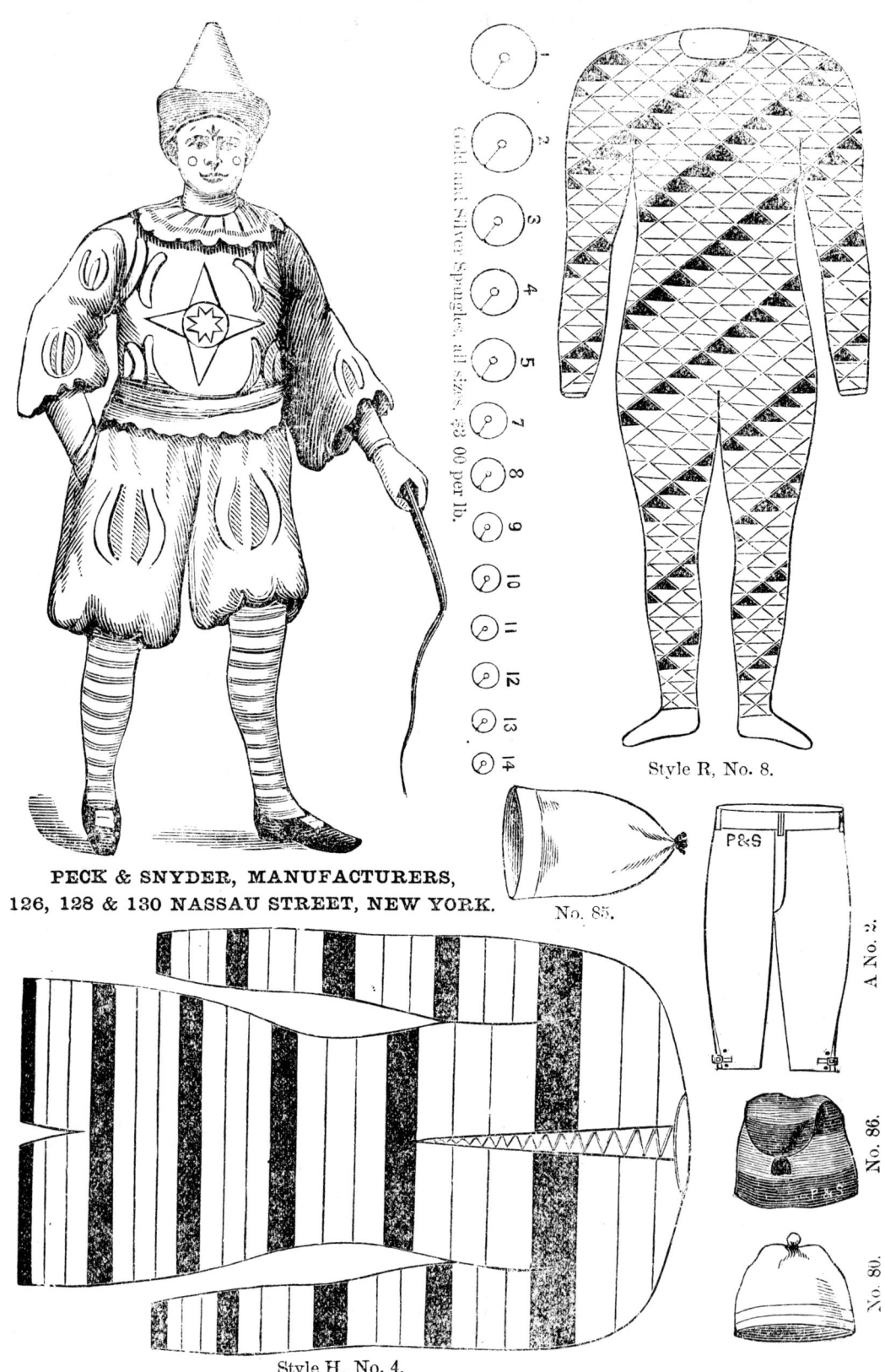

Style L.—Padded Tights, Shirts and Stockings.

We call special attention to our Padded Hosiery, made of finest brand of wool, by expert weavers. We can warrant them correct in every respect. Paddings made to order for any particular part of the body, at short notice.

No.	Item	Price
1.	Calf and Thigh Pads, (see cut)	per pair $10.00
2.	Calf Pads, (see cut)	" " 4.00
3.	Calf Padded Tights	" " 6.50
4.	Padded Sleeves	" " 5.00
5.	Padded Shirts, (see cut)	each 10.00
6.	Padded Hips	per pair 5.00

In ordering Paddings for any special imperfection be careful to state fully, just where and how heavy you want the Padding to be. Prices according to amount of work. Satisfaction guaranteed.

Style M.—Silk Opera Vests.

No.		Price
1.	All Silk Opera Vests, best quality, any color	each $9.00
2.	" " " " cotton bottoms, best quality, any color	" 8.00
3.	Fine Quality Worsted Opera Vests, any color, (see cut)	" 3 50

Style N.—Silk Thigh or Opera Hose.

No.		Price
1.	Best Quality Silk Opera Hose, any color	per pair $7.50
2.	" " " " " striped around	" " 8.50
3.	" " " " " perpendicular stripe	" " 18.00
4.	" " " " " fancy patterns	" " 16.00
5.	" " " " " perforated, any color, (see cut)	" " 14.00

Style O.—Worsted Thigh or Opera Hose.

No.		Price
1.	Best Quality Worsted Opera Hose, heavy weight, any color, (see cut)	per pair $2.50
2.	" " " " " light	" " 2.50
3.	" " " " " 2 colors, striped around	" " 3.00
4.	" " " " " perpendicular stripe, 2 inches wide	" " 10.00

Style P.—Silk Knee Hose.

No.		Price
1.	Best Quality Silk Knee Hose, any Color	per pair $5.00
2.	" " " " " 2 colors, striped around	" " 5.50
3.	" " " " " perpendicular stripe, 2 inches wide	" " 14.00

Style Q.—Worsted Knee Hose.

No.		Price
1.	Worsted Knee Hose, any color	per pair $1.75
2.	" " " 2 colors, striped	" " 2.00
3.	Worsted Knee Hose, special P. & S. brand	" " 1.00

In Colors, Black, Garnet, Brown, Navy, Grey, Blue, and Cardinal. The best and cheapest long Stockings ever offered to the profession. Fast Colors.

Style R.—Worsted Clown Suits. Animal Suits, &c.

No.		Price
1.	Worsted Clown Suits, two colors, striped around (see cut)	each $10.00
2.	" " " three " "	" 10.50
3.	" " " four " "	" 11.00
4.	" " " five " " (see cut)	" 12.00
5.	" " " block pattern " "	$20.00 to 25.00
6.	" " " diamond " " (see cut)	30.00
7.	" " " step " " (see cut)	20.00
8.	" Harlequin Suit, four colors, (see cut)	$24.00 to 32.00
9.	" " " five "	$26.00 to 34.00
10.	Monkey Dress	18.00
11.	" " with hood and gloves	20.00
12.	Frog Suit, plain green	10.00
13.	" " spotted, with gloves	15.00
14.	Demon Suit, plain	10.00
15.	" " with hood and horns	12.00
16.	Bear "	18.00
17.	Wild Man Suit	18.00
18.	Painted Skeleton Suit	15.00
19.	Cat Suit	18.00
20.	Gorilla Suit	18.00
21.	" " with hood and gloves	20.00
22.	Spangled Suits	$15.00 to 18.00

Special attention is given to these Suits, and each Suit when finished, is as correct, and as accurate a representation of what the animal would be in life.

No Masks go with above Suits. We can furnish any style Mask required.

Style S.—Worsted Clown Caps.

No.		Price
1.	Clown Cap, two colors, striped around	$0.85
2.	" " three " "	1.00
3.	" " four " "	1.15
4.	" " block pattern	1.25
5.	" " diamond pattern	2.00

N. B.—Any of the above goods can be sent either by mail or express. Persons wishing them in a hurry and to be sent by mail, will please remit 25 cents in addition to the advertised price, and for safety in carriage, 10 cents extra for registering package.

HALL'S STANDARD LUNG TESTER.

The public has long felt the necessity of a Spirometer (or Lung-tester) that would combine accuracy, beauty in form and shape, and pleasing and entertaining to the eye and mind, as well as ornamental and useful. Such is the one we take pleasure in presenting to our patrons for the first time. It is a beautiful instrument in every respect. It is highly decorated, has a silvery-toned patent gong attachment, which can be adjusted to ring at any desired figure upon the gauge, and is destined to become as popular as the piano or organ for parlor entertainment or amusement. So perfect are its workings that there is not the slightest pressure or weight upon the lungs, even the smallest child being able to register their lung capacity.

For parties who cannot get sufficient physical exercise to keep the outer cells of the lungs well open and well developed, these Spirometers are a mine of wealth. Air is life and vitality itself, and the lungs require as much, if not more, exercise than any other function of the body. Parties using these instruments will be surprised to notice the gradual increase of their lung capacity as they use it from day to day. This is because the outer cells of the lungs have become contracted and closed up (like a dry sponge) for the want of sufficient lung exercise. A man may walk, or hammer on an anvil all day, without exercising or expanding the respiratory organs. One of these machines has been in use in the *Police Gazette* office during the past year, to register the lung capacity of the sporting fraternity generally, and has given entire satisfaction.

These Spirometers are especially adapted for parlor entertainments, ladies' fairs, festivals, pleasure grounds, museums, hospitals, recruiting offices, armories, gymnasiums, club-houses, fire departments, hotels, saloons, workshops, etc. They are put upon the market at the lowest possible figure, consistent with a fair profit to the manufacturer and dealers, in order that no family or house who can afford it shall be without one.

Price, No. 1, patent gong, ornamented, &c.........$30 00
" No. 2, without gong, ornamented........ 20 00

PECK & SNYDER, Gen'l Agents, 128 Nassau St., N.Y.

THE NEW PARLOR QUOITS FOR YOUNG AND OLD.

Can be used in the Parlor without injury to Furniture.
Can be used on the Lawn without injury to Grass.

The extreme popularity with which this game has been received during the past season leads us to believe that it will rank in favor with the now popular lawn tennis, while at the same time, involving far less trouble and expense.

The Quoits used are covered with soft material, so that they will not mar the finest furniture, while they are at the same time of proper weight to be thrown with accuracy, and have no tendency to roll when they strike the floor.

For healthful recreation, without violent exercise, they bid fair to supersede any game yet placed upon the market.

Directions and Rules for the Game are printed upon the Box.
Ash Stand, 4 cloth-covered Rings...per set .75
Walnut Stand, 4 cloth-covered Rings.. " $1.00

Steam Propellers.—These propellers are all run direct by crank to shaft, and are as simple to handle as No. 1 Engine. The boilers are filled by removing a small screw stop. The lamps are filled with sponge, making them safe against overflow. *No adjustment of parts.* Any boy six years old, and of ordinary intelligence, can run them.

No. 76. THE LITTLE WONDER.

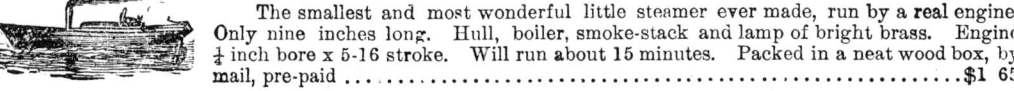

The smallest and most wonderful little steamer ever made, run by a real engine. Only nine inches long. Hull, boiler, smoke-stack and lamp of bright brass. Engine ¼ inch bore x 5-16 stroke. Will run about 15 minutes. Packed in a neat wood box, by mail, pre-paid $1 65

Sporting Goods
PECK & SNYDER
an historical introduction

"Sometimes, but not very often, we find in society a gifted individual who knows how to take the lead in a few round games, and is able to divert the company with a trick or two. His opportune talents are rewarded by a flattering prominence, and he steps out from the ranks to assume a well-deserved leadership. But his resources are, perhaps, soon exhausted. He has succeeded in raising a keen appetite for more of the same sort, which he is unable to appease. *His laurels fade—he relapses into his former insignificance.*"

The foregoing is from an 1873 guide to parlor games, *What Shall We Do To-Night?* by a jokester writing under the name of Leger D. Mayne. By consulting the pages of his book, you were guaranteed a bag full of rib-tickling stunts and games to make you the center and life of the party. Much the same result might be obtained, however, by having consulted and ordered from any one of the annual catalogs issued by Peck & Snyder of New York or from various other mail order dealers. In fact, *Cassell's Book of Sports and Pastimes,* offered just such advice:

"To those who can afford to procure a constant supply of new and original toys and games, no better means of learning of their appearance can be had than is supplied in the catalogues issued, for the most part gratuitously, or at a very small cost, from time to time, by the leading firms engaged in the toy trade."

Peck & Snyder was, of course, selling much more than toys. Its stock in trade would appear to have been sporting goods and clothing. Second in importance were magic and tricks, and, third, mechanical and scientific "recreative" amusements. The company manufactured some of the sporting supplies, imported a great variety of "conjuring tricks" and "magical apparatus," and stocked a wide assortment of novelties and books produced by other companies. They claimed to carry the "Largest Assorted Stock" of knit goods "of any dealer in the world."

Sporting goods was a term that covered a much wider scope in Victorian America than today. The "sporting gentlemen" of the early ninetennth century was by the 1880's a more common and varied figure. A whole new world of amusing pastimes—"manly" and sedentary—opened up in the years following the Civil War for the average American man, woman and child. "Many at first," a sports historian has written, "knew not the meaning of sportsmanship; some never learned." Aristocratic pastimes such as equestrian riding, polo, cricket and lawn tennis were to enjoy popularity in the period from 1870 to 1900, but this was truly the era of baseball, of establishing new rules and regulations, of "stealing home" to the plate. The sports heroes of the day were thoroughly democratic gentlemen.

The home was still the center for recreation. "Accumulating wealth and increasing leisure offered to some an opportunity to spend more time in the open," but parlor or yard games were the most common form of "sporting" activity. Some Christian groups still frowned on truly physical activity on Sunday, then the only day of rest, and had grave doubts about the sanctity of card playing and dancing. The childen of strict sabbatarians could, however, enjoy such a board game as "The Pilgrim's Progress." It is described in the catalog as "Going to Sunday-School, and Tower of Babel. Three Games in One Board. A triple combination of moral games. The Pilgrim's Progress illustrates Bunyan's great book. The Sunday-School Game, The Temptations of Youth, and The Tower of Babel is based on the biblical accounts of the great tower."

Many children had to make do without such explicit equipment, and must not have suffered too greatly. They invented their own games, and may have taken to the attic, or the garret. An 1881 book described the pleasures that might be found there.

"Happy the children who have inherited a garret! We mean the good old country garret, wherein have been stowed away the accumulations of many generations of careful housewives . . . A bright boy or girl will unearth many a pearl of price from those old trunks, those dilapidated bureau-drawers, those piles of old love-letters, those garments of the past, that broken-down guitar, that stringless violin, that too-reedy flute."

More energetic activity was, however, being strongly recommended at the time, especially for the children of the increasing number of city dwellers. Their sedentary parents, as well, were beginning to indulge the art of "physical culture." Grown women were escaping the front parlor for such lady-like pursuits as croquet, archery and lawn tennis. "We do not fear contradiction," a sports manual writer noted in 1886, "in asserting that manly sports, mirth, pastimes, and active exercise, are the physical laws of nature; and that without due regard to them, man cannot attain the perfection of his nature."

Baseball was *the* favored athletic activity in the 1880's for men and boys. In 1885 the first World Series match was held between teams from the National League and American Association. In 1886 Chicago (National League) and St. Louis (American Association) met and St. Louis won the championship. Newspapers and magazines devoted increasing amounts of column space to coverage of the sport. Football was also on the rise, but during the 1880's many of the rules and basic terminology were still to be worked out.

Other "manly" sports which gained in popularity following the Civil War and enjoyed special favor during the 1880's were riflery (in 1879 there were 144 clubs equipped with outdoor ranges or indoor galleries), boxing, and fencing. More "gentle" sports, favored by women as well, were lawn tennis (a national association was founded in 1881), bowling (tenpin alleys were built in several major cities during the mid-1880's) croquet, archery (the first national tournament was held in 1879), and bicycling. These latter activities drew "into the ranks of participants boys and girls as well as men and women . . . and served as the medium through which women entered into the sport life of the nation, and thereby took a long step forward in their struggle for equality with men."

The great craze for bicycling, however, was not to occur until the late 1880's and 90's after the introduction of the "safety" model. The reader will note that Peck & Snyler did not offer much in the way of bicycles or auxilliary equipment in 1886. They did present a few models of the high-wheeled variety, then popular, and several velocipedes or "bone shakers." The "safety," invented in 1885 in England, was introduced in this country in 1887. A League of American Wheelman had been founded in 1880, and most preferred the high-wheeled variety then produced by such manufacturers as Colonel Albert A. Pope of Boston. In the mid-1890's the League had over 100,000 members and all were riding the "safety," lower model.

Athletic clubs and gymnasiums were to be found in almost all major cities by the 1880's. Gentlemen who could not visit these institutions were, however, advised to purchase their own exercise equipment from firms such as Spalding or Peck & Snyder. The variety offered by the latter firm was extensive. Some gymnasium sets were especially recommended for "clergymen, literary men, and all persons of sedentary occupation. . . . The exercises are especially invigorating to the digestive and respiratory organs." The use of Indian clubs was widespread and highly touted. "Club swinging is a well tried and established institution and is universally recognized as one of the best methods for developing the muscles of the body, improving the circulation, digestion, etc."

One of the distinctive sports of the 1880's was roller skating. Special bearings for the wheels were patented at the time, and skates for both the expert and novice were available. The gigantic Olympia roller skating rink was opened in New York on 53rd Street in 1885. A. G. Spalding, famed baseball player and sports supplier opened another in Chicago in 1884, and published a *Manual of Roller Skating* the same year.

For rainy days and evening amusement, nothing, however, was guaranteed to fascinate more than "parlour magic." At the time, it was written, "Conjuring has its professors and teachers, and may be ranked as a science, if not as an art." Almost anyone could be a "professor" of magic by using a few of the many devices supplied by Peck & Snyder. Books on hocus-pocus and conjuring were extremely popular.

Peck & Snyder specialized in these amusing goods, and claimed that "the Conjuring tricks and Magical Apparatus sold by us for beauty of workmanship and mechanical skill, have never been equaled in the world. They are so handsomely finished that they are an ornament in any drawing-room, although, when used for performing they will cause both astonishment and admiration." The firm offered special boxes of assorted tricks, and a thousand and one separate items, including such curious numbers as "The Nose Trick," "The Novel and Extraordinary Conjuring Table," and "The Child Found in a Borrowed Hat" ("The performer borrows a hat [which is shown quite empty] and instantly produces from the Hat a 'Child' three-quarters-of-a-yard long; the 'child' is nicely dressed, with cap trimmed with lace and ribbon, a bib, &c. This 'Trick' is not only very astonishing, but always creates shouts of laughter; very easy to perform in a drawing-room or theater."

If these tricks didn't do the job, then a reader might select one of the many manuals on the subject which were listed: "Parlor Pastimes, or, The Whole Art of Amusing," "Tricks and Diversions with Cards," etc. These were offered along with self-improvement guides ("Marriage Made Easy," "Personal Beauty," "Wilson's Ball-Room Guide") designed to pep up any shy bachelor or maiden.

For the truly imaginative and dramatically inclined, Peck & Snyder supplied everything from costumes, wigs and scenery to the plays themselves. The theme, if not content, of many of these so-called "theatricals" was racist at best. Ethnic differences were stressed for "fun," and Black humor was dark and grim, indeed. Plays about Blacks were called "Darky" or "Ethiopian" dramas. Among the items offered was " 'Nigger Jokes and Stump Speeches,' being a collection of approved Nigger jokes, Stump Speeches, Conundrums, and the Essence of Minstrelsy." Fortunately, these offensive materials are now almost as antique as segregated waiting rooms.

Especially symbolic of the era in which they were introduced are the "educational" or "recreative" scientific kits and magic lanterns. "The daily growing army of men and boys who make science of some sort their hobby proceed in very different ways to gratify it," and Peck & Snyder more than supplied these needs. Of all "sporting" activities, these probably met with the greatest degree of approbation, for, as one writer of the period put it, "The lives of not a few of the greatest engineers and inventors the world has ever seen show that their peculiar genius was first roused to activity by their having access in boyhood to tools and workshops." Electric telegraph kits and model steam engines were among the more sophisticated items available to budding scientists.

It was the magic lantern which best captured the imagination: "Some of the tricks that can be managed with it are so wonderful, that it well merits the character of *magical*, which it has long sustained, and perhaps no class of entertainments has been so interesting to boys of the past, nor will be to boys of the future."

No truer words could have been spoken. One of those boy geniuses, Thomas Alva Edison, was to supply the whole world with a new and dominant form of recreation—the moving picture. In the 1880's and 90's, Americans still enjoyed a very vigorous, participatory life of recreation. Without movies, television and other push-button amusements, they were forced to use their legs and their minds in pursuit of leisure.

Suggestions for further reading

contemporary sources:
Athletic Sports for Boys. New York: Dick & Fitzgerald, 1866.
BENEDICT, GEORGE H. *Manual of Boxing, Club Swinging and Manly Sports.* New York and Chicago: A. G. Spalding & Bros., 1886.
Cassell's Complete Book of Sports and Pastimes. New York and London: Cassell & Company, Ltd., n.d.
MAYNE, LEGER D. (PSEUD.). *What Shall We Do To-Night?* New York: Dick & Fitzgerald, 1873.

useful secondary sources:
HEYL, EDGAR. *Cues for Collectors.* Chicago: Ireland Magic Company, 1964.
KROUT, JOHN ALLEN. *Annals of American Sport.* The Pageant of America series. New Haven: Yale University Press, 1929.
SMITH, ROBERT. *Baseball in America.* New York: Holt, Rinehart and Winston, 1961.
WEAVER, ROBERT B. *Amusements and Sports in American Life.* Chicago: The University of Chicago Press, 1939.

Public collections of late nineteenth-century sporting goods

The following public historical and art museums have indicated that they have within their holdings some of the items displayed in the 1886 Peck & Snyder catalog. A good proportion of the catalog offerings, however, would be best sought in antique and second-hand shops as they are "nostalgic" items usually relegated to the trivia category.

Arizona Pioneers' Historical Museum, Tucson, Ariz.
Chicago Historical Society, Chicago, Ill.
El Monte Historical Museum, El Monte, Calif.
Grand Rapids Public Museum, Grand Rapids, Mich.
Greensboro Historical Museum, Greensboro, N. C.
Henry Ford Museum and Greenfield Village, Dearborn, Mich.
Historical Museum and Institute of Western Colorado, Grand Junction, Colo.
Lane County Pioneer Museum, Eugene, Ore.
Missouri Historical Society, St. Louis, Mo.
Monmouth County Historical Society Museum, Freehold, N. J.
Museum of the City of Mobile, Mobile, Ala.
Museum of the City of New York, New York, N. Y.

Nassau County Historical Museum, Syosset, N. Y.
National Baseball Hall of Fame and Museum, Cooperstown, N. Y.
National Lawn Tennis Hall of Fame and Tennis Museum, Newport, R. I.
Nebraska State Historical Society, Lincoln, Neb.
Newark Museum, Newark, N. J.
New York Historical Society, New York, N. Y.
North Carolina State Department of Archives and History, Raleigh, N. C.
Oakland Museum, Oakland, Calif.
Orange County Historical Museum, Orlando, Fla.
Pioneer Woman Museum, Ponca City, Okla.
San Bernardino County Museum, Bloomington, Calif.
San Diego Historical Society, Serra Museum, San Diego, Calif.
South Dakota State Historical Society, Pierre, S. D.
Staten Island Historical Society, Richmond, S. I., N. Y.
Wadsworth Atheneum, Hartford, Conn.
William Penn Memorial Museum, Harrisburg, Penn.
Witte Memorial Museum, San Antonio, Tex.